The
New International
Lesson Annual

2011-2012

September–August

Abingdon Press
Nashville

THE NEW INTERNATIONAL LESSON ANNUAL 2011–2012

Copyright © 2011 by Abingdon Press

This book is printed on acid-free paper.

Scripture quotations marked NRSV are taken from the New Revised Standard Version of the Bible, copyright 1989, Division of Christian Education of the National Council of the Churches of Christ in the United States of America. Used by permission. All rights reserved.

Scripture quotations marked CEV are taken from the Contemporary English Version Copyright © 1991, 1992, 1995 by American Bible Society. Used by permission.

Scripture quotations marked GNT are taken from the Good News Translation in Today's English Version—Second Edition © 1992 by American Bible Society. Used by permission.

Scripture quotations marked KJV are taken from the King James or Authorized Version of the Bible.

Scripture quotations marked *"THE MESSAGE"* are taken from *THE MESSAGE*. Copyright © by Eugene H. Peterson 1993, 1994, 1995, 1996, 2000, 2001, 2002. Used by permission of NavPress Publishing Group.

Scripture marked NIV is taken from the Holy Bible, New International Version®, NIV®. Copyright © 1973, 1978, 1984 by Biblica, Inc.™ Used by permission of Zondervan. All rights reserved worldwide. www.zondervan.com.

Scripture quotations marked NJB are taken from THE NEW JERUSALEM BIBLE, copyright © 1985 by Darton, Longman & Todd, Ltd. and Doubleday, a division of Random House, Inc. Reprinted by Permission.

Scripture quotations marked REB are taken from the Revised English Bible © Oxford University Press and Cambridge University Press 1989.

Scripture quotations taken from the Amplified® Bible, Copyright © 1954, 1958, 1962, 1964, 1965, 1987 by Lockman Foundation. Used by permission. (www.Lockman.org)

ISBN 978-0-687-66031-5

ISSN 1084-872X

11 12 13 14 15 16 17 18 19 20—10 9 8 7 6 5 4 3 2 1

MANUFACTURED IN THE UNITED STATES OF AMERICA

PREFACE

Welcome to the global community of Bible students who study resources based on the work of the Committee on the Uniform Series, known by many as the International Lesson Series. Specifically designed for teachers who seek a solid biblical basis for each session and a step-by-step teaching plan that will help them lead their classes, no matter which student curriculum resource the adult students may use, *The New International Lesson Annual* is also a primary resource for many students.

During the September 2011 through August 2012 Sunday school year we focus on four themes: tradition, faith, creation, and justice. "Tradition and Wisdom," the study for the fall quarter, explores Proverbs, Ecclesiastes, Song of Solomon, and wisdom that Jesus taught in Matthew 5–6 as part of the Sermon on the Mount. The winter quarter, "God Establishes a Faithful People," examines selected passages from Genesis, Exodus, Luke, and Galatians. "God's Creative Word," the study for spring, begins with one lesson on Proverbs and then turns to the Gospel of John. The summer quarter, "God Calls for Justice," surveys the theme of justice in Exodus, Leviticus, Deuteronomy, 1 Samuel, 2 Samuel, 1 Kings, 2 Kings, 1 Chronicles, 2 Chronicles, Psalms, Isaiah, Jeremiah, and Ezekiel.

The following features are especially valuable for busy teachers who want to provide in-depth Bible study experiences for their students. Each lesson includes the following sections:

Previewing the Lesson highlights the background and lesson Scriptures, focus of the lesson, three goals for the learners, a pronunciation guide in lessons where you may find unfamiliar words or names, and supplies you will need to teach.

Reading the Scripture includes the Scripture lesson printed in both the New Revised Standard Version and the New International Version. By printing these two highly respected translations in parallel columns, you can easily compare them for in-depth study. If your own Bible is another version, you will then have three translations to explore as you prepare each lesson.

Understanding the Scripture closely analyzes the background Scripture by looking at each verse. Here you will find help in understanding concepts, ideas, places, and people pertinent to each week's lesson. You may also find explanations of Greek or Hebrew words that are essential for understanding the text.

Interpreting the Scripture looks at the lesson Scripture, delves into its meaning, and relates it to contemporary life.

Sharing the Scripture provides you with a detailed teaching plan. Written by your editor, who is a very experienced educator, this section is divided into two major sections: *Preparing to Teach* and *Leading the Class*.

In the *Preparing to Teach* section you will find a devotional reading related to the lesson for your own spiritual enrichment and ideas to help you prepare for the session.

The *Leading the Class* portion begins with "Gather to Learn" activities designed to welcome the students and draw them into the lesson. Here, the students' stories and experiences or other contemporary stories are highlighted as preparation for the Bible story. The next three headings of *Leading the Class* are the three "Goals for the Learners." The first goal always focuses on the Bible story itself. The second goal relates the Bible story to the lives of the adults in the class. The third goal prompts the students to take action on what they have learned. You will find a variety of activities under each of these goals to help the learners fulfill them. The activities are diverse in nature and may include the following among other strategies: listening, reading, writing, speaking, singing, drawing, interacting with others, and meditating. The lesson ends with "Continue the Journey," where you will find closing activities, preparation for the following week, and ideas for students to commit themselves to action during the week, based on what they have learned.

In addition to these weekly features, each quarter begins with the following helps:

- **Introduction to the Quarter** provides you with a quick survey of each lesson to be studied during the quarter. You will find the title, background Scripture, date, and a brief summary of each week's basic thrust. This feature is on the first page of each quarter.
- **Meet Our Writer**, which follows the quarterly introduction, provides biographical information about each writer, including education, pastoral or academic teaching experience, or both, previous publications, and family information.
- **The Big Picture**, written by the same writer who authored the quarter's lessons, is designed to give you a broader scope of the materials to be covered than is possible in each weekly lesson. You will find this background article immediately following the writer's biography.
- **Close-Up** gives you some focused information, such as a timeline, chart, overview, short article, map, or list that you may choose to use for a specific week or anytime during the quarter, perhaps even repeatedly.
- **Faith in Action** provides ideas related to the broad sweep of the quarter that the students can use individually or as a class to act on what they have been studying. These ideas are usually intended for use beyond the classroom.

Finally, two annual features are included:

- **List of Background Scriptures** is offered especially for those of you who keep back copies of *The New International Lesson Annual*. This feature, found immediately after the contents, will enable you to locate Bible background passages used during the current year at some future date.
- **Teacher enrichment article** is intended to be useful throughout the year, so we hope you will read it immediately and refer to it often. This year's article, "Stewards of God's Abundant Provisions," relates to the themes of our quarters and encourages readers to consider God's unfailing care for us. You will find this article following the List of Background Scriptures.

We welcome your input to help us make *The New International Lesson Annual* the first resource you consult when planning your lesson. Please send your questions, comments, and suggestions to me. I invite you to include your e-mail address or phone number, or both. I will respond as soon as your message reaches my home office in Maryland.

Dr. Nan Duerling
Abingdon Press
P.O. Box 801
Nashville, TN 37202

Your presence among *The New International Lesson Annual* community is a blessing. Our prayers are with you and those who study with you as you are guided by the Word of God and the Holy Spirit to be transformed and conformed to the image of our Lord and Savior Jesus Christ.

Nan Duerling, Ph.D.
Editor, *The New International Lesson Annual*

CONTENTS

FIRST QUARTER

Tradition and Wisdom
September 4, 2011–November 27, 2011

UNIT 1: TEACHING AND LEARNING
(September 4–October 23)

UNIT 2: JESUS TEACHES WISDOM
(October 30–November 27)

SECOND QUARTER

God Establishes a Faithful People
December 4, 2011–February 26, 2012

UNIT 1: GOD'S COVENANT
(December 4-25)

UNIT 2: GOD'S PROTECTION
(January 1-29)

THIRD QUARTER

God's Creative Word
March 4, 2012–May 27, 2012

UNIT 1: THE WORD WAS IN THE BEGINNING
(March 4–April 8)

UNIT 2: THE WORD IS HERE AND NOW
(April 15-29)

UNIT 3: THE WORD WILL BE
(May 6-27)

FOURTH QUARTER

God Calls for Justice
June 3, 2012–August 26, 2012

UNIT 1: JUSTICE DEFINED
(June 3-24)

UNIT 2: JUSTICE ENACTED
(July 1-29)

UNIT 3: JUSTICE PROMISED
(August 5-26)

List of Background Scriptures, 2011–2012

Old Testament

Genesis 12:1-9	December 4	2 Kings 4:1-37	July 22
Genesis 15:1-21	December 11	2 Kings 8:1-6	July 22
Genesis 22:1-14	December 18	1 Chronicles 18:14	July 8
Genesis 39:1-23	January 1	2 Chronicles 9:8	July 15
Genesis 41:1-52	January 8	2 Chronicles 18:28–19:11	July 29
Genesis 42:1-38	January 15	Psalm 146	August 5
Genesis 45:1-28	January 15	Proverbs 3:1-35	September 4
Genesis 50:1-26	January 22	Proverbs 4:1-27	September 11
Exodus 1:8-14	January 29	Proverbs 8	March 4
Exodus 15:1-27	January 29	Proverbs 10:1–15:33	September 18
Exodus 21–23	August 5	Proverbs 25:1-28	September 25
Exodus 22:1–23:9	June 3	Proverbs 28:1–29:27	October 2
Leviticus 19:9-18, 33-37	June 10	Ecclesiastes 9:13–10:20	October 9
Leviticus 25:8-55	June 17	Ecclesiastes 11:7–12:14	October 16
Numbers 21:4-8	March 25	Song of Solomon 4:8–5:1	October 23
Deuteronomy 10:1-22	June 24	Isaiah 9:1-7	August 12
Deuteronomy 16:18-20	June 24	Isaiah 58	August 5
1 Samuel 7:3-17	July 1	Jeremiah 23:1-6	August 19
2 Samuel 22:1–23:7	July 8	Jeremiah 33:14-18	August 19
1 Kings 3	July 15	Ezekiel 34	August 26

New Testament

Matthew 5:1-12	October 30	John 9	April 29
Matthew 5:17-26	November 6	John 10:1-18	May 13
Matthew 5:43-48	November 13	John 11:1-27	May 20
Matthew 6:5-15	November 20	John 14:1-14	May 27
Matthew 6:25-34	November 27	John 18–19	April 1
Luke 1:26-56	December 25	John 20:1-23	April 8
John 1:1-14	March 11	Galatians 1:1–2:21	February 5
John 2:1-12	March 18	Galatians 3:6-18	December 25
John 2:13-22	April 15	Galatians 3:1-14	February 12
John 3:11-21	March 25	Galatians 3:15-29	February 19
John 4:1-42	April 22	Galatians 4:1–5:1	February 19
John 6	May 6	Galatians 5:2–6:18	February 26

Teacher Enrichment: Stewards of God's Abundant Provisions

Citizens in the United States and around the world have been jolted by the global economic freefall of recent years. Some have lost their jobs, their homes, or both. Some may still be seeking employment commensurate with a former job, whereas others have taken major cuts in pay and responsibility, and still others have dropped out of the employment search completely. Stocks plummeted and although they are on the rebound as of this writing, the retirement accounts—and dreams—of many workers have had to change dramatically. Health-care costs have risen so astronomically that a single serious illness can wipe out the life savings of countless families. Life as many have known it will never be the same. Even those who have not been directly affected by this major downturn worry that they might be the next ones to receive a pink slip or to fall behind on their mortgage due to a job loss or serious illness. The days of living "the good life" are definitely over.

Or are they? The answer is a resounding yes if that phrase simply refers to material goods, conspicuous consumption, and financial security. But the answer could easily be no if we focus on the radical abundance that God wants to pour out upon us. In speaking about his role as "the gate for the sheep," Jesus said, "I came that they may have life, and have it abundantly" (John 10:7, 10, lesson for May 13). We experience this abundance as we walk with Jesus, trusting that he will provide all we need to live securely under God's care and protection.

God's radical abundance is evident throughout the Bible. The diversity of God's creation is apparent in Genesis 1. God might have been content with a limited creation, but instead God poured out an abundance of rocks, trees, animals, birds, waterfowl, plants, seas, rivers, and lakes upon the earth. Moreover, God clearly intended to share this creation with humanity. God said to Adam and Eve, "I have given you every plant yielding seed that is upon the face of all the earth, and every tree with seed in its fruit; you shall have them for food" (Genesis 1:29). Imagine! God's intention was that food would be bountifully provided not only for humanity but also for the animals (1:30). The psalmist was well aware of this abundance when he wrote in Psalm 104 about how God gave drink to every animal (104:11), caused grass to grow for cattle (104:14), provided food for humans (104:14-15), watered the trees "abundantly" (104:16), and exclaimed how the creatures look to God for food and their very life (104:28-29).

Even when hardship was to come in the days of Joseph (see Genesis 37–50, lessons for January 1, 8, 15, 22), God provided so that the people might live. God revealed information to Joseph so that he could interpret Pharaoh's dream about seven fat and seven lean cows and a second dream in which the ruler saw seven full ears of corn and seven withered ones (Genesis 41:17-24). Joseph had the God-given wisdom to discern that during the seven years of plenty, resources would need to be marshaled to provide for everyone during the famine. Pharaoh recognized Joseph's wisdom and understood that God was with Joseph. Consequently, Pharaoh put Joseph in charge so as to be well prepared for the crisis to come. When famine struck, the Egyptians fared well, and so did Joseph's own family, who made their way to Egypt in search of food.

God always provided for people's physical needs. Exodus 16 records that God sent manna from heaven for the entire forty years that the liberated Hebrew slaves sojourned in the desert (16:35). The food was there regularly each day, except for the sabbath. But on the day before, God provided enough extra so that people had plenty to eat on the sabbath. The key was that they were to gather enough for each day (two days' worth to be ready for the sabbath), but if they tried to hoard the food, it spoiled by the next day (16:20). God provided, but the people needed to trust that the manna would arrive. In the desert where no water seemed to be available, God supplied water from a rock (Exodus 17:1-7). The Hebrew people neither hungered nor thirsted, even though they wandered in an extremely inhospitable landscape. Moreover, as Moses gave his farewell speech in Deuteronomy, he reminded the people that neither their clothing nor sandals had worn out (29:5). God had met all of their needs, and so they survived in a desolate land.

In Isaiah 55:1-7 the prophet invites people to abundant life in God. The invitation is for "everyone," even and perhaps especially for those who "have no money" (55:1). God is throwing a huge party, a heavenly banquet, and all are invited to "listen" to God, to "eat what is good," and to delight themselves "in rich food" (55:2). People are called to "seek the LORD" by turning away from wickedness and returning to God, who "will abundantly pardon" them (55:6-7). That pardon reminds us that God's grace flows freely. God is willing and able to forgive and "have mercy" on us (55:7).

The beloved Twenty-third Psalm paints another picture of God's extraordinary abundance. There is no question about God's providential care: "The LORD is my shepherd" and because that is the case, "I shall not want" (23:1). God will provide all that we need, so much so that our "cup overflows" (23:5). This Good Shepherd meets not only physical needs but spiritual needs as well. Even as death hovers around us, God walks with and cares for us. We are not alone. God is present.

In the law, God provided ways for people to live abundant lives. Leviticus 25 institutes the Year of Jubilee, during which people receive ancestral property that may have been forfeited due to debt (25:10), and those who had no choice but to serve as laborers to pay debts are released (25:39-41). The land was to lie fallow for the Jubilee Year (25:11). As was true in the days of manna, when the bread from the sixth day fed the people on the seventh, so it was true during the Jubilee that God would ensure that the food from the preceding season, year six, would feed the people abundantly until the ninth year when new crops would be ready to reap (25:20-22).

God's law also provided ways for people to help those who did not have sufficient food. Leviticus 19:9-10 sets forth rules for gleaning. God commanded farmers to leave food at the edges of the field and the grapes that had fallen to the ground. Poor people and aliens were welcome to go into the fields and glean. We see an example of gleaning in the story of Ruth and Naomi. Two childless widows would have been in very desperate straits had God not provided a way for them to eat. They were entitled to this food by God's law, and did not have to depend on someone for a charitable handout.

One of the most extravagant examples of God's abundance in the New Testament is the story of Jesus feeding the five thousand. On May 6 we will study this story as it is told in John 6:1-14 as part of our background Scripture. This is one of the few stories that appears in all four Gospels (see also Matthew 14:13-21; Mark 6:30-44; and Luke 9:10-17). In each case, Jesus takes a small quantity of food and multiplies it so that five thousand men are fed. Women and children were not counted, so surely the number can be increased dramatically. They eat a simple meal of bread and fish, but they are not meagerly just "getting by." Instead, the meal is so abundant that all four Gospel writers report that there are twelve baskets filled with leftovers (Matthew 14:20; Mark 6:43; Luke 9:17; and John 6:13). God was unimaginably extravagant in providing for the people, who were physically and spiritually hungry.

Jesus knew that his listeners were living under the oppressive Roman rule, subject to exorbitant taxes, and living day-to-day without certainty of the day's wage that would enable them to feed their families. He addressed their concerns in the Sermon on the Mount (Matthew 6:25-34) when he urged them to seek God's kingdom first and promised that "all these things" (6:33)—the necessities of life—would be given to them as well. He later illustrated that message in the parable of the laborers in the vineyard (Matthew 20:1-16). Jesus spoke of a landowner who hired laborers throughout the day. Most would not have found employment for the day, probably indicating that unemployment was high among these unskilled workers. Jesus must have floored his listeners when he told how the reapers hired last received the same amount that the landowner had promised to those who had been hired first. In response to the grumbling of those who had worked all day, the landowner made clear that he could do as he pleased with what belonged to him. He asked, "Are you envious because I am generous?" (20:15).

Another example of such extravagance occurs when the resurrected Jesus appeared to his disciples, who had been fishing throughout the night without success. John 21:3 reports, "they caught nothing." A man called to the seven men in the boat and told them to put their net on "the right side of the boat" (21:6). Now, these were experienced fishermen plying their trade to earn money. They knew what they were doing, but since they were coming home empty-handed they decided to follow the man's instructions and give it one more try. When they did this, the net was so full of fish they could barely haul it in. They realized that Jesus was the man. Moreover, when they got to shore and examined their catch, they discovered that they had 153 large fish (21:11).

We could cite many other biblical examples to show how God provides abundantly for us. Yet the greatest example is God's sending the Beloved Son Jesus to us. We cannot begin to fathom the extravagant love revealed by Jesus' incarnation as a helpless babe, his simple life as an itinerant rabbi who taught and healed the multitudes, and his willingness to endure an agonizing death on the cross. As if all this were not enough, by the power of God, Jesus was raised from the dead on the third day. Because he lives, we know that we too not only have the joy of his presence now but will also spend all eternity with him. God's provisions for us are generous beyond belief.

As we examine these examples of God's abundant provisions for us, we can see a melding of the quarterly themes of this year's Bible studies: tradition, faith, creation, and justice. Throughout the Bible, we see a long and continuing tradition of God's care not only for humanity but also for all of creation. Such care is a matter of justice that is even encoded into God's law. Faith enters the picture as we consider times when we feel that our needs are not being met—at least not in the way or timeframe that we would prefer. Yet, somehow in the end, the promise of Philippians 4:19 is fulfilled: "And my God will fully satisfy every need of yours according to his riches in glory in Christ Jesus."

Think of it: God will provide for our every need. We can take that on faith, knowing that the Bible provides numerous illustrations of God's abundant provisioning. God provided not once but over and over again. Food appears from heaven not once or twice but dependably over the course of forty years—and in the lunchbox of a boy who had come to hear Jesus.

How then do we respond to the abundance of love, grace, and means to fulfill our basic needs that God so graciously provides? The Bible teaches us that we need to be stewards of God's bounty. Despite the ingrained notions that we can be self-made people and that whatever we earn or have is ours, the Bible emphatically tells us differently. In addition to Genesis

1 and 2, Job 38–41 declares that God is the creator of all that exists. Exodus 19:5-6 makes clear that God is also the owner: "Now therefore, if you obey my voice and keep my covenant, you shall be my treasured possession out of all the peoples. Indeed, the whole earth is mine, but you shall be for me a priestly kingdom and a holy nation." Psalm 24:1 teaches the same lesson: "The earth is the LORD's and all that is in it, the world, and those who live in it." In speaking about offerings with which to build the Temple, King David recognizes the ownership of God in 1 Chronicles 29:14: "But who am I, and what is my people, that we should be able to make this freewill offering? For all things come from you, and of your own have we given you."

In other words, God has graciously poured out God's own abundance upon us. We are not the owners; we are the caretakers, or administrators, or stewards. Look at these Greek words related to "steward," which are the roots for the English words *ecology*, *economy*, and *ecumenical*:

OIKOS (oy' kos)	household
OIKONOMOS (oy kon om' os)	household manager or overseer; steward
OIKONOMIA (oy kon om ee' ah)	administration of a household; stewardship
OIKOUMENE (oy kou men' ay)	whole world; God's entire household

God gives lavishly, but we have a responsibility to wisely use the resources entrusted to us, as Joseph did, so that God's whole household, the entire world, may benefit. And take note: The examples we have seen all relate to the basic needs of a simple lifestyle that everyone can enjoy. The resources are shared with all (as in the desert) and with the poor who have no money to buy, though they are welcome to come and glean. They are not hoarded by a few, as some tried to do in the desert only to find their stored manna was full of worms the next day (Exodus 16:20). In fact, God is quite displeased when we try to hold onto something that is not ours: "Will anyone rob God? Yet you are robbing me! But you say, 'How are we robbing you?' In your tithes and offerings!" (Malachi 3:8). God is equally clear about what happens when we let go of what we think is ours and trust God to take care of us: "Bring the full tithe into the storehouse, so that there may be food in my house, and thus put me to the test, says the LORD of hosts; see if I will not open the windows of heaven for you and pour down for you an overflowing blessing" (Malachi 3:10). We do not give to get more, but we do give in response to the mercy and grace of the One who loved enough to send the Beloved Son so that we might have eternal life. Now that's abundant living!

First Quarter
Tradition and Wisdom

SEPTEMBER 4, 2011–NOVEMBER 27, 2011

During the fall quarter we will survey the Wisdom Literature of the Old Testament in Proverbs, Ecclesiastes, and Song of Solomon. Then we will turn to the Sermon on the Mount in Matthew to discover how Jesus teaches this traditional wisdom. Unlike most quarters where our lessons are divided into three units, this quarter's sessions are contained in two units. These lessons all help us to discover God's principles for living purposeful and meaningful lives.

Unit 1, "Teaching and Learning," includes eight sessions that focus on human wisdom and the importance of passing on lessons learned from experience and tradition. As is characteristic of Wisdom Literature, the books we will encounter seldom refer to God's covenant or to spiritual life. Instead, they generally portray a teacher speaking to a student or a parent passing on words of wisdom to a child. "Righteousness and Wisdom," the opening session on September 4, looks at Proverbs 3:1-35 to discern wisdom for living. Proverbs 4:1-27, the background Scripture for September 11, considers the wise path and how the way to walk along that path is transmitted "From Generation to Generation." On September 18 we turn to Proverbs 10:1–15:33 to hear good advice concerning "Teaching Values." Proverbs 25:1-28, which we will encounter on September 25 in a session titled "Wisdom and Discernment," teaches the value of good relationships. The session for October 2, "An Ordered Life," examines Proverbs 28:1–29:27 to explore how we can experience safety and security by trusting in God. On October 9 we move from Proverbs to Ecclesiastes 9:13–10:20 to appreciate "The Superiority of Wisdom." Ecclesiastes 11:7–12:14, the basis for the lesson on October 16, looks at "Wisdom for Aging." The unit ends on October 23 with "Tradition and Love," a lesson from the love poetry of Song of Solomon 4:8–5:1.

In Unit 2, "Jesus Teaches Wisdom," we will look at portions of the Sermon on the Mount to see how Jesus used traditional wisdom in his own teachings. The first four lessons, based on Matthew 5 and 6, investigate what Jesus says to the disciples about living, forgiving, loving, and praying. In the fifth lesson Jesus teaches us how to live without worrying. We begin on October 30 with a study of the Beatitudes in Matthew 5:1-12 to learn how we can seek true happiness by "Living as God's People." "Forgiving as God's People," the session for November 6, delves into Matthew 5:17-26 to help us discern how we can live in harmony with other people. We learn how to adopt an attitude of love, even for our enemies, as we study Matthew 5:43-48 in the lesson for November 13 titled "Loving as God's People." In Matthew 6:5-15, the Scripture for November 20, Jesus teaches us how we are to be "Praying as God's People." The unit and quarter end on November 27 with "Facing Life Without Worry," a session based on Matthew 6:25-34 in which Jesus reminds us that we need not be anxious because God knows our needs and will care for us.

MEET OUR WRITER

THE REVEREND DR. STEPHEN C. RETTENMAYER

Steve Rettenmayer is an ordained United Methodist pastor who retired in 2009, having been a member of the Baltimore-Washington Conference since 1970. He served churches in that conference as well as an international, interdenominational congregation in London, England, for four years. While in London, Steve was a regular commentator on a popular BBC radio program where he was asked to give a Christian perspective on current issues and everyday events.

A native of Canton, Illinois, Steve attended Dickinson College in Carlisle, Pennsylvania, where he graduated magna cum laude with honors in Greek. His theological degrees are from Union Theological Seminary in Richmond, Virginia, including a year of theological studies at the universities of Bern and Basel in Switzerland. Before attending college, Steve played clarinet and saxophone with the United States Marine Band, "The President's Own," in Washington, DC. He still loves music, regularly plays his clarinet and piano, and teaches private music lessons. He is also an avid tennis fan and player and enjoys reading.

Steve's continuing passion in ministry is teaching and helping to support and train pastors. He has taught the Old Testament Prophets at Saint Mary's Seminary and University in Baltimore and is currently a faculty member of the Course of Study School of Wesley Theological Seminary in Washington, DC, where he teaches a course for local pastors in theology. He is also an adjunct faculty member of the Jerusalem Center for Biblical Studies, teaching and leading tours to the Holy Land. Whenever possible, Steve enjoys consulting with and leading continuing education opportunities with pastors and has done so internationally in Lithuania and Zimbabwe.

Steve's wife, Linda, is also a United Methodist pastor, and together they love to travel and spend time with their family. They are the parents of three grown boys: Wesley, Joshua, and Nathaniel.

THE BIG PICTURE: SURVEYING TRADITION AND WISDOM

The Scripture readings this quarter represent a unique combination of passages from both the Old Testament and the New Testament, all gathered together under the umbrella theme of "Tradition and Wisdom." As a noun, "wisdom" is defined in *The Oxford American College Dictionary* as "the quality of having experience, knowledge, and good judgment" as well as "the soundness of an action or decision" based on such "experience, knowledge, and good judgment." We might say of someone: "Her wisdom shone through in the decision she made or the advice she gave." Such a statement implies that the person being described demonstrated good knowledge of a particular subject as well as sound judgment and common sense. A second dictionary definition of wisdom is "the body of knowledge and principles that develops within a specified society or period." One such society and period that had an important "body of knowledge and principles" that was passed on through the generations was Israel in the Old Testament period.

In the context of the Bible, we speak of wisdom as both a tradition and a genre of literature. Narrowly defined, "Wisdom Literature" includes the biblical books of Job, Proverbs, Ecclesiastes, and Song of Solomon in the canonical Old Testament. In addition, we could include those psalms that are specifically called "Wisdom Psalms" (for example, Psalms 1, 37, 49, 73) and two of the apocryphal/deuterocanonical books that are found in some versions of the Bible: Wisdom of Solomon and Ecclesiasticus (The Wisdom of Jesus Son of Sirach). Understood more broadly, the wisdom tradition influenced many passages in the Bible; for example, the story of the wise man Joseph (Genesis 37–50), some of the prophets (especially Amos), the teachings of Jesus, and other parts of the New Testament (for example, James 3:17). Christians have traditionally understood Rabbi Jesus to be the Master Teacher, the wisest of all teachers. Five of the thirteen lessons in this quarter's material are from Jesus' Sermon on the Mount in Matthew 5–6.

Wisdom Literature is practical and concerns daily living. Most every culture has a wisdom tradition, if nothing more than proverbs and wise sayings passed down from generation to generation that teach valuable truths in everyday settings. For example, in our culture we have such popular proverbs as "the early bird catches the worm" and "a stitch in time saves nine." Parents and teachers pass on such proverbs to their children in the educational process of equipping them with practical wisdom to deal with life's challenges.

This would have been true in Israel as well. The origins of Israelite Wisdom Literature lie in the oral and written insights of family and clan, as well as in the teachings of professional "wise men" who would have provided training in a more formal educational process and in the courts of royal Jerusalem. Serving as counselors for the king, these wise men sometimes gave counsel that God's prophets rejected. Isaiah (29:14), Jeremiah (18:18), and Ezekiel (7:26) all make reference to such a group of wise men or elders and proclaim God's judgment against the false counsel they gave the king on particular occasions. On the whole, however, Israel's wisdom teachers were respected as they looked at life with discerning eyes and shrewd minds to observe what makes for a happy and successful life. Wisdom Literature is intended to pass on the lessons of life that are learned from living in God's world and observing the created order, so that others can find meaning in life and better cope with life's challenges.

Most ancient Near Eastern cultures had wisdom traditions. We know from ancient written sources that there were wise men in the courts of Egypt, Babylonia, Persia, and other neighboring lands whose function was to give wise counsel to the royal leaders and to educate their sons to be their successors, as well as to educate other young people in the ways of proper conduct in serving royalty for the good of the order of the kingdom. In 1 Kings 4:30-31, passing reference is made to the wise men of surrounding nations. The influence of such international wisdom on Israel's wisdom tradition can be seen in Proverbs 22:17–24:22 where scholars have seen many parallels to the *Instructions* of the famous Egyptian wise man Amen-em-ope, whose teachings can be dated to some time between 1000 and 600 B.C. The magi who traveled hundreds of miles to worship Jesus (Matthew 2:1-12) were probably members of the class of wise men from ancient Persia. We turn now to look at some of the basic themes or topics that were addressed in Israel's Wisdom Literature.

The Two Ways. At the heart of Wisdom Literature is the doctrine of the Two Ways: The way of the wicked leads to punishment and death; the way of the righteous leads to reward and life. The wise choose the righteous way, the outcome of which is blessing; and the fool chooses the wicked way, the outcome of which is disaster. In many of Israel's proverbs, as well as the wisdom psalms, the fool is set over against the wise person, and the righteous person is contrasted with the wicked. Jesus draws on this tradition in Matthew 7:13-14, 24-27, where he declares that the gate leading to destruction is wide, while the gate leading to life is narrow. He goes on to draw a contrast between the wise who hear his words and act on them by building their houses on solid rock and the foolish who ignore his words by building their houses on sand.

Choices. Wisdom Literature is very aware that life is a relentless series of choices, and each choice has consequences—good or bad. Over and over we find ourselves standing at the proverbial fork in the road, and we must choose which path to take. Not to choose, whether out of fear of the unknown or from a sense of helplessness, is a choice in itself. The wisdom teachers stood firmly in the theological tradition that honored both God's sovereignty and human freedom, the freedom to say yes or no to God. God freely chooses to love us, and as persons created in the image of God, we are given the freedom to choose whether we will love God in return. Of course, the wisdom tradition always urges us to choose the way of justice and faithful living, the way of obedience to God's commandments that leads to blessing. This is in keeping with many other Old Testament passages in which God invites us to choose life, to choose God's gracious way. (For example, see Deuteronomy 30:15-20; Joshua 24:15; Isaiah 55:1-7.)

The Order Inherent in Creation. The main core of Wisdom Literature assumes there is a divinely implanted order in the universe and that success in life comes when one discovers and accepts, not rebels against, one's place in that order. We find this even in the Book of Job, which is written as a protest against some of the teachings of traditional wisdom. After Job has spent most of the book complaining about what he perceives to be a divine miscarriage of justice, in chapters 38–41 God responds with a lengthy recitation of God's sovereignty and power in creating the universe, and God refutes Job's denial of divine order. In the Book of Proverbs, Wisdom is personified as a woman (Dame Wisdom) who was God's first act of creation and thereafter God's helper and daily delight in the process of creating the universe and bringing about cosmic order (Proverbs 3:19-20; 8:22-31).

Part of wisdom's task in ancient Israel was to teach people to know their place in the order of things. Israel understood its social order in a three-tiered fashion: God, king, and people.

For the most part that order provided security and assurance. The wisdom teachers taught that, as long as the people were obedient to God's covenant and the king was obedient to God and just in his governing, all would be well, and God would bless their community. Kings were charged with keeping moral order and preventing social chaos by removing evil and wickedness from the realm so that they could rule in righteousness (see Proverbs 25:4-5; 28:3-4, 16; 29:2, 4, 14). As kings were to be obedient to God in order to rule justly, so the people were to be obedient to God and the king, and children were to obey their parents.

It should be no surprise, therefore, that the concept of "discipline" appears over and over in Proverbs. The wisdom teachers speak both of the Lord's discipline of us and the discipline practiced by parents in raising their children (Proverbs 3:11-12). Teachers warn that discipline is the key to raising children in the "fear of the LORD," so that they might be successful and happy adults and citizens. Discipline can be understood in two senses in Israel's Wisdom Literature: as chastening or correcting someone and as instruction and learning in the school of wisdom.

The Fear of the Lord. At first glance, Wisdom Literature can seem quite secular. There are not nearly as many references to God and to the salvation themes typically found in the historical and prophetic books of the Old Testament, such as God's activity in history, the call to covenant faithfulness, and God's judgment of those who break the covenant. In their place in Wisdom Literature is an emphasis upon human reason, learning, experience, responsibility, and decision making in ordering human community. Look, for example, at the story of Joseph in Genesis 37–50, which was highly influenced by Israel's wisdom tradition. God is not mentioned often in the story, but at certain critical points we are reminded that God is constantly in the background guiding events, and it is God who gives Joseph his wisdom and directs his life (Genesis 39:21-23; 41:16; 45:4-9; 50:20).

The situation is similar in Proverbs, Ecclesiastes, and the rest of biblical Wisdom Literature. Although it had its origin in family and clan circles and the teaching of the elders, Israel's wisdom tradition was highly influenced by its monotheistic faith. The result is that, here and there, throughout Israel's Wisdom Literature are strong reminders that the real source of wisdom is the Lord. "The fear of the LORD is the beginning of knowledge" (Proverbs 1:7) or "wisdom" (9:10). "The LORD gives wisdom" (2:6) and "the fear of the LORD is instruction in wisdom" (15:33). The word "fear" can mean dread or terror, but used in relation to God, fear has more the sense of reverence, awe, and piety. In the biblical understanding, fearing God expresses a trusting relationship with God and a commitment to God that results in the worship of God and obedience to God's will. Proverbs 29:25-26 affirms that "one who trusts in the LORD is secure," and "it is from the LORD that one gets justice." Even the cynical Teacher in Ecclesiastes, whose understanding of God is that of a mysterious, inscrutable Being whose working and ways are beyond challenge and human understanding (3:11; 7:13-14; 8:16-17; 11:5), ultimately calls for faith and obedience to God (12:1, 13-14).

The Power of Words. Throughout Israel's Wisdom Literature, especially Proverbs, we find an understanding of the power of the tongue, and there are many directions about proper and improper speech. See Proverbs 15:23, 26, 28 and Ecclesiastes 9:17 as examples. Over and over Proverbs reminds us of the importance of weighing our words before we speak, for once a word is uttered it cannot be taken back. Wisdom urges us to give forethought and reflection before answering, so that we might employ our words for constructive rather than destructive purposes. We find particular warnings against speech that flows from rage or uncontrolled anger. Jesus understood the power of well-chosen words as well as the danger of uncontrolled anger (for example, see Matthew 5:21-26, 33-37).

Jesus and the Wisdom Tradition. I close with some comments about Jesus' relationship to the wisdom tradition of Israel and the manner in which he used wisdom concepts and images in his preaching and teaching. I have already noted Jesus' reference to the wide and narrow gates that lead, respectively, to destruction and life (Matthew 7:13-14) and Jesus' contrast between the "wise man" and the "foolish man" (7:24-27). Certainly Jesus is understood in the Gospels as a wise teacher. Mark records how astounded people were when they heard him speak: "Where did this man get all this? What is this wisdom that has been given to him?" (Mark 6:2). On another occasion Jesus made reference to the renowned wisdom of King Solomon, reputed to have been the wisest man in Israel's past, when Jesus said of himself, "Something greater than Solomon is here!" (Matthew 12:42; Luke 11:31). On yet another occasion Jesus speaks of "the Wisdom of God" (Luke 11:49) as a way of describing God's will and purposes.

Like a true wisdom teacher, Jesus used wisdom gained from life experience and his observation of the created order to teach valuable truths. Can we add a single hour to our life span by worrying (Matthew 6:27)? Clearly not. In Matthew 6:25-30 he drives home his point about God's providential care for us by drawing on his observation of nature (the "birds of the air" and the "lilies of the field" in verses 26, 28), a standard technique used by wisdom teachers. In Matthew 11:16-19 Jesus points to the everyday scene of children playing a game in the marketplace and then invites a comparison of his generation to that scene, in order to make his point that the religious leaders were looking for someone to fit into their mold and their expectations, which neither John the Baptist nor Jesus did. Jesus then compares himself with personified Wisdom by saying, "wisdom is vindicated by her deeds" (Matthew 11:19). We remember that the image of Dame Wisdom is found in Proverbs 8:1–9:6, where Wisdom is depicted as a hostess at a banquet who has prepared the finest meal and then invites those who are simple and humble to come partake of her food and enjoy her company (9:1-6). There are definite parallels between Dame Wisdom's invitation and Jesus' invitation to "come to me, all you that are weary and are carrying heavy burdens, and I will give you rest" (Matthew 11:28). These are just some of the Gospel references that express Jesus' relationship to and rootedness in the language and tradition of wisdom in Israel.

CLOSE-UP:
TEACHING WORDS
OF WISDOM

This quarter's sessions spotlight the traditional wisdom that the Bible considers essential for a sound relationship with God and other people. As we read both the Old and New Testaments we become aware of the importance of passing on traditions to children and to those who have never been exposed to these truths. After hearing the great commandment to love God in Deuteronomy 6, listeners are told not only to keep these words in their own hearts but also to "recite them to your children and talk about them" (6:7). As in biblical times, so today parents are still children's first and usually most influential teachers, both by their words and by their example.

As was true in the early Gentile church, many contemporary parents have not had encounters with God and experiences in the church that would enable them to teach their children how to live according to God's ways. Consequently, the church needs to be intentional about offering Sunday school, vacation Bible school, before and after school programs, choirs, and youth groups so that children and youth might learn about God and decide to enter into a personal relationship with Jesus. The church also has an opportunity to aid parents in deepening their relationship with and knowledge of God for their own benefit, which in turn can help their children. But the fact that many of today's parents have not participated in Christian education and worship themselves is also a potential crisis because they may see no need for their children to be involved with God and the church, which they may consider unimportant or irrelevant.

Church members will want to welcome parents and children alike and make them feel at home throughout the building. Newcomers would like to be invited to attend classes and activities. All who interact with children and youth, especially in leadership roles, must show by their words and example that these young people are respected and valued as part of the family of God. While the adage "children are the future of the church" is true, it is equally true that they are the present of the church. The congregation needs to treat them as such so that they may grow in their relationship with Jesus and learn how to live wisely as members of God's family.

While the biblical model of parents teaching children is still essential, a vibrant church will also offer "the old, old story" in fresh, exciting ways that children can relate to. Children and youth want to interact with their peers, not just listen to an adult talk. Today's young people want to see and experience the story, not just hear it. They need age-appropriate opportunities to learn, serve, fellowship, and worship. They can be encouraged to express themselves in song, dance, movement, art, poetry, and other means that allow them to more fully encounter the good news. Technology that is familiar to them can enhance learning and provide ways for them to keep in touch with one another. Teaching methods have changed over the centuries, but the message of God's unconditional love for us is still the same. We are called to share it.

FAITH IN ACTION: LIVING WISELY IN THE KINGDOM OF GOD

During the first unit of this quarter we are studying the wisdom passed on from teacher to student or parent to child, from one generation to the next. In the second unit we hear wise words from Jesus as he taught on the Mount. How, though, do we incorporate this wisdom into our own lives? Use this activity to help the adults do that.

Post a sheet of newsprint as the quarter begins. Create a list of key verses by adding the current week's key verse to the newsprint. Each week, encourage the students to memorize the key verse from a translation of their individual choosing. At the end of the quarter, recall what you have learned by discussing the following questions, either with the whole class or in small groups. If you choose to work in groups, post the questions on newsprint so that all may see them. If time allows, call on each group to report their findings for at least one question to the total class.

1. **Look at our key verses and recall what you have learned during this quarter. What do you believe to be the core ideas of wise living in God's kingdom?**
2. **Which of these verses represent a wise way that you find difficult to follow? Why?** (Recognize that some students will agree in principle with a verse but find it challenging to follow. Try to identify the stumbling blocks. For example, our first key verse, Proverbs 3:5, calls us to trust God with all our heart, but when the going gets tough we may want to trust our money, brains, education, position, or something else. What do we need to do to learn to let go and allow God to handle the situation?)
3. **How might the class help individuals to live more wisely? What might the church do to model wise living?** (Think, for example, about Matthew 6:33-34, the key verses for our last session. Here Jesus calls us to strive first for the kingdom of God *and* to set aside all worry about the future. If a situation is looming large in the congregation— let's say a financial crisis is on the horizon—what might the church do to show how to stay focused on the Kingdom without worrying about money?)
4. **As you look at the list of key verses and consider their implications, how do you think the lives of individual Christians and the congregation as a body would be different if we really put these teachings into practice?**
5. **If Christians put these teachings into practice, what opportunities might arise for authentic witnessing, particularly to unbelievers, about what it means to live in close proximity to the kingdom of God?**

Conclude your time together by challenging the adults to be alert for opportunities to teach these words of wisdom to others, especially those generations that follow them. Remind participants that they need to hear the Word, understand it, and set an example for others as to how to live out the Word.

UNIT 1: TEACHING AND LEARNING
RIGHTEOUSNESS AND WISDOM

PREVIEWING THE LESSON

Lesson Scripture: Proverbs 3:1-12
Background Scripture: Proverbs 3:1-35
Key Verse: Proverbs 3:5

Focus of the Lesson:
People want their lives to have purpose and meaning. Is there a way of living that really works toward that end? Proverbs is rooted in a tradition of instruction that encourages godly living.

Goals for the Learners:
(1) to recognize God's principles for living true and fulfilled lives.
(2) to honor God.
(3) to trust God with their whole hearts.

Pronunciation Guide:
hubris (hyoo' bris)
musar (moo sawr')
shalom (shah lohm')
Torah (toh' ruh)

Supplies:
Bibles, newsprint and marker, paper and pencils, hymnals

READING THE SCRIPTURE

NRSV
Proverbs 3:1-12
1 My child, do not forget my teaching,
but let your heart keep my
commandments;
2 for length of days and years of life
and abundant welfare they will give
you.

NIV
Proverbs 3:1-12
1My son, do not forget my teaching,
but keep my commands in your heart,
2for they will prolong your life many years
and bring you prosperity.
3Let love and faithfulness never leave you;
bind them around your neck,

3 Do not let loyalty and faithfulness
   forsake you;
    bind them around your neck,
    write them on the tablet of your heart.
4 So you will find favor and good repute
   in the sight of God and of people.
5 **Trust in the LORD with all your heart,**
   and do not rely on your own insight.
6 In all your ways acknowledge him,
   and he will make straight your paths.
7 Do not be wise in your own eyes;
   fear the LORD, and turn away from evil.
8 It will be a healing for your flesh
   and a refreshment for your body.
9 Honor the LORD with your substance
   and with the first fruits of all your
    produce;
10 then your barns will be filled with plenty,
   and your vats will be bursting with
    wine.
11 My child, do not despise the LORD's
   discipline
   or be weary of his reproof,
12 for the LORD reproves the one he loves,
   as a father the son in whom he delights.

   write them on the tablet of your
    heart.
4Then you will win favor and a good name
   in the sight of God and man.
5**Trust in the LORD with all your heart**
   and lean not on your own
    understanding;
6in all your ways acknowledge him,
   and he will make your paths straight.
7Do not be wise in your own eyes;
   fear the LORD and shun evil.
8This will bring health to your body
   and nourishment to your bones.
9Honor the LORD with your wealth,
   with the firstfruits of all your crops;
10then your barns will be filled to
    overflowing,
   and your vats will brim over with new
    wine.
11My son, do not despise the LORD's
   discipline
   and do not resent his rebuke,
12because the LORD disciplines those he
    loves,
   as a father the son he delights in.

UNDERSTANDING THE SCRIPTURE

Introduction. In chapters 1 through 9 of Proverbs is found a series of advice-giving compositions commonly referred to as instructions. These instructions make frequent use of the command form of the verb and are addressed to the student as if spoken by a mother or father to "my child" (for example, 1:8; 2:1; 3:1, 21) or "my children" (7:24; see also 4:1). The instructions provide a kind of moral map for living life with meaning and purpose based upon "trust in the LORD" (3:5, today's key verse). Chapter 3 includes two sections of instructions: verses 1-12 deal with the theme of trusting in the Lord, and verses 21-35 focus on right behavior toward other people. In contrast, verses 13-20 are written in the style of a poem or hymn that praises God's gift of wisdom and articulates the value and benefits of wisdom.

Proverbs 3:1-4. In verse 1 the Hebrew word translated as "teaching" is *torah*, the technical term for law or instruction in the Old Testament. In Hebrew thought the "heart" (see also verses 3 and 5) was understood as the center of emotions, feelings, and passions, as well as intellectual activity. In verse 3 are three commands related to two very important words at the core of Israel's understanding of their covenant with God: "loyalty" and "faithfulness." These words are often used together, as they are here, in describing God's steadfast love and faithfulness, God's utter reliability in word and deed to humans. Note the commandments to "bind them around your neck" and "write them on the tablet of your heart." The "them" can refer to both the "teaching and commandments" of verse 1 and the "loyalty and faithfulness" of verse 3. In ancient Israel, as in orthodox Judaism today, amulets containing sacred writing were bound about the neck and thus worn close to the heart as reminders to be obedient to God's covenant with Israel. (See Proverbs 1:9; 6:20-21; 7:1-3; and Deuteronomy 6:6, 8.) Note also that the commands found in verses 1 and 3 are followed by clauses in verses 2 and 4 describing the benefits that come from obeying the commands.

Proverbs 3:5-8. The three commands in verses 5 and 6a help define one another. To trust in the Lord with total commitment ("with all your heart") means not to rely on one's own cleverness and understanding but to acknowledge and confess God in all of our conduct ("all your ways"). The word "insight" in verse 5 is normally a positive term in Hebrew Wisdom Literature indicating an intellectual virtue of keen understanding given by God. But when it is set in opposition to trusting in the Lord, it becomes sinful hubris or pride. Verse 7 reinforces what is said in verse 5. If we trust only in our own wisdom and the work of our own hands, that leaves no room for the "fear of the LORD" (see 3:7) or trusting God to guide our lives. Verses 6b and 8 express the benefits that ensue from wholehearted trust in the Lord: a sense of health and well-being and the assurance and peace of knowing that God will guide our every step through life.

Proverbs 3:9-12. In verse 9 there are echoes of Deuteronomy 26:1-11, which speaks of honoring God by bringing the first fruits of the ground to the Temple priest. Verse 10 expresses the consequence of honoring and obeying God: God will faithfully and abundantly provide for our needs. In verses 11-12 God is likened to a father who lovingly disciplines and corrects his children when they need it. The wisdom teachers were realistic and knew that

perfect obedience was impossible. Therefore, God would need to discipline and correct even the most faithful from time to time. But always God's discipline is to be understood as an expression of God's love.

Proverbs 3:13-18. Verse 13 is a beatitude stating a blessing upon those who attain wisdom from God. "Understanding" is used often in Proverbs as a synonym for "wisdom," and the two words are frequently found together (see 3:19). Verses 14-18 contain a succession of motive clauses stating the rewards of wisdom and why the person who finds wisdom is blessed. Wisdom is of more value than gold or silver or precious stones (3:14-15). Whoever finds and practices wisdom is promised long life along with riches and honor (3:16; see also 3:2). Knowing that the word "honor" was used in 3:9, we are reminded that whoever in wisdom honors God with tithes and offerings receives honor in return. The "peace" mentioned in verse 17 as a further benefit of wisdom is a translation of the Hebrew *shalom*; thus it carries a holistic understanding of harmony, well-being, peace, and wholeness in life. In verse 18, wisdom is likened to a life-producing tree that offers the blessing of nourishing fruit.

Proverbs 3:19-20. With the blessings of wisdom having been enumerated, wisdom is now commended to the young by elevating it and linking it to God's work of creating the universe. Wisdom is pictured as a very important tool in God's creative hands. Creation through Wisdom is more fully elaborated and personified as a woman in Proverbs 8:22-31. If God, in using Wisdom, can accomplish the wonders of creation, just think what God can do in the lives of those who open their hearts and minds to receive God's wisdom.

Proverbs 3:21-26. Verse 21 begins another section of this chapter with a return to instruction signaled by "My child." The theme of this instruction is correct relations with other people. The command in verse 21 to "keep sound wisdom and prudence" is followed by a listing of benefits (3:22-26) that come to those who use sound discretion and make wise choices flowing from their trust in God. No matter what they face, God will be their confidence and security and will give them peaceful sleep.

Proverbs 3:27-31. These verses contain a series of negative admonitions all beginning with the command "Do not. . . ." The call is to "do no harm" but rather "do good," two of John Wesley's *General Rules*, in our relationships with neighbors.

Proverbs 3:32-35. These verses, which present reasons for not envying "the violent" of verse 31, are arranged as a succession of contrasts, with the second half of each verse beginning with "but." Those who are righteous and trust in the Lord are contrasted with those who are perverse and wicked. The former are wise and are blessed by the Lord, while the latter are "stubborn fools" (3:35) who will inherit disgrace.

INTERPRETING THE SCRIPTURE

The Benefits and Rewards of Wisdom

Proverbs 3:1-12 lists many rewards and benefits that accrue from trusting God and being faithful to God's Torah and commandments, which is what the Bible means by wise living. People find favor and good repute in the sight of God and others; they experience material abundance, God's daily guidance, peace, well-being, health, and long life. As suggested earlier, the very structure of Proverbs 3:1-12 prompts us to anticipate these benefits. In verses 1, 3, 5, 6a, 7, 9, and 11 the command form of the verb carries the weight of authority of the teacher instructing students in wise and godly living. The alternating verses 2, 4, 6b, 8, 10, and 12 are clauses that convey rewards or consequences that await those who are obedient.

The argument seems to be this: If you diligently seek wisdom and you trust in the Lord with all your heart, relying on God to guide you in all your endeavors, you will be rewarded with the variety of benefits listed. On the whole, probably most of us find this to be true in our life's experience. As we seek to live Christ-like lives, treating others with love, respect, and kindness, we experience many of the benefits spoken of in Proverbs 3: the joy of God's presence and guidance, peace, well-being, and wholeness

in our relationships. And when we seek to be good stewards of our bodies and financial or material resources, we may even experience material abundance and good physical health.

But can all of these benefits and rewards be guaranteed? I think the answer to that question is no. The wisdom tradition in the Old Testament (expressed primarily in Job, Ecclesiastes, Proverbs, and some of the Psalms) was largely based on what was known as the doctrine of retribution. This doctrine, which also provided the basis for much of the thinking in the Prophets, held that God punishes the wicked and rewards the righteous. Put in a simple formula, it said that sin equals suffering and disease, while righteousness (faithfulness and obedience to God) equals prosperity and health. Wisdom teachers traditionally taught, as we see here in Proverbs 3, that trusting in the Lord and practicing good conduct would inevitably lead to long life and many other benefits.

However, within the wisdom tradition itself are protests against an overly mechanistic interpretation of this doctrine based on the wisdom teachers' own observations. Their personal experience, especially Job's, told them that sometimes the wicked prosper and the righteous suffer. We, too, might lift our voices in protest against any tradition that teaches that these rewards and benefits are guaranteed or that they will always and automatically be there for us. For our experience tells us that the faithful and the God-fearing are not always rewarded with good health and long life; accidents happen, cancer strikes, and tragedies occur even in the lives of the most faithful believers.

Nevertheless, there is, in general, a correlation between happiness and wholeness in life and our trusting in God. Relying on God and living faithfully by God's commandments bring a positive outlook on life, fulfilling relationships, and many internal spiritual rewards not measured by outward standards. In this sense the wisdom tradition is correct. I think of Paul's words in Philippians 4 where he writes of a deep inner joy and peace promised to believers in even the most difficult of circumstances; such joy and peace, like wisdom, are of more value than all the silver and gold and precious jewels in the world. (See also the promises of Proverbs 3:22-26.)

The Limitations of Human Wisdom

In general, in the Bible's Wisdom Literature there is a strong focus on human responsibility, education, and decision making in ordering human community. Yet at the same time there is an intense awareness that the effectiveness of human wisdom is limited. Proverbs constantly urges us to seek understanding, wisdom, and insight (for example, Proverbs 3:1, 13, 21; 4:7; and many other places). Yet side by side with these commands are verses like Proverbs 3:5, 7: "Trust in the LORD with all your heart, and do not rely on your own insight. . . . Do not be wise in your own eyes." All the teaching, observation, and life experience in the world do not provide enough wisdom to guide us successfully through life if we do not primarily rely on God.

Throughout the Bible's Wisdom Literature are found warnings against the use of wisdom apart from faith in God. Historically, as Israel borrowed and adapted wisdom teachings and proverbs from Egypt and other more secular cultures, Israel incorporated them into the context of her faith in the living God. As a result, the starting point for true wisdom became the "fear of the LORD" (see 3:7 in our passage; see also 1:7; 9:10; 15:33; and 19:23). In the final analysis, if wisdom is to be a successful guide in directing us through life, it must always be used in relationship to our trusting in God with all of our heart (3:5). God is the giver of true wisdom (2:6). For other passages in Proverbs that express the spirit of Proverbs 3:5, 7, see 16:1, 9; 19:21; and 28:25-26.

The Lord's Discipline

Proverbs 3:11 reminds us to "not despise the LORD's discipline." The Hebrew term *musar*, translated here as "discipline," can mean discipline in the sense of chastening or correcting, which is the probable meaning in this verse in light of the verb "reprove" (NRSV) in verse 12. But *musar* can also mean discipline in the sense of instruction or learning in the school of wisdom. This same word is translated in the NRSV as "instruction" in Proverbs 1:2, 3, 7; 15:33; 23:23.

Persons who have achieved success in music or sports know how essential the discipline of regular practice is. A good student knows how vital the discipline of regular study habits is. When she was in school, my wife had a teacher who would remind the class over and over, "Discipline is the training that makes punishment unnecessary." And though we may not have appreciated it at the time, most of us are grateful for the discipline our parents dispensed, when our behavior deserved it, in order to help us grow into better women and men.

Here in Proverbs 3:11-12, God is likened to a loving parent who disciplines a child when that is necessary. According to the wisdom teachers, the presupposition behind the Lord's discipline is that God loves us, as a parent loves a child, and has our best interests in mind. Thus, we need not fear God's discipline. No matter how severe it may seem at the time, it is always an expression of God's love.

SHARING THE SCRIPTURE

Preparing Our Hearts

Explore this week's devotional reading, found in Psalm 115:3-11. In this liturgical prayer, the psalmist draws a sharp contrast between idols that can offer nothing and the steadfast God of Israel, who faithfully cares for the people. Israel is called to fear and trust in the Lord. Are you able to identify idols that you are now depending upon? If so, set them aside and renew your faith and trust in God.

Pray that you and the adult learners will be open to God's wisdom for living.

Preparing Our Minds

Study the background Scripture from Proverbs 3:1-35 and the lesson Scripture from Proverbs 3:1-12. Think about whether there is a way of life that leads toward purpose and understanding.

Write on newsprint:
❏ headings *Commands* and *Rewards* for "Recognize God's Principles for Living True and Fulfilled Lives."
❏ steps for "Trust God with One's Whole Heart."
❏ information for next week's lesson, found under "Continue the Journey."
❏ activities for further spiritual growth in "Continue the Journey."

Review the "Introduction" to the fall quarter, "The Big Picture," "Close-up," and "Faith in Action." Begin to decide how you will use this information during the coming thirteen weeks.

LEADING THE CLASS

(1) Gather to Learn

❖ Welcome the class members and introduce any guests.

❖ Pray that the students will seek a greater understanding of God's principles for living a true and fulfilled life.

❖ Read these quotations aloud and invite the adults to comment on how well a particular quotation reflects their ideas about finding meaning and purpose in life:
- **Many people have a wrong idea of what constitutes true happiness. It is not attained through self-gratification, but through fidelity to a worthy purpose.** (Helen Keller)
- **Focusing your life solely on making a buck shows a poverty of ambition. It asks too little of yourself. And it will leave you unfulfilled.** (Barack Obama)
- **Service is the rent we pay to be living. It is the very purpose of life and not something you do in your spare time.** (Marian Wright Edelman)
- **One needs something to believe in, something for which one can have whole-hearted enthusiasm. One needs to feel that one's life has meaning, that one is needed in this world.** (Hannah Senesh)
- **In the world to come, I shall not be asked, "Why were you not Moses?" I shall be asked, "Why were you not Zusya?"** (Rabbi Zusya)

❖ Read aloud today's focus statement: **People want their lives to have purpose and meaning. Is there a way of living that really works toward that end? Proverbs is rooted in a tradition of instruction that encourages godly living.**

(2) Recognize God's Principles for Living True and Fulfilled Lives

❖ Choose a volunteer to read Proverbs 3:1-12.

❖ Use the first paragraph of "The Benefits and Rewards of Wisdom" in Interpreting the Scripture and information from Understanding the Scripture to help the class see the relationship between the commands and rewards cited in the alternating verses. Post newsprint on which you create two columns, the one on the left labeled *Commands* and the one on the right labeled *Rewards*. Briefly write the *Commands / Rewards* as the students call them out. This chart may help the learners more easily see the relationship.

❖ Discuss: **What insights does this list offer to you for living today?**

❖ Form several small groups. Encourage each group to answer these questions:
> **(1) How do we as a congregation go about teaching God's wisdom to our young people?**
> **(2) What else could we do?**

❖ Bring everyone back together and encourage a speaker from each group to report their ideas.

❖ Conclude by reading the remainder of "The Benefits and Rewards of Wisdom" in Interpreting the Scripture.

(3) Honor God

❖ Invite several class members to read aloud Proverbs 3:9-10 from a variety of translations. Listen for nuances in meaning. Here are some translations you may not have readily available to add:

■ **Honour the LORD with your wealth and with the firstfruits of all your produce; then your granaries will be filled with grain and your vats will brim with new wine.** (Revised English Bible)

■ **Honour Yahweh with what goods you have and with the first-fruits of all your produce; then your barns will be filled with corn, your vats overflowing with new wine.** (New Jerusalem Bible)

■ **Honor the LORD by giving him your money and the first part of all your crops. Then you will have more grain and grapes than you will ever need.** (Contemporary English Version)

■ **Honor the Lord by making him an offering from the best of all that your land produces. If you do, your barns will be filled with grain, and you will have too much wine to store it all.** (Good News Translation)

■ **Honour the LORD with thy substance, and with the firstfruits of all thine increase: So shall thy barns be filled with plenty, and thy presses shall burst out with new wine.** (King James Version)

❖ Talk with the class about what it means to fulfill the command to "honor the LORD" (3:9). Also consider the rewards of fulfilling the command. (Be careful to distinguish between honoring God for God's own sake and doing so inappropriately in order to experience the benefits of God's radical abundance.)

❖ Provide a few moments of silence for the adults to contemplate this question:

How am I honoring God with the wealth and goods that I have?

(4) Trust God With One's Whole Heart

❖ Read aloud the first paragraph of "The Limitations of Human Wisdom" from Interpreting the Scripture.

❖ Reread the last sentence of that paragraph. Ask: **Why do you think Christians agree with this statement in theory but act as if it is untrue? Or, to phrase the question another way, why do you think we pay lip service to God while relying on our own limited human wisdom?**

❖ Distribute paper and pencils. Encourage the students to take the following steps, which you may wish to post on newsprint:

■ **Step 1: Identify a challenge or problem in your life that you have been trying to solve by relying mostly on human wisdom.**

■ **Step 2: Make a confidential commitment to turn this situation over to God.**

■ **Step 3: Offer a silent prayer that you will leave this situation in God's hands and trust God to set you on the right path.**

(5) Continue the Journey

❖ Break the silence by praying that today's participants will continue to grow spiritually so that they will trust God completely.

❖ Read aloud this preparation for next week's lesson. You may also want to post it on newsprint for the students to copy.

■ **Title: From Generation to Generation**
■ **Background Scripture: Proverbs 4:1-27**
■ **Lesson Scripture: Proverbs 4:10-15, 20-27**
■ **Focus of the Lesson: People want to live life to its fullest. Are there ways to live that will make that happen? Proverbs suggests that those who make good choices and keep a righteous path will find fulfillment in life.**

❖ Challenge the students to complete one or more of these activities for further spiritual growth related to this week's session. Post this information on newsprint for the students to copy.

(1) **Research the phrase "fear of the Lord," which is at the theological core of the teachings of Proverbs on wisdom. Where is this phrase used? What does it mean?**

(2) **List as many sayings or proverbs popular in your culture as you can within five minutes. Do any on your list reveal God's wisdom? What do they suggest about the behaviors considered important in your society?**

(3) **Consider the value of God's wisdom. How would your own life be different if you were to pay greater attention to this divine wisdom?**

❖ Sing or read aloud "Trust and Obey."

❖ Conclude today's session by leading the class in this benediction adapted from Proverbs 3:5 and 29:25: **Go forth trusting in the Lord with all your heart, knowing that one who trusts in the Lord is secure.**

UNIT 1: TEACHING AND LEARNING
FROM GENERATION TO GENERATION

PREVIEWING THE LESSON

Lesson Scripture: Proverbs 4:10-15, 20-27
Background Scripture: Proverbs 4:1-27
Key Verse: Proverbs 4:13

Focus of the Lesson:
People want to live life to its fullest. Are there ways to live that will make that happen? Proverbs suggests that those who make good choices and keep a righteous path will find fulfillment in life.

Goals for the Learners:
(1) to review the instruction from Proverbs about living a wise and balanced life.
(2) to reflect on the meaning of doing the right thing and following a straight path.
(3) to develop strategies of making good choices and living a godly life.

Pronunciation Guide:
musar (moo sawr')
Torah (toh' ruh)

Supplies:
Bibles, newsprint and marker, paper and pencils, hymnals, optional copy of Robert Frost's poem "The Road Not Taken"

READING THE SCRIPTURE

NRSV
Proverbs 4:10-15, 20-27
10 Hear, my child, and accept my words,
    that the years of your life may be many.
11 I have taught you the way of wisdom;
    I have led you in the paths of
      uprightness.

NIV
Proverbs 4:10-15, 20-27
10Listen, my son, accept what I say,
    and the years of your life will be
      many.
11I guide you in the way of wisdom
    and lead you along straight paths.

12 When you walk, your step will not be hampered; and if you run, you will not stumble.	12When you walk, your steps will not be hampered; when you run, you will not stumble.
13 **Keep hold of instruction; do not let go; guard her, for she is your life.**	13**Hold on to instruction, do not let it go; guard it well, for it is your life.**
14 Do not enter the path of the wicked, and do not walk in the way of evildoers.	14Do not set foot on the path of the wicked or walk in the way of evil men.
15 Avoid it; do not go on it; turn away from it and pass on. . . .	15Avoid it, do not travel on it; turn from it and go on your way. . . .
20 My child, be attentive to my words; incline your ear to my sayings.	20My son, pay attention to what I say; listen closely to my words.
21 Do not let them escape from your sight; keep them within your heart.	21Do not let them out of your sight, keep them within your heart;
22 For they are life to those who find them, and healing to all their flesh.	22for they are life to those who find them and health to a man's whole body.
23 Keep your heart with all vigilance, for from it flow the springs of life.	23Above all else, guard your heart, for it is the wellspring of life.
24 Put away from you crooked speech, and put devious talk far from you.	24Put away perversity from your mouth; keep corrupt talk far from your lips.
25 Let your eyes look directly forward, and your gaze be straight before you.	25Let your eyes look straight ahead, fix your gaze directly before you.
26 Keep straight the path of your feet, and all your ways will be sure.	26Make level paths for your feet and take only ways that are firm.
27 Do not swerve to the right or to the left; turn your foot away from evil.	27Do not swerve to the right or the left; keep your foot from evil.

UNDERSTANDING THE SCRIPTURE

Introduction. Unlike Proverbs 3, which we looked at in the last lesson, in chapter 4 any reference to "the Lord" is conspicuous by its absence. The main point being expressed about wisdom is not that the beginning of wisdom is "the fear of the LORD" (9:10), nor is there a call to trust in the Lord as opposed to relying on one's own insight (3:5). Rather, the focus is upon listening attentively to the wisdom that is passed on by the elders from generation to generation. Because Proverbs 4 is part of *Israel's* tradition, it can be assumed that what is stated explicitly elsewhere (for example, 2:6; 9:10) is implied here. However, there are no explicit references to God or the Lord in chapter 4. The chapter consists of three discourses (verses 1-9, 10-

19, and 20-27), each beginning with a command to "children" or "my child" to listen or be attentive to the wisdom that is being handed on from past generations.

Proverbs 4:1-4. The mention of "mother" in verse 3 along with "father" in verses 1 and 3 would seem to indicate the setting of a home with parents passing on wisdom to their children as opposed to the setting of a school with interaction between teachers and students. However, in either setting the point is the same: Wisdom, which shows us the right way to walk in the world, is passed on from parents to children and grandchildren, from generation to generation, from elders to the youth. As in many native cultures today, in ancient Israel elders were revered and were considered to be storehouses of great wisdom for the younger generation. Parental wisdom brought insight and life itself (2:1; 3:2; 4:1, 4).

Proverbs 4:5-9. These verses are both an encouragement and an admonition to "get wisdom; get insight: do not forget, nor turn away" (4:5). A certain synergy is implied. Parents are faithful teachers and mediators of wisdom, but the children have an active role to play in learning and applying what they learn. Successful application toward the living of a life of faithfulness to God is the ultimate empirical test of wisdom's validity. The personal pronouns "her" and "she" in verses 6-9 refer to wisdom. As in chapters 1:20-33 and 8:4-36, Wisdom is personified in these verses. Lady (or Dame) Wisdom, as she has been called, is a wonderful literary device used in Wisdom Literature. It's as though we can enter into a kind of personal relationship with Wisdom and hear her voice speaking to us. As God used wisdom as a tool to help create the world (3:19), so God continues to use wisdom to nurture creation and to help guide God's people into a faithful walk with God in everyday life. Wisdom is to be highly valued, and Lady Wisdom will honor and reward us as we are faithful to her (4:8).

Proverbs 4:10-19. One of the most prominent themes in Wisdom Literature is the theme of the "two ways" or "two paths." The way of the wicked, those who are insolent and who do not rely on God, leads to punishment and death; the way of the righteous, those who trust God and hold fast to the instruction of their wise elders, leads to a full, rich, rewarding life. This is the major theme of verses 10-19. Verses 10-13 describe the right path, the way of wisdom, which leads to life. The parent or teacher has done his or her job to impart wisdom; now it is up to the child or student to follow through in a disciplined way to apply that wisdom in the daily walk of life. The word "instruction" in 4:13 is a translation of the Hebrew *musar*, which, as we saw in the last lesson, can be translated also as "discipline." As

with the discipline of an athlete in training, it takes commitment and daily discipline to begin the walk and to continue down the path that wisdom forges, but the reward is worth it: It leads to life (4:13).

Verses 14-17 describe the wrong path, the way of the wicked, which leads to violence and destruction. The Hebrew verbs in 4:14-15 are strong in expressing a prohibition for us *not* to walk in this path. "Avoid it; do not go on it" (4:15). The image of insomnia in 4:16 is fascinating. Wrongdoing plays such a central role in the daily routine of the wicked that they cannot sleep if they have not committed evil during the day. As William McKane writes in *Proverbs: A New Approach*: "In their addiction to evil, they are like the sleeping-pill addict who has been denied his daily dose."

Verses 18-19 summarize a contrast between the two paths. The path of righteousness is full of light and leads to an even brighter day. The path of wickedness is darkness and leads to destruction, for the wicked "do not know what they stumble over" (4:19). This thought reflects Jesus' words from the cross: "Father, forgive them; for they do not know what they are doing" (Luke 23:34). In both passages it would seem that not knowing or understanding, because people do not really know God, is an essential part of sin.

Proverbs 4:20-27. As with the other two discourses in this chapter, these verses begin with a series of commands for the child to be attentive and listen to the wise teachings of the parent. Verse 22 is a motive clause giving the reason why the parents' words should be obeyed: Attentive listening and application of the words of wisdom will bring life and health and healing. As we saw in last week's lesson, the "heart" (4:23) in Hebrew thought was considered to be the center of intellectual activity as well as the center of a person's emotions, feelings, and passions. It is from the "heart" or "mind" that "flow the springs of life" (4:23). The implication of 4:23-27 is this: If we guard our heart and keep it pure, then all the other functions of our body—our speech, our vision, our walking—will be pure and straight, because they flow from the heart.

INTERPRETING THE SCRIPTURE

Voices From the Grave

Tradition. One of my favorite Broadway musicals is *Fiddler on the Roof*. Tevye, the lead character, is always singing and talking about "tradition." Tradition is a double-edged sword. It can be a positive thing, the solid foundation on which we stand to build a brighter future. Tradition can be understood as a gift from those who have gone before us and whose experience and teaching can guide our path as we journey onward in life. But tradition can also be a negative force. It can imprison us within its deathly grip, keeping us mired in the mud of its landscape and prohibiting us from taking a step forward. In other words, tradition can be the healthy launching pad that sends us into an exciting new future, or it can be the poison that kills our creative spirits by reminding us, "Don't try it. That's not the way we do things around here."

Matthew 15:1-9 reminds us that the religious leaders of his day often chastised Jesus for breaking "the tradition of the elders" (Matthew 15:2). Jesus had come to talk about the living spirit of God's Torah that leads to life, whereas the Pharisees were often champions of the dead letter of the law that only entangled people in the web of their human teachings and control.

Biblical Wisdom Literature affirms that tradition can be a positive force in our lives, something that can teach us and prepare us for the future without imprisoning us. G. K. Chesterton, one of the wisest of Christians, wrote: "Tradition means giving votes to the most obscure of all classes, our ancestors. It is the democracy of the dead. Tradition refuses to submit to the small and arrogant oligarchy of those who merely happen to be walking about. . . .We will have the dead at our councils." Yes, tradition at its best calls us to honor those voices from the grave that continue to speak wisdom to us and challenge us to live more purposeful lives. Somewhere in my years of training I heard the following maxim: "Something is not true simply because it's in the Bible. It's in the Bible because it's true." In other words, the Bible is a book full of wisdom and truth that has stood the test of time and proved itself in the crucible of everyday living to be genuine for every generation. That's why the Bible is called the living Word of God that transcends the barriers of time. Contrary to the popular thinking of a culture that worships youth, there is a grace and wisdom that comes with age and experience. Such grace and wisdom constitute tradition at its best.

A Lifelong Journey

In preparing couples for marriage, I always emphasize that a one-time "I do" at the altar will not last a lifetime of marriage. The expression of commitment needs to be affirmed again and again, day in and day out, for a rich and vibrant marriage to ensue. Like marriage, our spiritual walk is just that, a journey. Our commitment to God, as well as our experience of God's love for us, needs to be renewed over and over again in daily discipline and prayer, in Bible reading and regular worship.

Similarly, chapter 4 of Proverbs makes clear that seeking wisdom and walking in the path of wisdom is a lifelong pursuit, not a one-time occurrence. The command to listen and accept words of wisdom (4:10) ends with a purpose statement: "that the years of your life may be many." In 4:13 the call to "keep hold of instruction" and "guard her" suggests the daily discipline of continuing tenacity as we go through life. In 4:14 we are urged to "not walk in the way of evildoers." In the Bible "walking" is a metaphor for daily behavior and living everyday life. Then in 4:15 the call to "turn away from" evil and "pass on" again suggests an ongoing journey and daily vigilance as we seek God's way over the course of a lifetime. The same is true of the language of 4:25-27. As we walk the path of life, we are to keep our eyes focused on wisdom: "Do not swerve to the right or to the left" (4:27). Hearing and obeying the words of wisdom that are passed on to us by our parents and teachers is a lifelong pursuit, not a one-time event. It is like running a spiritual marathon, not a sprint. As Jesus said, "The one who endures to the end will be saved" (Matthew 10:22).

The Choice Is Yours

In his poem "The Road Not Taken" Robert Frost writes about coming to a fork in the road as he traveled through the woods. He had to make a choice, and that choice had consequences, for he did not expect to ever return to this place in the road again to make the same choice.

I took the one less traveled by,
And that has made all the difference.

Biblical Wisdom Literature is very aware that life is full of choices, and, as mentioned earlier, it constantly places before us the choice between two paths. The one path is the way of the wicked that leads to ruin and death; the other path is the way of the righteous that leads to a full, rich, and rewarding life. The wisdom teachers stood firmly in the theological tradition that honored both God's sovereignty and human freedom, the freedom to say yes or no to God. God did not create us as robots. God freely chooses to love us, and as persons created in the image of God, we are given the freedom to choose whether we will love God in return.

Of course, the wisdom tradition always urges us, in response to God's invitation, to choose life, to choose the way of God. This is in keeping with the rest of the Bible. In Deuteronomy 30:15 we find Moses' words to the Israelites: "See, I have set before you today life and prosperity, death and adversity," and he urges them to "choose life" (30:19). Later Joshua leads the Israelites in renewing their covenant with God as he calls for their ultimate decision: "Choose this day whom you will serve" (Joshua 24:15). In Isaiah 55:1-7 the prophet issues an invitation for the Jewish exiles to choose life by accepting God's offer of mercy and abundant life.

Likewise in the New Testament Jesus extends an invitation to life with him: "Come to me, all you that are weary and are carrying heavy burdens, and I will give you rest" (Matthew 11:28). And very much in keeping with the theme of the "two paths" that we see in Proverbs 4:10-27, Jesus also talked about two ways. Along one, "the gate is wide and the road is easy that leads to destruction" (Matthew 7:13). Along the other path "the gate is narrow and the road is hard," but this path leads to life (Matthew 7:14). We may learn wisdom from our elders, but ultimately the choice of paths is ours.

SHARING THE SCRIPTURE

Preparing Our Hearts

Explore this week's devotional reading, found in Jeremiah 31:7-11. Here we envision a grand family reunion as those who were scattered during the exile in Babylon return home. God will lead them along "a straight path in which they shall not stumble" (31:9). That image reflects the idea of the path of the righteous found in Wisdom Literature. Are you choosing to follow that straight path? If not, what prevents you from doing so? What changes do you want to make?

Pray that you and the adult learners will walk this path yourselves and help others to find and choose this path for themselves.

Preparing Our Minds

Study the background Scripture from Proverbs 4:1-27 and the lesson Scripture from Proverbs 4:10-15, 20-27. Think about how you can live life to the fullest.

Write on newsprint:

❑ discussion questions for "Review the Instruction from Proverbs about Living a Wise and Balanced Life."

❑ information for next week's lesson, found under "Continue the Journey."

❑ activities for further spiritual growth in "Continue the Journey."

Locate in a book or online "The Road Not Taken" by poet Robert Frost if you choose to use this option in the "Develop Strategies for Making Good Choices and Living a Godly Life" portion.

LEADING THE CLASS

(1) Gather to Learn

❖ Welcome the class members and introduce any guests.

❖ Pray that the students will seek to know more about living a wise and balanced life.

❖ Discuss this question: **What do you think of when someone says, "I want to live the good life to the fullest"?** List ideas on newsprint and then try to categorize them. For example, some things on the list may relate to wealth, material possessions, relationships, types of experiences, or good health. Try to identify categories that the class members seem to think of most when they try to define "good life."

❖ Read aloud today's focus statement: **People want to live life to its fullest. Are there ways to live that will make that happen? Proverbs suggests that those who make good choices and keep a righteous path will find fulfillment in life.**

(2) Review the Instruction From Proverbs About Living a Wise and Balanced Life

❖ Open this part of the session by reading "Voices from the Grave" from Interpreting the Scripture to set wisdom in the context of tried and true tradition.

❖ Choose two volunteers, one to read Proverbs 4:10-15 and another to read verses 20-27.

❖ Form two groups or an even number of groups if the class is large. Assign half the groups to verses 10-15 and the other half to verses 20-27. Post these questions for discussion.

(1) **Who is the wise person or teacher in this section? Who is the listener?**

(2) **What does the parent urge the child to do with his "words"?**

(3) **What benefits come to those who follow the way of wisdom?**

(4) **How does the way of wisdom differ from the way of the wicked?**

(5) **Although the parent strongly urges the "child" to follow the**

way of wisdom, the child must make the choice. What do you think motivates people to make the choice to follow the way of wisdom or to reject it?

❖ Call the groups together and invite each group to answer question 5.

❖ Ask: **How are the words of wisdom that you studied here similar to and different from the words of wisdom you live by and teach others?**

(3) Reflect on the Meaning of Doing the Right Thing and Following a Straight Path

❖ Read this case study: **Ellie Jones is the administrative assistant to a boss who likes to cut corners and inflate figures to present his work in the best possible light. Ellie is very uncomfortable with what she deems unethical behavior. Yet she is the one who distributes her boss's reports and often fields questions when readers call to inquire. Ellie must work, but she has trouble looking at herself in the mirror because she feels complicit in this unacceptable behavior. What words of wisdom would you have for Ellie?**

❖ Distribute paper and pencils. Invite the adults to think of a situation in which they feel caught in a situation that prevents them from following a straight path. Suggest that they describe this situation and then pinpoint the behavior(s) that rubs against the grain of their beliefs. Encourage them to analyze the situation to see how they may be able to do whatever they believe is right. Be sure to say at the outset that this information is confidential. Recognize that some adults may prefer to think about these ideas rather than write them.

❖ Encourage volunteers to state why doing the right thing is so important to them.

(4) Develop Strategies for Making Good Choices and Living a Godly Life

❖ Read "The Choice Is Yours" from Interpreting the Scripture.

❖ **Option:** Read aloud Robert Frost's "The Road Not Taken." Discuss how this poem reflects the choices we encounter in our spiritual lives.

❖ Encourage the students to identify criteria they use for making good choices. List their ideas on newsprint. These may include *Bible teachings, teachings of the church, sermons, advice of friends, insights from prayer and meditation, circumstances, past experience with similar decisions, personal beliefs, information garnered from classes or individual study.*

❖ Post newsprint and encourage the class to create affirmative statements to show the criteria by which they will make their choices. Here are several examples to read aloud:

- ■ **I will pray about choices and ask God to lead me.**
- ■ **I will speak with Christian confidants about the choices I need to make and seek their counsel.**
- ■ **I will list on paper the "pros" and "cons" of each decision that I face, asking God to show me which are the most important matters.**
- ■ **I will search the Scriptures to find divine guidance.**

❖ **Option:** Distribute paper and pencils and invite the students to jot down any strategies that they would like to try.

❖ Conclude by asking those adults who plan to use any of these strategies to raise their hands to signify their commitment to making good choices.

(5) Continue the Journey

❖ Pray that the adults will use strategies they have developed to make good choices and live godly lives.

❖ Read aloud this preparation for next week's lesson. You may also want to post it on newsprint for the students to copy.

- ■ **Title: Teaching Values**
- ■ **Background Scripture: Proverbs 10:1–15:33**
- ■ **Lesson Scripture: Proverbs 15:21-33**
- ■ **Focus of the Lesson: People need good and effective advice in order to live well. Where can we find good advice? Proverbs is full of advice that can guide us toward a godly life.**

❖ Challenge the students to complete one or more of these activities for further spiritual growth related to this week's session. Post this information on newsprint for the students to copy.

(1) **Read Robert Frost's poem "The Road Not Taken" and contemplate how you choose which path you will take.**

(2) **Share with a younger person some of God's wisdom that you have learned and experienced in** your own life. Be a mentor in the faith to this person and encourage him or her to choose the path that leads to abundant life.

(3) **Research labyrinths. You can find printable finger labyrinths online, as well as places to buy handheld labyrinths and directories that will help you locate a labyrinth you can walk. The labyrinth, seen by many as a metaphor for the journey of life, was used often during the Middle Ages by Christian pilgrims. Its use is experiencing a resurgence of interest among Christians as many people choose to walk the path of the labyrinth. Try using a labyrinth.**

❖ Sing or read aloud "I Want a Principle Within."

❖ Conclude today's session by leading the class in this benediction adapted from Proverbs 3:5 and 29:25: **Go forth trusting in the Lord with all your heart, knowing that one who trusts in the Lord is secure.**

UNIT 1: TEACHING AND LEARNING
TEACHING VALUES

PREVIEWING THE LESSON

Lesson Scripture: Proverbs 15:21-33
Background Scripture: Proverbs 10:1–15:33
Key Verse: Proverbs 15:32

Focus of the Lesson: People need good and effective advice in order to live well. Where can we find good advice? Proverbs is full of advice that can guide us toward a godly life.

Goals for the Learners:
(1) to become acquainted with sayings that promote effective living.
(2) to share their experiences of following wise teachings.
(3) to apply godly principles to daily life.

Pronunciation Guide:
Sheol (shee' ohl)

Supplies:
Bibles, newsprint and marker, hymnals

READING THE SCRIPTURE

NRSV
Proverbs 15:21-33

21 Folly is a joy to one who has no sense,
    but a person of understanding walks
        straight ahead.
22 Without counsel, plans go wrong,
    but with many advisers they succeed.
23 To make an apt answer is a joy to anyone,
    and a word in season, how good it is!
24 For the wise the path of life leads
        upward,
    in order to avoid Sheol below.

NIV
Proverbs 15:21-33

21Folly delights a man who lacks judgment,
    but a man of understanding keeps
        a straight course.
22Plans fail for lack of counsel,
    but with many advisers they succeed.
23A man finds joy in giving an apt reply—
    and how good is a timely word!
24The path of life leads upward for the wise
    to keep him from going down to
        the grave.

---

25 The LORD tears down the house of
the proud,
but maintains the widow's boundaries.
26 Evil plans are an abomination to
the LORD,
but gracious words are pure.
27 Those who are greedy for unjust gain
make trouble for their households,
but those who hate bribes will live.
28 The mind of the righteous ponders
how to answer,
but the mouth of the wicked pours
out evil.
29 The LORD is far from the wicked,
but he hears the prayer of the
righteous.
30 The light of the eyes rejoices the heart,
and good news refreshes the body.
31 The ear that heeds wholesome
admonition
will lodge among the wise.
32 **Those who ignore instruction
despise themselves,
but those who heed admonition
gain understanding.**
33 The fear of the LORD is instruction
in wisdom,
and humility goes before honor.

25The LORD tears down the proud
man's house
but he keeps the widow's boundaries
intact.
26The LORD detests the thoughts of
the wicked,
but those of the pure are pleasing to him.
27A greedy man brings trouble to his family,
but he who hates bribes will live.
28The heart of the righteous weighs
its answers,
but the mouth of the wicked gushes evil.
29The LORD is far from the wicked
but he hears the prayer of the righteous.
30A cheerful look brings joy to the heart,
and good news gives health to the bones.
31He who listens to a life-giving rebuke
will be at home among the wise.
32**He who ignores discipline despises
himself,
but whoever heeds correction
gains understanding.**
33The fear of the LORD teaches a man
wisdom,
and humility comes before honor.

UNDERSTANDING THE SCRIPTURE

Introduction. Chapters 10–15 of Proverbs are part of the second major section of the Book of Proverbs, commonly known as "The Proverbs of Solomon" (10:1). This section includes two collections of sentence proverbs that resemble the more traditional notion of a proverb—a short pithy saying that conveys practical wisdom for living, born out of everyday human experience. The first collection of Solomonic proverbs is 10:1–22:16, which can be divided into two subsections: 10:1–15:33 and 16:1–22:16. The second collection is 25:1–29:27. Our session focuses on chapters 10–15.

It should be noted that most of the proverbs in 10:1–15:33 are composed in antithetical parallelism, which means that the two halves of a verse state exactly opposite ideas, normally with a "but" beginning the second half of the verse. The majority of sayings composed in antithetical parallelism draw a contrast between the wise and the foolish, the righteous and the wicked (10:1-2). The other form of parallel structure found less frequently in these chapters is synonymous parallelism where, according to Kathleen Farmer in *Who Knows What Is Good?*, "two halves of a verse state a single idea phrased in two slightly different ways," often with the word "and" connecting the two halves of the verse (see 10:18 and 11:25).

Proverbs 10:2-3, 7, 16, 24, 28, 30; 11:3, 5-8, 18-19, 21, 23, 31; 12:3, 7, 13, 21; 13:6, 9, 25; 14:11, 32; 15:6, 9. In all of these proverbs a contrast is drawn between the consequences of righteous behavior and wicked behavior. There is a strong focus on the connection between act and consequence. For example, see 10:16, "The wage of the righteous leads to life, the gain of the wicked to sin," and 11:19, "Whoever is steadfast in righteousness will live, but whoever pursues evil will die." Over and over the sentence proverbs of 10:1–15:33 insist that one reaps what one sows. The general message is that the righteous (the wise who obey) will be rewarded with such recompense as security, gladness, protection from troubles, and a long, quality life, while the wicked will receive punishment and troubles and see their works brought to nothing. Although the name of "the LORD" is not mentioned with great frequency in Proverbs, the implication in 10:3 is that it is by the Lord's hand that such reward and punishment will come.

Proverbs 10:4-5, 26; 12:11, 24, 27; 13:4; 14:23; 15:19. All of these proverbs deal with the theme of laziness versus diligence and hard work. In 10:4-5, laziness is linked to poverty and hard work to success. There is a message here to the young: Although we know there are exceptions and mitigating circumstances, generally success comes to those who work hard. In 10:26 we confront a similar warning against laziness: As vinegar can cause discomfort when it comes in contact with decaying teeth (in the days before dental hygiene) and smoke can cause irritation to the eyes, so a lazy person can bring irritation to the person who employs him (literally in the Hebrew, "who sends him"). In a similar way, 12:24, 27; 13:4 contrast the consequences of the diligent hand and the lazy hand. We find the same thought in 14:23

where laziness is pictured as "mere talk," as in our phrase "all talk and no action." Proverbs 15:19 contrasts the way of the lazy person with the way of the upright or diligent person. The way of the lazy is strewn with thorns because she or he has not done the work of clearing the path, while the industrious person has done the work to clear the path and make a "highway." Indeed our actions have consequences.

Proverbs 10:3, 22, 27, 29; 11:1; 12:2, 22; 14:2, 26-27; 15:3, 11, 16, 25-26, 29, 33. These proverbs center around "the fear of the LORD" (14:26-27; 15:16, 33) and the specific mention of "the LORD" as the source or motivation for wise behavior. As noted elsewhere, explicit theological language is not commonly found in Wisdom Literature. However, in 10:1–15:33, "the LORD" is referenced with enough regularity to remind us that Israel's Wisdom tradition, although rooted in the more secular institutions of family and royal court, was deeply influenced by her faith in God. The Lord is strategically named at the beginning and end of this subsection of Solomon's sayings (10:3 and 15:33) and then several other places in these chapters in various contexts: God's concern for fairness and justice (11:1; 12:22; 15:25-26); God's blessing and gift of quality life to the righteous (10:22, 27, 29; 12:2; 14:2, 26-27; 15:16); God's all-seeing presence (15:3) and knowledge of the human heart (15:11); and God's nearness to the upright (15:29).

Proverbs 10:6, 11-14, 18-21, 31-32; 11:9, 11-13; 12:6, 13, 16-19, 22, 26; 13:3; 14:3, 5, 25; 15:1-2, 4, 7, 28. All of these proverbs deal with human speech and the power of words to do good or to do harm. Proverbs 10:11-14, 18-21, 32; 12:6, 13 contrast the speech of the righteous and the wicked and point to the consequences of both kinds of speech. The words of a righteous person can bring life to others (10:11, 21), but the deceptive speech and "lying lips" of a wicked person conceal violence and hatred (10:11, 18). Whole communities can be destroyed by the mouths of the wicked or blessed by the words of the righteous (11:9, 11). Several verses speak of the evil associated with gossip: 11:12-13; 13:3; 15:28. Proverbs 12:17 and 14:5, 25 deal with truthful witnesses and false witnesses. And several verses contrast the words that build up others and the words that destroy others: 12:18, 26; 15:1-2, 4, 7.

Proverbs 11:24-26; 14:20-21, 31. These proverbs focus on generosity and care for the poor. The beatitude in 14:21 and the special connection between God and the poor that is implied in 14:31 are reminiscent of the teachings of Jesus, in particular his parable of the great judgment in Matthew 25:31-46.

Proverbs 12:16; 14:17, 29-30; 15:1, 18. These proverbs focus on the importance of restraint and holding one's temper in check. They clearly point out the positive consequences of discipline and self-control while expressing the strife and negative consequences brought about by uncontrolled anger.

INTERPRETING THE SCRIPTURE

The Fear of the Lord

Where do you turn when seeking solutions to problems? To whom do you go for advice and wise counsel when you are feeling overwhelmed by a challenge? In our lesson Scripture (Proverbs 15:21-33), as well as throughout the Book of Proverbs, we are reminded over and over that "the fear of the LORD is the beginning of knowledge" (1:7) and "instruction in wisdom" (15:33). In John's Gospel is a passage that describes how several followers of Jesus turned away and no longer followed him when the going got tough and his teachings were difficult. "So Jesus asked the twelve, 'Do you also wish to go away?' Simon Peter answered him, 'Lord, to whom can we go? You have the words of eternal life' " (John 6:67-68).

Yes, to whom shall we go? Ultimately it is God who has the answer to the mysteries of life and the challenges that overwhelm us. We are reminded of this truth throughout the Book of Proverbs. Most of the wise sayings found throughout this book have their origin in family and court where elders and parents passed down to their children the wisdom gained from a lifetime of experience, and wise teachers in the royal court were employed to teach the young the right path to walk. But scattered throughout the Book of Proverbs are just enough reminders, one or two here and one or two there, that the *real source* of wisdom is the Lord. As mentioned previously, that idea begins in 1:7, "The fear of the LORD is the beginning of knowledge," and is essentially repeated in 9:10. In 2:6 we are told, "The LORD gives wisdom; from his mouth come knowledge and understanding." Then in 19:23 we read, "The fear of the LORD is life indeed." Our lesson Scripture for today culminates with the words of 15:33: "The fear of the LORD is instruction in wisdom."

In this context, the "fear of the LORD" is a positive reality; yet many people have difficulty with this phrase. In a Bible study I led, a woman told me that that idea turned her off totally, and she would not read any passages that contained that phrase. I imagine she speaks for others as well because of a misunderstanding of the word "fear" used in the biblical context. The Hebrew word can mean fear in the sense of dread or terror. But used in relation to God, it has more the sense of "reverence, awe, and piety." In the biblical understanding, fearing God expresses a trusting relationship with God and a commitment to God that results in the worship of God and obedience to God's will. We see this focus on the Lord in three other verses in today's lesson Scripture where God desires justice for the widow (15:25), hears the prayer of the righteous (15:29), and opposes evil plans that would hurt others (15:26). So it is that we are to "fear the Lord" in the sense of kneeling before God in reverence and awe, assured that God loves and cares for us, is compassionate to the vulnerable, and desires our trust and obedience.

Expanding the Circle

As we seek to answer the focus question of this lesson, "Where can we find good advice to live well?" the starting point is the Lord. The Bible is the primary source book of our faith, and it is in the Bible that we find the great teachings of our faith that can guide our lives. Prayer, as conversation and open communication with God, is also a powerful resource for listening to God and receiving guidance. But there is another resource that God gives to us as well: our relationships with our sisters and brothers in the faith community. God can speak to us and give guidance for our living through fellow Christians.

The Wesleyan tradition, in which I am rooted as a United Methodist pastor, has a strong conciliar focus. *The Oxford American College Dictionary* defines "conciliar" as "of, relating to, or proceeding from a council, especially an ecclesiastical one." The experience of my tradition, as well as four decades of experience as a pastor, tells me that wise decisions come from gathering with fellow Christians to pray and counsel with one another about the issues and challenges before us, especially as we trust one another and trust the Holy Spirit to speak through our differing perspectives. Such a practice is biblically based. We remember Jesus' words, "where two or three are gathered in my name, I am there among them" (Matthew 18:20). Then when the early church faced a crisis of faith that threatened its worldwide mission to the Gentiles, the famous Council of Jerusalem was called.

Acts 15 tells the story of this council as "the apostles and the elders met together to consider this matter" (15:6), trusting in the Holy Spirit to guide them to a wise decision.

Three proverbs in our lesson Scripture (15:22, 31, 32) focus on the importance of not making lone or rash decisions, but rather expanding the circle of trusted counselors and friends. The text of 15:22 is especially strong in its admonition to seek the counsel of many advisers and to look at any issue from different perspectives. The wise teachers of Israel realized that human beings are social creatures and the decisions we make need, in part, to be shaped by our fellow travelers. (See also 11:14 and 13:20 for similar advice.)

Be Careful What You Say

How often have we thought to ourselves, "I wish I had never said that to her. If only I had a magic wand and could take back those words." How often do we not think before we speak, and we say something rashly, foolishly, or in anger that we later regret? There are three proverbs in our lesson Scripture (15:23, 26, 28) that deal with speech and admonish us to be careful about what we say and how we say it.

Prayerfully weighing words and thinking before we speak can help us employ words for constructive rather than destructive purposes and to build up rather than tear down others. In the last section we reflected on the wisdom of having trusted counselors and friends from whom to seek advice. Proverbs 15:23 (NIV) admonishes us to be such trusted counselors ourselves and to make an "apt reply" and give a "timely word" when requested. In speech, as in other endeavors in life, timing is everything. An apt and timely word requires that we really listen and respond not just to hear ourselves talk but with an answer that is relevant and appropriate to the question being asked. Such an answer requires forethought and a capacity to reflect and measure our words, not just react emotionally. Proverbs

15:28 exhorts us to do just that, to ponder our thoughts before we speak, so that our mouth does not pour out evil, like an unrestrained rush of water, that needlessly hurts others. The modern proverbial admonitions to "count to ten" before responding to an insult or to "put the brain in gear before opening the mouth" are similar in character.

SHARING THE SCRIPTURE

Preparing Our Hearts

Explore this week's devotional reading, found in Proverbs 1:1-7. In these verses we find the prologue to the Book of Proverbs. Proverbs is directed toward young people but is also useful to those who are more mature. This book teaches certain attitudes and behaviors that will help readers live as wise people. We learn in verse 7 that "the fear of the LORD is the beginning of knowledge." Are you standing in fear (that is, awe, respect, and obedience) of the Lord? How do you embrace God's wisdom and share it with others?

Pray that you and the adult learners will follow the good advice given in Proverbs.

Preparing Our Minds

Study the background Scripture from Proverbs 10:1–15:33 and the lesson Scripture from Proverbs 15:21-33. Think about where you can find good and effective advice that will enable you to live well.

Write on newsprint:
❑ questions for "Share Experiences of Following Wise Teachings."
❑ information for next week's lesson, found under "Continue the Journey."
❑ activities for further spiritual growth in "Continue the Journey."

LEADING THE CLASS

(1) Gather to Learn

❖ Welcome the class members and introduce any guests.

❖ Pray that the students will become acquainted with proverbial sayings that promote effective living.

❖ Discuss this question: **Where do you turn when you need advice?** Some answers may be general, such as to an authority on the subject, whereas others may be specific, depending on the need at hand. For example, some may say that they will consult their auto mechanic if there is a problem with their vehicle. Other answers may focus on advice columns, such as Dear Abby. Some may turn to trusted family members and friends. Some students will suggest turning to the Bible.

❖ Read aloud today's focus statement: **People need good and effective advice in order to live well. Where can we find good advice? Proverbs is full of advice that can guide us toward a godly life.**

(2) Become Acquainted With Sayings That Promote Effective Living

❖ Invite each person to read aloud one verse from Proverbs 15:21-33. Before you begin, announce that anyone who chooses not to read may simply say "pass."

❖ Ask the students to determine which word often appears first in the second line of each proverb. (The word is "but.") Read the second paragraph under "Introduction" in Understanding the Scripture to explain antithetical parallelism. Look at what is being contrasted in each of these verses: 21, 22, 25, 26, 27, 28, 29, 32. Look next at the synonymous parallelism (also explained in the second paragraph under "Introduction") in verses 23, 30, 33 to discern how the first part of the proverb is being expanded or explained by the second part.

❖ Read or retell "The Fear of the Lord" from Interpreting the Scripture and the section in Understanding the Scripture that begins with "Proverbs 10:3, 22" to consider how "fear of the Lord" informs God's wisdom in our lives.

❖ Use the proverbs cited in the final paragraph of "Expanding the Circle" in Interpreting the Scripture to discuss the importance of the community in crafting wise advice.

❖ Look at the proverbs mentioned in "Be Careful What You Say" in Interpreting the Scripture to recognize both the power of words and the need to use our words responsibly.

❖ Conclude this portion of the lesson by inviting volunteers to state which proverb in verses 21-33 is most helpful to them and why they find it useful.

(3) Share Experiences of
Following Wise Teachings

❖ Form several small groups and invite all of them to discuss these questions, which you will post on newsprint:
   (1) **What is the best or most important advice someone ever gave you?**
   (2) **What benefits did you reap by following this advice?**
   (3) **If you heard the same advice from more than one person, was there one particular person who convinced you to follow it? How did your relationship or past experience with this person's guidance prompt you to accept his or her advice?**

❖ Call the groups together. Conclude by asking these questions: **Of the wise teachings you have followed, which would you recommend to someone else? Why?**

(4) Apply Godly Principles to Daily Life

❖ Read these case studies aloud and invite the group to respond. If time is short, either choose one study to focus on or form two groups and assign each one a study.

Study 1: Community Church is considering whether to open a soup kitchen for lunch on Saturdays. As the debate has heated up, people's positions have been galvanized. One group strongly supports the soup kitchen because God calls us to feed the hungry. Another group is concerned about having "outsiders" in the building. A third group likes the idea, but cannot see how the church will pay for such a program. A fourth group is suggesting that Community partner with other area churches to make this program happen. You have been called in as a consultant, since the groups can find no common ground. How will you apply some of God's principles for wise living to this situation?

Study 2: Little Brown Church in the Vale is in the midst of a conflict that you have been called in to help resolve. Certain members of the congregation are highly dissatisfied with their pastor, whereas others see her as a fine Christian and capable leader. Word is spreading throughout the community that things are nasty in this congregation. Those from the new housing community who might choose to visit are understandably reluctant to do so. What proverbs can you summon to help this church explore the problems and then solve them? What might you do to help the church change its negative image so as to draw in newcomers?

❖ Wrap up the session by providing a few moments of silence for the adults to contemplate this question: **In what situations in our own congregation do we need to discern and apply God's wisdom?**

(5) Continue the Journey

❖ Break the silence by praying that in the coming week the adults will apply the godly principles they have learned to their lives.

❖ Read aloud this preparation for next week's lesson. You may also want to post it on newsprint for the students to copy.

- ■ **Title: Wisdom and Discernment**
- ■ **Background Scripture: Proverbs 25:1-28**
- ■ **Lesson Scripture: Proverbs 25:1-10**
- ■ **Focus of the Lesson: People need principles by which to conduct their relationships in society. Where do we find such principles? The Proverbs of Solomon suggest principles for developing good and equitable relationships.**

❖ Challenge the students to complete one or more of these activities for further spiritual growth related to this week's session. Post this information on newsprint for the students to copy.

(1) Contact several appropriate advisers to guide you concerning a deci-sion that confronts you. Listen carefully to what each has to say. Weigh their words against the Scriptures. Make a wise decision.

(2) Read proverbs at random from chapters 10 through 15. Which ones grab your attention? Record these in your spiritual journal so that you can refer to them. How can you apply them to your life?

(3) Recall some biblical proverbs and wise sayings you heard as a child. Which of these have continued to guide you? Which no longer seem helpful to you? Why are they no longer useful?

❖ Sing or read aloud "Dear Lord, Lead Me Day by Day."

❖ Conclude today's session by leading the class in this benediction adapted from Proverbs 3:5 and 29:25: **Go forth trusting in the Lord with all your heart, knowing that one who trusts in the Lord is secure.**

UNIT 1: TEACHING AND LEARNING
Wisdom and Discernment

PREVIEWING THE LESSON

Lesson Scripture: Proverbs 25:1-10
Background Scripture: Proverbs 25:1-28
Key Verse: Proverbs 25:9

Focus of the Lesson:
People need principles by which to conduct their relationships in society. Where do we find such principles? The Proverbs of Solomon suggest principles for developing good and equitable relationships.

Goals for the Learners:
(1) to examine the wisdom of following godly advice in dealing with other people.
(2) to reflect on what it means to treat others as you desire to be treated.
(3) to take steps to live in humility before God and in harmony with others.

Pronunciation Guide:
Hezekiah (hez uh ki' uh)

Supplies:
Bibles, newsprint and marker, paper and pencils, hymnals

READING THE SCRIPTURE

NRSV

Proverbs 25:1-10

¹ There are other proverbs of Solomon that the officials of King Hezekiah of Judah copied.

² It is the glory of God to conceal things,
but the glory of kings is to search
things out.

NIV

Proverbs 25:1-10

¹These are more proverbs of Solomon, copied by the men of Hezekiah king of Judah:

²It is the glory of God to conceal a matter;
to search out a matter is the glory of
kings.

3 Like the heavens for height, like the
        earth for depth,
     so the mind of kings is unsearchable.
4 Take away the dross from the silver,
     and the smith has material for a vessel;
5 take away the wicked from the
        presence of the king,
     and his throne will be established
        in righteousness.
6 Do not put yourself forward in the
        king's presence
     or stand in the place of the great;
7 for it is better to be told, "Come up here,"
     than to be put lower in the presence
        of a noble.
     What your eyes have seen
8   do not hastily bring into court;
     for what will you do in the end,
        when your neighbor puts you
        to shame?
9 **Argue your case with your neighbor
        directly,
     and do not disclose another's secret;**
10 or else someone who hears you will
        bring shame upon you,
     and your ill repute will have no end.

3As the heavens are high and the earth
        is deep,
     so the hearts of kings are unsearchable.
4Remove the dross from the silver,
     and out comes material for the
        silversmith;
5remove the wicked from the king's
        presence,
     and his throne will be established
        through righteousness.
6Do not exalt yourself in the king's
        presence,
     and do not claim a place among great
        men;
7it is better for him to say to you, "Come up
        here,"
     than for him to humiliate you before a
        nobleman.
     What you have seen with your eyes
8   do not bring hastily to court,
     for what will you do in the end
        if your neighbor puts you to shame?
9**If you argue your case with a neighbor,
        do not betray another man's
        confidence,**
10or he who hears it may shame you
     and you will never lose your bad
        reputation.

UNDERSTANDING THE SCRIPTURE

Introduction and Proverbs 25:1. The second major collection of the Proverbs of Solomon is found in chapters 25–29. These proverbs have a more secular and self-reliant tone than the first collection in 10:1–22:16, where there is a more explicit theological orientation and language about "the fear of the Lord" and God's justice and direction in our lives. Proverbs 25:1 locates the editorial work and collection of these proverbs in the royal court of King Hezekiah of Judah, who reigned from 715–687 B.C.

Proverbs 25:2-3. These two verses are linked by the words "search" and "unsearchable," and they are meant to remind the hearer of the order of things in Israel with its three-tiered social hierarchy: God, king, and people. Israel had a strong belief in the ultimate inscrutability of God's ways. The king, sovereign though he was among the people (25:3), could only begin to investigate and search out those things that the unfathomable mind of God had chosen to conceal. But search them out he must. It was the king's royal duty to do so to the best of his ability in order to render sound decisions for the welfare of his subjects.

Proverbs 25:4-5. The metaphor in 25:4 of purifying a precious metal by smelting and removing the dross provides the key to understanding the process in 25:5 of cleansing society of wickedness so that the king can rule in righteousness.

Proverbs 25:6-7b. The theme of these two verses is humility, and they offer practical advice to young members of the royal court: Don't jockey for position or be pushy in seeking upward mobility because it may backfire. To overvalue our own importance is to risk the embarrassment of being "put lower" (25:7).

Proverbs 25:7c-10. There are two admonitions in these verses warning against the dangers of making rash accusations and entering into inadvisable legal entanglements with neighbors. The first warning is against speaking too hastily as a witness in court based only upon what one has "seen" without necessarily knowing the whole situation. The second admonition is against unnecessarily exposing details from a conversation that should be kept private.

Proverbs 25:11-15. These verses deal with speech and the blessing or harm it can bring. In 25:11-12 the beauty of well-chosen words is compared with well-crafted jewelry. Could the image of a "gold ring or an ornament of gold" (25:12) be purposely chosen in this cleverly crafted proverb to leave us with the mental impression of a beautiful gold earring that adorns a "listening ear"? The two proverbs in 25:13-14 are tied together by the weather images found in each. The "cold of snow" in 25:13 is a positive image expressing the point that reliable messengers are as refreshing as being cooled off on a sweltering day. The image in 25:14 is negative. Clouds that do not deliver what they promise, that is, rain for the parched earth, are like a person who boasts of giving a gift when, in fact, he has not given it. Such feigned generosity does not bring refreshment, as in 25:13, but rather a drought of truth. In 25:15 we are reminded that the virtues of patience and gentle speech are far more effective than pushiness and rash words when a person is seeking to persuade or influence someone.

Proverbs 25:16-17. The phrase "too much of" in the NIV helps to tie these two verses together thematically. They both warn against letting too much of a good thing turn into a bad thing. The warning against overstaying one's welcome in 25:17 reminds me of the modern proverb "Fish and company begin to stink after three days." These proverbs teach us to do all things in moderation and within proper limits.

Proverbs 25:18-20. These three proverbs deal with social relationships. Verse 18 admonishes us not to bear false witness against a neighbor. The point in verse 19 is that both a decaying tooth and a lame foot are useless in effectively performing their intended functions of chewing and walking, respectively. In the same way, it is useless to depend on persons who cannot be trusted in times of need. As a comparison between the NIV and NRSV shows, Proverbs 25:20 presents several problems in translation due to textual corruption in the Hebrew. Nevertheless, the intent is to show the damage done to a grieving heart by inappropriate levity.

Proverbs 25:21-22. These verses are quoted by Paul in Romans 12:20 as scriptural support in his encouragement for Christians to "overcome evil with good" (12:21). The language of Proverbs 25:21-22 is Christlike in its call to extravagant generosity, even for one's enemies (see Matthew 5:43-48). What is more difficult to explain is the motivational clause, "for you will heap coals of fire on their heads" (25:22). Perhaps it means to say that repaying acts of enmity with mercy and kindness is, in God's economy, a kind of punishment in that the enemy does not receive what the enemy expected: acts of vengeance that, in turn, can justify further acts of vengeance. Such mercy and kindness takes the enemy by surprise and stops the endless cycle of revenge. As David Hubbard suggests, the hope is to shame "the enemy into contrition and repentance so that his hatred dissipates."

Proverbs 25:23-24. Both of these proverbs have to do with unhealthy, destructive relationships whether caused by a gossiping "backbiting tongue" (25:23) or a "contentious wife" (25:24). The meaning of 25:24 is that it is better to live in solitude or even discomfort than to live in an atmosphere of constant irritation and contention.

Proverbs 25:25-26. These verses are linked by images of water. The cold water image of 25:25 is positive even as the polluted water image of 25:26 is negative, reflecting the negative impact on communal well-being when the righteous allow the wicked to prevail.

Proverbs 25:27. Honey certainly sweetens life, but by itself honey does not make a healthy meal, and too much of it can make one sick. Likewise, to arrogantly seek after too much honor is unhealthy for our souls and relationships.

Proverbs 25:28. This concluding proverb highlights the wisdom of having self-control. Without it we are vulnerable and exposed to emotional disaster, even as a city with no defensive walls is vulnerable to attack.

INTERPRETING THE SCRIPTURE

Order in the Court

Proverbs 25:1 reminds us that the proverbs found in chapters 25–29 originated in the court of King Solomon and were collected and edited in the court of King Hezekiah two centuries later. Indeed, 25:2-10 are all set in the royal court, and so I have called this section "Order in the Court." If you have ever watched a courtroom drama on television, you are familiar with that phrase. It's impossible for a judge to preside over legal proceedings if the environment is chaotic. Likewise in life, if we want to prevent social chaos and total disorganization, order is necessary, whether it is the daily schedule of chores we make in our families, the calendar we keep for social events, or the social order being enforced by a civic police force and fire department in the communities where we live.

Order can be both liberating and imprisoning, depending on how we understand it. For example, a prescribed social order can be enslaving if the place where I find myself in that order is demeaning or dehumanizing and I am there against my will. I think of the example of having been born a slave in the early 1800s in the United States or being born a member of a lower caste in India. There is a basic injustice inherent in such an order, and our faith calls us to do all we can to right such injustices.

On the other hand, order can bring comfort and security. When I know my place within the family or community of which I am a part and I am happy with my place, accept it, and find fulfillment in it, I can experience a sense of security and peace. It can also liberate me from having to spend precious time and energy rebelling and trying to change places or move to a higher place if I think the higher place is where I deserve to be.

As mentioned in Understanding the Scripture concerning 25:2-3, Israel understood its social order in a three-tiered fashion: God, king, and people. For the most part that order provided security and assurance to the people of Israel. As long as the people were obedient to God's covenant and the king was obedient to God and just in his governing, all would be well in the universe and God would bless their community.

Part of wisdom's task in ancient Israel was to teach people to know their place in the order of things. Thus kings, who were stewards of God's earthly kingdom, were charged with governing justly and wisely the affairs of their subjects by seeking out the wisdom of God that was concealed from the people (25:2-3). Likewise kings were charged with keeping moral order and preventing social chaos by removing evil and wickedness from the realm so that they could rule in righteousness (25:4-5). Wisdom also admonished people about the dangers of social climbing and arrogantly trying to push themselves ahead of others (25:6-7b) or using litigation and conflict to further their own ends (25:7c-10). The warning was to be careful, because things can quickly backfire (25:8, 10).

Order as a positive reality should be very familiar to us from our religious tradition. The apostle Paul often talked about the need for order in his correspondence with the young churches he had founded (for example, 1 Corinthians 14). John Wesley, the father of Methodism, spoke a lot about the importance of order and discipline in the life of the Christian community. And any of us who has ever been involved in a chaotic church council meeting knows how important order is if everyone is to be heard and feel secure in speaking his or her opinion. Order at its worst is misused and abused to demean and dehumanize people. Order at its best is God's gift to bring us peace and security in the context of which we can live out our lives fruitfully and faithfully as Jesus' disciples, in the assurance that God is in charge and we live within the boundaries of God's love.

The Wisdom of Humility

Though the setting is the royal court, the wise advice of 25:6-7 is appropriate for any setting. Self-accorded honor is never appropriate, whether in the presence of the king, the president, or one's spouse. Our importance in any situation should be determined not by our own self-estimate but rather by how others view us. Proverbs 25:7 provides us the motivation for not overvaluing our own importance: to avoid the risk of embarrassment at being "put lower." Probably most of us could tell more than one story about how our efforts at jockeying for position or pushing ourselves up the social ladder ended in embarrassment and humiliation for us.

There is no question in my mind that Jesus knew this proverb well. Its message is the basis for a very poignant parable (Luke 14:7-11) he told about those who scrambled for places of honor at a wedding banquet, only to be asked by the host to vacate those places in deference to someone more distinguished who had arrived. In disgrace they were moved lower. Jesus' teaching is that all "who exalt themselves will be humbled, and those who humble themselves will be exalted" (Luke 14:11). An early Christian hymn written about Jesus and quoted by Paul in Philippians 2:6-11 affirms the truth of his teaching.

Honoring Our Neighbors

In 25:7-10, as well as in 25:17-18, there is a focus on proper relationships with neighbors. The two proverbs in 25:7-10 concern discretion of speech and maintaining proper boundaries with neighbors. Note the sensory focus on "seeing" in the first proverb and "hearing" in the second. The warning is against jumping to conclusions based only upon what you have seen, without necessarily knowing the whole situation, and then bearing public witness to that, such as in court, thus possibly spreading rumors or committing slander, even unwittingly, that can come back to bite you.

Both these proverbs, which admonish against inadvisable legal entanglements or going too hastily to court with neighbors, anticipate Paul's warnings in 1 Corinthians 6:1-8 about Christians taking one another into public courts with lawsuits. The same concern is echoed in Matthew 18:15-17 as

Jesus encourages his disciples to work out their disagreements one-on-one if possible. Anytime we get more people involved than necessary in a situation or make public those matters that were meant to be private or confidential, there is a danger of gossip and slander being spread, whether intentionally or unintentionally. I once witnessed the tragic results of two people in a congregation who took a disagreement into a civil court rather than try to resolve their differences using the channels and resources of their faith community. Many people experienced deep hurt, and the congregation was split by gossip and people taking sides. No wonder there are so many proverbs that admonish us to honor both our relationships with our neighbors and our boundaries with them.

SHARING THE SCRIPTURE

Preparing Our Hearts

Explore this week's devotional reading, found in 1 Kings 3:5-14. King Solomon had a dream in which he asked God for "an understanding mind" to govern (3:9). In Israelite history, there was a clear connection between the king's relationship with God and his ability to rule with righteousness and wisdom. In a secular, democratic society we do not have such expectations. But think for a moment: If our elected leaders did rule according to God's wisdom, how would our society be different? Would you expect those who are now first to be last? Would you expect those who occupy seats of power and privilege to be asked to defer to others?

Pray that you and the adult learners will think carefully when choosing elected officials and then continue to hold them in prayer that they might act as God's representatives.

Preparing Our Minds

Study the background Scripture from Proverbs 25:1-28 and the lesson Scripture from Proverbs 25:1-10. Ask yourself this question: Where do you find principles by which to conduct good and equitable relationships within society?

Write on newsprint:
❏ information for next week's lesson, found under "Continue the Journey."
❏ activities for further spiritual growth in "Continue the Journey."

LEADING THE CLASS

(1) Gather to Learn

❖ Welcome the class members and introduce any guests.

❖ Pray that the students will open their hearts and minds to the wisdom of following godly advice when dealing with other people.

❖ Brainstorm with the class answers to this question: **What character traits are necessary for developing good relationships with other people?** Write ideas on newsprint. These ideas may include *trustworthiness, ability to keep confidences, fair-mindedness, good communication skills, instinct for setting appropriate boundaries, truthfulness, empathy,* and *self-control.*

❖ Read aloud today's focus statement: **People need principles by which to conduct their relationships in society. Where do we find such principles? The Proverbs of Solomon suggest principles for developing good and equitable relationships.**

(2) Examine the Wisdom of Following Godly Advice in Dealing With Other People

❖ Choose a volunteer to read Proverbs 25:1-10.

❖ Lead the class in a discussion of the Proverbs by looking at each one and using information from Understanding the Scripture in 25:2-3, 4-5, 6-7b, and 7c-10 to help the students understand the teachings of each of these sayings.

❖ Create three columns on a sheet of newsprint headed with these words: *Order, Humility, Neighbors*. Talk with the class about how these three concepts are reflected in the proverbs we are studying today. Use "Order in the Court," "The Wisdom of Humility," and "Honoring Our Neighbors" from Interpreting the Scripture to expand the discussion.

❖ Conclude this activity by distributing paper and pencils. Encourage the class members to write a proverb or two in their own words to help them remember some wise advice they have discussed today.

(3) Reflect on What It Means to Treat Others as You Desire to Be Treated

❖ Point out that although what we know as the Golden Rule is not specifically stated in today's proverbs, the idea of treating others equitably is very important to our study. Here are several incomplete stories. Invite volunteers to either roleplay the ending or simply state what they would say.

Scenario 1: You take great pride in your yard, particularly your flower garden. You look out the window to see your neighbor's Saint Bernard digging up your mums and rolling in the dirt. Sebastian is having a great time; you are not. You dial your phone and say: "Hi, George. This is Peter next door."

Scenario 2: You arrive at the mall for the huge sale only to find everyone else in the community is there as well. You start to pull into the only parking space you see when someone roars in ahead of you and damages your car. You get out, walk toward the other driver, and begin to speak.

Scenario 3: You are escorting your ninety-two-year-old mother into a restaurant. She is unable to move quickly, and the party behind you becomes very impatient and starts making rude remarks. At first you ignore them, but then you feel you must speak.

❖ Invite the students to comment on how the replies did or did not reflect how they believe we are taught to treat others. Perhaps some adults will have additional ideas for helpful responses.

(4) Take Steps to Live in Humility Before God and in Harmony With Others

❖ Select someone to read Jesus' parable in Luke 14:7-11. Choose someone else to read again Proverbs 25:6-7.

❖ Discuss these questions:
   (1) **Why do so many of us find it challenging to live with the kind of humility that both Jesus and Proverbs teach?**
   (2) **What are some ways that we can show our humility before God?** (There are many possibilities, but one answer might be to keep an open, teachable spirit. We want to learn and grow as Christian disciples, but none of us has all the answers.)

❖ Transition to a discussion of living in harmony with others by choosing someone to read again Proverbs 25:7-10.

❖ Read or retell Proverbs 25:7c-10 from Understanding the Scripture and then ask:
   (1) **What might happen when people spread stories that may have some basis in fact but lack the solid evidence of an eyewitness account?**
   (2) **Without going into the details of the situation, have you ever been**

the victim of someone spreading stories about you when they were not fully aware of what was going on? If so, how did you feel? What response did you make?

(3) Proverbs 25:9 tells us not to "disclose another's secret." Normally this is very sound advice. However, are there situations in which you feel that secrets must be disclosed? If so, what are they? (In cases of abuse or some sort of criminal activity, secrets may need to be told to the proper authorities to stop harmful and illegal behavior.)

❖ Distribute paper and pencils if you have not yet done so. Provide a few moments of quiet time for the students to describe one way that they will try to live more humbly before God and one way that they will work to promote harmony with a neighbor.

(5) Continue the Journey

❖ Break the silence by praying that the adults will take steps this week to live humbly before God and in harmony with others.

❖ Read aloud this preparation for next week's lesson. You may also want to post it on newsprint for the students to copy.

■ Title: An Ordered Life
■ Background Scripture: Proverbs 28:1–29:27
■ Lesson Scripture: Proverbs 29:16-27
■ Focus of the Lesson: People look for ways to live with some sense of security in their lives. Is there a

way to live with a sense of security? A life ordered by godly principles builds trust in God and brings a sense of security to life.

❖ Challenge the students to complete one or more of these activities for further spiritual growth related to this week's session. Post this information on newsprint for the students to copy.

(1) Do all in your power to mend fences with a neighbor with whom you have had a disagreement or falling out.

(2) Recall a time when you had a hasty reaction to a disagreement. How did you respond to the problem? What additional problems did your reaction cause? What lessons did you learn? How might some of the proverbs we are studying have been helpful to you when this incident occurred?

(3) Note that many proverbs teach us about what we say, how we listen, and when to keep silent. Observe your own behavior this week. When were your words healing? When were they hurtful? When did you speak when you should have remained silent, or speak when you should have been listening? How can the biblical proverbs help you?

❖ Sing or read aloud "Breathe on Me, Breath of God."

❖ Conclude today's session by leading the class in this benediction adapted from Proverbs 3:5 and 29:25: **Go forth trusting in the Lord with all your heart, knowing that one who trusts in the Lord is secure.**

UNIT 1: TEACHING AND LEARNING
AN ORDERED LIFE

PREVIEWING THE LESSON

Lesson Scripture: Proverbs 29:16-27
Background Scripture: Proverbs 28:1–29:27
Key Verse: Proverbs 29:25

Focus of the Lesson:
People look for ways to live with some sense of security in their lives. Is there a way to live with a sense of security? A life ordered by godly principles builds trust in God and brings a sense of security to life.

Goals for the Learners:
(1) to discover the relationship between an orderly life and trust in God.
(2) to reflect on what it means to live an ordered life.
(3) to reevaluate their priorities in light of God's wisdom.

Pronunciation Guide:
Torah (toh' ruh)

Supplies:
Bibles, newsprint and marker, paper and pencils, hymnals

READING THE SCRIPTURE

NRSV
Proverbs 29:16-27
16 When the wicked are in authority,
    transgression increases,
      but the righteous will look upon their
      downfall.
17 Discipline your children, and they will
      give you rest;
    they will give delight to your heart.
18 Where there is no prophecy, the people
      cast off restraint,

NIV
Proverbs 29:16-27
16When the wicked thrive, so does sin,
      but the righteous will see their downfall.
17Discipline your son, and he will give
      you peace;
    he will bring delight to your soul.
18Where there is no revelation, the
      people cast off restraint;
    but blessed is he who keeps the law.

but happy are those who keep the law.

19 By mere words servants are not
disciplined,
for though they understand, they will
not give heed.

20 Do you see someone who is hasty
in speech?
There is more hope for a fool than for
anyone like that.

21 A slave pampered from childhood
will come to a bad end.

22 One given to anger stirs up strife,
and the hothead causes much
transgression.

23 A person's pride will bring humiliation,
but one who is lowly in spirit will
obtain honor.

24 To be a partner of a thief is to hate one's
own life;
one hears the victim's curse, but
discloses nothing.

25 The fear of others lays a snare,
but one who trusts in the LORD
is secure.

26 Many seek the favor of a ruler,
but it is from the LORD that one gets
justice.

27 The unjust are an abomination to the
righteous,
but the upright are an abomination to
the wicked.

19A servant cannot be corrected by
mere words;
though he understands, he will
not respond.

20Do you see a man who speaks in haste?
There is more hope for a fool than
for him.

21If a man pampers his servant from youth,
he will bring grief in the end.

22An angry man stirs up dissension,
and a hot-tempered one commits
many sins.

23A man's pride brings him low,
but a man of lowly spirit gains honor.

24The accomplice of a thief is his own enemy;
he is put under oath and dare not testify.

25Fear of man will prove to be a snare,
but whoever trusts in the LORD is
kept safe.

26Many seek an audience with a ruler,
but it is from the LORD that man gets
justice.

27The righteous detest the dishonest;
the wicked detest the upright.

UNDERSTANDING THE SCRIPTURE

Introduction. A quick reading through Proverbs 28–29 will show a return to the style of antithetical parallelism that we saw in the sentence proverbs of chapters 10–15. The majority of the sentences in Proverbs 28–29 show a contrast between two ways of living, with the English conjunction "but" beginning the second half of each of the proverbs.

Proverbs 28:1, 5, 12-13, 24-26, 28; 29:2, 6, 8, 10-11, 16, 24, 27. All of these proverbs deal with the contrast between the "righteous"

and the "wicked," between "evil" people who "do not understand justice" and those "who seek the LORD" and do understand it (28:5), between those who "conceal transgressions" and those who confess them and seek God's mercy (28:13). In Proverbs 28:1 the wicked flee, even though no one pursues them, perhaps because of a troubled conscience and a secret fear that their evil ways will be found out. However, the righteous are bold and confident ("as a lion") and do not flee because their trust is in the

Lord. In contrast to righteous behavior, Proverbs 28:24 and 29:24 describe the behavior of evildoers, who are referred to as partners of thugs or thieves, whether their offense is stealing from their parents (28:24) or not volunteering to give evidence when they have witnessed a crime (29:24).

Other terms synonymous with "wicked" and "righteous" are used in several verses. In 28:25 the contrast is between the "greedy person" who "stirs up strife" and one who "trusts in the LORD"; in 28:26 between "those who trust in their own wits" and those "who walk in wisdom," presumably the wisdom of trusting in God; in 29:8 between "scoffers" who set a city on fire with conflict and "the wise" who restore order and peace; in 29:10 between the "bloodthirsty" and the "blameless," the latter being hated by the former; in 29:11 between a fool who unleashes his anger and a wise person who exercises self-control. As a group, Proverbs 28:12, 28; 29:2, 16 contrast the wicked and the righteous in terms of their governing. The phrase "when the wicked prevail, people go into hiding" is found in both 28:12 and 28:28 and speaks of fear in the larger community when those who are evil rise to power and oppress the people. The final verse (29:27) expresses the mutual abhorrence that the righteous and the wicked feel for each other.

Proverbs 28:10, 17-20, 22; 29:1. These proverbs remind us that we must bear the consequences of our actions. Similar to Jesus' teaching in Matthew 5:19, Proverbs 28:10 warns against leading others astray. The image of falling into a pit of one's own making reminds us of Western sayings such as "he who lives by the sword will die by the sword." Although the Hebrew of 28:17 is difficult to translate, the idea is clear: Anyone who has shed blood will be "burdened" in his conscience. Efforts to run away from his guilt will be futile. He will be a "fugitive until death," haunted by what he has done. In 28:18, walking in "integrity" is contrasted with walking in "crooked ways"; each path has its inevitable consequences.

Rooted in the values of agricultural life, 28:19-20 teaches that a farmer's faithful, honest labor in working the land will bring blessings and abundant food, while irresponsible behavior and the endeavors of "get rich quick" pursuits will end in poverty and futility. The "miser" of 28:22 is literally "bad of eye" in Hebrew, "apparently an idiom for a greedy person." Proverbs 29:1 reminds us of the negative consequences ("broken beyond healing") when we stubbornly refuse to accept wise counsel and discipline. Both 28:22 and 29:1 imply that although the greedy and the stubborn may not want to acknowledge that there are consequences for their actions, those consequences are inevitable.

Proverbs 28:2, 3, 15-16; 29:4, 12, 14, 26. These proverbs deal with rulers and proper governing. Proverbs 28:2 speaks of the chaos and instability that go hand-in-hand with weak government leadership; a strong, moral leader is needed to maintain benevolent order. The issue in 29:12 is likewise the importance of moral leadership, for when a ruler abdicates his responsibility to seek truth the result can be the corruption of other governing officials who work for the ruler.

The other proverbs referenced above center around the issue of governing with justice. Proverbs 28:3, 15; and 29:14 deal specifically with a ruler's responsibility to pay special attention to the needs of the vulnerable and not to abuse or oppress the poor. Proverbs 28:16 and 29:4 affirm that a sensitive ruler who seeks justice for his people will receive the reward of long life for himself and stability for his country. Proverbs 29:26 reminds us that, even though many will seek justice by currying the favor of human rulers, *genuine justice* ultimately comes from the Lord.

Proverbs 28:6, 8, 11, 27; 29:7, 13. These proverbs speak in a positive manner about "the poor." In a culture where the poor were often disparaged and many people believed that the wealthy were naturally blessed and favored by God, 28:6, 11 reverse that way of thinking; here the poor who walk in integrity and humility are lifted up. Proverbs 28:8 reflects Old Testament law (Exodus 22:25 and Leviticus 25:36-37) that forbids lending at interest, in order to protect the poor from exploitation. This proverb implies that any unjust profit gained by the lender will "presumably in a stroke of divine justice," according to David Hubbard, writing in *The Communicator's Commentary Series, Proverbs*, "fall into the hands of someone who will take 'pity' on 'the poor.' " Proverbs 28:27 and 29:7 admonish us to act compassionately and justly toward the poor.

Proverbs 28:4, 7, 9; 29:18. The Hebrew word *torah* ("law, teaching, instruction") appears five times in these four verses and likely refers to God's instruction as opposed to the instruction of the wise (see 1:8; 3:1; 4:2). Proverbs 28:4, 7, 9 draw a contrast between those who obey the Torah and those who do not. In 29:18, there is reference to "prophecy" and the Torah, perhaps reflecting the first two divisions of the Hebrew Scriptures: the Law and the Prophets. Without prophetic vision from the Lord to guide the people, there will be chaos and disorder. But security and happiness come to those who "keep the law" (29:18).

INTERPRETING THE SCRIPTURE

The Rewards of Discipline

As I wrote in the first lesson, discipline has different shades of meaning in Proverbs. It can have the sense of correcting or chastising someone; it can also be understood as instruction, learning, or training in the school of wisdom, where young people are prepared for life. In this week's lesson Scripture, the word "discipline" occurs in 29:17, 19, and the need for discipline is implied in 29:21.

Important to effective discipline are rewards that serve as motivation. When I started playing musical instruments as a child, I hated to take time from playing sports to practice. But through my mother's loving, persistent urging, I learned the discipline of regular practice. Eventually that discipline, which I dreaded at first, brought the rewards of enjoying the music I was playing and the success of accomplishments. These rewards transformed the discipline of practice from being drudgery into a joy because I could see and experience the positive results.

The importance of such positive rewards and proper motivation is seen in 29:17, 19. To parents who patiently and with self-discipline perform the hard work of consistently disciplining their children come the positive results of "rest" from worry and anxiety and "delight" in their hearts (29:17) at seeing the kind of well-behaved young people their children become. In 29:19 the focus is on the necessity of strong motivation in the disciplining of servants. Sometimes mere words are not enough to motivate proper behavior. In 29:17, 19 the administration of corporal punishment, a common mode of discipline in ancient Near Eastern cultures, is probably implied. Such proverbs as 13:24 and 29:15 would suggest this. However, because of the lack of specific instructions in 29:17, 19, other kinds of motivation could be intended, including encouragement and other material rewards for work well done. In 29:21 the meaning of the final word in Hebrew is unknown, but the sense of the proverb seems to be this: Failure to properly discipline a servant who is reared from childhood leads to a spoiled servant and an unsatisfactory relationship between master and servant.

When Fear and Chaos Reign

In October 2002 a tense drama played out in the Washington, DC, metropolitan area when a sniper named John Allen Muhammad, along with a younger accomplice named Lee Boyd Malvo, carried out a series of random attacks that killed ten people and wounded several others. The entire metropolitan area was terrorized for three weeks before the two men were arrested on October 24, 2002. Repeated interviews with bystanders expressed the deep-seated fears that gripped the population of the metropolitan area.

The focus of our lesson is the deep yearning that people have to live their lives with a sense of security and trust. This desire is heightened in our day and culture because of the many threats to peace and security all around us. Night after night news broadcasts pummel us with reports of violence on our city streets or suicide bombings in Afghanistan or Pakistan. Warnings about the threat of terrorist attacks are kept ever before us. Even television commercials seem to play upon our fears and insecurities with a plethora of commercials about everything from our need for home security systems to pharmaceutical ads stating our need for this drug or that drug to give us protection from some terrible disease that might strike us.

Several proverbs in our lesson Scripture relate to situations where such antisocial forces as fear, crime, chaos, and unchecked anger are present and threaten people's security. Proverbs 29:16 warns that lawlessness and disorder in society increase when evil rulers are in authority. Perhaps this is so because good people exhibit the paralysis of inaction out of fear of reprisal from their rulers. The phrase comes to mind that is attributed to the Irish philosopher Edmund Burke, "All that is necessary for the triumph of evil is for good men to do nothing," whether out of fear or apathy. Tragically, if good people do nothing, the danger is that "hotheads" will take the initiative, and anger will lead to a mob mentality resulting in further strife and chaos (see 29:22). In 29:18 we have a picture of a chaotic society where people do whatever they want with no restraint when God's prophetic word is not heard, and 29:24 witnesses to the reality of crime in the social order.

We could point to many examples throughout history when chaos and disorder prevailed in societies where evil persons were in authority. One actual situation in biblical history occurred during the last years of the Northern Kingdom of Israel just before Assyria conquered and exiled many of Israel's leaders and people in 722 B.C. From 746 B.C. until 722 B.C. there was a rapid succession of six kings, four of whom were assassinated in violent coups (see 2 Kings 15). The prophet Hosea described this period of virtual anarchy with these words: "All of them are hot as an oven, and they devour their rulers. All their kings have fallen; none of them calls upon me" (Hosea 7:7).

Trusting in the Lord

Of course, the remedy for such social disorder and fear lies in people's trust in God and their obedience to God's law (29:18). Here near the conclusion of the Proverbs of Solomon, in 29:25-26, we are reminded once again of the central place of God in Israel's Wisdom Literature and the importance of trusting in the Lord. Proverbs 29:25, our key verse, contrasts fear and trust. The deleterious effect of letting the fear of others guide our lives is contrasted with the blessed release from fear that comes from putting our trust in God. I think of the words of 1 John 4:18: "There is no fear in love, but perfect love casts out fear." In God's economy, love and trust are almost synonymous. If we say we love God, then that love must express itself in our day-to-day trusting of God. And the wonderful consequence of trusting God is deep peace and the assurance of God's strong presence that vanquishes our fears and anxieties.

How we wish our national and international leaders understood this and would try to put it into practice on a global scale. Ultimately, the answer to the world's violence is not more violence. It is not dropping bombs and launching missiles and seeking revenge. A saying attributed to various people, including Mahatma Gandhi, suggests that if people operate only by the law of retaliation ("an eye for an eye and a tooth for a tooth"), eventually the whole world will become blind and toothless. No, as 29:25-26 affirms, true justice and genuine security from the fears and violence that surround us will come only from putting our trust in the holy God of compassion and then seeking to be living reflections of God's love in all our relationships, local and global. Anything short of that will only protract the seemingly endless cycle of revenge.

SHARING THE SCRIPTURE

Preparing Our Hearts

Explore this week's devotional reading, found in Deuteronomy 1:9-17. As Moses recalls events of the forty-year sojourn with the liberated Hebrews, he reminds them about the appointment of tribal leaders to help him administer justice. These were to be "wise and reputable individuals" (1:15) who would judge with fairness and equity. They were not to show partiality but were to be mindful that "the judgment is God's" (1:17). Their presence would help to ensure law and order in the new society that was taking shape. How are law and order ensured in your community? What role do you play?

Pray that you and the adult learners will order your lives on godly principles.

Preparing Our Minds

Study the background Scripture from Proverbs 28:1–29:27 and the lesson Scripture from Proverbs 29:16-27. Consider how you can live with a sense of security.

Write on newsprint:

❏ information for next week's lesson, found under "Continue the Journey."

❏ activities for further spiritual growth in "Continue the Journey."

LEADING THE CLASS

(1) Gather to Learn

❖ Welcome the class members and introduce any guests.

❖ Pray that the students will discover the relationship between an orderly life and trust in God.

❖ Brainstorm answers to this question, and write the responses on newsprint: **Where do people turn to find security?** Try to address a broad range of possibilities, including home and vehicle security systems; locks; insurance policies to protect one's home, vehicle, and other possessions; life insurance to protect a family's financial well-being; tamper-resistant bottles for medications; vaccinations against diseases; home safes; computer firewalls and antivirus programs; and protective sports gear.

❖ Discuss briefly how effective the adults believe these various security measures are.

❖ Read aloud today's focus statement: **People look for ways to live with some** sense of security in their lives. Is there a way to live with a sense of security? A life ordered by godly principles builds trust in God and brings a sense of security to life.

(2) Discover the Relationship Between an Orderly Life and Trust in God

❖ Choose a volunteer to read Proverbs 29:16-27.

❖ Look at specific verses in that passage by following these steps:

- ■ **Step 1:** Invite the class to look again at verses 17, 19, and 21. Read aloud "The Rewards of Discipline" in Interpreting the Scripture. Use pertinent information from Understanding the Scripture. Encourage the adults to tell stories of discipline that challenged or rewarded them, such as the discipline of playing a musical instrument, playing a sport, or studying a subject.
- ■ **Step 2:** Invite the class to look again at verses 16, 18, 22, and 24. Read aloud "When Fear and Chaos Reign" in Interpreting the Scripture. Use pertinent information from Understanding the Scripture. Provide an opportunity for the class members to discuss circumstances in their lives that caused them to be fearful. Where did they turn for help?
- ■ **Step 3:** Invite the class to look again at verses 25-26. Read aloud "Trusting in the Lord" in Interpreting the Scripture. Use pertinent information from Understanding the Scripture. Challenge the students to identify situations in the community, nation, and world that keep them awake at night as they consider potentially damaging consequences.

❖ Conclude by leading the class in reading Proverbs 29:25, today's key verse, as a reminder that security is found in God.

(3) Reflect on What It Means to Live an Ordered Life

❖ Note that today's session falls under the category of law and order, which provides us with a sense of safety and security.

❖ Form several groups. Give each one a sheet of newsprint and a marker. Read this question and tell them they have three minutes to write as many answers as possible: **What does it mean to you to live an ordered life?**

❖ Call the groups together and hear their ideas. Ask each group to post its newsprint. See if the class can identify any broad categories. For example, some answers may point to a life that is "neat and tidy"; for example, the house is clean and tidy, the calendar is well organized, and the checkbook is balanced. Another category may include those who live what appear to be messier lives, but who store in their heads ways to catalog the information they have and keep things in order. An example here would be the person who piles papers on the desk and knows which "level" to look at to find the needed information. Another category may include those who just follow wherever God leads, trusting that God will keep them secure.

❖ Pause for a few moments so that the adults may reflect on how they define "an ordered life" and take stock of how well their own life measures up to the ideal definition they hold.

(4) Reevaluate Priorities in Light of God's Wisdom

❖ Distribute paper and pencils. Read the following questions aloud slowly, allowing time for the students to reflect on their answers and, if they choose to do so, write them.

(1) As you look back on the proverbs we have considered today, what do they say to you about what is important in light of God's wisdom? (pause)

(2) As we read earlier, "If people operate only by the law of retaliation ('an eye for an eye and a tooth for a tooth'), eventually the whole world will become blind and toothless." Where in the world do you see this "an eye for an eye" mentality? What do you think needs to be done to change this kind of thinking? (pause)

(3) Where do you see injustice right here in our own community? (pause)

(4) What actions are you willing to take to help get community priorities in line with God's wisdom? (pause)

(5) What changes would you expect to see in your community if all people were aware of and chose to model God's justice and mercy? (pause)

❖ Bring everyone together. Invite volunteers to comment on changes they believe the community needs to make in its priorities to be more faithful to God. Also encourage them to comment on what they believe the church might do to help the community make these changes.

(5) Continue the Journey

❖ Pray that the adults will spend time this week reevaluating their priorities in light of God's wisdom.

❖ Read aloud this preparation for next week's lesson. You may also want to post it on newsprint for the students to copy.

■ **Title: The Superiority of Wisdom**
■ **Background Scripture: Ecclesiastes 9:13–10:20**

■ **Lesson Scripture: Ecclesiastes 9:13-18**
■ **Focus of the Lesson: People are drawn in by loud voices that make an impression even though these voices lack true wisdom. To whom should we listen? Ecclesiastes teaches that we should not ignore the quiet, thoughtful words of the wise.**

❖ Challenge the students to complete one or more of these activities for further spiritual growth related to this week's session. Post this information on newsprint for the students to copy.

(1) **Be alert this week for situations in which you craved a sense of security. What prompted this need? Where did you turn to find help? How did God figure into your circumstances?**

(2) **Identify examples of how the actions of an evildoer have upset the orderly conduct of a society or community. For example, you may wish to consider how the decisions of powerful, greedy people have affected you.**

(3) **Take action this week to confront an injustice. Help an individual, write letters to elected officials as an advocate for a group, or volunteer for an agency that works for peace and justice.**

❖ Sing or read aloud "If Thou But Suffer God to Guide Thee."

❖ Conclude today's session by leading the class in this benediction adapted from Proverbs 3:5 and 29:25: **Go forth trusting in the Lord with all your heart, knowing that one who trusts in the Lord is secure.**

UNIT 1: TEACHING AND LEARNING
THE SUPERIORITY OF WISDOM

PREVIEWING THE LESSON

Lesson Scripture: Ecclesiastes 9:13-18
Background Scripture: Ecclesiastes 9:13–10:20
Key Verse: Ecclesiastes 9:16

Focus of the Lesson:
People are drawn in by loud voices that make an impression even though these voices lack true wisdom. To whom should we listen? Ecclesiastes teaches that we should not ignore the quiet, thoughtful words of the wise.

Goals for the Learners:
(1) to explore the story of a person, wise and poor, who delivered a city.
(2) to recognize the superiority of wisdom over force.
(3) to seek the great value of wisdom by asking God for it.

Pronunciation Guide:
qahal (kaw hawl')
Qoheleth (ko heh' leth)

Supplies:
Bibles, newsprint and marker, paper and pencils, hymnals

READING THE SCRIPTURE

NRSV
Ecclesiastes 9:13-18

¹³ I have also seen this example of wisdom under the sun, and it seemed great to me. ¹⁴There was a little city with few people in it. A great king came against it and besieged it, building great siegeworks against it. ¹⁵Now there was found in it a poor wise man, and he by his wisdom delivered the city. Yet no one remembered that poor man. ¹⁶So I said,

NIV
Ecclesiastes 9:13-18

¹³I also saw under the sun this example of wisdom that greatly impressed me: ¹⁴There was once a small city with only a few people in it. And a powerful king came against it, surrounded it and built huge siegeworks against it. ¹⁵Now there lived in that city a man poor but wise, and he saved the city by his wisdom. But nobody remembered that

"Wisdom is better than might; yet the poor man's wisdom is despised, and his words are not heeded."

17 The quiet words of the wise are more
  to be heeded
    than the shouting of a ruler among
    fools.
18 Wisdom is better than weapons of war,
    but one bungler destroys much good.

poor man. 16So I said, **"Wisdom is better than strength." But the poor man's wisdom is despised, and his words are no longer heeded.**

17The quiet words of the wise are more to
  be heeded
    than the shouts of a ruler of fools.
18Wisdom is better than weapons of war,
    but one sinner destroys much good.

UNDERSTANDING THE SCRIPTURE

Introduction. The name "Ecclesiastes" comes from the ancient Greek translation of the Hebrew title *Qohelet*, a word rendered in the NRSV as "the Teacher." Derived from the Hebrew word *qahal*, which means "to gather or assemble," Qoheleth is most likely "one who assembles" or "one who calls (people) together"; hence, the translation "Teacher." A later tradition, expressed in 12:9-10, remembered Qoheleth as one who "taught the people knowledge, weighing and studying and arranging many proverbs." Although Ecclesiastes 1:1 implies that the author of this book is Solomon, son of David, most scholars, based especially on the late style of the Hebrew, agree that the book was written well after Solomon's time. A date roughly in the vicinity of 300 B.C. can be assumed for the completion of the book.

Ecclesiastes 9:13-18. With a couple of exceptions, "the Teacher" in this book passes on his wisdom through first-person meditations based on his own experience. Many of his teachings begin with phrases like "I perceived" (2:14), "I saw" (1:14; 2:24; 3:16, 22; 4:1, 7; 9:11), or other verbs that express his own life experience. So 9:13 begins in a similar way with an example of wisdom that he has seen. The example here is a story about a "poor wise man" who, by his wisdom, saves his town from an attack by the army of a great king. There is a similar story in 4:13-16 about a "poor but wise youth." It's not surprising that in both these stories the descriptive word "poor" is associated with the adjective "wise," for elsewhere in Ecclesiastes the Teacher sees the vanity of chasing after money and seeking fulfillment in materialism (see 4:8 and 5:10-17).

In this story found in chapter 9, no details are mentioned about how the victory was accomplished. According to David Hubbard, writing in *The Communicator's Commentary: Ecclesiastes, Song of Solomon,* the spotlight is on wisdom and how indispensable it is to success "and how readily it can be shelved when the battle is over." Qoheleth is a realist. He knows the importance of wisdom, that it is "better than might" (9:16) and "better than weapons of war" (9:18). Yet if the wise person is not respected, the words can fall on deaf ears (9:16), and the "quiet words of the wise" can be overshadowed by the noisy shouts "of a ruler among fools" (9:17). Wisdom is fragile and vulnerable, and sadly much good can be undone by the deeds of "one sinner" (NIV) or "one bungler" (NRSV). This last thought in 9:18 is similar in meaning to the modern proverb that "one bad apple can spoil the whole barrel."

Ecclesiastes 10:1-3, 12-15. In 10:1-3, 12-15 there is a focus on the contrast between wisdom and folly. In meaning, 10:1 really belongs with 9:17-18. Just as unwanted dead flies can cause a foul odor in perfume or ointment, so tiny bits of folly can pollute an entire mass of "wisdom and honor." Even today we use the phrase "a fly in the ointment" to refer to the smallest of flaws or problems that can destroy the best-laid plans.

In 10:2 we see an example of antithetical parallelism as the "heart of the wise" is contrasted with "the heart of a fool." (Recall from the session for September 18 that *antithetical parallelism* means that the two halves of a verse state exactly opposite ideas, normally with a "but" beginning the second half of the verse. The majority of sayings composed in antithetical parallelism draw a contrast between the wise and the foolish, the righteous and the wicked.) With apologies to all persons who are left-handed, it must be noted that in the Hebrew language "left" is synonymous with what is ominous and awkward while "right" is synonymous with what is good and right. The "right hand" of God was considered to be a saving instrument. In Exodus 15:6 and Psalm 48:10 it is the right hand of God that wins the victory, while in Matthew 25:33 the Son of Man places the saved sheep on his right and the damned goats on his left. So "the heart of the wise inclines to the right, but the heart of a fool to the left" (Ecclesiastes 10:2).

In 10:12-15 the contrast between the wise and the foolish continues with a focus on the speech of fools. While the words of the wise are "gracious" (NIV) and "bring them favor" (NRSV), the speech of fools is self-destructive (10:12) and malicious; it ends in evil or "wicked madness" (10:13). Fools don't know when to stop speaking, and so their harangue goes on and on until they begin to speculate about the future, of which they know nothing (10:14). For Qoheleth this is the height of folly because the future is unknowable by humans (compare 6:12; 7:14; 8:7; 11:6). Fools work so hard at this futile exercise that they forget even the simplest of things, like how to get to town (10:15).

Ecclesiastes 10:4-7. Wisdom was meant to be a guide in governmental affairs as well as the affairs of everyday life. In 10:4 advice is given about prudent behavior in the presence of the king, especially when the king is angry. The wise person will remain calm and exercise self-control, not allowing himself or herself to be stampeded into a panic or a knee-jerk reaction even when his superior is out of control. In 10:5-7 the Teacher reminds us about the unpredictability of life and how easily the world can be turned upside down (slaves on horseback and princes on foot), frequently by the decisions and actions of rulers and government officials.

Ecclesiastes 10:8-11. Accidents are waiting to happen, and there are hazards in every task we undertake in the workaday world. That seems to be the theme of 10:8-9, and the way for us to be prepared to deal with such threats is to get wisdom, for "wisdom helps one to succeed" (10:10). Wisdom gives common sense and coaches us to be cautious and careful, thereby cutting down the possibility of such accidents. In 10:10 wisdom is likened, according to Kathleen Farmer in *Who Knows What Is Good?*, to "having a sharp edge on an axe: it reduces the effort one needs to expend and increases one's chances of success." Wisdom also has to do with timing, as 10:11 expresses. One needs wise foresight to charm the snake *before* it bites.

Ecclesiastes 10:16-20. These final verses deal with wise governance or the lack thereof. Verses 17 and 18 express a contrast between an unhappy land and a happy land. What makes the difference is whether the king uses his authority to rule wisely and do such things as keep the "feasting" of his "princes" under control. The phrase "at the proper time" (10:17) is important and reflects the Teacher's concern for timing and proper social order (compare 3:1-8). As a house can fall into disrepair when it is not properly maintained, so the king's "sloth" and "indolence" can weaken his house or kingdom (10:18).

The words of 10:20, like 10:4, urge us to exercise discretion and self-control in speech, lest our words, uttered in private, may become public and come back to haunt us.

INTERPRETING THE SCRIPTURE

Faithfully Serving

President Harry Truman is reported to have said, "It is amazing what you can accomplish if you do not care who gets the credit." A similar thought lies behind this story in Ecclesiastes 9:14-16 about the "poor wise man" who by his wisdom saved his town from an enemy's siege. In telling this story the Teacher is holding up the great value of wisdom to accomplish seemingly impossible tasks. Yet the irony is that, even though wisdom is of great value, wisdom is not valued by everyone. In fact, the Teacher warns that wisdom is often despised and not heeded, especially when it comes from an unexpected source, in this case a "poor" person. There was a strain of thought in conventional Wisdom Literature that identified folly with poverty and wisdom with wealth, on the assumption that wealth and wisdom went hand in hand as blessings from God. The surprise in this story would have been the fact that the wise man was an insignificant poor person, not someone of wealth and status to whom people generally looked for wise counsel.

As usual, the Teacher is a realist who has witnessed the unexpected ups and downs and inequities of life. He warns his hearers not to expect that the rewards of wisdom will automatically be fame and fortune. His point is that wisdom is of high value, and if one is wise enough to know the right thing to do, then one should do it regardless of whether one is given proper recognition or not. Wisdom is its own reward, as is the satisfaction of having done the right thing.

Jesus had some strong words to say about faithfully doing one's job as a servant of God and not worrying about rewards or credit: "Do you thank the slave for doing what was commanded? So you also, when you have done all that you were ordered to do, say, 'We are worthless slaves; we have done only what we ought to have done!'" (Luke 17:9-10). For us as Christian disciples, just having the privilege to serve and live in a daily, loving relationship with our Lord is its own reward. It is to God that honor and credit are due, not to us.

I've often told parishioners that God does not call us to be successful, only faithful. Our job is to faithfully and humbly do the tasks God has called us to do and not worry about success or failure. We can leave that in God's hands; in doing so there is great peace and freedom.

Still Water Runs Deep

We've all heard expressions like "the squeaky wheel gets the oil," or "the misbehaving child gets the attention." And it's generally true. The person who speaks the loudest or generates the most excitement usually draws the initial crowd and perhaps some "oohs" and "aahs," even as a loud, colorful, provocative cover on a book might grab initial attention. However, if the content of the book is weak, a flashy cover will not make up for it. There is an old preacher's joke about the pastor who wrote in the margins of his sermon manuscript: "Weak point. Shout like heck!" In other words, the intent was to use outward emotion and volume of voice to deflect attention away from the weak content in his sermon.

In the end, fire is more important than smoke, and substance is more important than style. It is to this issue that Ecclesiastes 9:17 is speaking: "The quiet words of the wise are more to be heeded than the shouting of a ruler among fools." It's true that the loudest voice often gets the attention, but the loudest voice is not necessarily the wisest. Retired United Methodist Bishop Joseph Yeakel used to issue sage advice during our annual conference sessions when we were voting on key issues. At times speeches would become impassioned and folks would get very emotional with their voices and clapping either in support of or against certain speeches or stands on issues. On more than one occasion Bishop Yeakel would need to remind us that critical issues were not decided by the heightened level of decibels but by the wisdom of words and reasoned votes.

I have always appreciated the old proverbial expression "Still water runs deep." How many of us know persons whose demeanor is quiet and reserved. They don't attract a lot of attention by their loud voices or flashy personalities. They are not the life of the party. But when we want wise counsel or have serious questions to talk over with somebody, it is to such persons that we go. They are deep-thinking people whose wisdom, gained from years of experience, we respect.

It was to just such a person that I turned when at the tender age of twenty I made a commitment of my life to be a disciple of Jesus. Harold was a man in my church who was three times my age and very different in personality from me. He was quiet, reserved, and unassuming; but in him I saw the spiritual wisdom that came from years of a close relationship with Christ and a deep prayer life. He became my unofficial mentor for several years, and God used him to teach me much. Still water *does* run deep.

Actions and Consequences

Our lesson Scripture concludes with a verse that once again reflects the Teacher's pragmatic understanding of life: "Wisdom is better than weapons of war, but one bungler destroys much good" (9:18). As mentioned earlier, 10:1 reiterates the same thought: "a little folly outweighs wisdom and honor." A parallel modern proverb would be "One bad apple can spoil the whole barrel." Experience tells us that it only takes one rash, unthinking act or a couple of ill-timed words to undo much that is good or that one has worked long and hard to accomplish. It could be a single act from long ago—a choice made in anger to get revenge on someone rather than forgive, a decision to cheat on an entrance exam that was later discovered, a sexual contact with an HIV-infected person.

As I was growing up, I can remember my mother telling me over and over, "Steve, every action you take has consequences sooner or later." That parenting advice was both true and effective. On more than one occasion it made me stop and think before I did something ill advised that could have resulted in disastrous consequences. It is so important to be wise in our choices because one bad decision, one decision made in haste without consideration of the consequences, can later come back to haunt us.

SHARING THE SCRIPTURE

Preparing Our Hearts

Explore this week's devotional reading, found in Psalm 33:13-22. Perhaps you remember the children's grace that begins, "God is great, God is good." This psalm describes the goodness and greatness of God, who created the earth and observes humanity from heaven. How do you feel knowing that "the eye of the LORD is on those who fear him" (33:18)? What evidence reveals that you truly trust God (33:21), rather than rely on human might (33:16-17)? Give thanks for God's steadfast love and presence in your life.

Pray that you and the adult learners will rely constantly on God.

Preparing Our Minds

Study the background Scripture from Ecclesiastes 9:13–10:20 and the lesson Scripture from Ecclesiastes 9:13-18. Ask yourself this question: With all of the voices clamoring for my attention, to whom should I listen?

Write on newsprint:
❑ information for next week's lesson, found under "Continue the Journey."
❑ activities for further spiritual growth in "Continue the Journey."

LEADING THE CLASS

(1) Gather to Learn

❖ Welcome the class members and introduce any guests.

❖ Pray that the students will recognize wisdom's superiority as they explore the story of a poor but wise person.

❖ Tell this story: **A scholar who was very learned in Buddhist studies came to a master to learn Zen. The scholar began waxing eloquent about his extensive knowledge and all that he knew. The Zen master listened to all these words and then went to make tea. She started to pour the tea and continued until the cup overflowed and water spilled everywhere. The scholar began yelling for the Zen master to stop, since the cup was full. The Zen master ceased pouring and said, "You come and ask for teaching, but your cup is full; I can't put anything in. Before I can teach you, you'll have to empty your cup."**

❖ Discuss these questions:
  (1) Which character in this story was truly wise?
  (2) If you had met these two characters individually without knowing this story, which one would you have thought wise? Why?
  (3) What might this story suggest about how we react to someone who seems to know so much?

❖ Read aloud today's focus statement: **People are drawn in by loud voices that make an impression even though these voices lack true wisdom. To whom should we listen? Ecclesiastes teaches that we should not ignore the quiet, thoughtful words of the wise.**

(2) Explore the Story of a Person, Wise and Poor, Who Delivered a City

❖ Select a volunteer to read Ecclesiastes 9:13-16.

❖ Read the first paragraph of "Faithfully Serving" from Interpreting the Scripture and invite the students to respond to these questions:
  (1) **Why do you suppose that we generally listen to the loud and powerful voices when it is so often the quiet ones that have the wisdom to steer us in the right direction?**
  (2) **Why do you suppose that wisdom is not valued by everyone?**
  (3) **What traits mark a wise person? How can you recognize these traits, especially if the person is quiet and does not choose to bask in the spotlight?**
  (4) **The Teacher tells us that a great king could not defeat "a little city with few people in it" (9:14) as a result of the wisdom of one man, who clearly had no wealth or power. What does this story suggest about how we might overcome seemingly impossible odds?**

(3) Recognize the Superiority of Wisdom Over Force

❖ Choose a volunteer to read Ecclesiastes 9:17-18.

❖ Read "Actions and Consequences" in Interpreting the Scripture.

❖ Invite the adults to talk about how bad choices can have disastrous consequences, particularly when the choice involves "weapons of war" (9:18). The class members may be able to give some examples. Affirm all comments, though be aware that one person may believe a particular decision was a wise one, whereas another will say that same decision led to disaster.

❖ Read verse 18 and relate it to 10:1 ("Dead flies make the perfumer's ointment give off a foul odor") and the more modern saying, "One rotten apple spoils the barrel." Discuss:

(1) Why does it seem that the "one bungler" or "rotten apple" has the power to destroy an entire group?

(2) Tell us about an experience in school when one class clown or unruly student caused an entire class to be punished. How did you feel about this treatment?

(3) What can the rest of the batch or group do to keep from being destroyed by one negative influence?

(4) Seek the Great Value of Wisdom by Asking God for It

❖ Read these words: **James 1:5 states, "If any of you is lacking in wisdom, ask God, who gives to all generously and ungrudgingly, and it will be given you." James 3:17 defines God's wisdom as "first pure, then peaceable, gentle, willing to yield, full of mercy and good fruits, without a trace of partiality or hypocrisy."**

❖ Raise these questions and invite the students to respond. There are no "correct" answers, so be sure to affirm whatever each person offers.

(1) What other words would you use to describe God's wisdom?

(2) James says that all we have to do is ask for God's wisdom, yet it appears that many people do not

do that. What reasons can you suggest to explain why more of us are not asking God for wisdom?

(3) What could we do to encourage people to seek God's wisdom rather than listen to the rabble of the crowd?

(4) How might we encourage those whose lives bear the marks of God's wisdom to share that wisdom, particularly if they are quiet, unassuming people?

❖ Conclude this activity by suggesting that each person makes a silent commitment to seek God's wisdom this week.

(5) Continue the Journey

❖ Pray that the adults will ask God for wisdom.

❖ Read aloud this preparation for next week's lesson. You may also want to post it on newsprint for the students to copy.

■ **Title: Wisdom for Aging**
■ **Background Scripture: Ecclesiastes 11:7–12:14**
■ **Lesson Scripture: Ecclesiastes 11:9–12:7, 13**
■ **Focus of the Lesson: All people experience the aging process. Is there a way to appreciate the fullness of life without regard to our age? Ecclesiastes concludes that the only thing that makes life worth living is to remember and honor our creator God all the days of our lives.**

❖ Challenge the students to complete one or more of these activities for further spiritual growth related to this week's session. Post this information on newsprint for the students to copy.

(1) **Become knowledgeable about a current issue. Which names continue to come to the forefront as authorities on this issue? Do you believe that they are the ones with**

the best wisdom on the topic? Why or why not?

(2) Listen for God's still small voice to guide you as you pray and meditate. Discern God's wisdom as it relates to your life.

(3) Be alert for words of wisdom coming from someone who may seem to you to be an unlikely source. Watch yourself as you evaluate speakers on the basis of their appearance, speaking ability, and other factors that may have nothing to do with the wisdom of their words.

❖ Sing or read aloud "Open My Eyes, That I May See."

❖ Conclude today's session by leading the class in this benediction adapted from Proverbs 3:5 and 29:25: **Go forth trusting in the Lord with all your heart, knowing that one who trusts in the Lord is secure.**

UNIT 1: TEACHING AND LEARNING
WISDOM FOR AGING

PREVIEWING THE LESSON

Lesson Scripture: Ecclesiastes 11:9–12:7, 13
Background Scripture: Ecclesiastes 11:7–12:14
Key Verse: Ecclesiastes 12:13

Focus of the Lesson:
All people experience the aging process. Is there a way to appreciate the fullness of life without regard to our age? Ecclesiastes concludes that the only thing that makes life worth living is to remember and honor our creator God all the days of our lives.

Goals for the Learners:
(1) to discover the wonder and futility of life expressed in Ecclesiastes.
(2) to reflect on the meaning of life even as we move toward death.
(3) to create and act on a plan to honor God with mind, body, and soul.

Pronunciation Guide:
hebel (heh' bel)
Qoheleth (ko heh' leth)

Supplies:
Bibles, newsprint and marker, paper and pencils, hymnals

READING THE SCRIPTURE

NRSV
Ecclesiastes 11:9–12:7, 13

⁹Rejoice, young man, while you are young, and let your heart cheer you in the days of your youth. Follow the inclination of your heart and the desire of your eyes, but know that for all these things God will bring you into judgment.

¹⁰Banish anxiety from your mind, and put away pain from your body; for youth and the dawn of life are vanity.

NIV
Ecclesiastes 11:9–12:7, 13

⁹Be happy, young man, while you are
    young,
    and let your heart give you joy in the
        days of your youth.
Follow the ways of your heart
    and whatever your eyes see,
but know that for all these things
    God will bring you to judgment.
¹⁰So then, banish anxiety from your heart

71

12:1Remember your creator in the days of your youth, before the days of trouble come, and the years draw near when you will say, "I have no pleasure in them"; 2before the sun and the light and the moon and the stars are darkened and the clouds return with the rain; 3in the day when the guards of the house tremble, and the strong men are bent, and the women who grind cease working because they are few, and those who look through the windows see dimly; 4when the doors on the street are shut, and the sound of the grinding is low, and one rises up at the sound of a bird, and all the daughters of song are brought low; 5when one is afraid of heights, and terrors are in the road; the almond tree blossoms, the grasshopper drags itself along and desire fails; because all must go to their eternal home, and the mourners will go about the streets; 6before the silver cord is snapped, and the golden bowl is broken, and the pitcher is broken at the fountain, and the wheel broken at the cistern, 7and the dust returns to the earth as it was, and the breath returns to God who gave it.

13The end of the matter; all has been heard. **Fear God, and keep his commandments; for that is the whole duty of everyone.**

and cast off the troubles of your body,
  for youth and vigor are meaningless.
12:1Remember your Creator
  in the days of your youth,
before the days of trouble come
  and the years approach when you
    will say,
  "I find no pleasure in them"—
2 before the sun and the light
and the moon and the stars grow dark,
and the clouds return after the rain;
3 when the keepers of the house tremble,
  and the strong men stoop,
when the grinders cease because they
    are few,
  and those looking through the windows
    grow dim;
4when the doors to the street are closed
  and the sound of grinding fades;
when men rise up at the sound of birds,
  but all their songs grow faint;
5when men are afraid of heights
  and of dangers in the streets;
when the almond tree blossoms
  and the grasshopper drags himself
    along
  and desire no longer is stirred.
Then man goes to his eternal home
  and mourners go about the streets.
6Remember him—before the silver cord
    is severed,
  or the golden bowl is broken;
before the pitcher is shattered at the
    spring,
  or the wheel broken at the well,
7and the dust returns to the ground it
    came from,
  and the spirit returns to God who gave it.
13Now all has been heard;
  here is the conclusion of the matter:
**Fear God and keep his commandments,
  for this is the whole duty of man.**

UNDERSTANDING THE SCRIPTURE

Introduction. As mentioned in the last lesson, the Teacher in Ecclesiastes is a realist about both the joys and the sorrows of life. "Vanity" is a word used often in this book, and its primary meaning in the context of the Teacher's thought is "transitory" or "fleeting"; life is transitory, and many of the joys in life are fleeting. Because life *is* full of uncertainties and sorrow, and death is coming for all of us, we are to make the most of each moment we have and live each moment to the fullest, seeking joy and happiness in the simple gifts and relationships that God gives us.

Ecclesiastes 11:7-10. The Teacher urges us to find joy by looking for beauty in such simple things as the sunlight in each new day, for such "light is sweet" (11:7). The Hebrew word translated as "sweet" is a strong word found elsewhere in the Old Testament in the context of images that help us understand its meaning here. The joy that sunlight can bring to us is sweet like the taste of honey (Judges 14:18), like a kiss (Song of Solomon 2:3), or like the attractiveness of God's commandments, which are "sweeter also than honey" (Psalm 19:10). We are to "rejoice" during a time of light, remembering that "the days of darkness" are coming (Ecclesiastes 11:8).

We are also to rejoice and appreciate the years of our youth (11:9). For the Teacher, the enjoyment of life is an imperative from God; it is God's will for us. We see this expressed even in the grammatical structure of 11:9-10 where the imperative mood is used four times in 11:9 and twice in 11:10. Qoheleth gives two reasons for the urgency of his message to enjoy life: Life is fleeting (11:8, 10; 12:1), and it is God's will that we enjoy life. This latter thought is the best interpretation of the Teacher's words that "for all these things God will bring you into judgment" (11:9). Such divine judgment is not meant, in a negative sense, to be a warning against a hedonistic understanding of following "the inclination of your heart and the desire of your eyes" (11:9). Rather, it is to be understood in a positive sense as an announcement that God holds us responsible to follow our passions and the callings of our heart that are given to us by God. In other words, God will judge us as to whether we have made the most of life's opportunities and lived each moment to the fullest. God will bring us to judgment, as Robert Gordis suggests in *Koheleth—The Man and His World*, based on "all the joys which He has extended to you and which it is His will that you enjoy." Verse 10 reinforces this thought by urging us to banish from our hearts anxiety and troubles, which only distract us from living fully in each moment. Surely the last phrase of 11:10 does not mean to say that youth is "meaningless" (NIV) or "vanity" (NRSV) in the sense that our years of youth are worthless; rather, as noted earlier, they are painfully brief and fleeting.

Ecclesiastes 12:1-8. Verses 1-7 are a description of the approach of old age with all of its limitations and debilitating conditions. A variety of images (meteorological, a house and estate in decline, nature, and animals) are used in 12:2-5 to describe the process of change and decay that takes place in the human body and its organs as persons grow older. Some have interpreted 12:3-4 as an allegory of a deteriorating human body, referencing the "guards" as arms, the "strong men" as legs, the "women who grind" as teeth, and the "windows" as eyes growing dim. Others see a similar body allegory in 12:4 with the "doors on the street" referring to deafness, the "sound of the grinding" meaning the digestive tract, the rising up "at the sound of a bird" as inability to sleep, and "all the daughters of song" being brought low as a reference to deafness again. In 12:5 the "blossoming almond tree" could perhaps refer to the white hair of old age, and the "grasshopper" dragging itself along could refer to the increasing difficulty of walking in old age.

Whatever images or combination of images one chooses to see in these verses, they surely describe the inevitable advent of death, which is explicitly referenced at the end of 12:5 and in 12:7. Knowing how swiftly and finally old age and death come, the Teacher in 12:1, as he did in 11:9, exhorts young people to enjoy every day of their youth while they have energy and vitality and to especially remember their Creator. Following this vivid description of old age and death in 12:1-7, verse 8 once again declares how transitory and fleeting ("vanity") life is, echoing what was stated earlier in 11:8, 10.

Ecclesiastes 12:9-14. These closing verses of Ecclesiastes constitute what is commonly referred to as the epilogue or really two epilogues (12:9-11; 12:12-14). They were probably added by an editor since they speak of the Teacher in the third person, while throughout the rest of the book Qoheleth refers to himself in the first person. The first epilogue (12:9-11) gives both valuable and favorable information about the Teacher. Not only was he a professional sage working in the royal court, as the word "wise" in verse 9 would suggest, but he "also taught the people" (12:9), apparently reaching out to an audience larger than the narrow circle of the governing elite. In 12:11 the word "shepherd" (note the capital "S" in the NIV) could well be a reference to God as the Shepherd of Israel. If so, this epilogue definitely points to God as the divine source for what the Jewish wisdom teachers learned and taught.

Such an understanding prepares us to hear the final two verses, where there is explicit language about God and God's intention for our lives. Our whole duty is to "fear God, and keep his commandments" (12:13). The spirit of this exhortation is in keeping with the Teacher's thoughts elsewhere about fearing God or standing in awe before God (3:14; 5:7; 7:18; 8:13). The reminder that "God will bring every deed into judgment" (12:14) is similar in tone to 8:12 and 11:9.

INTERPRETING THE SCRIPTURE

The Transitoriness of Life

How many times have we stood by the graveside of a loved one or wistfully looked back over the years and thought, "Where have the years gone? How fleeting life is." This is one of the themes that runs through Ecclesiastes. In this book the Teacher uses the Hebrew word *hebel* thirty-eight times to describe much of what happens in life. The NRSV translates *hebel* as "vanity" while the NIV translates it as "meaningless." Just in this week's lesson alone the word is found in 11:8, 10; and three times in 12:8. When the Teacher begins the book by saying in 1:2 that "all is *hebel*" and then repeats the same phrase at the end of the book in 12:8, what does he mean to convey? In its most basic sense *hebel* means "a puff of air," "a breath," or "a vapor." When I think of a puff of air or a breath, I think of something that is important for life (we have to breathe air to remain alive) and yet quite transitory and brief. In the Psalms *hebel* is used in several places to refer to the brevity and transitory nature of human life compared to the eternity of God (Psalms 39:5, 11; 62:9; 78:33; 94:11; 144:4).

It is in this sense that we should largely understand *hebel* in Ecclesiastes. The quality to which *hebel* primarily refers in this book is not a lack of worth or meaning, as the

English words "vanity" (NRSV) and "meaningless" (NIV) suggest, but rather a lack of permanence. This is especially true in the context of our Scripture for this lesson. As wonderful as light is, it is fleeting, and the days of darkness are coming (11:8). It is good to enjoy the days of our youth while we can because they, too, are fleeting and transitory (11:9-10). Then in 12:8 the triple use of *hebel* follows the metaphorical description of old age and death. Yes, life in this world is fragile and fleeting.

Is There a Positive Word?

As his frequent use of the Hebrew term *hebel* suggests, the Teacher was very much a realist, sometimes skeptical and often cynical, who knew how fleeting life's joyous moments could be and how, inevitably, darkness follows light. He was well acquainted with the capriciousness and injustices of life. He had seen the wicked prosper and the righteous suffer (7:15; 8:14). So it is that after reading through Ecclesiastes one is compelled to ask: Does the Teacher have any positive message about the meaning and purpose of life?

The answer is yes. We have a choice as to how we are going to respond to the seeming futility and transitoriness of life. We can sit around in our frustration cursing God and complaining about why life has to be so fragile and fleeting. Or precisely because life is brief and transitory and we don't know when death will come, we can choose to enjoy every moment as a gift from God and live each moment to the fullest. In no fewer than six chapters (2:24-26; 3:12-13, 22; 5:18-20; 6:3; 8:15; 9:7-10) the Teacher exhorts us to embrace life and receive the simple pleasures of life, such as knowledge and joy, eating and drinking, daily labor, marriage, and family and friendship, as gifts from the hand of God, the gracious Provider. Then in 11:9-10 we are urged to cast aside anxieties and cares in order to enjoy the years of our youth before the times of darkness and

death come. Since life is very unpredictable and we cannot control the future, by the grace of God we are free to enjoy the present.

Such is the positive word that the Teacher has for us: *Carpe diem!* (Seize the day!) Embrace each moment and each day as a gift from God and live it to the fullest!

Qoheleth and Jesus: Their Understanding of God

Over the centuries Christian thinkers have wondered if there is a connection between the teachings of Qoheleth and Jesus, between the Teacher and the Master Teacher. There are similarities in their teaching. Although Jesus brought a positive, hope-filled word in his ministry, Jesus was also a realist. He knew well the devastating consequences of human sin and selfishness; that is what put him on the cross. And with Qoheleth-like pragmatism Jesus admonished his followers to "not worry about tomorrow, for tomorrow will bring worries of its own. Today's trouble is enough for today" (Matthew 6:34). This is the context for Jesus' teaching in Matthew 6:25-33 that his disciples should not be anxious about life's basic needs; rather, they should daily trust God to provide for them. Thus both Jesus and Qoheleth taught that it was God's will for us to let go of our anxieties and enjoy life, to embrace relationships and live life to the fullest. Both believed that God will hold us accountable for our actions (Ecclesiastes 11:10; 12:14). Both admonished us to trust God ("fear God, and keep his commandments," Ecclesiastes 12:13) as the giver of life and true wisdom.

However, Jesus had a different motivation for his teaching, rooted in a different understanding of God. W. Sibley Towner observed that Jesus was not drawn, as Qoheleth was, by "a melancholy sense of the fleetingness of it all, but by the nearness and greatness of the kingdom of God and God's righteousness (Matthew 6:33)." In other words, Jesus did share with Qoheleth a sense of realism about life and a belief in God's working in the world. But whereas in Qoheleth's thought God was more of a mysterious, inscrutable Presence in the background, for Jesus God was front and center and actively present in everyday life. Jesus was exuberant in talking about God's reign and purpose for human affairs and God's active involvement in our lives, even numbering the hairs on our heads (Matthew 10:29-30).

I believe we can think of the teaching of Qoheleth as a kind of preparation to hear the gospel. The Teacher's warning about the emptiness and transitory nature of life anticipated Jesus' recognition of the vaporous quality of life; however, Jesus had an answer to fill the vacuum. The Teacher's somewhat depressing remarks about the advent of old age and death (12:1-8) prepare us to hear Jesus' glorious promise: "I am the resurrection and the life. Those who believe in me, even though they die, will live" (John 11:25). So it is that Ecclesiastes, with its cynical but realistic expression of the vicissitudes and injustices of life, helps prepare us to receive the hope-filled and life-affirming promises of the One who said, "I came that they may have life, and have it abundantly" (John 10:10).

It should be noted that the abundant life that Jesus promises, unlike Qoheleth's understanding, does not end after our years of youth, "before the days of trouble come, and the years draw near when you will say, 'I have no pleasure in them' " (12:1). Rather, with Jesus in our lives, we can speak of *growing old gracefully*: living with purpose and with commitment to serve and honor our Creator until we draw our last breath. We need to speak not of "aging" as a negative process but of "maturing" as a positive experience. And when the end comes, we can face death with great confidence and hope, assured that nothing in life or in death "will be able to separate us from the love of God in Christ Jesus our Lord" (Romans 8:39).

SHARING THE SCRIPTURE

Preparing Our Hearts

Explore this week's devotional reading, found in Psalm 71:1-12. In this prayer of an aging (71:9) musician, we hear a cry for help, for rescue from enemies. Yet we also hear words of hope and assurance, for God has been with the psalmist since before his birth (71:6). The words ring with testimony to the goodness and grace of God. Despite his situation, the psalmist continues to praise God. What words would you use to describe God? How would you describe your relationship with God? What situations prompt you to call on God now? Are you willing to trust God to be your rock and fortress?

Pray that you and the adult learners will walk closely with God, regardless of your age.

Preparing Our Minds

Study the background Scripture from Ecclesiastes 11:7–12:14 and the lesson Scripture from Ecclesiastes 11:9–12:7, 13. Think about whether there is a way to appreciate the fullness of life without regard to your age.

Write on newsprint:
❏ information for next week's lesson, found under "Continue the Journey."
❏ activities for further spiritual growth in "Continue the Journey."

LEADING THE CLASS

(1) Gather to Learn

❖ Welcome the class members and introduce any guests.

❖ Pray that the students will discover both the wonder and transitoriness of life as expressed in Ecclesiastes.

❖ Invite the participants to tell stories of someone they know who is aging well, enjoying life, and still filled with a sense of humor and ability to wonder. Next, invite the group to tell stories of someone they know (but will not name) for whom aging is a morose, debilitating experience.

❖ Ask: **Given that we all continue to age until the time of our death, why do you think that some older adults continue to experience joy in living whereas others are often depressed and complaining?**

❖ Read aloud today's focus statement: **All people experience the aging process. Is there a way to appreciate the fullness of life without regard to our age? Ecclesiastes concludes that the only thing that makes life worth living is to remember and honor our creator God all the days of our lives.**

(2) Discover the Wonder and Futility of Life Expressed in Ecclesiastes

❖ Select a volunteer to read Ecclesiastes 11:9–12:7, 13.

❖ Discuss these questions:

(1) The Teacher tells us in verse 10 to banish anxiety and put away pain. What challenges do we face and try to overcome as we try to live this way?

(2) What images of aging do you find in Ecclesiastes 12? (Use information under Ecclesiastes 12:1-8 from Understanding the Scripture to help identify ways in which people have understood these images.)

(3) Do you think these images accurately portray the aging process? Why or why not?

(4) How does the Teacher's idea that God wants us to enjoy life square with what you have been taught?

(5) On balance, do you see life as a wondrous joy, as a transitory futility, or something else? Why?

❖ Invite the adults to read in unison Ecclesiastes 12:13, which is today's key verse.

❖ Ask: **Do you think most people are in awe of God and keep God's commandments? Support your answer with evidence.**

(3) Reflect on the Meaning of Life Even as We Move Toward Death

❖ Post a sheet of newsprint on which you have written "+" on the left and "–" on the right. Title this sheet "The Effects of Aging." Encourage the adults to call out both pluses and minuses of the aging process. (Be aware that one person's plus may be someone else's minus, so list the idea in both columns if students suggest that.)

❖ Review the list to see if the adults gain a new appreciation for all stages of life as they realize the benefits of aging. Note that in the United States, we often view aging in a negative light because we are a youth-oriented society. Other societies, like many in Asia, for example, revere the wisdom and experience of their older adults. Suggest that the way a culture views aging will certainly have an impact on the way we see ourselves as we age.

❖ Encourage the students to talk about trade-offs they see. For example, an older person will likely not be able to play a hard game of soccer, but he or she may have many stories of life experiences to share. Ask the adults to name other trade-offs that to them are of equal value.

❖ Point out that one real plus older adults have is that they are often better equipped to zero in on what is important. The longer any of us lives, the better able we are to discern meaning and set priorities.

(4) Create and Act on a Plan to Honor God With Mind, Body, and Soul

❖ Recall that the Teacher tells us that God wants us to enjoy life. Read "Is There a Positive Word?" from Interpreting the Scripture.

❖ Distribute paper and pencils. Invite the adults to consider something they can do mentally, physically, spiritually, or all of these, to honor God. Here are some ideas: *be more mindful of what I eat, exercise regularly, read my Bible daily, pray without ceasing, investigate the lives of people who clearly obeyed God and try to find ways to do what they have done, serve others with a grateful heart.*

❖ Post newsprint and invite students to call out their ideas, which you will write down.

❖ Challenge the adults to select items from this list that work for them and create a plan as to what they will do to honor God with mind, body, and soul. Suggest that they write their plan on paper.

(5) Continue the Journey

❖ Pray that the adults will go forth committed to honoring God with their minds, bodies, and souls all the days of their lives.

❖ Read aloud this preparation for next week's lesson. You may also want to post it on newsprint for the students to copy.

■ **Title: Tradition and Love**
■ **Background Scripture: Song of Solomon 4:8–5:1**
■ **Lesson Scripture: Song of Solomon 4:8–5:1**
■ **Focus of the Lesson: People find it difficult to express their feelings about love and life. How can we find words to describe our feelings? Song of Solomon uses poetry and figurative language to talk about love and life.**

❖ Challenge the students to complete one or more of these activities for further spiritual growth related to this week's session. Post this information on newsprint for the students to copy.

(1) **Spend some time with an elderly person who seems to have a zest for living. Ask him or her to share secrets for such a positive, productive attitude.**

(2) **Write a journal entry in which you discuss what makes your life worth living. Be honest, since this is for your eyes only.**

(3) **Write your own obituary. Give thanks for your life. If there are contributions that you had hoped to make but have not yet done, do whatever you can to clear up these loose ends in your life.**

❖ Sing or read aloud "I Will Trust in the Lord."

❖ Conclude today's session by leading the class in this benediction adapted from Proverbs 3:5 and 29:25: **Go forth trusting in the Lord with all your heart, knowing that one who trusts in the Lord is secure.**

UNIT 1: TEACHING AND LEARNING
TRADITION AND LOVE

PREVIEWING THE LESSON

Lesson Scripture: Song of Solomon 4:8–5:1
Background Scripture: Song of Solomon 4:8–5:1
Key Verse: Song of Solomon 4:16

Focus of the Lesson:
People find it difficult to express their feelings about love and life. How can we find words to describe our feelings? Song of Solomon uses poetry and figurative language to talk about love and life.

Goals for the Learners:
(1) to recognize the music of love found in the Song of Solomon.
(2) to realize and accept the beauty and wonder of love shared in a committed relationship.
(3) to act on building a relationship that honors a marriage commitment.

Pronunciation Guide:
Amana (uh may' nuh)
calamus (kal' uh muhs)
Senir (see' nuhr)

Supplies:
Bibles, newsprint and marker, paper and pencils, hymnals

READING THE SCRIPTURE

NRSV
Song of Solomon 4:8–5:1
8 Come with me from Lebanon, my bride;
   come with me from Lebanon.
  Depart from the peak of Amana,
    from the peak of Senir and Hermon,
  from the dens of lions,
    from the mountains of leopards.

NIV
Song of Solomon 4:8–5:1
8Come with me from Lebanon, my bride,
   come with me from Lebanon.
  Descend from the crest of Amana,
    from the top of Senir, the summit of
   Hermon,
  from the lions' dens

9 You have ravished my heart, my sister,
  my bride,
    you have ravished my heart with
    a glance of your eyes,
    with one jewel of your necklace.
10 How sweet is your love, my sister,
  my bride!
    how much better is your love than
    wine,
    and the fragrance of your oils than any
    spice!
11 Your lips distill nectar, my bride;
    honey and milk are under your tongue;
    the scent of your garments is like the
    scent of Lebanon.
12 A garden locked is my sister, my bride,
    a garden locked, a fountain sealed.
13 Your channel is an orchard of
    pomegranates
    with all choicest fruits,
    henna with nard,
14 nard and saffron, calamus and cinnamon,
    with all trees of frankincense,
    myrrh and aloes,
    with all chief spices—
15 a garden fountain, a well of living water,
    and flowing streams from Lebanon.
16 Awake, O north wind,
    and come, O south wind!
  Blow upon my garden
    that its fragrance may be wafted
    abroad.
  **Let my beloved come to his garden,
  and eat its choicest fruits.**
5:1 I come to my garden, my sister, my bride;
    I gather my myrrh with my spice,
    I eat my honeycomb with my honey,
    I drink my wine with my milk.

and the mountain haunts of the
  leopards.
9 You have stolen my heart, my sister,
  my bride;
    you have stolen my heart
  with one glance of your eyes,
    with one jewel of your necklace.
10 How delightful is your love, my sister,
  my bride!
    How much more pleasing is your love
    than wine,
    and the fragrance of your perfume than
    any spice!
11 Your lips drop sweetness as the
    honeycomb, my bride;
    milk and honey are under your tongue.
    The fragrance of your garments is like
    that of Lebanon.
12 You are a garden locked up, my sister,
  my bride;
    you are a spring enclosed, a sealed
    fountain.
13 Your plants are an orchard of pomegranates
    with choice fruits,
    with henna and nard,
14 nard and saffron,
    calamus and cinnamon,
    with every kind of incense tree,
    with myrrh and aloes
    and all the finest spices.
15 You are a garden fountain,
    a well of flowing water
    streaming down from Lebanon.
16 Awake, north wind,
    and come, south wind!
  Blow on my garden,
    that its fragrance may spread abroad.
  **Let my lover come into his garden
  and taste its choice fruits.**
5:1 I have come into my garden, my sister,
    my bride;
    I have gathered my myrrh with my spice.
    I have eaten my honeycomb and my honey;
    I have drunk my wine and my milk.

UNDERSTANDING THE SCRIPTURE

Introduction. When we open our Bibles to the Song of Solomon, we encounter a content and language quite different from the rest of the Old Testament. Here there are no prophetic announcements of divine judgment or descriptions of heroism, tribal conflict, desert wanderings, royal intrigue, or the giving of the law. There are no proverbial sayings or lofty psalms of praise and thanksgiving to God. In fact, unique among all biblical books, with the exception of Esther, is the fact that God is not mentioned at all in this book. Nor are there any allusions to any of the overarching themes of Israel's history and religious traditions or covenant relationship with God. Rather, the focus is on the private relationship between an unnamed woman and man, who are very much in love, with occasional comments made by a group of companions, sometimes nameless while at other times referred to as the "daughters of Jerusalem" (Song of Solomon 8:4). The language of these eight chapters is the language of love that uses metaphors and images to express sensuality, longing, disappointment, human affection, and intimacy. According to Renita J. Weems, the Song of Solomon is a collection of lyrical poems filled with complex emotions, "candid longing and tender expressions of desire and desperation by both the lover and her beloved." The ongoing series of lyrical exchanges between the female protagonist and her shepherd suitor represents the only biblical book in which a female voice predominates.

Our lesson Scripture this week follows immediately after three passages that provide important background for our understanding. In 3:1-5 the woman recounts what appears to have been a dream describing her desperate search for her lover. This is followed in 3:6-11, as her reverie continues, by a description of an ornate wedding processional and ceremony—a vision of her wedding day when she can finally consummate her union with her beloved. Then in 4:1-7 the man extols his bride's beauty, describing in detail the loveliness and grace of her eyes and hair, her teeth and lips, her neck and breasts. In his eyes she is flawless (4:7), and her beauty draws him to her.

Song of Solomon 4:8. The above-mentioned verses prepare us for 4:8 when the groom issues an invitation for his bride to join him, perhaps for the honeymoon. But there are questions. Why are the mountainous regions of Lebanon, Amana, Senir, and Hermon (the dominant peak of Israel, 9,100 feet above sea level and the source of the Jordan River) specifically mentioned and in connection with dens of lions and leopards? As with the rest of the poetry in this book, the mention of these mountains and the predatory animals that roamed there in ancient times is meant to be metaphorical. A couple of interpretations have been suggested. One points to these ominous mountain locations as a way of talking metaphorically about the bride's inaccessibility. Certainly, a universal theme in love poetry in all cultures is that lovers are perpetually confronted by dangers and impediments that threaten to keep them apart. Another interpretation is that, whatever dangers and difficulties these place names may represent, the focus of the verse is the groom's invitation for his bride to come away from those dangers to be with him on a peaceful, remote honeymoon where the two of them can be alone and safe in order to share the intimacy of their marital union.

Song of Solomon 4:9-15. Having detailed the beautiful features of his bride in 4:1-7, the groom now employs graphic images from his first-century Palestinian culture to describe the impact of those features on him and how they have aroused him. "You have ravished my heart" ("stolen my heart," 4:9 NIV) expresses his feelings of arousal. In fact, the term "heart" is used in other Middle Eastern poetry as a description of the male sexual organ, which, in its aroused state, readies the husband for intercourse. It should be noted also that the word "sister" (4:9, 10, 12; 5:1) was used often in love poetry as a term of endearment promising the bride a place in her husband's life as close as that of a blood relative.

Beginning in 4:10 the talk leads to touching and caressing and then to passionate kissing in 4:11. Note the reference there to "lips" and "tongue" which denotes the depth and fullness of the kissing. "Milk and honey" is a favorite biblical metaphor for sweetness; the Promised Land was a land that "flows with milk and honey" (Numbers 13:27). Finally in 4:12-15 the metaphor of a garden with its "choicest fruits" suggests the consummation of their marital union as the couple enters fully into the passionate act of love making. Throughout these verses the images are erotic. The garden fruits, plants, fragrances, and spices that are mentioned (wine, honey and milk, pomegranates, henna, nard, saffron, calamus, cinnamon, frankincense, myrrh, and aloes) summon forth the taste and scents of romance. This poetry is quite evocative. It has been suggested that the garden metaphor is the ideal symbol of love. Renita J. Weems notes: "The garden is both the ideal place for sexual consummation and a metaphor for the woman's fertility."

Song of Solomon 4:16–5:1. In response to her husband's sexual advances and his words of adoration for her body, the aroused wife can remain silent no longer. She first invites the wind to blow upon her "garden" so that the scent of her womanhood will waft around her husband as a sign that she is ready to receive the fullness of his love for her. Then she invites her husband ("my beloved") to come to "his garden, and eat its choicest fruits" (4:16). She is aroused and ready to consummate their marital union. Her husband's willing response is expressed in 5:1. With the fragrance of her body wafting in the breeze, he gladly comes and immerses himself in the rapturous act of making love to his wife. This is not a picture of one person dominating another, but of two persons joyfully and willingly giving themselves to each other in an act of mutual love and commitment. The two "become one flesh" in fulfillment of God's intention (Genesis 2:24).

INTERPRETING THE SCRIPTURE

Mutual Love

When one reads through the Song of Solomon, the vivid imagery and the erotic nature of the language can initially be shocking, but the content is not lewd or obscene. In fact, the love that is described in these poems is quite beautiful. The dialogue between the protagonist and her beloved passionately expresses the longing, commitment, and consummation of genuine self-giving, mutual love. This is so different from much of what is written in our time about love and sex. Sadly, reports about rape, sexual and spousal abuse, and the abuse of power in exchange for sexual favors seem commonplace and are in the headlines almost daily.

Because sex and power seem to be virtually synonymous in our culture, it is a pleasure to read these love poems in the Song of Solomon that model an intimacy that does not abuse power and that celebrate self-giving love that seeks the fulfillment of the other. In 4:1–5:1 the two lovers each extend an invitation to the other; there is no coercion involved. Mutual love in covenant union is the context for their sharing with each other their bodies and their passion. The shepherd celebrates the body of his lover, according to Renita J. Weems, "without any attempt to dominate or subdue her. He just appreciates his beloved's beauty."

Exclusive Love

One of the central themes that runs through the Bible from Genesis 12 to the end of Revelation is the inclusive, redemptive love of God for all people. Such a focus on inclusiveness is especially strong in the Book of Jonah and the teachings of Jesus and Paul. But the Bible also places a strong emphasis on the *exclusive* nature of love between covenant partners, whether those partners be God and Israel or husband and wife. In the context of our culture where there is an implicit societal acceptance of casual sex and extramarital dalliances, it is extremely refreshing to see the focus in the Song of Solomon on commitment and the exclusiveness of love between our protagonist and her beloved shepherd. Over and over in our lesson Scripture the possessive pronoun "my" is emphatically used by both partners: "my bride," "my sister," "my garden," "my beloved." The phrases "a garden locked" and "a fountain sealed" in 4:12 are metaphors for a chaste woman who has not yet engaged in sexual relations. The garden gate of her womanhood is locked and sealed, to be opened only by her husband. There are other expressions of exclusive love found in the book as well, such as "My beloved is mine and I am his" (2:16). See 6:3 and 7:10 for similar expressions.

Marriage

Although the word "God" is not found once in the pages of this book, after reading these poems we realize that we are dealing with one of God's greatest gifts: the gift of sexual love expressed in the exclusive intimacy of a committed relationship that the Bible calls marriage. As mentioned earlier,

one of the important passages (3:6-11) leading into our lesson Scripture is the description of an ornate wedding processional and ceremony of which the woman dreams. Then four times within our brief lesson Scripture the man refers to his lover as "my bride" (4:8, 9, 10; 5:1). Finally, as mentioned in the previous section, the intimate relationship so graphically described in the Song of Solomon is that of mutual, exclusive love—the kind of love that is meant to be shared between marriage partners. All of this points to marriage as being the context within which the love between our protagonist and her beloved is consummated.

Throughout the Bible, the intimate sharing of life that we call marriage is celebrated and even viewed as a fitting metaphor to describe the relationship between God and human beings. The opening chapters of Genesis picture the union of the first man and first woman and say it was solemnized with a binding command: "they became one flesh" (2:24). Genesis 1:27 affirms that they were created in God's image, male and female. The theological implication is that "their capacity for strong interpersonal bonding with each other was a reflection of their union and communion with God," as David A. Hubbard suggests. Of course, in any marriage relationship there can be struggles and challenges as partners seek to live faithfully and lovingly within their covenant relationship. The Old Testament prophets understood that as well, and some of them (Hosea, Isaiah, and Ezekiel) employed the metaphor of marriage to talk about the relationship between God and Israel. Israel is meant to be God's faithful spouse, bound to God in covenant loyalty. However, Israel becomes the unfaithful partner who breaks her covenant with God and chases after other gods. Isaiah 62:4 looks to a day when Jerusalem, having been taken into exile and called "Forsaken" and "Desolate" in judgment, will be renamed "My Delight Is in Her" and "Married." The focus is on God's redeeming faithfulness and love that will take Israel back into the marriage.

In the New Testament, Jesus identifies himself as the Bridegroom who urges the wedding guests (his followers) to always be prepared for his arrival and to rejoice in his presence. (See Matthew 9:14-15; 25:1-13; John 3:29.) In Ephesians 5:21-33, Paul writes that human marriages are meant to be reflections of the divine faithfulness and love that Paul saw in Christ's marriage to the church. Finally, in the Book of Revelation the seer of Patmos uses the metaphor of marriage to describe the culmination of all that God has intended, as God has guided human history with a redeeming hand: "for the marriage of the Lamb has come, and his bride has made herself ready" (19:7). Such is the larger biblical context in which the soon-to-wed groom and love poetry we call the Song of Solomon fits.

In the Garden

The word "garden" is found six times in our lesson Scripture (4:12 [twice], 15, 16 [twice]; 5:1) and has symbolic meaning as a place of beauty and fertility where love is consummated. Gardens also have a prominent place in several other key biblical passages in which they become places of personal encounter where genuine love is expressed. One thinks of the garden in Genesis 2 where our first parents were placed to enjoy fellowship with God and each other as well as bountiful fruits and blessings. Of course, in Genesis 3 their love story in the garden goes awry because of their disobedience, and the innocence they enjoyed is replaced by guilt and shame and a diminishing of mutual sexual fulfillment; the woman feels subjugated to the man (Genesis 3:16). By contrast, in the garden of the Song of Solomon mutuality is reestablished.

I think of other biblical gardens as well. In the garden of Gethsemane Jesus was in agony and felt abandoned by his disciples; yet there he experienced the intimacy of his Father's love and presence. Then there was the garden of resurrection where, on the first Easter, Jesus encountered Mary Magdalene, and hope was born out of despair (John 20:11-18). Finally, the Revelation to John gives us a vision of that garden in the New Jerusalem in which will be found the tree of life with bountiful fruit and leaves that will bring God's healing to the nations (Revelation 22:1-2).

SHARING THE SCRIPTURE

Preparing Our Hearts

Explore this week's devotional reading, found in Genesis 2:18-24. Here we find the familiar story of the creation of *adam*, the human God created from the dirt, and the creation of a partner for *adam*. They were identified by their genders: man (*ish*) and woman (*ishshah*) (2:23). God's intention was that they would "become one flesh" (2:24). God certainly intended a loving, intimate partnership. How have we fallen short of God's ideal for us? What impact does our culture's portrayal of sex and romantic love, along with our rampant divorce rate and spousal abuse, have on our expectations for marriage?

Pray that you and the adult learners will give thanks for God's good gift of marriage.

Preparing Our Minds

Study the background Scripture and the lesson Scripture, both of which are found in

Song of Solomon 4:8–5:1. Where do you find words to express your deepest feelings about love and life?

Write on newsprint:
❑ information for next week's lesson, found under "Continue the Journey."
❑ activities for further spiritual growth in "Continue the Journey."

LEADING THE CLASS

(1) Gather to Learn

❖ Welcome the class members and introduce any guests.

❖ Pray that the students will be attuned to the music of love found in today's Scripture lesson from Song of Solomon.

❖ Read: **We have probably all heard stories of high school sweethearts who broke up, drifted apart, or went their separate ways to college and reconnected years later, often at a class reunion. Sometimes these couples just did not know how to express themselves as teens. But life experiences, frequently including a failed marriage, have taught them to be more articulate and open about their feelings. In some cases, these two who were sweethearts at one time are in a position to marry many years later. How tragic that a failure to communicate was the root cause of a breakup that could have resulted in many years of a happy marriage.**

❖ Read aloud today's focus statement: **People find it difficult to express their feelings about love and life. How can we find words to describe our feelings? Song of Solomon uses poetry and figurative language to talk about love and life.**

(2) Recognize the Music of Love Found in the Song of Solomon

❖ Read or retell "Introduction" in Understanding the Scripture to set the stage for encountering this biblical literature that is quite different from the rest of the Bible.

❖ Create a reader's theater by choosing two men to read Song of Solomon 4:8-15; 5:1 and two women to read 4:16.

❖ Invite the students to look in their Bibles and name images that convey the love story found in Song of Solomon. ("Song of Solomon 4:9-15" in Understanding the Scripture will be helpful, as will "In the Garden" in Interpreting the Scripture.) You may wish to list these images on newsprint.

❖ Discuss these questions:
　(1) How would you compare and contrast these images with the ones so often found in the media and society at large?
　(2) What can we learn from the description in Song of Solomon concerning a biblical view of romantic love and its appropriate expression?

(3) Realize and Accept the Beauty and Wonder of Love Shared in a Committed Relationship

❖ Read or retell as much as you choose from "Mutual Love" in Interpreting the Scripture, and be sure to make this point: The love poems of Song of Solomon "model an intimacy that does not abuse power and . . . celebrate self-giving love that seeks the fulfillment of the other." Similarly, read or retell information from "Exclusive Love" in Interpreting the Scripture, being certain to emphasize that for most relationships the Bible stresses inclusiveness but in the matter of romantic relationships "the Bible also places a strong emphasis on the *exclusive* nature of love between covenant partners."

❖ Ask these questions:
　(1) Why do you think the Bible emphasizes the exclusive nature of a romantic relationship?
　(2) What is at stake in this kind of relationship?
　(3) Without naming names or going into detail, what can you tell us about romantic relationships that are not based on exclusivity?

❖ **Option:** Invite several volunteers to tell stories of how they met and decided to marry their spouses. Use discretion with this option, particularly if there are unmarried adults in the group for whom such stories may evoke painful emotions.

(4) Act on Building a Relationship That Honors a Marriage Commitment

❖ Read "Marriage" from Interpreting the Scripture. Note biblical views on marriage.

❖ Form small groups. If possible, try to discreetly include currently married, previously married, and unmarried participants in each group. Distribute paper and pencils. Challenge each group to brainstorm at least ten things that a couple can do to build a relationship that honors their marriage commitment. Encourage them to focus on one or two ideas and suggest specific ways that their plan can be fulfilled. For example, if "spend more time together" is an idea for relationship building, what can be done to make that happen? Ideas that may promote greater time together include *reserving a date night at least twice a month; planning to have a quiet, twosome-only dinner once a month; cutting back on a volunteer project to free up time for the beloved; hiring someone to do a regular household chore so that you can spend more time together.*

❖ Call the groups together and invite them to report on their ideas.

❖ Challenge those who are married to use at least one of the ideas they have heard to build up their relationship. Recommend that others may want to share these ideas with those who are married if such an opportunity presents itself.

(5) Continue the Journey

❖ Pray that the adults will honor marriage commitments, both their own—if they are married—and the marriage commitments of others.

❖ Read aloud this preparation for next week's lesson. You may also want to post it on newsprint for the students to copy.

■ **Title: Living as God's People**
■ **Background Scripture: Matthew 5:1-12**
■ **Lesson Scripture: Matthew 5:1-12**
■ **Focus of the Lesson: People seek happiness in their lives. Is there a way to satisfy the search? In the Beatitudes, Jesus lists nine ways that God blesses those who seek first the kingdom of God.**

❖ Challenge the students to complete one or more of these activities for further spiritual growth related to this week's session. Post this information on newsprint for the students to copy.

(1) **Consider: What does a Christ-centered marriage look like to you? If you are married, how would you rate your marriage in relation to the ideal? If you are not married, what expectations do you have of yourself and a future partner if you plan to marry?**

(2) **Recall that in the Bible God is depicted as Israel's husband and the church is portrayed as the Bride of Christ. How do these images help you to understand God's intentions for a faithful marital relationship?**

(3) **Encourage engaged and newly married couples to make Christ the center of their relationship so that they might experience the kind of marriage that God wants for them.**

❖ Sing or read aloud "Your Love, O God, Has Called Us Here."

❖ Conclude today's session by leading the class in this benediction adapted from Proverbs 3:5 and 29:25: **Go forth trusting in the Lord with all your heart, knowing that one who trusts in the Lord is secure.**

UNIT 2: JESUS TEACHES WISDOM

LIVING AS GOD'S PEOPLE

PREVIEWING THE LESSON

Lesson Scripture: Matthew 5:1-12
Background Scripture: Matthew 5:1-12
Key Verse: Matthew 5:6

Focus of the Lesson:
People seek happiness in their lives. Is there a way to satisfy the search? In the Beatitudes, Jesus lists nine ways that God blesses those who seek first the kingdom of God.

Goals for the Learners:
(1) to examine Jesus' teachings on the Mount.
(2) to experience the blessings of God's reign already present on the earth.
(3) to look for the blessings of the Beatitudes in their everyday lives.

Pronunciation Guide:
makarios (mak ar' ee os)

Supplies:
Bibles, newsprint and marker, paper and pencils, hymnals

READING THE SCRIPTURE

NRSV
Matthew 5:1-12

¹When Jesus saw the crowds, he went up the mountain; and after he sat down, his disciples came to him. ²Then he began to speak, and taught them, saying:

³"Blessed are the poor in spirit, for theirs is the kingdom of heaven.

NIV
Matthew 5:1-12

¹Now when he saw the crowds, he went up on a mountainside and sat down. His disciples came to him, ²and he began to teach them, saying:

³"Blessed are the poor in spirit,
    for theirs is the kingdom of heaven.

4"Blessed are those who mourn, for they will be comforted.

5"Blessed are the meek, for they will inherit the earth.

6"Blessed are those who hunger and thirst for righteousness, for they will be filled.

7"Blessed are the merciful, for they will receive mercy.

8"Blessed are the pure in heart, for they will see God.

9"Blessed are the peacemakers, for they will be called children of God.

10"Blessed are those who are persecuted for righteousness' sake, for theirs is the kingdom of heaven.

11"Blessed are you when people revile you and persecute you and utter all kinds of evil against you falsely on my account. 12Rejoice and be glad, for your reward is great in heaven, for in the same way they persecuted the prophets who were before you."

4Blessed are those who mourn,
    for they will be comforted.

5Blessed are the meek,
    for they will inherit the earth.

6Blessed are those who hunger and thirst for righteousness,
    for they will be filled.

7Blessed are the merciful,
    for they will be shown mercy.

8Blessed are the pure in heart,
    for they will see God.

9Blessed are the peacemakers,
    for they will be called sons of God.

10Blessed are those who are persecuted
    because of righteousness,
    for theirs is the kingdom of heaven.

11"Blessed are you when people insult you, persecute you and falsely say all kinds of evil against you because of me. 12Rejoice and be glad, because great is your reward in heaven, for in the same way they persecuted the prophets who were before you."

UNDERSTANDING THE SCRIPTURE

Introduction. The first twelve verses of the Sermon on the Mount (Matthew 5–7) are commonly referred to as the Beatitudes. It's important to state what the Beatitudes are *not*. They should not be read as practical advice for successful living or as a list of nine easy steps on how to procure God's blessing. They are not a list of rules to follow, but rather a description of nine qualities that are to characterize the lives of Jesus' followers.

In general, the first four beatitudes (5:3-6) could be thought of as describing the disciples' relationship to God, while the last five beatitudes (5:7-12) describe the disciples' duties and relationships with others. Note that each beatitude begins with the adjective "blessed" followed by the subject of the sentence that expresses an attitude or behavior characteristic of Jesus' disciples

(for example, "those who mourn," "the meek," and so on). Then in each beatitude there is a second clause beginning with "for" that explains the blessing given by God, whether in the present or the future: Mourners are comforted, the hungry are satisfied, the merciful receive mercy.

Matthew 5:1-2. Matthew 5:1 tells us that Jesus "sat down," following the normal custom of a rabbi who would have sat down to teach, and "his disciples came to him." Our English word "disciple" comes from a Greek word that means "learner or pupil or apprentice." Matthew quite intentionally presents Jesus as a rabbi or teacher who "began to speak, and taught them" (5:2).

Matthew 5:3. The "poor in spirit" should not be confused with the economically poor, and certainly one should never read into this beatitude, or its parallel in Luke 6:20, that the state of economic poverty is being blessed or honored by God. That would go against all that we know about God's justice and special concern for the poor found throughout the Bible. The "poor in spirit" are those who acknowledge their spiritual poverty and their dependence on God. They are beggars before God who confess their need of God. Because of their openness to and desire for God, the blessings and gifts that come from a relationship with God are easily poured into their lives in the present ("for theirs is the kingdom of heaven"). "The kingdom of heaven" is Matthew's phrase for the reign of God or what Mark and Luke call the kingdom of God.

Matthew 5:4. This beatitude is often read at funerals, but the mourning mentioned here cannot be understood as relating only to the grieving process following a death. In the Bible the concept of lamentation also included mourning over sin and evil in the world and over the condition of God's people when they were oppressed. So it is here. The key to understanding any of the beatitudes lies in the life of the One who taught them. As Jesus wept over the sin of others and over the unrepentant city of Jerusalem that would not receive him (Luke 19:41), so are we, as Jesus' disciples, to weep over our sin and over the evil and violence of our world.

Matthew 5:5. The Greek word translated as "meek" can also mean "gentle, humble, considerate." However, meekness should not be confused with weakness, as it sometimes is. Being meek does not make one a wimp. Jesus used this term, "meek," to describe himself (Matthew 11:29 KJV), and he was anything but a pushover. His inner strength was incredible as he did battle with the powers of corruption and evil, while the whole time renouncing the violent methods of this-worldly power. To be meek does not mean to be self-deprecating but means to know our true worth as God's children and with inner strength to do God's will gently and humbly in the world.

Matthew 5:6. Those who "hunger and thirst for righteousness" are those who long for God and for God's kingdom to be established and God's will to be done. "Righteousness" is a key concept in Matthew's Gospel that refers both to God's activity of bringing us into a right relationship with God (God's gift of salvation to us) and our seeking to actively do the will of God (our ethical response to God).

Matthew 5:7. To be merciful is to show unconditional compassion for people in need. We see such mercy modeled in Jesus' life and teachings, especially in the Gospel of Matthew. In 9:13 and 12:7 Jesus quotes the prophet Hosea, who says that God "desires mercy, not sacrifice" (6:6 NIV). And in one of his parables about forgiveness, we find these words: "Should you not have had mercy on your fellow slave, as I had mercy on you?" (Matthew 18:33). It's all about grace. As we receive mercy from God, we, in turn, are to become channels to convey mercy to others. The blessing promised to those who show such compassion is that they "will receive mercy" from God (see 25:31-46).

Matthew 5:8. The word "pure" means unmixed, and this beatitude calls us to examine our motives to see whether they are unmixed or are tainted with self-serving aims. Jesus reminds us in Matthew 6:4, 6, 18 that God, who sees "in secret," looks into our hearts when judging us in order to see our motives as well as our outward actions. The "pure in heart" are not divided in loyalty but live with single-minded devotion to God. They are transparent before God and others, utterly sincere, genuine in commitment, and without hypocrisy.

Matthew 5:9. Being peacemakers should come naturally to us as followers of the One who has broken down the dividing wall of hostility and reconciled us to God and to one another, making peace by the blood of the cross (Ephesians 2:14-16). As it is with the "meek," being peacemakers does not suggest a passive attitude but rather a strong, positive action. Making peace and working toward reconciliation, whether between two persons or two opposing groups, can be hard work, but it is worth every effort, for it is divine work.

Matthew 5:10-12. The final beatitudes remind us that disciples may well face misunderstanding and unjust persecution because of their commitment to righteousness and to God's purposes, which are often antithetical to the world's purposes.

Certainly the One who spoke these beatitudes understood this. Jesus experienced tremendous suffering and persecution, and the disciple is not above his or her Master. Note how 5:11-12 is a transitional passage related in content to 5:10 but shifting from third-person to second-person speech as it leads into the rest of the Sermon on the Mount, which is largely instruction in the imperative mood.

INTERPRETING THE SCRIPTURE

To Be Blessed

The English word "blessed" begins each of the Beatitudes. It is translated from an original Greek word *makarios*, which can also be translated as "happy, fortunate, well-off." A few English versions (for example, the Good News Translation) translate *makarios* as "happy," but that can be misleading. For happiness is more of a subjective, psychological state of inward satisfaction, whereas Jesus is making an objective judgment declaring not what his disciples may feel like ("happy"), but how God sees them and what God is declaring them to be: They are blessed.

What does it mean to be blessed? It is clear that for the biblical writers, "being blessed" had its roots not in material things or circumstances that make us feel good, but rather in God, who loves and sustains us through all circumstances. In the end, happiness has too shallow a meaning for "blessing." For example, suppose I buy a new car and am very happy with the color and the way it runs before the first rattle. But in a few weeks, after it gets as muddy as every other car and loses that new-car smell, it becomes just a way to get around. That car has temporarily made me happy, but it has not blessed me.

On the other hand, I think of a time in my life when I was in deep grief. My father died when I was a young adult, and the emptiness was unbearable. But in my unhappiness and grief were those who listened to me, supported me, and held me when I cried. Above all, I felt God's sustaining strength, and I knew the truth of "Blessed are those who mourn, for they will be comforted" (Matthew 5:4). I experienced blessing in the midst of my unhappiness. The point is that blessing has its roots in God and in God's love for us. Being blessed has to do with our relationship with God, no matter what our outward circumstances may be. We can be blessed even when we mourn or are persecuted. We are blessed when we find the source of our life and strength in God.

What Will Satisfy Us?

In our culture we seem to have insatiable appetites for the newest, the biggest, and the best. Corporate America and Madison Avenue tell us we should not be satisfied with today's model when there is something bigger and better coming tomorrow. This is especially true in the field of technology, which is constantly producing faster computers, better televisions with higher-definition pictures, and cell phones that will do most everything except serve lunch. For years the fast-food restaurateurs have told us that we should not be satisfied with a normal-size meal when for a few pennies more we can super-size it. When and where will it ever stop? It seems that we are being consumed by our consumerism. Yet people seem no happier or more fulfilled because of all the new gadgets and things that they accumulate.

Jesus has an answer for our self-destructive consumerism in the Beatitudes. His wisdom lies in his understanding of what it means to be truly human. As finite human creatures, we are all created with a variety of needs, along with appetites to meet those needs. In order to develop as healthy persons, we have an appetite for food, water, and sleep to meet our physical needs. We have an emotional appetite for human contact and a sense of belonging, for caring and shared love. We have a spiritual appetite that can only be satisfied through a personal relationship with God, who calls us to live for a higher purpose than just satisfying our basic physical needs.

Knowing that our spiritual needs are the key to understanding our other needs, Jesus said, "Blessed are those who hunger and thirst for righteousness, for they will be filled [satisfied]" (Matthew 5:6). Our physical appetites seem to be insatiable. We have a wonderful meal that fills us, but only temporarily, for within a few hours we are hungry again. We buy "things" only to discover that within a short while we want something bigger, better, and newer. In the emotional arena we hunger for love and companionship, but if there is not also a spiritual dimension to direct our hunger, love easily becomes distorted into lust and self-centeredness rather than other-centered desire. No, Jesus knew that only a hunger and thirst for a right relationship with God and the doing of God's will ("righteousness") will fully satisfy us. Several of the other beatitudes echo this. Blessed are the "poor in spirit" (those who are beggars before God and depend on God), the

"meek," "the peacemakers" (the humble who seek to gently do God's will and the divine work of reconciliation), and the "merciful" (those whose lives reflect God's compassion).

A Reversal of Values

For those of us who are Christians in North America the final beatitude may seem strange, almost foreign. Most of us do not experience persecution for seeking to live as faithful disciples of Jesus, at least not the kind of extreme persecution (physical torture and death) that the early Christians faced or that Christians in other parts of the world face today. After all, we live in a country that practices freedom of religion and guarantees certain protections. However, we may well be able to identify with Jesus' comments on persecution in 5:11: "Blessed are you when people revile you . . . and utter all kinds of evil against you falsely on my account." It's very possible that as we seek to faithfully live out Jesus' teachings and values we may feel misunderstood at times and even reviled. This is so because the values expressed in the Beatitudes represent a radical reversal of the values of our secular and power-oriented society. For example, in the early days of the American invasion of Iraq in 2003, many who spoke out against the war on the basis of their Christian conscience were reviled as traitors or labeled as unpatriotic.

As we think about the values expressed in the Beatitudes, we see how radically different they are. The world typically judges the rich to be blessed, not the poor or the poor in spirit. Our society tends to admire the carefree, not those who take sin and evil so seriously that they mourn over it; the strong and the powerful, not those who are gentle and meek and seek to be peacemakers; those who grab for it all, not the empty-handed and hungry; those who get things accomplished, even if by questionable means, not the pure in heart who refuse to compromise their integrity and transparency. In the Beatitudes Jesus challenges the very self-centeredness, hedonism, and will to power that characterizes so much of our social and political behavior.

SHARING THE SCRIPTURE

Preparing Our Hearts

Explore this week's devotional reading, found in James 5:7-11. We are called to patiently endure until the day of God's judgment. If we do so, we will indeed be blessed. What does it mean to you to be blessed? What link do you see in James between suffering and blessedness? Do you think only in terms of material possessions, or does being blessed include something more, something different for you?

Pray that you and the adult learners will seek to patiently endure so that you may experience God's blessings.

Preparing Our Minds

Study the background Scripture and the lesson Scripture, both of which are found in Matthew 5:1-12. Consider what a successful "recipe" for happiness might look like.

Write on newsprint:
❑ information for next week's lesson, found under "Continue the Journey."
❑ activities for further spiritual growth in "Continue the Journey."

Familiarize yourself with the points in Understanding the Scripture for use in "Examine Jesus' Teachings on the Mount."

LEADING THE CLASS

(1) Gather to Learn

❖ Welcome the class members and introduce any guests.
❖ Pray that the students will be open to the meaning of Jesus' Beatitudes.

❖ Note that we will be studying the Beatitudes today. These teachings of Jesus at the beginning of the Sermon on the Mount use the Greek word *makarios*, which most Bibles translate as "blessed," but some, including the Good News Translation, render this word as "happy."

❖ Post a sheet of newsprint on which you have written the word *happy* at the top left. Invite the students to call out words or phrases that come to mind when they think about being happy. On the right side of the paper, write the word *blessed*, and encourage the adults to think about what it means to be blessed, in this case by God. You may wish to add information from the second and third paragraphs of "To Be Blessed" in Interpreting the Scripture.

❖ Ask: **Would you rather be happy or blessed? Why?**

❖ Read aloud today's focus statement: **People seek happiness in their lives. Is there a way to satisfy the search? In the Beatitudes, Jesus lists nine ways that God blesses those who seek first the kingdom of God.**

(2) Examine Jesus' Teachings on the Mount

❖ Choose eleven volunteers to read Matthew 5:1-12, with one person reading verses 11 and 12. Having different voices, if possible, will allow each beatitude to be heard individually.

❖ Read "Introduction" in Understanding the Scripture to set the stage for today's discussion.

❖ Review the list of beatitudes in order, stopping to discuss each one. Ask the adults to explain what they think each beatitude means. Add information you have studied from Understanding the Scripture for each verse. Continue through to verse 12.

❖ Discuss these questions:

(1) **What do the Beatitudes say to you about the kingdom of God?**

(2) **What are some of the marks of the alternative community that the Beatitudes portray?** (*The New Interpreter's Study Bible* suggests "justice, transformed social relationships, practices of piety, and shared and accessible resources.")

(3) Experience the Blessings of God's Reign Already Present on the Earth

❖ Brainstorm answers to this question and write them on newsprint: **What blessings of God's reign can we experience here on earth?**

❖ Read or retell "What Will Satisfy Us?" in Interpreting the Scripture.

❖ Form small groups to discuss or debate this statement, which you will want to read aloud several times: **Many Christians, particularly in the United States, chase after things that they think will satisfy them without recognizing the blessings of God that are already present here on earth.**

❖ Call everyone together. Ask a spokesperson for each group to comment on one or two observations that sparked discussion within the group.

❖ Discuss this question: **What steps can we, as a church family, take to help people experience the blessings of God's reign that are present here and now?** (Here is an example: People who are hungering and thirsting for God's righteousness can explore spiritual disciplines that will enable them to draw closer to God. They can make a commitment to pray for those who have not yet experienced God's salvation. They

can talk with others about what it means to be a child of God and encourage them in the faith. They can take action to bring about justice.)

❖ Distribute paper and pencils. Challenge the adults to continue thinking about the prior question and the suggestions that have been made. Encourage them to jot down steps they would be willing to take to implement ideas that have been broached.

❖ Invite volunteers to read their steps aloud. Try to link participants who have similar ideas so that they can work together to refine and implement a plan.

(4) Look for the Blessings of the Beatitudes in Everyday Life

❖ Read the following scenarios and invite class members to give multiple responses. After hearing several responses, ask the group to suggest the blessings that they may experience because of the stance they took.

■ **You are standing in line to make a purchase when the person ahead of you gets into a heated discussion with the cashier. How might you act as a peacemaker?**

■ **You supported an ethical decision at work that really annoyed those who were willing to cut corners. Now they are saying nasty things about you. How will you act?**

■ **You are aware that at least two gangs are operating in your local high school. You have no "in" at the school but want to make a difference. What can you do?**

■ **People in your community association have drawn battle lines because of your next-door neighbor's fence, which violates community covenants. Some expect you to stop speaking to your neighbor and take harsh action. What is your response?**

❖ Close by leading the group in a unison reading of today's key verse, Matthew 5:6.

(5) Continue the Journey

❖ Pray that the adults will look daily for the blessings set forth in the Beatitudes.

❖ Read aloud this preparation for next week's lesson. You may also want to post it on newsprint for the students to copy.

- ■ **Title: Forgiving as God's People**
- ■ **Background Scripture: Matthew 5:17-26**
- ■ **Lesson Scripture: Matthew 5:17-26**
- ■ **Focus of the Lesson: People wonder if good, harmonious relationships are possible. Can we all just get along? Jesus teaches us that forgiveness is crucial to Christian living.**

❖ Challenge the students to complete one or more of these activities for further spiritual growth related to this week's session. Post this information on newsprint for the students to copy.

(1) Choose one beatitude and try to enact it in your own life this week. **For example, if you choose verse 9, be alert for opportunities to act as a peacemaker. Do what you can to bring harmony to a specific situation.**

(2) Share the promise of God's blessing with someone who needs to hear this good news. Be careful to help this person understand that you are talking not about material goods but rather about spiritual blessings.

(3) Talk with some class members about opportunities for ministry that may arise from one or more of the Beatitudes. Is there a project that you can undertake that addresses any of the Beatitudes?

❖ Sing or read aloud "Sent Forth by God's Blessings."

❖ Conclude today's session by leading the class in this benediction adapted from Proverbs 3:5 and 29:25: **Go forth trusting in the Lord with all your heart, knowing that one who trusts in the Lord is secure.**

UNIT 2: JESUS TEACHES WISDOM

FORGIVING AS GOD'S PEOPLE

PREVIEWING THE LESSON

Lesson Scripture: Matthew 5:17-26
Background Scripture: Matthew 5:17-26
Key Verses: Matthew 5:23-24

Focus of the Lesson:
People wonder if good, harmonious relationships are possible. Can we all just get along? Jesus teaches us that forgiveness is crucial to Christian living.

Goals for the Learners:
(1) to explore Jesus' teaching about reconciliation.
(2) to experience the joy of forgiving and being forgiven.
(3) to make reconciliation a priority in their lives.

Pronunciation Guide:
Raca (rah' kah)
Sanhedrin (san hee' druhn)
Torah (toh' ruh)

Supplies:
Bibles, newsprint and marker, paper and pencils, hymnals

READING THE SCRIPTURE

NRSV
Matthew 5:17-26

¹⁷"Do not think that I have come to abolish the law or the prophets; I have come not to abolish but to fulfill. ¹⁸For truly I tell you, until heaven and earth pass away, not one letter, not one stroke of a letter, will pass from the law until all is accomplished. ¹⁹Therefore, whoever breaks one of the least of these commandments, and teaches others to do the same, will be called least in the

NIV
Matthew 5:17-26

¹⁷"Do not think that I have come to abolish the Law or the Prophets; I have not come to abolish them but to fulfill them. ¹⁸I tell you the truth, until heaven and earth disappear, not the smallest letter, not the least stroke of a pen, will by any means disappear from the Law until everything is accomplished. ¹⁹Anyone who breaks one of the least of these commandments and teaches

kingdom of heaven; but whoever does them and teaches them will be called great in the kingdom of heaven. ²⁰For I tell you, unless your righteousness exceeds that of the scribes and Pharisees, you will never enter the kingdom of heaven.

²¹"You have heard that it was said to those of ancient times, 'You shall not murder'; and 'whoever murders shall be liable to judgment.' ²²But I say to you that if you are angry with a brother or sister, you will be liable to judgment; and if you insult a brother or sister, you will be liable to the council; and if you say, 'You fool,' you will be liable to the hell of fire. **²³So when you are offering your gift at the altar, if you remember that your brother or sister has something against you, ²⁴leave your gift there before the altar and go; first be reconciled to your brother or sister, and then come and offer your gift.** ²⁵Come to terms quickly with your accuser while you are on the way to court with him, or your accuser may hand you over to the judge, and the judge to the guard, and you will be thrown into prison. ²⁶Truly I tell you, you will never get out until you have paid the last penny."

others to do the same will be called least in the kingdom of heaven, but whoever practices and teaches these commands will be called great in the kingdom of heaven. ²⁰For I tell you that unless your righteousness surpasses that of the Pharisees and the teachers of the law, you will certainly not enter the kingdom of heaven.

²¹"You have heard that it was said to the people long ago, 'Do not murder, and anyone who murders will be subject to judgment.' ²²But I tell you that anyone who is angry with his brother will be subject to judgment. Again, anyone who says to his brother, 'Raca,' is answerable to the Sanhedrin. But anyone who says, 'You fool!' will be in danger of the fire of hell.

²³"Therefore, if you are offering your gift at the altar and there remember that your brother has something against you, ²⁴leave your gift there in front of the altar. First go and be reconciled to your brother; then come and offer your gift.

²⁵"Settle matters quickly with your adversary who is taking you to court. Do it while you are still with him on the way, or he may hand you over to the judge, and the judge may hand you over to the officer, and you may be thrown into prison. ²⁶I tell you the truth, you will not get out until you have paid the last penny."

UNDERSTANDING THE SCRIPTURE

Introduction. Matthew 5:17 begins the main body of the Sermon on the Mount, the focus of which is a description of how life is to be lived and shared in the community of Jesus' disciples. In our lesson Scripture, Jesus is introduced as the One who fulfills the Old Testament law and calls his disciples to live with such moral and spiritual righteousness that it will exceed even the righteousness of the Jewish religious leaders. Matthew 5:21-26 contains the first of six antitheses or antithetical statements

characterized by the formula "you have heard . . . but I say to you." In these antithetical statements Jesus lays out his radical ethical demands that constitute the higher righteousness. It should also be noted that many of the verbs Jesus uses in our lesson Scripture, as well as throughout the Sermon on the Mount, to address his disciples and give them instruction are in the second-person plural form. His focus is on the *community* of disciples and their life together.

Matthew 5:17-20. These verses contain the general principles that will be illustrated in greater detail in the six antitheses that will follow. The first thing Jesus says, which is the fundamental principle of what is to follow, is that he has come to fulfill all that the Hebrew Scriptures taught and promised ("the law or the prophets"), not to abolish them (5:17). Jesus has come as the Messiah to embody and teach the definitive will of God that had been laid out in the Torah (the first five books of the Old Testament) and the larger body of the Hebrew Scriptures found in the prophetic and historical books.

Using emphatic first-person speech in 5:17, 18, and 20, Jesus speaks with great authority as he affirms the continuing validity of the Torah. He clearly seems to consider his own teaching to be as binding as the Torah because he, like the Torah, has been sent by God to mediate the will of God. Dietrich Bonhoeffer commented that Jesus adds nothing to the commandments of God "except this, that he keeps them." These verses may also reflect debates in the early church about the role of the Torah, especially the moral law, in the lives of the earliest Christians. Jesus' strong teaching in 5:19-20 is that his disciples must do or practice the commandments of God, not just teach them, in order that their "righteousness" might exceed that of the scribes and Pharisees. We see a similar emphasis upon "doing" the will of God, not just talking about it, in 7:21, 24, and 26 at the end of the Sermon on the Mount.

Matthew 5:21-22. Beginning in 5:21 is the first of the six antitheses that explain in more detail what Jesus means by the higher righteousness to which he calls his disciples. Each of these units (5:21-26, 27-30, 31-32, 33-37, 38-42, 43-48) begins with a juxtaposition of what "was said" by God through Moses "to those of ancient times" and what is *now* being said by Jesus. "You have heard" in 5:21 probably refers to people hearing the Torah read in the synagogue. The phrase "But I say to you" in 5:22 is a strong expression by which Jesus claims divine authority to reinterpret the Torah for the new community of his disciples and to clarify or correct any distortions and misinterpretations that may have been taught over the years. Notice that Jesus first reaffirms the command in the Torah against murder (5:21; Exodus 20:13). He does not countermand it, for he has come to fulfill the law, not to abolish it.

Then Jesus radically reinterprets the commandment. His point is that it is not just the outward act of murder about which God is concerned but also the inward passion of anger that can lead to murder. For murder has its birth in anger fostered by an uncontrolled spirit of revenge; therefore, Jesus says that such anger is also an infringement of God's commandment against murder. The other phrases in 5:22 reinforce the admonition about anger. The word *Raca* (found in the NIV but omitted in the NRSV) is actually an Aramaic word more or less equivalent to the English "nitwit," "numskull," or "worthless fool." To call someone *Raca* was not a playful jabbing at that person saying "you're foolish," but an insult of the most abusive kind, one that would have been expressed in a fit of anger.

Matthew 5:23-26. In these verses Jesus continues to illustrate what the higher righteousness looks like, what it means to go beyond the letter of the law to live in the spirit of God's liberating word. First, he speaks to us while we are at worship, an activity that is central in our lives as Christians. As important as it is to keep our focus on God during worship, Jesus teaches that we are to think also of our sisters and brothers and that reconciliation with someone from whom we have become estranged is even more important than worship at the altar. In fact, we might think of the act of reconciliation with an estranged brother or sister as itself being an act of worship. We read similar thoughts in the Old Testament prophets (Isaiah 1:10-17; Amos 5:21-24; Micah 6:6-8).

Second, Jesus says we are to seek reconciliation with someone from whom we are alienated *no matter whose fault it is*. The text says, "If you remember that your brother or sister has something against you" (5:23). That could be understood in two different ways. I may have been at fault in doing something to hurt another person, and she or he holds it against me. Or the other person may simply not like me and begin to spread gossip about me when I can think of nothing specific that I have done to deserve it. Either way, whether it is my fault or not, if I sense any estrangement, it is my responsibility as one of Jesus' disciples to take the initiative in seeking reconciliation. Verses 25-26 serve to heighten the urgency of seeking reconciliation before we find ourselves at the judgment seat of God. Of course, none of us knows when that will be. We must be ready at all times.

INTERPRETING THE SCRIPTURE

The Higher Righteousness

What does Jesus mean in 5:20 when he calls his disciples to practice a righteousness that "exceeds that of the scribes and Pharisees"? First of all, he wants his disciples to be genuine in their commitment to practice what they preach. In many places in Matthew's Gospel, including several passages in the Sermon on the Mount, Jesus speaks out against the hypocrisy of the scribes and Pharisees and admonishes his disciples not to be like them. Rather, his disciples are to "do" the will of God, not just talk about it or teach it. (See Matthew 6:2, 5, 16; 7:1-5, 21-27; 15:7-9; and chapter 23 where Jesus condemns the hypocritical actions of the scribes and Pharisees.)

This leads to a second observation about what Jesus meant. The righteousness of his disciples is to exceed that of the scribes and Pharisees in kind rather than in degree. The reference above to the hypocrisy of the scribes and Pharisees does not mean to say that all of them were all talk and no action. Jesus issued strong words at times against some of the Pharisees to make a point, but there would have been other Pharisees, such as Nicodemus (John 3:1), who would have sincerely sought to obey the commandments as they understood them. However, as we saw in last week's lesson on the Beatitudes, Jesus' concern was not just outward obedience of the commandments, but motive and inward sincerity of the heart.

The righteousness that Jesus demands of his followers, the righteousness that exceeds that of the Pharisees, is the deeper righteousness of the heart. For Jesus, what is important is not just the outward actions that others see, but our inner motives and attitudes that God sees. For example, in 5:21-22 Jesus condemns not only the outward act of murder but also the inward passion and attitude of anger that, at its worst, can lead to murder and, at its best, can be self-destructive and destructive of relationships. Or note in 5:28 how Jesus condemns not just the outward act of adultery but also the inward act of committing adultery "in [one's] heart" by looking lustfully at another person. For Jesus it is the inner motive that matters, for the higher righteousness comes from the heart.

Appropriate Anger

Most of us can probably say we have never murdered anyone. But who of us can say we have never been angry, maybe even angry enough that we felt as if we could have killed someone? Probably most of us can identify with that situation. We know that anger is a normal human emotion that needs to be expressed, and to suppress it or repress it can have unhealthy psychological consequences. Yet the opposite is also true; uncontrolled anger can turn into rage that, in turn, can lead to destructive behavior.

As with any other human emotion, the key is to learn how to express or channel our anger in healthy ways and for productive purposes. As one who had an issue with anger management when I was much younger, Jesus' words in 5:22 were a matter of great concern to me when I read them after first becoming a disciple in my early twenties. I took his admonition with great seriousness as I studied these verses, reflecting on my own issue of having a short fuse. Through prayer and the surrender of my turbulent feelings to God when something would happen to trigger my anger, by the grace of God I learned to control and manage my anger.

In time I came to understand Jesus' words in 5:22 in the context of his larger ministry. At various places in the Gospels we find Jesus angry and his passions stirred. Like the prophets before him, Jesus got angry about sin and the injustices he saw around him. He was deeply moved and upset when he saw people hurting from disease and demon possession (for example, Mark 1:41, where some ancient authorities use the word "anger" rather than "pity"). When he entered the Temple and overturned the tables of the money changers, driving out those who made it a "den of robbers" (Mark 11:17) and later issued his passionate, face-to-face rebuke of the scribes and Pharisees (Matthew 23), I can't imagine this was done in a passive, quiet-voiced manner. I like to characterize Jesus' passionate feelings as righteous indignation. Jesus channeled his anger into positive energy in his battle against injustice and all that opposed God's will.

This channeling of anger for productive purposes is what links Matthew 5:22 with 5:23-24. Jesus is not saying that we are never to be angry, for anger is a natural human emotion. Rather, he admonishes us not to come to the altar of sacrifice until we are reconciled to the person with whom we are angry. Paul says something similar in Ephesians 4:26: "Be angry but do not sin; do not let the sun go down on your anger."

Reconciliation Is Risky

In last week's Understanding the Scripture on Matthew 5:9, I said that peacemaking and working toward reconciliation can be hard work. It can also be risky. I vividly remember that dramatic November day in 1977 when Anwar El Sadat, president of Egypt, flew to Israel to meet with Israeli prime minister Menachem Begin. Against the advice of his own counselors and at a time when Israel and Egypt were sworn enemies, Sadat unilaterally and at great personal and political risk took the initiative for peace and announced that he was going to Jerusalem. His initiative, which ultimately cost him his life due to assassination, led eventually to the Camp David Accords and the subsequent Egypt-Israel peace treaty that, in spite of all the upheavals in the Middle East over the past thirty years, is still in effect as of this writing.

Whether it is seeking reconciliation between two estranged individuals or two opposing groups or nations, there are always risks in taking the initiative as a peacemaker. One takes the risk of rejection and hurt if the offer is rebuffed. There is the risk that one may appear weak or lose face in a society that admires aggressiveness and power. And, of course, there is the ultimate risk of losing one's life for the cause of peace, as Anwar Sadat, Mahatma Gandhi, Martin Luther King, Jr., Robert Kennedy, and a host of others who have been bold initiators of reconciliation, personally experienced.

Initiating forgiveness and seeking reconciliation with another person or group is also hard work. Striving to lay aside our prejudices and struggling to really listen and sincerely understand an opposing point of view is emotionally and physically draining. It takes continuing and focused commitment for two parties in a conflict to surrender their egos enough to acknowledge that neither of them has "the truth" (only God has that) but rather "a truth" seen from each other's perspective. All of these efforts demand real concentration, deep commitment to the task, and lots of energy, but the end goal of reconciliation and peace is worth every ounce of energy expended. And in the end we really have no choice, if we are to be faithful disciples of the One who exhausted himself on the cross to be our peace and to reconcile us to God (2 Corinthians 5:18-19; Ephesians 2:14-16). He promised us: "Blessed are the peacemakers, for they will be called children of God" (Matthew 5:9).

SHARING THE SCRIPTURE

Preparing Our Hearts

Explore this week's devotional reading, found in Psalm 32:1-5. The writer bears witness to the joy he experiences because he has confessed his sins and been forgiven by God. Use your devotional time to acknowledge your sins to God and receive forgiveness. You may wish to write about how you feel knowing the weight of sin has been lifted from you. How is this feeling different from what you experience when you keep sin locked within?

Pray that you and the adult learners will turn to God for forgiveness as soon as you realize that you have sinned.

Preparing Our Minds

Study the background Scripture and the lesson Scripture, both of which are found in Matthew 5:17-26. Consider what is necessary for living together harmoniously.

Write on newsprint:
❑ information for next week's lesson, found under "Continue the Journey."
❑ activities for further spiritual growth in "Continue the Journey."

LEADING THE CLASS

(1) Gather to Learn

❖ Welcome the class members and introduce any guests.

❖ Pray that the students will find new meaning for their lives in Jesus' teachings about reconciliation.

❖ Read: **Chaired by Bishop Desmond Tutu, the Truth and Reconciliation Commission was convened in South Africa to bring about reconciliation between black and white communities bitterly separated by apartheid. The Commission heard testimony concerning violations of human rights, offered reparation and rehabilitation, and in some cases granted amnesty to those who committed these violations. Most people thought the commission was successful in achieving its goal. In 2004, a dramatic film, *Forgiveness*, portrayed how a police officer who had killed a freedom fighter and was granted amnesty by the commission later went to the young man's family to ask forgiveness.**

❖ Ask: **What value do you see in a system that not only encourages people to state how they have been wronged but also opens doors for amnesty and forgiveness?**

❖ Read aloud today's focus statement: **People wonder if good, harmonious relationships are possible. Can we all just get along? Jesus teaches us that forgiveness is crucial to Christian living.**

(2) Explore Jesus' Teaching About Reconciliation

❖ Select a volunteer to read Matthew 5:17-20.

❖ Use information from "Introduction" and Matthew 5:17-20 in Understanding the Scripture to help the adults understand Jesus' message.

❖ Ask: **What does Jesus mean in 5:20 when he calls his disciples to practice a righteousness that "exceeds that of the scribes and Pharisees"?** Use information from "The Higher Righteousness" in Interpreting the Scripture to expand the \discussion.

❖ Call on another volunteer to read Matthew 5:21-26.

❖ Discuss these questions:

(1) **Jesus did not abolish the injunction against murder, but in this passage he ties physical killing to anger that leads to insults and judgment. What connection do you see between murder and anger?**

(2) **How would living in a faith community where anger is tantamount to murder challenge the norms of the society at large?**

(3) **Why do many people find it difficult to ask forgiveness from those closest to them—their church family and their own family?**

(4) **What might your congregation do to promote reconciliation among the body of Christ there?**

(3) Experience the Joy of Forgiving and Being Forgiven

❖ Invite the adults to listen as you read Psalm 32:1-5, which so poignantly describes the benefits of seeking forgiveness.

❖ Provide participants with an opportunity to experience God's forgiveness by leading them in this guided imagery activity. Invite them to sit comfortably in their chairs and close their eyes if they choose.

■ **Imagine yourself in a place where you feel peaceful and secure. Envision yourself settled into this place when Jesus comes and sits**

near you. **How do you feel?** (pause)

■ **He invites you to confess any sin, promising that he will never leave you or forsake you no matter what you have done. You start to pour out your heart to Jesus.** (pause)

■ **You have finished your confession when you hear him say, "Your sins are forgiven. Go and sin no more." How do you feel now?** (pause)

■ **Continue to commune with Jesus and open your eyes when you are ready.** (pause)

❖ Encourage the adults to imagine themselves in conversation with Jesus at any time they have something to confess. Assure them that he will hear and forgive them. Remind them that they need to forgive themselves as well.

(4) Make Reconciliation a Priority

❖ Lead the group in reading today's key verses from Matthew 5:23-24.

❖ Point out that just as we need to ask God's forgiveness, there are times when we need to ask forgiveness of others whom we have in some way harmed, although that is sometimes very difficult to do.

❖ Read "Reconciliation Is Risky" from Interpreting the Scripture.

❖ Distribute paper and pencils. Tell the adults that what they are about to write will not be shared with the group. Encourage them to think of someone with whom they want to be reconciled. Suggest that they recall the incident(s) that prompted the estrangement and any attempts they have made to bring about reconciliation. Recommend that they write the incident from the other people's perspective. Think of reasons why these aggrieved parties have thus far been unable to forgive. Jot down ideas as to what might be said or done to open the door to reconciliation.

❖ Challenge the students to take action over the next several weeks to try to bring about reconciliation with the persons they have identified.

(5) Continue the Journey

❖ Pray that the adults will make reconciliation a priority in their lives and go forth now to do whatever they can to bring about reconciliation.

❖ Read aloud this preparation for next week's lesson. You may also want to post it on newsprint for the students to copy.

- ■ Title: Loving as God's People
- ■ Background Scripture: Matthew 5:43-48
- ■ Lesson Scripture: Matthew 5:43-48
- ■ Focus of the Lesson: People usually find it hard to love—even to like—those who are their enemies. Is there any help that would encourage us to change our attitude toward those who hurt us? Jesus taught the disciples to pray for those who are unjust and evil.

❖ Challenge the students to complete one or more of these activities for further spiritual growth related to this week's session. Post this information on newsprint for the students to copy.

(1) **Contact someone from whom you need to seek forgiveness. Offer a genuine apology and promise to try to avoid giving offense in the future. Pray before you make this contact. Recognize that not all people are willing to forgive and some may need additional time to do so.**

(2) **Evaluate your ability to manage anger. Do you have "broad shoulders" or "a short fuse"? Listen to what people are telling you about how you react to situations that may cause tempers to flare. Seek help from someone who keeps a cool head. Pray that God will help you control your temper.**

(3) **Make amends with someone in your congregation with whom you have had a dispute. Reach out your hand in reconciliation, whether you or the other person caused the conflict.**

❖ Sing or read aloud "Forgive Our Sins as We Forgive."

❖ Conclude today's session by leading the class in this benediction adapted from Proverbs 3:5 and 29:25: **Go forth trusting in the Lord with all your heart, knowing that one who trusts in the Lord is secure.**

UNIT 2: JESUS TEACHES WISDOM
LOVING AS GOD'S PEOPLE

PREVIEWING THE LESSON

Lesson Scripture: Matthew 5:43-48
Background Scripture: Matthew 5:43-48
Key Verses: Matthew 5:44-45

Focus of the Lesson:
People usually find it hard to love—even to like—those who are their enemies. Is there any help that would encourage us to change our attitude toward those who hurt us? Jesus taught the disciples to pray for those who are unjust and evil.

Goals for the Learners:
(1) to explore Jesus' teachings concerning loving and praying for one's enemies.
(2) to recognize and appreciate the relationship between loving one's enemies and being a child of God.
(3) to commit to participate in activities, such as prayer, designed to show love and concern for our enemies.

Pronunciation Guide:
teleios (tel'-i-os)
Torah (toh' ruh)

Supplies:
Bibles, newsprint and marker, paper and pencils, hymnals

READING THE SCRIPTURE

NRSV
Matthew 5:43-48

⁴³"You have heard that it was said, 'You shall love your neighbor and hate your enemy.' **⁴⁴But I say to you, Love your enemies and pray for those who persecute you, ⁴⁵so that you may be children of your Father in heaven;** for he makes his sun rise

NIV
Matthew 5:43-48

⁴³"You have heard that it was said, 'Love your neighbor and hate your enemy.' **⁴⁴But I tell you: Love your enemies and pray for those who persecute you, ⁴⁵that you may be sons of your Father in heaven.** He causes his sun to rise on the evil and the good, and

on the evil and on the good, and sends rain on the righteous and on the unrighteous. [46]For if you love those who love you, what reward do you have? Do not even the tax collectors do the same? [47]And if you greet only your brothers and sisters, what more are you doing than others? Do not even the Gentiles do the same? [48]Be perfect, therefore, as your heavenly Father is perfect.

sends rain on the righteous and the unrighteous. [46]If you love those who love you, what reward will you get? Are not even the tax collectors doing that? [47]And if you greet only your brothers, what are you doing more than others? Do not even pagans do that? [48]Be perfect, therefore, as your heavenly Father is perfect.

UNDERSTANDING THE SCRIPTURE

Introduction. We turn now to the last of the six antithetical statements ("You have heard . . . but I say to you") that Jesus made describing how his disciples are to share their everyday lives together in community. Matthew 5:43-48, which deals with extending love to our enemies, is closely related in content and emphasis to 5:38-42, where Jesus teaches us that love does not retaliate. It is important to understand that when Jesus teaches us to turn the other cheek and not to resist an evildoer (5:39), he is not advocating that we just lie down in front of the steamroller of evil and let it run over us. Turning the other cheek is meant to be a sign not of weakness but of inner spiritual strength. It is not surrender but a positive course of action, a strategy for living boldly in God's love as we face the challenges and injustices of life. It is with such an understanding that we should read 5:43-48.

Matthew 5:43. As noted in last week's session, Jesus' words "You have heard" probably refer to hearing the reading of the Torah in the synagogue. They could also refer to the various teachings and Torah interpretations of rabbis, scribes, and Pharisees over the generations, as is probably the case in this verse.

Jesus' reference is to Leviticus 19:18: "You shall not take vengeance or bear a grudge against any of your people, but you shall love your neighbor as yourself: I am the

LORD." This verse implies that "neighbor" means fellow Israelite ("your people"), as was probably the common understanding in Jesus' day. This is reinforced by the phrase "your people" in 19:16 and "your kin" in 19:17, both of which are used as synonyms of "neighbor." However, earlier in the same chapter the Israelites are commanded to leave gleanings of their harvest and some of the grapes of their vineyards "for the poor and the alien," the resident foreigner (Leviticus 19:10). Later in 19:34 we read: "The alien who resides with you shall be to you as the citizen among you; you shall love the alien as yourself, for you were aliens in the land of Egypt: I am the LORD your God." Thus, even within the Torah itself we find the roots of an understanding of neighbor as being more than just a fellow Israelite.

The main point to emphasize, however, is that the phrase "and hate your enemy" is not found anywhere in the Torah. Also, the vital phrase "as yourself," which is part of the original commandment in Leviticus 19:18, is omitted in Jesus' quotation. Thus it would seem that when Jesus says, "you have heard," he is quoting a scribal or rabbinic addition to the law that was intended to interpret it, but in fact distorted the law in two ways. First, the distortion narrowed the standard of love by omitting the phrase "as yourself." Second, the scope of love that God intended in the original commandment was narrowed with the addition of the command to hate one's enemies. It was this distortion or perversion of the Torah that Jesus rejected, not the spirit of the original commandment.

Matthew 5:44-45. Speaking with divine authority as one who came to "fulfill" the law (5:17), Jesus expresses his bold interpretation of the original commandment. He expands the traditional understanding of "neighbor" and extends the scope of love to include enemies, at the same time calling on his disciples to pray for even those who persecute them. What Jesus teaches here is not totally unique, for in parts of the Old Testament we see elements and tendencies toward love for all people, including enemies. See, for example, Proverbs 25:21-22 and the Book of Jonah, especially 4:10-11. However, what is unique is that Jesus made this the core of his teaching, and he personally lived it out to his dying breath on the cross.

For Jesus, a neighbor is not limited to a fellow Jew, someone of "my own group," or the person who happens to live immediately next door. A neighbor is anyone who is near us, any fellow human being who is in need. Jesus clarified what he meant by "neighbor" in his parable of the good Samaritan (Luke 10:25-37). In Matthew 5:45 Jesus states both the motive and the purpose for loving our enemies: so that we may show ourselves to be sons and daughters of God, who loves all people, both the just and the unjust, impartially.

Matthew 5:46-47. In 5:46-47 Jesus reminds us that God's kind of impartial, unconditional love is not a mutual "you scratch my back and I'll scratch yours" kind

of love. Loving only those who love us or are kind to us can become self-serving, and the motives for such love can be highly questionable. "Tax collectors" were the paid underlings of the Roman tax contractors and were generally despised by the Jewish people as dishonest traitors because they worked for the hated Romans. "Gentiles" were non-Jews; in time the word "Gentiles" became synonymous with "unbelievers." After saying in these two verses what God's kind of love is *not*, Jesus went on throughout his ministry to describe what it is. See especially Luke 14:12-14 and also his parables of the great judgment (Matthew 25:31-46), the good Samaritan (Luke 10:25-37), and the prodigal son (Luke 15:11-32). Alongside his teaching, Jesus demonstrated in his life, ministry, and suffering for others what genuine love is. It is unconditional, selfless, and other-centered; it is willing to make sacrifices to meet others at their point of need and to seek their welfare.

Matthew 5:48. When Jesus says we are to be "perfect" as God is perfect, I don't think he means absolute moral perfection in the sense that we are faultless or never make any mistakes or commit any sins. Jesus knew that we are sinful creatures continuously in need of forgiveness. Rather, the context indicates that we are to be "perfect" in love. Our loving is to mirror the perfect love of God, which is impartial and all-embracing and shown even to those who do not return it. The parallel verse in Luke's version of the Sermon would seem to confirm this interpretation: "Be merciful [compassionate], just as your Father is merciful [compassionate]" (Luke 6:36).

INTERPRETING THE SCRIPTURE

Loving Neighbors and Enemies Alike

The world has shrunk, and the global community is now in our neighborhood.

Even those of us who live in more rural areas may have regular interaction with people from various cultures, religions, and ethnic groups. These interactions may well have challenged some of our beliefs and attitudes.

I share a story about someone we shall call Jim. Jim grew up in a conservative Christian family in small-town America. Words like "Islam," "Hinduism," and "Buddhism" were just concepts in a book; he had never met anybody who practiced those religions. After the horrible events of 9/11, like many Americans at the time, Jim started to become suspicious of Muslims and Arabs in general and anyone who even looked Middle Eastern. Little by little he began to see the world in black and white, good guys and bad guys, and he began to see Islam as "the enemy," a religion that he thought taught and practiced hatred and killing. He honestly struggled with his feelings because he knew that Jesus had commanded his followers to love even their enemies. But the atrocities of 9/11 were so terrible and he felt so frightened by the threat of terrorism and his association of Islam with terrorism, that he couldn't help his bitter feelings.

Then one day a Muslim family moved into the neighborhood just two houses away. He felt pulled in opposite directions. Part of him wanted to totally avoid meeting the family, but the other part believed that, as a Christian and a good neighbor, he should go and welcome them, which is what he finally did. Surprisingly, he discovered they were not at all like the stereotype he had imagined. They were peace-loving people who felt terrible about what had happened on 9/11 and said that such violence was against the tenets of their faith. Jim could see that they had a wonderful family life and their love for God was central to everything they did. In time, Jim discovered that many of his fears and stereotypes had been unfounded. His whole understanding of a group of people he used to call "the enemy" was being transformed.

How do we come to love our enemies? It doesn't happen at once; it's a step-by-step process. In Jim's case, it began with a nudging from his Christian background and a willingness to risk meeting this new family. Because the seed of Christ's love had been planted in his heart, he was given the courage to take a risk. In the process he discovered the truth of something Martin Luther King, Jr., said in a sermon about the creative and redemptive power of love: "Love is the only force capable of transforming an enemy into a friend."

So may it be in our lives as we are willing to take a risk. Our model, of course, is Jesus, who showed us what genuine love is. It is unconditional and unlimited, selfless and sacrificial. It has little to do with sentimentality and feelings and a lot to do with commitment, will, and action. I'm sure Jesus didn't "feel" like going to the cross, but out of deep commitment to God and others he went. Paul wrote, "While we were enemies, we were reconciled to God through the death of his Son" (Romans 5:10). As God has loved us, so are we, as God's reconciled sons and daughters, to love others, including our enemies; they are our neighbors also.

Moving Outside Our Comfort Zones

One of the characteristics of our postmodern culture is the hunger for genuine intimacy and human relationships. People who spend a lot of time within the virtual community of cyberspace communication hunger for the experience of genuine community and face-to-face interaction with others. Many people who visit our churches on Sunday mornings come seeking interpersonal relationships and an experience of genuine fellowship. Therefore, one of the most important ministries of any local church is the ministry of hospitality: welcoming persons, taking time to talk with them and listen to their stories, and then seeking to get them involved in small groups where they can be nurtured and meet other people.

My experience as a pastor has been that one of the most challenging tasks is to get parishioners to leave their familiar circles and friendship groups to intentionally seek out persons they don't know and welcome them. Jesus' words in Matthew 5:46-47 speak to this issue. It's hard for most of us to break out of our comfort zones. But, as Jesus said, if we greet only our brothers and sisters, what more are we doing than others? If we sincerely want Christ's love to be manifest in our congregations, we will need to be intentional about breaking out of the familiar in order to extend the hand of hospitality to the strangers in our midst. To love as Jesus loved demands it.

Are We Expected to Be Perfect?

The first time I seriously studied the Sermon on the Mount and read Matthew 5:48, I thought to myself, "Can Jesus be serious? Does he really expect me or any of his disciples to be *perfect*? He, of all people, knows our sinful nature and our many imperfections." Of course, my thoughts had been shaped by a certain dictionary definition of the word "perfect": "free from any flaw or defect in condition or quality; faultless." This is probably the common understanding of "perfect" that most people have in mind: something without flaw, an unattainable ideal toward which we aim but never quite reach, at least not on a daily or even regular basis. It's like a perfect score in bowling or a perfect game in baseball; it

may happen once in thousands of attempts, but never on a regular basis. So how can Jesus ever expect us to be "perfect" in this world and, as is implied in 5:48, to do so continuously, as God is perfect?

As I said previously, I don't think Jesus was referring to the Greek ideal of absolute moral perfection in the sense that we are faultless in our judgment and behavior and we never make any mistakes or commit any sins. Rather, the context of 5:43-48 suggests that we are to be *perfect in love*. As God is compassionate and loves impartially and selflessly, the good news is that we too can love impartially and selflessly. The Greek adjective *teleios*, which is translated here as "perfect," is derived from a verb that means "to complete or accomplish" and carries the meaning of "mature, fully developed, complete, having attained the end or purpose." Understood in this way, being perfect is not an unattainable ideal but a matter of spiritual maturity. At any given moment, it is possible to attain the goal of loving unconditionally and all-inclusively, as God loves us. The secret lies in what Paul said in Galatians 2:20: "It is no longer I who live, but it is Christ who lives in me." As we mature spiritually by taking our own egos off the throne of our hearts and, faltering step by faltering step, we let more and more of Christ and his love dwell in our hearts, we can become perfect in love. Our imperfect attempts at loving will be absorbed into Christ's perfect love flowing through us and out into the lives of others.

SHARING THE SCRIPTURE

Preparing Our Hearts

Explore this week's devotional reading, found in Matthew 22:34-40. Religious leaders gathered to test Jesus by asking him, "Which commandment in the law is the greatest?" (22:36). Without hesitation, Jesus responded that we are to love God with all of our being and love our neighbor as we love ourselves. This all-encompassing love, he insisted, is the foundation for "the law and the prophets" (22:40). Think about how you interact with others. What are the signs that you are—or are not—living out of a deeply rooted sense of love for God and neighbor? What changes might you need to make?

Pray that you and the adult learners will love God and neighbor, even those neighbors you consider enemies.

Preparing Our Minds

Study the background Scripture and the lesson Scripture, both of which are found in Matthew 5:43-48. Ponder how we might change our attitudes toward those who hurt us.

Write on newsprint:
- ❑ discussion starters for "Commit to Participate in Activities, Such as Prayer, Designed to Show Love and Concern for Our Enemies."
- ❑ information for next week's lesson, found under "Continue the Journey."
- ❑ activities for further spiritual growth in "Continue the Journey."

Familiarize yourself with the Understanding the Scripture portion so as to be prepared to do the study suggested in "Explore Jesus' Teachings Concerning Loving and Praying for One's Enemies."

LEADING THE CLASS

(1) Gather to Learn

❖ Welcome the class members and introduce any guests.

❖ Pray that the students will be led by the Spirit as they explore Jesus' teachings concerning loving and praying for one's enemies.

❖ Read the second and third paragraphs of "Loving Neighbors and Enemies Alike" in Interpreting the Scripture.

❖ Ask these questions:
   (1) **What does this story suggest to you about why we consider some people enemies, even if we do not know them personally?**

   (2) **What does this story suggest about what may happen to our preconceived notions when we come to know someone we had considered an enemy?**

❖ Read aloud today's focus statement: **People usually find it hard to love—even to like—those who are their enemies. Is there any help that would encourage us to change our attitude toward those who hurt us? Jesus taught the disciples to pray for those who are unjust and evil.**

(2) Explore Jesus' Teachings Concerning Loving and Praying for One's Enemies

❖ Choose a volunteer to read Matthew 5:43-48.

❖ Do a verse-by-verse study of this passage by reading or retelling the information in Understanding the Scripture.

❖ Discuss these questions:
   (1) **Why are we to love our enemies?** (Jesus teaches that God cares for the just and the unjust. We are to imitate God by doing likewise.)

   (2) **In what way does Jesus seem to be holding his followers to a higher standard than other people are expected to reach?** (See "Moving Outside Our Comfort Zones" in Interpreting the Scripture.)

   (3) **What might praying for those you deem enemies do for them? What might the act of praying for them do for you?**

   (4) **Do you think God expects us to be perfect? If so, what does "perfect" mean in this context?** (See "Are We Expected to Be Perfect?" in Interpreting the Scripture.)

(3) Recognize and Appreciate the Relationship Between Loving One's Enemies and Being a Child of God

❖ Lead the group in reading today's key verses, Matthew 5:44-45. Notice the relationship between loving enemies and being a child of God.

❖ Tie these verses to Matthew's community by reminding the class that these people lived under Roman occupation. Hatred for one's political, religious, and personal enemies could certainly be understood, but Jesus did not condone such behavior—and neither should we.

❖ Ask: **What is the basis for Jesus' command to love even our enemies?** After giving participants an opportunity to answer, read this quotation by M. Eugene Boring found in volume VIII of *The New Interpreter's Bible*: **"Jesus bases the command not on a humanitarian ideal, a doctrine of human rights, or a strategy or utilitarian purpose [to win the enemy over] but (a) only on his authority to set his own command in juxtaposition to the Law (5:43), (b) on the nature of God who loves all impartially (5:45), and (c) on the promise of eschatological reward (5:46)."**

❖ Conclude this portion of the session by asking: **How does your love for enemies affect the enemy, those who may observe what you do, and who you are?**

(4) Commit to Participate in Activities, Such as Prayer, Designed to Show Love and Concern for Our Enemies

❖ Brainstorm answers to this question and record ideas on newsprint: **Who are groups that some Christians may consider enemies?** (Note that you are asking for types of groups, not names of individuals.) Answers may include *gangs, criminals, substance abusers, those who take advantage of the powerless, companies or organizations that act unethically, those with whom we are at war.*

❖ Form small groups and ask each group to discern ways that the church can show love for such groups. Here are several discussion starters for you to read or post on newsprint:

■ Provide a safe haven at the church for teens where they are respected and have appropriate outlets for their creativity and energy so as to help keep them out of gangs.

■ Establish a prison ministry to help those who have committed crimes to see that there is a better, more loving way to live through Christ Jesus.

■ Open the church doors to meetings of Alcoholics Anonymous, Narcotics Anonymous, and other groups that try to help those whose lifestyle is likely abusive or harmful to others. Show hospitality to those who attend these meetings.

■ Pray together for those who are at war with us. Learn all you can about all sides so that you can better understand the reasons for hatred and violence. Do whatever you can to influence public policy that will create a lasting peace.

❖ Invite the groups to report back.

❖ Distribute paper and pencils. Challenge everyone to write a sentence or two about an activity they are willing to commit to that will show love for those who we may consider enemies.

(5) Continue the Journey

❖ Pray that the adults will pray for those who have hurt them or treated them unjustly.

❖ Read aloud this preparation for next week's lesson. You may also want to post it on newsprint for the students to copy.

■ Title: Praying as God's People
■ Background Scripture: Matthew 6:5-15
■ Lesson Scripture: Matthew 6:5-15
■ Focus of the Lesson: People want to make a good public appearance. What is the benefit of looking good on the outside? Jesus taught that it is more important to develop our inner relationship with God through prayer.

❖ Challenge the students to complete one or more of these activities for further spiritual growth related to this week's session. Post this information on newsprint for the students to copy.

(1) **Pray regularly for an individual or group of people that you consider your enemy. Notice over time how your prayers may change your attitude.**

(2) **Research how faith communities known as peace churches—such as Church of the Brethren, Mennonites, Amish, Quakers—practice love toward those whom others would call enemies.**

(3) **Ponder how Jesus' approach to those we label "enemies" is different from the "eye for an eye" relationship that many people, including some Christians, practice.**

❖ Sing or read aloud "Help Us Accept Each Other."

❖ Conclude today's session by leading the class in this benediction adapted from Proverbs 3:5 and 29:25: **Go forth trusting in the Lord with all your heart, knowing that one who trusts in the Lord is secure.**

UNIT 2: JESUS TEACHES WISDOM

PRAYING AS GOD'S PEOPLE

PREVIEWING THE LESSON

Lesson Scripture: Matthew 6:5-15
Background Scripture: Matthew 6:5-15
Key Verse: Matthew 6:6

Focus of the Lesson:
People want to make a good public appearance. What is the benefit of looking good on the outside? Jesus taught that it is more important to develop our inner relationship with God through prayer.

Goals for the Learners:
(1) to become familiar with Jesus' teaching about prayer.
(2) to enjoy the fruit of authentic prayer.
(3) to practice authentic prayer.

Pronunciation Guide:
abba (ab bah')
Aramaic (air uh may' ik)
tameion (ta mi' on)

Supplies:
Bibles, newsprint and marker, paper and pencils, hymnals

READING THE SCRIPTURE

NRSV
Matthew 6:5-15
⁵"And whenever you pray, do not be like the hypocrites; for they love to stand and pray in the synagogues and at the street corners, so that they may be seen by others. Truly I tell you, they have received their

NIV
Matthew 6:5-15
⁵"And when you pray, do not be like the hypocrites, for they love to pray standing in the synagogues and on the street corners to be seen by men. I tell you the truth, they have received their reward in full. ⁶But

reward. [6]But **whenever you pray, go into your room and shut the door and pray to your Father who is in secret; and your Father who sees in secret will reward you.**

[7]"When you are praying, do not heap up empty phrases as the Gentiles do; for they think that they will be heard because of their many words. [8]Do not be like them, for your Father knows what you need before you ask him.

[9] "Pray then in this way:
Our Father in heaven,
     hallowed be your name.
[10]   Your kingdom come.
     Your will be done,
          on earth as it is in heaven.
[11]   Give us this day our daily bread.
[12]   And forgive us our debts,
          as we also have forgiven our debtors.
[13]   And do not bring us to the time of trial,
          but rescue us from the evil one.
[14]For if you forgive others their trespasses, your heavenly Father will also forgive you; [15]but if you do not forgive others, neither will your Father forgive your trespasses.

when you pray, go into your room, close the door and pray to your Father, who is unseen. Then your Father, who sees what is done in secret, will reward you. [7]And when you pray, do not keep on babbling like pagans, for they think they will be heard because of their many words. [8]Do not be like them, for your Father knows what you need before you ask him.

[9]"This, then, is how you should pray:
" 'Our Father in heaven,
     hallowed be your name,
[10]your kingdom come,
     your will be done
          on earth as it is in heaven.
[11]Give us today our daily bread.
[12]Forgive us our debts,
          as we also have forgiven our debtors.
[13]And lead us not into temptation,
     but deliver us from the evil one.'
[14]For if you forgive men when they sin against you, your heavenly Father will also forgive you. [15]But if you do not forgive men their sins, your Father will not forgive your sins."

UNDERSTANDING THE SCRIPTURE

Introduction. Matthew 6:1 serves as an introduction to the whole of 6:2-18. In these verses Jesus admonishes us concerning the religious practices of almsgiving (deeds of mercy), prayer, and fasting. The Greek word that translates as "piety" in 6:1 is the same word that the NRSV translates as "righteousness" in 5:6 and 20. In those two verses the reference is to moral righteousness (qualities such as kindness, honesty, compassion, integrity), whereas in 6:1 Jesus is talking about what we might call "religious righteousness" or practices related to the proper worship of God. Our lesson Scripture, Matthew 6:5-15, deals with prayer.

Matthew 6:5. In his words about prayer, Jesus admonishes his disciples not to be "like the hypocrites." The Greek word translated as "hypocrites" in these verses was used in classical Greek culture to refer to players or actors on a stage. Thus, in referring to some of the Jewish religious leaders as "hypocrites," Jesus implies that they like to perform their religious acts in order to receive the notice and accolades of others rather than out of sincere devotion to God. So it is, Jesus says, that they have already "received their reward."

Through the centuries, some Christian interpreters have mistakenly understood this description of insincere and showy prayer as typical of Jewish prayer in general. But other Jewish writings also criticized such pretentious praying, indicating it was not the norm. And Jesus is not condemning public prayer in general; it was an important part of the synagogue service in which Jesus himself would have participated. What Jesus is condemning is the insincere motive behind praying "at the street corners" to be seen by others, as if prayer were a performance to be applauded.

Matthew 6:6. Jesus now instructs his disciples on the correct way to pray. The Greek word *tameion*, translated as "room," was used by the ancients to refer to a storeroom, closet, or any inner, hidden room in a house used for privacy or for the safekeeping of valuables and important items. The implication is that a disciple's prayer room is a safe sanctuary reserved for the treasure that is genuine prayer: honest, heartfelt, and humble conversation with God, not an ostentatious show to impress others. The phrase "in secret," found twice in 6:6 as well as twice in 6:4 and 6:18, only serves to highlight this fact. God is not impressed with outward show if the inner motive of the heart is insincere. For God sees "in secret" and knows our inner hearts.

Matthew 6:7-8. Jesus condemns not only the hypocrisy of the Jewish religious leaders but also the prayer habits of Gentiles. The "empty phrases" and "many words" probably refer to the ritual repetition and wordiness of prayer formulas used to impress and gain the attention of the many different gods of pagan religion. It should be noted that Jesus assumes that Gentiles pray. That should not surprise us since God has created all humans with an inherent desire for communion with God. That God desires an intimate relationship with God's children is implied in the last phrase of 6:8; as our "Father" who loves us, God knows our needs even before we ask. It is this assurance that gives us the comfort and the courage to pray as Jesus taught us.

Matthew 6:9-15. Matthew 6:9-13 contains the essence of what we call "The Lord's Prayer," the model prayer for all of our praying. It begins as all true prayer should: with God and the praise of God. The opening words are "Our Father," not "My

Father." Jesus wants this to be the prayer of the disciple community, reminding us that we are not alone but bound together when we pray. Undoubtedly, "Father" was the word Jesus used to describe his own intimate and loving relationship with God. The Aramaic word (Aramaic being the everyday language of first-century Palestine) that stood behind the Greek word for "father" was *abba*. This was a term of loving endearment like "Daddy" or "Papa" that would have been used by small children and adult children alike in addressing their fathers.

The heart of Jesus' prayer is made up of six petitions. The first three petitions focus on God and express our desire to honor God's name, which in biblical understanding represents the reality of a person, as being holy and exalted over every other name. We also pray for God's kingdom or reign to be fulfilled now "on earth as it is in heaven" (6:10), even as we offer ourselves to be living vessels through whom God's will and divine purposes will be accomplished.

The last three petitions focus on our needs as humans. "Daily bread" is to be understood literally as food and symbolically as the basic necessities, not luxuries, of life. The Greek word for "daily" could be understood as meaning either the current day or the following day, but the focus is on trusting God one day at a time. The second need is the forgiveness of debts or sins (see Luke 11:4). The burden of guilt and estrangement can weigh heavily on us, and forgiveness is a powerful redemptive force. Matthew 6:14-15 reinforces the meaning of the word "as" in 6:12, reflecting the important connection between human and divine forgiveness. Jesus is not saying that God's forgiveness of us is dependent on our forgiveness of one another. No, God's grace is unconditional and precedes human forgiveness. Jesus is simply saying that a heart that is intentionally unforgiving is not receptive to God's forgiveness. The key to understanding the final petition (6:13) is to know that the Greek word translated in the NRSV as "time of trial" can be translated as "test" or "temptation." The Bible tells us that God does not "tempt" us to do evil (James 1:13), but God does "test" us to strengthen our faith. Perhaps the best way to paraphrase this petition is as follows: "Do not lead us into testing or allow us to be led into temptation or a time of trial without being there to rescue us from the evil one." The primary focus is on God's presence and power to deliver us.

INTERPRETING THE SCRIPTURE

What Is Your Motive?

I remember reading somewhere about a news reporter who described a long pretentious prayer spoken at a civic gathering in Boston as "the most eloquent prayer ever offered to a Boston audience." The reporter's point was that this particular prayer was not offered sincerely from the heart to God but rather given to impress the political and social elite of the city. It is to such hypocritical behavior that Jesus' words in Matthew 6:5-8 speak. In God's economy, our inner thoughts and motives are just as important, if not more important, than our actions. As beauty is more than skin-deep, so God looks beyond and through our actions to see the motives behind them, to see why we do what we do.

It is very possible to do the right thing, or at least what others might perceive as a right or good thing, but for the wrong reasons. Imagine, for example, that I am really nice to you; I treat you with great kindness. Other people might say, "Gee, what a wonderful Christian Steve is." But they cannot look into my heart, as God can, to see my motives. It could be that I have an ulterior motive for being so kind to you. You have season tickets to my favorite sports team, and I am hoping to ingratiate myself with you in the hope that you will invite me to some games. Others might see pure kindness in my outward demeanor, but God, who sees "in secret," can peer through my pretense to see the motives behind my actions. It is about such hypocritical behavior as this that Jesus admonishes us.

I find it very important in my own spiritual journey to keep coming back to these verses in Matthew 5–6, because they remind me of the inward righteousness of the heart. One of my favorite spirituals is "Lord, I Want to Be a Christian." One verse says: "Lord, I want to be like Jesus in my heart, in my heart." Throughout the song the phrase "in my heart" is repeated over and over. That pretty well sums up Jesus' message about motive. We can fool other people much of the time, but we can never fool God. Why? Because God looks into our hearts to see our innermost thoughts and to examine our motives. Blessed are we when we remember this and, with God's grace working in us, do all in our power to keep our hearts and motives pure. Jesus promised that, even as God sees into our hearts, "blessed are the pure in heart, for they will see God" (5:8).

God as Our Father in Heaven

As a faithful Jew, Jesus would have worshiped God as the Creator of the universe and of Israel as a people. Jesus knew well the power of God, both historically as God had guided Israel through the centuries, and in his contemporary setting as Jesus saw God's power at work in his own ministry of healing and working miracles. But above all else, Jesus understood God as an intimate and loving Presence whom he referred to as "our Father in heaven" (6:9).

Jesus was not unique in addressing God as "Father." The epithet "Father" was used in many first-century Jewish prayers to address God. What was unique, however, was the way Jesus consistently lived out his understanding of God as his heavenly Father. We see it in the intimacy and constancy of his prayer relationship with God, in his heartfelt desire to do his Father's will at all cost to himself, and in the expression of his closeness with God at the times of his greatest suffering and challenge. See, for example, Matthew 26:36-46, where, in the agony of Gethsemane, Jesus addresses God in prayer as "My Father" (26:39, 42). In Mark's account of the same incident, Jesus' most intimate term for God is remembered: "Abba, Father" (Mark 14:36). As mentioned in Understanding the Scripture, the Aramaic word *abba* was a term of loving endearment used by children to speak to their fathers. To address God in this personal way is to acknowledge that God is not a whimsical, unpredictable tyrant whom we must fear and be ready to appease at any given moment, such as was the case with many pagan gods. Rather, it is to say that God is personal and gracious and, like a loving parent, is *for* us, not against us; God is one who lovingly disciplines, forgives, and knows how to give good gifts to beloved children (Matthew 7:11). To know that this was Jesus' perception of God helps us to understand why Jesus talked about and practiced prayer the way that he did.

Prayer: Our Lifeline to God

I was riding in an elevator recently when I glanced up to see the following sign posted on the elevator wall: "In case of emergency, please bang on the door, scream loudly and panic!" For too many people prayer is like that. They tend to use prayer only in panic situations, in times of crisis when their backs are to the wall and they don't know what else to do. In other words, prayer is practiced only as a last resort.

But for Jesus prayer was a first resort. It was not the last thing he tried when all else had failed. It was the first thing he did, assuring him of God's strength, presence, and love in the midst of all life's challenges. From all accounts, Jesus prayed regularly and often. Jesus would routinely withdraw to the Galilean hills for quiet time and prayer in the midst of the hectic demands made on him by the crowds (Luke 9:18, 28). He prayed all night before choosing his disciples (Luke 6:12). He prayed before confronting his disciples with the reality that his ministry would lead to suffering and rejection (Luke 9:18). He prayed fervently in the garden of Gethsemane the night before his crucifixion. While he was hanging on the cross, he was in prayerful conversation with his Father and even prayed for God's forgiveness of those who were murdering him (Luke 23:34). Throughout his ministry Jesus demonstrated that prayer is as much an attitude as it is words: an attitude of receptivity and constant openness to God's loving presence. Wherever we meet Jesus in the Gospels, he is persistently practicing prayer.

Of course, Jesus spent so much time in prayer because of the intimate relationship he shared with God. When two people love and trust each other deeply, they want to spend as much time together as they can. They exult in each other's presence. That's the way it was with Jesus and the One he called Abba. The presupposition behind all prayer is that we are dealing with "our Father in heaven" who loves us and knows what is best for us, not with some unpredictable tyrant. The highest purpose of prayer is not to get things that we think we need or to receive answers to hard questions; rather, it is to enter into God's very presence and to deepen our relationship with the One who cares for us and loves us unconditionally.

SHARING THE SCRIPTURE

Preparing Our Hearts

Explore this week's devotional reading, found in Isaiah 12. Read this psalm as your own prayer of praise and thanksgiving. List at least ten reasons you have to thank God today. Think also about what you say when you pray to God. Are you pleading for something, making a petition on behalf of someone else, praying for leaders, offering praise, making a confession, listening for God, or perhaps all of these?

Pray that you and the adult learners will value the importance of regularly conversing with God.

Preparing Our Minds

Study the background Scripture and the lesson Scripture, both of which are from Matthew 6:5-15. Think about the benefit of looking good to others as opposed to developing an inner relationship with God through prayer.

Write on newsprint:
❑ statements for "Gather to Learn."
❑ information for next week's lesson, found under "Continue the Journey."
❑ activities for further spiritual growth in "Continue the Journey."

LEADING THE CLASS

(1) Gather to Learn

❖ Welcome the class members and introduce any guests.

❖ Pray that the students will want to deeply explore Jesus' teachings about prayer.

❖ Post these statements about prayer on newsprint. Invite the adults to call out answers to complete them:

(1) I define "prayer" as _____ _____.

(2) **If called upon to lead a prayer during worship, Sunday school, or a church meeting, I feel** _____ _____.

(3) **I can pray silently or with a group for the purpose of** _____ _____.

(4) **I believe God does/does not hear my prayers because** _____ _____.

(5) **For me, the Lord's Prayer** _____ _____.

❖ Read aloud today's focus statement: **People want to make a good public appearance. What is the benefit of looking good on the outside? Jesus taught that it is more important to develop our inner relationship with God through prayer.**

(2) Become Familiar With Jesus' Teaching About Prayer

❖ Read Matthew 6:5-9a yourself, asking the students to join you for verses 9b-13. Finish by reading verses 14-15 yourself. The adults may use different versions of the Bible, but do ask them to read what is written, which may not be the exact words they normally say.

❖ Use information from Understanding the Scripture for Matthew 6:5 and 6:6 to contrast the way of prayer that Jesus calls hypocritical to the way that he teaches is appropriate for his followers. Focus on motivation by adding ideas from "What Is Your Motive?" in Interpreting the Scripture. Be sure to point out that Jesus was not calling all who pray in public "hypocrites." Also note his challenge to Gentile prayers in verses 7-8.

❖ Look carefully at Jesus' address to God and the six petitions included in his model prayer, as found in verses 9-13. Consider the meaning of each phrase. Information under Matthew 6:9-15 in the

Understanding the Scripture portion, as well as "God as Our Father in Heaven" in Interpreting the Scripture, will be helpful.

❖ Discuss these questions:

(1) Why do you suppose that the Lord's Prayer is so enduring?

(2) How has this prayer encouraged you in your own faith?

(3) Are there one or two phrases that you find especially meaningful? Which one(s)? Why?

(4) If someone asked you to describe what this prayer is about, what would you say?

(3) Enjoy the Fruit of Authentic Prayer

❖ Note that some prayers ring so true that Christians repeat them over and over for centuries. Read at least one such prayer and talk with the class about why the selected prayer continues to touch hearts long after it was penned. In other words, what is so authentic about this prayer?

■ **The Prayer of Saint Francis (Italy, thirteenth century)**

Lord, make me an instrument of thy peace;
where there is hatred, let me sow love;
where there is injury, pardon;
where there is doubt, faith;
where there is despair, hope;
where there is darkness, light;
and where there is sadness, joy.
O Divine Master,
grant that I may not so much seek
to be consoled as to console;
to be understood, as to understand;
to be loved, as to love;
for it is in giving that we receive,
it is in pardoning that we are pardoned,
and it is in dying that we are born to eternal life.

■ **The Prayer of Ignatius of Loyola (Spain, sixteenth century)**

Teach us, good Lord,
to serve you as you deserve;
to give and not to count the cost;
to fight and not to heed the wounds;
to toil and not to seek for rest;
to labor and not to ask for any reward,
except that of knowing that we do your will;
through Jesus Christ our Lord. Amen.

■ **Covenant Prayer in the Wesleyan Tradition (John Wesley, England, eighteenth century)**

I am no longer my own, but thine.
Put me to what thou wilt, rank me with whom thou wilt.
Put me to doing, put me to suffering.
Let me be employed by thee or laid aside for thee.
exalted for thee or brought low by thee.
Let me be full, let me be empty.
Let me have all things, let me have nothing.
I freely and heartily yield all things
to thy pleasure and disposal.
And now, O glorious and blessed God,
Father, Son, and Holy Spirit,
Thou art mine, and I am thine. So be it.
And the covenant which I have made on earth,
let it be ratified in heaven. Amen.

❖ Wrap up by encouraging the adults to name or offer prayers that have had a positive impact on their relationship with God.

(4) Practice Authentic Prayer

❖ Distribute paper and pencils. Ask the students to write a prayer in their own words that follows the model Jesus gave us.

❖ Form small groups and invite each

person to read his or her prayer to the group.

❖ Conclude the activity by suggesting that students continue to pray (and revise) their prayer during the coming week.

(5) Continue the Journey

❖ Pray that the adults will seek opportunities this week to practice authentic prayer.

❖ Read aloud this preparation for next week's lesson. You may also want to post it on newsprint for the students to copy.

- ■ **Title: Facing Life Without Worry**
- ■ **Background Scripture: Matthew 6:25-34**
- ■ **Lesson Scripture: Matthew 6:25-34**
- ■ **Focus of the Lesson: People often find that worry neither prevents nor solves life's problems. So why do we worry? Jesus taught that depending on God to meet our needs can relieve our worries.**

❖ Challenge the students to complete one or more of these activities for further spiritual growth related to this week's session. Post this information on newsprint for the students to copy.

(1) **Sing or think about some favorite hymns that relate to prayer, such as "Prayer Is the Soul's Sincere Desire," "Standing in the Need of Prayer," "Sweet Hour of Prayer," or "Take Time to Be Holy." What do you learn about prayer from the song(s) you selected? How might the hymn(s) enrich your prayer life?**

(2) **Pray the Lord's Prayer very slowly at least once each day. Linger over each phrase. Invite God to teach you how to come before the throne of grace through this model prayer.**

(3) **Teach a child or new Christian the words of the Lord's Prayer. Explain the meaning in terms appropriate to the person you are teaching.**

❖ Sing "The Lord's Prayer."

❖ Conclude today's session by leading the class in this benediction adapted from Proverbs 3:5 and 29:25: **Go forth trusting in the Lord with all your heart, knowing that one who trusts in the Lord is secure.**

UNIT 2: JESUS TEACHES WISDOM
FACING LIFE WITHOUT WORRY

PREVIEWING THE LESSON

Lesson Scripture: Matthew 6:25-34
Background Scripture: Matthew 6:25-34
Key Verses: Matthew 6:33-34

Focus of the Lesson:
People often find that worry neither prevents nor solves life's problems. So why do we worry? Jesus taught that depending on God to meet our needs can relieve our worries.

Goals for the Learners:
(1) to survey Jesus' teaching about God as the great provider.
(2) to explore feelings about the relationship between money and stress.
(3) to work out a plan to lean more and more on God to provide for needs.

Supplies:
Bibles, newsprint and marker, paper and pencils, hymnals

READING THE SCRIPTURE

NRSV
Matthew 6:25-34

25"Therefore I tell you, do not worry about your life, what you will eat or what you will drink, or about your body, what you will wear. Is not life more than food, and the body more than clothing? 26Look at the birds of the air; they neither sow nor reap nor gather into barns, and yet your heavenly Father feeds them. Are you not of more value than they? 27And can any of you by worrying add a single hour to your span of

NIV
Matthew 6:25-34

25"Therefore I tell you, do not worry about your life, what you will eat or drink; or about your body, what you will wear. Is not life more important than food, and the body more important than clothes? 26Look at the birds of the air; they do not sow or reap or store away in barns, and yet your heavenly Father feeds them. Are you not much more valuable than they? 27Who of you by worrying can add a single hour to his life?

life? ²⁸And why do you worry about cloth-ing? Consider the lilies of the field, how they grow; they neither toil nor spin, ²⁹yet I tell you, even Solomon in all his glory was not clothed like one of these. ³⁰But if God so clothes the grass of the field, which is alive today and tomorrow is thrown into the oven, will he not much more clothe you—you of little faith? ³¹Therefore do not worry, saying, 'What will we eat?' or 'What will we drink?' or 'What will we wear?' ³²For it is the Gentiles who strive for all these things; and indeed your heavenly Father knows that you need all these things. **³³But strive first for the kingdom of God and his righteous-ness, and all these things will be given to you as well.**

³⁴"So do not worry about tomorrow, for tomorrow will bring worries of its own. **Today's trouble is enough for today."**

²⁸"And why do you worry about clothes? See how the lilies of the field grow. They do not labor or spin. ²⁹Yet I tell you that not even Solomon in all his splendor was dressed like one of these. ³⁰If that is how God clothes the grass of the field, which is here today and tomorrow is thrown into the fire, will he not much more clothe you, O you of little faith? ³¹So do not worry, saying, 'What shall we eat?' or 'What shall we drink?' or 'What shall we wear?' ³²For the pagans run after all these things, and your heavenly Father knows that you need them. **³³But seek first his kingdom and his righ-teousness, and all these things will be given to you as well. ³⁴Therefore do not worry about tomorrow,** for tomorrow will worry about itself. **Each day has enough trouble of its own."**

UNDERSTANDING THE SCRIPTURE

Introduction. Matthew 6:25-34 is one of two units of thought in the larger section of 6:19-34. In 6:1-18 Jesus has dealt with three religious practices that are important to any disciple's expression of devotion to God and that are to be carried out with sincerity: almsgiving, prayer, and fasting. In the sec-ond half of the chapter (6:19-34) Jesus talks about important attitudes or perspectives on money, possessions, values, and anxi-eties associated with daily living. Matthew 6:25-34 deals specifically with the issue of "worry" (6:25, 27, 28, 31, 34), something that particularly plagues us in our highly mate-rialistic and competitive culture. In these verses we see the influence of Israel's wisdom tradition, for Jesus appeals to com-mon sense, rather than revelation, and makes his point by reference to the observa-tion of nature. He also contrasts the folly of worry and trusting in material things with the wisdom of trusting in God, who knows our needs and promises to care for us.

Matthew 6:25. This verse begins with the important adverb "therefore," implying that Jesus is drawing a conclusion from what has gone before. The previous passage dealt with the dangers of honoring a divided commitment (pulled between two masters, 6:24) and putting one's trust in wealth and material things rather than in God. If our god (that which we value most in our life) is money or material posses-sions, then we will experience much anxiety because we are seeking after things that can-not ultimately satisfy us. Jesus asks: "Is not life more than food, and the body more than clothing?" Verse 25 represents the first of several admonitions not to worry or be anx-ious about the basic material needs of life.

Matthew 6:26-30. Like 6:25, four of these verses contain personal and penetrating questions as Jesus presses his disciples to look inward and examine their lifestyle, val-ues, and their faith—or lack of faith—in God. Like a true wisdom teacher, Jesus urges his disciples to observe the simple things of nature—the birds, wild flowers, and grass—and learn from them about the providential care of God. Twice Jesus uses the argument of relative value from the lesser to the greater. Jesus says that God values all creation, but God's children have a special place. Referring to how God takes care of the "birds of the air," Jesus poses the question, "Are you not of more value than they?" (6:26). Then in 6:30, where Jesus recounts how God cares even for "the grass of the field," which is here one day and burned the next, he poses the question, "Will [God] not much more clothe you— you of little faith?" Throughout this whole passage, Jesus' call is to a stronger faith, a deeper trust in God. In 6:27 Jesus raises what may be for us moderns the most pertinent question, and, of course, we know the answer. Worrying will not lengthen our life by the smallest amount. In fact, medical studies indicate just the opposite, that stress, worry, and anxiety shorten our lives quantitatively and also lessen the quality of our lives.

Matthew 6:31-33. In 6:25 Jesus had raised the profound question with which each of us must struggle and ultimately seek to answer: "Is not life more than food, and . . . clothing?" In 6:31-33, which begins with that important word "therefore," suggesting that Jesus is going to draw a conclusion, he answers his own question. Life *is more* than food, clothing, and material things. Real life, not superficial life, has to do with God and our making the concerns of God's reign (justice, kindness, compassion) and a right relationship with God ("his righteousness") our top priority (6:33). Indeed, if our relationship with God is our top priority in life, then Jesus asks the logical question: Why in the world do we worry about food, drink, clothing, and other such material things of life? God already knows we have need of these things, and God will provide them for us as long as we trust God and keep God at the center of our focus (6:33).

Jesus hinted at this earlier in the chapter when he taught his disciples the model prayer. They were to pray first for the coming of the kingdom and for God's will to be done; then would follow the provision of their "daily bread" (6:11).

Of course, nowhere does Jesus say that his disciples are to sit idly by while God does all the work and provides for them. The call to trust in God's providence does not exclude the disciples' involvement and working. After all, the birds of the air work hard to build their nests and obtain food for their young, and they do it without complaining. It is in this manner that God provides for them. It should be noted that the verbs that Jesus mentions in 6:26 and 28 ("sow," "reap," "gather" [into barns], "toil," and "spin") are all activities of meaningful labor, ordained and blessed by God, in which his disciples would have been involved in their daily lives. The point Jesus is making is that daily life includes our performing these activities that help provide for our needs, but genuine life, the life that Jesus came to bring, is also much more than these activities. Abundant life, quality life, comes from striving "first for the kingdom of God and his righteousness" (6:33).

Matthew 6:34. Like "therefore" in 6:25 and 31, the adverb "so" prepares us to hear a conclusion that Jesus is drawing from what he has said before: "So do not worry about tomorrow. . . . Today's trouble is enough for today." I don't think Jesus suggests here that we should never think about or plan for the future. For elsewhere Jesus tells his disciples to "estimate the cost" (Luke 14:28) and to be prepared by planning ahead (Matthew 25:1-13). What Jesus does affirm is that in this world there are enough problems and challenges that we face each day; there is no need to borrow ahead. His disciples are to live one day at a time, assured that their lives are in the hands of a loving heavenly Father who knows their needs and cares deeply for them.

INTERPRETING THE SCRIPTURE

Why Do We Worry?

As I write this, a kind of pall hangs over the world. We are just coming out of the worst economic recession since World War II, and in the United States we still find ourselves with an unemployment rate above 9 percent nationally. Add to this the reality that our country is involved in two unpopular wars, and there is grave international concern about the threat posed by global warming. Indeed, many people are deeply worried not only about the present and whether they will have jobs and income to meet their families' needs but also about their children's future and even whether there will be a future for their children. "Angst" is the word that psychology has given us to describe this type of anxiety and malaise about the future. One dictionary defines "angst" as "a feeling of deep anxiety or dread, typically an unfocused one about the human condition or the state of the world in general."

Whether it is general angst or it is worry about specific personal issues, living with constant anxiety can drain people emotionally, spiritually, and physically; it is also destructive of human health and well-being. So why do we worry? Primarily, we become anxious when we are in situations where we feel we are not in control. Whether it is facing an unknown future (regarding our health, our children, our finances), an unexpected event such as a job loss, catastrophic illness, or a natural disaster that strikes us, or perhaps the scarcity of some substance that we believe we must have to survive, it is easy for anxiety, fueled by fear of the unknown, to set in and overwhelm us.

This is when we need to hear these simple but profound words of Jesus that can pull us out of our tailspins of worry and turn our spiritual eyes heavenward toward our Father. For Jesus wants his disciples to be filled with life and faith, not anxiety and dread that leads to spiritual death. In Matthew 6:25-34, Jesus reminds us that abundance, not scarcity, is the mark of God's economy and that, as our loving heavenly Father, God desires to give us everything that we can possibly need (6:33).

So why do we put ourselves through the agony of worry? It's so self-defeating and unnecessary when Jesus has given us the answer. Recently, I read some interesting statistics that someone had compiled about worry: 40 percent of our anxieties will never happen; 30 percent are things about the past that can't be changed; 12 percent are criticisms by others, most untrue; 10 percent are things about health, which will only get worse with stress and worry; 8 percent are real problems that will have to be faced. What this says is that 92 percent of our worries are unnecessary. Regarding the 8 percent that represent real problems, Jesus promises in Matthew 6:25-34 that God will give us the strength and wisdom to deal with those victoriously as we put our trust day-by-day in God. Indeed, if we are busy putting God's kingdom first in our lives and doing God's will, we won't have time to worry.

The Search for Meaning

The term "seekers" has been adopted into the language of the church to refer to those people who are searching and whose hearts are open to hear the gospel. Many churches even have "seeker services" oriented especially to people who are exploring the faith but have not yet made a Christian commitment. Certainly, Jesus understood that every human being is on a journey seeking that which will bring purpose and fulfillment to his or her life. In 6:25-34 Jesus challenges us to think about the meaning of life (see the question in 6:25), and he clearly lays out two alternative paths that humans can walk in search of fulfillment.

One is to look to material things and possessions to provide that meaning. We need only to glance at advertisements on television or in newspapers and magazines to see the path they lure us to follow. Supposedly, the good life can be ours with the purchase of the right clothing, jewelry, cars, cosmetics, vacation homes, or numerous other things that entice our hearts' yearning for gratification. But, alas, how unfulfilling material possessions can ultimately be. Rather than freeing us to enjoy life, they make us slaves; we become possessed by our possessions. We can have our homes, closets, and garages filled to overflowing with clothes and toys and yet be miserable and lonely, left with hungry hearts that are unsatisfied. Like a drug addict who is worried about getting his next fix, we become anxious about which purchase we need to make next to keep us happy. This is a path that leads to nowhere.

The alternate path that Jesus offers us, one that leads to fulfillment and meaning in life, is that of a relationship with our heavenly Father, who promises to provide all that we need, if we just live as trusting children and seek first God's kingdom and righteousness (6:33). Saint Augustine, after a long search for meaning in his own life, wrote in his autobiography that the greatest human adventure is to seek God. He also left us with this famous prayer: "Lord, you have made us for yourself, and our hearts are restless until they rest in you." Augustine points us all in the right direction.

Trust God and Work Hard

Years ago I saw a banner hanging in a church with the following words: "Pray as if everything depends on God and work as if everything depends on you." This counsel speaks to a kind of synergy between God and humans that I have found to be a dynamic reality in my own journey as a disciple. In Matthew 6:25-34 Jesus promises that, as God provides for the birds, wildflowers, and even the grass of the field, even more so will God care for us as we put our trust in God. But as mentioned in the commentary on 6:31-33, nowhere does Jesus say we can be totally passive while God is the active One in our relationship doing all the work. No, God expects us to be active copartners in our covenant relationship with God. God indeed cares for the birds of the air, but God does so through their participation as they work hard to build their nests, lay and incubate their eggs, and search for provisions to feed their young. Furthermore, Jesus does not condemn our involvement in thought and planning for the future. Rather, he condemns nervous anxiety about the future that betrays a lack of trust in God.

What Jesus calls for is a kind of synergy as we work with God, a balance in our lives between trusting God and working diligently to do God's will (striving first for God's kingdom and righteousness; 6:33). Paul was to echo this emphasis on synergy in Philippians 2:12-13: "Work out your own salvation with fear and trembling; for it is God who is at work in you, enabling you both to will and to work for his good pleasure." Such synergy and balance is the secret to living a fulfilled and meaningful life as disciples of Jesus.

SHARING THE SCRIPTURE

Preparing Our Hearts

Explore this week's devotional reading, found in Psalm 37:1-8. This psalm attributed to David is summed up in verse 1: "Do not fret." We are called to trust in the Lord and wait patiently. Verse 8 gives us a reason not to fret: "it leads only to evil." This psalm reinforces Jesus' teachings in Matthew 6:25-34, which we will study this week. Do you tend to worry and be anxious? If so, practice putting your trust in the Lord. Reread this psalm throughout the week, particularly if you feel yourself becoming upset and starting to worry.

Pray that you and the adult learners will consistently turn over life's problems and worries to the God who loves and cares for you.

Preparing Our Minds

Study the background Scripture and the lesson Scripture, both of which are from Matthew 6:25-34. Think about why we worry, even though worrying can neither prevent nor solve life's problems.

Write on newsprint:
- ❏ questions for "Work Out a Plan to Lean More and More on God to Provide for Needs."
- ❏ information for next week's lesson, found under "Continue the Journey."
- ❏ activities for further spiritual growth in "Continue the Journey."

LEADING THE CLASS

(1) Gather to Learn

❖ Welcome the class members and introduce any guests.

❖ Pray that the students will recognize that because God is the great provider they have no need to worry.

❖ Read aloud these sayings about worry:
- ■ **Don't tell me that worry doesn't do any good. I know better. The things I worry about don't happen.** (Anonymous)
- ■ **Happy is the man who is too busy to worry by day, and too sleepy to worry at night.** (Anonymous)
- ■ **One is given strength to bear what happens to one, but not the one hundred and one different things that might happen.** (C. S. Lewis, 1898–1963)
- ■ **When worry is present, trust cannot crowd its way in.** (Billy Graham, 1918–)
- ■ **Worry gives a small thing a big shadow.** (Swedish proverb)
- ■ **Worry is an indication that we think God cannot look after us.** (Oswald Chambers, 1874–1917)

❖ Encourage the adults to talk about how any of these quotations relates to their own attitudes toward worry.

❖ Read aloud today's focus statement: **People often find that worry neither prevents nor solves life's problems. So why do we worry? Jesus taught that depending on God to meet our needs can relieve our worries.**

(2) Survey Jesus' Teaching About God as the Great Provider

❖ Read the first two paragraphs of "Why Do We Worry?" from Interpreting the Scripture. Invite the adults to add other reasons people may worry.

❖ Select a volunteer to read Matthew 6:25-34.

❖ Look specifically at Jesus' words about worry in Matthew 6:25, 27, 28, 31, 34.

❖ Direct attention to the questions Jesus poses in verses 25-30. Use information from

Understanding the Scripture for 6:25 and 6:26-30 to help students see how Jesus is calling them to a greater trust in God.

❖ Read verse 33 and ask: **How can we as a church and as individuals seek God's righteousness first, especially when there are so many other things that clamor for our attention?**

(3) Explore Feelings About the Relationship Between Money and Stress

❖ Read aloud the following partial statements and invite the participants to fill in the blanks silently as they explore their feelings about the relationship between money and stress.

(1) **When I pay my bills each month I feel _____ _____.**

(2) **As I look at the money I have to live on, I wonder _____ _____.**

(3) **If something breaks down in my home or car, my first response is _____.**

(4) **If I rate my concerns about money on a scale of 1 to 10 with 1 being "no worry or stress at all" and 10 being "constantly stressed about money," I would rate myself as a _____.**

❖ Suggest that the adults spend several moments listening for God to assure them that like the lilies of the field and the birds of the air, they will be provided with life's basic needs.

(4) Work Out a Plan to Lean More and More on God to Provide for Needs

❖ Form groups of three. Encourage the adults to tell stories of times when God provided for their needs. Limit time and be certain that each person has a chance to speak. Recognize that some stories may be more dramatic than others, but everyone has a story to tell.

❖ Call the groups back together. Invite everyone to silently consider this question: **What do your story and the stories of your classmates teach you about God's ability to provide?**

❖ Distribute paper and pencils. Suggest that the adults list two or three situations they currently face that are causing them to worry. They will not be called on to share their lists, so encourage them to be as specific as possible. For example, instead of saying "war," write "my grandchild wants to enlist in the army, and I fear for his or her safety." Instead of listing "health," write, "I need medications that are becoming increasingly difficult for me to pay for." Post these questions for the adults to mull over or write about in relation to each situation they have identified.

(1) **What specifically causes me to feel anxious in this situation?**

(2) **What attitudes or actions on my part will show that I trust God to provide?**

(3) **What Bible verses or stories will remind me of God's ability and willingness to provide?**

❖ Bring the group back together and lead the group in reading today's key verses, Matthew 6:33-34. Encourage the adults to take Jesus' words seriously as they seek to live righteously before God and with full assurance and confidence in God. Suggest that they turn often this week to the Bible stories or verses they identified to help bolster their trust in God's ability to provide.

(5) Continue the Journey

❖ Pray that the adults will lean more and more on God to meet their needs.

❖ Read aloud this preparation for next week's lesson. You may also want to post it on newsprint for the students to copy.

■ **Title: A Blessing for All Nations**
■ **Background Scripture: Genesis 12:1-9**

- Lesson Scripture: Genesis 12:1-9
- Focus of the Lesson: Sometimes people are asked to do incredibly difficult things with only promises of reward to motivate them. How much are some people willing to endure and risk in exchange for promises? Abram and Sarai in their old age risked everything to move their family and all their possessions to a new land because of their faith in God's promises.

❖ Challenge the students to complete one or more of these activities for further spiritual growth related to this week's session. Post this information on newsprint for the students to copy.

(1) **Monitor your feelings this week. When situations arise that cause you to worry, stop for a moment and recall today's key verses from** Matthew 6:33-34. **Give thanks that you can rely completely upon God.**

(2) List five worries that you currently face. Which of these do you have any control over? Which are totally out of your hands? Take action where possible, but recognize that God is in charge. In prayer, turn all of these worries over to God.

(3) Write a poem, draw a picture, sing a song, or use some other artistic media to demonstrate what life can be like when you seek God first.

❖ Sing or read aloud "Seek Ye First."

❖ Conclude today's session by leading the class in this benediction adapted from Proverbs 3:5 and 29:25: **Go forth trusting in the Lord with all your heart, knowing that one who trusts in the Lord is secure.**

Second Quarter
God Establishes a Faithful People

DECEMBER 4, 2011–FEBRUARY 26, 2012

The lessons for the winter quarter, which emphasize faith, focus on God's covenant through Abraham. God promised Abraham that through him all the nations of the earth would be blessed. The covenant was passed down through generations and ultimately fulfilled in Jesus Christ.

Unit 1, "God's Covenant," delves into the story of God's promise to Abraham. On December 4 we hear about how Abraham will be "A Blessing for All Nations," according to Genesis 12:1-9. God made "A Promise to Abraham," which the patriarch believed, as we will read in Genesis 15:1-21 on December 11. Having been told to sacrifice his son Isaac, Abraham prepares to obey the command and as he does so learns that "The Lord Provides," as recounted in Genesis 22:1-14, which we will study on December 18. The first unit concludes on Christmas Day with a lesson from Luke 1:26-56 and Galatians 3:6-18, where we discover how Jesus' coming is "According to the Promise" that was made to Abraham centuries earlier.

Unit 2, "God's Protection," includes five sessions from Genesis and Exodus. The first four survey the story of Joseph in Genesis 39–50 to see how God's promise to Abraham continues through the generations and is carried into Egypt. The last lesson looks at the songs of Moses and Miriam in Exodus 15, where the newly liberated Hebrew people celebrate God's covenant faithfulness. The lesson for January 1 from Genesis 39:1-23 demonstrates how "God Watches over Joseph," a great-grandson of Abraham, who lived a life of integrity even when tempted. "Joseph Finds Favor" and real success in the eyes of Pharaoh, as recorded in Genesis 41:1-52, which is the basis for the lesson for January 8. Genesis 42:1-38 and 45:1-28 form the backdrop for "God Preserves a Remnant," the story of Joseph's family told in the lesson for January 15. The session for January 22 from Genesis 50:1-26 teaches that as a result of his forgiveness for the wrongs his brothers have done to him, "Joseph Transmits Abraham's Promise." The second unit ends on January 29 with a study of Exodus 1:8-14 and 15:1-27 that celebrates God's protection of the Hebrews who were led by Moses "Out of Egypt."

Unit 3, "God's Redemption," explores Paul's letter to the Galatians, which helps us to discern how Christians are to understand the law and justification by faith, and also see ourselves as heirs of God's promise to Abraham. On February 5 we learn about what it means to be "Justified by Faith in Christ" as we study Galatians 1:1–2:21. Galatians 3:1-14, the Scripture for the lesson on February 12, examines how we are "Freed from Law Through Christ." Paul teaches that we are "Heirs to the Promise" as he writes in Galatians 3:15-29 and 4:1–5:1, which we will study on February 19. The quarter concludes on February 26 as we examine the "Fruits of Redemption," found in Galatians 5:2–6:18.

MEET OUR WRITER

THE REVEREND VON W. UNRUH

Von W. Unruh is the pastor of Morton Memorial United Methodist Church in Monteagle, Tennessee. A member of the Tennessee Conference of The United Methodist Church since 1991, he has previously served pastorates in Tennessee and Kentucky. He was also appointed briefly as editor of *Adult Bible Studies* and *Adult Bible Studies Teacher* at The United Methodist Publishing House.

A former member of the Southeastern Jurisdiction Commission on Archives and History, Unruh has read and published a number of papers on United Methodist history. He has also edited *Methodism in the Tennessee Conference*, a quarterly historical journal of the Tennessee Conference of The United Methodist Church; taught several seminars on how to research one's local church history; and served for several years as archivist of the Tennessee Conference.

The author of a couple of books, Unruh has served as spiritual director of countless Walk to Emmaus and Chrysalis weekends, implemented morning prayer at each of his churches, enjoys teaching Bible studies, and leads workshops for local churches. A former conference secretary of the Tennessee Conference, he is a member of the Wesleyan Theological Society.

Von was blessed with a twenty-five-year marriage to Tammy Williams Unruh, a tireless community and social worker before her death in 2010.

THE BIG PICTURE: HUMAN FAITH AND DIVINE FAITHFULNESS

Each lesson this quarter provides us an opportunity to investigate one or more aspects of faith. By focusing our attention primarily on Abraham and Joseph and the church in Galatia, the lessons give us the opportunity to think about such questions as: What do we mean when we say we have faith? Where does faith come from? What do we mean when we say God is faithful? Is human faith different from divine faithfulness? How do our understandings of faith and faithfulness differ from those we find in Scripture?

We want our answers to these questions to be based on Holy Scripture, but our hymnody can also teach us the basic definitions of many words we use as well as concepts we hear in church. This is certainly true of faith. For instance, on the basis of Lamentations 3:22-23, the opening sentence in Thomas Chisholm's hymn "Great Is Thy Faithfulness" declares, "Great is thy faithfulness, O God my Father." That sentence doesn't define faithfulness, but it does make a value judgment about it. It is "great"; it is truly important. Faithfulness is a divine virtue, an attribute that God possesses. Drawing on the words of James 1:17, the second line in the hymn dares to give a preliminary description of divine faithfulness: God doesn't change or "turn." At least one aspect of divine faithfulness is therefore stability, dependability, surety, which has the capability of producing in us confidence. The rest of the first verse reinforces this meaning of changelessness, for God will be as God has always been. Faithfulness is, therefore, an aspect of who God is in Godself.

That's not all. The next to last clause in the refrain confesses that God meets our needs. When we speak of God's faithfulness we're really talking about God's providence. God not only knows us, God looks after us and cares for us. From God we receive all that we need (Philippians 4:19). And the last clause in the refrain states emphatically, "Great is thy faithfulness, Lord, *unto me!*" (italics added). So another aspect of faithfulness that this hymn highlights is how God relates to us.

Other hymns of the church, such as "I Know Whom I Have Believed," "Give to the Winds Thy Fears," or "Rock of Ages, Cleft for Me," explore other nuances of the meaning of divine faithfulness. A nice way to introduce this important theme in the lesson each week would therefore be to highlight one hymn from your hymnal. Meditate on the hymn throughout the week and then, at the beginning of class, share what God's Spirit has taught you about faith through the words of the hymn. There is most likely a topical index in the back of your hymnal to help draw your attention to those hymns that are focused specifically on God's faithfulness.

What Faith Is Not

Faith is not just a divine attribute, however. As God seeks to enter into relationship with us, we must eventually decide how we will respond to God. If we respond positively, God's faithfulness will elicit faith in us. In the sermon we know as the book of Hebrews, we are offered a succinct, albeit elusive definition of human faith. "Faith," we are told, "is the assurance of things hoped for, the conviction of things not seen" (Hebrews 11:1). This definition expands the discussion of faith from a divine attribute to one of the forms it takes in human beings. Because of words such as "assurance," "hope," "conviction," and "unseen," some Christians have decided that faith is not really very tangible. They might even agree with the little boy who was asked by his Sunday school teacher to explain what faith is. "Sure thing," he said. "Faith is believing in stuff you know isn't true." Well, no; faith has nothing to do with believing untrue stuff. Neither is faith what I once heard an adult in a Sunday school class say. "Faith," said this person, "is believing things you cannot prove." While "things you cannot prove" is marginally better than "things that are untrue," that's not faith, either. Faith would be a very useless gift if it merely encouraged us to believe lies or illusions.

These popular notions but wrong ideas about human faith approach faith as if it were primarily a mental judgment we make. It reduces faith to a theory we hold when we don't have all the information that we need to make a well-informed decision or to a private opinion we cling to when the so-called "facts" of our world overwhelm us.

What Faith Is

There is certainly much more to life than so-called objective facts. Relationships with other human beings are just as real as mathematical equations and we can be just as confident in describing another person's character as we can be when defining a word. God, who is truth, does not expect us to tether our lives to nonsense or to imaginary tales. Faith is not what we are left to cling to when we are unable to obtain "real" knowledge. The confidence we have in a friend, the belief we have in someone's goodness, the trust we place in a spouse—these are some of the forms that human faith takes.

But what does Scripture itself teach us about God's faithfulness and human faith? Beyond what we can learn from our hymns, beyond what the dictionary tells us is the definition of faith, what do the lessons this quarter tell us about God's faithfulness and the forms that our faithful response takes to God and other people? In two words, a lot.

All of the lessons in Unit 1 explore God's faithfulness to the covenantal promises God has made. In calling Abram to follow (Lesson 1), God made several promises to Abram (Genesis 12:1-3). These promises bound God to act in certain ways. Curiously, God made these promises to Abram even before Abram responded to God's call. That important fact about how God works remains true to this day. God initiates contact with us. God calls us and seeks us out. God in love invites us to respond with love.

At the same time, this lesson describes one form that a faithful response to God's call and God's promises looks like. God called Abram to "go" (Genesis 12:1) and so Abram "went" (12:4). At the heart of human faithfulness is obedience. In addition, Abram "took his wife Sarai, his brother's son Lot, . . . and the persons whom they had acquired in Haran" (12:5). Thus, yet another form that human faithfulness takes is the willingness to share God's blessings with others.

In Lesson 2, based on Genesis 15, God repeated earlier promises to Abram, this time binding Godself to Abram with a special oath known as a covenant (Genesis 15:18). That God's promises endure unchanged introduces the notion of stability to God's faithfulness. Likewise, when Abram discovered that God intended to remain bound by divine promises and that those promises would not be taken from him, he was encouraged to put his faith in God and trust God.

Abraham's trust in God was put to the test in Genesis 22 (Lesson 3) when God told Abraham to sacrifice his beloved son, Isaac, as a burnt offering to God (22:2). Abraham's willingness to trust God to provide (22:8) was rewarded when God did just that (22:13-14). God's faithfulness can take the form of providence as God looks after us and cares for us. On the human side, a faithful response can be the willingness to submit one's will and even one's future to God.

In the final lesson of the first unit, a major shift occurs when we move from Abraham in Genesis and turn to Mary's Magnificat in Luke 1. God's providential care is seen to extend to individuals as well as nations (Luke 1:48) and becomes a gospel proclamation of steadfast mercy (1:50). As for Mary, her submission to God's will resulted in much joy (1:47) and the willingness to praise and glorify God (1:49).

In the second unit, the lessons explore the various ways that God's faithfulness provides protection to God's people. Once again a major shift occurs as our attention is turned to Joseph, the great-grandson of Abraham. Already in Egypt, Joseph was purchased by Potiphar and placed in charge of his household, which began to thrive because God blessed both Joseph and Potiphar's household (Genesis 39:5). God's protective faithfulness did not render Joseph immune to hardship or attack, but it did take the form of constant presence with Joseph (39:3, 21). For Joseph, faith in God meant living a righteous life, a chaste life of sexual purity (39:7-8).

In Lesson 6, God's faithfulness was revelatory and generous, granting wisdom and insight that were not natural to Joseph (Genesis 41:16, 37-41), as well as administrative skills and discernment (41:33-36). In a side note, we learn that God's faithful promises to Abraham regarding posterity continued to be honored, as Joseph's wife bore him two sons (41:50). Joseph's faithful response to God's generous wisdom was to use that wisdom generously on behalf of those around him, mimicking God by providing and caring for them.

At its core, God's faithfulness means salvation and deliverance for human beings. While discussions of salvation in church today tend to default to discussions of eternal life and freedom from sin, Scripture also speaks of God's salvation in terms of such things as daily deliverance from enemies, provision of daily sustenance, and the resolve to address matters that concern us. Lesson 7 invites us to reflect on how God's faithfulness works through everyday events to "preserve life" and "preserve . . . a remnant" (45:5, 7). Human faith then takes the form of our willingness to be used by God as God sees fit to accomplish ends that God has designed. In the words of John Wesley, this is a prayerful willingness to "give up myself to [God's] will in all things . . . let me be employed for you, or laid aside for you." Joseph willingly consented to care for the people of God; that is, for his brothers and their families.

Another important aspect of God's faithfulness is God's desire to be reconciled to all human beings, as well as all creation. Lesson 8, based on Genesis 50:15-26, looks at the final story of Joseph and his brothers. It helps us explore what forgiveness and reconciliation look like, how they work, and why they matter so greatly. Similarly, human faith also concerns itself with extending forgiveness to and seeking reconciliation with persons with whom, for whatever reasons, our relationship has been broken. Faith is unwilling to let grudges, wrongs, and fears dictate the form that a relationship takes. It cannot create a friendship where none is desired, but it can restore civility and kindness.

God's intervention on behalf of God's people is the final form of divine faithful protection that is explored in the second unit. Lesson 9 calls our attention to Exodus 15 and the Red Sea crossing when God intervened on behalf of the Hebrews and rescued them from the hand of their enemies. Most of the time we are unaware of the ways that God intervenes in our lives on our behalf. But this lesson invites us to reconsider "coincidences" and "twists of fate" and even "dumb luck" as possible pointers to God at work among us. Might coincidences really be "a God thing"?

As for human faith, it is one thing to trust another person in the sense of believing that he or she is a person of integrity or good repute. It is quite another thing to trust another person with one's very life. And yet, we do this every day of our lives as we drive vehicles we didn't build, sit as passengers on buses driven by someone else, or eat food in restaurants prepared by people we do not know. Is it something we do in relation to God? In relation to God, still another aspect of human faith is the praise that wells up in us that we want to share with God (Exodus 15:1-2).

Unit 3 turns to the New Testament and consists of four lessons on Paul's letter to the church in Galatia. The lessons offer a fresh look at what a first-generation Christian theologian thought about God's faithfulness and the redemption God offers to all humanity. In Lesson 10, divine faithfulness is displayed most fully in the gracious justification God has made available to all people in Christ Jesus (Galatians 2:16). It is through Jesus that God has most fully loved us and given Godself for us (2:20). Through Jesus, God's reclamation project that began in earnest with Abraham has been extended to all people. Surprisingly, Paul declared that human faith is exhibited by putting our trust solely in Jesus, not by aligning ourselves with the Jewish race or adhering to the Law (2:16). Christ lives in those who live by faith in him (2:20).

In Galatians 3, the basis for Lesson 11, Paul reiterated his belief (which was also his experience) that God's faithfulness is revealed in God's love for and justification of all people, Gentiles as well as Jews. God's faithfulness is even able to "work miracles" among us (3:5). In extending the promise made originally to Abraham to all people through Christ, God has also extended the blessing pronounced on Abraham to all people. On the human side, faith that renounces "human effort" (3:3 NIV) and "believe[s] what [is] heard" (3:5 NIV) is reckoned as righteousness (3:6) and results in "the promise of the Spirit" (3:14).

In Lesson 12, based on Galatians 3–4, God's faithfulness is said to have resulted in the Incarnation of Jesus (4:4), which itself resulted in our release from "the elemental spirits of the world" (4:3). As we mature in faith, God faithfully "has sent the Spirit of his Son into our hearts" (4:6). Through faith, humans are redeemed from the law and "receive adoption as children" (4:5).

In the final lesson, which looks at Galatians 5–6, we are introduced to the fruit of the Spirit: "love, joy, peace, patience, kindness, generosity, faithfulness, gentleness, and self-control" (5:22-23). In response, faithful spiritual people (6:1) "work for the good of all" (6:10), "bear one another's burdens" (6:2), and "test their own work" (6:4).

Final Thoughts

We can learn much about faith by reading definitions in a dictionary. We can learn even more by reading an article on faith in a theological dictionary. But the answers we receive from these sources pale in comparison to what we learn from Scripture itself.

This quarter, listen as God's Spirit teaches you and your class that faith is not just a topic to discuss. It is a divine attribute to praise and a gift to receive graciously. It enables us to live at peace with God and one another.

CLOSE-UP: PAUL'S LETTER "TO THE CHURCHES OF GALATIA"

Consider presenting information from this outline to the students.

I. Purpose of the Letter
   A. To respond to a crisis within the Galatian churches brought about by unidentified missionaries, probably Jewish Christians, who disagreed with Paul's insistence that Gentiles need not become Jews by undergoing circumcision and following the Law in order to enter into a saving relationship with Christ.
   B. To explain justification by faith.

II. Author of the Letter
   A. Paul is identified as the author in 1:1 and 5:2.
   B. In 1:1, Paul further identifies himself as an apostle (that is, one sent) who has been divinely authorized by Jesus Christ.
   C. Scholars agree that Galatians is an authentic Pauline letter.

III. Recipients of the Letter
   A. The letter is addressed to "the churches of Galatia" (1:2).
   B. Scholars debate exactly who these recipients are because "Galatia" refers both to a territory and to a Roman province. Located in northern Asia Minor, the territory includes the cities of Ancyra, Pessinus, and Tavium where people of Celtic origins, known as Galatians, settled. The Roman province includes this same territory, along with cities to the south such as Antioch in Pisidia, Iconium, Lystra, and Derbe.

IV. Dating of the Letter
   A. If the letter was addressed to people in the Roman province, then it could have been written as early as A.D. 49 or 50. This dating is based on Paul's visit to these cities on his first missionary journey, according to Acts 13:4–14:28.
   B. If the letter was addressed to the ethnic Galatians in the territory, then the letter would likely have been written about A.D. 55. Paul passed through this territory on both his second (Acts 16:6) and third (Acts 18:23) missionary journeys.

V. Main Themes of the Letter
   A. Humans are set right with God (justified) through Jesus, not because of works of the Law that we perform. As those who are set right, we become God's adopted children.
   B. The cross, according to Paul's theology, changed everything by setting us free from the powers that bound us and bringing into being a new creation.
   C. Christ died on the cross. As a result, all who are "in Christ" have received the gift of the Holy Spirit. That gift confirms our adoption as children of God and empowers us to be transformed so that the community of those "in Christ" may produce good fruit.
   D. Distinctions between Jews and Gentiles no longer exist. There is now only one group of those "in Christ."
   E. Those who profess Christ and live in the Spirit experience freedom.

VI. Uses of the Letter
   A. In response to those who tried to convince the Gentile Christians in Galatia that they must first become Jews, Paul wrote this letter to argue for justification by faith.
   B. During the sixteenth century, both the Roman Catholic Church and Protestants used this letter to buttress their views concerning how one is made right with God.
   C. Today this letter remains one of the most essential texts in the New Testament.

FAITH IN ACTION: LIVING AS FAITHFUL PEOPLE

As we consider how God established a faithful people by creating a covenant with Abraham through whom the people of the earth would be blessed, our lessons continually emphasize faith. What is faith? How do we demonstrate faith? Although Hebrews 11:1 is not part of this quarter's study, it may contain the best biblical definition of faith: "Faith is the assurance of things hoped for, the conviction of things not seen." We believers often claim to have this faith, but do our actions really show it?

Share with the class these two illustrations. We may pray but do not really expect God to give an answer, or we do not recognize the answer when it comes. Perhaps class members have additional stories to share. Encourage them to comment on how these two accounts may reflect the behavior of some Christians.

- **A community beset by drought came together to pray fervently for rain. Yet only one small boy showed up with an umbrella.**

    A man caught in a flood beseeched God to save him. A rescue team came by in a boat, but the man assured them that God would save him. He would not get into the boat, so the crew left. A second boat came, but the man, now waist-deep in water, again refused help, saying God would save him. As the water continued to rise, the man climbed onto his roof, where a helicopter crew threw him a line, but again their attempt was rebuffed by this man who claimed to have faith. Finally, the man drowned. As he faced Saint Peter he expressed his disappointment that God had not saved him. Incredulously, Peter replied, "We sent two boats and a helicopter!"

Read aloud one example of the faith of J. Hudson Taylor (1832–1905), an English doctor and missionary to China:

- **While Dr. Taylor was aboard a sailing vessel heading for New Guinea in 1854, the wind stopped blowing. The captain was visibly shaken, because the boat was being carried by the current to some sunken reefs. Cannibals on the shore were already lighting fires in anticipation of the shipwreck. Although the captain thought that all had been done that could be done, Dr. Taylor refused to accept that verdict. He and three other Christians on board went to their cabins and fervently prayed for wind. A few minutes later, Dr. Taylor returned to the deck and told the first officer, a nonbeliever, to set the sail. The officer saw no useful purpose, and claimed there was no way one could "pray up a wind," but Taylor insisted. The captain came to the deck, felt the wind, and soon the ship was sailing away from the perilous reefs and certain death.**

Conclude this activity by discussing how Dr. Taylor manifested his faith in God, even as he faced a situation as potentially death-dealing as the one Moses and the Hebrews faced at the Red Sea. Invite the adults to share other stories of real people who by their actions have demonstrated their faith.

UNIT 1: GOD'S COVENANT
A BLESSING FOR ALL NATIONS

PREVIEWING THE LESSON

Lesson Scripture: Genesis 12:1-9
Background Scripture: Genesis 12:1-9
Key Verse: Genesis 12:2

Focus of the Lesson:

Sometimes people are asked to do incredibly difficult things with only promises of reward to motivate them. How much are some people willing to endure and risk in exchange for promises? Abram and Sarai in their old age risked everything to move their family and all their possessions to a new land because of their faith in God's promises.

Goals for the Learners:

(1) to delve into the story of God's promise to Abram and Sarai and of their faithful response.
(2) to imagine how it felt for Abram and Sarai to pick up and move to a faraway place.
(3) to name the promises that God holds out to them today and for the future.

Pronunciation Guide:

Achan (ay' kan)	Moreh (mor eh')
Ai (i) or (ay' i)	Nablus (nab' luhs)
Beersheba (bee uhr shee' buh)	Negeb (neg' eb)
Ebal (ee' buhl)	Negev (neg' ev)
Gerizim (ger' uh zim)	Shechem (shek' uhm)
Haran (hair' uhn)	Sychar (si' kahr)
Luz (luhz)	Terah (ter' uh)

Supplies:

Bibles, newsprint and marker, paper and pencils, hymnals, map of Canaan

---

READING THE SCRIPTURE

NRSV
Genesis 12:1-9

¹Now the LORD said to Abram, "Go from your country and your kindred and your

NIV
Genesis 12:1-9

¹The LORD had said to Abram, "Leave your country, your people and your father's

father's house to the land that I will show you. ²I will make of you a great nation, and **I will bless you, and make your name great, so that you will be a blessing.** ³I will bless those who bless you, and the one who curses you I will curse; and in you all the families of the earth shall be blessed."

⁴So Abram went, as the LORD had told him; and Lot went with him. Abram was seventy-five years old when he departed from Haran. ⁵Abram took his wife Sarai and his brother's son Lot, and all the possessions that they had gathered, and the persons whom they had acquired in Haran; and they set forth to go to the land of Canaan. When they had come to the land of Canaan, ⁶Abram passed through the land to the place at Shechem, to the oak of Moreh. At that time the Canaanites were in the land. ⁷Then the LORD appeared to Abram, and said, "To your offspring I will give this land." So he built there an altar to the LORD, who had appeared to him. ⁸From there he moved on to the hill country on the east of Bethel, and pitched his tent, with Bethel on the west and Ai on the east; and there he built an altar to the LORD and invoked the name of the LORD. ⁹And Abram journeyed on by stages toward the Negeb.

household and go to the land I will show you.
²"I will make you into a great nation
  and **I will bless you;**
I will make your name great,
  and you will be a blessing.
³I will bless those who bless you,
  and whoever curses you I will curse;
and all peoples on earth
  will be blessed through you."

⁴So Abram left, as the LORD had told him; and Lot went with him. Abram was seventy-five years old when he set out from Haran. ⁵He took his wife Sarai, his nephew Lot, all the possessions they had accumulated and the people they had acquired in Haran, and they set out for the land of Canaan, and they arrived there.

⁶Abram traveled through the land as far as the site of the great tree of Moreh at Shechem. At that time the Canaanites were in the land. ⁷The LORD appeared to Abram and said, "To your offspring I will give this land." So he built an altar there to the LORD, who had appeared to him.

⁸From there he went on toward the hills east of Bethel and pitched his tent, with Bethel on the west and Ai on the east. There he built an altar to the LORD and called on the name of the LORD. ⁹Then Abram set out and continued toward the Negev.

UNDERSTANDING THE SCRIPTURE

Genesis 12:1. By writing "Lord" in small caps (LORD), the NRSV and NIV are alerting readers that the Hebrew word is not the generic word for God (*el*) but the personal name of God (*Yahweh* or *Jehovah* [KJV]). This is true also in verses 4, 7, and 8. God's call of Abram was not an impersonal summons by an unknown person to a "Dear Occupant," as in a form letter; the call occurred within an intimate conversation.

God's call required of Abram an abrupt and complete break in his life. To fulfill

God's call, Abram would have to set aside the comfortable surroundings into which he had settled. From this time forward, Abram was destined to live as "a stranger in a foreign country" (Hebrews 11:9 NIV). Christians today, likewise, are "aliens and strangers in the world" (1 Peter 2:11 NIV). Our real "citizenship is in heaven" (Philippians 3:20).

Genesis 12:2-3. God's promise to Abram was presented in the form of five "I will" statements: (a) "make of you," (b) "bless you," (c) "make your name great," (d) "bless those who bless you," (e) curse those who curse you. Not only would Abram himself be blessed but God also promised that the divine blessings would come through Abram to "all the families of the earth."

Genesis 12:4-5. Abram was mostly, but not completely, obedient to God's call. God had told him to leave even "your father's house" (12:1), but Abram took with him his nephew Lot. The decision would later cause much consternation to Abram (Genesis 13:7; 14:11-16; 18:16–19:29) and his descendants (Genesis 19:36-38). The same would later be true of Moses, whose obedience to God's call was also incomplete (Exodus 3:11–4:17). As a result, God permitted Moses to take along his brother Aaron, a decision he surely rued (Exodus 32:1-9; Numbers 12:1).

Since Abraham lived to be 175 years old (Genesis 25:7) and Sarah 127 (Genesis 23:1), it seems disingenuous to continue declaring that they were "old" when they moved from Haran to Canaan. Given their long life spans, they weren't even middle-aged when Abram received his call at age 75.

The partial remains of a temple dedicated to the moon god Sin are extant in Haran, which was a major Mesopotamian commercial center located on the main east-west highway at an important crossroads where the southern route took traders to Damascus and on to Egypt. It is likely that Abram and his entourage traveled this commercial artery as they traveled toward Canaan.

Genesis 12:6-7. Notice that in verse 1, God simply told Abram to "go . . . to the land I will show you." No specific destination was named. Only in verse 5 did a destination become clear: Canaan. It was the same location to which Abram's father, Terah, had set out years before, but he had never arrived (11:31). It is something of a truism in the Christian faith that God doesn't shine more light on our path until we are obedient to the light we have already received. Only after Abram was obedient did God tell Abram that his

descendants would be given (12:7) the land that he was being shown (12:1).

Shechem, located near Nablus in the present West Bank, was (like Haran) a commercial center at the time of Abram. In Old Testament times, the fortified city lay north of Bethel between Mount Ebal and Mount Gerizim. When the Hebrews returned to Canaan following their enslavement in Egypt, Joseph's bones were buried at Shechem (Joshua 24:32). In the early years of the Northern Kingdom of Israel, Shechem was made its capital (1 Kings 12:25). After the exile, it remained an important Samaritan city. The New Testament town of Sychar, where Jesus had a conversation with a woman at Jacob's well (John 4), may well have been built on or near the site of ancient Shechem.

Genesis 12:8. Like Shechem, Bethel (Beth-El, "house of God") was situated in the area presently known as the West Bank. It was approximately twenty miles south-southeast of Shechem and ten miles north-northeast of Jerusalem. A contemporary thoroughfare connected Bethel to Shechem, which would have made Abram's trip much easier. Two generations later, Abram's grandson Jacob would have a dream at Bethel of "a ladder set up on the earth, the top of it reaching to heaven" (Genesis 28:12). Another name for the city was Luz (28:19; 35:6).

Ai, slightly east of Bethel, was first established about 3100 B.C. It underwent several transformations during its long history. By about 1125 B.C. when the Israelites were thought to have conquered Ai, it was a village peppered with storage granaries that reflected the town's agrarian economy. Ai is perhaps best known for being the site where Joshua and the Hebrew army were routed because Achan "transgressed [God's] covenant" (Joshua 7:11).

Why Abram chose not to settle down in either Bethel or Ai is not narrated. Instead, he sojourned ("pitched his tent") for a time in the countryside between the two cities.

Twice, in verses 7 and 8, it is noted that Abram "built an altar to the LORD." He built the first altar when God appeared and promised to give the land of Canaan to Abram's descendants. No rationale is given for the building of the second altar. Perhaps Abram erected it because he had seen the main part of the land that his heirs would receive as their own.

Genesis 12:9. The Negeb (Negev NIV) is the wilderness region south of the Dead Sea, west of Moab and Edom. Its principal city was Beersheba, in the vicinity of where Abraham's concubine (Sarah's maidservant, Hagar) and son (Ishmael) wandered after they were thrown out of Abraham's household (Genesis 21:14).

INTERPRETING THE SCRIPTURE

An Imperceptible Beginning

Often today new ministries are not started in local churches until they have been studied, vetted, poked, prodded, and studied some more. Target groups are polled. Funding is sought. Staff is hired. Space is secured. Publicity is purchased. Only when it can be proved, on paper, that the ministry can succeed is it given a green light to proceed.

In Scripture, God-ordained ministries take a very different form. Like mustard seeds or yeast (Matthew 13:31-33), they often start out small, almost imperceptible. There is nothing about them to draw anyone's attention. The only thing they have going for them is that, like God's Word, once they go forth, they do not return empty, but will successfully accomplish the purpose God intended (Isaiah 55:11).

God's decision to bless the entire world turned on an almost imperceptible, all-but-hidden calling of a man named Abram. There were no news feeds through the local media, no press conferences touting the benefits to be incurred. This one man and his wife, plus his nephew, simply pulled up stakes and moved all their possessions and household. In this act of obedience, the first sentence of a new chapter in humanity's relationship with God is written. As Martin Luther put it, "With Abram a new world . . . began."

In the same way, Jesus' first followers were not well-situated politicians or moneyed stockholders. They were an odd assortment of fishermen, tax collectors, zealots, and ne'er-do-wells. Had anyone paid Jesus' fledgling movement any mind, he or she would not have been impressed with his organizational skills. Who would ever have predicted that this small group would turn the world upside down and shower it with the blessings of God's love?

Few ministries formed in local churches today will grab headlines anywhere. Some begin as the Spirit-prodded tug on the heart of a single individual. Without fanfare, adequate funds, or any human hope for success, ministry after ministry gets off the ground and shares the love of God in amazing, transforming ways. As with Abram long ago, God has surely blessed these ministries to "be a blessing" (Genesis 12:2).

A Risky Departure

In my mind's eye, it is as clear as if it happened yesterday. Twenty-five years ago, I backed the moving trailer out of my parents' driveway and headed out to complete my last academic degree in a city several hundred miles away. As I looked back to wave good-bye, I expected to see my dad waving at me. I was startled to see his bottom lip quivering uncontrollably and large tears rolling down both cheeks. Dad understood, in ways I was still too young to fathom, that my departure was changing our lives forever. I would never again live near my parents. We would never again be able to drop in on each other easily. We both knew I was leaving in response to a divine call on my life. Dad was proud of that fact, but that didn't make my leaving any easier on him.

Five years ago my incredibly healthy dad discovered he had advanced colon cancer, to which he eventually succumbed. This time, he was the one leaving to inhabit the far country, and I was the one who couldn't come along. This time I was the one waving good-bye, lip quivering, as he set off to complete his journey. I knew where he was going, of course; but that didn't make his leaving any easier for me. I so miss him.

Responding to God's call as Abram did is always a risk precisely because we do not do so in a vacuum. One of the great difficulties in answering God's call is realizing that our response will affect those we love as surely as it affects us. They may, or may not, approve of, appreciate, or even understand our response. But as the prophet Jeremiah put it, once we hear the call of God on our lives, we feel "there is something like a burning fire shut up in my bones; I am weary with holding it in, and I cannot" (Jeremiah 20:9).

Not You but Your Offspring

We live in a time when it has become a truism to speak of instant gratification. Washing machines, digital cameras, microwave ovens, laptop computers, cell phones, credit cards, and lines of credit have fundamentally changed the way we live. Already on the second Sunday of Advent, we are singing Christmas hymns. The joy of waiting has fallen by the wayside. Anticipation has become a lost art.

Then we crack our shins on the words of God in Genesis 12:7: "To your offspring I will give this land." Not "to you" but "to your offspring." Abram, of course, did not

know at the time that he would live another hundred years. Even so, he knew that he would never possess the content of God's promise. Still he lived faithfully. Indeed, he lived the remainder of his life preparing for (but never enjoying) an inheritance that would only be received by those who came after him.

And yet, through the eyes of faith, maybe we discover that waiting and anticipating and living faithfully are not as much a lost art as we might at first suppose. Elementary school teachers rarely get to see the payoff on all the hours and hard work they put into the children in their classes. They simply trust that the next teachers to receive their students will faithfully teach the next levels of instruction. Pastors plant seeds and start programs and proclaim the gospel and teach Scripture and counsel the hurting and water the young Christians in the churches they serve, but often the harvest of all their hard work falls to someone else to enjoy. We plant trees we will never see mature. And the thing is that we do this without giving any of it a second thought. Whether we can articulate it or not, deep down we know there is great joy not only in being the blessing that others receive (Genesis 12:2) but also in knowing that God is caring providentially for those who follow us.

A Covenant Prayer

Scripture tells us that when God told Abram, "Go," Abram "went" (Genesis 12:1, 4). When Jesus told Simon and Andrew, "Follow me," they "followed him" (Matthew 4:19, 20). Yet some people hesitate to respond to God's call because they find it difficult to believe on a daily basis what the Scriptures and our hymns teach us about God: God "will take care of you, through every day, o'er all the way."

Anglican priest John Wesley adapted a 1663 Puritan prayer service by Richard Alleine for the Methodist movement Wesley led. First used by Wesley on August 11, 1755, the service is still used in United Methodist churches, often on New Year's Eve. One of the prayers in this covenant service implores God: "Let me be your servant, under your command. I will no longer be my own. I will give up myself to your will in all things." The worship leader then instructs the people, "Be satisfied that Christ shall give you your place and work."

The people then respond, "Lord, make me what you will. I put myself fully into your hands." Learning how to pray these submissive words may just be the most spiritually mature thing we ever do. Through these words, we follow in the footsteps of Abram, whose willingness to submit himself to God opened wide the floodgates for blessings not only for Abram but also "for all the families of the earth" (Genesis 2:3).

SHARING THE SCRIPTURE

Preparing Our Hearts

Explore this week's devotional reading, found in Hebrews 6:13-20. The writer refers to God's pledge to Abraham as an example of the reliability of God's promises. Abraham "patiently endured" (6:15) and in God's time the promise was fulfilled. What promises are you waiting for God to fulfill in your life? What memories do you have of God fulfilling promises? How do those memories—and the words of Scripture—assure that God will once again be a promise keeper? In your spiritual journal write a promise of God and how it was fulfilled.

Pray that you and the adult learners will continue to trust God to make and keep promises that bless you and all God's children.

Preparing Our Minds

Study the background Scripture and the lesson Scripture, both of which are from Genesis 12:1-9. Think about how much you would be willing to risk if you only had the promise of a reward to motivate you to undertake a difficult task.

Write on newsprint:

❏ information for next week's lesson, found under "Continue the Journey."

❏ activities for further spiritual growth in "Continue the Journey."

Study the map of Canaan you have located and information in Understanding the Scripture so as to be prepared to talk with the class about the places mentioned in Genesis 12:1-9. If possible, have a classroom map or map handouts available.

Review the "Introduction" to the fall quarter, "The Big Picture," "Close-up," and "Faith in Action." Begin to decide how you will use this information during the coming thirteen weeks.

LEADING THE CLASS

(1) Gather to Learn

❖ Welcome the class members and introduce any guests.

❖ Pray that the students will be willing to take risks for God, who promises us blessings.

❖ Read Dr. Bill Lawrence's story of the risks that South Hills Community Church took for God (http://mobile.crosswalk.com /spirituallife/archives/11624767.html): **Begun in 1969, this start-up church focused its energies on missions and worshiped in a rented space. After almost eight years the host congregation told South Hills it was time to vacate. The congregation bought** land and raised money, only to find out that due to steep price increases they were $100,000 short of their goal, not $10,000 short as they had thought. Moving ahead was very risky indeed. Although not a wealthy church, the leadership committed itself to raising $100,000 within three weeks. Without the money, the church would cease to exist. With it, they could continue their work for God. They took the risk—and have a fully paid-for campus that includes the original building plus two others. The congregation came to know God better because they trusted God completely.

❖ Discuss these questions:
   (1) **In what ways has our congregation been stretched to take risks for God?**
   (2) **How did we respond?**
   (3) **How did God respond to our trust?**

❖ Read aloud today's focus statement: **Sometimes people are asked to do incredibly difficult things with only promises of reward to motivate them. How much are some people willing to endure and risk in exchange for promises? Abram and Sarai in their old age risked everything to move their family and all their possessions to a new land because of their faith in God's promises.**

(2) Delve Into the Story of God's Promise to Abram and Sarai and of Their Faithful Response

❖ Choose a volunteer to read Genesis 12:1-9.

❖ Focus first on God's call and promise by looking at Genesis 12:1-3, these verses in Understanding the Scripture, and "An Imperceptible Beginning" in Interpreting the Scripture.
   (1) **Suppose you had been Abram. What questions would have come to your mind?**

   (2) **How would you have felt knowing that God had chosen to pour out blessings on "all the families of the earth" through you and your descendants?**

❖ Focus next on Abram's response by looking at verses 4-5, 6-7, 8, 9 in Understanding the Scripture and "A Risky Departure" in Interpreting the Scripture. Discuss these questions:
   (1) **Abram seemed to be well settled and wealthy. What do you suppose motivated him to pick up everything and leave, not even knowing where God was going to take him?**
   (2) **How might you have responded to such a call? Why?**
   (3) **Where did Abram's entourage go?** (Use information from Understanding the Scripture and any maps you have to acquaint the students with the places mentioned and the route Abram may have taken.)
   (4) **Abram built an altar to God not once but twice (12:7, 8). What does this action suggest to you about Abram's relationship with God?**

(3) Imagine How It Felt for Abram and Sarai to Pick Up and Move to a Faraway Place

❖ Invite the students to tell stories to the class or a small group of times when they moved from familiar surroundings. Why did they leave? Was this a leave-taking of their choosing, or were they forced into going by circumstances, such as a war or need to find a job? Did they move because of a life change, such as needing more space for a growing family, needing less space in retirement, or needing help that could be provided in an assisted-living or rehab center? What hassles were involved in making this move? How did they see this move as risky? How did they see God's hand upon this move?

❖ Encourage volunteers to state how they might have felt had they been Abram and Sarai as they moved away from their home—and had no means of easily communicating with those they left behind.

(4) Name the Promises That God Holds Out Today and for the Future

❖ Distribute paper and pencils. Suggest that the students write one or more promises that they believe God has made to them for the future. These may be scriptural promises, and some adults may want to quote them from their Bibles. Or they may be personal promises that they feel God has made to them, perhaps in conjunction with a call.

❖ Provide an opportunity for volunteers to share their promises.

❖ Conclude this portion of the lesson by reminding everyone of a pervasive promise in the Scriptures, stated in words such as "Be not afraid for I am with you." No matter where we are or what we are called to do, God does promise to be present with us.

(5) Continue the Journey

❖ Pray that the adults will recognize and hold fast to God's promises in their own lives.

❖ Read aloud this preparation for next week's lesson. You may also want to post it on newsprint for the students to copy.

■ **Title: A Promise to Abraham**
■ **Background Scripture: Genesis 15:1-21**
■ **Lesson Scripture: Genesis 15:1-6, 12-18**
■ **Focus of the Lesson: Sometimes people are asked to believe the unbelievable, even the impossible.**

How far can some people's ability to believe be stretched? Even though he and his wife were long beyond the age of childbearing, because of his faith in God, Abram believed God when told that he would have descendants more numerous than the stars.

❖ Challenge the students to complete one or more of these activities for further spiritual growth related to this week's session. Post this information on newsprint for the students to copy.

(1) **Think about past and current calls that God has made on your life. How did you respond? If you followed God, how did that choice affect you? How did it affect other people? Who needs to hear about your experiences as they are struggling with God's call on their lives? Talk with these persons.**

(2) **Remember that Abram built two altars to worship God. Set up a worship space in your home, if you do not already have one. Place symbols there that connect you to God.**

(3) **Consider barriers that may keep you and others from responding to God's call. What steps can you take to overcome these obstacles to obeying God's will?**

❖ Sing or read aloud "The God of Abraham Praise."

❖ Conclude today's session by leading the class in this benediction: **By the power of the Holy Spirit go forth to be a blessing to others even as God through Christ has blessed you.**

UNIT 1: GOD'S COVENANT
A PROMISE TO ABRAHAM

PREVIEWING THE LESSON

Lesson Scripture: Genesis 15:1-6, 12-18
Background Scripture: Genesis 15:1-21
Key Verse: Genesis 15:6

Focus of the Lesson:
Sometimes people are asked to believe the unbelievable, even the impossible. How far can some people's ability to believe be stretched? Even though he and his wife were long beyond the age of childbearing, because of his faith in God, Abram believed God when told that he would have descendants more numerous than the stars.

Goals for the Learners:
(1) to study God's promise to Abram that God would give him children and land.
(2) to contemplate the possibility that God can and will do the otherwise impossible.
(3) to demonstrate faith in accepting God's extravagant promises.

Pronunciation Guide:
Amorite (am' uh rite)
Eliezer (el ee ee' zuhr)
Euphrates (yoo fray' teez)

Supplies:
Bibles, newsprint and marker, paper and pencils, hymnals

READING THE SCRIPTURE

NRSV
Genesis 15:1-6, 12-18

¹After these things the word of the LORD came to Abram in a vision, "Do not be afraid, Abram, I am your shield; your reward shall be very great." ²But Abram said, "O Lord GOD, what will you give me, for I continue childless, and the heir of my house is Eliezer of Damascus?" ³And Abram

NIV
Genesis 15:1-6, 12-18

¹After this, the word of the LORD came to Abram in a vision:

"Do not be afraid, Abram.
   I am your shield,
   your very great reward."

²But Abram said, "O Sovereign LORD, what can you give me since I remain childless and

said, "You have given me no offspring, and so a slave born in my house is to be my heir." [4]But the word of the LORD came to him, "This man shall not be your heir; no one but your very own issue shall be your heir." [5]He brought him outside and said, "Look toward heaven and count the stars, if you are able to count them." Then he said to him, "So shall your descendants be." **[6]And he believed the LORD; and the LORD reckoned it to him as righteousness.**

[12]As the sun was going down, a deep sleep fell upon Abram, and a deep and terrifying darkness descended upon him. [13]Then the LORD said to Abram, "Know this for certain, that your offspring shall be aliens in a land that is not theirs, and shall be slaves there, and they shall be oppressed for four hundred years; [14]but I will bring judgment on the nation that they serve, and afterward they shall come out with great possessions. [15]As for yourself, you shall go to your ancestors in peace; you shall be buried in a good old age. [16]And they shall come back here in the fourth generation; for the iniquity of the Amorites is not yet complete."

[17]When the sun had gone down and it was dark, a smoking fire pot and a flaming torch passed between these pieces. [18]On that day the LORD made a covenant with Abram, saying, "To your descendants I give this land, from the river of Egypt to the great river, the river Euphrates."

the one who will inherit my estate is Eliezer of Damascus?" [3]And Abram said, "You have given me no children; so a servant in my household will be my heir."

[4]Then the word of the LORD came to him: "This man will not be your heir, but a son coming from your own body will be your heir." [5]He took him outside and said, "Look up at the heavens and count the stars—if indeed you can count them." Then he said to him, "So shall your offspring be."

[6]Abram believed the LORD, and he credited it to him as righteousness.

[12]As the sun was setting, Abram fell into a deep sleep, and a thick and dreadful darkness came over him. [13]Then the LORD said to him, "Know for certain that your descendants will be strangers in a country not their own, and they will be enslaved and mistreated four hundred years. [14]But I will punish the nation they serve as slaves, and afterward they will come out with great possessions. [15]You, however, will go to your fathers in peace and be buried at a good old age. [16]In the fourth generation your descendants will come back here, for the sin of the Amorites has not yet reached its full measure."

[17]When the sun had set and darkness had fallen, a smoking firepot with a blazing torch appeared and passed between the pieces. [18]On that day the LORD made a covenant with Abram and said, "To your descendants I give this land, from the river of Egypt to the great river, the Euphrates."

UNDERSTANDING THE SCRIPTURE

Genesis 15:1. Presumably several years have passed since God first promised Abram that he would become "a great nation" (Genesis 12:2). Abram and Sarai were still childless when God appeared to him in a vision and said, "Do not be afraid," which is the most common command in all of Scripture. God's command was both a challenge and a comfort. The challenge was to continue to take God's word in faith. The comfort was the discovery that God knew completely the anxiety Abram was facing. Similarly, in the seven letters contained in Revelation 2–3, seven times Jesus told the "angel" of the respective church, "I know" the situation you are facing.

Genesis 15:2-3. Abraham is rightly called the father of faith, but that does not mean that faith came quickly or easily to him. Like Mary at the Annunciation (Luke 1:34), Abram was not opposed to the word he received from God; but he knew enough basic biology to be puzzled by what he was hearing. Furthermore, he was saddened that the upshot of his childlessness was that God's blessing apparently would be transferred to one of the servants in his household after his death.

Eliezer of Damascus is not named again in Genesis, but he may well be the "senior servant" (Genesis 24:2) whom Abraham decades later would charge to "go to my country and my kindred and get a wife for my son Isaac" (24:4).

Genesis 15:4-5. God addressed Abram's disappointment by asserting that he would yet have a son. To "prove" the assertion, God told Abram to take note of the stars in the sky. The implication was that if God could create the vast lights in the sky, God could surely create a son for Abram. "So shall your descendants be" is less about the *quantity* of offspring Abram would have and more about the *certainty* that Abram would indeed have descendants.

Genesis 15:6. Abram knew no additional facts after God spoke than he had known before. What he obtained, however, was God's word on the matter. It was enough. Abram believed God's word because what God asserts inevitably comes to pass (see, for example, the creation story in Genesis 1 and Isaiah 55:10-11).

Genesis 15:7. Although this passage has historically been referred to as the report of a covenant God made with Abram, several contemporary scholars prefer to call it an "oath of promise." The difference may be more semantic than real.

Whether oath or covenant, the prologue identified the party establishing the legal relationship as Yahweh, who had already "brought you from Ur of the Chaldeans." But God's actions on Abram's behalf were not only past history. There were also promises of future blessing. God had larger and more expansive plans for Abram. Foremost was "to give you this land to possess."

Exodus 20:2 offers another example of a covenantal prologue rooted in the past actions of God.

Genesis 15:8. Abram did not doubt God's identity, which was asserted in verse 1. He did, however, ask God to do more than merely state intentions. God had "proved" that Abram would have descendants by showing him a sign: the stars in the sky (15:5). What sign would God offer Abram regarding the promise of land?

Genesis 15:9-11. In reply, God told Abram to secure three animals and two birds. The animals (heifer, goat, and ram) and birds (dove and pigeon) that God told Abram to obtain became the species of animals and birds that the Hebrew people later used as sacrifices for burnt offerings (Leviticus 1:10, 14), sin offerings (4:27-28), and guilt offerings (6:6).

The covenant ritual of cutting animals in half and walking between them appears also in Jeremiah 34:18. The Hebrew actually speaks of "cutting" a covenant rather than "making" a covenant, as our English translations put it (see Genesis 15:18).

Covenants, as well as promissory oaths, imposed binding legal and contractual obligations on the two parties involved. The terms of the covenant were typically stipulated by the stronger party and took the form of: I promise to do thus and so, and you in return promise to do thus and such. The terms of God's oath with Abram are spelled out in verses 13-16. The detail that God walked alone suggests to scholars that God placed no stipulations upon Abram, but rather, acted unilaterally.

The reference to unclean carrion or "birds of prey" in verse 11 may have a parallel in Ezekiel 17 and thus refer to Israel's enemies. The need to keep unclean carrion away from a sacrifice during the day, lest it make the offered sacrifice unclean, is inferred in Leviticus 11:13-19.

Genesis 15:12-16. The "deep and terrifying darkness" is a reference to God, who spoke to Abram via a nighttime vision. Rudolf Otto, a German theologian of a century ago, spoke similarly of God as the "mysterium tremendum," the "great mystery," the palpable authority in whose holy presence we recognize (and acknowledge) our own great inadequacy.

Instead of imposing obligations on Abram, the covenant consisted of four statements God made to Abram: (1) Although the land definitely belonged to Abram, only his descendants would enjoy its fruits (15:16); (2) before claiming the land as their own, Abram's descendants would first have to endure years of servitude apart from the land (15:13); (3) Abram's descendants would be compensated for their years of servitude (15:14); (4) Abram himself would not face servitude but would die in great peace as an old man (15:15).

The Amorites were the present occupants of the land of Canaan.

Genesis 15:17-21. To ratify a covenant, the weaker of the two parties would take upon itself the curses of the covenant. According to rituals associated with Near Eastern covenant ratification, the one who walked between the sacrifices was the one who was promising to bear the same fate as those animals for violating the covenant. Surprisingly, in this instance, it was God who walked the line.

The land of Canaan is described in terms of both its geography and its inhabitants. The river of Egypt was its southwestern border; the Euphrates was its northeastern border. The peoples inhabiting Canaan were variously described in the Old Testament (see, for instance, Genesis 10:15-18; Exodus 3:8).

INTERPRETING THE SCRIPTURE

Accomplishing the Unbelievable

It is a truism that God can do anything. Divinity students in their first theology class learn that one of God's primary attributes is omnipotence; God is all-powerful. In Scripture, Jesus is quoted in three Gospels as saying, "For God all things are possible" (Matthew 19:26; Mark 10:27; see also Luke 18:27). In fact, Scripture tells of God speaking creation into existence (Genesis 1). And, of course, there is the incarnation of Jesus, when God took on flesh (Luke 2); and the crucifixion and resurrection of Jesus, when God defeated evil and death (Matthew 27:32–28:10).

Yet we sometimes bemoan the situations we find ourselves in and wring our hands, wondering what we can possibly do to correct them. Pastors are as prone to this as anybody.

Several years back, I found myself increasingly frustrated with the parents in our church. They faithfully brought their children and teens to worship but weren't making much of an effort to bring them to Sunday school or midweek activities. How, I moped, could the church possibly compete against all the influences these children were receiving? How could one hour of worship effectively compete with more than thirty hours of school and thirty hours of television and who knows what else each week?

That's when God grabbed me by the collar and told me I ought to take God a bit more seriously. Furthermore, I ought to take better note of what God's Spirit was accomplishing in the teens and children I was so worried about. The kids were humble and honored their parents. They participated fully in worship with glad hearts. Their lives exhibited the fruit of the Spirit. Sure, the influence of the church could have been greater if they had participated in more church activities. But the point was clear: Through the Holy Spirit, God was having as great or greater an influence on their lives through one hour of church as they were receiving through multiple times that many hours elsewhere.

I still wish parents were more diligent about getting their kids to important events at the church, but I no longer moan about it. I fully believe God can do—and does—the impossible.

Learning to Wait

As important as Abram's willingness to believe God's word was his willingness to wait on God's timing. It is a trait many of us could work on. Today is only the third Sunday of Advent. The start of the twelve days of Christmas (December 25–January 5) is still two weeks away. Yet many of us, including many of our churches, have already started celebrating Christmas. Rather than develop the Advent discipline of waiting, we schedule our cantatas and children's Christmas programs in the middle of Advent. We wouldn't dream of singing Easter resurrection hymns in the middle of Lent or Holy Week, yet we hardly give a second thought to singing Christmas carols weeks before Christmas arrives.

Might a first step in the church's ability to free itself from its enslavement to our culture's penchant for instant gratification be as simple as learning to wait on Christmas before celebrating its arrival?

Bishop Will Willimon, in his book *Why I Am a United Methodist*, quotes *The Autobiography of Malcolm X* to show how he was finally able to free himself from jail. His brother told him to stop eating pork. "Malcolm said that . . . such abstinence was unthinkable, a denial of his whole culture, his whole way of life. . . . He had never said no to pork or anything else." But he tried it.

Willimon concludes, "The day that Malcolm said, 'I don't eat pork' was a day of rebirth, conversion, empowerment for him. For the first time in his life he was on the road to true freedom."

Abram's trust in God was so complete that he was willing to wait on God's timing, even though he personally would never see the promises completely fulfilled. Only in "the fourth generation" (Genesis 15:16) would Abram's "descendants" (15:18) finally obtain the land.

Signs

Signs, like oracles, are notoriously difficult to discern. But to those with "eyes to see," they appear patently obvious. Several years ago I was appointed to a church in which "Marie," an elderly lady, was a member. Marie was a wonderful person, always able to detect a silver lining, no matter how difficult or trying the present circumstances.

Knowing that her life had not been particularly easy, I asked her once how she was able to live with such grace. She smiled and said that whenever life grew difficult for her, she would ask for a sign that God was aware of this and taking care of her. Invariably, she said, God would show her a cross; usually scores of them. The puzzled look on my face apparently gave away the fact that I didn't have any idea where she was seeing so many crosses. That's when she educated me (a still-wet-behind-the-ears pastor) to the fact that our world is filled with crosses. "Pastor," she said, "do you not know that telephone poles are in the shape of a cross? And trees with their bent limbs look like crosses, too, you know. Even wooden fences reveal my Savior. So did every letter *t* I ever typed in a memo at work."

Twenty years later, I too am able to see crosses everywhere I look. I just needed someone like Marie to open my eyes to them.

Abram wanted to believe what God told him but he needed God to show him a sign. The sign he received was not a unique flash of light or something he had never before seen. God told him to look into the evening sky and take note of the stars. God told Abram that he could count on God's promise of an heir coming to pass as surely as he could depend on the stars appearing in the night sky. From that moment forward, his eyes now opened by God's sign to the certainty of God's promise, Abram believed.

God's Timing

Habakkuk 2:3 (NIV) could function as an exclamation point to the waiting that Abram had to do: "The revelation awaits an appointed time; it speaks of the end and will not prove false. Though it linger, wait for it; it will certainly come and will not delay." The prophet spoke of the certainty of God's word coming to pass. Yet, as we see with Abram, and have so often experienced ourselves, the timing is under God's control, not ours.

I struggled greatly with the actions of an older gentleman in one of the churches I pastored. His opposition to ministries that I thought were very important was very frustrating to me. Late in his life he developed terminal cancer. In his waning weeks I spent much time with him and cared for him and loved him as best I could as his pastor. Gradually, trust began to replace resentment and love overcame hurt and two men who were effectively enemies became friends. Many years later, I still mourn my friend, glad that we were granted the time we needed to reconcile before he died.

God told Abram that he would die and his descendants would be oppressed for 400 years. God also promised him that they would return to the Promised Land "in the fourth generation" (Genesis 15:16). Abram's descendants would be oppressed in Egypt, but in God's time they did return to take possession of their land. The impossible became reality—long after Abram affirmed his belief that with God all things are possible.

SHARING THE SCRIPTURE

Preparing Our Hearts

Explore this week's devotional reading, found in Hebrews 13:17-22. In these closing words of Hebrews, the writer admonishes readers to obey leaders and to pray. Verses 20-21 offer a "good word," a benediction, to the readers. Jesus' "blood of the eternal covenant" (13:20) is that which makes us "complete." Consider how this benediction relates to today's Scripture lesson from Genesis 15 in which God makes a covenant with Abram. What does it mean to you to live under God's covenant through Christ?

Pray that you and the adult learners will appreciate and give thanks for the covenants that God has made with humanity.

Preparing Our Minds

Study the background Scripture from Genesis 15:1-21 and the lesson Scripture from Genesis 15:1-6, 12-18. Consider how far you think most people are willing to go to believe something that seems impossible.

Write on newsprint:

❑ questions for "Demonstrate Faith in Accepting God's Extravagant Promises."

❑ information for next week's lesson, found under "Continue the Journey."

❑ activities for further spiritual growth in "Continue the Journey."

LEADING THE CLASS

(1) Gather to Learn

❖ Welcome the class members and introduce any guests.

❖ Pray that the students will find hope in God's seemingly unbelievable promise to Abram.

❖ Read these stories of survival following a major earthquake in Haiti in 2010: **Grocery store worker Wismond Extantus was trapped for eleven days, subsisting on Coca-Cola and biscuits. "It was God who was tucking me away in his arms. It gave me strength," the twenty-four-year-old survivor reported. Rescued from his collapsed home, twenty-one-year-old Emannuel Buso also credited his survival to God: "I am here today because God wants it." Two-week-old Elisabeth Joassaint was rescued in her home. "This wasn't the way Jesus wanted the baby to die," her grandfather said. "Everybody knew the baby was dead, except the Lord." The earthquake hit during a church meeting, trapping sixty-nine-year-old Ena Zizi. When a Mexican rescuer reached her and she grabbed his hand, he later said, "I felt that God had touched my hand." She attributed her miraculous survival to her faith and prayer.**

❖ Ask: **How do you respond when you hear stories such as these of faith and courage in the face of seemingly impossible odds?**

❖ Read aloud today's focus statement: **Sometimes people are asked to believe the unbelievable, even the impossible. How far can some people's ability to believe be stretched? Even though he and his wife were long beyond the age of childbearing, because of his faith in God, Abram believed God when told that he would have descendants more numerous than the stars.**

(2) Study God's Promise to Abram That God Would Give Him Children and Land

❖ Choose a volunteer to read Genesis 15:1-6, 12-18.

❖ Remind the group of God's promises to Abram in Genesis 12:1-3, which were made an unknown number of years before the covenant ritual we are studying today. Read aloud the first and last paragraphs of "God's Timing" from Interpreting the Scripture.

❖ Discuss these questions:
  (1) Why do you suppose that Abram believed God, even though the divine promises of descendants and prophecies of 400 years of oppression in a foreign land before returning to the Promised Land probably sounded unbelievable to him (and perhaps to us as well)?
  (2) In this early story of God's relationship with humanity, Abram's trust and obedience seem to be key features. How do these two themes play out as we so often must wait on God's timing?

❖ End this activity by inviting volunteers to state why they do (or do not) believe God to be not only a promise-maker but also a promise-keeper.

(3) Contemplate the Possibility That God Can and Will Do the Otherwise Impossible

❖ Read or retell "Accomplishing the Unbelievable" from Interpreting the Scripture.

❖ Invite the adults to tell stories of times when God "grabbed them by the collar" and showed them a new perspective on a situation or person they had given up on.

❖ Turn the discussion to biblical stories of Jesus' miracles. Recognize that although there are Christians who do not believe these miracles happened, many other Christians do believe and give God glory for doing what seems to be impossible.

❖ Conclude this discussion by encouraging volunteers to tell stories about their own lives when all they could see was a brick wall looming, and God made a way where there was no way.

(4) Demonstrate Faith in Accepting God's Extravagant Promises

❖ Read these words to the class: **Abram was clearly anxious because God's promise to him of an heir remained unfulfilled. The sign of the countless stars in the sky reassured Abram, who believed God's promise.**

❖ Invite the participants to read in unison today's key verse, Genesis 15:6.

❖ Point out that Paul cited this verse in Romans 4:3, 9, 22 and Galatians 3:6 to make the case that faith is the basis for salvation. Abram, of course, lived centuries before the Law existed, so he did not live under the Law. Note that James also cited Genesis 15:6 in his letter (2:23) to argue that works demonstrate one's faith.

❖ Distribute paper and pencils. Challenge the adults to respond in writing to these questions, which you will post on newsprint:

(1) In what situations are you currently awaiting God's fulfillment of a promise?

(2) What signs might help you believe that the promise will be fulfilled in God's time?

(3) How will you demonstrate your acceptance of that promise in faith?

(5) Continue the Journey

❖ Conclude the prior activity by praying that the adults will stretch their own faith as needed to accept God's extravagant promises.

❖ Read aloud this preparation for next week's lesson. You may also want to post it on newsprint for the students to copy.

■ Title: The Lord Provides

■ Background Scripture: Genesis 22:1-14

■ Lesson Scripture: 22:1-2, 6-14

■ Focus of the Lesson: Sometimes people's faith may be tested by others with demands to do things they could not normally imagine doing. Does faith require doing anything and everything requested? Abraham was unquestioning in his faith and devotion to God, who eventually rescinded his demand to kill Isaac.

❖ Challenge the students to complete one or more of these activities for further spiritual growth related to this week's session. Post this information on newsprint for the students to copy.

(1) Be supportive of a couple who wants children they have thus far been unable to have. If you are such a person, seek others who may be willing to support you.

(2) Pray for an answer to a problem that seems impossible to solve. Be willing to stretch your faith to believe that in God's time and in God's way an answer will come, even if it is not the answer you would prefer.

(3) Research the concept of "covenant." Where do you see God's covenants operating throughout the Bible and in our world?

❖ Sing or read aloud "All My Hope Is Firmly Grounded."

❖ Conclude today's session by leading the class in this benediction: **By the power of the Holy Spirit go forth to be a blessing to others even as God through Christ has blessed you.**

UNIT 1: GOD'S COVENANT
THE LORD PROVIDES

PREVIEWING THE LESSON

Lesson Scripture: Genesis 22:1-2, 6-14
Background Scripture: Genesis 22:1-14
Key Verse: Genesis 22:12

Focus of the Lesson:
Sometimes people's faith may be tested by others with demands to do things they could not normally imagine doing. Does faith require doing anything and everything requested? Abraham was unquestioning in his faith and devotion to God, who eventually rescinded his demand to kill Isaac.

Goals for the Learners:
(1) to explore the story of Abraham's willingness to sacrifice his one and only son in order to please God.
(2) to reflect on the bounds of faith and devotion.
(3) to determine their bounds of devotion and obedience within their faith.

Pronunciation Guide:
Moriah (muh ri' uh)
Søren Kierkegaard (sir' uhn keer' kuh gard)

Supplies:
Bibles, newsprint and marker, paper and pencils, hymnals

READING THE SCRIPTURE

NRSV
Genesis 22:1-2, 6-14

¹After these things God tested Abraham. He said to him, "Abraham!" And he said, "Here I am." ²He said, "Take your son, your only son Isaac, whom you love, and go to the land of Moriah, and offer him there as a burnt offering on one of the mountains that I shall show you."

NIV
Genesis 22:1-2, 6-14

¹Some time later God tested Abraham. He said to him, "Abraham!"
"Here I am," he replied.
²Then God said, "Take your son, your only son, Isaac, whom you love, and go to the region of Moriah. Sacrifice him there as a

⁶Abraham took the wood of the burnt offering and laid it on his son Isaac, and he himself carried the fire and the knife. So the two of them walked on together. ⁷Isaac said to his father Abraham, "Father!" And he said, "Here I am, my son." He said, "The fire and the wood are here, but where is the lamb for a burnt offering?" ⁸Abraham said, "God himself will provide the lamb for a burnt offering, my son." So the two of them walked on together.

⁹When they came to the place that God had shown him, Abraham built an altar there and laid the wood in order. He bound his son Isaac, and laid him on the altar, on top of the wood. ¹⁰Then Abraham reached out his hand and took the knife to kill his son. ¹¹But the angel of the LORD called to him from heaven, and said, "Abraham, Abraham!" And he said, "Here I am." ¹²He said, "Do not lay your hand on the boy or do anything to him; for now **I know that you fear God, since you have not withheld your son, your only son, from me."** ¹³And Abraham looked up and saw a ram, caught in a thicket by its horns. Abraham went and took the ram and offered it up as a burnt offering instead of his son. ¹⁴So Abraham called that place "The LORD will provide"; as it is said to this day, "On the mount of the LORD it shall be provided."

burnt offering on one of the mountains I will tell you about."

⁶Abraham took the wood for the burnt offering and placed it on his son Isaac, and he himself carried the fire and the knife. As the two of them went on together, ⁷Isaac spoke up and said to his father Abraham, "Father?"

"Yes, my son?" Abraham replied.

"The fire and wood are here," Isaac said, "but where is the lamb for the burnt offering?"

⁸Abraham answered, "God himself will provide the lamb for the burnt offering, my son." And the two of them went on together.

⁹When they reached the place God had told him about, Abraham built an altar there and arranged the wood on it. He bound his son Isaac and laid him on the altar, on top of the wood. ¹⁰Then he reached out his hand and took the knife to slay his son. ¹¹But the angel of the LORD called out to him from heaven, "Abraham! Abraham!"

"Here I am," he replied.

¹²"Do not lay a hand on the boy," he said. "Do not do anything to him. Now **I know that you fear God, because you have not withheld from me your son, your only son."**

¹³Abraham looked up and there in a thicket he saw a ram caught by its horns. He went over and took the ram and sacrificed it as a burnt offering instead of his son. ¹⁴So Abraham called that place The LORD Will Provide. And to this day it is said, "On the mountain of the LORD it will be provided."

UNDERSTANDING THE SCRIPTURE

Introduction. There are striking parallels between the sacrifice of Abraham's younger son, Isaac, and the "sacrifice" of Abraham's older son, Ishmael (Genesis 21:14-21). Both stories begin with Abraham getting up "early in the morning" to see a son off (Genesis 21:14; 22:3). In both cases Abraham burdened with supplies those leaving

(Genesis 21:14; 22:1). Despite art that portrays Abraham's sons as boys, both sons were probably young men at the time of their sacrifice. (Jewish tradition states that Isaac was thirty-seven years old.) And on both occasions, God ended up providing so that neither son died (Genesis 21:19-20; 22:13-14).

Genesis 22:1. Abram's name change to

Abraham is reported in Genesis 17:5. Taken at face value, God's "test" of Abraham suggests there were details about Abraham's character that God still needed to know: Did Abraham believe that he was a steward or the owner of the gifts God had given him?

Some people dismiss the idea that God would test the chosen people, but Scripture repeatedly shows that God did just that. After this verse, the next time that God tested the people is narrated in Exodus 15:25, which we will study in Lesson 9.

Genesis 22:2. As was true of God's call on Abram in Genesis 12:1 ("your country"; that is, "your kindred"; that is, "your father's house"), so here God's call to Abraham became increasingly specific and clear ("your son"; that is, "your only son Isaac"; that is, the son "whom you love"). Abraham's emerging clarity of God's demand is telescoped in this verse. He does continue to "see" (22:4, 13) as the journey progresses.

The meaning of the word "Moriah" is unclear, though it is similar to a verb form that means "see." Second Chronicles 3:1 names Moriah as the Temple Mount in Jerusalem. For Muslims, it is also the site from which Mohammed ascended to heaven. The large rock on which Abraham attempted to sacrifice Isaac is now inside the Muslim shrine known as the Dome of the Rock.

Genesis 22:3. The two servants are not identified, nor did they do anything except accompany Abraham. Abraham himself performed each of the preparations necessary to sacrifice Isaac. The "burnt offering" is one that is completely consumed by fire on the altar.

Genesis 22:4. Taken literally, "the third day" designates the amount of time it took Abraham to travel the fifty miles from Beersheba (Genesis 21:33) to Moriah. However, in Scripture "the third day" often draws attention to events suffused with God's presence, such as God's descent to the holy mountain (Exodus 19:11, 16) or the resurrection of Jesus (Matthew 16:21; 17:22; 20:19).

Genesis 22:5. Abraham ordered his servants to attend to the donkey while he (and Isaac) worshiped God. Abraham said "we" will return, perhaps foreshadowing what Abraham believed.

Genesis 22:6. As the story unfolds, Isaac emerges as a Christ figure. In this verse, as Jesus did later (John 19:17), Isaac carried the wood on which he was to be killed. The sentence "So the two of them walked on together," here and at the end of verse 8, frames the conversation between Abraham and Isaac.

Genesis 22:7. Isaac had apparently accompanied his father on previous occasions when Abraham offered sacrifices to Yahweh, for on this occasion he noted that his father had failed to bring with him the lamb that would be slain.

Genesis 22:8. Abraham's response to Isaac's question is ambiguous. Abraham is commonly understood by many Jewish and Christian interpreters to have told his son that there was yet time for God to provide the necessary lamb. If this is correct, Abraham's response was less than forthright. However, it is just as grammatically correct to read Abraham's response as completely forthright: "The lamb that God will provide for this sacrifice is . . . you, my son."

Genesis 22:9. Upon arriving at the site for the sacrifice, Abraham performed four acts. He built an altar, arranged the wood, bound his son, and laid Isaac on the altar. The mounting pathos in this verse is excruciating!

Considering Abraham's advanced age and Isaac's young manhood, the only rational explanation of how Abraham was able to bind Isaac is that Isaac must have willingly consented to be sacrificed (as Jesus himself would do centuries later). Many Jewish and early Christian interpreters of this story believe that Isaac willingly offered himself. As a result of this act, Christians, in retrospect, have seen in Isaac a figure who resembles Christ.

Genesis 22:10. The word for "knife" used here is a rare term in the Old Testament. It was not plunged into the heart of the sacrificial lamb but was used to slit its throat.

Genesis 22:11. In many Old Testament stories "the angel of the LORD" is effectively interchangeable with "God" (see Exodus 3:2, 4; Judges 6:12, 14).

The double call of Abraham by the angel of the Lord is the classic way a divine call is extended to a person in Scripture. Other examples include Moses (Exodus 3:4), Samuel (1 Samuel 3:4), and Saul (Acts 9:4).

Genesis 22:12. Much ink has rightly been spilled in recent years clarifying that the "fear of the Lord" refers primarily to worship of God, not to terror of God. However, notions of power and adoration cannot always be separated neatly. To their credit, neither Abraham nor the biblical writer shied away from offering his adoration to the God whose demands on us are sometimes terrifying.

Contrary to those who declare that God's omniscience demands that God know all things about the future, verses like this one suggest that there are things about us that God does not know but must learn.

Genesis 22:13. At the last possible instant, Abraham was provided the substitute offering of a ram for his son. Centuries later when God's own son was offered on our behalf, no substitute was provided; Jesus himself was the "lamb without blemish or defect" (1 Peter 1:19).

Genesis 22:14. In English, as in Hebrew, the words for "see" and "provide" (or "vision" and "provision") are related. Readers can discover this by comparing the NIV or NRSV translations of this verse with the KJV translation. A textual footnote in the NRSV for the Lord "will provide" is "will see." God's *providence* is God's willingness to *provide* what God *sees* we need.

INTERPRETING THE SCRIPTURE

Preparation for Worship

The carefulness and meticulousness with which we prepare for worship reveals how we value the encounter taking place between God and us. Do we meditate deeply on the lessons during the week prior to worship? Do we approach worship prayerfully, humbly? Do we have the sense when we enter the church sanctuary that we are standing on holy ground?

In his book *Reaching for the Invisible God*, Philip Yancey tells about a time when he, a friend, and an Orthodox priest visited an inmate in a chapel in a Russian jail. At the conclusion of the visit, Yancey's friend commented to the priest that they should offer a prayer before leaving. "You want a prayer?" asked the priest. Several minutes later, having assembled vestments, candles, incense, stoles, prayer books, and headpieces, and after following a highly ritualized order of kneelings, kisses, and manual acts, the priest was ready to pray.

Rather than being put off by what he witnessed, Yancey was convicted by the care with which the priest approached God, so different from the almost flippant attitude toward prayer often adopted in Western churches. He concluded that the priest's "tradition had taught him . . . that you do not approach the Other as you would approach your own kind."

Although Abraham enjoyed an intimate, long-term relationship with God, he did not dare to parlay his relationship into personal favors. Even when the divine summons demanded that he act in a way that would cause him to give up the great gift God had given to him previously, Abraham's response to God continued being "Thy will be done."

Suspension of the Ethical

Across the centuries, Abraham's attempted sacrifice of Isaac has captured the imagination of poets (Emily Dickinson), composers (Igor Stravinsky), artists (Rembrandt, Donatello), and writers (Søren Kierkegaard). In *Fear and Trembling*, Kierkegaard (writing under the pen name of Johannes de Silentio, John the Silent) explored four of the myriad ways possible to interpret what took place "on the three days' journey when Abraham rode with sorrow before him and with Isaac by his side."

(1) Abraham explained fully to Isaac that he planned to sacrifice him. When Isaac was unable to understand why, Abraham defended God by acting like a deranged madman, insisting that the idea of sacrificing Isaac was really his idea, causing Isaac to cry out to God for mercy. "After all [said Abraham to God], it is better for him to believe that I am a monster, rather than that he should lose faith in Thee."

(2) Abraham obediently did all that God required of him. When God provided a lamb as a substitute for Isaac, Abraham dutifully sacrificed the lamb, but he was never able to forget what God had demanded of him. Although he remained completely obedient to God, he ended up losing faith in God.

(3) Emotionally, Abraham was a torn man. He knew that the tight bonds that bind father to son and son to father must eventually be broken to permit the son to become his own person. And yet, he did not understand how it could ever be right to sever the bonds of love shared by two people.

(4) When the time came for Abraham to sacrifice Isaac, he momentarily hesitated. Abraham quickly recovered from his brief loss of faith, but Isaac, having witnessed his dad's hesitation and doubt, lost faith himself.

Kierkegaard argued that there are acts (such as Abraham's sacrifice of Isaac) that are not (by our definition) ethical yet are righteous because they are commanded by God. Instead of operating under our understanding of what is ethically appropriate and then using that definition to judge the thoughts and actions of others (including God), our understanding of righteousness emerges from a study of what God does and says. That is, we would not know what righteousness is had God not revealed it to us. There are times when God's righteous demands conflict with our understanding of what is ethically appropriate.

By way of illustration, Kierkegaard referred to a mother who hides her breast in order to wean her infant. Kierkegaard himself, knowing that he would not be able to be a good husband to her, let his fiancée think him a monster and thus break off their engagement. Other examples would include the tough love a family must show to an alcoholic or the willingness of a parent/teacher to permit a child/student to make a grievous mistake. The ultimate example of God's righteousness trumping human ethics is Jesus' death on the cross.

Isaac, the Child of Promise

God's call on Abraham to sacrifice his son seems impossible to obey. We're not told if Abraham shared God's words with Sarah, but Jewish interpreters say it was the shock of hearing what Abraham intended to do to Isaac that killed her (*Midrash Genesis Rabbah* 56:8).

It's hard for me to imagine the conversation that took place between Abraham and Isaac during their three-day trip. With every step Abraham must have relived the joy he saw on Sarah's face as she held their newborn son, heard again Isaac's first cry, remembered his first clumsy step. I suspect, too, that Abraham was arguing with God as passionately as he ever had.

In time, they reached Mount Moriah. Rock by rock, the old man and the son of promise built an altar. They arranged the wood atop the altar. All the time Abraham wondered how he could break the news to his son as to what must happen next. How would Isaac take the news? How could he, an aged man, wrestle his son into submission? And assuming he somehow accomplished these impossibilities, how could he bind to the altar his son, his only son, whom he loved, Isaac?

As it turned out, God provided a way. Jewish and Christian interpreters both suggest that, at some point, the father's great need of a lamb became clear to the child of promise. Sensing how important this sacrifice was to his father, realizing there was no lamb available, Isaac committed his soul to God and did for his dad what his dad could not bring himself to do. Early commentators believe that like a lamb led to the slaughter, Isaac scaled that rock-hewn altar himself and lay down, bound in place by the great love a promised son has for the dad he adores.

Abraham passed God's test, but not in the strength of his own faith, great as it was. He passed, assisted by Isaac, the child of promise. Today, we are able to pass the tests we encounter in life because in the fullness of another time there was another child of promise, another brokenhearted father, and another sacrifice atop Mount Moriah (where stands Golgotha). Accompanied by his father, this son, too, bore on his shoulders the wood for his sacrifice. He, too, ascended a hill, scaled the wood, and spoke the final word. But unlike the mercy shown the son of his friend, Abraham, God did not spare this son, his only son, whom he loved, Jesus. On the mount of "the skull," the lamb God provided was no ram caught in a thicket. It was an innocent lamb, an only begotten son whose shed blood still takes away the sin of the world.

SHARING THE SCRIPTURE

Preparing Our Hearts

Explore this week's devotional reading, found in Philippians 4:15-20. Paul had raised this issue of sharing in 1:7, but here he gives more specific details. Of all the churches with which Paul had a relationship, he regularly received assistance only from the Philippian congregation. The apostle referred to their gift as "a fragrant offering, a sacrifice acceptable and pleasing to God" (4:18). Think about the kinds of sacrifices you are willing to make. How are they pleasing to God? How does your sacrificial giving demonstrate your faith in God?

Pray that you and the adult learners will listen for God's voice and be willing to support others with sacrificial gifts.

Preparing Our Minds

Study the background Scripture from Genesis 22:1-14 and the lesson Scripture from Genesis 22:1-2, 6-14. Ponder this key question: Does faith require doing anything and everything that is requested?

Write on newsprint:
❑ information for next week's lesson, found under "Continue the Journey."
❑ activities for further spiritual growth in "Continue the Journey."

Recognize that the story of binding Isaac has a long history of interpretation. Some ideas presented may not appear directly in the biblical text but rather reflect the way scholars and commentators have wrestled with issues that this difficult story raises.

LEADING THE CLASS

(1) Gather to Learn

❖ Welcome the class members and introduce any guests.

❖ Pray that the students will consider the sacrifice Abraham was willing to make in light of their own desires to please God.

❖ Read this information from United Methodist News Service: **United Methodist Church of the Resurrection, a 12,000-member congregation in Leawood, Kansas, added Grand Avenue Temple, a struggling historic downtown church, to its two existing campuses. Spiritual and physical growth is occurring at the downtown campus, which was already heavily invested in ministries to the poor and draws 240 worshipers on a weekly basis (as of February 2010). Members of the Church of the Resurrection have made significant investments of time and money to embrace Grand Avenue, a magnificent structure that had lost membership as people moved from the city. But there is more: Six couples sold their suburban homes to move to the city to participate in the church and the revitalization of the city.**

❖ Discuss: **Imagine selling your home and moving from your community for the primary purpose of supporting a fledgling ministry. Explain why you would or would not take such sacrificial action.**

❖ Read aloud today's focus statement: **Sometimes people's faith may be tested by others with demands to do things they could not normally imagine doing. Does faith require doing anything and everything requested? Abraham was unquestioning in his faith and devotion to God, who eventually rescinded his demand to kill Isaac.**

(2) Explore the Story of Abraham's Willingness to Sacrifice His One and Only Son in Order to Please God

❖ Choose volunteers to read the parts of Abraham, Isaac, God, and a narrator for Genesis 22:1-2, 6-14.

❖ Invite the students to identify whatever surprises or troubles them in this story. You may want to list these concerns on newsprint and discuss them more fully. Use informa-

tion from Understanding the Scripture wherever it is helpful in providing answers. (Recognize that this story has long troubled readers. Thus, it is important to encourage the adults to raise their concerns, but they also need to be aware that some questions are and will remain unanswerable.)

❖ Discuss these questions:

(1) **What does this story tell you about Abraham?**

(2) **What does this story tell you about Isaac?** (Add information from "Isaac, the Child of Promise" in Interpreting the Scripture.)

(3) **What does this story tell you about God?** (Be sure the group considers not only God's demand but also how God provides a way out for Abraham and Isaac.)

(3) Reflect on the Bounds of Faith and Devotion

❖ Select two participants to roleplay a conversation between Abraham and Isaac as they descend the mountain. Have them consider the bounds of faith and devotion. Encourage the one who plays Abraham to share his emotions. He may, for example, have agonized about the loss of his son, while also believing that God would provide a way to spare him. Suggest that the Isaac character, thought to be age thirty-seven, think about his feelings toward both his father and God. What has he learned from this experience?

❖ Invite the class members to comment on insights they gleaned from the roleplay.

❖ Move to a discussion of their own understanding of the boundaries of faith and devotion by asking these questions:

(1) **Abraham acted on his belief that God had called him to sacrifice Isaac. Other parents/people have felt "led by God" to kill a child they believed was demon-possessed or in some other way not acceptable to God. The latter**

group faced criminal prosecu-
tion. What criteria do we use to
determine what God is—or is
not—calling us to do?

(2) Do you believe that there are
boundaries on faith, lines that
you would not cross in the name
of faith? If so, what are they?

*(4) Determine Bounds of Devotion and
Obedience Within the Learners' Faith*

❖ Read or retell "Suspension of the
Ethical" in Interpreting the Scripture. Invite
the class to comment on any ideas here that
help them to better understand Abraham's
situation, as well as guide them in choices
they may need to make.

❖ Distribute paper and pencils and read
these words: **Suppose you truly believed
that God asked you to sacrifice something
of great importance to you, such as leaving
familiar surroundings to serve as a missionary, or using a large chunk of your
money to support a particular ministry, or
changing your career to one that pays far
less than your current salary but enables
you to serve God more fully. Write about
what it might be that God may call you to
sacrifice and how you might respond.**

❖ Call the group together. Do not ask
people to tell their stories, but do encourage
volunteers to state how easy or difficult they
felt making a sacrifice for God might be.

❖ Conclude by asking this question for
silent reflection: **How might saying yes to
God's call for sacrificial action stretch the
boundaries of your faith?**

(5) Continue the Journey

❖ Pray that the adults will determine,
and if possible stretch, the bounds of their
faithful devotion and obedience.

❖ Read aloud this preparation for next
week's lesson. You may also want to post it
on newsprint for the students to copy.

■ Title: According to the Promise
■ Background Scripture: Luke 1:26-
56; Galatians 3:6-18
■ Lesson Scripture: Luke 1:46-55
■ Focus of the Lesson: Faithfulness
has timeless benefits. How can
acts of faithfulness be rewarded
in a time far from the actual acts?
Because Abraham was faithful to
God and God was faithful to the
promise to give Abraham many
descendants, God acknowledged
Mary's faithfulness to God by
choosing her to be mother of the
Savior.

❖ Challenge the students to complete
one or more of these activities for further
spiritual growth related to this week's session. Post this information on newsprint for
the students to copy.

(1) Encourage a young person to
come to belief in Christ and then
to grow in faith. Act as this person's mentor.

(2) Recall that Abraham took great
care as he prepared to worship
and sacrifice to God. Think about
your own preparations, particularly for worship on Sunday. Do
you really open your heart and
mind? If not, what might you do
to better prepare yourself to come
into the presence of God?

(3) Tell someone who is struggling
with difficult situations how God
has helped you to be faithful,
even when you would have chosen a different response.

❖ Sing or read aloud "When Our
Confidence Is Shaken."

❖ Conclude today's session by leading
the class in this benediction: **By the power
of the Holy Spirit go forth to be a blessing
to others even as God through Christ has
blessed you.**

UNIT 1: GOD'S COVENANT
ACCORDING TO THE PROMISE

PREVIEWING THE LESSON

Lesson Scripture: Luke 1:46-55
Background Scripture: Luke 1:26-56; Galatians 3:6-18
Key Verses: Luke 1:46-47

Focus of the Lesson:
Faithfulness has timeless benefits. How can acts of faithfulness be rewarded in a time far from the actual acts? Because Abraham was faithful to God and God was faithful to the promise to give Abraham many descendants, God acknowledged Mary's faithfulness to God by choosing her to be mother of the Savior.

Goals for the Learners:
(1) to hear anew Mary's song praising God's faithfulness.
(2) to observe the timelessness of faithfulness passed on through generations of descendants.
(3) to catalog stories of faithfulness that they will pass on to future generations.

Pronunciation Guide:
Esdraelon (ez druh ee' luhn)
Magnificat (mag nif' uh kat)
Sepphoris (sef' uh ris)

Supplies:
Bibles, newsprint and marker, paper and pencils, hymnals

READING THE SCRIPTURE

NRSV
Luke 1:46-55

⁴⁶And Mary said,
⁴⁷ "My soul magnifies the Lord,
and my spirit rejoices in God my
Savior,
⁴⁸ for he has looked with favor on the
lowliness of his servant.

NIV
Luke 1:46-55

⁴⁶And Mary said:
"My soul glorifies the Lord
⁴⁷ and my spirit rejoices in God my
Savior,
⁴⁸for he has been mindful
of the humble state of his servant.

Surely, from now on all generations
will call me blessed;
49 for the Mighty One has done great things
for me,
and holy is his name.
50 His mercy is for those who fear him
from generation to generation.
51 He has shown strength with his arm;
he has scattered the proud in the
thoughts of their hearts.
52 He has brought down the powerful from
their thrones,
and lifted up the lowly;
53 he has filled the hungry with good
things,
and sent the rich away empty.
54 He has helped his servant Israel,
in remembrance of his mercy,
55 according to the promise he made to our
ancestors,
to Abraham and to his descendants
forever."

From now on all generations will call me
blessed,
49 for the Mighty One has done great
things for me—
holy is his name.
50 His mercy extends to those who fear him,
from generation to generation.
51 He has performed mighty deeds with
his arm;
he has scattered those who are proud
in their inmost thoughts.
52 He has brought down rulers from their
thrones
but has lifted up the humble.
53 He has filled the hungry with good things
but has sent the rich away empty.
54 He has helped his servant Israel,
remembering to be merciful
55 to Abraham and his descendants forever,
even as he said to our fathers."

UNDERSTANDING THE SCRIPTURE

Luke 1:26-28. Gabriel, one of only two good angels who bear names in Scripture, made announcements also to Daniel (Daniel 8:16; 9:21) and Zechariah (Luke 1:19). The other named good angel is Michael (Daniel 12:1; Jude 9; Revelation 12:7).

In a foreshadowing of the way that Jesus' ministry would play out, the Annunciation took place in Nazareth (not Jerusalem). On the edge of the Esdraelon Plain, hilly Nazareth was a despised Galilean town (John 1:45-46) that was never even mentioned in the Old Testament. Joseph, Mary's betrothed, was a descendant of King David, but he lived in obscurity as a carpenter (Matthew 13:55) in Nazareth. Perhaps he supplemented his work by hiring out on construction projects in nearby Sepphoris, a burgeoning cosmopolitan city only five miles to the north.

Luke 1:29-33. Writing in *The Gospel of Luke*, I. Howard Marshall claims that it is quite possible that Mary was only eleven or twelve years old at the time of the Annunciation. Other commentators suggest different ages, but the Scriptures are silent as to her exact age. Given the customs of the day, she was likely no older than her early teens. Already betrothed, it is also likely that she was beginning to dream about the family that she would have with Joseph, so Gabriel's announcement that she would conceive and "give birth to a son" (1:31 NIV) would not have been particularly shocking news. Similarly, given Joseph's ancestry within the house of David, it is understandable that Mary might have dreamed about regal greatness for her first son and that he might enjoy an especially close relationship to God. Mary gleaned important and amazing information about her son from Gabriel.

Luke 1:34-37. When Mary asked Gabriel to explain himself more clearly, the angel told her two things. First, Gabriel said, "The Holy Spirit will come upon [her]" and "overshadow" her. Mary would bear a child to be called "Son of God" (1:35). Second, she was told that her barren kinswoman Elizabeth was herself now six months pregnant. Gabriel used Elizabeth's condition to demonstrate to Mary that "nothing will be impossible with God" (1:37).

Luke 1:38. Mary showed herself to be a true descendant of Abraham by receiving God's gift and pronouncing herself "the servant of the Lord." She was ready and willing to obey God.

Luke 1:39-45. Whether it was because of Gabriel's astounding visit and announcement or because she wanted to share in Elizabeth's joy, Mary left Nazareth and traveled more than seventy miles to "the hill country" of Judea, probably a reference to the district immediately surrounding Jerusalem, to the home of Zechariah and Elizabeth. In a reversal of social roles, Elizabeth immediately deferred to her young kinswoman, declaring twice that Mary was "blessed" (1:42, 45) and once that the child in Mary's womb was "blessed" (1:42). Even John, still in Elizabeth's womb but already filled with the Spirit (1:15), recognized the presence of the Christ and "leaped" to acknowledge him (1:41).

Luke 1:46-55. The song found in these verses has long been referred to as Mary's Magnificat. The term is taken from the verb "to magnify," in verse 46. The Magnificat is essentially a compilation of Old Testament quotations and allusions, many of which are from the Psalms. Many scholars see Hannah's Song (1 Samuel 2:1-10) as a possible model for the Magnificat. Beginning with verse 49, God is the subject of every verb. Although almost every verb is in the past tense, the actions named are not just deeds God did once upon a time; they are deeds God is actively performing this very moment.

In verses 46-50 Mary's song is personal and full of joy, for she is aware that God has looked favorably upon her and chosen to do amazing things through her. In verses 51-55, Mary's song expands its horizon to take in all Israel. In doing so, the song turns decidedly political. Mary praised a God who is active and involved with people. Seeking justice, God takes on the structures of power that have developed in this world and cuts the powerful down to size. Divine attention is intimately focused on the powerless for whom God cares. The rich seek satisfaction and joy in the things they gather around them, which prove to be elusive. Instead, God freely shares satisfaction and joy with the poor and those without worldly luxuries. Nation-states such as Israel, which cannot compete on the global scene, discover that God is on their side. God regularly does for them what they cannot accomplish for themselves.

Luke 1:56. Mary stayed with Elizabeth and Zechariah through the final trimester of Elizabeth's pregnancy and then returned home to Galilee.

Galatians 3:6-9. To set this passage in context, recall that the people to whom Paul was writing were experiencing a crisis of faith. After he left the area, some people (possibly Jewish Christians) arrived and taught that in order to become followers of Christ, people had to adhere to the Jewish law. For males, this included circumcision, a practice for Gentiles with which Paul vehemently disagreed. The point the false teachers made was that one must be circumcised in order to be a descendant of Abraham. To counteract this point, Paul reminded the Galatians that Abraham was justified by faith. God deemed him righteous long before the Mosaic law even existed. Therefore, argued Paul, those who have faith are in fact descended from Abraham. As he did in Romans 4:3, Paul quoted Genesis 15:6, drawing attention to

Abraham's faith and his explicit willingness to act on that faith by believing God. In this respect, Mary proved herself a worthy descendant of Abraham. By God's grace, the blessing that came to Abraham and to Mary because of their faith has been extended to all persons, including those who believe and thus become "descendants of Abraham" (3:7).

Galatians 3:10-14. While keeping God's

rules is important, what finally matters is whether we are willing to receive for ourselves the blessing of a relationship with God available to us in Christ Jesus.

Galatians 3:15-18. As important as the Mosaic law is to our relationship with God, it is subsidiary to the eternal covenant of relationship that God established with Abraham and extended to us through Christ.

INTERPRETING THE SCRIPTURE

The Lord Is With You

There are many liturgical acts, gestures, and words we employ in worship that are taken for granted by some and despised by others as the trappings of fallible human beings that should be dispensed with. Yet many of the acts, gestures, and words we use in worship come directly from the pages of Holy Scripture, just as Mary's Magnificat itself did.

A case in point is the sentence of greeting in worship, "The Lord is with you," or as some of us say "The Lord be with you." I have heard these words explained as a way for the preacher to get the attention of the congregation prior to offering a prayer. I have also heard the words used as if they were a wish for the hearers, that is, "May the Lord be with you."

In truth, these are the words of proclamation Gabriel spoke to Mary when he announced to her that God "highly favored" her (Luke 1:28). They are the words that "the angel of the LORD" spoke to warriors such as Gideon (Judges 6:12) and kings such as Jehoshaphat (2 Chronicles 20:17). They are the words that God has spoken to various forebears in faith time and time again, beginning with Isaac: "I will be with you" (Genesis 26:3; see Abimelek's words to Abraham in Genesis 21:22).

That fact should alert us to two things every time we hear or speak these words, especially on this Christmas Day. First, we are reminding one another of the faithful "Emmanuel" nature of Jesus, who throughout his earthly life incarnated God's promise to be with us always. Even today, he remains fully present with his church through the empowering and faithful presence of the Holy Spirit.

Second, it is vital that we hear these words as the daring declaration of faith that they are. When someone is spiritually down and unsure how to move forward, the most gracious words of courage we can speak to them are the reminder "The Lord is with you!" When someone is struggling against the powers of darkness and feeling overwhelmed by personal sin or corporate structures of evil, they need to hear us say to them, "The Lord is with you!" When the church is unsure what to do or how to address concerns or how to proclaim God's salvation, someone needs to speak loudly and confidently, "The Lord is with you." Few words have the ability to make us more resolute than these as we humbly serve God.

All this and more is embedded in this one pregnant sentence that we speak to one another every time we gather to worship God. The next time you hear or speak these words, let them hearten you and fill you with confidence and joy.

Mr. Tinker Plays Table Tennis

In the church of my youth, Mr. Tinker was an elderly widower. I never learned much about him. As I think about him (as I often do), that is my loss. I never learned much about him because he rarely spoke about himself. I know he had a son who was a clergyman in a town about 200 miles away. I do not know if he had other children or if he had any grandchildren.

Why Mr. Tinker took an interest in me, I don't know. We never talked about deep subjects, but he would make a point almost every Sunday of saying hello to me. On the other side of eternity, I am sure I will discover that he prayed for me daily.

Every Friday evening our church opened its gym for local teens to play basketball or just to hang out. I would often hold court playing table tennis. Most Friday evenings, Mr. Tinker would show up and await his turn to play a round of table tennis with me. Since most of the teens preferred the basketball court to playing table tennis, sooner or later the table would be left to Mr. Tinker and me, and we would often play upward of a dozen games each Friday before his weakened heart would force him to stop or before a passel of teens would make their way back from the basketball court.

As a teen, I tended to take Mr. Tinker for granted, although I certainly missed him on those rare Fridays when he didn't show. He died a couple years later while I was away at college.

Mr. Tinker has been gone now for more years than I care to admit. But I continue to honor him by treasuring his memory. In fact, my gratitude for him continues to deepen. With a bit of age on me now and some experience under my belt, I now recognize Mr. Tinker as one of the humble whom God lifted up, whom Mary sang about so beautifully (Luke 1:52).

Thankfully, the church is filled with Mr. Tinkers, humble men and women who pour what is left of themselves into someone like me, who may not recognize the great gift being offered until much later. That doesn't worry or frustrate them, however, for they seem to know, as did Gabriel, that no word from God will ever fail.

One of my ongoing prayers is that God would use me to touch the lives of others as deeply as humble Mr. Tinker continues to touch mine.

Red-Headed Firebrand

I have a goddaughter, a red-headed firebrand as intense as they come. From the time she was an infant, she would set her jaw and squint her eyes and her cheeks would turn fiery red, and you knew a burst of raw energy was about to strike. And heaven help whatever or whoever dared stand in her path. I don't think she knows the meaning of the word "demure."

Religious artists have consistently painted Mary as the icon of serenity, as demure as they come, submissive and meek. I don't understand why. That young lady who first spoke the Magnificat strikes me as one who was as volatile and defiant as they come. She knew her Scriptures as well as any rabbi and asserted them with an air of confidence and verve. She figuratively had her fist in the air, daring anyone within her hearing to take issue with her God who has consistently "performed mighty deeds . . . scattered [the] proud . . . brought down rulers" and "sent the rich away empty" (1:51-53 NIV).

At the same time, she knew how important it was that God had also elected to stand with the nameless masses, "lift[ing] up the humble" and "fill[ing] the hungry" and "help[ing] his servant Israel, remembering to be merciful" (1:52-54 NIV). The apostle Paul caught some of her bravado when he spoke of "God's foolishness" and "God's weakness" (1 Corinthians 1:25).

The artists are right to portray Mary as submissive, but her submissiveness was not that of a broken spirit. It was the submissiveness of an ox that gladly shoulders the yoke it has been given and plows ahead with all its strength, focused on the work it has been given, unafraid of the labor that stretches before it, determined to work all day long, content with the shelter, food, and care it receives from its master.

God, this Christmas, make me submissive like that humble ball of fire you chose to mother your Son.

SHARING THE SCRIPTURE

Preparing Our Hearts

Explore this week's devotional reading, found in 2 Corinthians 1:18-22. God is always faithful, declared Paul. And God's promises are always a yes. How have you experienced God's faithfulness in your life? Can you recall specific watershed moments when you knew without doubt that God was present and active in your life? Write about one or more of these experiences in your spiritual journal. Give thanks to God for faithfulness and resounding yeses to meet your needs.

Pray that you and the adult learners will recognize and celebrate the fulfillment of God's promises in your lives.

Preparing Our Minds

Study the background Scripture from Luke 1:26-56 and Galatians 3:6-18. The lesson Scripture for this Christmas Day is Mary's Magnificat from Luke 1:46-55. Consider how acts of faithfulness are rewarded long after the time of the acts.

Write on newsprint:

❑ information for next week's lesson, found under "Continue the Journey."
❑ activities for further spiritual growth in "Continue the Journey."

Be prepared for a different kind of class today. Worship schedules may change, leaving less time for Sunday school. Class members may be away, or may have company with them. Given the excitement of Christmas Day, people may not be as ready to focus as usual.

LEADING THE CLASS

(1) Gather to Learn

❖ Welcome the class members and introduce any guests.

❖ Pray that the students will join Mary in praising God's faithfulness for the gift of Jesus.

❖ Greet the class with the words "The Lord be with you." They may respond, "And also with you."

❖ Read or retell "The Lord Is with You" from Interpreting the Scripture. Talk informally about how God is with us, especially in Jesus, Emmanuel, whose very name means "God with us."

❖ Ask: **How do you experience God's presence?**

❖ Read aloud today's focus statement: **Faithfulness has timeless benefits. How can acts of faithfulness be rewarded in a time far from the actual acts? Because Abraham was faithful to God and God was faithful to the promise to give Abraham many descendants, God acknowledged Mary's faithfulness to God by choosing her to be mother of the Savior.**

(2) Hear Anew Mary's Song Praising God's Faithfulness

❖ Invite a volunteer to read Luke 1:46-49 and a second person to read verses 50-55.

❖ **Option:** If you have a hymnal that includes the Magnificat, read it responsively, using a sung response if available. (See *The United Methodist Hymnal*, page 199, "Canticle of Mary," if you have access to it.)

❖ Ask these questions to spark a theological discussion:

(1) **What does this passage tell you about God?**

(2) **What does this passage tell you about humanity in general?**

(3) **What does this passage tell you about Mary in particular?** (Add information from "Red-Headed Firebrand" in Interpreting the Scripture to help broaden the discussion.)

❖ Read or retell information from Luke 1:46-55 in Understanding the Scripture to help the group more fully understand this passage.

❖ Conclude by discussing this question: **How might you relate Abraham's faithfulness to Mary's faithfulness, and God's faithfulness to both of them?**

(3) Observe the Timelessness of Faithfulness Passed on Through Generations of Descendants

❖ Note that today's lesson stretches all the way back to the promise that God made to Abraham concerning descendants. God was faithful to Abraham and fulfilled that promise, beginning with Isaac and extending to the present. Jesus, of course, was the ultimate fulfillment of God's promise.

❖ Encourage the students to turn to Matthew 1:1-16, where they will find a list of Jesus' ancestors that begins with Abraham. Do not read this aloud, since many names may be difficult for a reader to pronounce. Ask the adults these questions:

(1) **Which of these names are familiar to you?**

(2) **What do you know about the people who are familiar?**

(3) **What does this long list of names suggest to you about how families help to form the faithfulness of their members?**

❖ Choose a volunteer to read 2 Timothy 1:3-7. Encourage the adults to observe how Paul was initially formed in his faith, found in Philippians 3:4-6. Compare that with how it appears that Timothy was formed in his faith. You will find an extra clue about Timothy in Acts 16:1.

❖ Wrap up this activity by talking about continuity. While it is clear that ways of reaching new generations may change, the good news of Jesus Christ remains constant from generation to generation. Write on newsprint ideas the class members may have for attracting people of all ages to the church. What new approaches need to be tried in order to reach more people? Pass these ideas on to the pastor and church leaders.

(4) Catalog Stories of Faithfulness to Pass on to Future Generations

❖ Form small groups. Invite the students to tell stories that have been handed on to them of how God has worked in their family, church, or community.

❖ Distribute paper and pencils. Challenge the adults to write a song of praise (or prose) in which they celebrate God's faithfulness to them, particularly through their families, church, or community. These may be songs of miracle, rescue, or healing, but they may also be songs extolling an ancestor who faithfully stood for God or left a legacy of obedient service to others on behalf of God.

❖ Provide time for several volunteers to read their praises.

❖ Commission today's participants to share their stories, especially as their family may gather for Christmas celebrations. Be sure that the rising generation hears how God has been faithful to the students and how they have responded in faith to God.

❖ **Option:** Suggest to the adults that they try to compile their stories in written form, on video, or through some other means that enable the stories to be recorded for posterity.

(5) Continue the Journey

❖ Pray that the adults will share their own stories of faith with those who are younger.

❖ Read aloud this preparation for next week's lesson. You may also want to post it on newsprint for the students to copy.
- Title: God Watches over Joseph
- Background Scripture: Genesis 39:1-23
- Lesson Scripture: Genesis 39:7-21
- Focus of the Lesson: Faithfulness and loyalty in our relationships determine our behavior in difficult situations. How do faithfulness and loyalty combine to help people make decisions about their life actions? Potiphar's complete faith in Joseph's integrity, Joseph's faith in and loyalty to God, and Joseph's loyalty to Potiphar led Joseph to decline the sexual demands of his master's wife.

❖ Challenge the students to complete one or more of these activities for further spiritual growth related to this week's session. Post this information on newsprint for the students to copy.

(1) **Compose a song of praise expressing your joy as to how God is working in your life.**

(2) **Do something special this week to help the vulnerable and oppressed. Consider taking action to provide short-term relief or serving as an advocate who works to change systemic ills within our society and political system.**

(3) **Reassess your own emphasis on material goods by taking stock of the gifts you gave. Did you spend more than you could afford? If so, why?**

❖ Sing or read aloud "Sing We Now of Christmas."

❖ Conclude today's session by leading the class in this benediction: **By the power of the Holy Spirit go forth to be a blessing to others even as God through Christ has blessed you.**

UNIT 2: GOD'S PROTECTION
GOD WATCHES OVER JOSEPH

PREVIEWING THE LESSON

Lesson Scripture: Genesis 39:7-21
Background Scripture: Genesis 39:1-23
Key Verse: Genesis 39:9

Focus of the Lesson:
Faithfulness and loyalty in our relationships determine our behavior in difficult situations. How do faithfulness and loyalty combine to help people make decisions about their life actions? Potiphar's complete faith in Joseph's integrity, Joseph's faith in and loyalty to God, and Joseph's loyalty to Potiphar led Joseph to decline the sexual demands of his master's wife.

Goals for the Learners:
(1) to investigate the details of Joseph's resistance to the attempted seduction of Potiphar's wife.
(2) to examine the intricate relationship of faith and loyalty as motivators for behavior.
(3) to review some of their behaviors in light of faithfulness and loyalty in their personal relationships.

Pronunciation Guide:
hesed (hee' sid)   Midianite (mid' ee uh nite)
inclusio (in kloo' zhee oh)   Potiphar (pot' uh fuhr)
Ishmaelite (ish' may uh lite)   Septuagint (sep too' uh jint)

Supplies:
Bibles, newsprint and marker, paper and pencils, hymnals

READING THE SCRIPTURE

NRSV
Genesis 39:7-21

⁷And after a time his master's wife cast her eyes on Joseph and said, "Lie with me." ⁸But he refused and said to his master's wife,

NIV
Genesis 39:7-21

⁷And after a while his master's wife took notice of Joseph and said, "Come to bed with me!"

"Look, with me here, my master has no concern about anything in the house, and he has put everything that he has in my hand. ⁹He is not greater in this house than I am, nor has he kept back anything from me except yourself, because you are his wife. **How then could I do this great wickedness, and sin against God?"** ¹⁰And although she spoke to Joseph day after day, he would not consent to lie beside her or to be with her. ¹¹One day, however, when he went into the house to do his work, and while no one else was in the house, ¹²she caught hold of his garment, saying, "Lie with me!" But he left his garment in her hand, and fled and ran outside. ¹³When she saw that he had left his garment in her hand and had fled outside, ¹⁴she called out to the members of her household and said to them, "See, my husband has brought among us a Hebrew to insult us! He came in to me to lie with me, and I cried out with a loud voice; ¹⁵and when he heard me raise my voice and cry out, he left his garment beside me, and fled outside." ¹⁶Then she kept his garment by her until his master came home, ¹⁷and she told him the same story, saying, "The Hebrew servant, whom you have brought among us, came in to me to insult me; ¹⁸but as soon as I raised my voice and cried out, he left his garment beside me, and fled outside."

¹⁹When his master heard the words that his wife spoke to him, saying, "This is the way your servant treated me," he became enraged. ²⁰And Joseph's master took him and put him into the prison, the place where the king's prisoners were confined; he remained there in prison. ²¹But the LORD was with Joseph and showed him steadfast love.

⁸But he refused. "With me in charge," he told her, "my master does not concern himself with anything in the house; everything he owns he has entrusted to my care. ⁹No one is greater in this house than I am. My master has withheld nothing from me except you, because you are his wife. **How then could I do such a wicked thing and sin against God?"** ¹⁰And though she spoke to Joseph day after day, he refused to go to bed with her or even be with her.

¹¹One day he went into the house to attend to his duties, and none of the household servants was inside. ¹²She caught him by his cloak and said, "Come to bed with me!" But he left his cloak in her hand and ran out of the house.

¹³When she saw that he had left his cloak in her hand and had run out of the house, ¹⁴she called her household servants. "Look," she said to them, "this Hebrew has been brought to us to make sport of us! He came in here to sleep with me, but I screamed. ¹⁵When he heard me scream for help, he left his cloak beside me and ran out of the house."

¹⁶She kept his cloak beside her until his master came home. ¹⁷Then she told him this story: "That Hebrew slave you brought us came to me to make sport of me. ¹⁸But as soon as I screamed for help, he left his cloak beside me and ran out of the house."

¹⁹When his master heard the story his wife told him, saying, "This is how your slave treated me," he burned with anger. ²⁰Joseph's master took him and put him in prison, the place where the king's prisoners were confined.

But while Joseph was there in the prison, ²¹the LORD was with him; he showed him kindness.

UNDERSTANDING THE SCRIPTURE

Genesis 39:1. This verse picks up the Joseph story line, which had been interrupted in Genesis 38. The Midianite/ Ishmaelite traders, who had brought Joseph to Egypt, recede and are now replaced by Potiphar, who purchased Joseph. The NIV translates the titles given to Potiphar as military positions. Other translations, such as the Septuagint (the Greek translation of the Hebrew Bible), refer to Potiphar as the head steward or "chief butcher" of Pharaoh.

Genesis 39:2-6a. Joseph, presumably still a young man in his early twenties (see Genesis 37:2; 41:46), did not take long to prove himself capable of overseeing duties in Potiphar's household. In short order, Potiphar made Joseph responsible for "all that he had" (39:6).

It is curious that even though Yahweh was not worshiped in Egypt, Potiphar recognized that Yahweh was working through Joseph. As a result of Potiphar blessing Joseph, Yahweh in turn blessed Potiphar and his household, illustrating how the divine promise that all of the families of the earth would be blessed by Abraham's family (Genesis 12:2-3) would be fulfilled through his descendants.

Genesis 39:6b-7. Because Potiphar was rarely at home, Joseph became the primary administrator both in the fields and in Potiphar's home. Apparently, Joseph was truly in charge, because verse 6 reports that Potiphar had "no concern for anything but the food that he ate." One day, Joseph's good looks (a feature according to 1 Samuel 16:12 that he shared with David, the regal descendant of his older brother, Judah) and constant presence led Potiphar's wife (who had taken "notice of Joseph," 39:7 NIV) to attempt to seduce him.

Genesis 39:8-10. Joseph rejected her advances, citing his loyalty to her husband, Potiphar. Although Potiphar's wife found opportunity almost daily to attempt to seduce him, Joseph continued to decline her repeated advances.

Genesis 39:11-12. "One day" lets the reader know that this day began as did all the rest before it, but it forebodes that it would not end as did those before it. With no other household servants present this day except Joseph, Potiphar's wife seized the opportunity finally to obtain the object

of her infatuation and desire: Joseph. Frustrated that Joseph had not yet consented to her repeated requests for sexual favors, this time Potiphar's wife tried to force herself upon Joseph. She grabbed his cloak to draw him close, but instead of submitting to her will, Joseph slipped out of his cloak and "ran." This was now the second time that Joseph was stripped of a garment (see Genesis 37:23).

Most Jewish commentators come to Joseph's defense when commenting on verses 11-12, declaring that he was above reproach. A small number, however, hint that Joseph's own will had weakened by this point and that he may even have encouraged the sexual advances of Potiphar's wife this day, only coming to his senses at the last possible moment and fleeing (see Babylonian Talmud, *Sotah* 36b). Such a reading cannot be ruled out, but the repeated references to Yahweh being "with" Joseph, both before and after this incident (39:2, 3, 21, 23), make the interpretation very unlikely.

Genesis 39:13-15. Spurned by Joseph and denied what she so greatly desired, Potiphar's wife became furious. Lust gave way to anger and she immediately acted to cover her tracks. Such quick thinking also denied Joseph any opportunity to speak of the matter with Potiphar.

The story that Potiphar's wife hatched and told to the household servants reversed the narrated order of events. Her story made it appear that Joseph was the aggressor. She also changed the location where Joseph left his cloak. According to her story, the cloak was left "beside me" rather than "in her hand." This change made it appear as if Joseph willingly undressed himself rather than being forcibly undressed by her. The detail concerning her quick decision in telling the servants is also curious, given the report that "no one else was in the house" (39:11).

Genesis 39:16-18. When Potiphar returned home, his wife immediately told him the carefully worded story she had first rehearsed to the household servants. Given their constant presence in and around the house, however, it seems certain that they would have been quite aware of her coquetry.

"Make sport" (39:17 NIV) can refer innocently to play or recreation. It can also connote sexual undertones, as it does in English. Similarly, "the food that he ate" in verse 6 can be taken as a literal reference to dinner cuisine, but it can also function as a locker room euphemism for Potiphar's wife.

Genesis 39:19-20. Upon hearing his wife's story, Potiphar "burned with anger" (30:19 NIV) and imprisoned Joseph. But the story is not as straightforward as it might first appear. Notice that the text does not say at whom Potiphar's anger burned. Was Potiphar angry with Joseph or his own wife? Granted, being thrown into prison was not a desirable turn of events for Joseph. But if Potiphar had fully believed his wife's report, it is difficult to understand why he did not have Joseph executed on the spot. Placing Joseph in prison would therefore seem to be a way for Potiphar to act on his wife's words yet protect the household steward whom "the LORD was with" (39:21).

Genesis 39:21-23. This interpretation seems justified since (1) verses 21 and 23 declare that Yahweh was "with" Joseph in prison just as he was "with" Joseph in Potiphar's household; (2) verse 21 says that Joseph found "favor in the eyes" (39:21 NIV) of the prison warden just as he had previously "found favor in [the] eyes" of Potiphar (39:4 NIV); (3) verse 22 relates that the prison warden immediately placed Joseph in the same relation over his fellow prisoners as he had had in Potiphar's household—namely, one of being "in charge" (39:22 NIV); and (4) the prison was in Potiphar's own home (40:3).

Given the subject matter of this lesson, it is important to point out that in verse 21, "kindness" in NIV and "steadfast love" in NRSV are the translations of the Hebrew word *hesed*, which refers to God's steadfast, loyal loving-kindness and mercy.

INTERPRETING THE SCRIPTURE

Yahweh Was With Joseph

Four times in Genesis 39 we are told that "the LORD was with Joseph," twice at the beginning of the chapter (39:2, 3) and twice at the end (39:21, 23). Thus, this phrase creates what scholars call an inclusio—a word or phrase that frames the story and provides the reader a built-in means of interpretation. In addition, as a kind of exclamation point, in verse 21 we are told that God's presence with Joseph was *hesed*, God's steadfast and loyal loving-kindness. Before we begin speaking of our need to be loyal to God, it is important to realize just how loyal to us God is.

Variations of this phrase, "The Lord is with you," occur over and over again in both the Old and New Testaments. We were introduced to the phrase last Sunday on Christmas Day as we reflected on Gabriel's Annunciation to Mary. We observed it was the same phrase we knew from worship as a greeting, but we may have no idea it appears as often as it does in the pages of Scripture.

There are two uses of "The Lord is with you" in the New Testament that many persons are familiar with. Both examples occur in the Gospel of Matthew. The first is in Matthew 1:23, where the angel of the Lord tells Joseph that Mary will bear a son, whom he is to name Jesus (Matthew 1:20-21). In the next verse, Matthew explains that this event fulfilled the words of Isaiah 7:14, in which a son will be given the name "Emmanuel" (which means "God is with us").

The second is in Matthew 28:20, which records the final earthly words that the resurrected Jesus spoke to his disciples: "Remember, I am with you always, to the end of the age." Just as God's loyal presence with Joseph forms an inclusio in Genesis 39, so the entire Gospel of Matthew is framed by God's loyal presence with us.

Similarly, there are a couple of well-known uses of the phrase in the Old Testament. One occurs in Psalm 23. After mentioning several ways in which God cared for him as a shepherd cares for his sheep, the psalmist forever put the lie to the idea that God is absent from us in times of trouble when he wrote: "Even though I walk through the darkest valley, I fear no evil, for *you are with me*" (Psalm 23:4, italics added).

A second Old Testament example occurs in Exodus 3:12. Having heard God call to him from within a bush that appeared to be on fire but wasn't, Moses tried to distance himself from God and reject God's call. The first of God's responses to Moses' objections was also the most direct: "I will be with you" (Exodus 3:12).

At a popular level, some people tend to think God is present with them in good times yet is absent from them in bad times (either because God is angry with them or because God becomes busy tending to other matters and momentarily forgets about them). Even church folk in their opening prayers in worship on Sunday morning often ask God to "be present with us." When you think about it, though, it is a strange request to make of a God who has repeatedly told us that "I will be with you," even when you "pass through the waters" (Isaiah 43:2).

"Everything Is Permissible" But . . .

Day after day with Potiphar's wife, Joseph had opportunity to break covenant with

Potiphar, who had "put [Joseph] in charge of all that he had" (Genesis 39:4). Joseph also had opportunity to break covenant with God, who "was with Joseph, and he became a successful man" (39:2). Instead, at much personal cost, he remained faithful both to Potiphar and to God. Why? We, too, have opportunities daily to display our loyalty to God and others, and to break or keep covenant. Why do we choose either path?

It is often said that our true character is displayed when we are not required to act in a certain way. So, for instance, what we do in private, which we think no one will learn about, often reveals more about who we really are than the public "face" we wear. Similarly, how we treat people we believe are beneath us—cashiers at the grocery store or waitresses in the restaurant, for instance—reveals much about our character. Some of us are old enough to remember Sunday "blue laws," which enforced a particular code of ethics by denying everyone the opportunity to do certain things, such as shop on Sunday. Similarly, when I was growing up, it would not have occurred to me to mow the grass or wash the car or do any other "work" on Sunday. However, with "blue laws" mothballed decades ago, do we still make any effort to "remember the Sabbath day [or, as Christians, the day of our Lord's resurrection], and keep it holy" (Exodus 20:8)?

There was a time when employee/employer relationships were governed by an implicit loyalty shown by the one party to the other. Employers did not release employees during slow sales periods or fire them to avoid paying benefits. Employees did not leave the company at which they learned the ropes so they could move up the corporate ladder with another company. There was also a time when marital covenants were understood to be "for better or for worse." So, too, with membership vows in a local church.

In 1 Corinthians 6:12, the apostle Paul quoted from a letter he had received from the church in Corinth. To their apparent position that they had the right to do anything, he indicated that that might be true. However, he quickly added, "not all things are beneficial." It was his not-so-subtle reminder that opportunity does not trump loyalty.

Church Membership Vows

When persons join the denomination of which I am a member, they vow to faithfully participate in the church's ministries with their prayers, presence, gifts, service, and witness. When this vow of loyalty is upheld faithfully, the result is often a vital, growing relationship with God and a willingness to live in peace and love with others. It does not produce Christians who think alike, but it does produce Christians who want to love God with all their heart, soul, mind, and strength; and to love their neighbors as themselves (Mark 12:30; Deuteronomy 6:4, 5; Leviticus 19:18).

Maturing Christians carry on a lifelong conversation with God and therefore are able to recognize God's voice. Just as faithful family members are not unaccountably absent from home, so faithful Christians can be counted on to be present in worship and study. God's generous and merciful Spirit gives thankful Christians a wonderful example to mimic as they give generously of their time and money and other resources to advance the kingdom of God. Obedient Christians acknowledge that God's call on their lives has indebted them to act humbly yet boldly in the name of Jesus Christ. Like Joseph, who was faithful to God in the midst of unimaginably difficult circumstances, we too are called to live with integrity—and we can do that because God is with us.

SHARING THE SCRIPTURE

Preparing Our Hearts

Explore this week's devotional reading, found in 1 Corinthians 10:1-13. Paul uses examples from Israel's history as cautionary tales. Those who believe in Christ are not to act as evildoers, idolators, complainers, or immoral people. We are, in other words, to live with integrity before God, recognizing that we will likely be tested but that God will give us strength to endure. Consider lessons you have learned from the negative examples of other people. How have their experiences helped you to avoid some of life's pitfalls?

Pray that you and the adult learners will seek Christ's example to enable you to live lives pleasing unto God.

Preparing Our Minds

Study the background Scripture from Genesis 39:1-23 and the lesson Scripture from Genesis 39:7-21. Think about how faithfulness and loyalty combine to help people make decisions about their actions.

Write on newsprint:
❑ information for next week's lesson, found under "Continue the Journey."
❑ activities for further spiritual growth in "Continue the Journey."

Recognize that since this is New Year's Day, attendance may be down and the Sunday morning schedule may be modified. Consider providing some breakfast refreshments.

LEADING THE CLASS

(1) Gather to Learn

❖ Welcome the class members and introduce any guests.

❖ Pray that the students will consider their own integrity in light of Joseph's.

❖ Talk with the class about society's expectations for faithfulness and loyalty, especially in marital relationships. Why are we especially disappointed and outraged when a politician, star athlete, or media personality commits adultery? What do such illicit relationships suggest to us about a person's integrity? (Be sure to keep the discussion focused on public personalities, not local people who may have committed similar indiscretions.)

❖ Read aloud today's focus statement: **Faithfulness and loyalty in our relationships determine our behavior in difficult situations. How do faithfulness and loyalty combine to help people make decisions about their life actions? Potiphar's complete faith in Joseph's integrity, Joseph's faith in and loyalty to God, and Joseph's loyalty to Potiphar led Joseph to decline the sexual demands of his master's wife.**

(2) Investigate the Details of Joseph's Resistance to the Attempted Seduction of Potiphar's Wife

❖ Use information from Genesis 39:1, 2-6a, 6b-7 in Understanding the Scripture to set the stage for today's reading.

❖ Invite volunteers for the parts of the narrator, Joseph, and Potiphar's wife. Read Genesis 39:7-21 as a drama.

❖ Discuss these questions:
   (1) **Given Potiphar's wife's actions, how would you describe her relationship with her husband?**
   (2) **Although Joseph had power, in the end he was a slave. What does his position suggest about the challenges he faced in guarding his integrity?**
   (3) **A slave facing the charges that were brought against Joseph would likely face immediate execution. What do Potiphar's actions suggest about his trust in Joseph? What do his actions sug-**

gest about his relationship with his wife?
   (4) **Four times in Genesis 39 the reader is told that the Lord was with Joseph (39:2, 3, 21, 23). What difference do you think God's presence made in how Joseph conducted himself even in the face of repeated temptation?** (Add information from "Yahweh Was with Joseph" from Interpreting the Scripture to augment the discussion.)

❖ Encourage the class to comment on how the conflicting values in this story are similar to competing values we experience in our own society.

❖ End this portion of the lesson by asking: **What prompts a person to remain true to his or her integrity when values are challenged?**

❖ **Option:** Invite volunteers to debate this statement, which you will read aloud: **All people, no matter what their gender, racial or ethnic background, or social, economic, or political status, have the power to choose to remain true to their values.**

(3) Examine the Intricate Relationship of Faith and Loyalty as Motivators for Behavior

❖ Brainstorm answers to this question, which you will list on newsprint: **What motivates human behavior?** (This is a very broad question with a lot of possible answers, including *fearing punishment, desiring to do the right thing, wanting to look good in the eyes of other people, wanting to obey God, looking out for oneself and one's family, seeking common good for the most people.*)

❖ Review the list, asking the students to identify those behaviors that seem consistent with how they believe God would want them to act.

❖ Form small groups. Challenge each group to identify strategies for encouraging people to behave in the ways you have just identified.

❖ Call everyone together and invite each group to report. Suggest that the adults begin to use whichever strategies seem most helpful to them.

(4) Review Some of the Learners' Behaviors in Light of Faithfulness and Loyalty in Their Personal Relationships

❖ Read or retell "Church Membership Vows" in Interpreting the Scripture. Invite the adults to recall any commitments they made when they joined your church.

❖ Distribute paper and pencils. Encourage the students to write answers to this question, telling them in advance that they will not be asked to share their answers: **How does my behavior demonstrate that I have been loyal to my membership vows, which in turn are a sign of my faithfulness to Christ?**

❖ Close by inviting the class to call out behaviors that they feel represent the kind of faithfulness and loyalty that church members should exhibit, not just among their faith community but in all personal relationships. List these ideas on newsprint.

❖ Provide a few moments for silent reflection as the adults ponder how what they have written about their own behaviors is similar to and different from the kinds of behaviors the group has suggested.

(5) Continue the Journey

❖ Break the silence by praying that the adults will continue to be aware of their faithfulness and loyalty to God as they make decisions.

❖ Read aloud this preparation for next week's lesson. You may also want to post it on newsprint for the students to copy.

■ **Title: Joseph Finds Favor**
■ **Background Scripture: Genesis 41:1-52**
■ **Lesson Scripture: Genesis 41:37-45, 50-52**
■ **Focus of the Lesson: Earning**

other people's faith in us can lead to great responsibility and honor. What results can we expect when others have faith in us? Because Joseph performed so well for the Egyptian king, Pharaoh had faith in Joseph's abilities, elevated him to the second position in all of Egypt, and gave him responsibility for ruling the day-to-day activities of the kingdom.

❖ Challenge the students to complete one or more of these activities for further spiritual growth related to this week's session. Post this information on newsprint for the students to copy.

(1) Check the media for stories about people who are wrongly imprisoned for crimes that they did not commit. Was this a case of mistaken identity, or was false evidence used? What happened to the one who was wrongly imprisoned? What happened to the accuser who was the victim of the crime?

(2) Recall a time when someone falsely accused you. What happened? How did you handle this situation? Were you able to forgive the accuser? If not, seek God's help in forgiving, and perhaps reconciling, with this person who treated you unjustly.

(3) Brainstorm ways that you can protect yourself from false accusers. For example, use a calendar to document your activities. Keep a journal in which you briefly detail what you have done, with whom, and when. Keep receipts to prove where and when you made purchases.

❖ Sing or read aloud "If Thou But Suffer God to Guide Thee."

❖ Conclude today's session by leading the class in this benediction: **By the power of the Holy Spirit go forth to be a blessing to others even as God through Christ has blessed you.**

UNIT 2: GOD'S PROTECTION
JOSEPH FINDS FAVOR

PREVIEWING THE LESSON

Lesson Scripture: Genesis 41:37-45, 50-52
Background Scripture: Genesis 41:1-52
Key Verse: Genesis 41:38

Focus of the Lesson:
Earning other people's faith in us can lead to great responsibility and honor. What results can we expect when others have faith in us? Because Joseph performed so well for the Egyptian king, Pharaoh had faith in Joseph's abilities, elevated him to the second position in all of Egypt, and gave him responsibility for ruling the day-to-day activities of the kingdom.

Goals for the Learners:
(1) to study Pharaoh's actions resulting from his faith in Joseph's abilities.
(2) to explore how superior performance can lead to greater responsibility and eventual honors by leaders and the community.
(3) to articulate a connection between their faith and the effort they put into their relationships and responsibilities.

Pronunciation Guide:
Asenath (as' uh nath)   On (on)
Ephraim (ee' fray im)   Potiphera (puh ti' fuh ruh)
Heliopolis (hee lee op' uh lis)   Zaphenath-paneah (zaf uh nath puh nee' uh)
Manasseh (muh nas' uh)

Supplies:
Bibles, newsprint and marker, paper and pencils, hymnals

READING THE SCRIPTURE

NRSV
Genesis 41:37-45, 50-52
  ³⁷The proposal pleased Pharaoh and all his servants. **³⁸Pharaoh said to his servants, "Can we find anyone else like this—one in whom is the spirit of God?"** ³⁹So Pharaoh

NIV
Genesis 41:37-45, 50-52
  ³⁷The plan seemed good to Pharaoh and to all his officials. **³⁸So Pharaoh asked them, "Can we find anyone like this man, one in whom is the spirit of God?"**

said to Joseph, "Since God has shown you all this, there is no one so discerning and wise as you. 40You shall be over my house, and all my people shall order themselves as you command; only with regard to the throne will I be greater than you." 41And Pharaoh said to Joseph, "See, I have set you over all the land of Egypt." 42Removing his signet ring from his hand, Pharaoh put it on Joseph's hand; he arrayed him in garments of fine linen, and put a gold chain around his neck. 43He had him ride in the chariot of his second-in-command; and they cried out in front of him, "Bow the knee!" Thus he set him over all the land of Egypt. 44Moreover Pharaoh said to Joseph, "I am Pharaoh, and without your consent no one shall lift up hand or foot in all the land of Egypt." 45Pharaoh gave Joseph the name Zaphenath-paneah; and he gave him Asenath daughter of Potiphera, priest of On, as his wife. Thus Joseph gained authority over the land of Egypt.

50Before the years of famine came, Joseph had two sons, whom Asenath daughter of Potiphera, priest of On, bore to him. 51Joseph named the firstborn Manasseh, "For," he said, "God has made me forget all my hardship and all my father's house." 52The second he named Ephraim, "For God has made me fruitful in the land of my misfortunes."

39Then Pharaoh said to Joseph, "Since God has made all this known to you, there is no one so discerning and wise as you. 40You shall be in charge of my palace, and all my people are to submit to your orders. Only with respect to the throne will I be greater than you."

41So Pharaoh said to Joseph, "I hereby put you in charge of the whole land of Egypt." 42Then Pharaoh took his signet ring from his finger and put it on Joseph's finger. He dressed him in robes of fine linen and put a gold chain around his neck. 43He had him ride in a chariot as his second-in-command, and men shouted before him, "Make way!" Thus he put him in charge of the whole land of Egypt.

44Then Pharaoh said to Joseph, "I am Pharaoh, but without your word no one will lift hand or foot in all Egypt." 45Pharaoh gave Joseph the name Zaphenath-Paneah and gave him Asenath daughter of Potiphera, priest of On, to be his wife. And Joseph went throughout the land of Egypt.

50Before the years of famine came, two sons were born to Joseph by Asenath daughter of Potiphera, priest of On. 51Joseph named his firstborn Manasseh and said, "It is because God has made me forget all my trouble and all my father's household." 52The second son he named Ephraim and said, "It is because God has made me fruitful in the land of my suffering."

UNDERSTANDING THE SCRIPTURE

Genesis 41:1-8. With little hope that things might change, Joseph was languishing in prison as a result of Potiphar's wife's charge that he had attempted to seduce her. Two years had elapsed since he had correctly interpreted dreams for the cupbearer and the baker with whom he had shared a jail cell. Unfortunately, the cupbearer failed to remember his promise to Joseph (Genesis 40:23).

Pharaoh had a dream that awakened him twice in the night (41:4, 7). Greatly troubled, he called for his dream interpreters. They either would not or could not interpret the dream for him.

Genesis 41:9-13. Pharaoh's conversation with his dream interpreters was overheard by his cupbearer, who suddenly remembered that two years previously Joseph had correctly interpreted dreams for him and for the baker. He promptly related this information to Pharaoh.

Genesis 41:14-16. Pharaoh lost no time summoning Joseph, who first had to get cleaned up after languishing for more than two years in prison. Curiously, he also shaved, choosing to appear before Pharaoh looking more as an Egyptian than as a Hebrew. When Pharaoh mentioned his dreams, he mentioned Joseph's reputation as one who could correctly interpret them. Joseph quickly and boldy made clear that he could not interpret dreams but that it was God who would "give Pharaoh a favorable answer" (41:16).

Genesis 41:17-24. In the retelling of his dreams it was obvious that the elusive meaning was weighing heavily on Pharaoh's mind. Although he could not interpret his own dreams, Pharaoh could clearly recount the two dreams: one with both seven "fat and sleek" cows and seven "poor, very ugly, and thin" cows (41:18-19); the other with seven "full and good" ears of grain and seven "withered, thin, and blighted" ears of grain (41:22-23). Since there were two dreams with the same type of message and symbolism, there could be no doubt that these dreams were to be understood as a communication from God.

Genesis 41:25-32. The meaning of Pharaoh's dream was immediately apparent to Joseph. The double sevens referred to years; the cows and ears of grain represented both bountiful harvests and severe famines. By emphasizing the bitter years of famine, Joseph hoped to make clear to Pharaoh that time was of the essence in addressing this important matter about which God had graciously forewarned him.

Genesis 41:33-36. To further emphasize the gravity of the matter revealed in Pharaoh's dreams, Joseph dared to suggest that an immediate plan of action needed to be put into place. Before another cycle of sowing and harvesting went by, Pharaoh must create a wise harvest czar, divide his country into agricultural districts, and place overseers over each of these districts. Although he does not suggest himself, Joseph certainly must have hoped that he would be chosen for this position of authority. One can imagine an empire builder like Pharaoh being intrigued by Joseph's plan, which would effectively gain and consolidate imperial control over Egypt's entire farming industry.

Genesis 41:37-40. Joseph's proposal "pleased Pharaoh and all his servants" (41:37), so presumably others heard what Joseph had to say. Impressed with Joseph's plan, Pharaoh wasted no time in implementing it. His very first act was to make Joseph the harvest czar with wide-ranging powers. As they already did toward Pharaoh, so the people were to submit humbly and fully to Joseph when they heard him speak. Pharaoh's reason for selecting Joseph is indeed amazing, given that this Egyptian ruler would not have worshiped God. Pharaoh does, however, recognize that the spirit of God is upon Joseph. Pharaoh attributes Joseph's ability to be "discerning and wise" (41:39) to God's spirit. No questions are asked about Joseph's skill, education, or experience in overseeing such a large agricultural project. He is selected solely on the basis of God's unmistakable working within him.

Genesis 41:41-43. During an installation ceremony Pharaoh gave to Joseph three tools he would need to accomplish his new work: Pharaoh's own signet ring, which Joseph would use to seal official documents; a royal wardrobe, which would enable Joseph to look the role he now assumed; and a royal chariot and driver, which permitted Joseph fast and safe travel throughout Egypt.

Genesis 41:44-45. After reminding Joseph that Pharaoh himself would still be in charge, Pharaoh concluded the installation ceremony with two final executive orders. First, Joseph was given an Egyptian name, Zaphenath-paneah, the meaning of which is debated. Second, Joseph was given an Egyptian wife from a noble family, which provided him with important familial connections into the Egyptian hierarchy. Potiphera, "the priest of On," is not the same person as Potiphar, the captain of the guard whose wife attempted to seduce Joseph. The city of On, later known as Heliopolis, was located just a few miles northeast of Cairo.

Genesis 41:46-49. Joseph's age is listed as thirty in verse 46. He was seventeen when he received "a richly ornamented robe" from his father (37:2-3 NIV). Two years elapsed between Joseph's interpretation of the cupbearer's dream and the dream of Pharaoh (Genesis 41:1). Those designations tell us that Joseph spent roughly ten years either in the employ of Potiphar or in Potiphar's prison. In other words, he has spent about one-third of his life in Egypt.

"During the seven plenteous years" (41:47) Joseph performed as he was charged by Pharaoh. He oversaw the collection and warehousing of the unnaturally large harvests that occurred in Egypt. Three phrases in verse 49 hint at the vastness of the annual harvests. They consisted of "grain in such abundance" they were "like the sand of the sea." And they were so far "beyond measure" that Joseph actually "stopped measuring."

Genesis 41:50-52. Also during the years of abundance, Joseph started his own family. Two sons, Manasseh and Ephraim, were born to Asenath, Joseph's wife. Curiously, even though Joseph received an Egyptian name when he was placed in the employ of Pharaoh, he gave to his two sons Hebrew names. These names seem to mirror Joseph's experiences: helping him to forget his hardships (Manasseh) and recognizing his good fortune (Ephraim). Joseph's life in Canaan was long over but his heart still resided there.

INTERPRETING THE SCRIPTURE

Pharaoh and Joseph

The pharaoh of the Exodus is not treated kindly by the writers of Scripture. He is pictured as a brutish, simpleminded ruler; he is outwitted by servants and lowly women; and he is not even granted the dignity of a name. The pharaoh in Genesis 41 is not given a name, either; but, in contrast, he manages to appear as a good-hearted man with a keen, discerning eye for administrative ability. This pharaoh recognized not only that the spirit of God was present in Joseph but also that Joseph's wisdom and discernment were directly due to God's favor (Genesis 41:38-39).

Across the years, I have led many retreats and workshops on spiritual gifts. Consistently, the one aspect of these workshops that has proved the most troubling to participants is the distinction made between spiritual gifts and natural talents or skills. Christians are not born with these Spirit-gifts; they are marks of our salvation. They are given in baptism when God's Holy Spirit comes to dwell in us. However, instead of being grateful that God generously and abundantly enables the church to accomplish amazing feats of faith, workshop participants often want to argue that these gifts are not God-given; they are innate abilities. We have no reason to suspect that Pharaoh would have known anything about the God of the Bible, yet he immediately grasped that Joseph's abilities were God-given.

Equally amazing is Pharaoh's complete lack of envy toward Joseph, which made it possible for him to provide generous assistance to Joseph, enabling Joseph to succeed at his administrative post far beyond anyone's reasonable expectations. Instead of being envious of Joseph's God-given wisdom and administrative prowess, Pharaoh was so pleased by them that he amply rewarded him with every gift he had in order to help Joseph accomplish the tasks he had charged him to accomplish.

Greater Responsibility, Greater Service

The first time I can remember being given responsibility for anything was in fourth grade. My teacher placed me in charge of organizing the science cabinet, a large multi-shelved metal cabinet in the front of the room into which all the remains of half-completed science projects from time immemorial had been tossed. I now realize that this "honor" was simply my teacher's way of keeping me busy, out of trouble, and (perhaps most important) very much in plain sight; but at the time, I approached my new responsibility with much pride. That said, from the moment I first opened that cabinet and looked at the disorganized heap of junk jutting out amid piles of ancient who-knows-what, I knew I was in over my head.

Years later, appointed by the bishop to my first parish, I moved my computer and several boxes of books into the makeshift room that would serve as my office for the next twelve years. I sat down, turned on my computer . . . and an ominous, overwhelming wave of inadequacy washed over me. It dawned on me that at any moment, someone in that church might walk in, sit down, strike up a conversation, and expect me to know a thing or two about God, church, or life in general.

At its simplest, responsibility is response-ability, the ability to respond. It is the capacity to address issues that arise in dependable, conscientious ways. More often than not, responsibility is not something we grasp for ourselves; it is often bestowed upon us by others who see in us possibilities we may be only dimly aware

exist in ourselves. Think, for instance, of Abraham, whom God made to be a blessing for others (Genesis 12:2-3); or Moses, whom God sent "to bring my people, the Israelites, out of Egypt" (Exodus 3:10).

Thus, responsibility is a gift of leadership bestowed on us by others. As the gift is practiced and lessons are drawn from the experience, a disciplined ability to accomplish measurable results is formed. This is true whether one is responsible for emptying trash cans, sewing a hem, performing a delicate surgery, or investing large sums of money. Pharaoh listened to Joseph's interpretation of his dream, weighed his suggestions as to how the ravaging effects of the famine could be avoided, and gave him the authority to accomplish the task.

Faith, Effort, and Honor

Having always worked hard, received good grades, and played on good sports teams when I was in high school and college, I came to believe that accolades and career advancements were earned by the superior performances a person turned in. Imagine, then, my surprise (and consternation) when I discovered as an adult that there is just as often little or no connection between ability and advancement.

This fact became unavoidably clear to me the day in grad school when I received yet another form letter that began "Thank you for your application but. . . ." The job I had applied for was entry-level and part-time. It required correctly delivering company mail to approximately thirty employees twice a day. I realize the letter I received was a standard, boilerplate form letter, but I was still rather incredulous when I read the line that said, "We have hired the person most qualified for the position." That was the day it truly began to dawn on me that if I expected to obtain a job because I was qualified, had excellent skills, or a good work ethic, I might very well starve.

Of course, if I had paid better attention to

the Scriptures I read daily, the creeds I recited regularly, and the hymns I sang on Sundays, I would have known this already. Jesus was "true God of true God, Light from Light Eternal" ("O Come, All Ye Faithful," verse 2); yet "he was despised and rejected by others" (Isaiah 53:3). Although "he came to what was his own, . . . his own people did not accept him" (John 1:11). Qualifications are important, as is ability, but jobs, friendships, promotions, and even love are often extended to us (or withheld from us) for reasons that may have nothing to do with either.

The excellence we strive to achieve, both in life and in work, is wasted if the primary point is only to draw attention to ourselves. As Christians, we want every relationship we have, every word we speak, every attitude we exhibit, every act we perform to glorify God. We not only think about "whatever is true . . . noble . . . right . . . pure . . .

lovely . . . admirable . . . excellent . . . praiseworthy" (Philippians 4:8 NIV), we "put it into practice" (Philippians 4:9 NIV). In short, the excellence we strive to achieve is to be an expression of our faith.

Interestingly, today's Scripture text does not say that it was Joseph's abilities that caught Pharaoh's imagination or his wisdom that gained Pharaoh's favor. Pharaoh surely listened carefully to Joseph's interpretation of his dream, but he never referred to it. What won Joseph his job at Pharaoh's court was Pharaoh's awareness that "God . . . made all this known to you" (Genesis 41:39 NIV). His relationship with God, the gifts that God gave him, and the eagerness to credit God in all things led to the amazing success that Joseph experienced. This success was not for himself alone but, more important, for the multitude whose lives were saved because he obediently prepared for hard times.

SHARING THE SCRIPTURE

Preparing Our Hearts

Explore this week's devotional reading, found in Genesis 49:22-26. In speaking his final words to his sons, Jacob pours blessings out upon Joseph. These blessings relate specifically to fertility, agricultural bounty, and the military strength of the tribes of Joseph's sons, Ephraim and Manasseh. Think about the blessings that have been bestowed upon you. How have you found favor with a person or with God? Try listing at least ten blessings on a sheet of paper and offer thanks for them in prayer.

Pray that you and the adult learners will be aware of God's blessings in your lives and find ways to share them with others.

Preparing Our Minds

Study the background Scripture from Genesis 41:1-52 and the lesson Scripture

from Genesis 41:37-45, 50-52. Think about the sorts of results we can expect when other people have the kind of faith in us that leads to greater responsibility and honor.

Write on newsprint:
❑ information for next week's lesson, found under "Continue the Journey."
❑ activities for further spiritual growth in "Continue the Journey."

Plan to retell Genesis 41:1-36 so that the students will be able to better understand the entire story.

LEADING THE CLASS

(1) Gather to Learn

❖ Welcome the class members and introduce any guests.
❖ Pray that the students will appreciate the abilities of others.

❖ Encourage the adults to think about their elected leaders by raising these questions for the entire class or discussing in smaller groups:

(1) **What criteria do you use to select a candidate for office?**

(2) **If one does well in a local office, are you willing to vote for that person for an office that requires greater skills and more responsibility? Why or why not?**

(3) **Why do you continue to have faith in this person?**

(4) **What might happen to cause you to lose faith in him or her?**

❖ Read aloud today's focus statement: **Earning other people's faith in us can lead to great responsibility and honor. What results can we expect when others have faith in us? Because Joseph performed so well for the Egyptian king, Pharaoh had faith in Joseph's abilities, elevated him to the second position in all of Egypt, and gave him responsibility for ruling the day-to-day activities of the kingdom.**

(2) Study the Pharaoh's Actions Resulting From His Faith in Joseph's Abilities

❖ Retell briefly the events of Genesis 41:1-36 to provide a framework for today's Scripture lesson.

❖ Choose a volunteer to read Genesis 41:37-45, 50-52.

❖ Discuss these questions:

(1) **Why do you think Pharaoh, who would have identified himself as a god, believed Joseph's interpretation of his dreams?**

(2) **What criteria did Pharaoh use for making Joseph, an imprisoned foreigner, second-in-command in all of Egypt?**

(3) **How do the gifts Pharaoh gave to Joseph during the installation ceremony set him apart from others?**

(4) **Had you been Joseph, how would you have responded to these gifts and your new position, which was very much a reversal of your life as an enslaved prisoner?**

(5) **What do the names of Joseph's children tell you about his life experiences?**

❖ Conclude this portion of the lesson with a brief debate on this topic: **Since God was clearly "with" Joseph, he should be considered as a model that Christians can follow.** (The students may rightly point out that in some ways Joseph is a good role model, but in other ways, he is not.)

(3) Explore How Superior Performance Can Lead to Greater Responsibility and Eventual Honors by Leaders and the Community

❖ Read or retell "Greater Responsibility, Greater Service" in Interpreting the Scripture.

❖ Form several small groups. Invite the adults to tell stories of times when they did well at a certain level and then were given greater responsibilities. How did that change work out? Why? These stories may relate to school, the workplace, a club or civic organization, or an arts organization.

❖ Bring the groups together and discuss these questions:

(1) **What kinds of attributes enable a person to achieve a superior performance?** (Consider innate talents, practice, perseverance, desire or drive to achieve, ability to set and meet goals, belief that God has called you to do a certain task.)

(2) **How does the community (or congregation, workplace, or team) select persons for greater responsibilities?**

(3) **"Superior performance" may be defined in different ways, depending upon the organization. What do you believe constitutes "superior performance" among volunteers in the church?**

(4) Articulate a Connection Between the Learners' Faith and the Effort They Put Into Their Relationships and Responsibilities

❖ Read these slogans that the adults may have heard, even during childhood: "Whatever you do, do it well." "Give of your best to the Master." "Work hard for the kingdom of God." "Give of your first-fruits to God, not what you have left." "You only get out of something what you put into it." Invite the class to add sayings containing similar ideas.

❖ Ask: **What do these slogans say to you about the relationship between one's faith in God and the effort one puts forth to please God?**

❖ Distribute paper and pencils. Encourage the learners to state in their own words what they believe to be the relationship between their own faith and the effort they put into whatever responsibilities they take on for God. Do they take on volunteer church jobs halfheartedly, to be done whenever they get around to them? Or do they take their responsibilities seriously and give a full effort? These brief essays will not be shared.

❖ Wrap up by encouraging everyone to respond to the idea that there is a definite relationship between one's faith and the effort one gives to fulfilling responsibilities. Perhaps some volunteers will give specific examples to support their statements.

(5) Continue the Journey

❖ Pray that the adults will make a connection between their faith and the effort they make to sustain their relationships.

❖ Read aloud this preparation for next week's lesson. You may also want to post it on newsprint for the students to copy.

■ **Title: God Preserves a Remnant**
■ **Background Scripture: Genesis 42:1-38; 45:1-28**

■ **Lesson Scripture: Genesis 45:3-15**
■ **Focus of the Lesson: When people are mutually faithful, they support and protect one another. What can faithful people expect from other faithful people? Because Jacob and Joseph were both faithful to God, God remained faithful to God's promise to Abraham by putting Joseph in a position to save the entire family from death by starvation.**

❖ Challenge the students to complete one or more of these activities for further spiritual growth related to this week's session. Post this information on newsprint for the students to copy.

(1) **Give someone a compliment this week for a job well done. Include a word about how you see the gifts of God working in this person's life.**

(2) **Look up the meaning of the names of some Bible people. What do these names tell you about each person's gifts, personality, or the work to which God has called them? What does your own name mean? How does this name reflect (or fail to reflect) who you are?**

(3) **Survey jobs in your church that need to be done. Do you feel that God has called and equipped you to do any of them? If so, which one(s)? If you have not already stepped forward to do this job, what is holding you back?**

❖ Sing or read aloud "Give Me the Faith Which Can Remove."

❖ Conclude today's session by leading the class in this benediction: **By the power of the Holy Spirit go forth to be a blessing to others even as God through Christ has blessed you.**

UNIT 2: GOD'S PROTECTION

GOD PRESERVES A REMNANT

PREVIEWING THE LESSON

Lesson Scripture: Genesis 45:3-15
Background Scripture: Genesis 42:1-38; 45:1-28
Key Verse: Genesis 45:8

Focus of the Lesson:
When people are mutually faithful, they support and protect one another. What can faithful people expect from other faithful people? Because Jacob and Joseph were both faithful to God, God remained faithful to God's promise to Abraham by putting Joseph in a position to save the entire family from death by starvation.

Goals for the Learners:
(1) to point out Joseph's acts of faithfulness to God and family, as recorded in the story of Joseph welcoming his brothers and caring for their families.
(2) to experience mutuality and its positive results in faithfulness.
(3) to make mutual commitments of faithfulness to God and in their families and communities.

Pronunciation Guide:
agape (uh gah' pay)
Goshen (goh' shuhn)

Supplies:
Bibles, newsprint and marker, paper and pencils, hymnals

READING THE SCRIPTURE

NRSV
Genesis 45:3-15

³Joseph said to his brothers, "I am Joseph. Is my father still alive?" But his brothers could not answer him, so dismayed were they at his presence.

⁴Then Joseph said to his brothers, "Come

NIV
Genesis 45:3-15

³Joseph said to his brothers, "I am Joseph! Is my father still living?" But his brothers were not able to answer him, because they were terrified at his presence.

⁴Then Joseph said to his brothers, "Come

closer to me." And they came closer. He said, "I am your brother, Joseph, whom you sold into Egypt. [5]And now do not be distressed, or angry with yourselves, because you sold me here; for God sent me before you to preserve life. [6]For the famine has been in the land these two years; and there are five more years in which there will be neither plowing nor harvest. [7]God sent me before you to preserve for you a remnant on earth, and to keep alive for you many survivors. [8]**So it was not you who sent me here, but God;** he has made me a father to Pharaoh, and lord of all his house and ruler over all the land of Egypt. [9]Hurry and go up to my father and say to him, 'Thus says your son Joseph, God has made me lord of all Egypt; come down to me, do not delay. [10]You shall settle in the land of Goshen, and you shall be near me, you and your children and your children's children, as well as your flocks, your herds, and all that you have. [11]I will provide for you there—since there are five more years of famine to come—so that you and your household, and all that you have, will not come to poverty.' [12]And now your eyes and the eyes of my brother Benjamin see that it is my own mouth that speaks to you. [13]You must tell my father how greatly I am honored in Egypt, and all that you have seen. Hurry and bring my father down here." [14]Then he fell upon his brother Benjamin's neck and wept, while Benjamin wept upon his neck. [15]And he kissed all his brothers and wept upon them; and after that his brothers talked with him.

close to me." When they had done so, he said, "I am your brother Joseph, the one you sold into Egypt! [5]And now, do not be distressed and do not be angry with yourselves for selling me here, because it was to save lives that God sent me ahead of you. [6]For two years now there has been famine in the land, and for the next five years there will not be plowing and reaping. [7]But God sent me ahead of you to preserve for you a remnant on earth and to save your lives by a great deliverance. [8]**"So then, it was not you who sent me here, but God.** He made me father to Pharaoh, lord of his entire household and ruler of all Egypt. [9]Now hurry back to my father and say to him, 'This is what your son Joseph says: God has made me lord of all Egypt. Come down to me; don't delay. [10]You shall live in the region of Goshen and be near me—you, your children and grandchildren, your flocks and herds, and all you have. [11]I will provide for you there, because five years of famine are still to come. Otherwise you and your household and all who belong to you will become destitute.' [12]"You can see for yourselves, and so can my brother Benjamin, that it is really I who am speaking to you. [13]Tell my father about all the honor accorded me in Egypt and about everything you have seen. And bring my father down here quickly." [14]Then he threw his arms around his brother Benjamin and wept, and Benjamin embraced him, weeping. [15]And he kissed all his brothers and wept over them. Afterward his brothers talked with him.

UNDERSTANDING THE SCRIPTURE

Genesis 42:1-5. The famine about which Pharaoh dreamed, which Joseph foresaw and planned for, came to pass. Its effects were far-reaching and stretched into Canaan.

Joseph's brothers are portrayed as passive in the face of the famine. Jacob had to spur them to act. Declaring that he had heard there were ample stores of grain in Egypt, he told his sons to "go down and buy grain" (42:2).

Only ten of his sons traveled to Egypt. Although it had been at least twenty years since Joseph's "death," Jacob kept Benjamin close to home because he was afraid of losing him.

Genesis 42:6-17. Joseph's brothers arrived in Egypt and eventually found the person in charge, Joseph. At least twenty years had passed since they had last seen Joseph as a seventeen-year-old. The authority seated before them looked and spoke like an Egyptian. The brothers did not recognize Joseph, but he recognized them immediately.

Having "learned" that the brothers were from Canaan and had another brother who had not made the trip with them, Joseph charged them three times with being spies, a charge they loudly denied. Joseph ignored their denials, declaring that the only way to clear their name was for one of them to go home and return to Egypt with their other brother. To give them time to think things over, Joseph then threw them all in prison.

Genesis 42:18-28. Joseph retrieved his brothers from prison after three days but stipulated that one of them must remain behind while the others returned to Canaan to get their "youngest brother" (42:20).

Joseph used an interpreter through which to speak to his brothers. Unaware that he could understand them, the brothers debated whether what was now happening to them was divine justice for what they had done to Joseph twenty years previously. It speaks volumes that, two decades later, that evil deed still retained such a stranglehold on their relationships.

Finally hearing them speak honestly among themselves, Joseph found it difficult to retain an emotional distance from them. Nevertheless, he bound Simeon and had him returned to prison, and sent the other brothers on their way with their grain. Unbeknownst to them, he had their coins with which they had purchased their grain returned to them—a fact they discovered to their dismay when they made camp and retrieved some grain with which to feed their animals.

Genesis 42:29-38. Upon returning home, the brothers told Jacob all that had happened, including why Simeon was not with them and why Benjamin would need to accompany them when they returned to

Egypt. Perhaps Jacob was sympathetic until his sons opened their bags of grain and each discovered his pouch filled with money. At that point, Jacob accused them of tearing the family apart. Reuben's attempted response—he personally would assume responsibility for Benjamin or Jacob could kill his two sons—was heartfelt, but how the murder of two of Jacob's grandsons would help ease the possible loss of Benjamin is unclear.

The scene ended with Jacob resolved not to let Benjamin be taken to Egypt.

Genesis 45:1-2. In the intervening chapters, the brothers returned to Egypt with Benjamin (43:1-15), Simeon was released (43:16-23), the brothers dined with Joseph (43:24-34), they received their grain (44:1-2), and they left for Canaan (44:3) only to be tracked down and accused of stealing Joseph's divining goblet (44:4-6). They denied the charge but the goblet was found in Benjamin's grain bag (44:7-12), forcing the brothers to return to Joseph's house (44:13-15), where Judah offered himself sacrificially in place of Benjamin (44:16-34). Judah's act and words so moved Joseph that he "could no longer control himself" (45:1). When he finally gave vent to his pent-up emotions, Joseph's sobs were so loud they could be heard in "the household of Pharaoh" (45:2), which must have been nearby.

Genesis 45:3. Joseph addressed his brothers in Hebrew, revealed himself to them, and inquired as to Jacob's health. Not surprisingly, the disclosure unnerved Joseph's brothers.

Genesis 45:4-7. Joseph repeated his revelation to his brothers, adding a note (that he alone would know) as to how he ended up in Egypt, and invited them to draw near. Because his self-revelation further troubled (rather than comforted) his brothers, Joseph tried to calm them by declaring that all that happened had occurred by the will of God "to preserve . . . a remnant" (45:7).

Genesis 45:8-13. Joseph reiterated that God, not his brothers, had sent him to Egypt and enabled him to gain a position that would keep alive many survivors. He entreated his brothers to tell Jacob that his son Joseph was held in high honor in Egypt and that he was to move immediately to Goshen. This move would make it easier for Joseph to care for Jacob and his family.

Genesis 45:14-15. Only when Joseph's words gave way to touch and tears were his brothers convinced of all that he had said. Repentance and reconciliation that had waited more than twenty years to come to pass is hinted at in the words "his brothers talked with him" (45:15).

Genesis 45:16-20. Meanwhile, word of the commotion at Joseph's home reached Pharaoh's ears. When he learned of the arrival of Joseph's brothers, Pharaoh sent official word to Joseph to invite his brothers to return to Canaan and to bring their father and their families and return to settle in Egypt. They were not to worry about "possessions, for the best of all the land of Egypt" would be theirs (45:20).

Genesis 45:21-24. As the brothers prepared to return to Canaan, Joseph distributed gifts to each. A special gift of twenty laden donkeys was sent to Jacob.

Genesis 45:25-28. Upon their return to Canaan, the brothers told their aged father that Joseph was alive. Disbelief gave way to belief when Jacob saw the carts arrive. The pathos is thick as Jacob, struggling to come to terms with such good news, could only manage to say, "My son Joseph is still alive" (45:28).

INTERPRETING THE SCRIPTURE

Love One Another

When Joseph caught the first glimpse of his brothers after more than twenty years, he had little reason to believe that the young men who had sold him into slavery had changed much. He tried to hold onto whatever residual anger he felt toward them as he "spoke harshly to them" (Genesis 42:7). But before that first meeting had concluded, Joseph was aware that the foul deed they had committed against him had deeply scarred his brothers and haunted them for two decades (42:21-23). Seeing the hurt they had experienced awakened in him the burning embers of love he still had for his birth family (42:24).

When next Joseph saw his brothers several months later, those burning embers of love were fanned into flame by the unexpected sacrifice of his brother, Judah. When Joseph stated that he intended to enslave Benjamin (44:17), Judah offered himself instead. He explained to Joseph that if they returned home without Benjamin, it would probably cause the death of their aged father, Jacob (44:29, 31).

Generations later, Judah's expression of *agape* love took root and bore fruit in his most celebrated descendant. Showing himself to be a true son of Judah, Jesus—whose birth we celebrated just three weeks ago— told his disciples, "No one has greater love than this, to lay down one's life for one's friends" (John 15:13). A few hours later, he went out and did just that. His example led the apostle John to eventually write, "We know love by this, that he laid down his life for us—and we ought to lay down our lives for one another" (1 John 3:16).

The Power of Forgiveness

One of the central tenets of scriptural Christianity is the power and importance of forgiveness. The act is critical if the church is truly to be a holy family that is able to live together and imitate God's mercy. While there is no one way to forgive, the beliefs we hold about forgiveness do make it easier or more difficult to forgive.

One of the less helpful notions about

forgiveness, a notion that is pervasive in the church today, is the idea that forgiveness follows (rather than precedes) repentance. It isn't always stated that bluntly, of course, but folks who have been wronged will often justify their withholding of forgiveness by saying, "When he repents, I'll forgive him." This belief may well help to explain why repentance and reconciliation are so rarely practiced in local churches today. Joseph illustrated another way.

Joseph reversed the forgiveness/repentance order often followed today. He forgave his brothers first, which provided them both the space and the grace they needed to demonstrate their repentance. That is not to say that he overlooked the wrong they had done to him and "let bygones be bygones." Nor did he pretend it had not happened. Nor did he say, "That's all right; just forget it." To forgive another is not to excuse another. Forgiveness is the acknowledgment that what the other person did or said was indeed inappropriate and hurtful. It is also the decision to not allow the hurtful word or deed to dictate the form that the relationship next takes.

As is usually true when forgiveness is offered, Joseph forced his brothers to face the wrong they had done to him and take responsibility for it. At the same time, he refused to be bound personally by their past action. That is, he refused to let their act dictate how he would treat them. Despite what they had done to him, he remained committed to their well-being. He continued to love them, even if he didn't always like them or what they did to him. And he understood that persons who do wrong are often more bound by the evil deed they commit than are the people they hurt. As a result, more often than not it is the "victim" who holds the key to repentance.

By forcing his brothers to take responsibility for their past act, he placed them under conviction. Once they were willing to acknowledge the inappropriateness of their act, if they wanted reconciliation to happen, they then needed to confess that what they had done was wrong. The act of confession, which is very important, is not yet repentance, however. Repentance, which is more than saying "I'm sorry," is the determination to provide restitution, if possible, for the wrongful act, and to refrain from committing the harmful action in the future. It is the desire to have the relationship with the victim restored and healed.

This is, of course, the order of divine forgiveness and human repentance too. God does not forgive those of us who repent. God forgives us *so that* we can repent. The apostle Paul said it best in his letter to the church in Rome: "Christ died for the ungodly" (Romans 5:6). And in case we didn't quite grasp his meaning, he immediately repeated himself. "God proves his love for us in that while we still were sinners, Christ died for us" (Romans 5:8).

Mama "Nell"

Mama "Nell" is a dearly loved member of one of the churches to which I was appointed as a young pastor. She is a hard worker who can be counted on to carry more than her share of the work in any situation. She also is not afraid to confront the preacher when he needs to be confronted. The word "toleration" is not in her vocabulary. As a result of her willingness to speak directly, I am today a better pastor and a better person.

Several times during the years I was appointed to that church, Mama "Nell" would come to the church office and shut the door behind her. After the first time or two that happened, I knew I was about to "get a talking to." She was never mean about what she said. And, bless her, she never conducted her confrontations publicly in the fellowship hall or in the sanctuary. She was always gracious; she would just corner me in my office.

I don't recall her ever raising her voice at me. She would simply lay out for me what she saw me doing, what she believed was happening, or what she had heard. Then she would pause, effectively giving me the opportunity either to acknowledge the truth of what she had said or to correct her impression of what was going on. I don't recall ever being able to take that second option and correct her; her analysis was typically dead-on.

After I had acknowledged what she had pointed out, Mama "Nell" typically offered a suggestion as to how best to proceed. Sometimes that required offering an apology to someone. Sometimes it required that I either start or stop doing something. Always

it was more than advice she was offering me. By confronting me, Mama "Nell" was loving me. By confronting me, she was forgiving me. She was truly living out the baptismal vows of the church and forcing me to come to terms with how I was not helping (or how I was actually hurting) someone.

Would that we all had a bevy of Mama Nells in our lives to keep us walking faithfully the straight and narrow.

SHARING THE SCRIPTURE

Preparing Our Hearts

Explore this week's devotional reading, found in Psalm 81:1-10. This psalm, which was perhaps originally used for the Feast of Tabernacles, calls people to remember the God of the covenant. Joseph, the subject of today's Bible lesson, is mentioned in verse 5. The people had cried out in distress and God "rescued" them (81:7). God wants the people to listen, but they will not. When have you acted stubbornly before God? What past events did God remind you of to help you recall all that God has done and is able to do for you, even in the midst of distress?

Pray that you and the adult learners will recognize the many blessings of God.

Preparing Our Minds

Study the background Scripture from Genesis 42:1-38; 45:1-28. The lesson Scripture is from Genesis 45:3-15. Think about what faithful people can expect from other faithful people.

Write on newsprint:
❑ information for next week's lesson, found under "Continue the Journey."
❑ activities for further spiritual growth in "Continue the Journey."
Use information from Understanding the Scripture to plan a brief lecture for Genesis

42:1-38 to help the adults put today's lesson in context.

LEADING THE CLASS

(1) Gather to Learn

❖ Welcome the class members and introduce any guests.

❖ Pray that the students will see Joseph's acts of faithfulness as a model for their own lives.

❖ Read this information from http://www.sowingseedsoffaith.com/courage.htm: **Eddie was a talented musician who also had a gift for ministry. He and his wife, Laurie, were the creative force behind a congregation's music program. Suddenly, Eddie was seriously ill due to a parasite in his brain that caused him to lose motor skills and his ability to talk and eat. Eddie was allergic to the one drug that could combat this parasite, so the medical community could offer him no hope. Yet there was also no bitterness on the part of Eddie and his family. Even in his hospital room, the family continues to praise God in song as they support their beloved Eddie.**

❖ Read aloud today's focus statement: **When people are mutually faithful, they support and protect one another. What can faithful people expect from other faithful people? Because Jacob and Joseph were** both faithful to God, God remained faithful to God's promise to Abraham by putting Joseph in a position to save the entire family from death by starvation.

(2) Point Out Joseph's Acts of Faithfulness to God and Family, as Recorded in the Story of Joseph Welcoming His Brothers and Caring for Their Families

❖ Present the brief lecture you have created on background Scripture to set the stage for today's lesson.

❖ Select a volunteer to read Genesis 45:3-15.

❖ Discuss these questions:

(1) **Put yourself in the place of the brothers. What is your first reaction to Joseph's revelation of his identity?**

(2) **Put yourself in Joseph's place. How do you feel about welcoming brothers who have seriously harmed you and even wanted you dead?**

(3) **Put yourself in Joseph's place. How would you feel knowing that your elderly father is still alive and will know that you not only are alive but also have been quite successful?**

(4) **Jacob's family was riddled with conflict, in part because he so strongly favored Joseph, the first-born of his beloved Rachel. Does the conflict continue now that Joseph has identified himself? If not, what has changed? If so, what still needs to change?**

(5) **Do you agree or disagree with Joseph's interpretation of events in terms of God working out all these circumstances as part of a divine plan? Support your position.**

❖ **Option:** Invite at least three volunteers to roleplay a conversation between Joseph and his brothers. Conclude by asking the observers to comment on how this interaction demonstrated God's grace and faithfulness in action.

(3) Experience Mutuality and Its Positive Results in Faithfulness

❖ Read aloud this fictional case study: **Community Church recently had a conflict that caused hard feelings among several members. Adele and Jonathan proposed that the now-vacant parsonage be renovated to use as a shelter for one or two families in need. Zoning regulations would allow for such use, but certain prominent members were highly offended to think that "their" parsonage would become a home for transients. While the Adele/Jonathan coalition argued that such a usage would be in keeping with God's will to care for the vulnerable, other members were very convinced that such people had not lived properly and therefore did not deserve the use of their lovely parsonage.**

❖ Ask: **Suppose you had been asked to serve as a mediator in this dispute. What kinds of alternatives could you suggest to enable the parties to discern and do God's will? What would be your preferred outcome? Why?**

❖ Read "Mama Nell" from Interpreting the Scripture. Encourage the group to talk about how she was able to work mutually with her pastor to bring about positive results for the congregation.

❖ List these attributes on newsprint and consider what role they played in her effectiveness:

■ willingness to work hard.

■ carefulness about stating her concerns in private.

■ speaking rationally in a normal tone of voice.

■ offering opportunities for the pastor to respond.

■ suggesting ideas as to how to proceed.

❖ Spend a few moments contrasting Mama Nell's attributes to those that are sometimes seen in the church. For example, a person who is not willing to work may be the first to complain. Or someone who does not like the way a situation is handled has criticism but not helpful ideas as to how to proceed. Be careful to keep the discussion general by not mentioning any names.

❖ Wrap up by suggesting that the group embrace Mama Nell's attributes and encourage others to do likewise.

(4) Make Mutual Commitments of Faithfulness to God and in the Learners' Families and Communities

❖ Distribute paper and pencils. Assure the students that this activity is "for their eyes only." Suggest that each person think of one family member (or other person close to them) with whom she or he has a broken relationship. Preferably, this person will still be alive, but if there is a deceased person who still holds sway over the student because of past conflicts, suggest that she or he choose this person. Challenge the adults to write a letter to the person selected. In this letter the student is to include:

■ possible reasons for the broken relationship.
■ an assessment of why this break occurred. (Be sure that the adults look at their own responsibility for the problem.)
■ an offer of forgiveness or an apology, or both, for the writer's behavior.

❖ Encourage the adults to edit their letters and rewrite them on nice stationery, and send them, if possible. Point out that even if the recipient is dead or living at an unknown address, the very act of writing to this person can dispel negative emotions. Writing helps to bring clarity to situations, and the writers may even recognize that they had a sizable role to play in creating this broken relationship.

(5) Continue the Journey

❖ Pray that the adults will commit themselves in faithfulness to God, family, and their community.

❖ Read aloud this preparation for next week's lesson. You may also want to post it on newsprint for the students to copy.

■ **Title: Joseph Transmits Abraham's Promise**
■ **Background Scripture: Genesis 50:1-26**
■ **Lesson Scripture: Genesis 50:15-26**
■ **Focus of the Lesson: Even though some people commit acts of faithlessness, they may be overcome by acts of others' faithfulness. Who can forgive acts of faithlessness? Because Jacob and Joseph were both faithful to God, Joseph was able to forgive his brothers' treachery of so many years before.**

❖ Challenge the students to complete one or more of these activities for further spiritual growth related to this week's session. Post this information on newsprint for the students to copy.

(1) **Investigate agencies in your community, including churches, that provide food for hungry people. Assist in whatever you can to enable more people to get the food they need.**

(2) **Work toward reconciliation with a family member, if you are estranged from one. If this person is an adult sibling, be willing to discuss how sibling rivalry played a part in the rupture of your relationship. Do whatever you can to create a new, loving relationship.**

(3) **Research an immigrant population in your area. What factors have prompted these people to leave their homeland? How has your community been a welcoming—or inhospitable—place?**

❖ Sing or read aloud "God Will Take Care of You."

❖ Conclude today's session by leading the class in this benediction: **By the power of the Holy Spirit go forth to be a blessing to others even as God through Christ has blessed you.**

UNIT 2: GOD'S PROTECTION

Joseph Transmits Abraham's Promise

PREVIEWING THE LESSON

Lesson Scripture: Genesis 50:15-26
Background Scripture: Genesis 50:1-26
Key Verse: Genesis 50:20

Focus of the Lesson:

Even though some people commit acts of faithlessness, they may be overcome by acts of others' faithfulness. Who can forgive acts of faithlessness? Because Jacob and Joseph were both faithful to God, Joseph was able to forgive his brothers' treachery of so many years before.

Goals for the Learners:

(1) to observe the acts of faithlessness and faithfulness in the story of Joseph and his treacherous brothers after their father's death.
(2) to realize that acts of faithlessness can be surpassed by later faithfulness.
(3) to find hope in taking corrective actions in unsatisfactory situations.

Pronunciation Guide:

Abel Mizraim (ay buhl miz' ray im)   Machpelah (mak pee' luh)
Atad (ay' tad)   Mamre (mam' ree)
Ephraim (ee' fray im)   Manasseh (muh nas' uh)
Goshen (goh' shuhn)   Shechem (shek' uhm)
Machir or Makir (may' kihr)

Supplies:

Bibles, newsprint and marker, paper and pencils, hymnals

READING THE SCRIPTURE

NRSV

Genesis 50:15-26

15Realizing that their father was dead, Joseph's brothers said, "What if Joseph still bears a grudge against us and pays us back

NIV

Genesis 50:15-26

15When Joseph's brothers saw that their father was dead, they said, "What if Joseph holds a grudge against us and pays us back in full for all the wrong that we did to him?" [16]So they approached Joseph, saying, "Your father gave this instruction before he died, [17]'Say to Joseph: I beg you, forgive the crime of your brothers and the wrong they did in harming you.' Now therefore please forgive the crime of the servants of the God of your father." Joseph wept when they spoke to him. [18]Then his brothers also wept, fell down before him, and said, "We are here as your slaves." [19]But Joseph said to them, "Do not be afraid! Am I in the place of God? [20]**Even though you intended to do harm to me, God intended it for good, in order to preserve a numerous people, as he is doing today.** [21]So have no fear; I myself will provide for you and your little ones." In this way he reassured them, speaking kindly to them.

[22]So Joseph remained in Egypt, he and his father's household; and Joseph lived one hundred ten years. [23]Joseph saw Ephraim's children of the third generation; the children of Machir son of Manasseh were also born on Joseph's knees.

[24]Then Joseph said to his brothers, "I am about to die; but God will surely come to you, and bring you up out of this land to the land that he swore to Abraham, to Isaac, and to Jacob." [25]So Joseph made the Israelites swear, saying, "When God comes to you, you shall carry up my bones from here." [26]And Joseph died, being one hundred ten years old; he was embalmed and placed in a coffin in Egypt.

for all the wrongs we did to him?" [16]So they sent word to Joseph, saying, "Your father left these instructions before he died: [17]'This is what you are to say to Joseph: I ask you to forgive your brothers the sins and the wrongs they committed in treating you so badly.' Now please forgive the sins of the servants of the God of your father." When their message came to him, Joseph wept.

[18]His brothers then came and threw themselves down before him. "We are your slaves," they said.

[19]But Joseph said to them, "Don't be afraid. Am I in the place of God? [20]**You intended to harm me, but God intended it for good to accomplish what is now being done, the saving of many lives.** [21]So then, don't be afraid. I will provide for you and your children." And he reassured them and spoke kindly to them.

[22]Joseph stayed in Egypt, along with all his father's family. He lived a hundred and ten years [23]and saw the third generation of Ephraim's children. Also the children of Makir son of Manasseh were placed at birth on Joseph's knees.

[24]Then Joseph said to his brothers, "I am about to die. But God will surely come to your aid and take you up out of this land to the land he promised on oath to Abraham, Isaac and Jacob." [25]And Joseph made the sons of Israel swear an oath and said, "God will surely come to your aid, and then you must carry my bones up from this place."

[26]So Joseph died at the age of a hundred and ten. And after they embalmed him, he was placed in a coffin in Egypt.

UNDERSTANDING THE SCRIPTURE

Genesis 50:1-3. Genesis 49:33 records the death of Jacob. Joseph acknowledged his father's death with a display of grief that has changed little despite the passage of the centuries.

Jacob was one of two people in the pages

of Scripture who were embalmed. His son, Joseph, was the other (Genesis 50:26). The narrator says that Jacob received the full embalming procedure, which took forty days to complete. That all Egypt mourned Jacob for "seventy days" speaks of the deep friendship that existed between Pharaoh and Joseph.

Genesis 50:4-6. Despite the close relationship Joseph had with Pharaoh, Joseph made his request to bury Jacob in Canaan through intermediaries. He vowed that once he completed the task, he would return. Pharaoh consented readily to Joseph's request.

Genesis 50:7-9. The funeral procession from Goshen to Mamre in Canaan was "very large" (50:9 NIV). It included Joseph's entire family, his brothers, and surviving members of his "father's household," (50:8) as well as many Egyptian dignitaries and heads of state. Curiously, the same members of the Egyptian army who would later pursue Jacob's descendants—"chariots and charioteers" (Genesis 50:9; see also Exodus 14:17, 18)—also accompanied the procession.

Goshen is very likely the area known as Wadi Tumilat, east of the Nile delta region. Archaeological discoveries of slave dwellings at Tell el-Daba, and at Medinet Habu (near Luxor), do not confirm that the Hebrew people lived there but they lend credence to the biblical account.

Genesis 50:10-14. Atad is not mentioned elsewhere in Scripture. Its location cannot be identified any more precisely than somewhere on the western side of the Jordan River, probably south of Mamre. At Atad, Joseph and his family mourned Jacob for seven days, the common length of time for mourning (see 1 Samuel 31:13). The Egyptian members of the funeral procession joined in the rites of mourning, causing local residents to refer to the site as Abel Mizraim, the "mourning of the Egyptians."

When the seven days of mourning were completed, the funeral procession continued on to "the cave of the field at Machpelah, the field near Mamre" (50:13), just north of Hebron. There Jacob was buried next to Abraham (25:9-10) and Sarah (23:10-20), Isaac (35:27-29), Rebekah (49:31), and Leah (49:31).

The burial of Jacob complete, Joseph and his family returned to Egypt.

Genesis 50:15-18. Given the events narrated in Genesis 45, which were discussed in the previous lesson, the concerns of Joseph's brothers seem strange. For more than seventeen years (see Genesis 47:28) they had been the recipients of Joseph's gracious forgiveness of the heinous act they committed when he was a youth (37:18-28). Why were they nervously now desiring Joseph to forgive them?

According to the NIV, the brothers made their request of Joseph through a third party, who informed Joseph that it was their father's wish that he, Joseph, forgive his brothers for "treating you so badly" (50:17). The NRSV, following the wording of the (Greek) Septuagint, makes no mention of messengers; Joseph's brothers speak to him themselves. When he received this request, "Joseph wept" (50:17). Before he had a chance to respond, the brothers arrived and prostrated themselves before him, subjecting themselves to his mercy.

Genesis 50:19-21. Joseph did not do as his brothers requested. That is, he did not forgive them . . . because he did not need to do so. He had already done so years before. Instead of pretending to do something he had already done, Joseph acknowledged the great fear that continued to gnaw at his brothers' consciences and addressed that fear: "Do not be afraid." In fact, he twice told them not to fear (50:19, 21). Joseph then restated the theological meaning he had discovered about the evils he had endured, a meaning he had already shared with his brothers (45:7-8) but which they needed to hear again: "Even though you intended to do harm to me, God intended it for good" (50:20). Finally, Joseph reassured his brothers that the good care they had received from his hand for the previous seventeen years would continue.

Genesis 50:22-23. Joseph lived 110 years, which means he died as a much younger man than Abraham (175; Genesis 25:7), Isaac (180; Genesis 35:28), or Jacob (147; Genesis 47:28). In our culture, a number is normally understood as its face value. There are exceptions to this rule, as for example, "just a second" doesn't mean "one" second but rather a short period of time.

In Scripture, numbers often signify more than their face value. Their symbolic meaning is often as important as or more so than their literal meaning. Such may well be the case here. Several scholars have noted that Abraham's age (175) is equivalent to 7×5^2, Isaac's age (180) is 5×6^2, Jacob's age (147) is 3×7^2, and Joseph's age (110) is $1 \times 5^2 + 6^2 + 7^2$. Writing in *The Book of Genesis, Chapters 18–50*, Victor P. Hamilton asserts: "The years of the patriarchs are formed as square numbers that constitute a succession." Hamilton further argues that Joseph's 110 years would be considered ideal in Egyptian culture, and so Joseph's death brings to a symbolic close the stories of the patriarchs.

Joseph lived long enough to see his great-grandchildren. The phrase "to place on the knees" means that Joseph claimed them as his descendants. Just as Ephraim and Manasseh, Joseph's sons, were adopted by Jacob (Genesis 48:12), so Joseph adopted his great-grandchildren, "the children of Machir son of Manasseh" (50:23).

Genesis 50:24-26. Before he died, Joseph declared that God's covenant promise to the patriarchs was still in effect. The day would come when they would return to Canaan. When they did, he charged his kindred to "carry up my bones from here" (50:25).

At his death, Joseph, like his father, Jacob, was embalmed. Unlike his father, his body was placed in a sarcophagus. Centuries later, when the Hebrew people left Egypt to return to Canaan, they took Joseph's bones with them (Exodus 13:19), which means they carried Joseph's embalmed body with them throughout the forty years they spent in the wilderness. He was eventually buried at Shechem (Joshua 24:32).

INTERPRETING THE SCRIPTURE

With People, This Is Impossible

In 1994, Rwanda was awash in genocidal bloodshed as neighbors turned on each other. Families were rent and entire villages were wiped out. Violence seemed to take on a life of its own. For a season, there was no good news in Rwanda. Or so it seemed.

Over time, however, it became clear that God had not left without witness, even in Rwanda. Over time, good news stepped into the breach, made itself known, and pointed out another way.

By 1995, the killing had mostly stopped, but ethnic tensions remained poised to break out again in renewed violence. Because the violence had been so widespread and involved as many people as it did, it quickly became obvious that the government would never be able to prosecute more than a tiny fraction of the offenders. It was also clear, however, that the country could not simply brush the violence under the rug and attempt to move forward as if nothing had happened. If there was to be any hope of healing the terrible wound the Rwandan population had received, justice needed to be meted out. But if the courts were not the answer, how could they bring justice to bear?

Taking a cue from a previous experiment used so effectively in South Africa following the abolition of apartheid, Rwandan officials instituted a program similar to the Truth and Reconciliation Commission. The premise was simple. Lower village courts, known as Gacaca courts, would allow respected village leaders to hear testimony and assign restitution. Sentences depended on the severity of the crime and whether accused persons readily confessed their complicity.

Church-sponsored ministries, such as Rwanda Partners, have also provided a forum for victims and perpetrators to speak honestly with each other and move toward forgiveness and reconciliation. A stirring compilation of stories, titled "Reconcilable Differences," is available at http://www.christianitytoday.com/ct/2009/june/26.28.html.

Reconciliation is never easy, even when both parties want it to happen, even when both parties are Christians. However, it can and does happen . . . all the time.

Passing the Peace

Growing up, I pitched on a summer baseball team for several years. I wanted to do well, so I practiced the craft daily, regularly pitching two or three hours a day. As is true of most jobs, pitching is a craft that involves precision mechanics, honed skill, learned expertise, ingrained habits, long familiarity with the rules of the craft, and a willingness to be inculcated into the craft. Had I not practiced or taken the role of pitcher seriously, I never would have learned the skills, much less developed the nuances necessary to play the position well.

Like pitching, woodworking, or detailing a car, learning to forgive and practice reconciliation is a craft that requires discipline and practice. How can Christians learn this discipline? Where can we practice it? One place is at home with our family. A second place is at church during the time often referred to as "the peace" or "the passing of the peace."

The act of extending "peace" to other Christians is an ancient liturgical rite based on the instructions of Paul (Romans 16:16; 1 Corinthians 16:20; 2 Corinthians 13:12; 1 Thessalonians 5:26) and Peter (1 Peter 5:14), and linked to Jesus' words to his disciples in John 20:21-23, "Peace be with you" (20:21).

Although the form it takes in some churches is equivalent to a greeting, "the peace" is meant to be the time in a worship service when a congregation practices the craft of forgiveness and reconciliation. That is why its placement in the liturgy is immediately after prayers of confession and words of absolution or pardon. Passing the peace every Sunday teaches us to extend to others the forgiveness we have received from God. It teaches us to take care of hurts and tiffs before they escalate into grudges or open conflict. It teaches us to speak honestly—and hear lovingly—words of mercy and grace. Assuming we learn through practice in worship how to extend and receive words of confession and forgiveness, we will know how to act in a similar way with persons outside of worship.

God's Forgiveness, Our Repentance

After twenty years of preaching in local churches, I am convinced that many Christians today are as uncertain of God's forgiveness as Joseph's brothers were of his forgiveness (Genesis 50:15-17). That is, they act as if it has never been offered them or perhaps was withdrawn. Consequently, they are constantly asking God for it. How is forgiveness good news if God may at any time renege on the offer? The psalmist was certain that "as far as the east is from the west, so far he removed our transgressions from us" (Psalm 103:12). Similarly, how is forgiveness good news if God only stingily shares it with us *after* we have effectively earned it? Paul argued long ago, "Now that we have been justified by his blood, we will be saved through him from the wrath of God. For . . . while we were God's enemies, we were reconciled to God through the death of his Son" (Romans 5:9-10). God's forgiveness never has been contingent on us first cleaning ourselves up enough to be worthy of receiving it.

The good news that the church has consistently proclaimed for centuries, the good news that we have received, is not that God *can* forgive our sin but that God *has already* forgiven our sin. Scripture is clear that our sins were forgiven two thousand years ago when Jesus died on the cross (John 3:16).

That is the radical meaning of the atonement and the incredible good news we rejoice in. It is also the gospel proclamation we joyfully sing in hymns such as "Come, Sinners, to the Gospel Feast" ("for God hath bid all humankind"), "Sinners, Turn: Why Will Ye Die" ("he hath brought to all the race full salvation by his grace"), or "Blow Ye the Trumpet, Blow" ("Jesus, our great high priest, hath full atonement made").

Indeed, through the atoning death of Jesus at Calvary, we believe that God has forgiven every human being who has ever lived or who will ever live. There is no such thing as an unforgiven human being. All have sinned, yes (Romans 3:23), but all are forgiven, too (1 John 2:12).

This is not to declare a version of universal salvation. It is to declare the wonder of universal grace. That is to say, while all human beings have been forgiven, not all persons have elected to receive God's offer of forgiveness as good news. Some persons have openly rejected it. But that is an entirely different matter. These persons may not appreciate God's forgiveness. Nor will they receive any eternal benefit from it. But that does not change the fact that they remain forgiven.

There are many Christians today who think they must request God's forgiveness again and again because it is contingent on their repentance (see the lesson for January 15), even though that belief reverses the biblical order of atonement and forgiveness preceding repentance. More serious, however, is the fact that some people try to sidestep their own continual need to repent by instead speaking of God's continual need to forgive.

SHARING THE SCRIPTURE

Preparing Our Hearts

Explore this week's devotional reading, found in Deuteronomy 7:6-11. God loves Israel and keeps covenant loyalty with those who love God and keep divine commandments. They are God's "treasured possession" (7:6). How do you see yourself as treasured by God? What does God's sending of Jesus into the world say about God's love for you and desire to be in a relationship with you? Meditate on these questions and give thanks to God for Jesus.

Pray that you and the adult learners will recognize and give thanks for God's covenant promises to them.

Preparing Our Minds

Study the background Scripture from Genesis 50:1-26 and the lesson Scripture from Genesis 50:15-26. Think about how and why someone would forgive acts of faithlessness.

Write on newsprint:
❑ information for next week's lesson, found under "Continue the Journey."
❑ activities for further spiritual growth in "Continue the Journey."

Prepare the suggested lecture for the section titled "Observe the Acts of Faithlessness and Faithfulness in the Story of Joseph and His Treacherous Brothers After Their Father's Death."

LEADING THE CLASS

(1) Gather to Learn

❖ Welcome the class members and introduce any guests.

❖ Pray that the students will be aware of acts of faithlessness and how they can counter and forgive such acts.

❖ Read this story taken from "Reconcilable Differences" by Mark Moring that appeared in the June 2009 issue of *Christianity Today*: **During the horrific genocide in Rwanda in 1994, friends and neighbors Felicita Mukabakunda and Marc Sahabo suddenly became bitter enemies when Sahabo killed her father, uncle, and four other family members. Sahabo fled the country but was later returned, arrested, and jailed for seven years. After his release, Sahabo was invited to attend a reconciliation workshop where he reports: "My heart was changed by Jesus. I wanted to ask the victims for forgiveness." Mukabakunda resisted attending such a workshop, but finally decided it was time. When Sahabo confessed his crimes on bended knees to her, Mukabakunda laid her hand on his shoulder and while looking him in the eyes said, "I forgive you."**

❖ Ask: **Where do people find the strength and courage to offer such forgiveness?**

❖ Read aloud today's focus statement: **Even though some people commit acts of faithlessness, they may be overcome by acts of others' faithfulness. Who can forgive acts of faithlessness? Because Jacob and Joseph were both faithful to God, Joseph was able to forgive his brothers' treachery of so many years before.**

(2) Observe the Acts of Faithlessness and Faithfulness in the Story of Joseph and His Treacherous Brothers After Their Father's Death

❖ Present the lecture you have prepared, based on Genesis 50:1-3, 4-6, 7-9, 10-14 in Understanding the Scripture. Your purpose is to set the context for today's lesson.

❖ Choose volunteers to read the parts of the narrator, Joseph, and at least two of Joseph's brothers. Read Genesis 50:15-26 as a drama.

❖ Select four volunteers to roleplay a discussion among Joseph's brothers prior to their meeting with him. Suggest that they

address these two questions in particular: What are their fears? Why are they so concerned, given all that Joseph has done for them and their families?

❖ Choose four other volunteers to role-play another conversation as Joseph's brothers after they have heard what he had to say. Suggest that they address these questions: What surprised them about their brother Joseph's speech? How has he changed from the upstart dreamer that they remember? How have they changed?

❖ Conclude this portion of the session by using material from Understanding the Scripture to clarify the meaning of Genesis 50:22-23, 24-26.

(3) Realize That Acts of Faithlessness Can Be Surpassed by Later Faithfulness

❖ Recall that although Joseph's brothers acted faithlessly toward him, Joseph later was faithful to them. In retrospect, Joseph had realized that God had a larger plan for his life that came to fruition as a result of his brothers' acts of betrayal.

❖ Invite the adults to tell stories in small groups about similar encounters they have had. Have they ever felt betrayed by someone, only to later demonstrate God's goodness and forgiveness to this person? The stories need not be very detailed, and the students should not name names. Here is an example: **I had a friend who betrayed me by telling others about a personal situation that I had told to her (or him) in strictest confidence. Our friendship ended for some time when the gossip got back to me, but when I heard that she (or he) was seriously ill, I knew I needed to reach out and offer forgiveness in the hope that we could be reconciled. I am still reticent about sharing confidential information with anyone, but we are working to rebuild our previously close friendship.**

❖ Conclude by reading "With People, This Is Impossible" from Interpreting the Scripture. Talk about how the acts of faithlessness here were later surpassed by faithfulness.

(4) Find Hope in Taking Corrective Actions in Unsatisfactory Situations

❖ Read the following scenarios, as time permits. Encourage the adults to finish them in a way that would be pleasing to God.

■ **Scenario 1: A professional colleague has been assisting you on a project. You have done the lion's share of the work, but she has let on to everyone that these ideas are hers and that you have helped her to implement them. When it comes time for a raise, you hear that she has gotten one, but you did not. What can you do to let her know how you feel? Are you willing to offer forgiveness? If so, how will you approach that conversation?**

■ **Scenario 2: Your teenager was riding in the car with another teenage driver who decided to show off for his carload of friends. Tragically, he veered off the road, striking a telephone pole. His injuries were minor, but your child was left paralyzed. Are you willing to offer forgiveness? If so, how will you approach that conversation?**

❖ Distribute paper and pencils. Provide a few moments of quiet time for the adults to think about any corrective actions they need to take in a difficult situation facing them. Some adults may choose to write their thoughts, but these are not to be shared aloud.

(5) Continue the Journey

❖ Break the silence by praying that the adults will freely offer forgiveness to, and willingly receive forgiveness from, those with whom they have a severed relationship.

❖ Read aloud this preparation for next week's lesson. You may also want to post it on newsprint for the students to copy.

■ **Title: Out of Egypt**
■ **Background Scripture: Exodus 1:8-14; 15:1-27**
■ **Lesson Scripture: Exodus 15:1-3, 19, 22-26**
■ **Focus of the Lesson: People will often follow a trusted leader even into dangerous places. What inspires such trust? Because Moses had faith in God, the Israelites followed him into the Red Sea, where God saved them from the Egyptians and from drowning.**

❖ Challenge the students to complete one or more of these activities for further spiritual growth related to this week's session. Post this information on newsprint for the students to copy.

(1) **Offer forgiveness to someone you have wronged. If possible, do something tangible to make restitution.**

(2) **Recall that Joseph's brothers imagined the worst after Jacob died, even though Joseph had cared for his brothers and their families. When have you imagined the worst only to discover that God was in charge and that what you dreaded did not come to pass? How did that incident affect your outlook?**

(3) **Recall that Joseph made preparations so that he could be buried in the Promised Land. What preparations have you made for your own bodily remains? Have you expressed your wishes to your family? If not, do so as soon as possible.**

❖ Sing or read aloud "This Is a Day of New Beginnings."

❖ Conclude today's session by leading the class in this benediction: **By the power of the Holy Spirit go forth to be a blessing to others even as God through Christ has blessed you.**

UNIT 2: GOD'S PROTECTION
OUT OF EGYPT

PREVIEWING THE LESSON

Lesson Scripture: Exodus 15:1-3, 19, 22-26
Background Scripture: Exodus 1:8-14; 15:1-27
Key Verse: Exodus 15:19

Focus of the Lesson:
People will often follow a trusted leader even into dangerous places. What inspires such trust? Because Moses had faith in God, the Israelites followed him into the Red Sea, where God saved them from the Egyptians and from drowning.

Goals for the Learners:
(1) to investigate the story of the Israelites' dangerous journey of faith through the Red Sea and into the wilderness.
(2) to recognize that faithfulness will not always keep them out of danger, but it will ultimately bring them to safety.
(3) to find strategies to remain faithful when times and situations are difficult or perilous.

Pronunciation Guide:
Elim (ee' lim)
Marah (mair' uh)
Meribah (mer' i bah)
Noadiah (noh uh di' uh)
Pithom (pi' thom)

Rameses (ram' uh seez)
Seti (se' ti)
Shur (shoor)
Thutmose (thyoot' mohs)

Supplies:
Bibles, newsprint and marker, paper and pencils, hymnals

READING THE SCRIPTURE

NRSV
Exodus 15:1-3, 19, 22-26
  ¹Then Moses and the Israelites sang this song to the LORD:

NIV
Exodus 15:1-3, 19, 22-26
  ¹Then Moses and the Israelites sang this song to the LORD:

"I will sing to the LORD, for he has
　triumphed gloriously;
　horse and rider he has thrown into
　the sea.
2　The LORD is my strength and my might,
　and he has become my salvation;
　this is my God, and I will praise him,
　my father's God, and I will exalt him.
3　The LORD is a warrior;
　the LORD is his name."

19When the horses of Pharaoh with his
chariots and his chariot drivers went into the
sea, the LORD brought back the waters of the
sea upon them; **but the Israelites walked
through the sea on dry ground.**

22Then Moses ordered Israel to set out
from the Red Sea, and they went into the
wilderness of Shur. They went three days in
the wilderness and found no water. 23When
they came to Marah, they could not drink
the water of Marah because it was bitter.
That is why it was called Marah. 24And the
people complained against Moses, saying,
"What shall we drink?" 25He cried out to the
LORD; and the LORD showed him a piece of
wood; he threw it into the water, and the
water became sweet.

There the LORD made for them a statute
and an ordinance and there he put them to
the test. 26He said, "If you will listen carefully to the voice of the LORD your God, and
do what is right in his sight, and give heed
to his commandments and keep all his
statutes, I will not bring upon you any of the
diseases that I brought upon the Egyptians;
for I am the LORD who heals you."

"I will sing to the LORD,
　for he is highly exalted.
The horse and its rider
　he has hurled into the sea.
2The LORD is my strength and my song;
　he has become my salvation.
He is my God, and I will praise him,
　my father's God, and I will exalt him.
3The LORD is a warrior;
　the LORD is his name."

19When Pharaoh's horses, chariots and
horsemen went into the sea, the LORD
brought the waters of the sea back over
them, **but the Israelites walked through the
sea on dry ground.**

22Then Moses led Israel from the Red Sea
and they went into the Desert of Shur. For
three days they traveled in the desert without finding water. 23When they came to
Marah, they could not drink its water
because it was bitter. (That is why the place
is called Marah.) 24So the people grumbled
against Moses, saying, "What are we to
drink?"

25Then Moses cried out to the LORD, and
the LORD showed him a piece of wood. He
threw it into the water, and the water
became sweet.

There the LORD made a decree and a law
for them, and there he tested them. 26He
said, "If you listen carefully to the voice of
the LORD your God and do what is right in
his eyes, if you pay attention to his commands and keep all his decrees, I will not
bring on you any of the diseases I brought
on the Egyptians, for I am the LORD, who
heals you."

UNDERSTANDING THE SCRIPTURE

Exodus 1:8. Over time, political realities
change in countries. Such was the case with
the dynasties in Egypt. Unfortunately, since
the pharaohs are not given names in the
Pentateuch, it is not possible to know which

pharaoh or even which dynasty was in
power at this time.

Working backward from the date given
in 1 Kings 6:1, it is possible that the
Eighteenth Dynasty was in power. If so, the

pharaoh is probably Thutmose III (1479 B.C.–1425 B.C.). On the other hand, the name of the store cities in Exodus 1:11 leads some scholars to believe that the Nineteenth Dynasty was in power. If so, the pharaoh is probably Seti I (1294 B.C.–1279 B.C.).

Exodus 1:9-10. Unlike the pharaoh who discerned the hand of God on Joseph's life, this pharaoh was unable to see God at work in the faithfulness of the Hebrews. Whereas he saw only a rapidly growing population of resident aliens, the Hebrew people were merely expressing their faithfulness (see Exodus 1:7) to God's creation order to "be fruitful and multiply" (Genesis 1:28)—a command God subsequently renewed with Noah (Genesis 9:1) and Jacob (Genesis 35:11).

Exodus 1:11. To counter the perceived threat of the Hebrew people, Pharaoh enslaved them. They were put to work in the Nile Delta erecting buildings at Pithom and Rameses. While the general location of these two "store cities" in the Wadi Tumilat area is certain, their exact location remains unknown.

Exodus 1:12-14. Despite their change in civic status, the Hebrew people continued to be faithful to God's command: "They multiplied and spread" (Exodus 1:12). The inability of the government to break the will or the faithfulness of the Hebrew people frustrated the Egyptians, and they redoubled their efforts to make life miserable for the Hebrews. The Hebrews were forced to work in urban settings as common day laborers ("mortar and brick") and in rural/agricultural settings as farm hands ("field labor").

Exodus 15:1. From its opening words, the song in 15:1-18 is focused on God. It praises God for defeating the mighty Egyptian army that had pursued the fleeing Hebrew people and caught up with them at the Red Sea. For the narration of this event, see Exodus 13:17–14:31. There are at least twenty references to the Red Sea crossing scattered throughout the Old Testament. Most are in

Exodus, Numbers, Deuteronomy, and Joshua but they are also found in other books, such as Psalms (106; 136).

The site of the Red Sea crossing is traditionally identified with the northern tip of the Gulf of Suez, although many persons make a case for it being through the "Reed Sea." These persons link the Reed Sea with the Bitter Lakes area (north of the Gulf of Suez, near Lake Timsah) or with Lake Sirbonis, a swampy region near the Mediterranean Sea. Still others, believing Mount Sinai to be in Saudi Arabia, place the crossing through the Gulf of Aqaba.

Exodus 15:2-12. As in Hebrew poetry generally, each verse of this song is a couplet or a pair of couplets. The first line of each couplet states an idea that is then repeated, deepened, or advanced in the second line using different words.

In verse after verse, God is praised for being "a warrior" who came to the defense of the Hebrew people. Mighty Egypt "boasted" of all it would do to the Hebrews (15:9 NIV). But Egypt failed to factor in God, who snorted in derision at its hollow threats. The Egyptian army subsequently disappeared like so much chaff in the wind.

Exodus 15:13-18. In the second half of the song the focus shifts from the strength God exercised on behalf of the Hebrews to the steadfast, "unfailing" (15:13 NIV) love God displayed toward them.

Four of Israel's traditional enemies are named anachronistically in verses 14-15. Philistia, home of the sea people who settled along the Mediterranean coast, was west of Judah. It would eventually give its name to the land of Canaan (Philistine → Palestine). Edom, home of the descendants of Esau (Genesis 25:30; 36:8-9), was south of Judah. Moab, home of the descendants of Lot (Genesis 19:36-37), was east of the Jordan River. Canaan referred to the land of the people who populated Judah and Israel prior to the arrival of the Hebrews.

Exodus 15:19-21. Moses' sister is mentioned in Exodus 2:4, but this is the only place Miriam is named in the book of Exodus. She was the eldest, Aaron was the second child, and Moses the third. Exodus 7:7 tells us that Aaron was three years older than Moses, but we cannot be sure of Miriam's exact age. She died a few months before they did, just as the wilderness journey was drawing to a close (Numbers 20:1). Like her brother Moses, Miriam was a "prophet" (15:20), one of five female prophets in the Old Testament. The others are Deborah (Judges 4:4), Isaiah's wife (Isaiah 8:3), Hulda (2 Kings 22:14), and Noadiah (Nehemiah 6:14).

Exodus 15:22-24. The Desert of Shur, which means "fortress" or "wall," was a wilderness in the (probably northern) Sinai Peninsula, just east of the Egyptian border. Having spent forty years in the general vicinity tending sheep for his father-in-law (Exodus 3:1), Moses would have known the location of watering holes along the roads that traversed the peninsula. Three days after leaving the Red Sea, the Hebrew people arrived at this site ready to replenish their water skins, only to discover that the water was *marah*, "bitter."

As is often seen during the sojourn in the wilderness, the people "complain," "grumble," or "murmur" (see, for example, Exodus 16:2; 17:3; Numbers 14:2). The Hebrew word used often in connection with the complaints voiced in the wilderness refers not to a negative comment but rather describes a rebellion against God.

Exodus 15:25-26. While the piece of wood that Moses threw into the water may have functioned as a natural filtering device, the point is probably theological (God's providential care of the people), not scientific (how it worked).

For God's testing of the people, see the lesson for December 18. The Hebrew people tested God at Meribah (Exodus 17:1-7), but the psalmist later declared that it was God who tested them at Meribah (Psalm 81:7).

Exodus 15:27. Elim, a lush oasis with multiple springs and palm trees, has traditionally been identified with the Wadi Gharandel, about sixty miles southeast of the Suez.

INTERPRETING THE SCRIPTURE

The Red Sea Crossing

For Christians, the biblical salvation story is the story of Jesus' passion and resurrection. We understand Jesus' arrest and beating and subsequent crucifixion as the event when God acted decisively on behalf of human beings to defeat evil. It is not, however, the only salvation story in the Bible.

For Jews, the biblical salvation story is the story of the Exodus of the Hebrew people from Egypt. They understand the plagues, the flight from Egypt, and the destruction of Egypt's army at the Red Sea as the events when God acted decisively on their behalf (see Exodus 2:24-25).

While God's salvation is celebrated in Exodus 15, it is in Exodus 13:17–14:31 that the story is told of the Hebrew people's dangerous journey of faith that ultimately led them through the Red Sea. The story is told in six parts.

In part one (Exodus 13:17–14:4), God's master plan is unveiled. Knowing the strengths and weaknesses of both the Hebrews and the Egyptians, God plotted a course designed to protect his people.

In part two (Exodus 14:5-9), Egypt's counterassault against the Hebrews is unveiled. However, nestled in the midst of Egypt's strategy is the statement that God was aware of their intentions and actively working on behalf of the Hebrew people (14:8).

In part three (Exodus 14:10-12), the initial response of the Hebrews is to cry out in great fear. Their relationship with God had not yet matured to the point that they were willing to trust God.

In part four (Exodus 14:13-14), the Hebrews learn that, with God on their side, they need no longer fear. God truly is faithful to "Israel . . . my firstborn son" (Exodus 4:22).

In part five (Exodus 14:15-18), a plan of action is adopted that will (1) rescue the Hebrew people, (2) glorify God, and (3) reveal to Egypt who the one, true God is.

In part six (Exodus 14:19-31), the actual crossing of the Red Sea by the Hebrews and the destruction of the Egyptian army is narrated.

This momentous event is celebrated by Moses in Exodus 15:1-19. There he sings a song of praise for God's amazing deeds that enabled the Hebrew people to escape their oppressors.

Faith Development

Rarely do shortcuts pay off. This is as true of our relationship with God as it is of life generally. Cutting corners is not the way to build vital trust. Nor is there anything about the Christian faith to suggest that our relationship with God secures for us a privileged position free of trouble or heartache. The Hebrew people discovered these facts immediately upon leaving Egypt.

As they marched out of Egypt with the spoils of Egypt under their arms (Exodus 12:36), there were undoubtedly many persons who thought all their problems were solved. Yet only days later, the Hebrews realized they were being pursued by Egypt's army, which caught up with them and pinned them down with their backs to the Red Sea.

No sooner were the Hebrew people miraculously saved from Egypt's army and again on their way to Canaan than they hit a "wall" in the Desert of Shur. (The Hebrew word *Shur* means "wall.") Then they had

nothing to drink. Then they had nothing to eat (Exodus 16:3). Then they were attacked by bands of marauding Amalekites (Exodus 17:8). So it went.

There were, of course, more direct routes that ran between Egypt and Canaan than the one the Hebrew people took. While the northern route that ran along the Mediterranean coast would have seemed very attractive to Hebrew slaves who wanted to move as quickly as possible from point A to point B, it was also heavily fortified by at least twelve Egyptian strongholds. Had they taken this route, they would have been overwhelmed militarily.

As it was, God led them by a circuitous route that did not promise speed; it promised God's providential oversight and protection (see Exodus 14:1-4). Along the way, they then had opportunity after opportunity to learn how God would care for them daily, sustaining them in situations that were beyond them.

Like the Hebrew people who "hit a wall," Jesus faced similar crises in his faith. No sooner was he baptized than he was forced to endure severe temptation that tested his resolve to rely on God (Matthew 4:1-11; Luke 4:1-13).

We, too, quickly discover that a change in our relationship with God does not magically solve other crises we are facing in life. If anything, the struggles we face tend to intensify in the weeks and months following the faith commitment we enter into with God in Jesus Christ.

We do young Christians a terrible disservice when we suggest that coming to Jesus will solve their problems. We would be more honest if we were to alert them that spiritual attack often follows on the heels of one's conversion.

Yet seeing the Christian faith as a long journey from one faith crisis to the next is only one way to view it. It is much more helpful to exercise humble trust that the same God who sought us out will providentially see us through the situations we face in life. Isn't this the mature witness of the psalmist in Psalm 23?

Marah and Faith

John Wesley liked to say that God's salvation produces in us a relative change before it produces a real change. That was his way of explaining the difference between justification (being made right with God) and sanctification (becoming the holy one God intended each of us to be). When persons are justified, the way they relate to God changes. Whereas previously their relationship with God was marked by enmity and strife, now it is built on love and friendship. When persons are sanctified, they themselves become different. They are no longer the people they once were.

On the far side of the Red Sea, the Hebrew people found themselves the recipients of a new relationship with God. However, they themselves were not yet new people. They still were as they had always been. So when they discovered that the defeat of the Egyptian army was not the last of their problems, they acted as they always had. They quickly grew frustrated and blamed Moses for the bitter situation they now found themselves in (Exodus 14:10-12).

God's response to the lack of gratitude displayed by the Hebrew people was once again gracious yet pointed (Exodus 15:22-26). It was gracious in that God made clear that Yahweh is the God who sees and provides (see Lesson 3; Genesis 22:14). God told Moses that he could fix the problem by throwing a tree limb into the watering hole. It was pointed in that God told the people that they could not stay as they had been. God then "put them to the test" (15:25) with four conditions. Henceforth, according to verse 26, they needed to (1) "listen carefully" to God; (2) do what God deems righteous; (3) heed God's commands; and (4) keep all God's decrees. In short, God told the Hebrew people, "Trust me."

Entering into a saving relationship with God typically has little noticeable effect on the type of situations we find ourselves in. However, it is important to understand that God does not foist bitter, Marah situations on us. We can recognize that in these Marah situations God is faithful to lead us through. The test itself is not the bitter situation; the test is our response to the bitter situation. Shall we or shall we not trust God to see us through?

SHARING THE SCRIPTURE

Preparing Our Hearts

Explore this week's devotional reading, found in Psalm 77:11-20. As the psalmist remembers God's deeds, he recalls that Moses followed God's directions to lead the Hebrew people safely across the Red Sea. The psalmist describes a furious storm that blew up, allowing a path through the waters to open for the fleeing slaves. When in your life has God made a way when there seemed to be no way? What paths has God cleared for you, when all you could see was a brick wall in front of and behind you?

Pray that you and the adult learners will follow leaders whom you believe are acting under the direction of God.

Preparing Our Minds

Study the background Scripture from Exodus 1:8-14; 15:1-27. The lesson Scripture is found in Exodus 15:1-3, 19, 22-26. Ponder what prompts people to follow a trusted leader even into a dangerous place.

Write on newsprint:
❏ information for next week's lesson, found under "Continue the Journey."
❏ activities for further spiritual growth in "Continue the Journey."
Familiarize yourself with the segments from Understanding the Scripture and Interpreting the Scripture that you are asked to share.

LEADING THE CLASS

(1) Gather to Learn

❖ Welcome the class members and introduce any guests.

❖ Pray that the students will recognize that our faith journeys sometimes lead us into dangerous places.

❖ Ask the class to identify characteristics of leaders they can trust and list their ideas on newsprint. Here are some possible answers: *integrity* (what the leader says and does match); *consistency* (people know what to expect); *courage* (willingness to stand firm in the face of difficult situations and unfair criticism); *motivation* (wanting to serve others, not being out for themselves); *wisdom* (ability to lead with discernment); *credibility* (acting in ways that are authentic and believable); *reliability* (will do what they promise to do when they promise to do it); *communication* (ability to converse well and truthfully with others so that everyone understands); *vision* (ability to see the big picture and lead people in that direction).

❖ Discuss for a few moments why people who have such characteristics inspire trust.

❖ Read aloud today's focus statement: **People will often follow a trusted leader even into dangerous places. What inspires such trust? Because Moses had faith in God, the Israelites followed him into the Red Sea, where God saved them from the Egyptians and from drowning.**

(2) Investigate the Story of the Israelites' Dangerous Journey of Faith Through the Red Sea and into the Wilderness

❖ Use information from "The Red Sea Crossing" in Interpreting the Scripture to set the context for today's lesson.

❖ Choose a volunteer to read Exodus 15:1-3, 19.

❖ Discuss these questions:
   (1) What do you learn about God?
   (2) What do you learn about Moses' relationship with God?
   (3) What new insights do you gain about God's activity on behalf of the people?
   (4) What questions does this passage raise for you?

❖ Select another volunteer to read Exodus 15:22-26.

❖ Read or retell information pertaining to these verses from Understanding the Scripture.

❖ Consider these questions. Refer to "Marah and Faith" in Interpreting the Scripture to augment the discussion.
   (1) What do you learn about the Hebrew people?
   (2) In what ways are we like them?
   (3) Where do you see evidence of God's grace?
   (4) What are the four conditions that would allow the people to pass God's test? (See Exodus 15:26.)
   (5) What will happen if the people pass the test? (They will not face the diseases that came upon the Egyptians.)

(3) Recognize That Faithfulness Will Not Always Keep the Learners Out of Danger, but It Will Ultimately Bring Them to Safety

❖ Read paragraphs six through nine from "Faith Development" in Interpreting the Scripture.

❖ Read again these sentences: **Yet seeing the Christian faith as a long journey from** one faith crisis to the next is only one way to view it. It is much more helpful to exercise humble trust that the same God who sought us out will providentially see us through the situations we face in life.

❖ Form several small groups. Invite the students to talk in their groups about times when the God who sought them out also saw them through a challenging situation.

❖ Call everyone together and ask: **As you listened to these stories, what conclusions can you draw about the relationship of faith to difficult, perhaps dangerous, situations?**

❖ Provide a few moments of quiet time for the learners to reflect on difficult situations that currently confront them or someone dear to them. Suggest that they offer prayer for faith to trust that God will see them through.

❖ Break the silence by reading today's key verse, Exodus 15:19, which gives us assurance that just as the escaping slaves walked on dry ground to flee their enemies, so too God makes available a way for us to deal with the Red Sea crises of our own lives.

(4) Find Strategies to Remain Faithful When Times and Situations Are Difficult or Perilous

❖ Encourage the students to turn to Hebrews 11 in their Bibles and read this chapter silently.

❖ List on newsprint the names of at least some of the faithful ones mentioned here.

❖ Encourage the adults to comment on reasons why each person is commended. Point out that these figures all faced stressful situations, many of which involved matters of life and death.

❖ Ask: **Knowing what you do about the individuals we have listed, what do you think enabled them to remain faithful even in death-defying circumstances?** You may wish to list these ideas on newsprint.

❖ Distribute paper and pencils. Invite the adults to review the list of ideas they have generated and select the ones they

believe would help them remain faithful in a difficult situation, particularly those that currently confront them.

(5) Continue the Journey

❖ Pray that the adults will remain faithful even in difficult circumstances.

❖ Read aloud this preparation for next week's lesson. You may also want to post it on newsprint for the students to copy.

■ **Title: Justified by Faith in Christ**
■ **Background Scripture: Galatians 1:1–2:21**
■ **Lesson Scripture: Galatians 2:15-21**
■ **Focus of the Lesson: People yearn to follow someone who can help them connect with God. In whom can we put our faith to achieve this goal? Paul taught that through his death and resurrection Jesus is able to make those who have faith in him right with God.**

❖ Challenge the students to complete one or more of these activities for further spiritual growth related to this week's session. Post this information on newsprint for the students to copy.

(1) **Write a song or poem commemorating something that God has done in your life.**

(2) **Look up "warrior" in an NRSV or NIV concordance. Select references that relate to God, including Exodus 15:3. What can you learn about the role and nature of God from this research?**

(3) **Tell good news to someone who needs to hear that God is a deliverer who cares for us even in seemingly impossible situations.**

❖ Sing or read aloud "O Mary, Don't You Weep."

❖ Conclude today's session by leading the class in this benediction: **By the power of the Holy Spirit go forth to be a blessing to others even as God through Christ has blessed you.**

UNIT 3: GOD'S REDEMPTION
Justified by Faith in Christ

PREVIEWING THE LESSON

Lesson Scripture: Galatians 2:15-21
Background Scripture: Galatians 1:1–2:21
Key Verses: Galatians 2:19-20 (NRSV); 2:20 (NIV)

Focus of the Lesson:
People yearn to follow someone who can help them connect with God. In whom can we put our faith to achieve this goal? Paul taught that through his death and resurrection Jesus is able to make those who have faith in him right with God.

Goals for the Learners:
(1) to listen to Paul's argument against salvation by works.
(2) to identify their perspective on the relationship between salvation and works.
(3) to confirm and deepen their faith in Jesus Christ as Savior.

Pronunciation Guide:
Barnabas (bahr' nuh buhs)
Cephas (see' fuhs)
Tiberius (ti bihr' ee uhs)

Supplies:
Bibles, newsprint and marker, paper and pencils, hymnals

READING THE SCRIPTURE

NRSV
Galatians 2:15-21

15We ourselves are Jews by birth and not Gentile sinners; 16yet we know that a person is justified not by the works of the law but through faith in Jesus Christ. And we have come to believe in Christ Jesus, so that we might be justified by faith in Christ, and not by doing the works of the law, because no

NIV
Galatians 2:15-21

15"We who are Jews by birth and not 'Gentile sinners' 16know that a man is not justified by observing the law, but by faith in Jesus Christ. So we, too, have put our faith in Christ Jesus that we may be justified by faith in Christ and not by observing the law, because by observing the law no one will be justified.

one will be justified by the works of the law. [17]But if, in our effort to be justified in Christ, we ourselves have been found to be sinners, is Christ then a servant of sin? Certainly not! [18]But if I build up again the very things that I once tore down, then I demonstrate that I am a transgressor. [19]For through the law I died to the law, so that I might live to God. **I have been crucified with Christ; [20]and it is no longer I who live, but it is Christ who lives in me. And the life I now live in the flesh I live by faith in the Son of God, who loved me and gave himself for me.** [21]I do not nullify the grace of God; for if justification comes through the law, then Christ died for nothing.

[17]"If, while we seek to be justified in Christ, it becomes evident that we ourselves are sinners, does that mean that Christ promotes sin? Absolutely not! [18]If I rebuild what I destroyed, I prove that I am a lawbreaker. [19]For through the law I died to the law so that I might live for God. **[20]I have been crucified with Christ and I no longer live, but Christ lives in me. The life I live in the body, I live by faith in the Son of God, who loved me and gave himself for me.** [21]I do not set aside the grace of God, for if righteousness could be gained through the law, Christ died for nothing!"

UNDERSTANDING THE SCRIPTURE

Galatians 1:1-5. His apostleship and the gospel he preached being seriously questioned, Paul began this letter with a defense of the gospel. New life, he said, is found only in Jesus Christ, "who gave himself for our sins" (1:4).

Galatians 1:6-10. Paul broached in passing the purpose of his letter in these verses. Christians in Galatia were beginning to follow presentations of the gospel other than that preached by Paul while he was among them. Paul was so certain that these alternative presentations of the gospel were perversions of the one, true faith that he declared that their proponents should be under God's curse.

Galatians 1:11-12. Unlike the alternative gospels being taught by others in Galatia, the gospel Paul preached was the real thing. He didn't dream it up nor was he taught it. It came "through a revelation of Jesus Christ" (1:12) himself.

Galatians 1:13-17. This was a startling development that no one could have predicted, least of all Paul himself, who was "zealous for the traditions of [his] ancestors" (1:14). But such is the mystery that

God should reorient the thinking of one such as Paul. Coming to terms with his new beliefs took time, however. Like Elijah before him, Paul sojourned for a time in the wilderness of Arabia.

Galatians 1:18-24. Eventually, Paul felt that he should speak to church leaders, such as Cephas and James, the Lord's brother, which he did. Then he returned to the province where he was reared as a child.

Galatians 2:1-5. After years in seclusion, during which time Paul honed his understanding of the gospel that he had begun preaching "among the Gentiles" (2:2), he consented to let church leaders in Jerusalem weigh in on his new way of thinking.

Galatians 2:6-10. After listening to Paul describe the gospel message he preached to Gentiles, church leaders in Jerusalem affirmed his preaching and his calling. As was true of Peter's preaching among Jews, Paul's preaching among Gentiles was deemed a fruitful, God-ordained ministry. Church leaders encouraged Paul to continue as he was doing, noting only that he should "remember the poor," which Paul was quite "eager to do" (2:10).

Galatians 2:11-14. Paul was dumbfounded by a sad incident that then unfolded in Syrian Antioch. In a robust expression of the freedom we receive in Christ, Cephas (Peter) was mixing freely with Gentiles and eating with them. But when word arrived that some observers sent by James, the Lord's brother, were coming to Antioch, Cephas suddenly reversed course and resumed his prior practice of maintaining certain distinctions from non-Jews, even from non-Jewish Christians. His influence was so great that it caused ripples throughout the Christian community in Antioch, even affecting Barnabas, the other main leader of the church in the city.

Galatians 2:15-16. Adopting for a moment the common Jewish-Christian point of view, Paul attempted an answer to the question he had posed to Peter (2:14). Justification before God, the act of being made right, a legal term akin to "acquittal," is obtained by throwing ourselves on the mercy of Jesus Christ, not by trying to perform certain acts (in the Mosaic law) that will gain God's approval. Not even Jews believe that keeping the law earns God's favor. They, too, understand that keeping the law is the response a godly person makes to the prior grace received from God. This "prior grace" takes the form of covenant or law for Jews; for Christians, it takes the form of Jesus Christ.

The final phrase in verse 16, "no one will be justified by the works of the law," an idea also found in Romans 3:20, appears to be Paul's appropriation of Psalm 143:2.

Galatians 2:17. Persons, including Jews who throw themselves on the mercy of Jesus Christ for their justification before God, inevitably discover the extent of their sinfulness. That does not mean that Christ is therefore the cause of their sin. It simply means that Christ has opened their eyes to a prior truth about themselves.

Galatians 2:18. Some persons attempt to escape this unwelcome truth about themselves by turning back to the naiveté of their past, reclaiming beliefs they once affirmed. Unfortunately, reclaiming past beliefs (for instance, choosing to believe that observing the law gains God's approval) renders no one righteous. Instead, it merely proves that these persons are truly guilty of the charge they sought to avoid. That is, by reverting to their previous beliefs, either they are declaring that they fell into sin (became a lawbreaker) during the time they believed in Christ, or (since Christ *is* the only means available to us by which we may be saved) they are opting for the comfortable sin of their past rather than the gracious freedom they had begun to enjoy in Christ.

Galatians 2:19. The long and the short of it is that when one abandons a prior set of beliefs and throws oneself upon the mercy of Jesus Christ, it is not a simple matter of tearing down one belief system and reconstructing another; it is a matter of death and resurrection. Unlike Paul's argument in Romans 6:2, his point here is not just that Christians are now dead to sin. Instead, he goes further by asserting that they are also dead to alternative systems of *goodness* and *morality*, including the law and other moral systems they may trust.

Galatians 2:20. Like the thief on the cross, persons who throw themselves on the mercy of Christ are "crucified with Christ"; as a result, they no longer live. New life comes by way of death. "The old has gone; the new has come!" (2 Corinthians 5:17 NIV). New life is entirely a divine gift and not in the least the result of personal accomplishment. Charles Wesley echoed Paul's understanding in the hymn "And Can It Be That I Should Gain": "Amazing love! How can it be that thou, my God, shouldst die for me?"

Galatians 2:21. Paul's concluding thought summarizes the intent of his argument in the previous paragraphs: "if righteousness could be gained through the law, Christ died for nothing" (2:21 NIV).

INTERPRETING THE SCRIPTURE

Salvation by Works

Since at least the time of Martin Luther (1483–1546), it has been common to oppose justification by grace through faith to the notion of "works righteousness." However, the contrast is not as straightforward as some suggest. For instance, as Luther himself pointed out, good works are acknowledged and encouraged in the Epistle of James. Unfortunately, that fact earned the epistle Luther's dismissive charge of being "an epistle of straw."

As might be expected in the "occasional" letters that Paul wrote to different churches facing very different situations, Paul used the term "works" in different ways. At least three different kinds of works can be delineated in Paul's writings. Two of the works are acts that Paul rejected; a third is actually encouraged by Paul.

The worst kind of work is performed by persons who think they can obtain God's approval by doing (or not doing) certain things. The attempt fails at two levels. First, it fails to understand that our sin has fundamentally separated us from God. The resulting gulf between us and God is so deep and broad that no amount of "good works" can ever bridge it, much less repair what has been broken in our relationship with God. Second, it fails to understand that God's law does not tell us how to obtain entry into God's kingdom; reconciliation has always been by grace. Rather, it reveals to us what God's kingdom looks like when it takes shape in human lives. As God's renovating work takes hold in our lives and remolds us (Jeremiah 18:4) and God purifies us (Malachi 3:2-4), we discover we are no longer abusing the name of God to achieve our own purposes (Exodus 20:7). In addition, various desires such as coveting (Exodus 20:17) and the attempts we make to protect ourselves by blaming others (Exodus 20:16) fade away.

A second kind of work that Paul rejected was the type that substituted a particular (ethnic) identity for a deepening relationship with God. Instead of pointing others to God, these works were intended to draw the attention of others to oneself.

The third kind of work is not only helpful, it turns out to be essential to our faith. We are "created in Christ Jesus for good works" (Ephesians 2:10). These good works are not acts we do to atone for past mistakes; they are acts we do that exhibit our new standing with God. Paul's notion is basically the same as that of Jesus when Jesus declared that "every good tree bears good fruit" (Matthew 7:17; see also Matthew 12:33).

Conversion: A Radically New Way

I grew up in a state that today would be known as a red state. Thus, when I had an opportunity to write a lengthy op-ed piece on capital punishment for my high school newspaper, I wrote in defense of it.

As I researched facts to bolster my argument in favor of the death penalty, to my chagrin I discovered that the data actually supported the position I wanted to attack. There was nothing to do but falsify the data in the editorial, which (I am ashamed to admit) I did.

A few years later, now in college, I had an opportunity to revisit the subject of capital punishment, this time in a speech class. Again I took a position in support of the death penalty. Again I found it necessary, even though I conducted additional research, to falsify my findings, which I did. More guilt.

A Christian friend in the class, after hearing my speech, asked me not long afterward how I, who claimed to be a Christian, could hold such a position. I attempted to argue with him, but I knew in my heart of hearts that I had been found out. Like Paul on the Damascus Road, I was struck by a blinding light (Acts 9:3-4). I realized I could no longer support a position I had to lie about to defend. That day, a belief to which I had always subscribed died, and a new belief was born.

In Paul's day there were honest differences of opinion among Christians about whether one could eat with Gentiles and even what it meant to follow Christ. There are similar differences of opinion between Christians today on a variety of topics, including capital punishment. I would not claim that the position we take on capital punishment is as vital to our standing with God as justification by faith in Christ is. Still, the analogy to the argument Paul made about the gospel of Jesus Christ to the churches in Galatia holds true. My conversion from the one opinion to the other was total. I died to the one belief and was reborn to the other. Today, I cannot fathom returning to my previous beliefs. They no longer hold any desire for me.

Our Savior Jesus Christ

The Nicene Creed has it exactly right. It is not enough to say that Jesus "was incarnate . . . and became truly human." Rather, it was *"for us and for our salvation* he . . . was incarnate and became truly human" (italics added). Similarly, it is not enough to say that Jesus was crucified, died, and was buried. Rather, it was *"for our sake* he was crucified under Pontius Pilate" (italics added). In traditional theological terms, the person of Christ cannot be separated from the work of Christ.

The term we use today for Jesus when we want to draw attention to his saving work on our behalf is "savior." However, that hasn't always been the case. It may surprise many to learn that the word "savior" is not a common term in Scripture. It occurs only twenty-four times in the NRSV New Testament. Almost half of those occurrences are in the Pastoral Epistles. Eight times the term is applied to God; sixteen times it is used of Jesus.

Perhaps one reason the church did not quickly adopt the term "savior" was due to the fact that Roman emperors, including Caesar Augustus (who reigned from 31 B.C. to A.D. 14), were already heralded as "savior." Upon Augustus's death, his son and successor Tiberius (who ruled during Jesus' life from A.D. 14–37) was also declared a "son of god" and "savior." The word had politically charged connotations and so was not trumpeted as being linked to Jesus early on. In late biblical passages, such as 2 Peter 1:11; 2:20; 3:2, which are thought to have been written at the end of the first century A.D. or the beginning of the second century A.D., the term was more freely used in relation to Jesus. By the time the creeds of the church were hammered out in the fourth century, the term "savior" was even more widely applied to Jesus.

Although Paul in Galatians did not refer to Jesus as our "savior," he did refer repeatedly to the saving work of Christ. That is important, for Jesus accomplished for us what we could never have accomplished for ourselves. Through his death he made forgiveness and reconciliation with God the Father possible. We had, indeed, been justified by faith in him; he was and is our Savior. Thanks be to God.

SHARING THE SCRIPTURE

Preparing Our Hearts

Explore this week's devotional reading, found in Luke 18:9-14. Here we encounter Jesus' parable about the Pharisee and the tax collector. Both men were in the Temple, talking with God. The Pharisee was touting his exemplary behavior, whereas the tax collector humbly acknowledged his sinfulness. In a reversal of what his listeners would have expected to hear, Jesus commended the tax collector, saying that he was "justified" (18:14), that is, made right with God. The Pharisee who relied on his own righteousness was not commended. What does it mean to you to be "justified"? How do you believe justification occurs? What surprises you about this parable?

Pray that you and the adult learners will recognize that those who humble themselves and walk in the way of Christ are made right with God.

Preparing Our Minds

Study the background Scripture from Galatians 1:1–2:21 and the lesson Scripture from Galatians 2:15-21. Ask yourself: Who can help us connect to God?

Write on newsprint:

❑ questions for "Confirm and Deepen the Learners' Faith in Jesus Christ as Savior."

❑ information for next week's lesson, found under "Continue the Journey."

❑ activities for further spiritual growth in "Continue the Journey."

Plan the suggested lecture for "Listen to Paul's Argument Against Salvation by Works."

LEADING THE CLASS

(1) Gather to Learn

❖ Welcome the class members and introduce any guests.

❖ Pray that the students will be open to the word that God has for them today.

❖ Read and discuss: **Throughout the Bible, people followed leaders such as Moses, Deborah, David, Peter, and Paul. Clearly, people thought that these leaders had something of value to offer them.**

    (1) What is it that people were hoping to find?

    (2) How did these leaders, and many others, enable the people to find what they were seeking?

    (3) What do you hope to find when you look toward church leaders?

❖ Read aloud today's focus statement: **People yearn to follow someone who can help them connect with God. In whom can we put our faith to achieve this goal? Paul taught that through his death and resurrection Jesus is able to make those who have faith in him right with God.**

(2) Listen to Paul's Argument Against Salvation by Works

❖ Use information from Galatians 1:1-5 through 2:11-14 in Understanding the Scripture to present a brief lecture to set the context for today's session.

❖ Invite a volunteer to read Galatians 2:15-21.

❖ **Option:** Call on two or three other volunteers who have different translations of the Bible to read the same verses. Hearing different translations may help the adults grasp Paul's teaching more clearly.

❖ Ask: **What arguments do you hear Paul making against working your way toward a saving relationship with God?**

❖ Suggest that the group read in unison today's key verses, Galatians 2:19-20 (NRSV) or 2:20 (NIV).

❖ Ask these questions:

    (1) What does this passage mean to you?

    (2) How have you experienced being crucified with Christ?

    (3) In what ways do you experience Christ living in you?

(3) Identify the Learners' Perspective on the Relationship Between Salvation and Works

❖ Ask this question: **What relationship do you see between salvation and works?**

❖ Retell "Salvation by Works" in Interpreting the Scripture.

❖ Add this information gleaned from Volume 11 of *The New Interpreter's Bible:*

■ **Luther's teaching has been very influential, especially in Protestant theology, but more recent scholarship finds it to be based on a faulty understanding, a "caricature" of Judaism, as Richard B. Hays writes in summarizing the currently accepted view of many scholars.**

■ **In his book *Paul and Palestinian Judaism,* E. P. Sanders argues that Judaism has never taught that one needed to work one's way into the covenant community. By God's grace, Jewish people are already part of the covenant. Instead, obedience to the law is the means by which one stays in the community.**

■ **In *The Epistle to the Galatians,* J. D. G. Dunn proposes that "works of Law" does not refer to good works in general, but is far more specific, referring to circumcision, keeping dietary laws, and observing the sabbath, all of which are distinctive features of Jewish ethnic identity.**

■ **With these thoughts in mind, Richard B. Hays suggests that Paul's teaching could be expressed this way: "We ourselves are Jews by birth and not Gentile sinners; yet, knowing that a person is rectified not by wearing the badges of ethnic identity but through the faith of Jesus Christ, even we have trusted in Christ Jesus."**

■ **In summary, Richard B. Hays points out that the target of Paul's teaching is not the idea of earning salvation through works, but rather the claim that salvation is based on one's ethnic or racial group.**

❖ Ask this question: **How do these additional ideas affirm or modify your ideas about the relationship between salvation and works?**

(4) Confirm and Deepen the Learners' Faith in Jesus Christ as Savior

❖ Read these words by Oswald Chambers (1874–1917): **Beware of worshiping Jesus as the Son of God and professing your faith in him as the Savior of the world, while you blaspheme him by the complete evidence in your daily life that he is powerless to do anything in and through you.**

❖ Distribute paper and pencils. Challenge the adults to answer these questions, which you will post on newsprint:

(1) **What evidence does your life give that you do have faith in Jesus as your Savior?**

(2) **What might you do to deepen your faith in Jesus?**

❖ Call everyone together. Discuss the second question. Talk about spiritual disciplines, such as *Bible study, prayer, meditation, worship, fasting, tithing, journaling, walking a labyrinth,* and so on. Invite those who have tried certain disciplines to discuss them. Also consider how doing works that reflect one's love for Christ can help deepen one's faith. Think about acts of mercy to those who are sick, poor, imprisoned, or otherwise vulnerable.

❖ Conclude this part of the session by challenging the adults to confirm and deepen their love for Christ by allowing him to work through them mightily so that they may grow in faith.

(5) Continue the Journey

❖ Pray that the adults will confirm and deepen their faith in the crucified and risen Christ.

❖ Read aloud this preparation for next week's lesson. You may also want to post it on newsprint for the students to copy.

- **Title: Freed from Law Through Christ**
- **Background Scripture: Galatians 3:1-14**
- **Lesson Scripture: Galatians 3:1-14**
- **Focus of the Lesson: To know and accept the ultimate object of faith is to make everything else subordinate, if not useless. In what should we place this ultimate faith? According to Paul, faith in Jesus Christ's sacrifice for us makes adherence to the Law foolishness.**

❖ Challenge the students to complete one or more of these activities for further spiritual growth related to this week's session. Post this information on newsprint for the students to copy.

(1) **Review your motivation for doing works in the name of Christ. Do you do what you do out of a desire to be recognized by others, an attempt to earn your** way to salvation, a response to God's love for you, or for some other reason? Consider jettisoning some jobs that you discern you are doing for the wrong reasons.

(2) **Research the word "justification" as it is used in a theological sense. What does being justified mean to you? How does its reality affect your life?**

(3) **Recall that in Galatians Paul is writing to counter the effects of false teachers. Use your Bible and other references to figure out how you can discern a false teacher.**

❖ Sing or read aloud "Thou Hidden Love of God."

❖ Conclude today's session by leading the class in this benediction: **By the power of the Holy Spirit go forth to be a blessing to others even as God through Christ has blessed you.**

UNIT 3: GOD'S REDEMPTION
Freed From Law Through Christ

PREVIEWING THE LESSON

Lesson Scripture: Galatians 3:1-14
Background Scripture: Galatians 3:1-14
Key Verses: Galatians 3:13-14 (NRSV); 3:14 (NIV)

Focus of the Lesson:
To know and accept the ultimate object of faith is to make everything else subordinate, if not useless. In what should we place this ultimate faith? According to Paul, faith in Jesus Christ's sacrifice for us makes adherence to the law foolishness.

Goals for the Learners:
(1) to understand Paul's contrast between adherence to the law and trusting in Jesus Christ.
(2) to explore the role of faith in their lives.
(3) to act on their claims to faith in Jesus Christ.

Pronunciation Guide:
Septuagint (sep too' uh jint)

Supplies:
Bibles, newsprint and marker, paper and pencils, hymnals

READING THE SCRIPTURE

NRSV
Galatians 3:1-14
¹You foolish Galatians! Who has bewitched you? It was before your eyes that Jesus Christ was publicly exhibited as crucified! ²The only thing I want to learn from you is this: Did you receive the Spirit by doing the works of the law or by believing

NIV
Galatians 3:1-14
¹You foolish Galatians! Who has bewitched you? Before your very eyes Jesus Christ was clearly portrayed as crucified. ²I would like to learn just one thing from you: Did you receive the Spirit by observing the law, or by believing what you heard? ³Are

what you heard? [3]Are you so foolish? Having started with the Spirit, are you now ending with the flesh? [4]Did you experience so much for nothing?—if it really was for nothing. [5]Well then, does God supply you with the Spirit and work miracles among you by your doing the works of the law, or by your believing what you heard?

[6]Just as Abraham "believed God, and it was reckoned to him as righteousness," [7]so, you see, those who believe are the descendants of Abraham. [8]And the scripture, foreseeing that God would justify the Gentiles by faith, declared the gospel beforehand to Abraham, saying, "All the Gentiles shall be blessed in you." [9]For this reason, those who believe are blessed with Abraham who believed.

[10]For all who rely on the works of the law are under a curse; for it is written, "Cursed is everyone who does not observe and obey all the things written in the book of the law." [11]Now it is evident that no one is justified before God by the law; for "The one who is righteous will live by faith." [12]But the law does not rest on faith; on the contrary, "Whoever does the works of the law will live by them." [13]**Christ redeemed us** from the curse of the law by becoming a curse for us—for it is written, "Cursed is everyone who hangs on a tree"—[14]**in order that in Christ Jesus the blessing of Abraham might come to the Gentiles, so that we might receive the promise of the Spirit through faith.**

you so foolish? After beginning with the Spirit, are you now trying to attain your goal by human effort? [4]Have you suffered so much for nothing—if it really was for nothing? [5]Does God give you his Spirit and work miracles among you because you observe the law, or because you believe what you heard?

[6]Consider Abraham: "He believed God, and it was credited to him as righteousness." [7]Understand, then, that those who believe are children of Abraham. [8]The Scripture foresaw that God would justify the Gentiles by faith, and announced the gospel in advance to Abraham: "All nations will be blessed through you." [9]So those who have faith are blessed along with Abraham, the man of faith.

[10]All who rely on observing the law are under a curse, for it is written: "Cursed is everyone who does not continue to do everything written in the Book of the Law." [11]Clearly no one is justified before God by the law, because, "The righteous will live by faith." [12]The law is not based on faith; on the contrary, "The man who does these things will live by them." [13]Christ redeemed us from the curse of the law by becoming a curse for us, for it is written: "Cursed is everyone who is hung on a tree." [14]**He redeemed us in order that the blessing given to Abraham might come to the Gentiles through Christ Jesus, so that by faith we might receive the promise of the Spirit.**

UNDERSTANDING THE SCRIPTURE

Galatians 3:1. Using characteristically strong language, Paul was baffled by the Galatian church's decision to turn from the one, true gospel of the cross that he had preached to an alternative one. He openly wondered if someone had cast a spell on them. Paul could not understand how anyone who had been made alive in Christ could be enticed to desire another gospel.

Galatians 3:2. Paul boiled down his incredulity to a single question: When the Galatian church received God's Spirit, was it because they had carefully observed the law or was it because they heeded the gospel that Paul preached to them? Paul was there and already knew the answer, so this was a rhetorical question. Twenty years after Pentecost, the reception of the Spirit was still the proof of the reception of new life in Jesus Christ.

Galatians 3:3. Pained as a parent who has just watched his child make a particularly bad choice, Paul could not contain himself. "What are you thinking?" he essentially blurted out. "Do you really believe you can perfect the work God has begun in you by reverting to human means?" Their decision was so unthinkable that it was beyond comprehension to Paul.

Galatians 3:4. On the basis of this verse alone, it is impossible to tell whether the "experience" of the Galatian Christians referred to something positive (the work of God's Spirit among them) or something negative (suffering they had endured). Either way, unless they changed the direction they were headed, Paul was afraid the experience would end up being for naught.

Galatians 3:5. In both the NRSV and the NIV it is clear that the giving of the Holy Spirit and the working of miracles were not events that used to occur among the Galatians but had now ceased. Rather, they were still-happening realities. In fact, they were not even separate events. The giving of the Spirit is an apt description of the new relationship with God that the church enjoys. And the working of miracles is the result of this new relationship; it is what the church is now empowered by God to do.

Pressing home the point he scored in verse 2, Paul drew attention to the fact that these were new realities the Galatians were experiencing. They were not known among those who were merely "doing the works of the law" (3:5).

Galatians 3:6. Six times in the next nine verses Paul proved his argument by citing Old Testament Scripture. The experience of the Galatian Christians in entering into a new relationship with God by faith (rather than works) was nothing new. That was Abraham's experience too (Genesis 15:6; see Lesson 2 for December 11).

Galatians 3:7. Just as it was Abraham's faith rather than his works (circumcision)

that "was reckoned to him as righteousness" (Galatians 3:6), by extension it is those who believe rather than those who observe the law or those who descend biologically who are credited as being "descendants of Abraham" (3:7).

Galatians 3:8. Justification of the entire world (not only Jews) by grace through faith (not works) has always been God's offer. This gospel covenant was fulfilled in Jesus Christ but it was already manifest in the divine promises made to Abraham in Genesis 12:3 (see Lesson 1 on December 4) and 18:18.

Galatians 3:9. Our entry into this covenant promise is by faith, which secures for us the same blessing it secured for Abraham: justification.

Galatians 3:10. Given the importance of Deuteronomy 27–28 in Jewish thought, it was natural for Paul, having just spoken of blessing, to turn his attention to curse. However, in citing the last of the twelve levitical curses (Deuteronomy 27:26), Paul turned the plain meaning of the text on its head. Whereas the text says that one is cursed *for not* observing the law, Paul said that one is cursed *for* observing the law.

One explanation for Paul's interpretation hinges on the word "all" ("all the things written" [NRSV] or "everything written" [NIV]), which appears in the Septuagint but not in the Hebrew version of Deuteronomy 27:26. Anything less than *perfect* obedience condemns those who try to live by the law. The problem with this explanation is that it appears elsewhere in Philippians 3:6. There Paul believed that it was quite possible to keep the law blamelessly.

A more compelling (and simpler) explanation is simply to remember that Paul equated observing the law with Jewish ethnic identity (Galatians 2:16; see Lesson 10 for February 5). To hold such a belief was ultimately to deny God's salvation to non-Jews, a belief that Paul's interpretation of Genesis 12:3; 18:8 (see Galatians 3:6, 8)—and the Galatians' experience of salvation—ruled out.

Galatians 3:11. On the basis of all that he had said in the last several verses, Paul turned readily to Habakkuk 2:4 (as he had done in Romans 1:17), to summarize his argument. Because the "righteous will live by faith," the law has nothing to do with one's standing before God.

Galatians 3:12. Having made his case that justification is based on faith, not law, Paul finally was able to speak a word in favor of law. Referring to Leviticus 18:5, the same passage he cited in Romans 10:5 and to which Jesus alluded when speaking to the expert in the law (Luke 10:28), Paul acknowledged that the righteous keep the law. That, however, is not the same thing as saying it is how the unrighteous "become" righteous.

Galatians 3:13. Returning to his quotation of Deuteronomy 27:26 in verse 10, Paul now proclaimed a word of gospel truth. Although there is no way for us to counter "the curse of the law," God could and did in Christ Jesus. Paul cited Deuteronomy 21:23 as a prophetic description of Jesus' death, a death that fully released us from the curse of the law.

Galatians 3:14. The result of Christ's death was that the "blessing of Abraham might come to the Gentiles" and that as both Jews and Gentiles we "might receive the promise of the Spirit."

INTERPRETING THE SCRIPTURE

Faith and Experience

Despite Paul's best attempts to spell out how God's salvation becomes operable in our lives, the relationship between faith and works remains a heated topic within the church. Historically, Christians have accused Jews of not taking grace or faith seriously. Protestants have accused Catholics of the same. Reformed Christians have made the same accusation of Arminian Christians, that is, those who believe that salvation is initiated by God and offered to everyone but is only effective for those who of their free will say yes to Jesus through God's grace. A careful reading of this Scripture lesson suggests that the key to moving beyond this matter of contention is experience.

After becoming a Christian, Paul did not deny the value of the law. Nor did he dispense with it. He did, however, understand it in light of his experience of Jesus Christ. In the series of rhetorical questions he asked the Galatian Christians in 3:1-5, it is clear that Paul believed that their experience paralleled his own.

What exactly was Paul's experience? Although he had kept the law blamelessly (Philippians 3:6), Christ's call on his life had nothing to do with what he had accomplished. Nor did it have anything to do with his Jewishness, cultural standing, intelligence, ability, or morality. Christ's call was an extension of God's grace. And Paul's receipt of that grace was a matter of faith or trust. The Galatian Christians had had the same experience.

By extension, when we understand the gospel rightly, the shocking yet gratifying truth is that our salvation has nothing to do with how well or how poorly we have conformed to God's desire for us. It has nothing to do with our nationality, zip code, skin color, or gender. It doesn't matter if we're charismatic or belong to a particular denomination, laid-off or fully employed, high school dropout or college-educated, straitlaced or immoral or criminal. God's grace is not contingent on anything about us. It is solely contingent on the life and death of Jesus (Galatians 3:13).

That said, the fact that God's grace is

universally extended to everyone does not mean that everyone receives God's salvation. Indeed, many reject it. However, insofar as God's grace becomes operative in our lives, it is as a result of our willingness to trust (that is, have faith in) God for it. As was true for Paul and the Galatian Christians, so too this is our experience.

Faith and Scripture

When we marry into a family, one of the first things that happens is we are introduced to our new family's stories. We learn the story of Uncle Ned at the zoo, of Aunt Sally on her wedding day. And who could forget Peggy's first crush? Or the time Bill got sprayed by a skunk? Every time the family gets together—at Thanksgiving or Christmas, for an anniversary or funeral—the well-worn stories are trotted out and everyone grins and laughs and cries.

Over time, the stories become ours. No, we weren't there when they happened, but we might as well have been. We end up hearing the stories so many times it feels like we were there. We know the stories so well we can now tell them ourselves. We know when to pause, what to exaggerate, how to make Cousin George's face. Yes, the stories are ours.

The same is true of Holy Scripture. Reading and reflecting on the stories and praying the psalms week after week after month after month after year after year the texts eventually become a part of us. The words of the prophets become ours. The stories of Jesus frame the way we think. The letters of Paul teach us the mind of God.

That's how it worked for Paul too. Day after day, across the course of a lifetime, he reflected on those "wonderful words of life." He considered their meaning. He pondered their insights into God's being. Over time, the words became so familiar to him that they became his words.

Six times in the final nine verses of our Scripture lesson, Paul quoted passages of Holy Scripture. (In one quotation from Genesis, Paul actually conflated two passages.) Two quoted passages are from Genesis (12:3/18:8; 15:6), one from Leviticus (18:5), two from Deuteronomy (21:23; 27:26), and one from Habakkuk (2:4). As a result of his knowledge of Scripture, Paul was able to make sense of the Gentiles' experience in the early church. He realized that their experience of receiving the Holy Spirit was legitimate and to be expected.

I wonder what experiences as well as insights we are missing out on today due to our lack of familiarity with the Bible. Faith continues to take many important forms in Christians. This person becomes an advocate for social reform. That person takes cut flowers from her garden to ill persons at church. Still another person regularly visits prisoners at the county jail. All the same, I often wonder how we can become a part of God's family and not know the stories of our new family any better than we do.

Faith and Trust

The following story may be apocryphal but it has appeared in print for nearly 150 years. It beautifully illustrates the difference between faith as "belief" and faith as "trust."

When word spread that a gentleman planned to walk across a rope that was strung high above Niagara Falls, a crowd gathered to watch the high-wire balance act. Many verbal and monetary wagers were made as to whether the man would succeed or plummet to his death.

To the great relief of those who watched, the man successfully walked the entire length of the rope across Niagara Falls and then returned. Upon returning to his starting point, the man announced that he now intended to push a wheelbarrow the full length of the rope. More wagers were made as to whether he would succeed or fail. One person in particular told his friend that he had no doubt whatsoever that the high-wire artist would succeed. And, indeed, he did. The man pushed the wheelbarrow the full length of the rope across Niagara Falls and then back again without incident.

This time, upon arriving back at his starting point, the man asked for a volunteer to sit in the wheelbarrow as he pushed it across the rope high above Niagara Falls. Even though they had just watched the man successfully complete this feat, the crowd fell silent. Not a single person volunteered to ride in the wheelbarrow—not even the gentleman who had told his friend that he had no doubt whatsoever that the high-wire artist would succeed.

When discussing theoretical questions that pose minimal or no risk to us, it is easy to declare our "belief" that God exists, answers prayer, or heals. It is another matter entirely when the risk is great and faith-as-belief must become faith-as-trust. When the issue that lies before us requires that we commit ourselves entirely—and not just verbally declare our belief about something—we learn how authentic our faith really is.

If Christ were that high-wire artist and the wheelbarrow he was pushing represented our salvation, would we have enough faith in his ability to take the risk of climbing into that wheelbarrow and letting him push us across that rope? If not, can we honestly say that we have committed our life into his safekeeping?

SHARING THE SCRIPTURE

Preparing Our Hearts

Explore this week's devotional reading, found in Matthew 19:16-23. This familiar story records the questions of a rich man to Jesus as to how he can gain eternal life. Note that Jesus does not denigrate the man for keeping the commandments. Rather, he challenges the man to go further—to sell what he has, give the proceeds to the poor, and follow Jesus. In response, the man "went away grieving, for he had many possessions" (19:22). The implication is that as righteous as this man seemed, he would not put his trust in Jesus; instead, he relied on his wealth. Who or what do you rely on? What is the source of your security?

Pray that you and the adult learners will recognize that Jesus is the one in whom you can place your trust.

Preparing Our Minds

Study the background Scripture and the lesson Scripture, both of which are from Galatians 3:1-14. Think about where you are willing to place your ultimate faith.

Write on newsprint:

❏ information for next week's lesson, found under "Continue the Journey."
❏ activities for further spiritual growth in "Continue the Journey."

Familiarize yourself with the points made about Paul's teaching in the Understanding the Scripture portion.

LEADING THE CLASS

(1) Gather to Learn

❖ Welcome the class members and introduce any guests.

❖ Pray that the students will invite the Spirit to illuminate Paul's teachings about trusting in Jesus.

❖ Invite the adults to imagine themselves among the spectators as you read "Faith and Trust" from Interpreting the Scripture.

❖ Discuss this question: **How does this**

story of the high-wire artist accurately—or inaccurately—reflect the way many Christians respond when challenged by life's circumstances to put their faith in Jesus?

❖ Read aloud today's focus statement: **To know and accept the ultimate object of faith is to make everything else subordinate, if not useless. In what should we place this ultimate faith? According to Paul, faith in Jesus Christ's sacrifice for us makes adherence to the law foolishness.**

(2) Understand Paul's Contrast Between Adherence to the Law and Trusting in Jesus Christ

❖ Choose a volunteer to read Galatians 3:1-14.

❖ Ask these questions. As the group responds, add pertinent information from the Understanding the Scripture portion.

(1) **Why is Paul upset with the Galatian Christians?**

(2) **What point is he making by using Abraham as an example?**

(3) **What point is he making about those who rely on the law?**

(4) **How would you summarize Paul's argument?** (Expect that Paul's strong language may lead some adults to conclude that Paul had no use for the law. Use information from "Faith and Experience" in Interpreting the Scripture to clarify that Paul did not deny the value of the law; rather, his experience was that the law could not bring one into a right relationship with God. Only Jesus could do that.)

❖ Conclude by pointing out that Paul made extensive use of the Bible in his argument. (You may want to give examples from "Faith and Scripture" in Interpreting the Scripture.) Ask: **What can we do as a congregation to help everyone become more biblically literate, more able to know and express how God has worked and**

continues to work in our world and in our individual lives?

(3) Explore the Role of Faith in the Learners' Lives

❖ Distribute paper and pencils. Encourage the adults to rate themselves on these statements using a scale of 1 to 4, with 1 being *never*, 2 being *seldom*, 3 being *sometimes*, and 4 being *always*. Read each statement aloud, pausing to allow the students time to write their answers.

(1) **My faith in God through Jesus Christ is strong in times of crisis.**

(2) **My faith in God is strong in good times when I apparently do not need to rely on God so much.**

(3) **I rely on God and my financial resources to take care of me.**

(4) **My relationship with Christ gives me life.**

(5) **When friends, family, and possessions fail me, I turn to Christ.**

(6) **I feel assured that God loves me.**

(7) **I feel assured of God's love but also abide by the law so as to be certain to have eternal life.**

(8) **I can be persuaded to follow novel points of view if the speaker is sincere.**

❖ Call the group together. Students will not be asked to reveal their specific answers. However, do ask them to comment on this statement: **Putting one's total faith and trust in Jesus is easy to agree to but far more difficult to do when confronting real-life situations.**

❖ Provide a few moments of quiet time for the adults to reflect on the role that faith in Jesus Christ truly plays in their lives. Break the silence by saying, "Thanks be to God."

(4) Act on Claims to Faith in Jesus Christ

❖ Form two small groups (or multiples of two) and assign each one of the following fictional scenarios, which you will read aloud. Each group may choose either to discuss how they would handle this situation or to do a roleplay to demonstrate how they would respond to the question.

(1) **The Westins had a considerable stock portfolio prior to a severe economic downturn. They are Christians who regularly attend church, yet their whole sense of peace and well-being was shattered when their investments shrank considerably. What could you say to help the Westins focus their trust for today and tomorrow on Jesus?**

(2) **Bonnie Hartford was so severely injured by a hit-and-run driver that she was no longer able to work in her beloved profession as an artist. She claimed faith in Christ prior to the accident and believes that he pulled her through this near-fatal experience. Yet she now sees no future for herself and no longer believes that Christ is really there for her. What might you say or do to help her reclaim her faith and trust in Christ?**

❖ **Option:** Debrief the roleplay by inviting those who witnessed each one to add other ideas that may be useful in helping the Westins or Bonnie Hartford.

(5) Continue the Journey

❖ Pray that the adults will live out their claim of faith in Jesus.

❖ Read aloud this preparation for next week's lesson. You may also want to post it on newsprint for the students to copy.

■ **Title: Heirs to the Promise**
■ **Background Scripture: Galatians 3:15-29; 4:1–5:1**

■ **Lesson Scripture: Galatians 3:15-18; 4:1-7**
■ **Focus of the Lesson: Sometimes a person inherits a system of values without personally investigating the appropriateness of such values. Why is it important to understand, rather than merely inherit, the values by which we live? Paul stated that Gentiles received God's blessing as heirs of Abraham, but had to accept the promise for themselves by maturing in their faith in Jesus Christ.**

❖ Challenge the students to complete one or more of these activities for further spiritual growth related to this week's session. Post this information on newsprint for the students to copy.

(1) **List five ways that you can demonstrate your faith in Jesus this week. Take action.**

(2) **Observe your own thoughts and actions. Does what you think and do reflect an ultimate trust in Jesus Christ, or are you placing your trust in something or someone else? What changes do you want to make?**

(3) **Consider how the Holy Spirit is moving among your congregation. Paul wrote in Galatians 3:5 about God working miracles among the Galatians. Where do you see miracles occurring? If few miraculous blessings are discernible, what needs to change within the congregation?**

❖ Sing or read aloud "Spirit of Faith, Come Down."

❖ Conclude today's session by leading the class in this benediction: **By the power of the Holy Spirit go forth to be a blessing to others even as God through Christ has blessed you.**

UNIT 3: GOD'S REDEMPTION
HEIRS TO THE PROMISE

PREVIEWING THE LESSON

Lesson Scripture: Galatians 3:15-18; 4:1-7
Background Scripture: Galatians 3:15-29; 4:1–5:1
Key Verse: Galatians 4:7

Focus of the Lesson:
Sometimes a person inherits a system of values without personally investigating the appropriateness of such values. Why is it important to understand, rather than merely inherit, the values by which we live? Paul stated that Gentiles received God's blessing as heirs of Abraham, but had to accept the promise for themselves by maturing in their faith in Jesus Christ.

Goals for the Learners:
(1) to encounter Paul's statements about being heirs of Abraham in the faith.
(2) to appreciate the value of their inherited faith.
(3) to confess the faith they have inherited as their own.

Pronunciation Guide:
Abba (ah' buh) or (ab' uh)

Supplies:
Bibles, newsprint and marker, paper and pencils, hymnals

READING THE SCRIPTURE

NRSV
Galatians 3:15-18

¹⁵Brothers and sisters, I give an example from daily life: once a person's will has been ratified, no one adds to it or annuls it. ¹⁶Now the promises were made to Abraham and to his offspring; it does not say, "And to offsprings," as of many; but it says, "And to your offspring," that is, to one person, who is Christ. ¹⁷My point is this: the law, which

NIV
Galatians 3:15-18

¹⁵Brothers, let me take an example from everyday life. Just as no one can set aside or add to a human covenant that has been duly established, so it is in this case. ¹⁶The promises were spoken to Abraham and to his seed. The Scripture does not say "and to seeds," meaning many people, but "and to your seed," meaning one person, who is

came four hundred thirty years later, does not annul a covenant previously ratified by God, so as to nullify the promise. [18]For if the inheritance comes from the law, it no longer comes from the promise; but God granted it to Abraham through the promise.

Galatians 4:1-7

[1]My point is this: heirs, as long as they are minors, are no better than slaves, though they are the owners of all the property; [2]but they remain under guardians and trustees until the date set by the father. [3]So with us; while we were minors, we were enslaved to the elemental spirits of the world. [4]But when the fullness of time had come, God sent his Son, born of a woman, born under the law, [5]in order to redeem those who were under the law, so that we might receive adoption as children. [6]And because you are children, God has sent the Spirit of his Son into our hearts, crying, "Abba! Father!" [7]**So you are no longer a slave but a child, and if a child then also an heir, through God.**

Christ. [17]What I mean is this: The law, introduced 430 years later, does not set aside the covenant previously established by God and thus do away with the promise. [18]For if the inheritance depends on the law, then it no longer depends on a promise; but God in his grace gave it to Abraham through a promise.

Galatians 4:1-7

[1]What I am saying is that as long as the heir is a child, he is no different from a slave, although he owns the whole estate. [2]He is subject to guardians and trustees until the time set by his father. [3]So also, when we were children, we were in slavery under the basic principles of the world. [4]But when the time had fully come, God sent his Son, born of a woman, born under law, [5]to redeem those under law, that we might receive the full rights of sons. [6]Because you are sons, God sent the Spirit of his Son into our hearts, the Spirit who calls out, "Abba, Father." [7]**So you are no longer a slave, but a son; and since you are a son, God has made you also an heir.**

UNDERSTANDING THE SCRIPTURE

Galatians 3:15. Paul continued to buttress his argument that the law was subordinate to faith. In addition to the scriptural proof texts already cited in 3:6-14 (see Lesson 11 for February 12), Paul now offered an everyday example that illustrated his point: an irrevocable last will.

Galatians 3:16. God's covenant with Abraham, now referred to as a promise, was also made to Abraham's "offspring" (Genesis 12:7). Noting that "offspring" (or "seed," NIV) was a singular noun, Paul ignored the apparent extension of the promise to the Jewish people as a whole and established a link between Abraham and Christ.

Galatians 3:17. Even more to the point, Paul reminded his readers that the promise

preceded the giving of the law by 430 years (see Exodus 12:40).

Galatians 3:18. The bottom line of Paul's argument is that the promise was not only given to Abraham (thus linking it to faith, not law) but was also a matter of divine grace, not human accomplishment.

Galatians 3:19-22. One could legitimately ask: What is the purpose of the law? Until Christ appeared, it provided a temporary means of addressing human sinfulness. It was never contrary to God's covenant with Abraham, but neither was it designed to "make alive" (3:21) or make someone righteous. Only God can do these things, which are available to us in Christ Jesus and which we can appropriate by faith. Had the law been able to justify us,

Jesus would not have needed to die for our sins.

Galatians 3:23-25. In short, the law was designed to be a kind of custodial parent for the Jews. The law protected them by restraining them from the excesses of sin until such time as "Christ came" (3:24) and he was able to fulfill the covenantal promises made to Abraham. Once Christ came, the custodial role of the law was no longer necessary for those who exercise faith in Christ.

Galatians 3:26-29. It is by faith and not through the law (mediated by Moses) that we become "children of God" (3:26). The means by which this trust in Christ or identification with Christ ("clothed . . . with Christ," 3:27) is made explicit is baptism. As a result of this new relationship with God, our relationships with other Christians change too. Old law-based distinctions that resulted in privilege and advantage for some (and inferiority and disadvantage for others) are supplanted by new relationships that no longer recognize such distinctions as worthy even of comment. All that matters is that we "belong to Christ" (3:29).

Galatians 4:1. Paul uses the theme of inheritance to address the same material that he just covered in 3:23-29. Jewish "heirs" may think that they are divinely privileged in ways that Gentile "slaves" are not. However, as long as they are underage (that is, as long as their relationship to God is based on mediated law, not faith in God's covenantal promise), such distinctions are a figment of their imagination.

Galatians 4:2. Underage heirs do not determine for themselves the date or conditions of their inheritance. Such matters are at the sole discretion of their fathers. In the meantime, prior to their coming of age, they live under the restrictions imposed by their legal guardians (that is, the law).

Galatians 4:3. Previously (3:23-25), "we" seemed to refer to Jews or Jewish Christians. In this verse, "we" seems to refer to Gentiles or Gentile Christians. Just as underage Jews were subject to all the vagaries of the law

(4:1-2), so underage Gentiles were subject to various forms of "the elemental spirits of the world."

Galatians 4:4. This verse is often taken out of context to prove beliefs such as predestination ("when the fullness of time had come") or virgin birth ("born of a woman"). In context, its meaning is both simpler and more profound. When God decided the time was optimal, God's own son was born as a Jew.

Galatians 4:5. The purpose of God sending "his Son" (4:4) was to redeem both Jews (those "under the law") and Gentiles (those receiving "adoption as children"). Paul uses the verb "to redeem" only twice in his uncontested letters—here and in 3:13. Paul alone among New Testament writers uses "adoption" as a metaphor for salvation.

Galatians 4:6. The proof that both Jews and Gentiles have been redeemed is the presence of the Holy Spirit with each. And the proof that each has the Spirit is that God's adopted children call God "Abba! Father!"

Galatians 4:7. Paul concluded this section of his argument by personalizing his conclusion: You (not Gentiles generally but the reader/hearer of these words) are no longer a slave to fate ("the elemental spirits of the world," 4:3) but an adopted child who is heir to the promises made to Abraham and realized in Christ Jesus (3:14).

Galatians 4:8-11. Paul asks the Galatian Christians why they would even consider "turning back" to the slavish past from which they had been released now that they know God. Paul also laments that, given the current behavior of the Galatians, his ministry on their behalf may have been wasted.

Galatians 4:12-16. Paul apparently once had a cordial relationship with the Galatian Christians. When he came among them, they accepted him despite "a physical infirmity," which is unspecified. Moreover, they were once willing to do anything for Paul. Now, however, their attitude has changed so much that he asks if he has become an enemy to them because he has proclaimed the truth of the gospel.

Galatians 4:17-20. The zealous desire of those who were (apparently) convincing the Galatians to consider the Jewish law as paramount served "no good purpose." Instead of building up the body of Christ, they were tearing it down.

Galatians 4:21-23. As for the Galatian Christians who were turning to the law, it would behoove them to think again.

Galatians 4:24-31. Employing an allegory drawn from the life of Abraham in Genesis and interpreted through the lens of Isaiah 54:1 and Genesis 21:10, Paul declared that a life based on faith in God's covenantal promise is much preferred to one based on the works of the law.

Galatians 5:1. Paul pleaded with the Galatians: Having been set free, don't subject yourselves again to the enslaving effects of the law.

INTERPRETING THE SCRIPTURE

Children of God

What constitutes a child of God? The Judaizers in Galatia said it was keeping the Jewish law. At a minimum, that meant adhering to certain practices, such as being circumcised, maintaining a particular diet, and keeping the Sabbath and several annual feasts. Paul had no inherent problem with any of these practices. Still, he argued strongly that keeping them did not make one a child of God.

On the basis of Scripture, Paul declared to the Galatian Christians that long before the law was given to Moses, God had already made a promise to Abraham. Reflecting on the fact that Abraham trusted in God's promise and God thereby said that Abraham was righteous, Paul concluded that both Jews and Gentiles become children of God by faith, not by keeping the law (works). To think or do otherwise was to revert to a position of spiritual immaturity.

One might think that after two thousand years of reflecting on Paul's words and attempting to live as he taught, the church would have a pretty clear understanding of what it means to be a child of God. Unfortunately, we remain as prone as ever to the error that was plaguing the Galatian church. At the risk of greatly oversimplifying matters, the church today is struggling to maintain its identity against *two* groups of "Judaizers" that would bind us to new forms of "law."

At one extreme are those who reduce the Christian faith to the keeping of certain practices and the avoiding of certain sins, both of which have varied from time to time and culture to culture, but most relating to personal behavior. In each case, their Christian journey could be tallied as a scorecard. Individuals check off those behaviors and attitudes that must be practiced, and mark an X by those that must be avoided. They can use their scorecards to rate themselves as Christians.

At the other extreme are those who focus on social activism. They believe that all they have to do is stand up for specific issues and take care of certain vulnerable populations, and then they can claim to be true Christians.

Both extremes may include actions and attitudes that are appropriate for Christians, but the problem is that neither personal morality nor social activism in and of itself can bring about salvation. Only faith in Jesus Christ can put us right with God. Once we have been justified, our personal behaviors and our actions on behalf of others become an expression of our faith in

Christ. On the basis of his letter to the Galatians, Paul would say that both of these contemporary "Judaizing" extremes are guilty of substituting childish works of law for the covenantal promise made to Abraham, fulfilled by Christ Jesus, and made operative in our lives through faith.

Adoption as God's Children

Probably the most common phrase used in the church today to describe our salvation is "born again." Interestingly, the phrase occurs only twice in the entire Bible. Both times the phrase was spoken by Jesus, and both occurrences are in his conversation with Nicodemus: "In reply Jesus declared, 'I tell you the truth, no one can see the kingdom of God unless he is born again'" (John 3:3 NIV; compare 3:7 NIV). The NRSV translates the Greek word "from above," rather than "again." Both translations are correct.

The point Jesus was driving home to Nicodemus was that God's salvation is not the result of a natural relationship with God we enjoy. It is not enough even to be born Jewish. Jew or non-Jew, we must be born *again*, born *from above*.

Paul alone among New Testament writers referred to our salvation as "adoption" (Galatians 4:5). What he meant by "adoption" was essentially the same thing that Jesus meant by "born again." Paul used the term five times in his letters (Romans 8:15, 23; 9:4; Galatians 4:5; and Ephesians 1:5) to describe a relationship with God we can enjoy, but which is not based on anything we can do or merit. Nor is it a relationship based on who we are. Based solely on God's grace (and received by us by faith), adoption is the result of a divine decision to extend to us a familial bond we could not enjoy otherwise.

An expression of God's love, adoption has always been God's plan (Ephesians 1:5). Activated for us and in us by God's Holy Spirit (Romans 8:15), it sets us free from "the elemental spirits of the world" as surely as it frees us from "the law" (Galatians 4:3, 5). Given first to Jews (Romans 9:4), adoption was ultimately extended to all people. The full extent of our adoption will not become clear until after the resurrection of our bodies (Romans 8:23).

Confessing Our Inherited Faith

Several years ago, my aunt died. She and her husband, who died before she did, never had any children. Imagine my surprise when I received a letter in the mail alerting me that I would shortly be receiving from her an inheritance. It wasn't much; only a few hundred dollars. But I had done nothing to receive that money. I certainly hadn't worked for it or earned it. It came to me purely as a gift.

In matters of faith, there are many things that we inherit. Three items that come immediately to mind are Scripture, creeds, and the hymnody of the church. These are not things we created, worked for, earned, or deserved. They belonged, if you will, to others who preceded us. They have come to us purely as gifts.

Despite the fact that the creeds of the church come to us as an inheritance, I recall some of my fellow students in seminary saying that they could not and would not confess the creeds because they didn't believe what they said about (for instance) the virgin birth or the resurrection of the body.

Their lack of belief may well have been true, but it was beside the point and frankly didn't matter. By making such comments, those students were acting as if the creeds were theological dictums that they had written, statements that needed to express their beliefs. Neither was true. The creeds were, and are, an inheritance. They convey to us the beliefs of the church. They come to us as a gift. Their value is not contingent on our agreement with them or lack thereof.

When we confess the creeds, we are declaring the faith of the church, a communal reality much larger and greater than us, but one into which we have been confirmed. We are expressing our thanks to God in the traditional words of those who preceded us and who made this gift available to us. We may or may not be confessing our own beliefs.

When I received that inheritance from my aunt, my receipt of the money was not contingent on my knowing how she earned the money. Nor was it contingent on anything I had accomplished in life, done for her, or said about her. It was completely and solely contingent on her desire to share it with me. To make it mine, all I ultimately had to do was acknowledge its receipt. That I did by cashing the check.

We make the inheritance of faith our own by receiving it as the gift it is and living the freedom of Jesus Christ that it extends to us.

SHARING THE SCRIPTURE

Preparing Our Hearts

Explore this week's devotional reading, found in Romans 4:1-8. Here Paul uses the example of Abraham, who was made right with God not because of any works he performed but because he had faith. Paul points to Abraham more frequently than he does to any other biblical figure, except Jesus. To use Abraham as an example in this way was both bold and counter to the prevailing rabbinical teachings that Abraham was justified by works. The point of Paul's example here is to show that Gentiles can be put right with God (4:9-12) through faith in the resurrected Christ, which fulfills the faith of the then-uncircumcised Abraham (4:12-25). Contemplate what you believe about how you are put right with God. How is Abraham an example for you?

Pray that you and the adult learners will recognize salvation as a gift, rather than as something you must work to earn.

Preparing Our Minds

Study the background Scripture from Galatians 3:15-29; 4:1–5:1. Today's lesson Scripture is from Galatians 3:15-18; 4:1-7. Think about why it is important to understand, rather than merely inherit, the values by which we live.

Write on newsprint:

❑ steps for the "Gather to Learn" values activity.
❑ information for next week's lesson, found under "Continue the Journey."
❑ activities for further spiritual growth in "Continue the Journey."

Plan the suggested lecture for "Encounter Paul's Statements About Being Heirs of Abraham in the Faith."

LEADING THE CLASS

(1) Gather to Learn

❖ Welcome the class members and introduce any guests.

❖ Pray that the students will give thanks for the faith they have inherited as descendants of Abraham.

❖ Help the adults think about the values they have inherited by doing this activity. Distribute paper and pencils. Set a time limit for the students to work. Post these steps on newsprint:

■ Draw vertical lines to make three columns. Across the top of the paper, write the names of three people who have had a major impact on your values.
■ List several values in your life that you attribute to each person in the column under each name.
■ Think for a few moments about

how each of these values has affected you. Put a check mark by those that have had a positive impact and an X by those that have had a negative impact.

■ Write two or three sentences about how you have examined these values and made them real in your own life, or chosen to ignore them because they did not seem appropriate to who you are.

❖ Read aloud today's focus statement: **Sometimes a person inherits a system of values without personally investigating the appropriateness of such values. Why is it important to understand, rather than merely inherit, the values by which we live? Paul stated that Gentiles received God's blessing as heirs of Abraham, but had to accept the promise for themselves by maturing in their faith in Jesus Christ.**

(2) Encounter Paul's Statements About Being Heirs of Abraham in the Faith

❖ Choose a volunteer to read Galatians 3:15-18.

❖ Use information from Understanding the Scripture to help the adults understand Paul's example. You may need to explain the argument concerning the use of the singular "offspring" (or "seed," NIV).

❖ Ask: **How is Paul's understanding of God's promise to Abraham similar to or different from your own view of God's promise?**

❖ Present the lecture you developed from Understanding the Scripture for Galatians 3:19-22, 23-25, 26-29 to fill in background information about Paul's teachings on the purpose of the law.

❖ Select a volunteer to read Galatians 4:1-7.

❖ Discuss these questions:
  (1) **What point is Paul trying to make in referring to heirs who are minors?**
  (2) **How did the coming of Jesus change our standing with God?**

(3) **How would you describe the relationship between the Father, the Son, the Holy Spirit, and the believer as depicted in verse 6?**

(3) Appreciate the Value of the Faith the Learners Have Inherited

❖ Read "Adoption as God's Children" from Interpreting the Scripture.

❖ Form groups of three or four. Invite each person in the groups to answer this question, which you will read aloud: **What difference does it make in your life to know that you are an adopted child of God who has inherited the faith first promised to Abraham and fulfilled in Jesus?**

❖ Bring the adults back together. Encourage them to comment on recurrent themes that they heard discussed within their groups.

(4) Confess the Faith the Learners Have Inherited as Their Own

❖ Distribute hymnals and invite the adults to turn to the section that contains affirmations of faith. (If you have *The United Methodist Hymnal*, check pages 880–89.)

❖ Select two of these affirmations for the students to review by reading them silently.

❖ Discuss these questions:
  (1) **Look at one creed** (which you will specify). **What does this creed confess about the Father, about the Son, and about the Holy Spirit?**
  (2) **Look at another creed** (which you will specify). **What does this creed confess about the Father, about the Son, and about the Holy Spirit?**
  (3) **What similarities do you note between these two creeds?** (List ideas on newsprint.)
  (4) **What differences do you note between these two creeds?** (List ideas on newsprint.)

(5) While we recognize that these are creeds of the church, not of individuals, which of the two that we have studied best confesses your own faith? Why? (Some adults may find the two equal in terms of expressing their beliefs.)

❖ **Option:** Read or retell "Confessing Our Inherited Faith" from Interpreting the Scripture.

❖ Conclude this portion of the lesson by inviting the students to read in unison one of these creeds aloud as a confession of their faith.

(5) Continue the Journey

❖ Pray that the adults will confess their faith to others in the week ahead.

❖ Read aloud this preparation for next week's lesson. You may also want to post it on newsprint for the students to copy.

- ■ Title: Fruits of Redemption
- ■ Background Scripture: Galatians 5:2–6:18
- ■ Lesson Scripture: Galatians 5:22–6:10
- ■ Focus of the Lesson: While faith in something or someone must come first, acts beneficial to others will follow. Why is it important to act on faith? Paul said faithfulness is one of the gifts of the Holy Spirit and whenever possible we should work for the good of all, especially for those in the family of faith.

❖ Challenge the students to complete one or more of these activities for further spiritual growth related to this week's session. Post this information on newsprint for the students to copy.

(1) Create or update a last will and testament. Talk with your family about your wishes so that they may know what you want done. If you have minor children, be sure to appoint trustworthy guardians for them.

(2) Use a Bible dictionary or other resource to research the meaning of "covenant." Notice the people with whom God made a covenant, such as Noah, Abraham, and David. What purposes do covenants serve?

(3) Share your understanding of being an adopted child and heir of God. Some people view Christianity as very legalistic. Your conversation can help them to see another very different side, one of God as a loving, gracious parent.

❖ Sing or read aloud "Our Parent, by Whose Name."

❖ Conclude today's session by leading the class in this benediction: **By the power of the Holy Spirit go forth to be a blessing to others even as God through Christ has blessed you.**

UNIT 3: GOD'S REDEMPTION
FRUITS OF REDEMPTION

PREVIEWING THE LESSON

Lesson Scripture: Galatians 5:22–6:10
Background Scripture: Galatians 5:2–6:18
Key Verses: Galatians 5:22-23

Focus of the Lesson:
While faith in something or someone must come first, acts beneficial to others will follow. Why is it important to act on faith? Paul said faithfulness is one of the gifts of the Holy Spirit and whenever possible we should work for the good of all, especially for those in the family of faith.

Goals for the Learners:
(1) to hear Paul's teaching to the Galatians about the faithfulness of bearing one another's burdens.
(2) to reflect on the connection between grace expressed in faith and supporting others in the faith.
(3) to support one another in the faith.

Pronunciation Guide:
agape (ah gah' pay)
eros (air' ose)
Judaizer (joo' day iz uhr)
kairos (ki' rohs)
philia (fih lee' ah)
storge (store gay')

Supplies:
Bibles, newsprint and marker, paper and pencils, hymnals, fruit or pictures of fruit, box or collection plate

---

READING THE SCRIPTURE

NRSV	NIV
Galatians 5:22–6:10	Galatians 5:22–6:10
²²By contrast, the fruit of the Spirit is love, joy, peace, patience, kindness, generosity,	²²But the fruit of the Spirit is love, joy, peace, patience, kindness, goodness,

faithfulness, [23]gentleness, and self-control. There is no law against such things. [24]And those who belong to Christ Jesus have crucified the flesh with its passions and desires. [25]If we live by the Spirit, let us also be guided by the Spirit. [26]Let us not become conceited, competing against one another, envying one another.

[1]My friends, if anyone is detected in a transgression, you who have received the Spirit should restore such a one in a spirit of gentleness. Take care that you yourselves are not tempted. [2]Bear one another's burdens, and in this way you will fulfill the law of Christ. [3]For if those who are nothing think they are something, they deceive themselves. [4]All must test their own work; then that work, rather than their neighbor's work, will become a cause for pride. [5]For all must carry their own loads.

[6]Those who are taught the word must share in all good things with their teacher.

[7]Do not be deceived; God is not mocked, for you reap whatever you sow. [8]If you sow to your own flesh, you will reap corruption from the flesh; but if you sow to the Spirit, you will reap eternal life from the Spirit. [9]So let us not grow weary in doing what is right, for we will reap at harvest time, if we do not give up. [10]So then, whenever we have an opportunity, let us work for the good of all, and especially for those of the family of faith.

faithfulness, [23]gentleness and self-control. Against such things there is no law. [24]Those who belong to Christ Jesus have crucified the sinful nature with its passions and desires. [25]Since we live by the Spirit, let us keep in step with the Spirit. [26]Let us not become conceited, provoking and envying each other.

[1]Brothers, if someone is caught in a sin, you who are spiritual should restore him gently. But watch yourself, or you also may be tempted. [2]Carry each other's burdens, and in this way you will fulfill the law of Christ. [3]If anyone thinks he is something when he is nothing, he deceives himself. [4]Each one should test his own actions. Then he can take pride in himself, without comparing himself to somebody else, [5]for each one should carry his own load.

[6]Anyone who receives instruction in the word must share all good things with his instructor.

[7]Do not be deceived: God cannot be mocked. A man reaps what he sows. [8]The one who sows to please his sinful nature, from that nature will reap destruction; the one who sows to please the Spirit, from the Spirit will reap eternal life. [9]Let us not become weary in doing good, for at the proper time we will reap a harvest if we do not give up. [10]Therefore, as we have opportunity, let us do good to all people, especially to those who belong to the family of believers.

UNDERSTANDING THE SCRIPTURE

Galatians 5:2-6. Christians gain nothing by trying to become Jews. To the contrary, we lose much. The righteousness we seek is obtained by grace through faith, not by becoming Jewish. And we do not prove that our faith in God is alive and well by willingly adhering to the law and being circumcised. We do this only by expressing to others the divine love we have received.

Galatians 5:7-12. Paul's exasperation

with the Judaizers, who seemed fixated on foreskins, finally boiled over. If they were so intent on using knives, why stop with the foreskin?

Galatians 5:13-15. Paul now addressed the flip side of his comments regarding the law. The freedom that Christians experience in the Spirit is not permission to live as libertines. It is freedom to "serve one another in love" (5:13 NIV).

Galatians 5:16-18. When we decide to live in the freedom of the Spirit, the resources that the Spirit provides us enable us to overcome the selfish desires of the "sinful nature" (5:16 NIV) that we are never entirely rid of.

Galatians 5:19-21. Paul's catalog of representative vices practiced by those who are controlled by the "sinful nature" names fifteen acts that few Christians would question. None are acts that Spirit-led Christians would want to do, for they do not enable us to love and serve our neighbor (5:13).

Galatians 5:22-23. In stark contrast to the multiple vices exhibited by those who are self-indulgent is the communal fruit of the Spirit. The nine virtues listed are, in fact, aspects of the one virtue that heads the list: love. In a context in which the "enmities, strife, . . . dissensions, factions, envy" (5:20-21) of the Judaizers were threatening the unity and integrity of the Christian community in Galatia, Paul drew attention to the community building that occurs in those who are "led by the Spirit" (5:18).

Galatians 5:24. The new life produced in us by the Spirit is able to take shape as we actively participate in the death of the "sinful nature" (NIV). It is certainly true that the destruction of the "old self" (Romans 6:6) is primarily the work of God done in us on our behalf, but it is equally true that God will not do this against our will. We must by faith cooperate with God's Spirit.

Galatians 5:25-26. The new life that began in us when we received the Spirit is not a once-and-done elixir that solves all our past and present problems and fixes us for the future. It is, in fact, a living relationship that requires our active participation. As the Spirit makes us aware of inappropriate prejudices and offensive attitudes and hurtful actions, we need to "live by the Spirit" (5:25). That is, we need to act in accordance with what the Spirit is telling us.

At the very least, that means that the community-destroying forms of selfishness—such as vain conceit and meaningless provocation and corrosive envy—that oppose the fruit of the Spirit must become a thing of the past.

Galatians 6:1. That is not to suggest that Paul had perfectionist leanings. He was too much the realist to fall prey to such expectations. In keeping with the communal concerns he had voiced in the last several verses, Paul made it clear that when persons in a church community fall prey to sin, the Spirit will call others in that communion to effect a restoration. Such work should be done with a humble, not a haughty, spirit.

Galatians 6:2. What Paul said in particular about the community coming to the aid of one caught in sin is equally true in general about the community assisting any who are suffering unduly under the weight of a burden. Such assistance is clearly one way we "fulfill the law of Christ" by loving our neighbors as ourselves.

Galatians 6:3-5. The bottom line is simply to remember that we are part of a community that is much more than the sum of its parts. None of us is more or less important than anyone else. We are each essential to the whole.

Consequently, no one who assists another should thereby think that she is better than the person she is assisting. And no one should adopt an attitude of entitlement and think that because he is so great, everyone else must drop what they are doing and come to his assistance. We are each ultimately responsible for how we conduct ourselves.

Galatians 6:6. That said, those persons in the community of faith who have responded to God's call to become teachers are entitled to material support from that community.

Galatians 6:7. Paul's final advice to the Christians in Galatia begins with a straightforward reminder that the personal and communal choices they were making had consequences.

Galatians 6:8. Those who put their best efforts into looking after the things of the flesh—including circumcision and ethnic identities—cannot hope in the end to receive anything but death. On the other hand, those who attend to God's Spirit will receive eternal life.

Galatians 6:9. Because the Christian life is not a one-and-done event but a relationship with God, its completion requires sustained effort on our part across our entire lifetime. We simply cannot "coast" or settle into thinking that we have done all the good we need to do.

Galatians 6:10. While it is especially appropriate for Christians to act kindly toward fellow Christians, there is nothing about our faith that encourages segregation from the world. To the contrary, we are to live as lights to the nations (Isaiah 49:6), treating all persons as neighbors whom we should love (Galatians 5:14) and treat well (Matthew 7:12; Luke 10:25-37, especially verses 27-28, 37).

Galatians 6:11-18. Paul's conclusion and farewell were written in his "own hand" in expensive and papyrus-wasting "large letters" to emphasize their importance (6:11). He reiterated his earlier arguments about circumcision and Jewish ethnic identity being supplanted by "a new creation" (6:15) and "the cross of our Lord Jesus Christ" (6:14).

INTERPRETING THE SCRIPTURE

Fruit of the Spirit

By coming at the end of Galatians 5, Paul's listing of the acts of the flesh (5:19-21) and the fruit of the Spirit (5:22-23) offers an apt conclusion to his discussions of law/promise, circumcision/uncircumcision, and flesh/Spirit. Whereas the acts of the flesh are self-centered and destructive to communities, the fruit of the Spirit is focused on the good of the community.

Although the title of this lesson might lead one to think otherwise, there is only one fruit of the Spirit. The nine virtues Paul listed in verses 22-23 are all facets of the first virtue: love. Thus, Thomas Langford was right on the money in his book *The Harvest of the Spirit*, when he titled each chapter as an aspect of love: "Love: Freedom's Embodiment"; "Joy: Love Released for Loving"; "Peace: Love Expressing Its Depth"; "Patience: Love Enduring over Time"; "Kindness: Love as Thoughtfulness"; "Goodness: Love Going Bone Deep"; "Fidelity: Love as Persistent Presence"; "Gentleness: Love as Tender Strength"; and "Self-Control: Life Shaped by Love."

Unlike English, which requires the word "love" to cover a vast range of semantic nuances (*The Oxford English Dictionary* lists thirty definitions for love), Greek employed four words for love. *Eros* was a catchall term for various forms of physical love. *Storge* described the love that family members have for one another. *Philia*, the most exalted form of love, described the love shared between friends. A fourth word, *agape*, was so rarely used as a noun that it was almost nonexistent. This is the term that the Christian church made its own and used to describe the sacrificial love of God.

Joy is not a fleeting emotion like happiness. It is a deep-seated satisfaction with life that grows out of our relationship with God. Peace is more than the absence of conflict or the detached calm that accompanies apathy. It is good health and contentment, security and serenity. Patience is that steadfastness that refuses to react to provocation or slight. Kindness is a form of mercy, the willingness to forgive and treat well. Goodness is a generosity of spirit. Faithfulness is reliability, dependability. Gentleness is strength yoked to grace, that is, a humble spirit, a courteous disposition. Self-control is the refusal to be ruled by one's passions. It is the reasoned grip on life that enables one to live a chaste, pure life.

Bearing Burdens

We are living at a time when the church as an institution is struggling both with its identity as a Spirit-led community of faith and with its actions as a people called to a life of sanctity. This makes for an interesting interplay both of excuses and finger-pointing.

On the one hand, it has become commonplace for both clergy and laity to dismiss the topic of sin by declaring that we are all sinners. True enough. Unfortunately, the declaration is not intended to be a lament that leads to the confession of sin and greater dependence on the grace of God. Instead, it is used as a catchall excuse, often delivered (it seems) with a wink and a nod: "We are, after all, only human."

In addition, the privatization of faith, the underscoring of "personal rights," and the retreat from scriptural truths has created a situation in which those who sin can effectively excuse their sin by saying that the issue in question is a matter "between God and me," the implication being that it is no one else's business. As long as no one is hurt, what they do in private is off limits for discussion or critique.

On the other hand, the inability to humbly acknowledge sin has led to a furious backlash across all sectors of society. It has become equally commonplace for persons to replace conversation with accusation, to exchange blame for dialogue. The ills of society, the graying of the church, the (lack of) morals among the youth—and countless other matters, large and small, ethical and theological—are not matters of concern that break hearts and lead to an intense desire to do whatever it might take to help. Instead, they lead to even more finger-pointing and faultfinding.

Paul offers us another option, the option of burden bearing. Were the church to commit itself to bearing burdens (Galatians 6:2), it could cut through this Gordian knot. To bear one another's burdens, we must (and must be permitted to) point out sin. However, the purpose is not to judge guilt; the purpose is to "restore . . . in a spirit of gentleness" (6:1). At the same time, we must once again exercise personal responsibility for our sin and "carry [our] own loads" (6:4-5).

Dietrich Bonhoeffer's *Life Together* offers an excellent exploration of what it means for us to bear one another's burdens. And through the figure of Raskolnikov in *Crime and Punishment*, Fyodor Dostoyevsky offered a penetrating analysis of what happens to individuals who "deceive themselves" (Galatians 6:3) by thinking they are something when really they are not, and who sin as they please and refuse to take responsibility for their actions.

At the Proper Time

Greek speakers generally, and writers of Scripture in particular, mark an important difference between the simple passage of chronological time and God-infused moments when time seems alive with new possibilities. Hidden in English translation in Galatians 6, Paul twice referred to God-infused *kairos* moments as the reason we should persevere in doing good—in verse 9 ("at the proper time," NIV; "at harvest-time," NRSV) and in verse 10 ("whenever we have an opportunity").

Imagine how sad it would be if a person who had trained for an Olympic race all her life were running and winning her event, only to suddenly grow tired of the race and drop out. Or consider a farmer who carefully tended the soil, planted the best seeds, weeded and sprayed the young plants, but failed to harvest the ripe fruit, letting it rot on the vine. The failures of the athlete and of the farmer to persevere "at the proper time" and as they "have an opportunity" would render both their work and their commitment suspect.

Parents and teachers know well that the payoff on instruction to children and students is sometimes long in coming. Patiently and repeatedly, a teacher will explain how to add and subtract, and rejoice when the student finally "gets it." Ditto with the parent teaching a child to tie her shoes or catch a ball. More than one teacher has despaired of a student ever learning a concept but, rather than forsake the student, has tried yet another approach, which ended up working. How sad for everyone involved if they had not exercised the patience and love necessary to make one more attempt to reach that child. The same could be said of students who, unable to make sense of an idea, keep struggling with it until it finally makes sense.

The church understands these God-infused moments to be "the time of God's favor, . . . the day of salvation" (2 Corinthians 6:2 NIV). Because of the faithfulness of Christ Jesus, God's *kairos* is no longer a future event we still await; it is here, "now" (2 Corinthians 6:2), "at hand" (Mark 1:15 KJV).

SHARING THE SCRIPTURE

Preparing Our Hearts

Explore this week's devotional reading, found in 2 Peter 1:3-8. God wants us to participate in "the divine nature" (1:4). Christ has provided for us all that we need to live as godly people who walk in the way of the Lord. Through faith in Christ we increasingly obtain the virtues listed in verses 5-7. These blessings, which rest on faith, enable us to be fruitful. Meditate on how you express the goodness, knowledge, self-control, endurance, godliness, mutual affection, and love that faith in Christ makes possible for you.

Pray that you and the adult learners will live so as to experience and allow others to witness the fruits of redemption.

Preparing Our Minds

Study the background Scripture from Galatians 5:2–6:18 and the lesson Scripture from Galatians 5:22–6:10. Ask yourself: Why is it important to act on faith?

Write on newsprint:

❑ information for next week's lesson, found under "Continue the Journey."

❑ activities for further spiritual growth in "Continue the Journey."

LEADING THE CLASS

(1) Gather to Learn

❖ Welcome the class members and introduce any guests.

❖ Pray that the students will open their hearts to bearing one another's burdens in faith.

❖ Read this information aloud: **If you've ever watched the Tour de France bicycle race, you're likely aware that riders stay as close to one another's back wheel as possible. They are drafting, that is, taking advantage of the wind blocking that the cyclist ahead is doing for them. Since approximately 80 percent of a cyclist's energy is expended on cutting through the air, one who is drafting can conserve considerable energy. Similarly, geese fly in a V formation for the same reason. In the world of cycling and in the natural world, no one individual is always in the lead. They take turns so as to share the workload. If a cyclist or goose falls away from** the main group, that individual quickly tires and lags farther and farther behind.

❖ Ask: **What lessons can cyclists and geese teach us about working for the good of all and bearing one another's burdens?**

❖ Read aloud today's focus statement: **While faith in something or someone must come first, acts beneficial to others will follow. Why is it important to act on faith? Paul said faithfulness is one of the gifts of the Holy Spirit and whenever possible we should work for the good of all, especially for those in the family of faith.**

(2) Hear Paul's Teaching to the Galatians About the Faithfulness of Bearing One Another's Burdens

❖ Choose a volunteer to read Galatians 5:22-26.

❖ Read "Fruit of the Spirit" from Interpreting the Scripture.

❖ **Option:** Bring nine pieces of fruit or pictures of fruit. Label each with one of the nine expressions of the "fruit of the Spirit." Note that "fruit" is singular, signifying different ways in which the "spiritual fruit" is manifested in each person who is made right with God through Jesus. Set the fruit on a table where it can be a visual representation of Paul's teaching.

❖ Select another volunteer to read Galatians 6:1-10.

❖ Look at the imperative (command) verb forms in this passage. List the verbs the students find in their Bibles on newsprint. These will vary by translation, but important ones in the NRSV include *restore, take care, bear, test, carry, share, do not be deceived, (do) not grow weary, do not give up, work.*

❖ Discuss these questions:
(1) **How do you see the church trying to restore those who have strayed?** (Be sure to keep this discussion general and not focused on specific people.)

(2) **What evidence can you cite to demonstrate that the people in your congregation bear one another's burdens?**

(3) **What examples can you give of people reaping what they sow?** (Again, be careful about pointing fingers toward specific individuals within the congregation or community if the example is negative. Public figures may be cited if their stories are well known.)

(4) **How are you as a community of faith working "for the good of all" (6:10)?**

❖ Conclude with this question for silent reflection: **How are you carrying your own load within the church?**

(3) Reflect on the Connection Between Grace Expressed in Faith and Supporting Others in the Faith

❖ Distribute hymnals. Look at "Blest Be the Tie That Binds," a familiar hymn in most congregations.

❖ Invite the adults to identify ways that songwriter John Fawcett envisions the church supporting each member. List those ideas.

❖ Look again at the list. Ask the group to identify specific ways that your congregation enacts the kind of support Fawcett writes about. For example, sharing one another's woes might include intercessory prayer, hands-on assistance, and visiting the sick and bereaved.

❖ Brainstorm additional ways that the church could support its members in faith. List these ideas on newsprint.

❖ Challenge the adults to make a commitment to implement one or more of these ideas. They may work with classmates to create a new ministry that will express God's grace to others who, for whatever reason, need support in their faith journey.

(4) Support One Another in the Faith

❖ Distribute slips of paper and pencils to half of the class. Ask those who have a paper to write their name on the paper, fold it, and put it in a collection plate, box, or other handy container.

❖ Pass the container around the room and ask each person who did not receive a paper to draw a slip from the container and read aloud the name. What the class has just done is create spiritual journey partners. (Pairs should not be related to each other, if at all possible.)

❖ Tell the adults that each half of the pair is to support the other in his or her faith as a prayer partner, an assistant in a service project, a Bible study colleague, or in some other way.

❖ Provide a few moments for pairs to meet together, exchange contact information if necessary, and talk about how they might be able to help each other in their spiritual journeys. Some people may have an immediate need they can express, whereas others may need some time to think over how the other person might offer helpful support.

(5) Continue the Journey

❖ Pray that the adults will support one another in the faith during the coming week.

❖ Read aloud this preparation for next week's lesson. You may also want to post it on newsprint for the students to copy.
   ■ **Title: Wisdom's Part in Creation**
   ■ **Background Scripture: Proverbs 8**
   ■ **Lesson Scripture: Proverbs 8:22-35**

■ **Focus of the Lesson: People appreciate wisdom and yearn for a depth of wisdom for themselves and others. What is the root of this longing for wisdom? The writer of Proverbs speaks about Wisdom having a divine origin, being present as God created all things, and having a role with God in creation.**

❖ Challenge the students to complete one or more of these activities for further spiritual growth related to this week's session. Post this information on newsprint for the students to copy.

   (1) **Memorize Galatians 5:22-23. Call this passage to mind often as you think about how the Spirit is manifested in your life.**

   (2) **Assist someone who needs help in bearing burdens. Do whatever you can, perhaps taking some tangible action, providing financial assistance, or offering moral support.**

   (3) **Thank someone who has been a burden-bearer for you. A heartfelt note and perhaps a small gift can let someone know how much you appreciate the kindness that was extended to you at a time when you really needed support.**

❖ Sing or read aloud "Spirit of God, Descend upon My Heart."

❖ Conclude today's session by leading the class in this benediction: **By the power of the Holy Spirit go forth to be a blessing to others even as God through Christ has blessed you.**

THIRD QUARTER
God's Creative Word

MARCH 4, 2012–MAY 27, 2012

During the spring quarter we will do an in-depth study of John by exploring this Gospel through the theological lens of creation. We often think of creation as a singular event in which God brought the world into existence. Yet creation also involves God's ongoing action of reconciling and recreating, both now and in eternity. God's creating word was, is, and shall be making all things good.

Unit 1, "The Word Was in the Beginning," features six sessions that spotlight the creative power of God's Word. On March 4 we consider "Wisdom's Part in Creation" by examining Proverbs 8, where wisdom is personified as a woman. Part of the Prologue of the Fourth Gospel, John 1:1-14, is the focus of our study on March 11 as we consider the amazing news that "The Word Became Flesh." We observe Jesus creating wine from water as we turn to John 2:1-12 on March 18 to read the story of "The Wedding at Cana." As we overhear Jesus' conversation with Nicodemus during the lesson for March 25 from John 3:11-21 and Numbers 21:4-8, we discover that "God's Word Saves." On April 1, Palm Sunday, we investigate the events leading to Jesus' crucifixion as recorded in John 18–19 in which "Jesus Testifies to the Truth." The first unit ends on Easter, April 8, as the empty tomb is discovered, as reported in John 20:1-23, and the disciples begin to become aware of "The Living Word."

Unit 2, "The Word Is Here and Now," includes three sessions in which we can see the power of the incarnate Jesus' words to purify the Temple, restore human life, and heal. The familiar story of him "Cleansing the Temple," rooted in John 2:13-22, begins this unit on April 15. As a result of Jesus' conversation with the "Woman of Samaria," which we will study on April 22 from John 4:1-42, the woman was able to turn her life around. John 9 is the basis for the session on April 29 in which we witness Jesus "Healing the Blind Man."

Unit 3, "The Word Will Be," explores several of the "I am" sayings of Jesus. On May 6 we examine John 6 to hear Jesus state that he is "The Bread of Life" and recognize that by eating this bread we will never be hungry. John 10:1-18, which we will encounter on May 13, presents us with the tender image of Jesus as "The Good Shepherd." On May 20, within the story of the death of Lazarus that is found in John 11:1-27, we hear Jesus comfort Martha with the words that he is "The Resurrection and the Life." The quarter closes on May 27 with a portion of Jesus' farewell address to his disciples from John 14:1-14, in which he assures them that he is "The Way, the Truth, and the Life" through whom they can find direction for life both now and forever.

MEET OUR WRITER

THE REVEREND DAVID KALAS

David Kalas is the pastor of First United Methodist Church in Whitewater, Wisconsin, where he has served since 2004.

David grew up as the son of a United Methodist minister, first in Madison, Wisconsin, and later in Cleveland, Ohio. After graduating from high school in Cleveland, he attended the University of Virginia, where he earned his bachelor's degree in English.

Having felt his call to the ministry as a young teenager, he began his ministry while a college student, serving as the student pastor of two little rural churches outside of Charlottesville, Virginia. He recalls with great fondness and gratitude the sweet and patient saints of Bingham's and Wesley Chapel United Methodist churches.

Because it was during his own teenage years that David came to Christ, began reading the Bible, and felt his calling, he has always had a heart for teens and for youth ministry. During the latter half of his college years and throughout his seminary training, David served as a youth minister in Cleveland, Ohio, and then in Richmond, Virginia.

David began his seminary work at Pittsburgh Theological Seminary in Pittsburgh, Pennsylvania, where he spent two years. After moving to Virginia, he completed his work at Union Theological Seminary in Richmond, Virginia, earning his M.Div. in 1991.

After seminary, David entered full-time pastoral ministry, serving a rural two-point charge in Virginia. A move to Wisconsin in 1996 was a happy return to his childhood home. For eight years, David served as pastor of Emmanuel United Methodist Church in Appleton, Wisconsin, before moving to his current appointment in Whitewater.

In his local church ministry, David emphasizes individual and corporate Bible study as key to spiritual growth and congregational strength. He places a premium on both preaching and teaching within the church, and he continues to cherish opportunities to work with youth.

In addition to *The New International Lesson Annual*, David has also contributed to a number of published collections of sermons, and is a regular writer for *Emphasis*, a lectionary-based resource for preachers.

David and his wife, Karen, have been married for nearly thirty years. They met in their home church youth group when they were just teenagers in Cleveland and have been together ever since. David and Karen are the proud parents of three daughters. Angela is a high school student, while Lydia and Susanna are both in elementary school.

Another one of the great loves of his life is the Holy Land. He has made six trips to that part of the world, and is planning another pilgrimage soon. David has found that his own reading of the Bible has been enriched by getting to know the land from which it came, and he encourages the members of his congregations to make the trip if they are able.

David is also an avid sports fan. He loves to play sports as recreation and to watch sports as relaxation. He enjoys traveling, walking, tinkering with around-the-house projects, and spending as much time with his family as possible.

THE BIG PICTURE:
THE GOSPEL OF JOHN

Five times in the Fourth Gospel, the author refers to himself as "the other disciple" (18:16; 20:2-4, 8). In each instance, he is distinguishing himself from Peter, who is also on the scene.

Perhaps we might likewise refer to his book as "the other Gospel," distinguishing it from Matthew, Mark, and Luke. For John is unmistakably different.

New Testament scholars commonly refer to the first three Gospels together as a group. They are called the "Synoptic Gospels," which alludes to their many similarities in content and organization.

John, however, is the other Gospel. It is the book that stands on its own, the one that does not lend itself to a side-by-side viewing with the other three. Each Gospel has its own distinctive characteristics, of course. But John's organization, content, and style set it apart as truly unique among the four.

While we will begin by looking at a passage from Proverbs, and we will certainly borrow insight from Matthew, Mark, and Luke along the way, John is the real focus of our study.

The Gospel's Purpose

Near the end of John's Gospel, he tells us his reason for writing it: "These are written so that you may come to believe that Jesus is the Messiah, the Son of God, and that through believing you may have life in his name" (20:31). In that succinct statement of purpose, John captures for us three great themes of his book.

First, there is the central issue of Jesus' identity: "the Messiah, the Son of God." As we will discover, John's entire Gospel is organized around the purpose of revealing who Jesus is. Moses, John the Baptist, the Father, and the Spirit all bear witness to Jesus. The signs that Jesus performs disclose his identity. And his words—most dramatically his "I am" statements—reveal who Jesus is.

Second, there is the importance of believing: "that you may come to believe." To foster such belief in Jesus was the very purpose of John the Baptist's ministry (1:7). And in the passages from John's Gospel that we will study together, we will see the disciples (chapter 2), a whole Samaritan village (chapter 4), a man born blind (chapter 9), the other disciple (chapter 20), and Thomas (chapter 20) all come to believe in Jesus.

And, finally, there is the result of believing: "that through believing you may have life." In our day, belief has turned into a kind of poll question. To say that you believe in something or someone is to affirm it, to endorse it. In the Fourth Gospel, however, believing in Jesus is not an endorsement of Jesus; it is a recognition of Jesus. And that recognition frees one from death (5:24; 11:26) and condemnation (3:18), resulting in eternal life (3:14-16; 6:40, 47).

The Gospel's Pace and Place

Among the many distinctive features of John's Gospel is his own unique sense of stagecraft. His handling of the narrative details of Jesus' story sets him apart from his peers.

First, John places the story more in Jerusalem and Judea than the Synoptic writers do. Matthew, Mark, and Luke portray the bulk of Jesus' early ministry in the northern region called Galilee, named for the lake that is at the center of so many cherished stories. Those three Gospels turn their attention to Jerusalem only for Jesus' final trip there, which we recall during Holy Week. John, on the other hand, gives us much more insight into Jesus' larger ministry in Jerusalem. Indeed, in his account, Jerusalem is the centerpiece of Jesus' activity, whereas Galilee is visited only occasionally.

The two different portrayals of Jesus' ministry should probably be embraced as complementary, rather than contradictory. As an adult Jewish man, Jesus would have been expected to participate in certain annual observances in Jerusalem. John reports a number of such festivals (for example, 2:23; 5:1; 7:10; 10:22-23; 13:1), which become the backdrop for Jesus' frequent presence in Jerusalem.

Meanwhile, just as John's geography is different from that of Matthew, Mark, and Luke, so is his chronology. Because John cites so many different festivals, it is easier to track his story on the Jewish calendar. And with his references to three different Passovers (2:13; 6:4; 11:55), it appears that John's story of Jesus' public ministry unfolds over the course of two to three years. The accounts in the Synoptic Gospels do not necessarily contradict such a chronology, but neither is a three-year ministry as explicit in those as in John.

And, finally, John demonstrates a different storytelling pace in where he spends his greatest time. The Fourth Gospel has twenty-one chapters, and John devotes five of them to the Last Supper episode. It's a phenomenal indulgence, especially when compared with the twenty-four-verse average of the Synoptic accounts.

To Make a Long Story Short

On two different occasions near the end of his Gospel, John makes reference to all the other things that he is not telling us. Not that he is being secretive; there is just a limit to time and space.

Shortly after his initial accounts of Jesus' resurrection appearances, John concedes, "Now Jesus did many other signs in the presence of his disciples, which are not written in this book" (20:30). We know, therefore, that there is more to be told, some portion of which may be found in Matthew, Mark, and Luke.

Then, in his final chapter, John shares one more extended episode from the disciples' time with the risen Lord. And then, as his conclusion to the whole Gospel, John writes, "But there are also many other things that Jesus did; if every one of them were written down, I suppose that the world itself could not contain the books that would be written" (21:25).

We do not read the Gospels with the assumption that they record every single thing that Jesus said and did. It's important for us to stop and ponder John's admission on this point, however, because it reminds us that he had to make some editorial decisions.

John knew more stories than he included. He knew more details than he shared. He had to be selective, and so we may give some thought to why he chose the things he did.

John knew of many miracles of Jesus, for example, but he chose to report relatively few. This is one of the most obvious differences between John and the Synoptic Gospels. John is selective about the miracle stories—he calls them "signs"—and he is more deliberate about attaching specific meaning to them. Again, since the author's central purpose is to reveal who Jesus is, he chooses the miracle stories that serve that end.

The Gospel in Black and White

From the very first verses of his book, we see a certain dualism in John. "The light shines in the darkness," he declares, "and the darkness did not overcome it" (1:5). And with that first clue, we begin to trace the contrasting themes of light and dark, life and death, truth and falsehood.

The author is not unsophisticated, but he sees reality in stark, either-or terms. There are no shades of gray in the spiritual matters of sin and salvation. Whoever sins becomes a slave of sin (8:34). Whoever believes becomes a child of God (1:12-13).

John thinks in broad categories. Hence he makes frequent use of group terms like "the Jews" (for example, 1:19; 2:18; 6:41; 18:14; 20:19), "the twelve" (for example, 6:67; 20:24), and "the world" (for example, 1:9-10; 3:16-17; 12:46-47; 15:18-19).

Meanwhile, part-and-parcel with his dualism and categorical thinking is a high degree of symbolism. John's Gospel does not feature the parables of Jesus so familiar from Matthew and Luke, yet it is full of a different kind of symbolic teaching. The new birth of chapter 3, the water of chapter 4, the bread of chapter 6, and the blindness of chapter 9 all have double meanings. There is the physical reality, which is typically the focus of Jesus' audience, and then there is the deeper, spiritual reality to which he points.

Finally, John's Gospel understands reality as having two planes: the earthly and the heavenly. Jesus expresses the dichotomy to Nicodemus: "If I have told you about earthly things and you do not believe, how can you believe if I tell you about heavenly things?" (3:12). The world—that is, the earthly realm—is where the Gospel's drama is being played out, for Jesus is the one who has "come into the world" (3:19; 6:14; 16:28; see also 12:46). He has come from heaven (6:38) and speaks of heaven (3:12-13, 31-32), but he was sent into the world because "God so loved the world" (3:16).

A Love-Hate Relationship

That relationship between God and the world is a fascinating study in John. That "God so loved the world" is not only a most familiar phrase, it is also a most fundamental truth. God's love for the world is the predicate upon which the salvation story is built.

Yet it is an unrequited love.

From the start, we read that the world did not manage to identify Jesus (1:10). Though he himself had made the world in the beginning, and though he had now come into the world in its own flesh, he was unrecognized here.

As the Gospel unfolds, we discover that the problem is deeper than just an identification problem, however. The issue is not merely recognition, but opposition.

The world is enemy territory (12:31; 16:11). Jesus portrayed it as a realm that was apart from—and even hostile to—God. He did not belong to the world (8:23) and neither did his disciples (17:16). The world did not know him (1:10), his Father (17:25), or the Holy Spirit (14:17). Jesus said that his ultimate kingdom was not from this world (18:36), and that the world hated him (7:7; 15:18) and would hate his disciples (15:19).

Yet for all of its antagonism and rejection, see the Lord's gracious policy toward the world. Jesus came as its light (8:12; 9:5) and to give it life (6:33). He came not to condemn it but to save it (3:17) and to take away its sins (1:29).

This love-hate relationship is not the sort that runs hot and cold. Rather, God's love for the world is constant, and the world's rejection of God is chronic. Yet it is emblematic of divine grace that those who rejected God are not rejected. Instead, God pursues them in love. Accordingly, God sent the Beloved Son into the world (10:36), sent the Holy Spirit (16:7-8), and sent the disciples (17:18).

All That Jesus Is

Perhaps the most famous feature of John's Gospel is the collection of "I am" statements found there. Over the course of the book, John records for us these seven statements of self-identification by Jesus: I am the bread of life (6:35, 48, 51); I am the light of the world (8:12; 9:5); I am the gate (10:7, 9); I am the good shepherd (10:11, 14); I am the resurrection and the life (11:25); I am the way, and the truth, and the life (14:6); and I am the vine (15:1, 5). We will have opportunity to consider in detail four of these statements during the weeks of our study.

The "I am" statements go to the heart of John's stated purpose. He is eager for the reader to come to believe in Jesus, and that means recognizing who Jesus is.

This component of John is a particular treasure for us.

First, these "I am" statements are what Jesus said about himself. We welcome the testimonies of others about Jesus—Peter and Paul, the four Evangelists, and the writer of Hebrews—but these statements are of a different order. We believe that God cannot be known by sinful human beings except to the extent of God's self-revelation to them. And in these seven statements, Jesus reveals himself to us.

Second, the language of the statements is meaningfully picturesque. The often sterile and esoteric terminology of philosophy and theology can sometimes leave us cold. But Jesus communicates profound truths in simple pictures: shepherds and gates, bread and vines. If a picture is indeed worth a thousand words, then Jesus was most clever to use word pictures.

Third, these statements are the stuff of meditation. Like a panoramic view off to the side of the highway, we find it is insufficient to drive by these words of Jesus at 60 miles per hour. They beckon to us to back up and park. To get out and look. To meditate on the meaning, as we endeavor to take in all the beauty and the truth.

Fourth, these teachings are essential to our witness. Near the end of the Gospel, Jesus prays "not only on behalf of [the disciples], but also on behalf of those who will believe in me through their word" (17:20). So it is that those who know Jesus are to bear witness to him in order that others may come to believe in him, too. And since he is the message we share, then these priceless truths about him are the heart of that message.

Finally, the "I am" teachings remind us of the relentlessly personal nature of the gospel message. Dogma and doctrine are not at the heart of Christianity. Neither ritual nor tradition, neither rules nor works are its essence. The Christian faith, first to last, is about a person. And the "I am" statements reveal to us who he is.

Face to Face

Finally, another evidence of the personal nature of the gospel message is the personal portrayals of Jesus. This is another distinctive element of John's Gospel—and part of its enduring appeal for us as individuals.

More than any other Gospel, John emphasizes the one-on-one encounters with Jesus. In the accounts of Jesus' ministry found in the Synoptic Gospels, one senses a ubiquitous crowd (for example, Matthew 9:25; Luke 8:45; 9:10-11). John focuses his lens more tightly, however, offering us many pictures of Jesus dealing with individuals.

Over the course of the Fourth Gospel, we see Jesus in one-on-one dialogues with Nicodemus (chapter 3), the Samaritan woman (chapter 4), the paralyzed man by the pool (chapter 5), the woman caught in the act of adultery (chapter 8), Martha and then Mary (chapter 11), Pilate (chapters 18 and 19), Mary Magdalene and then Thomas (chapter 20), and Peter (chapter 21).

More than Matthew, Mark, or Luke, John gives us a glimpse of Jesus dealing with people individually. And we cherish those images, for they reflect both our desire and our experience. We long for that personal relationship with him, and we rejoice in it when we find it.

And so, as we begin our study of the Gospel of John together, we can expect to see a unique and powerful portrait of Jesus. We will come to believe through the testimony of the witnesses. We will discover all that he is. And we will behold his glory, full of grace and truth.

CLOSE-UP:
THE FOURTH GOSPEL

All but the first session of our spring quarter examines the Gospel of John. "The Big Picture: The Gospel of John" article provides you with much information about this Gospel's focus, theological perspectives, and special accents. In this "Close-up" article, we will consider some background concerning John's Gospel. You may wish to use this information in a brief introductory lecture to help orient the class to this Gospel. If you have access to *The New Interpreter's Bible*, volume 9, the introduction to John by Gail R. O'Day will enable you to plumb these ideas in greater depth.

Writer: As is true of the other three Gospels, John was written anonymously. Not until the second century was the Fourth Gospel referred to as "The Gospel According to John." The John referred to here was understood to be the son of Zebedee, an apostle of Jesus. His status as an apostle gave this work authority and legitimacy. John 19:35 and 21:24 claim that eyewitness testimony undergirds this Gospel. This witness is not identified by name, but in 21:20 is called "the disciple whom Jesus loved." While the identification of John with this beloved disciple is conjecture, this notion dates back to the mid-second century.

Date and Audience: Based on the evidence of the text itself and references to John's Gospel within the early traditions of the church, this Gospel was presumably written no earlier than A.D. 75–80 and no later than 100. The term "put out of the synagogue," which appears in John 9:22, 12:42, and 16:2, suggests that the struggle within Judaism among those who followed Christ and those who did not had reached the point where heretics were banned from the synagogue. A document titled "Benediction Against Heretics" became part of the Jewish liturgy, probably sometime between 85 and 95. The people to whom this Gospel was addressed were likely Jewish Christians who had been "put out," because the Gospel itself includes harsh words about "the Jews" and relates to them in an adversarial way. John's community was apparently a persecuted minority that had been expelled from the larger Jewish community because they had accepted Christ.

Location: While scholars are uncertain as to where the Gospel of John was written, Ephesus is a strong contender because, according to Acts 18–19, that city hosted a large group of active Jews. Two other places with large Jewish populations, Antioch and Alexandria, are also possibilities, as is Palestine.

Outline (as proposed by Gail R. O'Day):

John 1:1-51	The Prelude to Jesus' Ministry
John 2:1–5:47	"The Greater Things": Jesus' Words and Works
John 6:1–10:42	Jesus' Words and Works: Conflict and Opposition Grow
John 11:1–12:50	The Prelude to Jesus' Hour
John 13:1–17:26	The Farewell Meal and Discourse
John 18:1–19:42	"The Hour Has Come": Jesus' Arrest, Trial, and Death
John 20:1-31	The First Resurrection Appearances
John 21:1-25	Jesus' Resurrection Appearance at the Sea of Tiberius

FAITH IN ACTION: WITNESSING TO GOD'S CREATIVE WORD

Throughout this quarter we are witnesses to "God's Creative Word," particularly as it manifests itself in the words and signs of Jesus. As we study John's Gospel we see Jesus interacting with diverse people as he shares the word of truth with them: Nicodemus, Pilate, the woman of Samaria, the money changers in the Temple, Martha, the blind man who is healed. Just as Jesus testified to God in these exchanges, so we can draw others to him by sharing our words of witness.

Challenge the class to consider how they might witness to others by following these steps, which you may wish to list on newsprint.

(1) Identify someone you already know who has not yet met Jesus.

(2) Think about and be prepared to tell several important milestones in your own faith journey. Make a timeline.

(3) Practice telling highlights of your own faith journey.

(4) Look for opportunities to find a natural way to make a connection between an issue facing this person and an issue you have faced with God's help. What difference did having Jesus in your life make as you dealt with this situation?

(5) Be aware of church events to which you could invite this person that he or she might consider nonthreatening. For example, could you invite her to help with a Habitat for Humanity build? Or ask him to help pack and deliver food to those in need? Or invite your friend to a church league softball game?

Schedule time during the quarter to do these activities in class:

(1) Distribute paper and pencils. Suggest that each participant draws a horizontal line and place his or her birthdate at one end of the paper and today's date at the other end. In between they are to write a few words concerning important milestones in their faith journeys. Examples include *baptism; confirmation; camp, retreat, or other event(s) that had a lasting impact; meeting a teacher, pastor, or someone else who greatly influenced your relationship with God; walking with God through illness, the death of a loved one, or another major event in which you clearly knew God was present.*

(2) Form groups of three. One person is to tell an important faith event to another person, who will assume the role of a nonbeliever. The second person may ask questions or challenge the testimony. The third person is to comment on the exchange after it is completed. What did the believer say that might have drawn in the unbeliever? Did the believer say anything that seemed to be a "turnoff"? How might the observer have handled the situation differently? All three adults will each have a turn to play all three roles.

(3) Brainstorm with the group steps they could take to help new believers grow in faith and become part of the community of faith. List ideas on newsprint. Some ideas include *teaching others to pray regularly; reading the Bible; attending worship; engaging in service and fellowship activities with other believers.* Work together to find ways to strengthen areas where class members themselves feel they need to grow before they can help others.

UNIT 1: THE WORD WAS IN THE BEGINNING
WISDOM'S PART IN CREATION

PREVIEWING THE LESSON

Lesson Scripture: Proverbs 8:22-35
Background Scripture: Proverbs 8
Key Verse: Proverbs 8:33

Focus of the Lesson:
People appreciate wisdom and yearn for a depth of wisdom for themselves and others. What is the root of this longing for wisdom? The writer of Proverbs speaks about Wisdom having a divine origin, being present as God created all things, and having a role with God in creation.

Goals for the Learners:
(1) to explore the origin of Wisdom and the importance of her presence in the creation of the world.
(2) to connect the importance of Wisdom with their lives.
(3) to express joy in the wisdom and wonder of God's creation.

Pronunciation Guide:
Bezalel (bez' uh lel)
Oholiab (oh hoh' lee ab)

Supplies:
Bibles, newsprint and marker, paper and pencils, hymnals

READING THE SCRIPTURE

NRSV
Proverbs 8:22-35
22 The LORD created me at the beginning
    of his work,
      the first of his acts of long ago.
23 Ages ago I was set up,
    at the first, before the beginning of
      the earth.

NIV
Proverbs 8:22-35
22"The LORD brought me forth as the first of
    his works,
      before his deeds of old;
23I was appointed from eternity,
    from the beginning, before the
      world began.

24 When there were no depths I
  was brought forth,
    when there were no springs abounding
    with water.
25 Before the mountains had been shaped,
  before the hills, I was brought forth—
26 when he had not yet made earth
  and fields,
    or the world's first bits of soil.
27 When he established the heavens,
  I was there,
    when he drew a circle on the face of
    the deep,
28 when he made firm the skies above,
  when he established the fountains
  of the deep,
29 when he assigned to the sea its limit,
  so that the waters might not transgress
  his command,
    when he marked out the foundations
    of the earth,
30 then I was beside him, like a master
  worker;
  and I was daily his delight,
    rejoicing before him always,
31 rejoicing in his inhabited world
  and delighting in the human race.
32 "And now, my children, listen to me:
  happy are those who keep my ways.
33 **Hear instruction and be wise,**
  and do not neglect it.
34 Happy is the one who listens to me,
  watching daily at my gates,
    waiting beside my doors.
35 For whoever finds me finds life
  and obtains favor from the LORD.

24When there were no oceans, I was given
  birth,
    when there were no springs abounding
    with water;
25before the mountains were settled in place,
  before the hills, I was given birth,
26before he made the earth or its fields
  or any of the dust of the world.
27I was there when he set the heavens in
  place,
    when he marked out the horizon on the
    face of the deep,
28when he established the clouds above
  and fixed securely the fountains of
  the deep,
29when he gave the sea its boundary
  so the waters would not overstep
  his command,
and when he marked out the foundations
  of the earth.
30 Then I was the craftsman at his side.
  I was filled with delight day after day,
    rejoicing always in his presence,
31rejoicing in his whole world
  and delighting in mankind.
32"Now then, my sons, listen to me;
  blessed are those who keep my ways.
33**Listen to my instruction and be wise;**
  do not ignore it.
34Blessed is the man who listens to me,
  watching daily at my doors,
    waiting at my doorway.
35For whoever finds me finds life
  and receives favor from the LORD.

UNDERSTANDING THE SCRIPTURE

Introduction. Our selection from the Old Testament Book of Proverbs features two characteristic elements of that book.

First, it is written as poetry. Unlike most of the poetry with which we are familiar, however, ancient Hebrew poetry did not depend upon rhyming of sounds or a metrical pattern. Rather, the chief feature of poetry in the Old Testament is parallelism: sometimes understood as the rhyming of ideas rather than the rhyming of sounds. In parallelism, a statement is echoed, expanded, or contrasted in the succeeding statement(s). The Hebrew use of parallelism might remind us of the development of a motif in a piece of music.

Second, our selected passage deals with the central theme of the entire book: wisdom. From the outset, the author identifies wisdom as the goal of his instruction (1:2-6). He also understands wisdom as the key to safety from all of the troubles that follow in the wake of folly and wickedness, to success in every kind of endeavor, and to personal fulfillment.

Most of the wisdom contained in the book, as the name suggests, comes in the form of proverbs—brief, pithy sayings that offer counsel and understanding. The earliest chapters, however, comprise longer discourses, including this passage, which is wisdom's soliloquy.

Proverbs 8:1-3. As a literary technique, the writer personifies wisdom here, just as he does at the beginning of his book (1:20-33). Wisdom is portrayed as a woman, and she stands in contrast to the adulterous woman, who also calls out an appeal of her own (7:10-27). If wisdom is embraced, she will keep one from that seductress (7:4-5). And while both women summon the young man for his attention and his love, what they promise in the end is night-and-day different.

Proverbs 8:4. Wisdom is seen as a kind of street preacher, calling out an urgent exhortation to anyone who will listen. She knows that her message will make all the difference to any soul who heeds her words. Hers is an open invitation: No prerequisites prevent a hearer from receiving all that she has to offer.

Proverbs 8:5. Proverbs is unapologetic about the reality that some people are "simple ones." In our day, we would resist any teacher or preacher who addressed himself to an audience so condescendingly. For the no-nonsense writer of Proverbs, however, it is a fact of life, but it need not be a permanent condition. Wisdom offers the antidote.

Proverbs 8:6-9. As we read the larger book from which this passage comes, we find that Proverbs features a clear-eyed dualism. On the one hand, a person may be honest, prudent, righteous, and wise. Or, on the other hand, a person may be deceitful, lazy, wicked, and foolish. These are recurring characteristics in the book, which we are encouraged to cultivate or reject, respectively. Here, by her attributes, wisdom is portrayed as Proverbs' ideal person.

Proverbs 8:10-11. Proverbs is a highly pragmatic book. It offers counsel on such practical day-to-day matters as commerce and relationships, eating and sleeping, working and resting, success and failure. And even here, in the midst of a more esoteric discussion of wisdom, the pragmatist still comes through. In the author's judgment, choosing wisdom is a simple calculation, and anyone should know enough to select the choice that has the greatest value and payback. The logic of these verses may remind us of two of Jesus' parables about the kingdom of heaven (Matthew 13:44-46).

Proverbs 8:12-13. If a person may be known by the company he keeps, then wisdom is endorsed by her choice of companions. She holds close to herself prudence, knowledge, and discretion, while she shuns pride, arrogance, evil ways, and perverted speech.

Interestingly, a certain mathematical equivalency is implied by the author. At the beginning of his book, he says that "the fear of the LORD is the beginning of knowledge" (1:7), and here he asserts that "the fear of the LORD is hatred of evil" (8:13). The implicit connection between the beginning of knowledge and the hatred of evil sheds new light on Eden's infamous "tree of the knowledge of good and evil" (Genesis 2:9).

Proverbs 8:14-16. We, in turn, are encouraged to keep company with wisdom. Her advice and insight, we are told, are resources fit for a king.

Proverbs 8:17-21. We observe again the author's pragmatism put to poetry. It may well be that righteous living is its own reward, but wisdom promises still more. Her way is not merely right; it is also prosperous. This message is not to be confused with the "prosperity gospel" of our day, which teaches that God is obliged to bless us materially when we do certain things. Rather, the author simply believes in a cause-and-effect paradigm of life. Namely, to live wisely is to position oneself for every good thing. To cut across the grain of God's wisdom, however, is to invite disaster.

Proverbs 8:22-26. The theme takes a dramatic turn here. Previously, the central issue was the relationship of a human being to wisdom. Now, however, the focus turns upward, and the author imagines for us the relationship between wisdom and God.

Apropos to the book's theme and paradigm, wisdom is identified as God's first creation, "the first of his acts of long ago" (8:22). Poetically, the voice of personified wisdom recalls how she preceded all the other marvelous elements of creation.

Proverbs 8:27-31. The distinctive importance of wisdom is illustrated as she accompanies God in creative work. The text recalls another piece of Wisdom Literature, as God amazes Job with the wonders of God's creation (Job 38:4–39:30). Wisdom is also referenced there, though as an attribute of God rather than as a separate being (38:36-37; 39:26).

Proverbs 8:32-36. The text returns now to its original emphasis—and, indeed, its primary focus throughout the book—namely, the invitation for humanity to embrace wisdom. That exhortation has a new quality now, however, for wisdom has been specially endorsed by the preceding verses. It is one sort of endorsement to say that wisdom is utilized by kings and nobles in their work (8:15-16), but it is a whole other magnitude of importance to say that wisdom was utilized by God in divine work (8:22-31).

INTERPRETING THE SCRIPTURE

A New Character in the Story?

Read the Genesis account of Creation, and you quickly get a sense of the major characters in the story. First, there is God, the Creator. Eventually, we meet Adam and Eve. And shortly after, they and we are introduced to the serpent.

By God's design, it would seem that the serpent should not get such special mention. After all, there were a great many other creatures present in the garden. The serpent's distinctive importance is derivative, however, like a vandal who defaces a work of art. The serpent becomes important primarily because he interferes with something important.

So we have four major characters: the Creator, the two human beings, and the subtle serpent. But then, many chapters and books later, we come to Proverbs 8, and we are introduced to another character in the Creation story: Wisdom.

Here in our passage, Wisdom claims to have been a player in Creation. She is the first thing God created (8:22-26), and evidently she was instrumental in the rest of the act of creation (8:27-31). So who is she?

This passage has led some Bible commentators and students into a great deal of mischief. Some elevate "wisdom" to the status of a demigod or a goddess. Theologically, some of these interpretations can be a bit reckless. And the true irony comes when the very readers who otherwise resist a literal interpretation of texts that purport to be historically factual will jump to a literal interpretation of a passage that features a patently poetic device. Wisdom is personified by the author, but that does not make her a person.

We may recall Wisdom and her role in Creation next week when John introduces us to the Word who was present and active with God in creation. But we need not add a new member to the cast of characters in the Creation story. Rather, our task is to explore and understand just what Proverbs is teaching us—and offering us—about wisdom.

Raphael Revisited

In 1510, the Italian Renaissance painter Raphael painted a work known to us as *The School of Athens*. The artist, according to Frederick Hartt, "presents under an ideal architecture the chief philosophers from all periods of Greek antiquity engaged in learned argument." Plato and Aristotle are there. So are Socrates, Pythagoras, and Euclid. It is the team picture for ancient Greek wisdom.

But what of ancient Hebrew wisdom? If Raphael had undertaken a different project—one rooted in Israel rather than in Greece—who would have appeared in his portrait?

Solomon comes immediately to mind, of course, for he was reputedly the wisest man in the world (1 Kings 4:29-34). Yet who will stand with Solomon in our imaginary *The School of Jerusalem*? Who are the other wise men and women of the Old Testament?

Let Raphael paint into this new portrait a man named Bezalel (Exodus 31:1-5), and next to him another man named Oholiab (Exodus 35:30-35). Hiram (1 Kings 7:13-14) should be in the picture, too, as well as a great many unnamed women (Exodus 35:25-26). These lesser-known (or altogether anonymous) Israelites do not have Solomon's enduring reputation for wisdom, yet wisdom is what they are known for in the Hebrew Scriptures.

A contemporary translation of the verses cited to introduce the characters named above might throw us off our course. The New Revised Standard Version, for example, tells us that Hiram was "full of skill"

(1 Kings 7:14). Similarly, the New International Version calls him "highly skilled." And in *The Message* Eugene Peterson describes him as "a real artist—he could do anything with bronze."

What we must understand about Hiram, however—along with the others mentioned above with him—is that the Hebrew Bible attributes to them "wisdom." The underlying Hebrew word that is personified as a woman in our text is the same word used to describe the artisans and craftsmen who were so skillful with their hands.

Hebrew wisdom is, above all, practical. It is not detached from daily life; it is not merely theoretical. The ants, with their native prudence and organization, are considered wise (Proverbs 6:6-8). They—along with badgers, locusts, and lizards—are all applauded for their wisdom, which is demonstrated by their capacity to make their way in the world beyond the limitations of their size and strength (Proverbs 30:24-28). And whatever men and women were capable of rolling up their sleeves and skillfully contributing to preparations of the Tabernacle were likewise known for their wisdom (for example, Exodus 28:3).

What we might call craftsmanship, therefore, the Old Testament called wisdom. So it is, then, that it was by wisdom that God made the universe and all the world's wonders. God is the ultimate artist, the original artisan. And just as surely as you and I would marvel at a magnificently chiseled statue, a beautifully painted picture, or some breathtaking feat of engineering, so too we may marvel at God's creation and all the amazing wisdom that lies behind it.

Wisdom for All

Generations of immigrants coming to the United States were greeted on their horizon by the hallmark statue of the New York Harbor, the Statue of Liberty. We sometimes call her "Lady Liberty," and we are familiar with her open invitation: "Give me your tired, your poor, your huddled masses yearning to breathe free. . . ." She does not stand as an imposing guard, preventing entry. Rather, she stands as a symbol of welcome and opportunity to all.

Meanwhile, thousands of years before Lady Liberty was erected, Lady Wisdom also called out an open invitation.

She is so attractive and so famous, a person might be reluctant to approach her. We see her first at a great distance, there at the beginning with God, fabulous in skill and creativity. We look at her and we think to ourselves, "What would she ever have to do with us?"

But, look! She turns toward us and beckons. She calls out to us. Indeed, she calls us her own children (8:32), and she extends her gracious summons to you and me. We are invited to find her, to heed her, to follow her, and to love her.

We observe that Lady Wisdom is no elitist, surrounding herself exclusively with the rich and famous. Neither is she cloistered off in some ivory tower, far removed from the lives of ordinary men and women. Rather, her invitation is to all (8:4), and perhaps especially the "simple ones" (8:5). What she offers is available to anyone who will listen to her (although surprisingly few do).

Wisdom is like all of the gifts of God: freely bestowed. She is beautiful, to be sure, but it is not a distant and unavailable sort of beauty. Rather, as we welcome her in, we find that she beautifies us. And as we embrace her words, the same order and loveliness that characterize the rest of her works will characterize our lives too.

SHARING THE SCRIPTURE

Preparing Our Hearts

Explore this week's devotional reading, found in Psalm 8. In this song of David, we hear both praise of God's divine majesty and a celebration of the distinctive role that humans play in God's kingdom. What is our role within God's creation? What emotions does this psalm evoke as you consider where God has placed you amid the universe? Respond to this psalm by finding some way to care for creation today.

Pray that you and the adult learners will give thanks for the exalted place the Sovereign God has given you.

Preparing Our Minds

Study the background Scripture from Proverbs 8 and the lesson Scripture from Proverbs 8:22-35. Think about why people yearn for wisdom.

Write on newsprint:
❑ questions for "Explore the Origin of Wisdom and the Importance of Her Presence in the Creation of the World."
❑ information for next week's lesson, found under "Continue the Journey."
❑ activities for further spiritual growth in "Continue the Journey."

Be prepared to use the Understanding the Scripture entries from Proverbs 8:1-3 through 17-21 to introduce Wisdom personified as a woman in the section titled "Explore the Origin of Wisdom and the Importance of Her Presence in the Creation of the World."

Review the "Introduction" to the spring quarter, "The Big Picture," "Close-up," and "Faith in Action." Begin to decide how you will use this information during the coming thirteen weeks. You may want to present the "Close-up" information next week.

LEADING THE CLASS

(1) Gather to Learn

❖ Welcome the class members and introduce any guests.

❖ Pray that the students will experience the awe of Wisdom that was present at creation.

❖ Read this excerpt from a sermon on Proverbs by Saint Bernard of Clairvaux (1090–1153): **Let us work for the food which does not perish—our salvation. Let us work in the vineyard of the Lord to earn our daily wage in the wisdom which says:** *Those who work in me will not sin.* **Christ tells us:** *The field is the world.* **Let us work in it and dig up wisdom, its hidden treasure, a treasure we all look for and want to obtain. . . . Look for wisdom while it can still be found. Call for it while it is near. Do you want to know how near it is?** *The word is near you, in your heart and on your lips,* **provided that you seek it honestly. . . . While wisdom is near and while it can be found, look for it and ask for its help. . . .** *Happy is the man who has found wisdom.* **Even more happy is the man** *who lives in wisdom,* **for he perceives its abundance. There are three ways for wisdom or prudence to abound in you: if you confess your sins, if you give thanks and praise, and if your speech is edifying.** *Man believes with his heart and so he is justified. He confesses with his lips and so he is saved.* **(www.crossroadsinitiative.com/ library_article/890/Seek_Wisdom_Bernard _of_Clairvaux.html)**

❖ Ask: **Why do you think people yearn for wisdom?**

❖ Read aloud today's focus statement: **People appreciate wisdom and yearn for a depth of wisdom for themselves and others. What is the root of this longing for wisdom? The writer of Proverbs speaks about Wisdom having a divine origin, being present as God created all things, and having a role with God in creation.**

(2) Explore the Origin of Wisdom and the Importance of Her Presence in the Creation of the World

❖ Use information extending from Proverbs 8:1-3 through 17-21 in Understanding the Scripture to introduce wisdom personified as a woman.

❖ Choose a volunteer to read Proverbs 8:22-35.

❖ Form several small groups and post these questions for discussion:
  (1) **From these verses, what do you discern about Wisdom's role in creation?**
  (2) **Wisdom here is definitely personified as a woman. How do you respond to that idea?**

❖ Call the groups together. Invite each one to report on one point the group agreed strongly about and another point about which they could not reach consensus.

(3) Connect the Importance of Wisdom With the Learners' Lives

❖ Read "Raphael Revisited" from Interpreting the Scripture and discuss these questions:
  (1) **If Raphael were to paint a contemporary portrait of wise people, who would you want to see included? What makes each of these individuals wise in your view?**
  (2) **Hebrew wisdom was described in this Interpreting the Scripture reading as "practical." How would you describe the wisdom that most people you know rely on today?**
  (3) **How would you describe the wisdom that the church relies on?**

❖ Look again at Proverbs 8:32-35, noting that 33 is today's key verse, and ask:
  (1) **Why is finding wisdom such a positive experience?**

(2) What role does God's wisdom play in your own life? Give specific examples.

(3) In verse 32 Wisdom calls people to listen, promising that those who "keep her ways" are "happy" (NRSV) or "blessed" (NIV). Verse 35 goes on to say that those who find Wisdom find life. Given all the benefits, why do some people consistently ignore God's Wisdom?

(4) Express Joy in the Wisdom and Wonder of God's Creation

❖ **Option:** Take a brief nature walk. If your church property, the time for the session, the weather, and the physical abilities of the class members allow, consider walking around the church grounds and marveling at the wonder of God's creation.

❖ Distribute paper and pencils. Point out that for those in the Northern Hemisphere, spring is almost here. As individuals contemplate the rebirth of nature, what are some changes that prompt them to rejoice in God's creation? Encourage participants to write about these changes. Select volunteers to read their comments.

❖ Read Psalm 8:3-8 as a reminder that human beings are very much part of God's creation. We are not only creatures but also caregivers for all else that God has created. Ask:

(1) How would you rate the way humanity has handled its unique role within creation? What evidence can you give to support your rating?

(2) What do you believe God is now saying about the way in which humans are listening to Wisdom in terms of the way we are handling creation?

(3) What changes do we need to make to treat creation wisely?

(5) Continue the Journey

❖ Pray that the adults will express joy in the wonder of God's creation.

❖ Read aloud this preparation for next week's lesson. You may also want to post it on newsprint for the students to copy.

■ **Title: The Word Became Flesh**
■ **Background Scripture: John 1:1-14**
■ **Lesson Scripture: John 1:1-14**
■ **Focus of the Lesson: People are often curious about how things began. How are we to answer our questions about the origins of faith? Jesus, who was fully human and fully involved in human society, was also personally divine from the beginning, and was God's agent in the world, creating and redeeming.**

❖ Challenge the students to complete one or more of these activities for further spiritual growth related to this week's session. Post this information on newsprint for the students to copy.

(1) Write a prayer in which you express joy for God's wisdom. Offer this prayer daily during the coming week.

(2) Take a child on a nature walk this week. If that is not possible, visit an aquarium, planetarium, botanical garden, or another facility where you can experience some aspect of creation together. Take note of the child's reaction to new discoveries. How do the child's responses influence your own?

(3) Share an aspect of God's wisdom with someone this week. Encourage that person to act wisely.

❖ Sing or read aloud "Creating God, Your Fingers Trace."

❖ Conclude today's session by leading the class in this benediction: **Go forth rejoicing that God, out of infinite love for the world, gave us Jesus, through whom we have eternal life.**

UNIT 1: THE WORD WAS IN THE BEGINNING

THE WORD BECAME FLESH

PREVIEWING THE LESSON

Lesson Scripture: John 1:1-14
Background Scripture: John 1:1-14
Key Verse: John 1:14

Focus of the Lesson:
People are often curious about how things began. How are we to answer our questions about the origins of faith? Jesus, who was fully human and fully involved in human society, was also personally divine from the beginning, and was God's agent in the world, creating and redeeming.

Goals for the Learners:
(1) to discover God's presence in heaven and on earth from creation.
(2) to examine how God's presence in the Word affects how they live.
(3) to use John's description of the origin of Jesus found in the Fourth Gospel to inform and strengthen their faith.

Supplies:
Bibles, newsprint and marker, paper and pencils, hymnals

READING THE SCRIPTURE

NRSV
John 1:1-14

¹In the beginning was the Word, and the Word was with God, and the Word was God. ²He was in the beginning with God. ³All things came into being through him, and without him not one thing came into being. What has come into being ⁴in him was life, and the life was the light of all people. ⁵The light shines in the darkness, and the darkness did not overcome it.

⁶There was a man sent from God, whose name was John. ⁷He came as a witness to

NIV
John 1:1-14

¹In the beginning was the Word, and the Word was with God, and the Word was God. ²He was with God in the beginning.

³Through him all things were made; without him nothing was made that has been made. ⁴In him was life, and that life was the light of men. ⁵The light shines in the darkness, but the darkness has not understood it.

⁶There came a man who was sent from God; his name was John. ⁷He came as a witness to testify concerning that light, so that

testify to the light, so that all might believe through him. [8]He himself was not the light, but he came to testify to the light. [9]The true light, which enlightens everyone, was coming into the world.

[10]He was in the world, and the world came into being through him; yet the world did not know him. [11]He came to what was his own, and his own people did not accept him. [12]But to all who received him, who believed in his name, he gave power to become children of God, [13]who were born, not of blood or of the will of the flesh or of the will of man, but of God.

[14]And the Word became flesh and lived among us, and we have seen his glory, the glory as of a father's only son, full of grace and truth.

through him all men might believe. [8]He himself was not the light; he came only as a witness to the light. [9]The true light that gives light to every man was coming into the world.

[10]He was in the world, and though the world was made through him, the world did not recognize him. [11]He came to that which was his own, but his own did not receive him. [12]Yet to all who received him, to those who believed in his name, he gave the right to become children of God— [13]children born not of natural descent, nor of human decision or a husband's will, but born of God.

[14]The Word became flesh and made his dwelling among us. We have seen his glory, the glory of the One and Only, who came from the Father, full of grace and truth.

UNDERSTANDING THE SCRIPTURE

John 1:1-5. John chooses to begin his Gospel with the exact same phrase as the Book of Genesis: "in the beginning." He thereby identifies his testimony with the story of Creation, affirming both the pre-existence of Christ and his role in creation.

John identifies Jesus as the source of life from the start (1:4). And that truth is not limited to the act of creation, as though we merely owed our existence to him. No, for he continues to be the source of and key to life (6:33, 35; 11:25; 14:6), abundant (10:10) and eternal (3:16, 36; 6:54).

John's Gospel functions with both a strong sense of dualism and a high degree of symbolism. Accordingly, we see here the author's assumption that darkness is hostile to the light. The triumphant claim, meanwhile, that "the light shines in the darkness, and the darkness did not overcome it" (1:5) also recalls the creation story that John echoes at the beginning. We recall that the prior state of things was darkness (Genesis 1:2) and that God's first act was to speak light into it (1:3).

John 1:6-9. All four Gospel writers prominently include the ministry of John the Baptist as an ordained precursor to Jesus. That is not a small detail when we consider some of the cherished elements of the gospel story that are not included in all four of those books (for example, the Christmas story, the Transfiguration, the Sermon on the Mount, the Lord's Prayer, the Golden Rule).

That John was "sent from God" is a statement of great importance for the narrator. Within the context of the Fourth Gospel, this designation puts John in the company of Jesus and the Holy Spirit (see 8:42; 14:26).

Likewise, John's role as a witness—one who testifies—also puts John in significant company. In addition to John, this Gospel also mentions Jesus, Jesus' works, the Father, the Holy Spirit, the Scriptures, Moses, the disciples, and the author testifying about Jesus (5:30-47; 8:14-18; 15:26-27; 19:35; 21:24).

The author makes a point of distinguishing between John and the light to which he testified. That may not seem to us like a necessary disclaimer, but it was an important word at that time. A great deal of speculation and expectation surrounded John during his ministry, and so he himself had to make a point of clarifying who he was and who he was not (for example, Luke 3:15-17; John 1:19-27).

John 1:10-13. We recall the Old Testament prophet's sober admission about the suffering servant, confessing that "we esteemed him not" (Isaiah 53:3 NIV). This is the sense of irony and tragedy at work here in John. The very one who gave existence—light and life—to the world was unrecognized and unwelcomed by that world.

When Jesus prayed for his tormentors' forgiveness on the cross, he said, "They do not know what they are doing" (Luke 23:34). Perhaps the essence of their ignorance was that they did not know to whom they were doing it.

The statement in verse 12 about "becom(ing) children of God" may surprise us. We operate with an assumption that we begin as children of God, that it is our starting point as humanity. "All people are God's children" is the common creed.

The more overt testimony of Scripture, however, is that God has one "begotten" Son. Strictly speaking, we begin not as God's children, but as God's creatures. So it is that we are God's children not by nature, but by adoption (see Romans 8:14-17; Galatians 4:4-7; Ephesians 1:3-6). This is God's gracious choice, and it is made operative in the work of Christ.

John 1:14. The final verse of the passage is truly the climactic statement, for this is the grand expression of the Incarnation.

At the outset, John established the preexistence of the Word. Now he proclaims that that divine Word "became flesh." Likewise, that Word was originally "with God" (1:1) but now he has "lived among us." Thus John tracks for us the magnificent demotion of grace.

Christina Rossetti famously penned, "Love came down at Christmas." Down, indeed. Down into flesh. Down to live among us. We have no means of calculating how far down love came.

Another hymn writer elegantly expresses the distance that separates sinful humanity from God: "Holy, holy, holy! Though the darkness hide thee, though the eye of sinful man thy glory may not see." Yet the God whom we could not reach by ourselves was willing and able to reach us. We could not cross the chasm to God, and so God crossed it into flesh and blood.

Later epistles reiterate the importance of this fundamental affirmation: "Every spirit that confesses that Jesus Christ has come in the flesh is from God" (1 John 4:2) is the straightforward, positive conclusion. Meanwhile, on the negative side, we read this dramatic verdict: "Many deceivers have gone out into the world, those who do not confess that Jesus Christ has come in the flesh; any such person is the deceiver and the antichrist!" (2 John 2:7).

We typically associate the term "antichrist" with apocalyptic beasts and hellish world leaders. Not so, however. Instead, the term is applied to a rather ordinary group that we might otherwise overlook as harmless: namely, those who deny the truth of the Incarnate Word, the humanity of Jesus.

We sometimes say of a message that has been inadequately passed from one recipient to another that "something got lost in the translation." In the case of Christ's Incarnation, however, we observe that nothing was lost in translation. He became flesh, yet still he was marked by glory. He lived in this fallen world among us, yet still his person and life were filled with grace and truth.

How right and true it was, then, for Jesus later to declare, "Whoever has seen me has seen the Father" (John 14:9).

INTERPRETING THE SCRIPTURE

Participant in Creation: The Preexistent Word

"In the beginning was the Word." With that opening statement, the Gospel writer lays the essential groundwork for the good news he is about to report. The good news is about Jesus, and John's task in his Gospel is to explore and proclaim just who this Jesus is. Jesus' identity will be revealed by the signs that he performs, by the words that he speaks (especially his familiar "I am" statements), and by those who testify to him. And the first testimony to Jesus is this statement about the preexistent Word.

"Preexistence" is not a word that makes its way into our everyday conversation. And while the word itself does not appear in John's Gospel, the concept is a recurring one.

The Jews of Jesus' day had many expectations about the promised Messiah, but not all of those expectations were entirely accurate. One of the most common misconceptions was that the Messiah would serve as a deliverer in the same way that previous heroic figures had. Israel of the first century was a conquered and occupied land, and so the natural longing was for a figure who would lead a military revolt, throw off the shackles of Rome, and reestablish political independence for the people of God.

Given their history, this was not an unreasonable expectation. Moses, Joshua, Deborah, Gideon, and David had all been such instruments of God. And, more recently, Judas Maccabeus had led an effective revolutionary movement that briefly restored Israel's independence during a time of oppression.

The deficiency with all these previous models, however, was that they were all human. They were ordinary men and women; people whom God had chosen and used, to be sure, but being chosen by God is not quite the same as being sent by God.

And it is a different matter entirely from actually being God.

We are familiar with the trajectory of other biblical heroes' stories. We know about baby Moses in the basket on the Nile (Exodus 2:1-10). We know about the shepherd boy, David, from Bethlehem (1 Samuel 16:6-13; 17:12-37). We know about Samson's Nazirite vow (Judges 13:2-24) and Samuel's answer-to-prayer birth (1 Samuel 1:1-28).

The trajectory of Jesus' story is different, however. It does not begin with his eventful baptism (Mark 1:9-11), his promising childhood (Luke 2:41-52), or even his specially heralded birth (Matthew 1:18–2:12; Luke 1:26-38; 2:1-20). Rather, as John reports, Jesus' story begins "in the beginning." Before he was born on this earth, he was with God. Indeed, he was God.

This preexistence theme is a recurring element in John (for example, 3:31-36; 6:46; 8:39-59; 13:3; 16:28), as well as a provocative question in the other three Gospels (for example, Matthew 22:41-45). Yet John does not merely affirm the preexistence of Christ: He specifically testifies to the work of the preexistent word in Creation.

At first blush, this may surprise us, for it seems somewhat removed from the saving work that we associate with Christ and with the gospel message. Yet before we learn that he came to save the world (3:17), we discover first that he created it (1:3-5, 10).

Participant in Creation: The Incarnate Word

The centerpiece of our study this week is John's declaration that "the Word became flesh and lived among us" (John 1:14). Here, then, is the other half of our Christology. The first affirmation was Christ's divinity as the preexistent Word. Now we also affirm his humanity as the Incarnate Word.

Charles Wesley marvelously captures this two-part truth in a familiar Christmas carol: "Veiled in flesh the Godhead see; hail th'incarnate Deity, pleased with us in flesh to dwell, Jesus our Emmanuel."

We noted that previous heroes from Israel's history were human beings whom God chose for work. The truth of the Incarnate Word, however, is on a different plane. This is not God choosing a human being for specific work, but rather God choosing to *become* a human being in order to do God's own work.

Because it is a challenging concept to affirm that Jesus was, in Anselm's language, both "very God and very man," the natural tendency is to slip off to one theological side or the other. One group gladly embraces the humanity of Jesus and extols him as an exemplary human being, but they are uneasy with claims of Christ's divinity. They resist the supernatural, and they avoid ascribing any uniqueness to the person and work of Christ. A different group, meanwhile, celebrates the divinity of Jesus and gladly calls him Lord and God, but they struggle with his full humanity. For them he is a kind of Superman, who could not really have been tempted as we are (compare Hebrews 4:15), experienced ordinary human need (for example, Matthew 4:2; John 19:28), or required any human assistance along the way (Matthew 26:37-40).

Yet this is the witness of the Gospel, as well as the doctrinal insistence of the church through the centuries. From the first generations of Christianity, there were those who argued against Jesus' divinity and those who disputed his humanity. Both positions were rejected, however, as heretical. For Jesus was, in the language of the ancient Nicene Creed, "true God from true God," and yet also "was incarnate of the Holy Spirit and the Virgin Mary and became truly human."

The Word did not merely deign to appear on earth in heavenly splendor. Nor did he condescend simply to put on a costume and pay a brief visit. Rather, he "became flesh" (John 1:14). And so the Creator literally entered into the stuff of Creation. It is an incalculable demotion (see Philippians 2:5-8), as well as an indescribable beauty.

First, he created. When that creation rebelled, however, it spiraled into a lost condition from which it could not save itself. The Creator sought to save the lost creation, and did so by entering into it. So the pre-existent word "became flesh and lived among us" (1:14).

Participant in Creation: The Neighboring Word

Genesis gives us the close-up view of the creation that John recalls. We see in that account a surprising willingness by the ineffable God to get his hands dirty (Genesis 2:7). And the same Lord who put hands and breath into the dust at creation now puts Godself into that dust at the Incarnation.

The testimony in John 1:14 that he "lived among us," therefore, is an extension of the intimacy that we already saw in the creation. The Lord does not stay at arm's length from humanity. God does not send an angel in to do the dirty work, or hover above, like some rescue helicopter. No, God, in the person of Jesus, moves into the neighborhood with us.

The bystanders and critics noted Jesus' fearless contact with lepers and his willingness to sup with sinners. But those were only the details of the larger choice. For whether he was dining with the publicans or the Pharisees, it was an act of incarnate grace either way.

And that same grace continues to this day. The One who moved into the neighborhood of Bethlehem or Nazareth, of Galilee or Judea, also willingly moves into the neighborhood of our hearts and our homes. He's still not afraid to get his hands dirty or to sup with sinners, and that's good news for us. So we join the evangelist, declaring that the Word still lives among us, full of grace and truth.

SHARING THE SCRIPTURE

Preparing Our Hearts

Explore this week's devotional reading, found in Isaiah 40:21-26. Here, we see reference to "the beginning" (as we will in our text from John 1) and to the "Holy One" responsible for all creation. What do you believe about God's role in creation? What does this passage from Isaiah suggest to you about the nature of God? Ponder creation and give thanks for its marvels and for the Creator.

Pray that you and the adult learners will recognize that God's creating Word has become flesh and lived among us.

Preparing Our Minds

Study the background Scripture and the lesson Scripture, both of which are from John 1:1-14. Think about how you answer questions related to the origins of faith.

Write on newsprint:
❑ information for next week's lesson, found under "Continue the Journey."
❑ activities for further spiritual growth in "Continue the Journey."

LEADING THE CLASS

(1) Gather to Learn

❖ Welcome the class members and introduce any guests.
❖ Pray that the students will praise God, whose Word has been present from creation.
❖ Prompt the adults to think about beginnings that are important to them and share them with the class. Which of these beginnings do they know about because they were actually present? Which have they reconstructed from stories they have heard? What are the most memorable aspects of each beginning? Here are some ideas: *the beginnings of one's family history in the country where you live, your early life, early interactions with your spouse, first days on your first job, first days in your residence, the birth of a child or grandchild, the start-up of a company.*

❖ Read aloud today's focus statement: **People are often curious about how things began. How are we to answer our questions about the origins of faith? Jesus, who was fully human and fully involved in human society, was also personally divine from the beginning, and was God's agent in the world, creating and redeeming.**

(2) Discover God's Presence in Heaven and on Earth From Creation

❖ Invite two volunteers to read Genesis 1:1-2 and John 1:1-14.
❖ Do a comparative Bible study by forming three groups and assigning one group to Philippians 2:5-11, a second to Colossians 1:15-20, and a third to Hebrews 1:1-13. Ask each group to compare their reading to the first fourteen verses in John 1. Provide time for each group to give a brief report.
❖ Discuss these questions with the entire class:
  (1) **What do you learn about the Word from John 1:1-14?** (List these ideas on newsprint.)
  (2) **How does the way John introduces Christ differ from the way Matthew and Luke introduce him?**
  (3) **How do these different introductions expand your understanding of the Word who came into the world?**
  (4) **As you read this passage, do you feel that the Word is very near you—or very far away? Why?** (You may wish to retell "Participant in Creation: The Neighboring Word" from Interpreting the Scripture.)

❖ Distribute hymnals and tell the students to turn to "The Nicene Creed." Read the creed in unison and then ask: **Where do you hear echoes of the first chapter of John?**

❖ Wrap up this section by reading "Participant in Creation: The Incarnate Word" from Interpreting the Scripture and inviting the adults to comment on their understanding of the Incarnate Word.

(3) Examine How God's Presence in the Word Affects How the Learners Live

❖ Read: **Although we have learned much about God's presence in the Word, who was both active in creation and also a flesh-and-blood human being who lived among us, these fourteen verses do not say much about how the presence of God's Word affects our daily lives. Thus, the question becomes, so what? What difference does this creating, enlightening presence make in your life? To answer this question, each person will have an opportunity to bear witness as to how you believe your life is influenced by the power and presence of the Word.** (Try to encourage everyone to participate, but recognize that some will be reluctant to speak. Do not pressure them; simply move on to the next person. If the class is large, do this activity in groups of three or four.)

❖ Ask: **Did you hear any common themes among our testimonies? If so, what were they?**

(4) Use John's Description of the Origin of Jesus Found in the Fourth Gospel to Inform and Strengthen Faith

❖ Distribute paper and pencils. Suggest that the adults listen again as you read John 1:1-14. This time, they are to jot down words, phrases, or images that grab their attention. Once they have done that, challenge them to consider how their choices might inform or strengthen their faith. Here are some possibilities to spark ideas:

■ **The Word as Creator:** What difference would it make in your life and faith if you recognized that the created world was fashioned by the same One who came to save the world?

■ **The Word as Light:** Do you honestly see yourself as living in the Light, or are there aspects of your life that you prefer to hide in the shadows of darkness? How would your life and faith be different if your whole being could stand in the Light?

■ **The Word Rejected by the World:** Have you accepted the Word as the center of your entire life, or have you, at least in part, rejected the Word? What do you do to help those who have not yet received the Word to do so?

■ **The Word as Flesh and Blood:** How does the fact that Jesus was truly human, with the same needs and desires as all people, empower you to enter into a relationship with him?

■ **The Word as Divinity:** How does the fact that the Word was with God and was God reveal God's love, grace, and truth to you?

❖ Conclude by leading the class in a unison reading of today's key verse, John 1:14.

(5) Continue the Journey

❖ Pray that the adults will invite Jesus, the Word of God, to continue to work in their lives.

❖ Read aloud this preparation for next week's lesson. You may also want to post it on newsprint for the students to copy.

■ **Title: The Wedding at Cana**
■ **Background Scripture: John 2:1-12**
■ **Lesson Scripture: John 2:1-12**

■ Focus of the Lesson: When faced with possibly embarrassing or difficult situations, many people hope for a miracle to bring order out of chaos. Where and how can we find these miracles? Jesus' first miracle during the wedding at Cana revealed his power by creating something good, and the disciples believed in him.

❖ Challenge the students to complete one or more of these activities for further spiritual growth related to this week's session. Post this information on newsprint for the students to copy.

(1) Recall that "light" is an image that John often used. Check chapters 1, 3, 5, 8, 9, 11, and 12 of John to learn what this image conveys to you about Christ and the people who follow him.

(2) Try to memorize John 1:1-18, often referred to as the Prologue to John's Gospel. Notice the four parts of this theologically rich passage: verses 1-5, the creating Word is the light and life of creation; verses 6-8, John the Baptist came to testify to the light; verses 9-13, the light came into the world; verses 14-18, the Word became flesh and lived among us.

(3) Create your own testimony, based solely on John's Prologue. Share this witness with someone.

❖ Sing or read aloud "Christ Is the World's Light."

❖ Conclude today's session by leading the class in this benediction: Go forth rejoicing that God, out of infinite love for the world, gave us Jesus, through whom we have eternal life.

UNIT 1: THE WORD WAS IN THE BEGINNING
THE WEDDING AT CANA

PREVIEWING THE LESSON

Lesson Scripture: John 2:1-12
Background Scripture: John 2:1-12
Key Verse: John 2:11

Focus of the Lesson:
When faced with possibly embarrassing or difficult situations, many people hope for a miracle to bring order out of chaos. Where and how can we find these miracles? Jesus' first miracle during the wedding at Cana revealed his power by creating something good, and the disciples believed in him.

Goals for the Learners:
(1) to examine all that was created good in the story of the Cana wedding, including wine from water, goodwill for the host, and believing disciples.
(2) to recognize and appreciate God's power to continue creating calm and order out of chaos as a miracle in the world.
(3) to express what leads them to believe in Jesus.

Pronunciation Guide:
Cana (kay' nuh)

Supplies:
Bibles, newsprint and marker, paper and pencils, hymnals

READING THE SCRIPTURE

NRSV
John 2:1-12

¹On the third day there was a wedding in Cana of Galilee, and the mother of Jesus was there. ²Jesus and his disciples had also been invited to the wedding. ³When the wine gave out, the mother of Jesus said to him, "They have no wine." ⁴And Jesus said to her, "Woman, what concern is that to you and to

NIV
John 2:1-12

¹On the third day a wedding took place at Cana in Galilee. Jesus' mother was there, ²and Jesus and his disciples had also been invited to the wedding. ³When the wine was gone, Jesus' mother said to him, "They have no more wine."

me? My hour has not yet come." [5]His mother said to the servants, "Do whatever he tells you." [6]Now standing there were six stone water jars for the Jewish rites of purification, each holding twenty or thirty gallons. [7]Jesus said to them, "Fill the jars with water." And they filled them up to the brim. [8]He said to them, "Now draw some out, and take it to the chief steward." So they took it. [9]When the steward tasted the water that had become wine, and did not know where it came from (though the servants who had drawn the water knew), the steward called the bridegroom [10]and said to him, "Everyone serves the good wine first, and then the inferior wine after the guests have become drunk. But you have kept the good wine until now." **[11]Jesus did this, the first of his signs, in Cana of Galilee, and revealed his glory; and his disciples believed in him.**

[12]After this he went down to Capernaum with his mother, his brothers, and his disciples; and they remained there a few days.

[4]"Dear woman, why do you involve me?" Jesus replied. "My time has not yet come."

[5]His mother said to the servants, "Do whatever he tells you."

[6]Nearby stood six stone water jars, the kind used by the Jews for ceremonial washing, each holding from twenty to thirty gallons.

[7]Jesus said to the servants, "Fill the jars with water"; so they filled them to the brim.

[8]Then he told them, "Now draw some out and take it to the master of the banquet."

They did so, [9]and the master of the banquet tasted the water that had been turned into wine. He did not realize where it had come from, though the servants who had drawn the water knew. Then he called the bridegroom aside [10]and said, "Everyone brings out the choice wine first and then the cheaper wine after the guests have had too much to drink; but you have saved the best till now."

[11]This, the first of his miraculous signs, Jesus performed at Cana in Galilee. He thus revealed his glory, and his disciples put their faith in him.

[12]After this he went down to Capernaum with his mother and brothers and his disciples. There they stayed for a few days.

UNDERSTANDING THE SCRIPTURE

John 2:1-2. It is interesting to note that John includes the detail about the timing of this event. He begins his story of Jesus' first miracle—and the occasion when the disciples came to believe (2:11)—as happening "on the third day" (2:1). Perhaps, as one of Jesus' closest followers, John had in mind all the times he had heard his Lord refer to "the third day" as pivotal (for example, Matthew 16:21; 17:23; 20:19).

Cana was a small village in the northern region of Palestine known as Galilee. It was near enough to Nazareth that Jerome once wrote that he could see Cana from Nazareth. It is perhaps not surprising, therefore, that Mary and Jesus were known to the bride, the groom, or their families.

No personal details are offered about the bride and groom. Some very old traditions suggest more information about the relationships between Jesus' family and the groom's, but John himself does not satisfy our curiosity about who the happy couple was.

John 2:3. Three women named Mary are mentioned by name in John's Gospel (Mary the sister of Martha and Lazarus, Mary the wife of Clopas, and Mary Magdalene), but

Jesus' mother is not named in this Gospel. Instead, John refers to her exclusively as Jesus' mother, and she appears in his Gospel in three separate stories (2:1-5, 12; 19:25-27).

Interestingly, Jesus' mother does not ask Jesus for anything specific; she simply alerts him to the need. In this respect, she may be a model for our prayers. Perhaps it is not necessary for me to lay out the program that God should follow. I only need to take to God the concerns I know about and the needs I have.

John 2:4. Some translations of this verse can make Jesus sound rather curt. To capture the way that the vocative "woman" would have been used in that day, the NIV and the Amplified Bible both translate it "Dear woman."

This is the first instance of a recurring emphasis in John on Jesus' "hour" (7:30; 8:20; 12:23, 27; 13:1; 17:1) or "time" (7:6, 8). Perhaps the best insight into Jesus' understanding of that hour is found in his statement about a woman's "hour" at the time of labor and birth (16:21). The hour is extremely difficult to endure, yet its result is a wonder.

John 2:5. Though Jesus' words had given no indication that he was going to do anything at this moment, his mother seemed to proceed with a certain confidence. Her instructions to the servants surely indicate that she expected Jesus to act. The persistence of Mary's certainty is reminiscent of the Canaanite woman, to whom Jesus did not speak encouragingly, yet who was undeterred in her faith (Matthew 15:22-28).

At a purely human level, it is interesting to note that Mary gave instructions to the servants. After all, they were not her servants. And presumably it would have been equally authoritative for Jesus to give them his instructions directly, with or without this preface from his mother. Perhaps this additional word was a mother's gentle nudge to her son.

John 2:6. A reading of the Old Testament Book of Leviticus acquaints us with the

Jewish emphasis on cleanliness. The old saying that "cleanliness is next to godliness" is not found in the Bible, but it could be. The Old Testament law put a great emphasis on ritual cleanness, and these large jars furnished a Jewish household with the water it needed for the ritual washing of hands before and during a meal.

John 2:7-8. We routinely refer to this as the occasion when Jesus changed water into wine. In fact, however, we never actually see him make that change. Some miracles occur right before our eyes—Jericho's walls fall down, Jesus walks on the water, and the leper is cleansed. In this case, however, you could keep your video camera trained on the scene the entire time, yet never see the change occur.

This miracle bears a resemblance to certain others. We observe that Jesus gives instructions, which are accompanied by no explanation, and which contain no apparent solution to the problem. Yet when the instructions are followed, the problem is solved. This outline reminds us of numerous other miracles in Scripture, including the Lord's curious provision for healing in the wilderness (Numbers 21:4-9), as well as a number of events from Elisha's life (2 Kings 2:19-22; 4:38-41; 5:9-14; 6:1-7). Our inclination might be to shrug our shoulders and say, "I can't see what good this is going to do." Yet we discover that our capacity to see is not identical with God's capacity to do.

John 2:9-10. The testimony of the steward is characteristic of how God works. We observe that the Lord did not merely lead the Israelites through the wilderness; he even preserved their clothes and sandals (Deuteronomy 29:5). Shadrach and company were not merely saved from the fire; they did not even smell like smoke (Daniel 3:27). Likewise, here, Jesus' work in Cana is not limited merely to the changing of the substance or the meeting of the need. Instead, typical of the above-and-beyond quality of his work, the wine he provides is superior wine.

John 2:11. As mentioned at the beginning of our study, John is very conscious of Jesus' "signs." He is the only Gospel writer to record this particular miracle, and the only one to number Jesus' miracles (see also 4:54). That this was "the first of his signs" indicates both that something special has begun and that something more is to come.

For John, each miracle of Jesus reveals something about him. This sign in Cana "revealed his glory."

One story after another in the Fourth Gospel reports that people came to believe in Jesus. Here, early in the Gospel, his disciples begin to believe.

John 2:12. Capernaum was another town in the region of Galilee. It was located right on the lake for which the region was named, and the Synoptic Gospels portray it as a kind of headquarters for Jesus' Galilean ministry. Indeed, Matthew seems to suggest that Capernaum became Jesus' adopted hometown (9:1). John's Gospel, on the other hand, devotes more attention to Jesus' activity in the southern region of Judea and in Jerusalem, which is where he goes after staying in Capernaum for "a few days."

INTERPRETING THE SCRIPTURE

Ordinary Need

When you think of the miracles recorded in the Bible, which ones come to mind first? It may come naturally to us to think in terms of the big, special-effects spectacles of the Old Testament—like the Nile turning to blood (Exodus 7:14-21), the parting of the Red Sea (Exodus 14), the sudden demolition of Jericho's walls (Joshua 6), or the sun standing still in the sky (Joshua 10:7-14).

Events like those seem far removed from us. Not only far removed in terms of time and space but also far removed from our experience. After all, most of us have not encountered an occasion when a body of water needed to be parted, or immense fortifications needed to fall down. Those occasions, therefore, simply become metaphors for us, and so we speak figuratively of the "walls" in our lives that God can bring down.

What Jesus does in Cana, however, is of a different order, and we may find as a result that this miracle is a very refreshing one for us. After all, consider the nature and the size of the need that Jesus meets.

The events of the Exodus were public spectacles, witnessed by both the Egyptians and the Israelites. What happened in Cana, by contrast, was observed by only a very few people. Indeed, it is the bridegroom, rather than Jesus, who receives the credit for the wine (2:9-10).

Likewise, the miracle-filled deliverance from Egypt became the stuff of an entire nation's testimony. The water-to-wine miracle, on the other hand, would only have been part of one anonymous couple's story, were it not recorded for us in this Gospel.

This miracle of Jesus, you see, was not an answer to some mammoth need. Indeed, for us today, this would be just a run to the grocery store to pick up a few more bottles. And so the beauty of Jesus' work here is not merely his power, but his sweetness. We marvel, therefore, not only at his capacity to change the water into wine; we marvel, too, at his willingness to do it.

Extraordinary Deed

The narrator of our story does us a great favor by reporting the quantities involved in this miracle. He tells us in verse 6 that there were six large jars available, that each one's capacity was between twenty and thirty gallons, that Jesus instructed that they (plural) should be filled, and that they were filled "up to the brim" (2:7). John does not do the math for us, but we are left with the strong impression that Jesus generated between perhaps 120 and 180 gallons of fine wine.

The proportions are astonishing. I do not drink wine, and so I can't speak very intelligently about this matter, but it seems to me that one hundred-plus gallons is super-abundant. Jesus has not just met the need; he has oversupplied.

Once again, we are reminded of an episode from Elisha's life and ministry. When miraculously assisting a poor widow to provide for her family's needs, he instructed her to borrow empty vessels from all of her neighbors. Then the prophet added, "and not just a few" (2 Kings 4:3).

Gospel songwriter Leila Morris captured Elisha's instructions and made them a bold chorus of promise: "He will fill your heart today to overflowing. As the Lord commandeth you, 'Bring your vessels, not a few.' He will fill your heart today to overflowing with the Holy Ghost and power."

Such is the nature of the Lord's provisions. The five thousand are not just miraculously fed; there are twelve baskets of leftovers too (John 6:12-13). The psalmist testified that his cup "runneth over" (Psalm 23:5 KJV). Paul bore witness to the Lord who "is able to accomplish abundantly far more than all we can ask or imagine" (Ephesians 3:20). Jesus came for his sheep not only to have life, but to "have it abundantly" (John 10:10). And he promised blessings provided in "good measure, pressed down, shaken together, running over" (Luke 6:38).

It is instructive to note that the enemy's first words to humankind were to question God's generosity: "Did God say, 'You shall not eat from any tree in the garden'?" (Genesis 3:1). But, no, God didn't say that. So much the contrary, the Lord had provided in free abundance for Adam and Eve. And so, from the beginning, we see both the generous nature of our God and the deceitful nature of our antagonist.

John reports that Jesus' disciples came to believe in him that day. Let us never lose sight of the truth that the Lord we have come to believe in is, as Leila Morris sings, the one who "will fill your heart today to overflowing."

Coming to Believe

The purpose of John's Gospel was to help people "come to believe" in Jesus (20:31). Encouraging people to believe is also why John the Baptist came to testify (1:6-7). Indeed, belief is what Jesus himself wants (for example, 5:24; 6:29, 40; 11:15; 14:1, 11, 29). And so the climax of this story is not the miracle, but the belief that follows it.

"Jesus did this, the first of his signs, in Cana of Galilee, and revealed his glory," John concludes, "and his disciples believed in him" (2:11).

But belief is not a one-episode phenomenon. And belief is not fully accomplished by just chapter 2 of the story. So while this miracle led to belief, that belief was not complete.

We recall that the writer of Hebrews calls Jesus "the author and perfecter of our faith" (12:2 NIV). Or, as the Amplified Bible helpfully interprets it, Jesus is both the One who is "giving the first incentive for our belief" and the One who is "bringing it to maturity and perfection."

Clearly prior to this event in Cana, Andrew (1:40-41) and Nathanael (1:49-50) had already come to significant belief in Jesus. Meanwhile, well after the Cana wedding, Jesus indicates that he anticipates his disciples coming to still further belief (11:15). Even on the eve of his crucifixion, those disciples are wrestling with their belief (14:10; 16:29-31). On Easter morning, we read about yet another epiphany of belief (20:8), and yet after that event we discover still another struggle with disbelief (20:25-29).

When John reports at the end of the wedding, therefore, that "his disciples believed in him" (2:11), what exactly does that mean?

I suspect that it means the same thing it means when you and I talk about coming to believe in Jesus. When did it happen for you? Perhaps there is a single day, a particular night, a watershed event. Yet the seeds of faith were probably planted before that red-letter day, and no doubt your faith has needed to grow and mature since then.

We rejoice in the events—like the sweet and abundant miracle in Cana—that help us come to believe in Jesus. They are the highlights of our testimony. Yet they are always plural. For, thankfully, God keeps working, and we keep growing.

SHARING THE SCRIPTURE

Preparing Our Hearts

Explore this week's devotional reading, found in John 17:1-5. Jesus' prayer for his disciples comes near the close of their final meal together. In contrast to his comment in John 2:4 that his "hour has not yet come," in John 17:1, Jesus acknowledges in his prayer that "the hour has come." He prays that God will glorify him, even as he has glorified God by doing the work he was sent to do. What time is it in your life? What work has God called you to do? How are you glorifying God?

Pray that you and the adult learners will recognize the unity among God the Father, God the Son, God the Holy Spirit, and the community of faith.

Preparing Our Minds

Study the background Scripture and the lesson Scripture, both of which are from John 2:1-12. As you study, evaluate your beliefs about miracles.

Write on newsprint:

❑ information for next week's lesson, found under "Continue the Journey."
❑ activities for further spiritual growth in "Continue the Journey."

Plan a lecture based on Understanding the Scripture to help the adults understand this story.

LEADING THE CLASS

(1) Gather to Learn

❖ Welcome the class members and introduce any guests.

❖ Pray that the students will be open to the positive impact that miracles can have on people's lives.

❖ Invite the adults to tell stories of embarrassing moments at weddings they have attended, even their own weddings. What happened? How were the situations resolved? If you need a discussion starter, here is a snafu that your editor witnessed: **The bride had hired a brass ensemble to provide the music for her special day. The musicians began to play several preludes, as instructed, when suddenly they saw that the nervous bride had begun to walk down the aisle with her attendants. She was coming forward at the wrong time to the wrong music. Moreover, no groom or pastor was awaiting her. Finally realizing her error, the bride and her retinue returned to the back of the church by the side aisle and marched down the aisle again at the appropriate time. Fortunately, she was able to laugh about this "memorable" moment.**

❖ Read aloud today's focus statement: **When faced with possibly embarrassing or difficult situations, many people hope for a miracle to bring order out of chaos. Where and how can we find these** miracles? Jesus' first miracle during the wedding at Cana revealed his power by creating something good, and the disciples believed in him.

(2) Examine All That Was Created Good in the Story of the Cana Wedding, Including Wine from Water, Goodwill for the Host, and Believing Disciples

❖ Read John 2:1-12 as a drama by selecting volunteers to read the words of the narrator, Mary, Jesus, and the chief steward.
   ❖ Discuss these questions:
      (1) What does the fact that Jesus, his mother, and his disciples were at a wedding suggest to you about Jesus?
      (2) Why do you think Jesus seemed reluctant to fulfill his mother's request?
      (3) Why do you suppose that even after he told his mother he would not honor her request, he did so anyway?
      (4) What do the chief steward's comments to the groom about the wine reveal about Jesus' miracle?
      (5) What good came from this miracle?
      (6) What might this sign have suggested to you about who Jesus was?
❖ Present the brief lecture that you have prepared from Understanding the Scripture. Invite the students to raise questions or make comments to wrap up this portion of the session.

(3) Recognize and Appreciate God's Power to Continue Creating Calm and Order Out of Chaos as a Miracle in the World

❖ Note that Jesus' turning water into wine was a sign that had the effect of creating order out of what could have been an embarrassing, chaotic situation for the bridal party.

❖ Call on volunteers to give examples of other biblical stories in which Jesus created order out of chaos. (Here are two examples: calming the sea, healing a man who lived among the tombs in Gerasene).
❖ Distribute paper and pencils. Invite the adults to write about a time when their inner peace was shattered by an external cause. Perhaps a fire or natural disaster left them homeless or temporarily displaced. Possibly the loss of a job dislocated their identity and their ability to survive.
❖ Draw the class together, but do not ask anyone to read his or her comments. Instead, ask everyone to continue to think about whatever incident each individual has recorded and give thanks for whatever way God was able to bring order out of this situation.

(4) Express What Leads the Learners to Believe in Jesus

❖ Read "Coming to Believe" from Interpreting the Scripture to accentuate that the sign of this story, as well as all the signs Jesus did, were done to help people come to believe in Jesus and grow in that belief.
❖ Go around the room inviting each person to state one reason why he or she believes in Jesus. Insist that each person just give one reason per turn, but go around as often as necessary to let everyone state all of their reasons. These should be short answers, such as "believe what the Bible says about Jesus" or "saw how certain Christians live and wanted that kind of life." List all the ideas on newsprint.
❖ Encourage the adults to talk in more detail, perhaps in a small group, about why they believe. For example, someone may have a story to tell about how Jesus was instrumental in helping during a family crisis. Another may have experienced God's power in the midst of a serious illness.
❖ **Option:** Invite students who have been moved by any of these stories to provide feedback. For example, someone who

is in the midst of a similar kind of situation may comment on how a story has helped them see that there is hope and light at the end of what currently feels like a dark tunnel.

❖ Challenge the students to tell their stories to others who do not have a personal relationship with Jesus.

(5) Continue the Journey

❖ Pray that the adults will tell others why they believe in Jesus.

❖ Read aloud this preparation for next week's lesson. You may also want to post it on newsprint for the students to copy.

■ **Title: God's Word Saves**

■ **Background Scripture: John 3:11-21; Numbers 21:4-8**

■ **Lesson Scripture: John 3:11-21**

■ **Focus of the Lesson: People understand that their behavior has consequences. How can we be saved from the consequences of our poor choices? The writer of John gives assurance that, regardless of our choices, God loves us and sent Jesus so the world might be restored to a right relationship with God.**

❖ Challenge the students to complete one or more of these activities for further spiritual growth related to this week's session. Post this information on newsprint for the students to copy.

(1) Recall that the story of the wedding in Cana, like many other stories, portrays Jesus as being involved in the daily affairs of our lives. Is there any particular place in which you need Jesus to be involved in your life right now? Pray about that, inviting him to come and take charge of that situation.

(2) Use a concordance to research "signs" that Jesus did according to John's Gospel. Read several of these. How do they help you to believe in Jesus? With whom might you share at least one of these stories?

(3) Call upon Jesus for assistance for yourself or, as Mary did, for someone else who has a need.

❖ Sing or read aloud "Jesus, Joy of Our Desiring."

❖ Conclude today's session by leading the class in this benediction: **Go forth rejoicing that God, out of infinite love for the world, gave us Jesus, through whom we have eternal life.**

UNIT 1: THE WORD WAS IN THE BEGINNING
GOD'S WORD SAVES

PREVIEWING THE LESSON

Lesson Scripture: John 3:11-21
Background Scripture: John 3:11-21; Numbers 21:4-8
Key Verse: John 3:16

Focus of the Lesson:
People understand that their behavior has consequences. How can we be saved from the consequences of our poor choices? The writer of John gives assurance that, regardless of our choices, God loves us and sent Jesus so the world might be restored to a right relationship with God.

Goals for the Learners:
(1) to examine the way in which Jesus demonstrates God's unconditional love for us.
(2) to become sensitive to the effects of God's saving act through Jesus Christ.
(3) to claim God's unconditional love for themselves.

Supplies:
Bibles, newsprint and marker, paper and pencils, hymnals

READING THE SCRIPTURE

NRSV
John 3:11-21

[11]"Very truly, I tell you, we speak of what we know and testify to what we have seen; yet you do not receive our testimony. [12]If I have told you about earthly things and you do not believe, how can you believe if I tell you about heavenly things? [13]No one has ascended into heaven except the one who descended from heaven, the Son of Man. [14]And just as Moses lifted up the serpent in the wilderness, so must the Son of Man be lifted up, [15]that whoever believes in him may have eternal life.

NIV
John 3:11-21

[11]I tell you the truth, we speak of what we know, and we testify to what we have seen, but still you people do not accept our testimony. [12]I have spoken to you of earthly things and you do not believe; how then will you believe if I speak of heavenly things? [13]No one has ever gone into heaven except the one who came from heaven—the Son of Man. [14]Just as Moses lifted up the snake in the desert, so the Son of Man must be lifted up, [15]that everyone who believes in him may have eternal life.

¹⁶"For God so loved the world that he gave his only Son, so that everyone who believes in him may not perish but may have eternal life. ¹⁷"Indeed, God did not send the Son into the world to condemn the world, but in order that the world might be saved through him. ¹⁸Those who believe in him are not condemned; but those who do not believe are condemned already, because they have not believed in the name of the only Son of God. ¹⁹And this is the judgment, that the light has come into the world, and people loved darkness rather than light because their deeds were evil. ²⁰For all who do evil hate the light and do not come to the light, so that their deeds may not be exposed. ²¹But those who do what is true come to the light, so that it may be clearly seen that their deeds have been done in God."

¹⁶"For God so loved the world that he gave his one and only Son, that whoever believes in him shall not perish but have eternal life. ¹⁷For God did not send his Son into the world to condemn the world, but to save the world through him. ¹⁸Whoever believes in him is not condemned, but whoever does not believe stands condemned already because he has not believed in the name of God's one and only Son. ¹⁹This is the verdict: Light has come into the world, but men loved darkness instead of light because their deeds were evil. ²⁰Everyone who does evil hates the light, and will not come into the light for fear that his deeds will be exposed. ²¹But whoever lives by the truth comes into the light, so that it may be seen plainly that what he has done has been done through God."

UNDERSTANDING THE SCRIPTURE

Introduction. The brief passage from Numbers comes from Israel's wilderness period—the forty years of wandering between their deliverance from slavery in Egypt and their conquest of the land of Canaan. Moses was their leader, and manna was their daily bread, which they had come to regard as "this miserable food" (Numbers 21:5).

Meanwhile, the excerpt from John's Gospel is part of a larger scene featuring Nicodemus, a Pharisee and member of the Jewish ruling council. He had approached Jesus "by night"—a detail that the narrator considers revealing enough to include twice (3:2; 19:39)—and his exit is even more shrouded, for it is unclear in the text when Nicodemus leaves. He simply no longer says anything after his expressions of bewilderment in verses 4 and 9. Jesus marvels at Nicodemus's inability to understand, which leads to our selected passage of Jesus' teaching.

Numbers 21:4-5. That the people grew impatient with their journey and its circumstances is not unique to this episode. The complaining and rebelling displayed here are typical of the people's behavior all along the way (for example, Exodus 14:11-12; 16:1-3; 17:1-3; Numbers 11:1-6).

Numbers 21:6-8. The pattern here is also typical. The people's complaints evoke God's chastening, which in turn prompts the people to repent. In this particular instance, the punishment from God came in the form of poisonous snakes, from which the people pleaded for relief. God's prescribed relief is the image to which Jesus alludes in our Gospel text.

John 3:11-13. Jesus' use of personal pronouns in these verses is somewhat perplexing. In keeping with the preceding one-on-one dialogue, Jesus begins with two singulars: "I" and "you." In the next breath, however, he shifts into plural references. "We speak," "we know," and "we have seen," are followed by a plural "you" that does not receive "our testimony." And, as though that were not curious enough, he mixes the singular and the plural in the next verse: "If I (singular) have told you (plural) . . . how can you (plural) believe if I (singular) tell you (plural) about heavenly things?"

If all of the references were singular, then we would simply understand it as Jesus speaking to Nicodemus. The plural pronouns, however, prompt us to wonder what group of people is speaking to what other group of people.

It may be that Nicodemus is addressed in the plural as a representative of his people, which is consistent with Nicodemus's own use of "we" in 3:2. Jesus' use of "we," meanwhile, may reflect his understanding of multiple witnesses, which is reflected throughout the Gospel (5:30-47; 8:14-18; 10:25; 15:26-27; see also 12:38).

The juxtaposition of "earthly" and "heavenly" things, as we observed earlier, is truly central to John's Gospel and the teachings of Jesus found there. It is not surprising, therefore, to find Jesus make explicit reference to the two realms in this dialogue with Nicodemus.

Meanwhile, Jesus presents himself as uniquely qualified to reveal heavenly things since he is the one who has descended from heaven (3:13; see also 1:18; 6:46).

John 3:14-15. The episode from Numbers 21, to which Jesus makes quick reference, is brief and obscure, yet Jesus elevates it to a position of great prominence and meaning.

At God's direction, Moses had fashioned an image of a snake out of bronze and raised it up on a pole in the midst of the camp. Whoever had been bitten could look at that bronze snake and be healed.

Jesus points back to that strange episode, and draws a line connecting that bronze snake to himself. Christians understand this teaching to be an allusion to the cross—the pole on which Jesus was lifted up in order that those who were dying might be saved and live.

John 3:16-18. Sometimes called "the gospel in a nutshell," John 3:16 has been memorized, recited, and cherished by untold millions of Christians across the generations. But as with anything familiar, we run the risk of passing by this verse without giving it much attention. Accordingly, we will give it careful attention here.

John 3:17 is not nearly as familiar as John 3:16, but the news is just as good. The teaching suggests two possible responses to the world's fallen condition: condemnation or salvation. The gospel is that, in Christ, God has opted and provided for salvation.

Still, in the following verse, we discover that condemnation remains an issue. Yet condemnation appears to be something that we choose rather than something that God enacts. Condemnation is not so much the future prospect for some unfortunate souls, but rather the present choice of those who do not believe.

In this moment, it all comes down to how one responds to the Son of God—a theme that is revisited in the following verses about how one responds to the light.

John 3:19-21. As noted at the beginning of our study, light and dark are recurring thematic categories in John's Gospel. At the outset, John echoes the initial language of Genesis—"in the beginning"—and we are reminded that the first creative act of God was to speak light into darkness. Likewise, in John's view of Christ's coming into the world, God has again sent light into darkness (1:4-5).

Darkness is associated with being lost (8:12; 12:35) and with hazard (6:17). Darkness is also understood in John not only as the opposite or absence of light but also as the antagonist of light (1:5).

Light, meanwhile, is associated with life (1:4), as well as clarity and freedom (11:10; 12:46). A person can be in the light (5:35; 12:35) or a person can have the light within (11:10). Most of all, light is associated with Jesus (8:12; 9:5; 12:46). Consequently, the light can be loved or hated (3:19-21), testified to (1:7-8), and believed in (12:36).

Accordingly, within this context in John 3, the light-dark dichotomy is about choosing sides—or, perhaps more accurately, showing which side one is on. The light has come into the world, and people either run to it or run from it. Hence, just the light coming into the world serves as a means of judgment.

INTERPRETING THE SCRIPTURE

Human Choices

In the 2003 comedy *Bruce Almighty*, the main character, Bruce Nolan, is given a small taste of God's power, as well as God's challenges. At one desperate moment, Bruce asks God, "How can you make a person love you without interfering with that person's free will?" God simply smiles and responds, "Welcome to my world."

Our key verse for this week's study declares God's great love for the world, and we will explore together the nature and implications of that love. As we begin, however, we should observe that God's love for human beings was demonstrated long before Christ's Incarnation. Indeed, God's love for us was evident from the very beginning in how the Lord chose to create us: free.

God's choice to make us free is an indication of divine love. Indeed, to put it baldly, our free will is tacit proof that love is more important to God than obedience. After all, if obedience were the most important thing to God, then we would have been designed to obey. That was certainly within God's power. Just as creation was designed to obey the laws of nature, so people could have been designed to obey the laws of God.

Such a design, of course, would have done away with our free will. And, more significantly, it would have disabled our capacity to love, for we cannot love unless we are free. And we know from Jesus' own words that love is what is most important to God (Matthew 22:36-40).

In our freedom, however, lies not only our capacity to love but also our capacity to sin. That has been our choice since our first parents in Eden; and it has remained the ever-present choice of humanity, both collectively and individually, ever since.

God's Choices

What's an omnipotent God to do? All the beauty and majesty of nature honors God, and the entire, splendid heavenly host worships and obeys. But human beings—evidently the most cherished part of God's creation—live at a self-imposed distance. Sometimes in malignant rebellion, and sometimes in ignorant self-absorption, humanity stays stubbornly lost. The righteous Creator would be justified in scrapping the whole project, but instead, God "so loved the world."

If the Lord had made no previous overtures toward fallen humanity, perhaps the Incarnation would be slightly less astonishing. If sending the Beloved Son into the world was the Father's very first effort to woo the lone rebels made in God's image (Genesis 1:26-27), perhaps it would be somewhat less remarkable. But the Lord had matched human stubbornness every step of the way (compare Matthew 23:37; Luke 20:9-16). God's love was no less persistent than our recalcitrance. Yet we remained entrenched in sin.

What's an omnipotent God to do? Just this: "He gave his only Son."

If God had sought the advice of almost any human consultant on this move, that expert would have replied that this was a clear case of throwing good money after bad. Given the lack of return on nearly every previous investment of divine love and grace, why spend more on this human experiment? Certainly, they don't deserve it. And all the evidence suggests that they won't respond properly to it.

Evidently, you see, the Lord had two choices in responding to a sinful world: to condemn it or to save it. The former would have been the easy and obvious choice. The latter, however, reflects the true heart and perfect will of God. And so "God did not send the Son into the world to condemn the world, but in order that the world might be saved through him" (3:17).

Here is where we meet with a caveat in human free will. Individual human beings are capable of choosing their way into sin, but they cannot simply choose their way out of it: "Very truly, I tell you," Jesus said, "everyone who commits sin is a slave to sin" (John 8:34).

By choosing sin, humanity has jumped into a depth and ferociousness of water in which we cannot survive. We are in over our heads. We are drowning, and we need to be rescued. Enter Jesus, the Savior.

Our Choices

By coming into the world to save us, Jesus renews our capacity to choose. For while salvation is offered, it is not imposed.

In my denomination, parents usually have their children baptized as babies and then confirmed as teenagers. I met recently with the parents of an incoming confirmation class, and I shared with them the design and meaning behind our confirmation tradition. When they brought their infants to be baptized thirteen years ago, those children didn't have a choice. When it comes time for them to be confirmed, however, it needs to be their choice. If the parents simply insist on it at the end of the year, then confirmation will be no different from the baptism event: a parental decision without the voluntary and faithful participation of the child.

God is the parent who leaves the choice up to the children. God encourages, but does not require; invites, but does not insist.

In love, God chose to send the Beloved Son into the world "so that everyone who believes in him may not perish but may have eternal life" (3:16). "Everyone who believes" is an open invitation, to be sure. There is no one who is ineligible for this salvation. Yet that salvation remains only an offer: It can be accepted or rejected. The choice to believe in the Son is necessarily as free as the choice to love.

Even in the midst of declaring the good news of God's gracious initiative and invitation, Jesus recognizes the potential tragedy involved. Just as the freedom to choose turned tragic in Eden, so it may be with God's salvation offer, as well.

Jesus says, "The light has come into the world" (3:19). Inasmuch as darkness means being lost, confused, and doomed, the light is good news. But what will be the response to that light?

When we are feeling our way along a dark hallway or through a dark room, we are relieved finally to find the light switch or the lamp. As soon as the light comes on, we relax. We move freely and confidently with the light on, whereas we are tentative and scared in the dark.

Not everything responds to the light switch that way, however. If you've ever had to share a living space with cockroaches, then you know the distasteful sight that comes with the light switch. Turn the lights on in the formerly dark kitchen, and watch the uninvited guests scurry for their cracks and crevices. They do not welcome the light.

And according to Jesus, not all human beings welcome his light coming into the world, either. If a person's reflex is to cling to evil, then the light is an intrusion and an embarrassment.

The Savior has come to rescue drowning humanity. We may grab hold of the saving hand he extends to us, or we may push it aside. The choice is ours.

SHARING THE SCRIPTURE

Preparing Our Hearts

Explore this week's devotional reading, found in Matthew 5:13-16. Here in the Sermon on the Mount Jesus refers to his followers as "the salt of the earth" (5:13) and "the light of the world" (5:14). In speaking about himself, Jesus says, "The light has come into the world" (John 3:19). Imagine! According to Jesus, both he and we are the world's light. Whose path are you lighting? Where can you let your light shine so that others may see God in you?

Pray that you and the adult learners will be salt and light to a world that needs to taste and see God.

Preparing Our Minds

Study the background Scripture from John 3:11-21 and Numbers 21:4-8. The lesson Scripture is from John 3:11-21. Think about how we can be restored to a right relationship with God.

Write on newsprint:

❏ information for next week's lesson, found under "Continue the Journey."
❏ activities for further spiritual growth in "Continue the Journey."

Become very familiar with information in Understanding the Scripture so as to add to the discussion as suggested in "Examine the Way in Which Jesus Demonstrates God's Unconditional Love for Us."

LEADING THE CLASS

(1) Gather to Learn

❖ Welcome the class members and introduce any guests.

❖ Pray that the students will experience God's unconditional love as expressed through Jesus.

❖ Form groups of three or four and invite the students to tell stories from their childhoods or teen years when they made poor choices and had to deal with the consequences of their actions. Here is an example: **Newly licensed driver "Jim" took his dad's car without permission. He gathered some of his guy friends to go cruising where girls often gathered. As he was rounding one corner a bit too quickly, "Jim" sideswiped another car, leaving a long red paint streak on his dad's car. Although he hoped his dad would not notice immediately, he was not so lucky and did have to confess. He lost driving privileges for three months until he could pay for the damage.**

❖ Read aloud today's focus statement: **People understand that their behavior has consequences. How can we be saved from the consequences of our poor choices? The writer of John gives assurance that, regardless of our choices, God loves us and sent Jesus so the world might be restored to a right relationship with God.**

(2) Examine the Way in Which Jesus Demonstrates God's Unconditional Love for Us

❖ Choose a volunteer to read John 3:11-21.

❖ Encourage the adults to read this passage again silently from their own Bibles. Suggest that they underline (or write on paper you have distributed) any words or phrases that jump off the page at them.

❖ Bring everyone together and invite

volunteers to say which words or phrases "spoke" to them. Talk with the group about the meanings they derived from their chosen words. Use ideas from Understanding the Scripture as they help to illuminate the meanings.

❖ Take a few moments to discuss the allusion in John 3:14-15 to Moses lifting up the snake in the wilderness, as first described in Numbers 21:4-8. Encourage the class to state connections they see between this story and Jesus being lifted on the cross. Note that the Greek word translated as "saved" in 3:17 also means "make well" or "heal."

❖ Discuss these questions:
(1) **What do you learn about Jesus from this passage?**
(2) **What do you learn about God's intentions for humanity?**
(3) **How do people judge and condemn themselves?**
(4) **How could you use this passage to help someone come to believe in Jesus? What would you say about how God's word saves?**

(3) Become Sensitive to the Effects of God's Saving Act Through Jesus Christ

❖ Invite one volunteer to read John 1:4-5, 9-11 and another to read John 3:19-21. Ask:
(1) **What effect did Jesus' coming into the world have on people?**
(2) **If people prefer to live in darkness, as these passages indicate, how can we as the church help them to become sensitive to the saving light of Jesus?** (Think here about how your congregation is—or could be—sharing the love of God within the community. How are you helping the poor, the marginalized, and others in need? In what ways do you proclaim the gospel in both words and deeds? What does the congregation do to help newcomers feel welcome? In

other words, how are people outside of the church seeing the light of Christ in those who profess to be his followers?)

❖ Recognize that there are those in the community who follow a religion other than Christianity—or no religion at all. Discuss how, without being offensive or sounding superior, you could present Christ to others so that they may see the effects of God's saving act. This quotation from D. T. Niles may be a helpful way to frame the discussion: **"Christianity is one beggar telling another beggar where he found bread."** As witnesses, we are not beating people over the head with our beliefs, but rather, offering food to a fellow seeker.

❖ End this portion by challenging participants to offer the bread of Christ to someone else this week.

(4) Claim God's Unconditional Love

❖ Read or retell "Our Choices" in Interpreting the Scripture.

❖ Remind the group that although God gave Jesus to the world, each person is free to accept or reject the unconditional love God showed through this gift.

❖ Distribute hymnals if they contain a service of confirmation. ("The Baptismal Covenant III" in *The United Methodist Hymnal*, pages 45-49, is an example of such a service.) Invite the class to read silently or aloud the parts of the service, looking specifically for what the candidates are assenting to as they present themselves for confirmation (and possibly baptism). How does the congregation respond?

❖ **Option:** Check with the pastor prior to the session if your hymnal does not contain a service of confirmation. Invite the pastor to attend class to explain what candidates are asked to agree to and how the congregation promises to support them. If the pastor is unable to attend, borrow a copy of this service so that you can walk the class through it.

❖ Provide quiet time for the participants to reflect on how their own experience of confirmation (or baptism) empowered them to claim God's unconditional love. Encourage those who want to reaffirm that commitment to offer silent prayer about this reaffirmation of faith.

❖ Conclude this portion of the lesson by leading the group in reciting today's key verse, John 3:16.

(5) Continue the Journey

❖ Pray that the adults will claim God's unconditional love for themselves.

❖ Read aloud this preparation for next week's lesson. You may also want to post it on newsprint for the students to copy.

- **Title: Jesus Testifies to the Truth**
- **Background Scripture: John 18–19**
- **Lesson Scripture: John 18:28-37**
- **Focus of the Lesson: Amid the good and bad things that happen to us, we wonder what our real purpose in life is. Why are we here, and what is our purpose? Even after his betrayal, arrest, and inquisition by Pilate, Jesus was clear that his purpose was to testify to the truth of God's love.**

❖ Challenge the students to complete one or more of these activities for further spiritual growth related to this week's session. Post this information on newsprint for the students to copy.

(1) **Take some action this week to be God's light in someone else's life. What difference can you see in that person because of your action?**

(2) **Sit in total darkness and meditate on the world that God loves. Bring light into the room and ponder how God's love through Christ changes everything.**

(3) **Research the phrase "eternal life." What does this mean? How does Jesus make eternal life possible?**

❖ Sing or read aloud "Because He Lives."

❖ Conclude today's session by leading the class in this benediction: **Go forth rejoicing that God, out of infinite love for the world, gave us Jesus, through whom we have eternal life.**

UNIT 1: THE WORD WAS IN THE BEGINNING
JESUS TESTIFIES TO THE TRUTH

PREVIEWING THE LESSON

Lesson Scripture: John 18:28-37
Background Scripture: John 18–19
Key Verse: John 18:37

Focus of the Lesson:
Amid the good and bad things that happen to us, we wonder what our real purpose in life is. Why are we here, and what is our purpose? Even after his betrayal, arrest, and inquisition by Pilate, Jesus was clear that his purpose was to testify to the truth of God's love.

Goals for the Learners:
(1) to examine how the encounter between Jesus and Pilate testified to God's redeeming love.
(2) to recognize how one's purpose in life may be challenged by others.
(3) to bear witness to Jesus, who came to testify to the truth.

Pronunciation Guide:
Annas (an' uhs)
Caiaphas (kay' uh fuhs)
Hasmonean (haz muh nee' uhn)

Supplies:
Bibles, newsprint and marker, paper and pencils, hymnals

READING THE SCRIPTURE

NRSV
John 18:28-37

²⁸Then they took Jesus from Caiaphas to Pilate's headquarters. It was early in the morning. They themselves did not enter the headquarters, so as to avoid ritual defilement and to be able to eat the Passover. ²⁹So

NIV
John 18:28-37

²⁸Then the Jews led Jesus from Caiaphas to the palace of the Roman governor. By now it was early morning, and to avoid ceremonial uncleanness the Jews did not enter the palace; they wanted to be able to eat the

Pilate went out to them and said, "What accusation do you bring against this man?" [30]They answered, "If this man were not a criminal, we would not have handed him over to you." [31]Pilate said to them, "Take him yourselves and judge him according to your law." The Jews replied, "We are not permitted to put anyone to death." [32](This was to fulfill what Jesus had said when he indicated the kind of death he was to die.)

[33]Then Pilate entered the headquarters again, summoned Jesus, and asked him, "Are you the King of the Jews?" [34]Jesus answered, "Do you ask this on your own, or did others tell you about me?" [35]Pilate replied, "I am not a Jew, am I? Your own nation and the chief priests have handed you over to me. What have you done?" [36]Jesus answered, "My kingdom is not from this world. If my kingdom were from this world, my followers would be fighting to keep me from being handed over to the Jews. But as it is, my kingdom is not from here." [37]**Pilate asked him, "So you are a king?" Jesus answered, "You say that I am a king. For this I was born, and for this I came into the world, to testify to the truth. Everyone who belongs to the truth listens to my voice."**

Passover. [29]So Pilate came out to them and asked, "What charges are you bringing against this man?"

[30]"If he were not a criminal," they replied, "we would not have handed him over to you."

[31]Pilate said, "Take him yourselves and judge him by your own law."

"But we have no right to execute anyone," the Jews objected. [32]This happened so that the words Jesus had spoken indicating the kind of death he was going to die would be fulfilled.

[33]Pilate then went back inside the palace, summoned Jesus and asked him, "Are you the king of the Jews?"

[34]"Is that your own idea," Jesus asked, "or did others talk to you about me?"

[35]"Am I a Jew?" Pilate replied. "It was your people and your chief priests who handed you over to me. What is it you have done?"

[36]Jesus said, "My kingdom is not of this world. If it were, my servants would fight to prevent my arrest by the Jews. But now my kingdom is from another place."

[37]**"You are a king, then!" said Pilate. Jesus answered, "You are right in saying I am a king. In fact, for this reason I was born, and for this I came into the world, to testify to the truth. Everyone on the side of truth listens to me."**

UNDERSTANDING THE SCRIPTURE

John 18:1-3. Following John's long account of the Last Supper, Jesus leads his disciples to the garden that Matthew (26:36) and Mark (14:32) identify as Gethsemane. The Kidron Valley lies east of Jerusalem, the same side of the valley as the Mount of Olives. And on the other side of the Mount of Olives is the town of Bethany. It is possible that Jesus and his disciples were staying in Bethany during the festival. If so, they

may have made this walk together each morning and evening. Perhaps it was Jesus' custom to stop and pray in this garden, and so his location was familiar and predictable for Judas.

John 18:4-9. While it might be the natural instinct to flee from those coming to apprehend you, Jesus goes to meet them. He asks them for whom they are looking, and identifies himself as that person, effectively surrendering himself to them. The initial response of the posse—"they stepped back and fell to the ground" (18:6)—is reminiscent of similar detachments' inability to arrest Elijah (2 Kings 1:9-15) and Elisha (2 Kings 6:8-23), as well as the Nazarenes' mysteriously frustrated effort to kill Jesus (Luke 4:28-30).

John 18:10-11. Jesus' reference to "the cup that the Father has given me" (18:11) has no precedent within John's Gospel, but we do get a sense for the image from other sources. In both Matthew (20:22) and Mark, Jesus asks the ambitious sons of Zebedee, "Are you able to drink the cup that I drink?" (Mark 10:38). And in Matthew 26:39, Jesus prays in Gethsemane, "Let this cup pass from me" (see also Mark 14:36; Luke 22:42). The image may find it scriptural origins in some of the judgment prophecies in the Old Testament (for example, Jeremiah 25:15-28; Ezekiel 23:32-34; Habakkuk 2:15-16).

John 18:12-14. The office of the High Priest, introduced by Moses and first held by Aaron, was originally a spiritual and ritual responsibility. Perhaps inevitably, it was used by some occupants as a position with political clout, and this was especially true during the Hasmonean Dynasty of the intertestamental period. Initially, it was an inherited office held for life (Exodus 40:12-15; Numbers 25:10-13). Under Rome, however, the office was appointed by the local Roman governor. Annas had served in that capacity A.D. 6–15. His son-in-law, Caiaphas, held the position A.D. 18–36, including the time of Jesus' crucifixion.

John 18:15-27. Peter and the other disciple, traditionally assumed to be the author of this Gospel, are also linked together in the story of the Last Supper (13:23-25), in the account of the empty tomb (20:3-10), and in a conversation with Jesus at the conclusion of the Gospel (21:20-24).

John 18:28. John's reference to "the Jews" is not solely an ethnic designation. After all, John himself was Jewish, as was Jesus. The phrase "the Jews" appears seventy times in the Fourth Gospel, and Raymond Brown observes that it is used "almost [as] a technical title for *the religious authorities, particularly those in Jerusalem, who are hostile to Jesus.*"

Meanwhile, two elements from the Old Testament law are at work in this moment. First, ritual cleanness was a strong theme in the law, and many causes could make a person ritually unclean. The Mosaic law does not include entering the home of a Gentile among those causes of uncleanness, but that became a later Jewish tradition. Second, an episode in the law indicated that a ritually unclean person could not participate in the Passover meal, but rather had to delay his or her celebration until the following month (Numbers 9:1-14). This combination of concerns prevented the Jewish leaders from entering Pilate's residence.

John 18:29-32. The Old Testament law provided for stoning to death a person guilty of a capital offense. Roman occupation in Israel, however, had curtailed the Jews' judicial jurisdiction. When Pilate suggested that the Jews handle for themselves the trial and punishment of Jesus, therefore, they complained that they were "not permitted to put anyone to death."

John 18:33-40. The phrase "King of the Jews" does not appear before this in John's Gospel, though it reappears five times in short succession after this. It is the very title that made Herod so afraid of Jesus' birth (see Matthew 2:1-4), and it was the charge Pilate ultimately opted to post on Jesus' cross (John 19:19), in spite of objections (19:20-22). Pilate was preoccupied with Jesus' kingship (see also 18:37, 39; 19:14-15), perhaps because it was a category he understood. "King" was from the kind of political lexicon in which Pilate was conversant. When the claim that Jesus was God's Son was mentioned, however, Pilate was clearly uncomfortable with it (19:7-8). For a passing moment, "truth" is the topic of Pilate's dialogue with Jesus. Jesus says that he came to testify to the truth, prompting Pilate to ask, "What is truth?" (18:38). Pilate "would not stay for an answer," however, as Francis Bacon sharply observed in his essay "Of Truth," and so cut short the conversation. Still, his question prompts us to recall the larger theme of truth in the Gospel of John (for example, 1:14, 17; 8:32; 14:6; 16:13; 17:17).

John 19:1-5. Flogging was a notorious method of punishment. The Jewish law placed restrictions on it (Deuteronomy 25:2-3), though the abusive Roman soldiers operated without such limits. Historical evidence suggests that the Romans used leather whips, which included pieces of bone and lead at the ends, effectively tearing the flesh as part of the torture.

John 19:6-16. Here is the first explicit reference to crucifixion in John's Gospel. Interestingly, the prospect is raised by the Jewish leaders rather than by Pilate, even though it was specifically Rome's method of execution. Roman citizens who were guilty of some capital offense were afforded a less torturous method of execution (beheading), while crucifixion was the marathon of public humiliation, bleeding, and suffocation designed for noncitizens.

John 19:17-30. The quotation about casting lots for clothing comes from Psalm 22 (22:18), which has sometimes been called "The Psalm of the Cross" because of its striking resemblances to Jesus' crucifixion. Jesus himself quoted that psalm from the cross when he cried out, "My God, my God, why have your forsaken me?" (Matthew 27:46).

John 19:31-42. "Day of Preparation" was a reference to the day before the Jewish Sabbath. Because no work was to be done on the Sabbath, Jewish families had to anticipate all that needed to be done in advance. The approaching Sabbath, with its numerous restrictions on activity, accounts for the urgency in removing Jesus' body from the cross and burying it.

INTERPRETING THE SCRIPTURE

The People Who Didn't Get It

See them standing outside of Pilate's palace. They are so careful and deliberate in their devotion to God's law. And so, in order to avoid contaminating themselves by entering the home of a Gentile, they stay outside on his doorstep. Bravo.

Yet see what agenda it is that brings them to this doorstep. They have come with Jesus in tow, seeking a death sentence for him from the local governor. They are careful with God's law, but they are reckless with God's Son.

Earlier that week, Jesus had accused them of straining a gnat and swallowing a camel (Matthew 23:24), and that is the very foolishness embodied in this scene. They are like superstitious children, who won't step on a sidewalk crack, yet they disobey and dishonor their mother to her face.

We should be careful, of course, not to lump all of the Pharisees and other Jewish leaders into a single generalization. Perhaps some individuals within their group were not hypocrites. Perhaps a few were able still to see the big picture and were not legalistically fixated on small, external details. But Jesus' many indictments of the scribes and Pharisees (for example, Matthew 23:1-36) surely lead us to conclude that they had regressed into an unwholesome lot.

Pilate naturally asked these leaders what charges they were bringing against their prisoner, to which they tartly responded, "If this man were not a criminal, we would not have handed him over to you" (John 18:30). Their evasive answer betrays the weakness of their case.

While they were unable to be specific about Jesus' crimes, however, they were quite specific about his punishment. For when Pilate suggested that they deal with Jesus themselves, they complained, "We are not permitted to put anyone to death" (18:31).

These men, who were so meticulous in their observance of external religiosity, turn irony into tragedy in this moment. They professed themselves to be the ones most careful about the things of God, and yet they were blind to the incarnate presence of God right there in their midst. And not only blind to him, but opposed to him.

These men, so versed in the Scriptures, had heard Jesus teach, and they had witnessed his miracles. They had enjoyed front-row seats for his power, his wisdom, and his compassion. Still, they did not perceive.

The Man Who Didn't Recognize It

Unable to achieve their dastardly will on their own, the Jewish leaders took Jesus to Pilate, the Roman governor. He was likely the only one who could give the order for Jesus' execution. And inasmuch as they were afraid of the popular response of the crowds, the members of the Sanhedrin no doubt recognized that the deed was better done by Rome than by them.

From what we know of Pilate from extrabiblical sources, we certainly have no reason to accuse him of being soft on crime. Yet he shows a notable reluctance to do what the Jewish leaders want him to do and sentence Jesus to death. As Herod earlier had been hesitant to execute John the Baptist, so now Pilate seems squeamish about putting to death this Jesus.

Ancient records report that Pilate was recalled from his post in Judea by Vitellius, then governor of Syria, because of his extortion and excessive cruelty. How is it that such a hardened magistrate would be so timid in dealing with Jesus? Yet the larger text reveals a man who seemed most eager to let Jesus go free.

Pilate's interrogation of Jesus begins with a question that seems to come out of the blue: "Are you the King of the Jews?" (John 18:33). The story does not report that the Jewish leaders had made any related accusation, and so one wonders why Pilate began with this question rather than the later, broader inquiry, "What have you done?" (18:35).

Yet we should give Pilate credit for his perception. His instincts were exactly right: The central issue was not Jesus' deeds but his identity. What he has done is merely a testimony to the more crucial truth of who he is (see, for example, Matthew 11:2-6; John 1:47-50; 14:11).

On the surface, there was nothing about Jesus that should have made Pilate spend any time on him—nothing to cause this agent of Rome to take Jesus seriously. After all, Jesus was not part of the current power structure in Israel, whether the religious leaders, Herod's family tree, or the aristocracy. He had not allied himself with a revolutionary movement or party, like the Zealots. And he showed no sign of having effectively mobilized his followers for insurrection. Why, then, would Pilate give him the time of day? And why suspect that he was some sort of king?

While there was nothing on the surface to commend Jesus, evidently Pilate sensed something below the surface. And he was right. His failure was that he came close to the truth about Jesus—closer than the Jewish leaders did—but he did not get all the way there. He was thinking "King of the Jews," but that was too small, too narrow. How could he have known that this nobody from Nazareth was the very King of the Universe? "He was in the world . . . yet the world did not know him" (John 1:10).

The One Who Testified to It

The action and dialogue in our scene begin with the Jewish leaders and then move to Pilate, but the scene ends with Jesus. And that is appropriate for, contrary to all human appearances, he is the real star of the show.

To a contemporary observer, Jesus would have appeared to be the powerless one—the victim, the weakling, the pawn. Yet that is not his posture in this scene, is it?

While the Jewish leaders are scrambling and maneuvering, Jesus seems still and tranquil. While Pilate is uncertain and torn, Jesus is confident and sure. William Barclay observed, "When a man faces him, it is not Jesus who is on trial; it is the man." This is, indeed, the feel of this majestic episode.

In the face of the Jews' opposition, Jesus is full of courage. In the midst of Pilate's confusion, Jesus is full of clarity. Surely, it requires a certain poise to be the center of an adoring crowd's attention, as on Palm Sunday, but this moment is a test of a completely different magnitude. When all fingers point at him, when the tide of events is entirely against him, and when the stakes are life-and-death, Jesus exhibits in that moment an uncommon serenity.

Jesus confirms that he is, indeed, a king, but not of the sort that Pilate imagined. The kings "from this world," after all, come and go. Their realm is limited and their reign is brief. But that is not the nature of Jesus' kingship: "my kingdom is not from here" (18:36). When it appears in this scene that Jesus is above it all, therefore, that's because he is.

Jesus' declaration about his kingdom is powerful, but it raises a question. If his kingdom is not of this world, then what is he doing here? Jesus seems to anticipate that question, for he answers it: He came "to testify to the truth" (18:37).

Testifying, of course, is the language of a trial. Yet Jesus suggests a larger court than Pilate's little chamber. Jesus may be the defendant at this particular moment, but it is the world's fate that is at stake. And so, on behalf of that world, he came to testify, so that they might know the truth, and the truth would set them free (8:32).

SHARING THE SCRIPTURE

Preparing Our Hearts

Explore this week's devotional reading, found in John 8:28-38. Here Jesus foretells his death and talks about what it means to be a true disciple. Do you see yourself as a true disciple now? If not, what do you need to ask God to do in your life?

Pray that you and the adult learners will seek the truth that sets you free.

Preparing Our Minds

Study the background Scripture from John 18–19 and the lesson Scripture from John 18:28-37. As you study, think about your purpose in life.

Write on newsprint:
❏ information for next week's lesson, found under "Continue the Journey."
❏ activities for further spiritual growth in "Continue the Journey."

LEADING THE CLASS

(1) Gather to Learn

❖ Welcome the class members and introduce any guests.

❖ Pray that the students will hear a message of God's redeeming love.

❖ Read this quotation about purpose in life by renowned Swiss psychiatrist Carl Jung (1875–1961), and invite the students to state why they agree or disagree with his ideas about purpose. **"The vast neurotic misery of the world could be termed a neurosis of emptiness. Men cut themselves off from the root of their being, from God, and then life turns empty, inane, meaningless, without purpose. So when God goes, goal goes. When goal goes, meaning goes. When meaning goes, value goes, and life turns dead on our hands."**

❖ Ask: **What does this quotation suggest about the importance of having purpose and meaning in life?**

❖ Read aloud today's focus statement: **Amid the good and bad things that happen to us, we wonder what our real purpose in life is. Why are we here, and what is our purpose? Even after his betrayal, arrest, and inquisition by Pilate, Jesus was clear that his purpose was to testify to the truth of God's love.**

(2) Examine How the Encounter Between Jesus and Pilate Testified to God's Redeeming Love

❖ Help the group learn more about Pilate by reading "The Man Who Didn't Recognize It" from Interpreting the Scripture.

❖ Call on five volunteers to read John 18:28-37 as a drama. One reader will act as the narrator, another as Pilate, a third as Jesus, and two others as Jesus' accusers.

❖ Invite the adults to imagine that they had been present as observers and ask:

(1) In light of the historical record and the biblical report, did Pilate act true to form or was he behaving in unexpected ways?

(2) Based on Jesus' testimony, would you have expected Pilate to condemn him to death? Why or why not?

(3) What would you have wanted to ask Jesus about his kingdom?

(4) When you heard Jesus' responses and observed his demeanor, what did you think about him?

(5) Would you have wanted to join his followers? Why or why not?

❖ Wrap up this activity by encouraging the adults to suggest reasons why people today are still unable to recognize Jesus.

(3) Recognize How One's Purpose in Life May Be Challenged by Others

❖ Read or retell "The One Who Testified to It" from Interpreting the Scripture. Ask: **How was Jesus' life purpose challenged, and how did he respond?**

❖ Point out that people may challenge what we believe to be our life's purpose as well.

❖ Distribute paper and pencils. Encourage everyone to complete this sentence: **The purpose of my life is to . . .**

❖ Ask the adults to recall a time when someone challenged this purpose. Write about what happened and how they responded. Here is an example you may wish to read: (The purpose) **The purpose of my life is to worship and serve Jesus Christ.** (The challenge) **During a heated discussion with a neighbor about his messy yard, he said that he didn't know why I went to church if I was going to act this way. As angry as I was, his words brought me up short. Now I think seriously about what I say and how I say it so as not to devalue my witness as a Christian.**

❖ Invite volunteers to tell about their purpose, a challenge to it, and how they responded. This is sensitive information, so do not prod anyone.

(4) Bear Witness to Jesus, Who Came to Testify to the Truth

❖ Lead the class in a unison reading of today's key verse, John 18:37.

❖ Select two volunteers. Assign one person to the role of Pilate and the other the role of Jesus. Note that in verse 38 Pilate asks, "What is truth?" Encourage the two to have a dialogue about truth. The person playing Jesus might offer information about the kingdom of God to answer Pilate's question.

❖ Form groups of three or four. Invite the adults to roleplay how they might answer a question about truth raised by someone who is a nonbeliever. People may not ask, "What is truth?" but they may ask, "How do you know that Jesus really is God's Son?" "What makes you think these Bible stories are true?" "I don't believe anything that cannot be proved, so why should I think what you are telling me is true?" If possible, have two people raising the questions and the other two providing answers based on what Jesus has said and done.

❖ Bring everyone together to talk about their experiences. Was it easy to carry on such a conversation? What hurdles did they have to clear? What do they need more information about in order to be better prepared?

❖ Challenge the adults to bear witness to Jesus, especially during this Holy Week.

(5) Continue the Journey

❖ Pray that the adults will go forth to bear witness to Jesus as the One sent by God to testify to the truth.

❖ Read aloud this preparation for next week's lesson. You may also want to post it on newsprint for the students to copy.

■ **Title: The Living Word**
■ **Background Scripture: John 20:1-23**
■ **Lesson Scripture: John 20:1-10, 19-20**
■ **Focus of the Lesson: People have always wondered about what happens to our human spirit after our physical death. Is there a life after death? Jesus' followers were confused when his body was missing, but when the resurrected Jesus appeared to them, they rejoiced.**

❖ Challenge the students to complete one or more of these activities for further spiritual growth related to this week's session. Post this information on newsprint for the students to copy.

(1) **Investigate the accounts of Jesus' trial before Pilate as found in Matthew 27:1-2, 11-14; Mark 15:1-5; and Luke 23:1-5. Compare these reports to the one in John 18:28-38. What do you learn about Jesus and Pilate from each of these accounts?**

(2) **Demonstrate God's love by doing something to serve others this week.**

(3) **Tell someone what you believe to be the truth about Jesus. If the person seems receptive, invite him or her to join you for Easter worship next Sunday.**

❖ Sing or read aloud "Rejoice, Ye Pure in Heart."

❖ Conclude today's session by leading the class in this benediction: **Go forth rejoicing that God, out of infinite love for the world, gave us Jesus, through whom we have eternal life.**

UNIT 1: THE WORD WAS IN THE BEGINNING
THE LIVING WORD

PREVIEWING THE LESSON

Lesson Scripture: John 20:1-10, 19-20
Background Scripture: John 20:1-23
Key Verse: John 20:20

Focus of the Lesson:

People have always wondered about what happens to our human spirit after our physical death. Is there a life after death? Jesus' followers were confused when his body was missing, but when the resurrected Jesus appeared to them, they rejoiced.

Goals for the Learners:

(1) to study the resurrection story as told in the Fourth Gospel.
(2) to reflect on feelings about death and resurrection.
(3) to express joy about resurrections (re-creation or new birth) in their lives.

Supplies:

Bibles, newsprint and marker, paper and pencils, hymnals

READING THE SCRIPTURE

NRSV
John 20:1-10, 19-20

¹Early on the first day of the week, while it was still dark, Mary Magdalene came to the tomb and saw that the stone had been removed from the tomb. ²So she ran and went to Simon Peter and the other disciple, the one whom Jesus loved, and said to them, "They have taken the Lord out of the tomb, and we do not know where they have laid him." ³Then Peter and the other disciple set out and went toward the tomb. ⁴The two were running together, but the other disciple outran Peter and reached the tomb first. ⁵He bent down to look in and saw the linen

NIV
John 20:1-10, 19-20

¹Early on the first day of the week, while it was still dark, Mary Magdalene went to the tomb and saw that the stone had been removed from the entrance. ²So she came running to Simon Peter and the other disciple, the one Jesus loved, and said, "They have taken the Lord out of the tomb, and we don't know where they have put him!"

³So Peter and the other disciple started for the tomb. ⁴Both were running, but the other disciple outran Peter and reached the tomb first. ⁵He bent over and looked in at the strips of linen lying there but did not go in.

wrappings lying there, but he did not go in. ⁶Then Simon Peter came, following him, and went into the tomb. He saw the linen wrappings lying there, ⁷and the cloth that had been on Jesus' head, not lying with the linen wrappings but rolled up in a place by itself. ⁸Then the other disciple, who reached the tomb first, also went in, and he saw and believed; ⁹for as yet they did not understand the scripture, that he must rise from the dead. ¹⁰Then the disciples returned to their homes.

¹⁹When it was evening on that day, the first day of the week, and the doors of the house where the disciples had met were locked for fear of the Jews, Jesus came and stood among them and said, "Peace be with you." ²⁰After he said this, he showed them his hands and his side. **Then the disciples rejoice when they saw the Lord.**

⁶Then Simon Peter, who was behind him, arrived and went into the tomb. He saw the strips of linen lying there, ⁷as well as the burial cloth that had been around Jesus' head. The cloth was folded up by itself, separate from the linen. ⁸Finally the other disciple, who had reached the tomb first, also went inside. He saw and believed. ⁹(They still did not understand from Scripture that Jesus had to rise from the dead.)

¹⁰Then the disciples went back to their homes.

¹⁹On the evening of that first day of the week, when the disciples were together, with the doors locked for fear of the Jews, Jesus came and stood among them and said, "Peace be with you!" ²⁰After he said this, he showed them his hands and side. **The disciples were overjoyed when they saw the Lord.**

UNDERSTANDING THE SCRIPTURE

John 20:1. Mary Magdalene is one of the most prominent women in the New Testament, appearing in all four Gospels. She is a woman from whom Jesus cast out seven demons (Mark 16:9) and one of the female followers of Jesus (Luke 8:2). She is among the witnesses of Jesus' crucifixion (Matthew 27:56) and burial (Mark 15:47). All four Gospels include Mary among the visitors to the tomb, though John is the only Gospel to focus exclusively on her.

In this scene, Mary is a picture of urgency. She would have been unable to visit the tomb on the Sabbath, but she went to the tomb "early on the first day of the week"—the day after the Jewish Sabbath. That she went "while it was still dark" also indicates her urgency, as she went to the tomb at her earliest opportunity.

John 20:2. "The other disciple" is identified here as "the one whom Jesus loved." That disciple is also mentioned as reclining next to Jesus at the Last Supper (13:23),

standing near the cross with Jesus' mother (19:26), recognizing Jesus at a postresurrection appearance (21:7), the object of some speculation (21:20-23), and the author of the Gospel (21:24). In keeping with tradition, therefore, we will identify "the other disciple" as John.

Mary does not specify who "they" are. Perhaps she did not have anyone specific in mind, and so this was the equivalent of saying, "Someone has taken the body." Or perhaps "they" referred generally to that entire conglomerate of bad actors who had orchestrated the terrible events of the past few days.

If this were a fabricated story, I think it would have featured a public and spectacular resurrection. Instead, the first Easter experience is only the bewilderment of an empty tomb.

John 20:3-9. These verses feature the sort of details that suggest an eyewitness account. John evidently outran Peter to the tomb. Perhaps it is typical of Peter's personality, however, that he went bursting in ahead of John.

The presence of the grave cloths is significant. If Jesus' body had been stolen, there would have been no reason to unwrap it. Instead, the linen wrappings have been discarded as though no longer needed. We recall that the denouement of Lazarus's resurrection was the instruction to "unbind him, and let him go" (John 11:44). A man who has been raised no longer needs to be wrapped up in burial cloths.

It is at this moment that "the other disciple . . . saw and believed" (20:8). This Gospel makes more than eighty references to believing. It is the reason John the Baptist came (1:7) and the Gospel was written (19:35; 20:31). It is key to becoming children of God (1:12), having eternal life (3:15-16; 5:24; 6:47), receiving what God has for us (6:35; 11:40; 20:31), and continuing the work of Jesus (14:12). We note that seeing is often the key to believing (2:11, 23; 4:48; 6:30; 11:45; 20:25), though not invariably (6:36; 12:37). And, in the end, there is a special blessing for those who believe without seeing (20:29).

John 20:10-11. At the outset, Mary went to the tomb, while the disciples remained at home. Now even in the absence of Jesus' body, Mary remains at the tomb, while the disciples return home. Clearly, Mary was drawn to that place: She had hurried there at her first opportunity, and now she was reluctant to leave.

John 20:12-13. Her encounter with the angels is a testimony to Mary's grief. Typically, an angelic appearance is an overwhelming experience for a human being (for example, Luke 1:12-13; 2:9-10). Yet Mary is so full of grief that she is unmoved by the presence of angels. And her preoccupation with finding Jesus' body allows her to converse very naturally with them, invoking their help in her quest.

John 20:14-16. Jesus asks Mary the same question the angels had asked her: "Woman, why are you weeping?" (20:15,

13). Perhaps this is the question that the Lord and his angels have been asking us ever since Easter morning.

It is unclear in the text why Mary did not recognize Jesus. Although she does not recognize him at first, she recognizes him instantly when he calls her by name. The familiar C. Austin Miles hymn based on this episode emphasizes the significance of Jesus' voice: "The voice I hear falling on my ear, the Son of God discloses."

There is something sweet about the recognition being not merely his voice (for he had already spoken several words to her), but specifically his voice calling her name. It's a personal moment, and it bears witness to a personal relationship.

John 20:17-18. The meaning of this encounter between Mary and Jesus is unclear, and commentators offer varying interpretations. R. Schnackenburg suggests that Jesus was not so much refusing Mary's embrace as hurrying her on her essential errand: "Go to my brothers and say to them . . ." The emphasis on Jesus going to God the Father resonates with what we see in John's Last Supper scene (for example, 13:1-3; 14:12, 28; 16:10, 28).

John 20:19-20. "Fear of the Jews" is a motivation we see elsewhere in John's Gospel (7:13; 9:22). The detail of the locked doors sets the stage for us to recognize that Jesus' appearance was miraculous. As the stone could not keep him in, the locked door could not keep him out.

Jesus shows his disciples his hands and side, both of which had been pierced. It is sweet victory that the marks of crucifixion should become the proofs of resurrection. They were the proofs that Thomas later insisted on seeing for himself (20:24-25).

John 20:21. In John, Jesus emphasizes the fact that he had been sent, and now reiterates the consequent mission of the disciples (see 17:18). In this formula, the disciples' work is an extension of Jesus' own work, and thus of the Father's work.

John 20:22-23. George Beasley-Murray

observes in this breathing on the disciples a parallel with both the creation of humankind (Genesis 2:7) and the resurrection of the dry bones (Ezekiel 37:9-10).

The teaching on forgiving or retaining sins echoes a teaching from earlier in his ministry about binding and loosing (Matthew 18:18). If we are uncomfortable with the implied authority vested in human beings, we must at least acknowledge the responsibility entrusted to believers. As representatives of Christ and bearers of the gospel, we are, more or less, vessels of his grace. If more, then sins will be forgiven; if less, then they will be retained.

INTERPRETING THE SCRIPTURE

Anatomy of a Doctrine

From the first account of God breathing into the molded dust to make "a living being" (Genesis 2:7), we recognize that human beings are a composite creation. We are not a single component or element, like iron, through and through. Rather, we have within us both some earthly and some heavenly stuff. And throughout our lives, we may be able to identify the signs of our "dust," as well as the evidence of our "breath of life" from God.

Throughout human history, various philosophies have taken different approaches to the composition of a human being. Some are inclined to deny the spiritual altogether, attributing every part of human existence and experience to the physical body. At the other end of the spectrum, others cannot deny the existence of the physical, but they deny its value. Some have elevated the importance of the body to a kind of idolatry, while others have been so suspicious of the body that they have made every effort to subordinate it.

Scripture freely admits the weakness of the flesh and the limitations of the present body. At the same time, however, the physical body is celebrated as part of God's creation, as well as part of God's plan for resurrection.

In the West, we are natural heirs to a Greek notion of the immortality of the soul, independent of any scriptural revelation. We may naturally, therefore, think more in terms of an entirely spiritual afterlife than a tangible, physical one. Yet Sunday after Sunday, we declare that we believe in "the resurrection of the body and the life everlasting."

The Christian faith has a remarkably high view of the body. We do not disparage it as a burden to be jettisoned as we enter eternity. Rather, we affirm it as part of God's design and plan, both in the beginning and in the end.

A Love-Hate Relationship

The apostle Paul argued: "No one ever hates his own body" (Ephesians 5:29). That statement may paint with too broad a brush, but it is fair to say that the instinct of a psychologically healthy person is to care for one's body rather than to harm it.

Even so, many people have something of a love-hate relationship with their bodies. We naturally protect and provide for our bodies, yet we may feel displeasure at what we see in the mirror. We work to guarantee the health of our bodies, while at the same time feeling dismayed by the deterioration of our physical abilities.

Meanwhile, we evidence another layer of our love for the body when it comes to our love for other people's bodies. I don't mean that in a prurient or promiscuous way. The simple truth is that human beings express their love for one another physically. In addition to the obvious facet of the romantic love between a man and a woman, there are also other forms of physical affection that people share. Hugging friends, snuggling siblings, lap-sitting children, giving hearty handshakes, providing pats on the back, and even wrestling playfully are all physical expressions of love and affection between people.

And, in our Easter morning story from John, we see yet another instance of physical expression of love. Mary went to Jesus' tomb, according to other Gospel references, in order to care for his body (Mark 16:1; Luke 24:1). This is what we human beings do: We care for the corpses of the people we love.

In many cultures, including ours, a great deal of time and money is invested in such postmortem care. It is the reflex of love to do whatever we can for our loved one. And once that loved one has died, all that seems to remain for our love to do is to care for the body.

I remember being called to a hospital room in the middle of the night to be with a man who had gone into cardiac arrest. The family lived some distance out of town, however, and so they did not arrive before he expired. Indeed, the widow was delayed so long that her husband's body had finally been moved out of his hospital room and into the temporary morgue in the basement.

Evidently, it was against hospital policy to let visitors into that portion of the building, but when I saw the woman's pleading face, I intervened on her behalf with the hospital staff. I accompanied her to the room where her husband's body lay, and I watched as she said her touching good-bye to a man who wasn't there.

Something within that grieving woman needed to see—indeed, to drape herself on—the body. And I suspect the same need was at work in Mary.

God's Body of Work

All sorts of people, with a wide variety of beliefs, console themselves with the prospect of an afterlife. They are not necessarily informed by Scripture, and their beliefs may be rather vague, but they cling to a conviction that the soul lives on after the body has died. When a loved one dies, therefore, they find comfort in the notion that the person is not really "gone." Rather, he or she just lives on in a different form.

That is not the testimony of Scripture, however. The Bible does not have a single, exhaustive teaching on the subject of death and what comes after it; rather, we are treated to a multiplicity of witnesses to God's good plan. And at the very center of our faith and understanding is the profound event recorded in this week's passage from John's Gospel: the resurrection of Jesus.

Easter Sunday is not about mere afterlife. Mary is not weeping over Jesus' corpse when suddenly she hears some disembodied voice calling her by name. "Don't worry, Mary," it says reassuringly. "Go and tell my brothers that, even though my body is dead, I continue to exist."

The resurrection of Jesus is not about a soul that survives the death of the body, but rather about a body that is raised from death. God does not bypass death, but instead conquers it.

What happens on Easter is all about the body. Mary goes to tend to it. She and the disciples are dismayed by its absence. When she recognizes the risen Lord, Mary wants to cling to him. That evening, Jesus appears bodily to his disciples. And the proofs of his identity and his life are found on his body. So they were overjoyed when they saw the Lord.

The God who gave us life in the beginning offers us new life. And the God who offers us new life raises us to eternal life. So we give all of our life—and all of our death—to God.

SHARING THE SCRIPTURE

Preparing Our Hearts

Explore this week's devotional reading, found in Psalm 31:1-5. In this prayer the writer expresses confidence that God will deliver him from his enemies. Notice the words "refuge" (used three times), "rock," and "fortress" (both used twice) describing how the psalmist feels about God's ability to care for him. Also note that part of verse 5 is quoted by Jesus as he dies on the cross (Luke 23:46) and is called to mind again by the first Christian martyr, Stephen, as he dies from stoning (Acts 7:59). From whom or what do you need protection today? Call upon God to save you.

Pray that you and the adult learners will find refuge in God.

Preparing Our Minds

Study the background Scripture from John 20:1-23 and the lesson Scripture from John 20:1-10, 19-20. Today's lesson prompts you to consider this question: Do you believe that there is life after death?

Write on newsprint:
❑ chart for "Study the Resurrection Story as Told in the Fourth Gospel."
❑ Scriptures for "Express Joy About Resurrections in the Learners' Lives."
❑ information for next week's lesson, found under "Continue the Journey."
❑ activities for further spiritual growth in "Continue the Journey."

LEADING THE CLASS

(1) Gather to Learn

❖ Welcome the class members and introduce any guests.
❖ Pray that the students will hear afresh the story of Jesus' resurrection and consider its meaning for their lives.

❖ Discuss these questions:
(1) **What do you say to people who want to know what you believe about life after death?**
(2) **What have people said to you about their beliefs in life after death?**
(3) **Why do you suppose there are so many different beliefs, not only from one religion to another but also among different Christian denominations?** (One reason is that different denominations emphasize ideas from different passages. Some read a particular passage more or less literally than others.)

❖ Read aloud today's focus statement: **People have always wondered about what happens to our human spirit after our physical death. Is there a life after death? Jesus' followers were confused when his body was missing, but when the resurrected Jesus appeared to them, they rejoiced.**

(2) Study the Resurrection Story as Told in the Fourth Gospel

❖ Choose one volunteer to read John 20:1-10 and another to read verses 19-20. (Point out that the familiar story of Mary Magdalene conversing with Jesus is in verses 11-18 but not part of our lesson today.)

❖ Encourage the adults to fill in this chart, which you will post on newsprint.

Verses	Time	Place	Characters	Action
John 20:1-10				
John 20:19-20				

❖ Discuss these questions:
  (1) **What did Mary think had happened when she realized the tomb was empty?**
  (2) **What did the other disciple think had happened when he saw the empty tomb?**
  (3) **Today's background Scripture includes the story of Mary Magdalene telling the disciples that she had seen the Lord (20:18). Their response to her announcement was to cower behind locked doors because they were afraid of what the Jewish leaders might do to them. What does their response suggest about their understanding of what had happened?**
  (4) **How do you think Jesus' appearance changed the disciples' outlook (except for Thomas, who was not present)?**

(3) Reflect on Feelings About Death and Resurrection

❖ Read the final three paragraphs of "A Love-Hate Relationship" from Interpreting the Scripture. Talk with the group about how the widow's response does (or does not) reflect their own response to the death of a loved one.

❖ Distribute paper and pencils. Give the adults one minute to write down words or phrases to describe how they feel about death. Select several volunteers to read their lists. See if the class can come to a consensus concerning their attitudes toward death.

❖ Invite the students to write what they believe about the resurrection. What is it? Do they believe Jesus was raised? How do they expect to experience resurrection?

❖ Close this portion of the session with quiet time so that the adults can ponder their attitudes and feelings about both death and resurrection. Suggest that they also think about how they might prepare spiritually for this experience.

(4) Express Joy About Resurrections (Recreation or New Birth) in the Learners' Lives

❖ Read "God's Body of Work" from Interpreting the Scripture.

❖ Read together today's key verse, John 20:20, which emphasizes the disciples' joy.

❖ Post the following Scriptures on newsprint. Form small groups and assign at least one Scripture to each group. The groups are to find and read the passage to discern how people respond to the illness, death, and new life of their loved one.

■ Elijah revives a woman's son	1 Kings 17:17-24
■ Elisha raises the son of a Shunammite woman	2 Kings 4:8-37
■ Elisha's bones raise up a dead man	2 Kings 13:21
■ Jesus raises a synagogue leader's daughter	Matthew 9:18-19, 23-26 Mark 5:21-24, 35-43 Luke 8:40-42, 49-56
■ Jesus raises a widow's son at Nain	Luke 7:11-17
■ Jesus heals a boy with a spirit	Mark 9:14-29
■ Jesus raises Lazarus	John 11:1-44
■ Peter raises Dorcas	Acts 9:36-42
■ Paul raises Eutychus, who fell from the window	Acts 20:7-12

❖ Call the learners together and ask them to report on what they learned about death and new life from their assigned passage. Try to identify commonalities among the mourners, among those who did the raising, and among the responses. Point out that as wonderful as all of these experiences were, only Jesus was actually raised from the dead to continuing new life. All of these other people did eventually die.

❖ Conclude by discussing this question: **How do these reports, along with the reports of Jesus' resurrection, give you hope or raise questions for you?**

(5) Continue the Journey

❖ Pray that the adults will joyously celebrate the resurrection of our Lord Jesus Christ.

❖ Read aloud this preparation for next week's lesson. You may also want to post it on newsprint for the students to copy.

■ **Title: Cleansing the Temple**
■ **Background Scripture: John 2:13-22**
■ **Lesson Scripture: John 2:13-22**
■ **Focus of the Lesson: Many people stray from their central purpose in life and need restoration. What can help people recognize their need for restoration and re-creation? Jesus' action in cleansing the Temple was intended to restore God's central place in worship and in the lives of the people.**

❖ Challenge the students to complete one or more of these activities for further spiritual growth related to this week's session. Post this information on newsprint for the students to copy.

(1) **Identify several favorite Easter hymns. What good news is proclaimed in each hymn? How does the music reflect the joy of the day? Sing praise.**

(2) **Imagine Jesus coming to you and saying, "Peace be with you" (John 20:19). Where in your life are you experiencing turmoil or uncertainty? Hear Jesus speak peace to you and rest in his care.**

(3) **Recall that the disciples saw Jesus' pierced hands and the gash in his side. They rejoiced because they knew it was Jesus. How are you aware of Jesus' living presence in your life? How might you share the assurance of his presence with someone else?**

❖ Sing or read aloud "He Rose."

❖ Conclude today's session by leading the class in this benediction: **Go forth rejoicing that God, out of infinite love for the world, gave us Jesus, through whom we have eternal life.**

UNIT 2: THE WORD IS HERE AND NOW
CLEANSING THE TEMPLE

PREVIEWING THE LESSON

Lesson Scripture: John 2:13-22
Background Scripture: John 2:13-22
Key Verse: John 2:16

Focus of the Lesson:
Many people stray from their central purpose in life and need restoration. What can help people recognize their need for restoration and re-creation? Jesus' action in cleansing the Temple was intended to restore God's central place in worship and in the lives of the people.

Goals for the Learners:
(1) to explore the story of the cleansing of the Temple.
(2) to relate Jesus' teachings and actions in this story to their lives.
(3) to make a commitment to reorder what is important in their lives so that God is central.

Pronunciation Guide:
emporion (em-por'-ee-on)

Supplies:
Bibles, newsprint and marker, paper and pencils, hymnals, pictures of animals or stuffed animals, coins, rope

READING THE SCRIPTURE

NRSV
John 2:13-22

¹³ The Passover of the Jews was near, and Jesus went up to Jerusalem. ¹⁴In the temple he found people selling cattle, sheep, and doves, and the money changers seated at their tables. ¹⁵Making a whip of cords, he drove all of them out of the temple, both the sheep and the cattle. He also poured out the

NIV
John 2:13-22

¹³When it was almost time for the Jewish Passover, Jesus went up to Jerusalem. ¹⁴In the temple courts he found men selling cattle, sheep and doves, and others sitting at tables exchanging money. ¹⁵So he made a whip out of cords, and drove all from the temple area, both sheep and cattle; he scattered the coins

coins of the money changers and overturned their tables. **¹⁶He told those who were selling the doves, "Take these things out of here! Stop making my Father's house a marketplace!"** ¹⁷His disciples remembered that it was written, "Zeal for your house will consume me." ¹⁸The Jews then said to him, "What sign can you show us for doing this?" ¹⁹Jesus answered them, "Destroy this temple, and in three days I will raise it up." ²⁰The Jews then said, "This temple has been under construction for forty-six years, and will you raise it up in three days?" ²¹But he was speaking of the temple of his body. ²²After he was raised from the dead, his disciples remembered that he had said this; and they believed the scripture and the word that Jesus had spoken.

of the money changers and overturned their tables. **¹⁶To those who sold doves he said, "Get these out of here! How dare you turn my Father's house into a market!"** ¹⁷His disciples remembered that it is written: "Zeal for your house will consume me." ¹⁸Then the Jews demanded of him, "What miraculous sign can you show us to prove your authority to do all this?" ¹⁹Jesus answered them, "Destroy this temple, and I will raise it again in three days." ²⁰The Jews replied, "It has taken forty-six years to build this temple, and you are going to raise it in three days?" ²¹But the temple he had spoken of was his body. ²²After he was raised from the dead, his disciples recalled what he had said. Then they believed the Scripture and the words that Jesus had spoken.

UNDERSTANDING THE SCRIPTURE

Introduction. By the start of the New Testament, Jews were living in many countries other than just Israel. During the major Jewish festivals, therefore, the Temple was filled with pilgrims from around the Mediterranean world. Pentecost was one such festival, and Acts' account of it bears witness to the broad map represented in Jerusalem at that time (Acts 2:5-11).

Because worship at the Temple always included some transaction at the altar (for example, Exodus 23:15), worshipers needed to have in hand some offering or sacrifice. It was impractical to travel from some distant land with a sheep, goat, or pigeon in tow, and so such animals were available for purchase at the Temple site. Also as a concession to practicality, people were on hand to exchange foreign currencies as well.

John 2:13. Passover was one of the three major Jewish holy days. (Pentecost and the Feast of Tabernacles are the other two.) Accordingly, it was a time when the Jews

from all of Judea, as well as many from outlying areas and other countries, would flock to Jerusalem as commanded in Exodus 23:17. Some scholars estimate that more than two million people were gathered in Jerusalem at that time, and Jesus was among those who journeyed there for the festival.

John 2:14. As previously noted, both the changing of currencies and the selling of animals for sacrifice were practical necessities, especially during the occasional festivals when people would be coming to the Temple from great distances. That necessity had been perverted, however, into a corrupt operation. Pernicious fees were charged for the animals that were made available for purchase, and visiting foreigners were further exploited by unfavorable exchange rates on their currency.

John 2:15. This is not the picture of Jesus that we cherish in song or hang on our Sunday schoolroom walls. This is not the serenity we associate with Warner Sallman's famous portraits of Christ. Jesus demonstrates violent opposition to what he sees going on in the Temple. It may make for an unpleasant picture, but not nearly so distasteful as the alternative: a picture of a Jesus who is indifferent to sin, or blasé about blasphemy.

John 2:16. Jesus' identification of the place is extremely personal. It is not merely "the Temple," or "the house of God," but "my Father's house."

The Greek word that we translate "marketplace" is *emporion*, in which we recognize our English word "emporium." It suggests to us not merely the presence of financial transactions, but a busy mall crowded with merchants and merchandise. It is a fine environment for the streets outside, but an unseemly array within the Temple.

John 2:17. Psalm 69 was written by a righteous man who was evidently being unjustly persecuted. In his condition, he called out to God for deliverance and justice. In the midst of stating his case, he wrote, "It is zeal for your house that has consumed me; the insults of those who insult you have fallen on me" (69:9).

By recalling a line from that psalm, not only are we given insight into this episode in the Temple, but the larger context of the psalm may also give us deeper insight into Jesus' experience, in general (for example, compare Psalm 69:21 with Mark 15:36).

John 2:18. By human standards, Jesus had no authority to come into the Temple and cause this sort of disruption. We recognize his authority in that setting, of course, but he had no civil or clerical office to authorize him to change practices or procedures in the Temple. The Jews, therefore, sought some supernatural evidence—a sign—that he had divine authorization for what he was doing.

The demand for a sign was a recurring phenomenon in Jesus' encounters with the Jewish authorities (for example, Matthew 12:38; 16:1; Mark 8:11; Luke 11:16). He never complied with the request (for example,

Mark 8:12), and often condemned it (for example, Matthew 12:39; 16:4).

John 2:19. Jesus' antagonists no doubt wanted an immediate, tangible sign. Instead, Jesus offered them something that sounded more like a riddle. While they did not understand Jesus' words, they did remember them, for when he was on trial they used a perversion of this statement against him (Matthew 26:59-61).

John 2:20-21. The Temple to which the Jews referred was the Temple in Jerusalem, the most recent renovation of which had been undertaken by Herod the Great. It was a grand and fabulous edifice, and so, on the surface, Jesus' words seemed preposterous.

Characteristically, however, Jesus was not talking about the same thing that his audience was talking about. Just as he was not talking about entering again into the mother's womb (John 3:3-4) or the actual water from the well (John 4:7-12), he was not speaking literally of the Temple building there in Jerusalem. Rather, the reference was to his body—they would execute it, and he would raise it up in three days.

In other requests for a sign, Jesus sometimes offered "the sign of Jonah" (for example, Matthew 12:39-40; 16:4), which similarly anticipated his death, burial, and resurrection.

John 2:22. The disciples' learning curve was not a steady one. We see fits and starts of understanding and faith (for example, Matthew 16:15-17; John 1:49), but the larger share of evidence suggests mostly a lack of understanding and a little faith. Indeed, at times Jesus is expressly disappointed by his disciples' faithlessness and cluelessness (for example, Matthew 8:24-26; 14:29-31; 16:6-8; 17:14-20; Mark 16:12-14). They misunderstood what it meant for him to be the Messiah (Matthew 16:20-23) and what true greatness meant in the kingdom (Mark 9:33-35). And even toward the conclusion of his earthly time with them, still the disciples were marked by failures (for example, Matthew 26:38-45, 56; Mark 14:66-72).

By the time we get to the end of the New Testament, however, the disciples whose stories we can follow have earned an entirely different reputation. They are marked by great faith, so as to work miracles and withstand opposition, as well as deep understanding, so as to instruct and correct others. But their development was not a steady incline from the day Jesus called them. Rather, it seems that their faith and understanding jumped dramatically "after he was raised from the dead" (2:22). We assume that it was not only this incident, therefore, that they came later to remember and understand. We suspect that virtually everything that had gone before suddenly led to new understanding and belief "after he was raised."

INTERPRETING THE SCRIPTURE

Jesus in the Temple

Luke is the Gospel writer who gives us our first glimpse of Jesus in the Temple. It comes when Jesus is still an infant, brought there by his parents to be presented to the Lord (Luke 2:22-23). Then, not too many years later, Luke offers a second and more revealing peek into Jesus' relationship to the Temple. When he was a still a boy, Jesus accompanied his parents to Jerusalem, but on the way back home to Nazareth the family discovered that young Jesus was not traveling with them. They returned to Jerusalem to look for him. After three days of panicked searching, they finally found their missing twelve-year-old in the Temple. When his parents conveyed to him their fear and frustration, Jesus matter-of-factly asked, "Why were you searching for me? Did you not know that I must be in my Father's house?" (Luke 2:49).

It is interesting to note that Jesus says nothing about the men with whom he was engaged in discussion (2:46-47). The narrative detail about that dialogue speaks to his wisdom, but evidently not to his purpose. He was not there because of the teachers; he was there because of his Father.

From quite a young age, therefore, Jesus had a very specific view of the Temple. It is his "Father's house." That's not institutional religion, you see; that's a personal relationship.

That same language in reference to the Temple appears here in our episode from John's Gospel. Jesus' lament over what has been going on in the Temple is not an arm's-length unhappiness; it is personal. It's about his Father's house.

I imagine an out-of-towner shaking his head in disapproval as he drives quickly through some city's worst neighborhood. It is a detached dismay, sorrow once removed. But this is a scene closer to home. This is the son observing what has become of his own Father's neighborhood and home. Personally and forcefully, therefore, he insists on change. "Stop making my Father's house a marketplace," he cries (John 2:16). It is deeply personal for Jesus: an all-consuming zeal.

Destructive Behavior

The scene is an easy one to misunderstand. I have heard people refer to this moment as the occasion when Jesus lost his temper, as though there is some weakness or vice on display. But that interpretation of events may be projecting our own frailties onto Jesus.

We know what it looks like for some individual—perhaps even ourselves—to lash out in frustration. We have seen people pound their fists on tables in aggravation, or slam doors in anger, or perhaps even throw things.

All of those analogies are misplaced, however, when examining this episode from Jesus' life.

In this scene, Jesus is manifestly angry, to be sure. His anger has hands and feet, as he swings a makeshift whip and turns over tables. Yet his behavior should not be misdiagnosed as a rant or a loss of control.

Perhaps we welcome such aggressiveness only to the degree that we also oppose whatever is being combated. And so if we attach certain labels to those tables that Jesus overturned, we may discover that the scene looks quite different. Call one table "drug abuse," for example, and we will have no problem with it being upended. Call another table "drunk driving," and we will cheer its demolition. Replace the moneychangers with child molesters, and suddenly we relish seeing them driven out with whips.

As soon as we recognize the badness of what Jesus found in the Temple, then we will recognize the strength, the goodness, and the beauty of his reaction to it. His conduct is not a rant; it is heroism. And his behavior is not destructive, but cleansing.

We traditionally call this event Jesus' "cleansing of the Temple." The language reminds us of the strong cleansing anticipated by the prophet: "He will sit as a refiner and purifier of silver, and he will purify the descendants of Levi and refine them like gold and silver, until they present offerings to the LORD in righteousness" (Malachi 3:3).

What's Wrong With This Picture?

Children's puzzle books often include a certain exercise in observation. The child is presented with a rather ordinary picture, which includes a few out-of-place details. Perhaps the car has a square wheel, or a fish nests in the tree. Then the child is asked to identify what's wrong with the picture.

That is our task within the context of this episode. Can we look at the scene that Jesus found in the Temple and identify what's wrong with that picture? Do we have enough sense of how it ought to be—how God wanted it to be—to recognize how disappointing it was?

I picture the walking vendors at a professional baseball or football game. They patrol throughout the stadium, loudly hawking their hot dogs, beers, and peanuts. But now imagine them taking their business and their style to the aisles of your church on a Sunday morning.

Or think of how the sacrament of the Lord's Supper is observed in your church. Now add to it the image of your ushers haggling with each member about the price of his or her piece of the bread, or your clergy charging you for your sip from the cup.

These are imperfect analogies, but they give us some sense of the revulsion Jesus felt when he saw all that was going on in his Father's house.

In the Old Testament, the prophet Ezekiel gives us a glimpse into God's displeasure at an earlier generation's misuse of the Temple (Ezekiel 8). Supernaturally, Ezekiel was given the ability to see what was wrong with that picture. And then, in a chilling scene, he also saw the terrible consequence, as God's glory abandoned his Temple (Ezekiel 10).

Meanwhile, the apostle Paul directs our attention to a still different Temple: "Do you not know," he asks the believers in Corinth, "that your body is a temple of the Holy Spirit within you, which you have from God, and that you are not your own?" (1 Corinthians 6:19).

I cannot stand at a distance from this story, you see. I cannot just shake my head disapprovingly at the officials who had let that Temple become a marketplace, for this story is more personal than that. I have to take a closer look at the temple for which I am responsible.

Can I look in the mirror and see what's wrong with my picture? Can I look at my life and see it as Jesus sees it, discerning the differences between what my life is and what he intended it to be?

Perhaps some things go on in me that displease and disappoint him. If so, then let me welcome him in, and let me cherish his cleansing.

SHARING THE SCRIPTURE

Preparing Our Hearts

Explore this week's devotional reading, found in Psalm 122. The words in verse 1, "Let us go," reflect the use of this psalm by pilgrims on their way to Jerusalem to celebrate one of the three major Jewish festivals: Passover, Pentecost, and Tabernacles. The song includes a call to prayer for "the peace of Jerusalem" (122:6). This was the locale of "the thrones of the house of David" (122:5), a rather small city situated on the western slope of the Kidron Valley. Offer praise to God today. Go, if possible, to your own church to pray for peace.

Pray that you and the adult learners will regularly pray for peace, particularly for areas in turmoil and places that hold special meaning for you.

Preparing Our Minds

Study the background Scripture and the lesson Scripture, both of which are from John 2:13-22. Think about what can help people recognize their need for restoration when they have strayed from their central purpose in life.

Write on newsprint:
- ❏ information for next week's lesson, found under "Continue the Journey."
- ❏ activities for further spiritual growth in "Continue the Journey."

Arrange a worship table with symbols related to this story, such as pictures of animals or stuffed animals, coins, and rope, prior to the session. If possible without creating a safety hazard, turn the table on its side and have the items strewn around it.

LEADING THE CLASS

(1) Gather to Learn

❖ Welcome the class members and introduce any guests.

❖ Pray that the students will find meaning for their lives in today's lesson.

❖ Invite the group to listen as you read Luke 15:11-24, the first portion of the story of the prodigal son. Discuss these questions:

(1) **Why did the son stray from his true identity and his purpose in life?**

(2) **What prompted him to see the need for reconciliation with his family?**

(3) **What events occurred to bring about that restoration?**

❖ Read aloud today's focus statement: **Many people stray from their central purpose in life and need restoration. What can help people recognize their need for restoration and re-creation? Jesus' action in cleansing the Temple was intended to restore God's central place in worship and in the lives of the people.**

(2) Explore the Story of the Cleansing of the Temple

❖ Draw attention to the worship table you set up prior to the session. Encourage the students to focus on it as you read John 2:13-22.

❖ Use information for John 2:13 and 2:14 from Understanding the Scripture to help the adults understand the laws and customs related to the selling of sacrifices and the currency used.

❖ Discuss these questions:

(1) What does this story tell you about the Temple leadership?

(2) What does this story demonstrate to you about Jesus? (Read "Destructive Behavior" from Interpreting the Scripture to help the class members see Jesus' behavior in an appropriate context.)

(3) What do the disciples remember? (Verse 17 refers to Psalm 69:10. Verse 22 indicates the importance of this incident, for after Jesus' resurrection the disciples' memory of it prompted belief.)

(4) Jesus' words in verse 19 cause misunderstanding. Where else in John do you recall his words being misinterpreted because they have been taken literally? (for example, Nicodemus—born again; woman of Samaria—living water.)

❖ **Option:** Compare this story in John to the way it is presented in the other Gospels by assigning one group to research Matthew 21:12-17; another, Mark 11:15-19; and a third, Luke 19:45-48. What differences in details do the students notice? Point out that only John places this story at the beginning of his Gospel. Prod the adults to formulate ideas as to why the story might be here, rather than near the end of Jesus' life.

(3) Relate Jesus' Teachings and Actions in This Story to the Learners' Lives

❖ Read "What's Wrong with This Picture?" from Interpreting the Scripture to help the adults begin to think about this biblical story in light of their own church practices.

❖ Post a sheet of newsprint on which you have sketched the outline of a church. Invite the participants to call out "tables" in today's church that they believe Jesus would want to overturn. Write their answers inside the sketch. Here are some

possible answers: *bickering, power struggles, racism, ageism, sexism, factions, groups that try to exclude others, pride.*

❖ Identify at least one "table" that the group agrees needs to be overturned in their own church: **What could we as a congregation do to overturn this table?** (Avoid any finger-pointing but instead try to focus on positive ideas. As an example, suppose the group indicated that exclusion seems to be an issue. Discuss how people might be invited into the congregation and made to feel welcomed, cared for, and loved. Ideas here include *encouraging folks to participate in the small groups within the church so as to have opportunities to know people through worship, fellowship, study, and service; making it a point to speak to visitors; having greeters and clear signs so that people know where to go.*)

❖ Agree together that you will do whatever you can to overturn this table so that others may see Christ and believe.

(4) Make a Commitment to Reorder What Is Important in Life So That God Is Central

❖ Distribute paper and pencils. Challenge the adults to write the ten most important things (these may be people, ideas, or something else aside from things) in their lives. Suggest that they rank each item, by putting a 1 next to that which is most important and numbering down until 10, which is the least important item on the list.

❖ Provide quiet time for the participants to think about how they spend their time and money. Ask the adults to rate themselves a second time to determine how they are really spending these treasures.

❖ Challenge the class members to make a commitment to reorder their priorities so that God is central.

(5) Continue the Journey

❖ Pray that the adults will be aware of commitments so as to order their lives in such a way that God is central.

❖ Read aloud this preparation for next week's lesson. You may also want to post it on newsprint for the students to copy.

- ■ **Title: Woman of Samaria**
- ■ **Background Scripture: John 4:1-42**
- ■ **Lesson Scripture: John 4:7-15, 23-26, 28-30**
- ■ **Focus of the Lesson: Our lives can be shaped by public perception and reputation. How can our lives be turned around? In his acceptance of the Samaritan woman, Jesus restored her life.**

❖ Challenge the students to complete one or more of these activities for further spiritual growth related to this week's session. Post this information on newsprint for the students to copy.

(1) Recall Paul's words in 1 Corinthians 6:19: "Your body is a temple of the Holy Spirit." Ponder what "housecleaning" Jesus would like to do within you. Open yourself to this holy cleansing.

(2) Note that Jesus' cleansing of the Temple was an event so significant that all four Gospels include it, though in different places in the narrative. What events have been so important for your congregation that you want to share them with others? Tell your story.

(3) Check books or the Internet for pictures depicting Jesus cleansing the Temple. Select a few of these works for study. How do the colors, depiction of action, and placement of the characters bring to life the biblical story?

❖ Sing or read aloud "Majesty, Worship His Majesty."

❖ Conclude today's session by leading the class in this benediction: **Go forth rejoicing that God, out of infinite love for the world, gave us Jesus, through whom we have eternal life.**

UNIT 2: THE WORD IS HERE AND NOW
WOMAN OF SAMARIA

PREVIEWING THE LESSON

Lesson Scripture: John 4:7-15, 23-26, 28-30
Background Scripture: John 4:1-42
Key Verse: John 4:14

Focus of the Lesson:
Our lives can be shaped by public perception and reputation. How can our lives be turned around? In his acceptance of the Samaritan woman, Jesus restored her life.

Goals for the Learners:
(1) to explore Jesus' restorative power in giving people "living water."
(2) to experience the redemptive presence of Christ in their lives.
(3) to witness to others about the re-creating presence of Jesus in their lives.

Pronunciation Guide:
Gerizim (ger' uh zim)

Supplies:
Bibles, newsprint and marker, paper and pencils, hymnals, water, several clear jars or pitchers, additives for water

---

READING THE SCRIPTURE

NRSV
John 4:7-15, 23-26, 28-30

7A Samaritan woman came to draw water, and Jesus said to her, "Give me a drink." 8(His disciples had gone to the city to buy food.) 9The Samaritan woman said to him, "How is it that you, a Jew, ask a drink of me, a woman of Samaria?" (Jews do not share things in common with Samaritans.) 10Jesus answered her, "If you knew the gift of God, and who it is that is saying to you, 'Give me a drink,' you would have asked him, and he

NIV
John 4:7-15, 23-26, 28-30

7When a Samaritan woman came to draw water, Jesus said to her, "Will you give me a drink?" 8(His disciples had gone into the town to buy food.)

9The Samaritan woman said to him, "You are a Jew and I am a Samaritan woman. How can you ask me for a drink?" (For Jews do not associate with Samaritans.)

10Jesus answered her, "If you knew the gift of God and who it is that asks you for a would have given you living water." [11]The woman said to him, "Sir, you have no bucket, and the well is deep. Where do you get that living water? [12]Are you greater than our ancestor Jacob, who gave us the well, and with his sons and his flocks drank from it?" [13]Jesus said to her, "Everyone who drinks of this water will be thirsty again, [14]but those who drink of the water that I will give them will never be thirsty. **The water that I will give will become in them a spring of water gushing up to eternal life.**" [15]The woman said to him, "Sir, give me this water, so that I may never be thirsty or have to keep coming here to draw water."

[23]"But the hour is coming, and is now here, when the true worshipers will worship the Father in spirit and truth, for the Father seeks such as these to worship him. [24]God is spirit, and those who worship him must worship in spirit and truth." [25]The woman said to him, "I know that Messiah is coming" (who is called Christ). "When he comes, he will proclaim all things to us." [26]Jesus said to her, "I am he, the one who is speaking to you."

[28]Then the woman left her water jar and went back to the city. She said to the people, [29]"Come and see a man who told me everything I have ever done! He cannot be the Messiah, can he?" [30]They left the city and were on their way to him.

drink, you would have asked him and he would have given you living water."

[11]"Sir," the woman said, "you have nothing to draw with and the well is deep. Where can you get this living water? [12]Are you greater than our father Jacob, who gave us the well and drank from it himself, as did also his sons and his flocks and herds?"

[13]Jesus answered, "Everyone who drinks this water will be thirsty again, [14]but whoever drinks the water I give him will never thirst. **Indeed, the water I give him will become in him a spring of water welling up to eternal life.**"

[15]The woman said to him, "Sir, give me this water so that I won't get thirsty and have to keep coming here to draw water."

[23]"Yet a time is coming and has now come when the true worshipers will worship the Father in spirit and truth, for they are the kind of worshipers the Father seeks. [24]God is spirit, and his worshipers must worship in spirit and in truth."

[25]The woman said, "I know that Messiah" (called Christ) "is coming. When he comes, he will explain everything to us."

[26]Then Jesus declared, "I who speak to you am he."

[28]Then, leaving her water jar, the woman went back to the town and said to the people, [29]"Come, see a man who told me everything I ever did. Could this be the Christ?" [30]They came out of the town and made their way toward him.

UNDERSTANDING THE SCRIPTURE

John 4:1-6. John sets the stage in terms of time and place. The time is "about noon" (4:6). That detail alone is enough to make us thirsty. We can imagine having walked a long time in that climate and then, at midday, sitting down and needing a drink. Meanwhile, the place is Samaria. Jesus is leaving Judea, in the south, and heading back to Galilee, which was in the north. In

between the two was this third region: Samaria.

The Samaritans traced back to the Assyrian conquest of the Northern Kingdom in the eighth century B.C. The Assyrians deposed many of the original inhabitants, replacing them with foreigners imported from other conquered territories. What evolved was a mixed-race people and a syncretistic religion. Both developments were repugnant to the devout Jews of the postexilic and New Testament periods.

John 4:7-9. Jews regarded Samaritans as half-breeds and heretics. Centuries of antipathy between the two groups resulted in an environment in which it was shocking for a Samaritan to be the hero in a parable (see Luke 10:30-37) and for a Jew to initiate the encounter here at the well.

John 4:10. Here the encounter takes on new meaning. At first Jesus and the woman talked about regular water, but now he talks about "living water." What follows is a typical parallel conversation, as Jesus speaks of spiritual things, while his audience still thinks in physical terms.

John 4:11-12. As part of their parallel conversation, the woman wonders how Jesus can access the water without benefit of a bucket. Her question reflects that she doesn't really understand what he is talking about, much like Nicodemus's question about rebirth (3:4).

The question whether Jesus is greater than Jacob is part of the larger quest in John to recognize who Jesus is. Later, Jesus will also be challenged about whether he is greater than Abraham (8:52-53). Elsewhere, he teaches that he is greater than the Temple, Jonah, and Solomon (Matthew 12:6, 41, 42).

John 4:13-14. The familiar material-spiritual dichotomy continues. Jesus juxtaposes the water the woman can access with the water he can provide. The former offers temporary satisfaction, while the latter permanently quenches a deeper thirst. This teaching mirrors what Jesus will say later about bread (6:31-35).

As with the bread in chapter 6, what is at stake is not merely human hunger and thirst. Rather, Jesus offers eternal life. As ordinary bread and water are essential to ordinary life, the bread and water Jesus provides are essential to eternal life.

Jesus extends the metaphor. Not only does the physical water have a spiritual counterpart; so does the well. The living water becomes a spring within—a continuous source of life and refreshment.

John 4:15. The woman continues to think and speak at a different level than Jesus. While he offers something spiritual and eternal, she remains fixated on the daily chore of fetching well water.

John 4:16-20. Here the conversation takes a turn. Jesus invites the woman to get her husband, evidently knowing what her personal situation is. When she answers with part of the truth, Jesus tells the rest of the story. This is one of several occasions when Jesus demonstrates that he knows things without being told (Luke 6:7-8; John 2:23-25; 6:64; 13:10-11).

Historically, the woman's question about worship dates back to two events. First, before the Israelites entered the Promised Land, Moses cited Mount Gerizim as a location of central, national, spiritual significance (Deuteronomy 11:29; 27:12). Centuries later, when the postexilic Jews were rebuilding the Temple in Jerusalem, they declined Samaritan participation. The Samaritans, in turn, selected Mount Gerizim as the site for their temple.

John 4:21-24. Jesus affirms the Jews' unique role in salvation history, yet he does not insist on the Jewish place of worship. Instead, he points to an imminent time when location will no longer be an issue. Consistent with his recurring emphasis on spiritual over physical, true worship is identified in terms of "spirit and truth" (4:23) rather than a physical location.

John 4:25-26. This conversation is reminiscent of Martha's later conversation with Jesus (11:20-27). Here, the woman anticipates the Messiah who will come someday (4:25). Later, Martha anticipates the resurrection that will come on the last day (11:24). In both instances, Jesus indicates that there is no more wait: He is the Messiah (4:26) and the resurrection (11:25).

John 4:27-30. People were reluctant to ask Jesus a question on several occasions

(Matthew 22:46; Mark 9:32; Luke 20:40; John 21:12).

John mentions that the woman left her jar, which represented her errand, her reason for coming to the well. The abandoned jar symbolizes the fact that she had a new errand and a new reason now.

The woman says to the people of her town, "Come and see a man who told me everything I have ever done!" (4:29). The invitation to come and see is a recurring motif in John (1:39, 46; 11:34).

John 4:31-34. Just as Jesus was speaking on a different plane than the Samaritan woman, we see the same pattern with his disciples. They press the issue of physical food, while he refers to a different sort of nourishment.

We must not misunderstand Jesus. He was not oblivious to physical needs (compare Matthew 4:2; John 19:38). Doing his Father's work was not a literal replacement for breakfast, lunch, and dinner. At the same time, he models for us a different hierarchy of need and of satisfaction. He does not live by bread alone, and neither should any human being (Matthew 4:4).

In our day, we recognize the pattern of people eating when they are unhappy. Perhaps the truly contented person feels less need to eat. And inasmuch as Jesus found his truest fulfillment in doing his Father's work, he was not as hungry as people so often think they are.

John 4:35-38. The work that Jesus was sent to do was not solely his: That work is extended to his disciples. Just as Jesus was sent by his father to do work (4:34), so he sends his disciples to do work (4:38). The physical image of a harvest is used to illustrate a spiritual reality (compare Matthew 9:37-38).

John 4:39-42. Within the context of that first-century Jewish world, a Samaritan woman would have been a doubly improbable heroine. Yet she plays the role of an effective evangelist in this episode, and in a Gospel where the disciples themselves are not seen functioning in that way.

INTERPRETING THE SCRIPTURE

Lord Knows

We human beings are uneasy with the truth about ourselves. We may welcome the truth in most other areas of life, but we are skittish about truth's spotlight when it is turned on us. We have been hiding from it since our first parents scurried behind the bushes in Eden.

We struggle to hide our blemishes, to keep our secrets, and to cover our faults. We fear that if so-and-so really knew the whole truth, then he wouldn't respect me, she wouldn't love me, or they would reject us.

At the same time, however, something within us sincerely longs to be known. We grow tired of hiding the dirty laundry and sweeping things under the rug. We wish someone would know the whole truth, and yet still love and accept us anyway.

The hostess spends hours making her house immaculate for her guests. When they comment on how lovely everything is, however, she jokes, "Oh, you should have seen it this morning" or "Just don't look in the back bedroom." She doesn't want them to see her messes, on the one hand, but she wants them to know about them, on the other.

Well, the Samaritan woman at the well had her own collection of secrets and messes. And it appears that she, too, toggled between hiding her secrets and longing to be known.

In the midst of her conversation with this Jewish stranger, he suddenly asked her to go and get her husband. It was an abrupt intrusion into her personal life, and her personal life resisted intrusions.

We discover that this woman had been married five times, which already raises eyebrows. And, beyond that, she was currently living with a man outside of marriage. Traditional Jewish teaching forbade a woman to be married more than two or three times. This woman's track record of five marriages, plus an out-of-wedlock relationship, was truly scandalous.

When Jesus asked her to get her husband, the woman was less than forthcoming. "I have no husband," she said to Jesus (4:17).

This is the sort of answer that qualifies as factually correct, though still rather misleading. If a politician gave a comparable answer to some public-interest question, he would be criticized as the worst sort of liar.

Jesus welcomes the woman's answer as an honest one, however. He does not condemn her less-than-full disclosure. Nor does he overtly condemn the rest of her story, which he proceeds to tell.

The moment is a lovely illustration of what it looks like when we confess our sins to the Lord. We aren't going to tell him anything that shocks him—anything that he doesn't already know. And we discover that, for all of our accumulated fear and shame, he is not the one who makes us feel that way.

The woman's reaction to Jesus' surprising knowledge of her situation is mixed. In the immediate moment, she maneuvers to steer the conversation from the personal to the theoretical. It is a clever transition, taking his knowledge as proof that he is a prophet, and then presenting him with a theological question.

Later, however, we discover that Jesus' personal knowledge was a meaningful and important turning point for the woman. Her declaration to her friends and neighbors was not about an unprejudiced Jew or living water, but about "a man who told me everything I have ever done!" (4:29).

If We Only Knew

Jesus knew all about the Samaritan woman, and that was impressive, but it was not the real issue. Rather, the crux of the matter was what the woman knew—or needed to know—about Jesus.

He raises this point with the woman very early in their encounter. He had initiated the whole conversation by asking for a drink, which caught the woman by surprise. It seemed to her a strange thing that he, a Jew, should be asking her, a Samaritan, for a drink.

The Lord spends no time, however, addressing that concern or the centuries of conflict that lay behind it. Instead, he makes the point that the water should be flowing in the other direction. Rather than him asking her for a drink, she should be asking him.

The woman misunderstands what Jesus is saying, and so begin the parallel conversations about spiritual and material things. But we return to consider precisely the words he said: "If you knew the gift of God, and who it is that is saying to you, 'Give me a drink,' you would have asked him" (4:10).

If she had only known with whom she was dealing, you see, she would have responded differently.

This has been the recurring tragedy in humanity's relationship with God: We forget—or never knew—with whom we are dealing. It was the flaw of every fearful, faithless soul, from the panicking Israelites (Exodus 14:10-14) to the frightened disciples (Matthew 8:24-27). And it was the terrible ignorance of those who "esteemed him not" (Isaiah 53:3 KJV). So Jesus' prayer for his tormentors was profoundly true: "They do not know what they are doing" (Luke 23:34).

In the case of this woman from Samaria, Jesus says that if she only knew with whom she was dealing, she would have asked him for something. Indeed, she would have asked him for something ultimately and eternally satisfying.

You and I may pick up the conversation with Jesus at precisely that point. Let us hear him say to us, "If you only knew, you would ask." And so we turn to him in faith and ask him for two things. First, to help us understand with whom we are dealing. And, second, to give us all the beauty, blessing, refreshment, and life that he has for us.

The Others Who Need to Know

The story of the Samaritan woman would be a beautiful one even if it were limited to Jesus' contact with her alone. But the beauty overflows her individual container, pouring out into the lives of those around her.

The woman's witness is not a calculated evangelism plan, nor is it the drudgery of mere duty. On the contrary, she finds it irresistible to tell her whole town about Jesus. So urgent is her discovery that she leaves behind her jar, wanting to be unencumbered as she hurries off on her new errand. So she tells them, and they begin to believe.

Ultimately, we read that the townspeople's faith in Christ is the result of firsthand, personal experience with him. Initially, however, they only come to meet him and know him because of another person's testimony about him.

We thank God for the people who first told us about Jesus. And then we thank him for the privilege of being that Samaritan woman in someone else's life.

SHARING THE SCRIPTURE

Preparing Our Hearts

Explore this week's devotional reading, found in Revelation 22:10-17. This passage near the end of Revelation closes with these words: "Let anyone who wishes take the water of life as a gift" (22:17). This same image of life-giving water appears in today's lesson from John 4. Make a list of the many ways you perceive water. Some of those ways will be very positive, but others will be negative. Think about how "the water of life" that Jesus gives affirms your life.

Pray that you and the adult learners will accept the life-giving water and do all in your power to share it with others.

Preparing Our Minds

Study the background Scripture from John 4:1-42 and the lesson Scripture from John 4:7-15, 23-26, 28-30. How can lives be turned around once public perception has tainted one's reputation?

Write on newsprint:
❑ information for next week's lesson, found under "Continue the Journey."
❑ activities for further spiritual growth in "Continue the Journey."

Bring several clear jars or pitchers. Fill the containers with water prior to class. One container should remain pristine, but add soap, dirt, stones, food coloring, or something else to the other jars.

LEADING THE CLASS

(1) Gather to Learn

❖ Welcome the class members and introduce any guests.

❖ Pray that the students will thirst for the living water that Jesus so willingly offers.

❖ Set out the jars or pitchers you have prepared so that everyone can see them. Invite the adults to talk about the jar they would be least likely to drink from.

Different students may have different choices. Invite them to identify the jar from which they would want to drink. Discuss why some of the water seems appealing while water in other containers does not. Mention that there are water-treatment processes that can restore the undesirable water to that which people would find appealing and safe. (Note: If you want further details about this process, check: www.nytimes.com/2007/11/27/us/27conserve.html or http://bluelivingideas.com/2009/03/14/toilet-to-tap-orange-county-turning-sewage-water-into-drinking-water/.) Encourage the adults to comment on how they would feel about drinking once-contaminated water that had been treated. What prompted the change in their perception?

❖ Read aloud today's focus statement: **Our lives can be shaped by public perception and reputation. How can our lives be turned around? In his acceptance of the Samaritan woman, Jesus restored her life.**

(2) Explore Jesus' Restorative Power in Giving People "Living Water"

❖ Read "John 4:1-6" from Understanding the Scripture to provide background for today's lesson.

❖ Choose three volunteers to read John 4:7-15, 23-26, and 28-30.

❖ Help the students understand that "living water" has two meanings: (1) fresh, running water, as from a spring (as opposed to water stored in a cistern); and (2) life-giving water.

❖ Make a list on newsprint of the issues that the woman raises with Jesus. These include *why he, a Jew, would speak with her, a Samaritan, which represented a serious breach of socially accepted behavior; her misinterpretation of Jesus' words about living water, which she took literally; the woman knowing the Messiah is coming, but not recognizing Jesus until he announced himself.*

❖ Ask: **As you review this list, what impact would you say that Jesus had on this woman's life?** (Be sure to include that she moved from a state of unbelief to being a believer to being a witness.)

❖ Select one volunteer to roleplay the woman and several other volunteers to be residents of her city who listen to what she has to say about Jesus. Encourage the residents to raise questions about what the woman has to say. (She need not have all the answers.) Suggest that one of the residents remains skeptical about Jesus. This person is to ask the others why they believe the woman's testimony.

❖ Conclude by asking:
   (1) **What influence would you say that this woman, who had been an outsider because of her multiple marriages, had on her community?**
   (2) **If this outsider could make such a difference in the lives of many because of her witness, what might we, as individuals or a group, be able to do to bring others to Christ?**

(3) Experience the Redemptive Presence of Christ in the Learners' Lives

❖ Read "If We Only Knew" from Interpreting the Scripture. Repeat the final paragraph, inviting the adults to ponder the statement, "If you only knew, you would ask." Provide a few moments for them to ask Jesus about whatever is on their hearts.

❖ Distribute hymnals and invite the students to look at hymns that speak about redemption. Possibilities include "Amazing Grace," "I Know Whom I Have Believed," "There Is a Fountain Filled with Blood," and "Victory in Jesus." Suggest that they choose one hymn—even a single verse—that is particularly meaningful for them. Encourage them to memorize this verse by repeating one phrase at a time. Recommend that at times when they feel they need a spiritual lift, they sing or recite their selected hymn so as to experience Christ's redemptive presence more fully.

(4) *Witness to Others About the Re-creating Presence of Jesus in the Learners' Lives*

❖ Point out the importance of the woman's testimony by reading "The Others Who Need to Know" from Interpreting the Scripture.

❖ Distribute paper and pencils. Recall that the woman of Samaria went to tell others because Jesus was able to tell her "everything I have ever done" (4:29). Suggest that they consider reasons they have to tell others about him. For example, they may believe he has healed them, provided a way out of a financial crisis, or taken care of a loved one in need. Invite them to make a list of those reasons. Form groups of two and ask each partner to tell the other his or her story as a means of witnessing about Jesus in their lives.

❖ Call the groups back together. Encourage each person to assess his or her comfort level in sharing a word of witness with someone else. Suggest that those who feel uncomfortable (especially if they normally have no problems in talking with others) examine themselves in the coming week to discern why they are uncomfortable and to take steps to overcome their unease.

❖ Challenge them to tell others about the presence of Christ in their lives and how his presence has changed them.

(5) *Continue the Journey*

❖ Pray that the adults will witness to others about the re-creating presence of Jesus in their lives.

❖ Read aloud this preparation for next week's lesson. You may also want to post it on newsprint for the students to copy.
- ■ **Title: Healing the Blind Man**
- ■ **Background Scripture: John 9**
- ■ **Lesson Scripture: John 9:1-17**
- ■ **Focus of the Lesson: People's critical personal needs often outweigh the rules and regulations made by other human beings. How do we decide which priorities in life come first? Jesus put the blind man's need to see before the Jewish rules about Sabbath observance.**

❖ Challenge the students to complete one or more of these activities for further spiritual growth related to this week's session. Post this information on newsprint for the students to copy.

(1) Tell at least one person this week about the life-changing effects that Jesus has had on your life.

(2) Look for opportunities to show hospitality this week. Try to find someone who is unable to return the favor. For example, buy lunch for a homeless person and, if possible, eat with that individual.

(3) Befriend someone who seems to be an outsider. Once you become better acquainted, encourage this person to attend church or another activity with you.

❖ Sing or read aloud "The First One Ever."

❖ Conclude today's session by leading the class in this benediction: **Go forth rejoicing that God, out of infinite love for the world, gave us Jesus, through whom we have eternal life.**

UNIT 2: THE WORD IS HERE AND NOW
HEALING THE BLIND MAN

PREVIEWING THE LESSON

Lesson Scripture: John 9:1-17
Background Scripture: John 9
Key Verse: John 9:16

Focus of the Lesson:
People's critical personal needs often outweigh the rules and regulations made by other human beings. How do we decide which priorities in life come first? Jesus put the blind man's need to see before the Jewish rules about Sabbath observance.

Goals for the Learners:
(1) to examine the healing ministry of Jesus.
(2) to reflect on their need for healing.
(3) to develop priority plans.

Pronunciation Guide:
Siloam (si loh' uhm)

Supplies:
Bibles, newsprint and marker, paper and pencils, hymnals

READING THE SCRIPTURE

NRSV
John 9:1-17

¹As he walked along, he saw a man blind from birth. ²His disciples asked him, "Rabbi, who sinned, this man or his parents, that he was born blind?" ³Jesus answered, "Neither this man nor his parents sinned; he was born blind so that God's works might be revealed in him. ⁴We must work the works of him who sent me while it is day; night is coming when no one can work. ⁵As long as I am in the

NIV
John 9:1-17

¹As he went along, he saw a man blind from birth. ²His disciples asked him, "Rabbi, who sinned, this man or his parents, that he was born blind?"

³"Neither this man nor his parents sinned," said Jesus, "but this happened so that the work of God might be displayed in his life. ⁴As long as it is day, we must do the work of him who sent me. Night is coming,

world, I am the light of the world." [6]When he had said this, he spat on the ground and made mud with the saliva and spread the mud on the man's eyes, [7]saying to him, "Go, wash in the pool of Siloam" (which means Sent). Then he went and washed and came back able to see. [8]The neighbors and those who had seen him before as a beggar began to ask, "Is this not the man who used to sit and beg?" [9]Some were saying, "It is he." Others were saying, "No, but it is someone like him." He kept saying, "I am the man." [10]But they kept asking him, "Then how were your eyes opened?" [11]He answered, "The man called Jesus made mud, spread it on my eyes, and said to me, 'Go to Siloam and wash.' Then I went and washed and received my sight." [12]They said to him, "Where is he?" He said, "I do not know."

[13]They brought to the Pharisees the man who had formerly been blind. [14]Now it was a sabbath day when Jesus made the mud and opened his eyes. [15]Then the Pharisees also began to ask him how he had received his sight. He said to them, "He put mud on my eyes. Then I washed, and now I see." [16]**Some of the Pharisees said, "This man is not from God, for he does not observe the sabbath." But others said, "How can a man who is a sinner perform such signs?" And they were divided.** [17]So they said again to the blind man, "What do you say about him? It was your eyes he opened." He said, "He is a prophet."

when no one can work. [5]While I am in the world, I am the light of the world."

[6]Having said this, he spit on the ground, made some mud with the saliva, and put it on the man's eyes. [7]"Go," he told him, "wash in the Pool of Siloam" (this word means Sent). So the man went and washed, and came home seeing.

[8]His neighbors and those who had formerly seen him begging asked, "Isn't this the same man who used to sit and beg?" [9]Some claimed that he was.

Others said, "No, he only looks like him." But he himself insisted, "I am the man."

[10]"How then were your eyes opened?" they demanded.

[11]He replied, "The man they call Jesus made some mud and put it on my eyes. He told me to go to Siloam and wash. So I went and washed, and then I could see."

[12]"Where is this man?" they asked him.

"I don't know," he said.

[13]They brought to the Pharisees the man who had been blind. [14]Now the day on which Jesus had made the mud and opened the man's eyes was a Sabbath. [15]Therefore the Pharisees also asked him how he had received his sight. "He put mud on my eyes," the man replied, "and I washed, and now I see."

[16]**Some of the Pharisees said, "This man is not from God, for he does not keep the Sabbath."**

But others asked, "How can a sinner do such miraculous signs?" So they were divided.

[17]Finally they turned again to the blind man, "What have you to say about him? It was your eyes he opened."

The man replied, "He is a prophet."

UNDERSTANDING THE SCRIPTURE

John 9:1-3. It was a well-established principle in the Hebrew Scriptures that obedience to God brought blessings, while disobedience brought troubles (for example, see Leviticus 26). This paradigm led to a kind of reverse logic: If a person has troubles, he or she must have disobeyed (for example, Job 4:7-9). This was the understanding behind the disciples' question.

While the disciples sought a spiritual explanation for the man's physical condition, our instinct would be to understand it in medical terms. Jesus corrected the disciples' misunderstanding, yet still offered a fundamentally spiritual perspective: "so that God's works might be revealed in him" (9:3). Purpose should not necessarily be confused with cause, and we are encouraged by the thought that our difficulties may serve the purpose of revealing the work of God.

John 9:4-5. George Beasley-Murray observes the significant collection of personal pronouns used by Jesus. "We must work the works of him who sent me," Jesus says (9:4). The affirmation that Jesus was sent by his Father is a recurring theme in John (for example, 4:34; 6:38-39; 17:18-25), but here we see that the Father's purpose is not accomplished solely by the Son. Rather, as Beasley-Murray notes, "Jesus associates his disciples with him in his mission in the present, as he will do in the future (14:12; 20:21)."

Jesus had already identified himself as "the light of the world" in the preceding chapter (8:12). In this context, however, he brings light into personal darkness by healing the man born blind.

John 9:6-7. This is one of three episodes in the Gospels when Jesus used spit in the process of healing (see also Mark 7:33; 8:23). The notion seems repugnant to us, although it may remind us of the homey image of a mother using her saliva to wet down a cowlick or scrub chocolate off a cheek. Furthermore, we are reminded of the servants' questions to Naaman when he recoiled at Elisha's method of healing (2 Kings 5:10-14). If we really want to be healed, will we bicker with God over the technique?

Interestingly, Jesus required this man to participate in his own healing. He was not a passive recipient; he had to do something, although a small thing, like the Israelites who were required to look at the snake on the pole in order to be healed (Numbers 21:8-9).

Because the man did not receive his sight until he had gone to wash the mud off his eyes, he still had not seen Jesus, who healed him. He knew Jesus' name (9:11), but he did not see Jesus until later in the episode (9:35-37).

John 9:8-12. Jesus' healing miracle was so astonishing that it provoked a practical concern for verification. We can imagine the people nudging and pointing, whispering and speculating about the formerly blind man. He was within earshot, and so he insisted, "I am the man" (9:9). The people were predictably incredulous, and so they kept asking questions. Eventually, they took him to their leaders in order to have the whole case investigated by the authorities.

John 9:13-17. For the second time, the formerly blind man tells his story. Rather than having those around him rejoice with him, however, the man discovers that they are more troubled than pleased by what has happened.

It's a bad sign when you can't be happy about a good thing. This was clearly a problem for the prodigal's older brother (Luke 15:25-32), as well as for the prophet Jonah (Jonah 3:10–4:3). And here we see the Pharisees similarly unable to rejoice in the work of God in this man's life.

The detail of when the healing occurred—that is, the Sabbath day—proves to be a sticking point for the Pharisees. We see this same dynamic at work in other healings of Jesus (Matthew 12:9-14; Luke 13:10-16; 14:1-6; John 5:1-18; 7:23). It is not clear whether Jesus' antagonists are so zealous for God's Sabbath, or simply seeking a basis for criticizing and condemning Jesus.

This episode is one of three in John's Gospel where Jesus is identified as the cause of division (compare 7:43 and 10:19). This is consistent with Jesus' own estimation of his effect (Matthew 10:34-36).

The blind man's conclusion that Jesus was a prophet (9:17) recalls the earlier assessment of the Samaritan woman (4:19).

John 9:18-23. The Pharisees were determined to be unhappy about this healing. They summoned the blind man's parents into the investigation, seeking confirmation that he was their son and that he had, in fact, been blind from birth. The parents were fearful of the inquisition (compare 7:13; 19:38; 20:19), and so they participated in the process as little as possible. Meanwhile, the threat of being put out of the synagogue is not limited to this episode (12:42; 16:2).

John 9:24-34. The interrogation of the blind man becomes even tenser, and he is not as reticent as his parents about crossing the authorities.

The command to "give glory to God" (9:24) is understood by some translators as an exhortation to be an honest witness (as in the Contemporary English Version). Alternatively, it may be that the Pharisees were insisting that God should be given credit for the healing, not "this man [who] is a sinner" (9:24).

The ensuing debate over just who and what Jesus is strikes at the heart of John's Gospel. From beginning (1:10-11) to end (20:31), recognizing Jesus is the central issue.

The back-and-forth over whose disciple a person is (9:27-29) echoes the earlier dispute about fathers (8:37-44).

John 9:35-38. There is a certain sweetness in the image of Jesus seeking out someone he had already healed (compare John 5:14). It bears witness to the fact that there was more to accomplish than the mere physical healing: There remained the pivotal question of faith. "Do you believe?" Jesus asks, echoing a central theme (1:12; 3:15-18; 4:39-42; 11:25-26; 17:20-21; 20:25-29, 31). When the formerly blind man comes to believe, he responds by worshiping Jesus—a scandalous thing for one man to do to another man within that first-century Jewish context.

John 9:39-41. As is always the case in John, the physical anticipates the spiritual. The healing of a man who was physically blind now prompts a teaching about spiritual blindness. Jesus' table-turning judgment regarding sight and blindness is reminiscent of other teachings (Luke 13:23-30; 16:19-25). Meanwhile, the Pharisees have a double problem: They are blind, and they don't recognize it.

INTERPRETING THE SCRIPTURE

A Proper Diagnosis

The first step is always the diagnosis. If you can't diagnose the problem, you stand little chance of solving it. And if you misdiagnose the problem, you stand an excellent chance of complicating it. And so the first step is to diagnose what's wrong.

In this week's story, the problem seems obvious enough: The man in question is blind. Evidently, he has been blind for his entire life. Yet right from the start, Jesus' disciples misdiagnose the situation.

"Rabbi," they ask Jesus, "who sinned, this man or his parents, that he was born blind?" (John 9:1).

Human beings have an instinct for cause-and-effect. We are loath to believe that some things—especially bad things—"just happen," and so we labor to discover the "why" behind events. For prescientific generations, superstition got the better of people, and the "why" was attributed to the gods and ghosts that populated their understanding of the world. Our generation is committed to finding different sorts of answers, to be sure, but the struggle to find answers continues, nevertheless.

At its most rudimentary expression, the quest to identify a cause for undesirable effects is captured in the question "Whose fault is it?" It's a central issue in business, sports, politics, and the legal system. We need to identify who is to blame. Of course, that reflex is nothing new, for even in Eden we see Adam and Eve scrambling to assign blame (see Genesis 3:11-13).

When the disciples saw the blind man, they assumed that someone was to blame, and they wanted to know who. In their logic, it must be the fault of either the man's parents or the man himself. And that fault was identified as sin. But the disciples were wrong. They had misdiagnosed the situation, and Jesus corrected them about it.

The Pharisees, meanwhile, were a different—and more unfortunate—case. At least the blind beggar recognized his own blindness. The Pharisees, however, suffered from a different sort of blindness, but they didn't realize it (9:39-41). And their blindness prevented them from seeing what was most important of all: Jesus.

Identity Issues

We say that seeing is believing, but the sighted people couldn't believe their eyes.

The blind beggar had been a fixture in their community for years. With no other way to support himself, begging had been his profession. Of necessity, he was always out in the public eye, extending his hand, exhorting the generous.

Was there anyone from that region who hadn't seen him along the way? Anyone who couldn't recognize him? Yet once he was able to see, suddenly they weren't sure who he was.

It's a certain brand of blindness when you are unable to see what's right in front of you simply because you believe "it can't be." Such blindness continues to afflict our skeptical generation. And that was the condition of the crowd that surrounded the formerly blind man.

If he had still been blind, not a person there would have doubted or denied that it was he. But just because he could see, some of the folks were no longer able to recognize

him. Did he look so different? No, but they presumed that it is impossible for a man born blind to gain his sight. And that conclusion-in-advance about what is and is not possible blinded some from recognizing the man who had been healed.

It turns out, however, that the blind beggar was not the only character whose identity was at issue. The real question—and the concern at the heart of John's Gospel—is the identity of Jesus. Was Jesus from God (9:30-33) or not (9:16, 29)? Was he a sinner (9:16, 24) or a prophet (9:17)? Or could he possibly be the Messiah (9:22)?

We remember the pivotal question that Jesus asked his disciples: "Who do you say that I am?" (Mark 8:29). And that is the pivotal question here, as well. Who does the blind man say that Jesus is? Who do his parents say that he is? And who do the Pharisees say that he is?

In the end, of course, it's not a vote. The speculating and debating does not determine or change who he is. The Pharisees cannot assign him an identity. Rather, they—and we—can either recognize him, or not.

Our Ordered Lives

In John Greenleaf Whittier's lovely hymn, "Dear Lord and Father of Mankind," he prays, "Let our ordered lives confess the beauty of thy peace."

An orderly desk, kitchen, or workshop is an area where everything is in its proper place. Likewise, we envision an "ordered life" as one in which every part of life is also in its proper place. That's not as easy as putting away one's books, utensils, or tools, but it is far more important.

What are the elements of my life or yours? And what is the proper place for each?

The custodian of a church where my father was the pastor tried to do him a favor one day. While my dad was out of town, this well-meaning man came into my dad's office and reorganized all of his books. Those books had been arranged in categories: biography, church history, biblical studies, and such. The man who tidied up the shelves, however, reorganized all the books in order of size. In the end, it was a very nice look, but it was a disaster for my dad. He couldn't find any book he needed without first trying to recall how big it was.

If the elements of my life are not in their proper place, then they are effectively lost. Indeed, I am lost, until God has been given the proper place in my life.

The Pharisees, so meticulous about everything being just so, had not managed to keep the big things of life in their proper places (see Matthew 23:23).

Earnest devotion to God always seeks practical application. Practical application necessarily concerns itself with details. And a certain misplaced zeal can elevate those details to an undesirable importance. So it was that the Pharisees' concern for God's law had declined into legalism. Earnest devotion to God became earnest devotion to details, including nitpicking about the Sabbath.

God was at work in Jesus, and the healing of the blind man was a marvelous work of God. Unfortunately, a narrow interpretation of the Sabbath law had come to prevail among the Pharisees. Under their influence, the Sabbath was no longer a gift, but a shackle. And so, rather than celebrate the healing, they called it a crime. They did not recognize God's work because they were bound up in some joyless protection of God's Sabbath.

An ordered life has everything in its proper place. And the proper place is defined by God. If it's important to God, then it should be important to us.

SHARING THE SCRIPTURE

Preparing Our Hearts

Explore this week's devotional reading, found in Isaiah 29:17-21. In this chapter where the prophet discusses the siege of Jerusalem, verses 17-21 sound a hopeful note. After judgment is over, the deaf will hear and the blind will see. This week's lesson also concerns the restoration of sight. Let's consider our own sight for a moment. How well do you "see" God's people, especially those who are living on the fringes? How well do you "see" God's will for your own life? What do you "see" in the near future for your own congregation in terms of its mission and ministry?

Pray that you and the adult learners will clearly see the contours of the kingdom of God and order your lives so as to make it your number one priority.

Preparing Our Minds

Study the background Scripture from John 9 and the lesson Scripture from John 9:1-17. Think about how you set priorities.

Write on newsprint:
- ❏ list for "Reflect on the Learners' Needs for Healing."
- ❏ steps for "Reflect on the Learners' Needs for Healing."
- ❏ information for next week's lesson, found under "Continue the Journey."
- ❏ activities for further spiritual growth in "Continue the Journey."

LEADING THE CLASS

(1) Gather to Learn

❖ Welcome the class members and introduce any guests.

❖ Pray that the students will be curious to learn more about Jesus' ministry of healing.

❖ Read this true story to the class: **A medic who was rushing his wife to the hospital in their car as she was having a stroke was arrested by a police officer and charged with multiple offenses. With his emergency flashers on, the man "proceeded cautiously through a red light," prompting the officer to follow him and try to pull him over. The husband continued on to the hospital, knowing how critical it was to get medical attention for his wife immediately. Upon arriving at the emergency room, the man, who was carrying his wife, was blocked at the entrance by the officer who was trying to arrest him. Unaware that the driver had phoned ahead and that staff was awaiting the patient, the officer barged into the treatment area and had to be told to leave by hospital staff. The medic was charged with "assaulting a police officer, disorderly conduct, reckless endangerment, evading arrest, two red light violations, and registration violation."**

❖ Ask: **If you had read this article in your local paper, what observations might you make in a letter to the editor about your opinion of this event?**

❖ Read aloud today's focus statement: **People's critical personal needs often outweigh the rules and regulations made by other human beings. How do we decide which priorities in life come first? Jesus put the blind man's need to see before the Jewish rules about Sabbath observance.**

(2) Examine the Healing Ministry of Jesus

❖ Select one volunteer to read John 9:1-12 and another to follow with verses 13-17.

❖ Finish the story by reading or retelling information from Understanding the Scripture, beginning with John 9:18-23.

❖ Discuss these questions:
   (1) Why do you think people were unwilling or unable to state conclusively that the man who was blind and the man who was now healed were one and the same

person? (You may want to draw ideas from "Identity Issues" in Interpreting the Scripture.)
   (2) Why did the Pharisees have trouble "seeing" what Jesus was doing?
   (3) How did the different characters in the story identify or describe Jesus?

❖ Assign three groups to investigate other stories of Jesus giving sight to the blind: Matthew 9:27-31; Mark 10:46-52; Luke 18:35-43. Suggest that the groups note similarities and differences between their assigned story and the account in John. Call the groups to report back answers to this question: **What have you learned about Jesus' healing ministry from this Bible study?**

(3) Reflect on the Learners' Needs for Healing

❖ Point out that in the story the main character was physically blind and the Pharisees were spiritually blind. Likely, each of us has some sort of blind spot that we need healed.

❖ Post this list on newsprint, which you will have written prior to the session.
   ■ Inability to see the needs of a neighbor.
   ■ Prejudice toward people of a different racial or ethnic background.
   ■ Lack of hospitality toward the stranger or immigrant.
   ■ Feelings of superiority over those who have less money or social standing.
   ■ Sense of holding more correct religious beliefs than others.
   ■ Unwillingness to help those in need.
   ■ Unforgiving spirit toward one who has wronged you.
   ■ "Know it all" attitude.
   ■ Tightfistedness with money.
   ■ Willingness to cut ethical and moral corners.

❖ Invite the participants to choose one of the items listed that they feel reflects a "blind spot" in their own lives and write it on paper you will distribute. They will not be asked to share their choice. Suggest that they take the following steps, which you will have written on another sheet of newsprint prior to the session:

■ **Step 1:** Identify specific situations in which this blind spot has become evident in your life.

■ **Step 2:** Think about Bible stories or teachings that show what Jesus would do in such a situation. For example, the good Samaritan showed hospitality toward the stranger.

■ **Step 3:** Meditate and pray, asking God to heal you of the blind spot you have identified.

■ **Step 4:** Begin to act in ways that demonstrate that you have been healed.

❖ Conclude this activity by challenging the adults to repeat it at home, focusing on another blind spot they have identified.

(4) Develop Priority Plans

❖ Recall that what riled the Pharisees so much was not that Jesus healed a man; they were upset because he healed on the Sabbath, thereby breaking a Jewish law.

❖ Ask: **What kinds of situations do you believe call us to break laws or buck the tide of accepted attitudes in order to put God first?** (Here are some ideas: *laws or attitudes that make some persons second-class citizens because of their religion, race, sexual orientation, or other marker; attitudes that prevent older adults from being hired; anything that detracts from the dignity of persons created in God's own image.*)

❖ Review the list to determine if any of these laws or attitudes exists in your community. Think of actions you can take to change these skewed priorities so that all people will feel welcomed as people of God.

(5) Continue the Journey

❖ Pray that the adults will recognize their blind spots and will, with God's help, begin to see clearly.

❖ Read aloud this preparation for next week's lesson. You may also want to post it on newsprint for the students to copy.

■ **Title: The Bread of Life**
■ **Background Scripture: John 6**
■ **Lesson Scripture: John 6:22-35**
■ **Focus of the Lesson: Many people are hungering for what will make their lives complete. Where do we find what is missing in our lives? Jesus promised his followers that they would never be hungry or thirsty if they would come to him.**

❖ Challenge the students to complete one or more of these activities for further spiritual growth related to this week's session. Post this information on newsprint for the students to copy.

(1) **Pray for someone who is ill or otherwise needs a physical healing from God.**

(2) **Watch one of these movies: *Rain Man, Field of Dreams, Mr. Holland's Opus.* How are "seeing" and "understanding" important concepts in these films?**

(3) **Experience physical blindness by wearing a blindfold and moving around your home. Why is it difficult to navigate without visual clues? Ponder how this physical activity might relate to your spiritual life.**

❖ Sing or read aloud "When Jesus the Healer Passed Through Galilee."

❖ Conclude today's session by leading the class in this benediction: **Go forth rejoicing that God, out of infinite love for the world, gave us Jesus, through whom we have eternal life.**

UNIT 3: THE WORD WILL BE
THE BREAD OF LIFE

PREVIEWING THE LESSON

Lesson Scripture: John 6:22-35
Background Scripture: John 6
Key Verse: John 6:35

Focus of the Lesson:
Many people are hungering for what will make their lives complete. Where do we find what is missing in our lives? Jesus promised his followers that they would never be hungry or thirsty if they would come to him.

Goals for the Learners:
(1) to explore in detail the meaning of the "bread of life."
(2) to discover how the living bread fills the gaps in our lives.
(3) to name ways in which they can provide the bread of life to the world.

Pronunciation Guide:
Capernaum (kuh puhr' nay uhm)
Tiberias (ti bihr' ee uhs)

Supplies:
Bibles, newsprint and marker, paper and pencils, hymnals, one or more loaves of bread

MAY 6

READING THE SCRIPTURE

NRSV
John 6:22-35

²²The next day the crowd that had stayed on the other side of the sea saw that there had been only one boat there. They also saw that Jesus had not got into the boat with his disciples, but that his disciples had gone away alone. ²³Then some boats from Tiberias came near the place where they had eaten the bread after the Lord had given thanks.

NIV
John 6:22-35

²²The next day the crowd that had stayed on the opposite shore of the lake realized that only one boat had been there, and that Jesus had not entered it with his disciples, but that they had gone away alone. ²³Then some boats from Tiberias landed near the place where the people had eaten the bread after the Lord had given thanks. ²⁴Once the

²⁴So when the crowd saw that neither Jesus nor his disciples were there, they themselves got into the boats and went to Capernaum looking for Jesus.

²⁵When they found him on the other side of the sea, they said to him, "Rabbi, when did you come here?" ²⁶Jesus answered them, "Very truly, I tell you, you are looking for me, not because you saw signs, but because you ate your fill of the loaves. ²⁷Do not work for the food that perishes, but for the food that endures for eternal life, which the Son of Man will give you. For it is on him that God the Father has set his seal." ²⁸Then they said to him, "What must we do to perform the works of God?" ²⁹Jesus answered them, "This is the work of God, that you believe in him whom he has sent." ³⁰So they said to him, "What sign are you going to give us then, so that we may see it and believe you? What work are you performing? ³¹Our ancestors ate the manna in the wilderness; as it is written, 'He gave them bread from heaven to eat.'" ³²Then Jesus said to them, "Very truly, I tell you, it was not Moses who gave you the bread from heaven, but it is my Father who gives you the true bread from heaven. ³³For the bread of God is that which comes down from heaven and gives life to the world." ³⁴They said to him, "Sir, give us this bread always."

³⁵**Jesus said to them, "I am the bread of life. Whoever comes to me will never be hungry, and whoever believes in me will never be thirsty."**

crowd realized that neither Jesus nor his disciples were there, they got into the boats and went to Capernaum in search of Jesus.

²⁵When they found him on the other side of the lake, they asked him, "Rabbi, when did you get here?"

²⁶Jesus answered, "I tell you the truth, you are looking for me, not because you saw miraculous signs but because you ate the loaves and had your fill. ²⁷Do not work for food that spoils, but for food that endures to eternal life, which the Son of Man will give you. On him God the Father has placed his seal of approval."

²⁸Then they asked him, "What must we do to do the works God requires?"

²⁹Jesus answered, "The work of God is this: to believe in the one he has sent."

³⁰So they asked him, "What miraculous sign then will you give that we may see it and believe you? What will you do? ³¹Our forefathers ate the manna in the desert; as it is written: 'He gave them bread from heaven to eat.'"

³²Jesus said to them, "I tell you the truth, it is not Moses who has given you the bread from heaven, but it is my Father who gives you the true bread from heaven. ³³For the bread of God is he who comes down from heaven and gives life to the world."

³⁴"Sir," they said, "from now on give us this bread."

³⁵**Then Jesus declared, "I am the bread of life. He who comes to me will never go hungry, and he who believes in me will never be thirsty."**

UNDERSTANDING THE SCRIPTURE

John 6:1-4. The Gospel writer sets the stage for what follows in three important details. First, all the action occurs on and around the Sea of Galilee. Second, we are introduced right away to the two primary groups of people involved: the large crowd that followed Jesus and the small group (that is, the Twelve) that followed him. And, third, we are told something about the timing: namely, that it was nearly the time for "the Passover, the festival of the Jews" (6:4).

John 6:5-9. All four Gospel writers tell

the story of the multiplication of loaves and fishes, but only John includes these four details: (1) Jesus' question to Philip, (2) Andrew's role in finding the familiar five loaves and two fish, (3) the boy who was the source of that food, and (4) the type of bread used. John specifies that the loaves were barley bread, which was regarded as poor man's bread (compare the relative prices of barley and wheat in 2 Kings 7:1).

John 6:10-13. In the previous section, Andrew is quick to observe that the boy's small supply of bread and fish would be woefully inadequate for the hungry multitude. Nevertheless, Jesus proceeds to have the people sit down, as though preparing for a meal. Then he gives thanks—a detail John mentions again in verse 23—and begins to distribute the elements. In the end, Andrew's very reasonable calculation proves to be completely wrong. Not only were the five loaves and two fish enough, in Jesus' hands, they were more than enough. Meanwhile, the abundance of leftovers proves that the miracle was not that the people were satisfied with a little, but rather that Jesus had turned a little into a lot.

John 6:14-15. The reference to "the prophet" as an anticipated figure is perhaps unfamiliar to us, for we think in terms of the people awaiting the Messiah. Earlier in the Fourth Gospel, the crowds speculate that John the Baptist may be "the prophet" (1:21), and later in the Gospel that speculation surrounds Jesus again (7:40).

The entire issue stems from Moses' prediction that the Lord would one day send a prophet like himself (Deuteronomy 18:15). John does not illuminate for us what the contemporary expectations about that prophet were, except that contextually "the prophet" is clearly distinct in people's minds from "the Messiah" (see 1:20-21; 7:40-41).

Within this episode, we observe that the mere suspicion that Jesus might be "the prophet" was evidently sufficient qualification for the crowd to make him their king.

The other three Gospel writers do not include this detail about a popular effort to coronate Jesus, but Jesus' resistance of that human movement to make him a human monarch resonates with his later conversation with Pilate (compare John 18:33-37).

John 6:16-21. The disciples were perhaps somewhat disoriented from the beginning because Jesus had gone off by himself (6:15) and still "had not yet come to them" (6:17) when they left for Capernaum. Also, John reports that it was dark, which is always an unsettling circumstance for human beings. And in that preelectric world, we imagine how completely dark it might have been. Add to that the strong winds that made for rough sailing, and the disciples were no doubt anxious and on edge. Then came the specter of a figure walking toward them on the water. It must have been terrifying. Jesus' command not to be afraid (6:20) is one of at least fourteen times in the Gospels that he tells people not to fear or be afraid.

John 6:22-25. The crowds are manifestly fascinated by Jesus. Earlier, they had wanted to make him their king. Now they are curious about his comings and goings. And, ultimately, they pursue him from one place to the next.

John 6:26-29. Jesus has a low estimation of what motivates the crowds. Reminiscent of the lost souls about whom Paul says, "Their god is the belly" (Philippians 3:19), Jesus urges this people to a more enduring loyalty. The juxtaposition of "perish" with "eternal life" occurs two other times in John (3:16; 10:28). His repudiation of working "for the food that perishes" (6:27) echoes the invitation of God in Isaiah 55:1-2.

John 6:30-40. The immediate context is the bread that Jesus had miraculously provided for the hungry multitude. The curious crowds introduce the comparison to the miraculous bread provided for their ancestors in Moses' day. Jesus then trumps both by identifying himself as "the true bread" and "the bread of life" (6:32, 35). The promise of never hungering or thirsting, including the crowd's eager (though misunderstanding) response, follows the same trajectory as Jesus' earlier conversation with the Samaritan woman (John 4:13-15). The people are predictably preoccupied with physical life and physical bread, while Jesus directs their attention to "the true bread" and eternal life.

John 6:41-42. The complaint of the Jews echoes the response of the folks in Jesus' hometown (Mark 6:2-3), as well as the reported bewilderment of the Jews concerning Jesus' origins and preexistence (John 8:56-58).

John 6:43-51. Thematically, the complaints of verses 41-42 are an interruption in a larger teaching of Jesus, connecting the earlier miracle to his identity and issues of eternity. Jesus' evaluation of and response to the Jews' complaints leads him back to that primary theme of belief in him and eternal life.

John 6:52-66. Even on this side of the Last Supper and the sacrament of Communion,

we may still find this teaching by Jesus a little grisly to read or hear. How much more so must it have seemed to that original audience? Jesus as "the bread of life" is a welcome metaphor, but when he expands on it to talk about eating his flesh and drinking his blood, we recoil a bit. And that was the prevailing response of many who heard him.

Interestingly, though the teaching seems graphically tangible, Jesus still returns to a characteristic emphasis on spirit rather than flesh: "It is the spirit that gives life; the flesh is useless," (6:63). Meanwhile, the twin emphases on his flesh (6:53-58) and his word (6:63) as sources of life resonate with our churches' pairing of "word and sacrament."

John 6:67-71. As we observed earlier, "the Twelve" is an important category for John. Here they are distinguished from the larger crowd by (1) their unwavering commitment to Jesus, and (2) their status as chosen.

INTERPRETING THE SCRIPTURE

Compound Creatures

At the graveside, the pastor is likely to say something like this: "Forasmuch as the spirit of the departed has returned to God who gave it, we commit his body to the ground, earth to earth, ashes to ashes, dust to dust." These familiar words of committal reflect our biblical paradigm that a human being is a two-part composition: spirit and flesh.

The story of creation tells how those two parts came together to form a single compound. "The LORD God formed man from the dust of the ground, and breathed into his nostrils the breath of life; and the man became a living being" (Genesis 2:7). Jesus, likewise, bore witness to our two ingredients when he lamented, "The spirit indeed

is willing, but the flesh is weak" (Mark 14:38).

Some of us have sensed this human composition when we have sat at the bedside of a dying person. One moment the person is there; the next moment, he is not. The "flesh" part is all still there, yet somehow the person is gone. The change seems more significant than just the cessation of organ functions. It is a departure: Something that was there has left.

But that which is suddenly divided at death is intricately intertwined in life. Where do we draw the line between spirit and flesh in a living person? How do we know where one leaves off and the other one begins?

When our bodies are sick or needy, we find it difficult for our spirits to soar. And when our spirits are weary and discouraged, we discover that it takes a toll on our bodies. "A cheerful heart is a good medicine," observed the ancient sage, "but a downcast spirit dries up the bones" (Proverbs 17:22). This combination of spirit and flesh is a complicated marriage.

Because our two ingredients are so closely knit together, we human beings often confuse their needs. We speak of "comfort food," and we observe how frequently people seek physical remedies (eating, drinking, smoking, sex) for inner turmoil.

The people who sought out Jesus were motivated by some hunger. But what was the true nature of that appetite? They had a perceived need, but had they perceived it correctly?

Our Bodies and Our God

The God who created us the way that we are continues to deal with us according to our makeup. The sacraments are an excellent example. On the surface, they are purely physical elements and acts, and as such they interface with our flesh. Yet we are assured that those elements and acts are spiritually infused, and so through those material things God mysteriously provides for our spirits.

Likewise, in providential care for creation, God does not dismiss or minimize the needs of either our bodies or our spirits. Individuals, movements, and entire cultures may become preoccupied with one aspect of human existence or the other, but God celebrates and provides for both. And that dual concern is evident in the larger context of our story from John.

The crowd on the far side of Galilee was physically hungry. Jesus did not pooh-pooh that need, nor did he refer it to someone else. He met the need, and met it with characteristic abundance.

Beyond that, we are aware of the other physical needs that Jesus met throughout his ministry. The feeding of the five thousand was not the exception; it was the rule. He healed their diseases (Matthew 8:14-17); provided fish (Luke 5:4-7), food (Mark 8:1-10), and wine (John 2:1-10); and taught his followers to meet all manner of physical needs, as well (Matthew 25:31-46).

In the wake of the miraculous provision of bread and fish, the crowds pursued Jesus to the other side of the lake. When they found him, however, he chided them for being solely motivated by their physical hunger (John 6:26). As we noted previously, the physical need was not unimportant to Jesus; evidently, it was just too important to the people.

We remember how Esau sold his birthright for a serving of stew (Genesis 25:29-34). The human creature so often subordinates all else to physical appetites. But not Jesus. Even when physically famished, he knew that "one does not live by bread alone" (Luke 4:4). Accordingly, he sought to redirect the hungry crowd's attention to a new and better bread.

The True Bread

"Do not work for food that perishes" (John 6:27), Jesus told the hungry crowd, which sounds like good advice, if only there were an alternative. But what other kind of food is there?

The fact is that so much human endeavor is devoted to things that perish: temporal causes and impermanent achievements. The writer of Ecclesiastes had observed this fact, and he nearly despaired of life's meaning as a result (Ecclesiastes 1:3-11). So Jesus encouraged his followers not to invest themselves too much in perishable things (Matthew 6:19), but not merely because they are perishable. Rather, because there are eternal alternatives, which are much more worth our while (Matthew 6:20).

Such was the nature of his counsel to those hungry Galileans. They had been both impressed and filled by the bread Jesus had provided one day earlier. Yet the very fact that they were hungry again was an indictment of that bread. It had not truly satisfied, for the bread was gone but the need remained.

Even the miraculous manna—so cherished by their forebears that they preserved a sample in the ark of the covenant (Exodus 16:33-34)—was ultimately inadequate. That bread from heaven had sustained its beneficiaries for a time; yet still they died (John 6:49, 58). Manna kept the Hebrews from starving to death, but it did not keep them from death altogether.

As an alternative, Jesus said, God was now providing a superior bread. It is a bread that truly satisfies, for the partaker is never hungry again (6:35), and a bread that truly nourishes, for it gives life eternal (6:27, 33, 50-51, 58).

The crowd was understandably eager. "Sir," they said to Jesus, "give us this bread always" (6:34). But they were surprised—even dismayed—to discover just what "this bread" was.

"I am the bread of life," Jesus told them. "Whoever comes to me will never be hungry" (6:35).

This truth stands at the heart of the gospel message: God has provided for our needs, and that provision is a person. It is not an object or an event; not a religion or a dogma; not a philosophy, a system, or a structure; but a person: Jesus Christ.

Human beings have a hunger, and it growls within us. But it is no mere craving for chocolate or carbs, nicotine or caffeine. Deeper than the appetites of our flesh, there is the longing of our spirits. And, not surprisingly, that need is only satisfied by the one who created both.

SHARING THE SCRIPTURE

Preparing Our Hearts

Explore this week's devotional reading, found in Psalm 107:1-9. Here the psalmist thanks God for saving him from trouble and distress. All are invited to praise and thank God for "steadfast love" and "wonderful works to humankind" (107:8). Verse 9 reports that God satisfies those who are hungry and thirsty. How does God satisfy your hunger, both physically and spiritually? How does Holy Communion figure into your answer? Give thanks to God for meeting your needs.

Pray that you and the adult learners will seek the bread that God wants to give you.

Preparing Our Minds

Study the background Scripture from John 6 and the lesson Scripture from John 6:22-35. Given that many people are hungering for what will make their lives complete, where do you find what is missing in your life?

Write on newsprint:
❑ question for "Gather to Learn."
❑ information for next week's lesson, found under "Continue the Journey."
❑ activities for further spiritual growth in "Continue the Journey."

Set up a worship table prior to the session. Arrange the loaf (loaves) of bread you have brought so that it looks appealing.

LEADING THE CLASS

(1) Gather to Learn

❖ Welcome the class members and introduce any guests.

❖ Pray that the students will come to appreciate Jesus as the bread of life.

❖ Post one or more sheets of newsprint

on which you have written: **What makes life complete?** Set markers nearby so that as students enter the learning area they may write their answers as if they were writing graffiti on a wall. They may answer both for themselves and as they think others might answer.

❖ Spend a few moments looking together at what the class members have written. See if any categories emerge, such as love, meaningful work, purposeful life, or material possessions. Is there a dominant theme in the answers?

❖ Read aloud today's focus statement: **Many people are hungering for what will make their lives complete. Where do we find what is missing in our lives? Jesus promised his followers that they would never be hungry or thirsty if they would come to him.**

(2) Explore in Detail the Meaning of the "Bread of Life"

❖ Select a volunteer to read aloud John 6:22-35. Ask someone else to hold up the bread on the worship table so that the adults may focus attention here as the Scripture is read.

❖ Help the students become aware of how Jesus is using and reinterpreting Hebrew Scripture by assigning individuals to look up and read the following passages:
- John 6:27   Exodus 16:18-21
- John 6:31-33   Exodus 16:4, 15; Psalm 78:24; Psalm 105:40

❖ Read "The True Bread" from Interpreting the Scripture. Ask: **What do you learn about the true bread?**

❖ Discuss these questions:
(1) **Why was the crowd so anxious to find Jesus?**
(2) **How would you restate Jesus' words to the crowd in verse 27 in your own words?** (This "Special Note" from *The New Interpreter's Study Bible*, page 1919, may be

helpful: "'Eternal life' does not speak of immortality or a future life in heaven, but is a metaphor for living now in the unending presence of God.")

(3) **How do the people understand "work"? What meaning does Jesus attach to the same word?** (Verses 28, 30 indicate that they see work as doing a particular act. In contrast, according to verse 29 and 4:34, Jesus refers to "work" as faith in God.)

(4) **In the retelling of the story of manna, what is Jesus saying about the sign the people are requesting?** (They already have the sign—"that which comes down from heaven and gives life to the world" (6:33). In other words, God's presence with them in the person of Jesus is the sign they seek.)

(3) Discover How the Living Bread Fills the Gaps in Our Lives

❖ Read or retell "Our Bodies and Our God" from Interpreting the Scripture. Invite the group to notice how Jesus fills both physical and spiritual needs.

❖ Brainstorm with the class answers to this question: **How do you perceive our church to be providing "bread of life" that fills gaps in our lives?** Post ideas on newsprint. These ideas may include *sacraments of baptism and Holy Communion; fellowship with God's people; help from the faith community to weather life's storms; opportunities to serve others, worship, study the Scriptures; groups that provide support; guidance in becoming and growing as a disciple.* The students may want to name specific groups within the church that help to fill gaps.

❖ Distribute paper and pencils. Encourage the adults to list "gaps" in their own lives, spaces that are looking to be filled with new ideas, more energy, or deeper connections. Invite them to review the previous list and write down several ideas that could help fill their own gaps. For example, if parents are having challenges with a teen, perhaps joining the parent support group that the church sponsors would be helpful to them. Or if an adult feels the need to do something for others, possibly working with the church's food pantry ministry would help to fill that gap.

❖ Conclude this activity by making an "I Wish" list. Post newsprint. Invite the learners to suggest ministries that the church does not currently offer but which may be helpful to them. For example, perhaps the church needs to start a support group for parents of teens, or maybe it needs to stock a food pantry and enlist volunteers to be available at specified times to distribute the food to those in need. See which ideas resonate with the group and assign several students the task of seeing how these ideas might become reality and be incorporated into the life of the church.

(4) Name Ways in Which the Learners Can Provide the Bread of Life to the World

❖ Use paper and pencils that have already been distributed. Based on the discussion so far, and any other ideas the class may have, challenge the students to list ways that they can help others to be fed by "the bread of life."

❖ End this activity by suggesting that each student write one step that he or she will take this week to begin providing God's "bread of life" to the world.

(5) Continue the Journey

❖ Pray that the adults will go forth to provide the bread of life to the world.

❖ Read aloud this preparation for next week's lesson. You may also want to post it on newsprint for the students to copy.

■ **Title: The Good Shepherd**
■ **Background Scripture: John 10:1-18**
■ **Lesson Scripture: John 10:7-18**
■ **Focus of the Lesson: People often follow strong leaders who may or may not have their best interests at heart. How do we know which leaders have our best interests at heart? Jesus was a strong leader whom people followed and who was willing to give up his life to save them from harm.**

❖ Challenge the students to complete one or more of these activities for further spiritual growth related to this week's session. Post this information on newsprint for the students to copy.

(1) **Bake a loaf of bread this week and share it with someone who needs to hear that Jesus is "the bread of life."**
(2) **Memorize today's key verse, John 6:35. Repeat it daily so that you will be able to call it to mind immediately when you feel there is a gap in your life.**
(3) **Ponder the significance of Jesus as "the bread of life," especially as you partake of the bread of Holy Communion.**

❖ Sing or read aloud "You Satisfy the Hungry Heart."

❖ Conclude today's session by leading the class in this benediction: **Go forth rejoicing that God, out of infinite love for the world, gave us Jesus, through whom we have eternal life.**

UNIT 3: THE WORD WILL BE

THE GOOD SHEPHERD

PREVIEWING THE LESSON

Lesson Scripture: John 10:7-18
Background Scripture: John 10:1-18
Key Verse: John 10:4

Focus of the Lesson:
People often follow strong leaders who may or may not have their best interests at heart. How do we know which leaders have our best interests at heart? Jesus was a strong leader whom people followed and who was willing to give up his life to save them from harm.

Goals for the Learners:
(1) to explore the image of the Good Shepherd.
(2) to discern the difference between a good and bad leader.
(3) to critically evaluate their leaders and choose to follow good leaders.

Supplies:
Bibles, newsprint and marker, paper and pencils, hymnals

READING THE SCRIPTURE

NRSV
John 10:4, 7-18

⁴When he has brought out all his own, he goes ahead of them, and the sheep follow him because they know his voice.

⁷So again Jesus said to them, "Very truly, I tell you, I am the gate for the sheep. ⁸All who came before me are thieves and bandits; but the sheep did not listen to them. ⁹I am the gate. Whoever enters by me will be saved, and will come in and go out and find pasture. ¹⁰The thief comes only to steal and kill and destroy. I came that they may have life, and have it abundantly.

NIV
John 10:4, 7-18

⁴When he has brought out all his own, he goes on ahead of them, and his sheep follow him because they know his voice.

⁷Therefore Jesus said again, "I tell you the truth, I am the gate for the sheep. ⁸All who ever came before me were thieves and robbers, but the sheep did not listen to them. ⁹I am the gate; whoever enters through me will be saved. He will come in and go out, and find pasture. ¹⁰The thief comes only to steal and kill and destroy; I have come that they may have life, and have it to the full.

11"I am the good shepherd. The good shepherd lays down his life for the sheep. 12The hired hand, who is not the shepherd and does not own the sheep, sees the wolf coming and leaves the sheep and runs away—and the wolf snatches them and scatters them. 13The hired hand runs away because a hired hand does not care for the sheep. 14I am the good shepherd. I know my own and my own know me, 15just as the Father knows me and I know the Father. And I lay down my life for the sheep. 16I have other sheep that do not belong to this fold. I must bring them also, and they will listen to my voice. So there will be one flock, one shepherd. 17For this reason the Father loves me, because I lay down my life in order to take it up again. 18No one takes it from me, but I lay it down of my own accord. I have power to lay it down, and I have power to take it up again. I have received this command from my Father."

11"I am the good shepherd. The good shepherd lays down his life for the sheep. 12The hired hand is not the shepherd who owns the sheep. So when he sees the wolf coming, he abandons the sheep and runs away. Then the wolf attacks the flock and scatters it. 13The man runs away because he is a hired hand and cares nothing for the sheep.

14"I am the good shepherd; I know my sheep and my sheep know me—15just as the Father knows me and I know the Father—and I lay down my life for the sheep. 16I have other sheep that are not of this sheep pen. I must bring them also. They too will listen to my voice, and there shall be one flock and one shepherd. 17The reason my Father loves me is that I lay down my life—only to take it up again. 18No one takes it from me, but I lay it down of my own accord. I have authority to lay it down and authority to take it up again. This command I received from my Father."

UNDERSTANDING THE SCRIPTURE

Introduction. Sheep and shepherds were part of the daily life and landscape of ancient Israel. For Jesus' original audience, therefore, this was not merely a sentimental image. Rather, it was highly practical and personally familiar.

Sheep and shepherd imagery was also part of Israel's theological life. The image of God as a shepherd for the people was firmly established in the Old Testament (for example, Psalm 23; Isaiah 40:11; Ezekiel 34:11-17). Also, the people cherished a memory of their greatest leader, David, being a shepherd (2 Samuel 5:2), and so there was a prophetic anticipation of the promised messiah being a shepherd like David (Ezekiel 34:23-24). Finally, Israel's deficient leaders had also been understood as inadequate shepherds (Jeremiah 23:1-2; Ezekiel 34:1-10).

When Jesus used shepherd imagery, here and in the familiar story of the lost sheep (Luke 15:4-7), he was building on a well-established foundation.

John 10:1-3. Ancient Near Eastern towns often had common folds where numerous people's flocks would be kept at night. These folds were enclosed structures, including gates that could be closed and locked. A shepherd could leave his flock there for the night with a reasonable sense of security. Meanwhile, a gatekeeper held the key to the gate. He would only permit entrance to one of the known shepherds.

John 10:4-6. Because the setting of Jesus' imagery is a communal fold, other flocks are implicit. This sets the stage for the shepherd "[bringing] out all his own" (10:4). That some but not all of the sheep in the fold follow him should not necessarily be understood here as an indictment of those other sheep, but merely an illustration of the intimate familiarity between this shepherd and the sheep of his flock.

John 10:7-10. In contrast to the formal, secure structure of the communal fold, Jesus turns now to the smaller, makeshift folds that were sometimes established out in the fields. Rocks were easy to come by in the hills and fields of ancient Israel, and so it was not a great engineering feat to create a makeshift fold enclosed by a small, stone wall. In that sort of arrangement, one opening was left in the wall as a place for the sheep to enter and exit. And when the sheep were in for the night, the shepherd would lie down in the opening. He himself became the gate.

The phrase "come in and go out" (10:9) is an image of routine, and therefore security. Furthermore, it echoes a recurring theme from the Old Testament, which may be part of the backdrop both for Jesus' language and for his original audience's understanding.

Jesus makes one reference to the "thieves and bandits" (10:8) who came before him, as well as a later reference to "the thief [who] comes only to steal and kill and destroy" (10:10). The exact interpretation of these references is not entirely clear. He may have had in mind the long history in Israel of false prophets, as well as the more recent spate of false messiahs. William Barclay characterizes the latter phenomenon as "adventurers who were continually arising in Palestine and promising that, if people would follow them, they would bring in the golden age." Meanwhile, R. V. G. Tasker suggests that, following on the heels of Jesus' indictment of the Pharisees at the end of chapter 9, they may be the thieves and robbers that Jesus has in mind. This interpretation surely resonates with other critiques Jesus made of the contemporary religious leaders (for example, Matthew 23:13-15). And, finally, the singular reference to "the thief" may allude to the devil

himself, with whom Jesus associates the misguided and misguiding people of his day (John 8:44).

In dramatic contrast to the intent and effect of "all who came before" (10:8) is the work of Jesus. While the thief comes to kill and destroy, this good shepherd comes "that they may have life, and have it abundantly" (10:10).

The underlying Greek root, used here as the adverb "abundantly," appears more than twenty times in the New Testament. Perhaps the most telling use is found in 2 Corinthians: "Now it is not necessary for me to write you about the ministry to the saints" (9:1). What the NRSV renders "not necessary," the King James Version translates "superfluous." Such is the nature of this good shepherd: He provides far beyond what is needed. So the ancient psalmist bore witness to this shepherd, saying, "My cup overflows" (Psalm 23:5).

John 10:11-13. The image of the shepherd laying down his life for the sheep follows naturally on the image of the shepherd as a gate. He lies down to serve as a gate in the entryway of the makeshift fold.

In this section, however, the image takes on a new layer of meaning. He does not merely lie down in the entryway to protect them by keeping them from wandering out. He lays down his very life in order to save them. The strong implication is that this shepherd sacrifices his own life for the sake of his flock.

In this respect, the good shepherd stands in contrast to "the hired hand" (10:12-13). The first sign of danger sends the hired hand running, while the self-sacrificing shepherd stays with his flock.

John 10:14-18. This portion of Jesus' teaching about the good shepherd now introduces the Father. The camera lens is widened, and we see a new vista. Previously, the focus had been entirely on the relationship between the shepherd and the sheep. Now we see that relationship in its larger context, namely, the relationship between Jesus and the Father. For what the good shepherd does for the sheep is a function of the Father's love and command.

Furthermore, the relationship between the shepherd and the sheep is identified in terms of Jesus' relationship to his Father. Just as he knows the Father and the Father knows him, so it is between Jesus and his flock. This reflects a larger theme in John (for example, 15:9; 17:20-21).

Finally, the image of the good shepherd laying down his life for his sheep, which was introduced in verse 11, is revisited in verses 16-18. As verse 18 makes clear, this shepherd who lays down his life must not be misunderstood as a victim ("no one takes it from me"); he is a volunteer ("I lay it down of my own accord") and a victor ("I have the power to take it up again").

INTERPRETING THE SCRIPTURE

The Shepherd and His Sheep

Pet lovers will not find this difficult to envision. It is a picture of a human being in a warm and familiar relationship with an animal.

I don't have any firsthand knowledge of sheep, but I know all about having dogs and cats, as well as a little bit about birds. And in my own experience, as well as what I have witnessed among others, I know how close a human being and an animal can become. In some homes, the death of a pet is a time of sincere grief. Dear friends of mine, who have no children of their own, care for their dogs with the love and affection of parents.

We have seen the movies and shows about the so-called "horse whisperers." Likewise, we've seen documentaries about those rare individuals who move out into some natural habitat and manage to establish a relationship of trust—even affection—with the wild animals among whom they live: bears, gorillas, tigers, and more. And, much closer to home, I knew a man some years ago who had developed quite a rapport with the chipmunk that lived near his patio.

With this in mind, we read Jesus' words about the nature of the good shepherd. For him, shepherding is not merely a job; it is a relationship. He knows his sheep, and his sheep know him. That relationship is the key to everything that follows—including the sheep.

The Others

The image of the Lord as shepherd is not unique to John 10. On the contrary, as indicated in the Understanding the Scripture portion, we should read this teaching of Jesus against the larger Old Testament backdrop that would have been familiar to both Jesus and his audience. Furthermore, in addition to those Old Testament images of shepherds, we also have the other significant teaching of Jesus about a good shepherd: the one who retrieves his one lost lamb (Luke 15:4-7).

For all of that backdrop, however, Jesus develops several themes in this passage that are minimally present or altogether absent from those other sheep-and-shepherd passages.

Prominent in this teaching is the theme of "others." There are "other sheep" for whom this good shepherd is concerned. And there are other characters besides the shepherd who may have some interest in or responsibility for the sheep.

The "other sheep" is almost certainly a reference to the Samaritans and Gentiles. Beyond that historical context, it is vital for those of us "inside" the fold to remember the Shepherd's love for the others "that do not belong to this fold" (10:16).

Meanwhile, all sheep need also to be mindful of the other characters Jesus references. He mentions thieves, bandits, hired hands, and a wolf. All of these have some point of contact with the sheep, but none of them is to be trusted or followed like the good shepherd.

We observe this fundamental difference between the good shepherd and all the others: selflessness versus selfishness. The self-interest of the thieves, bandits, and wolf draws them to the flock for their own gain. Meanwhile, the self-interest of the hired hands drives them away from the flock for their own preservation. But the good shepherd operates selflessly in his relation to his sheep. His interest in them is for their welfare, not his own. And his care for them extends even to the point of self-sacrifice.

What Makes This Shepherd Different

This teaching is not only about the shepherd and his sheep, it is also a testimony to how this particular shepherd is different. He is different, as we have observed, from the hired hand, as well as from the thieves and bandits. Yet on this matter of self-sacrifice, we also discover that this shepherd is different even from all the other good shepherds who have come before.

The good shepherd of Psalm 23 is tender, strong, and provident, yet there is never any sense in which that shepherd is endangered. Likewise, the exemplary shepherd of Ezekiel 34 is wise, caring, and just, but invulnerable. And in Luke 15, while there is implicit danger for the lost lamb, the shepherd seems invincible.

In John 10, however, we meet a different magnitude of good shepherd. He not only provides all the necessary guidance, care, and protection for his sheep; he dies for them. This shepherd saves his sheep at his own expense. It is a shepherd unknown to the writers of Psalm 23 and Ezekiel 34, but

well known to the sheep who live on this side of the cross.

Personal Gate

Andraé Crouch wrote a song that declared, "Jesus is the answer for the world today." It was a simple statement, but one that the Fourth Gospel writer would probably endorse. For all of the theological sophistication of John's Gospel, we observe that the "I am" statements distill to this simple truth: Jesus is, in fact, the answer.

As we have seen, those statements fall into two different categories. Some "I am" statements identify Jesus with abstract concepts; for example, truth, life, and light. Others, meanwhile, offer very tangible images; for example, bread, shepherd, and vine. And here we meet another rather concrete picture: a gate.

"I am the gate" (10:7) does not have the sentimental quality of "I am the good shepherd" (10:11). Portraits of Jesus as a gate do not grace the walls of our Sunday school classrooms. Yet the underlying truth is every bit as precious as the more picturesque truth of the shepherd.

First, as we have already observed, the role of gate was part and parcel of the role of the shepherd. In the makeshift folds out in the countryside, the shepherd necessarily served as a gate. In him, therefore, we find our security.

Beyond that, we also find in him our entrée. The same wall that prevents a lamb within the fold from getting out would also prevent him from getting in. If he would enter the safety of the fold, therefore, he would have to enter by the gate.

Imagine that the gate was a mechanism, like the protective child gates of homes with toddlers. The sheep would have no hope of entering. A closed gate would be, for him, a hopelessly locked gate.

Not in this fold, however. This gate is not a contraption, but a person. And not just any person: It is the familiar and beloved shepherd who knows his sheep and whose sheep know him.

"Whoever enters by me will be saved," Jesus promises (10:9). Salvation is a central issue in Jesus' ministry (Matthew 1:21; Luke 19:10) and in John's Gospel (3:17; 5:34; 12:47), and salvation is found in Christ. Again, we observe that the answer is a personal one. It's not a system, a dogma, or a checklist of rules by which one is saved, but by entering through the gate—our personal gate. Jesus is the answer.

SHARING THE SCRIPTURE

Preparing Our Hearts

Explore this week's devotional reading, found in Psalm 28. In this psalm we hear an individual pray for God's help and give thanks for receiving it. The song closes in verse 9 with a prayer for God to be the shepherd of the people forever. How do you, especially if you do not have firsthand experience with sheep, connect with the image of the shepherd? Is the image familiar and helpful, or unfamiliar and irrelevant? If you do not connect with this image, is there another relational image that might be more useful? If so, what?

Pray that you and the adult learners will yearn for caring, competent leadership, such as that provided by a faithful shepherd.

Preparing Our Minds

Study the background Scripture from John 10:1-18 and the lesson Scripture from John 10:7-18, noting that the key verse is 10:4. Ask yourself: How do we know which leaders have our best interests at heart?

Write on newsprint:
❑ information for next week's lesson, found under "Continue the Journey."
❑ activities for further spiritual growth in "Continue the Journey."

Find a picture depicting Jesus as the Good Shepherd. Many churches have such a picture. Check http://www.biblical-art.com/biblicalsubject.asp?id_biblical subject=789&pagenum=1 or books for recommendations. If the sanctuary has a stained glass window with this image, and if the class could meet there for one week, consider doing so.

Prepare a brief lecture from Understanding the Scripture as suggested under "Explore the Image of the Good Shepherd."

LEADING THE CLASS

(1) Gather to Learn

❖ Welcome the class members and introduce any guests.

❖ Pray that the students will connect with the image of the good shepherd.

❖ Read: **In his book *Servant Leadership*, Robert K. Greenleaf states: "A leader initiates, provides the ideas and the structure, and takes the risk of failure along with the chance of success." Although Greenleaf is a strong proponent of those leaders who serve others, history teaches us that some leaders will take the initiative, provide the ideas and structure, all while leading people in a direction that is surely not in their best interest.**

❖ Post a sheet of newsprint and draw a line down the center. On the left write *Good Leaders*; on the right write *Bad Leaders*. Encourage the students to call out names of well-known figures who have led people in positive, life-giving directions. Also encourage them to name those who have led people into circumstances that were not in their best interest. Leave the list posted for a later activity.

❖ Read aloud today's focus statement: **People often follow strong leaders who may or may not have their best interests at heart. How do we know which leaders have our best interests at heart? Jesus was a strong leader whom people followed and who was willing to give up his life to save them from harm.**

(2) Explore the Image of the Good Shepherd

❖ Display the picture(s) of Jesus as the Good Shepherd that you have located. Go around the room and invite the adults to say what the image of the Good Shepherd means to them. For example, some may see a gentle person, others a strong protector; some may be inspired to loyalty or trust.

❖ Read or retell "Introduction," "John 10:1-3," and "John 10:4-6" from Understanding the Scripture to set the scene for today's lesson. Be sure to include how the image of the shepherd was used throughout the Bible.

❖ Select a volunteer to read John 10:4, 7-18. Encourage the class to listen for words that comfort them.

❖ Call on volunteers to identify those words of comfort. Prompt them to say why they find these words so comforting.

❖ Give a brief lecture from Understanding the Scripture, beginning with verses 7-10 and continuing through to verse 18, to help students explore the setting and meaning of Jesus' teachings.

❖ Add information from "The Others" in Interpreting the Scripture to show that Jesus is concerned not only with the sheep currently in his fold but also with others.

❖ Invite the class to add any other observations about the image of the Good Shepherd.

(3) Discern the Difference Between a Good and Bad Leader

❖ Refer to the list created during the "Gather to Learn" segment. Post another sheet of newsprint that you will label *Traits of Good Leaders* and *Traits of Bad Leaders*. Suggest that the adults think about the traits of leaders they have already listed and use those traits to create these two lists.

❖ Probe the class to determine additional differences in traits they perceive between good and bad leaders.

❖ End this portion of the session by soliciting two volunteers, one to read Ezekiel 34:1-10 and the other to read Ezekiel 34:11-16. Through the prophet, God explains the difference between Israel's false shepherds and God, the Good Shepherd. Invite the class to add any traits from these passages to their list.

(4) Critically Evaluate the Learners' Leaders and Choose to Follow Good Leaders

❖ Point out that on November 6, 2012, voters in the United States will be going to the polls to elect national and local leaders. Without getting into a debate about parties or particular candidates, invite the class members to list on newsprint traits that they would like to see in their leaders.

❖ Observe, too, that congregations in some denominations have a say as to whom they would recommend for ordained ministry. Discuss any traits that you would add or subtract from the "good trait" list when considering a potential candidate for ministry.

❖ Challenge the adults to do the following:

■ Get to know a current or prospective leader (or pastor) who wants your support. If it is not possible to personally know that individual, read and talk with others about his or her qualifications.

■ Check this individual's voting record, if one exists, particularly in respect to issues that reflect your values as a Christian. Determine the organizations this prospect supports and find out what he or she has contributed to them. Also discern how well these organizations reflect your New Testament values.

■ Make an informed decision to back a particular candidate and do all in your power to support this person.

(5) Continue the Journey

❖ Pray that the adults will evaluate their leaders critically.

❖ Read aloud this preparation for next week's lesson. You may also want to post it on newsprint for the students to copy.

■ **Title: The Resurrection and the Life**
■ **Background Scripture: John 11:1-27**
■ **Lesson Scripture: John 11:17-27**
■ **Focus of the Lesson: People often think that death separates us from everything we know. How can we have confidence that death is not the end but a transformation? Jesus promised that those who believe in him will—even though they die—have a new relationship with God.**

❖ Challenge the students to complete one or more of these activities for further spiritual growth related to this week's session. Post this information on newsprint for the students to copy.

(1) **Observe your own dog or cat. See how your pet responds to your voice, the voice of other family members, and the voice of a stranger. What differences do you note? How would you compare your pet's response to you and your response to the Good Shepherd?**

(2) **Take action to support a good leader in the church, workplace, or community. Send a thank you, work on a project under this person, encourage others to vote for this person, or whatever else you can do.**

(3) **Do some research on the qualities of sheep and shepherds. How do these traits help you to better understand our relationship with Jesus? What qualities do not seem to fit? Why?**

❖ Sing or read aloud "Savior, Like a Shepherd Lead Us."

❖ Conclude today's session by leading the class in this benediction: **Go forth rejoicing that God, out of infinite love for the world, gave us Jesus, through whom we have eternal life.**

UNIT 3: THE WORD WILL BE

THE RESURRECTION AND THE LIFE

PREVIEWING THE LESSON

Lesson Scripture: John 11:17-27
Background Scripture: John 11:1-27
Key Verse: John 11:25

Focus of the Lesson:
People often think that death separates us from everything we know. How can we have confidence that death is not the end but a transformation? Jesus promised that those who believe in him will—even though they die—have a new relationship with God.

Goals for the Learners:
(1) to explore Jesus' promise of the resurrection and the need for belief in that promise.
(2) to relate the statement of Jesus, "I am the resurrection," to their lives.
(3) to share with others our confidence that we can believe in Jesus' promises and that he can make a difference in our lives.

Supplies:
Bibles, newsprint and marker, paper and pencils, hymnals

READING THE SCRIPTURE

NRSV
John 11:17-27

¹⁷When Jesus arrived, he found that Lazarus had already been in the tomb four days. ¹⁸Now Bethany was near Jerusalem, some two miles away, ¹⁹and many of the Jews had come to Martha and Mary to console them about their brother. ²⁰When Martha heard that Jesus was coming, she went and met him, while Mary stayed at home. ²¹Martha said to Jesus, "Lord, if you

NIV
John 11:17-27

¹⁷On his arrival, Jesus found that Lazarus had already been in the tomb for four days. ¹⁸Bethany was less than two miles from Jerusalem, ¹⁹and many Jews had come to Martha and Mary to comfort them in the loss of their brother. ²⁰When Martha heard that Jesus was coming, she went out to meet him, but Mary stayed at home.

335

had been here, my brother would not have died. ²²But even now I know that God will give you whatever you ask of him." ²³Jesus said to her, "Your brother will rise again." ²⁴Martha said to him, "I know that he will rise again in the resurrection on the last day." **²⁵Jesus said to her, "I am the resurrection and the life. Those who believe in me, even though they die, will live,** ²⁶and everyone who lives and believes in me will never die. Do you believe this?" ²⁷She said to him, "Yes, Lord, I believe that you are the Messiah, the Son of God, the one coming into the world."

²¹"Lord," Martha said to Jesus, "if you had been here, my brother would not have died. ²²But I know that even now God will give you whatever you ask."

²³Jesus said to her, "Your brother will rise again."

²⁴Martha answered, "I know he will rise again in the resurrection at the last day."

²⁵Jesus said to her, "I am the resurrection and the life. He who believes in me will live, even though he dies; ²⁶and whoever lives and believes in me will never die. Do you believe this?"

²⁷"Yes, Lord," she told him, "I believe that you are the Christ, the Son of God, who was to come into the world."

UNDERSTANDING THE SCRIPTURE

John 11:1-2. John's is the only Gospel to mention Lazarus, though the name is also applied to a character in one of Jesus' parables (Luke 16:19-31). His sisters, Mary and Martha, are featured together in an encounter with Jesus recorded by Luke (Luke 10:38-42). And John's identification of Mary as "the one who anointed the Lord" (11:2) ties her to the episode reported in John 12:1-8, where she is named, as well as Matthew 26:6-13 and Mark 14:3-9, where she is not.

John 11:3. Love is perhaps more central a theme in John's Gospel than any other. It is God's reason for sending his Son (3:16), the new commandment (13:34), the chief hallmark of Jesus' followers (13:35), and the ultimate question (21:15-17). We observe also that the author identifies himself as the disciple Jesus loved (19:26; 20:2; 21:7, 20). This reference to Lazarus as "he whom you love" (11:3), plus the absence of Lazarus's story from every other Gospel, have prompted some to speculate that Lazarus was the author of the Fourth Gospel. That is not the consensus of New Testament scholarship, however. Rather, this designation of

Lazarus is better recognized as characteristic of this Gospel's emphasis on love.

John 11:4-6. In human terms, Lazarus's illness did in fact lead to death. Ultimately, however, it led to God's glory. That sense of purpose in illness recalls an earlier episode in John, when Jesus explains the purpose of a certain man's blindness (9:1-3).

The narration strongly suggests that Jesus deliberately waited for Lazarus to die. The sisters obviously expected that Jesus would come to heal their brother, and thus prevent his death, but the purpose of God was better served by Lazarus's death.

John 11:7-10. Just one chapter earlier (10:22-39), the Jewish leaders in Judea had been so offended by Jesus that they endeavored to stone him. To return so quickly to the place where antagonism was so high seemed to the disciples a reckless choice.

Jesus' reference to "twelve hours of daylight" in verse 9 alludes to the ancient reality that there was a natural limit on working hours each day. His statement here recalls his earlier instruction: "We must work the works of him who sent me while it is day; night is coming when no one can work"

(9:4). It also reminds us of the larger theme of proper timing for Jesus' work (compare 2:4; 7:6-8; 12:27).

John 11:11-15. We see elsewhere the pattern of Jesus speaking metaphorically and being misunderstood (for example, Matthew 16:5-12; John 3:3-4). So, here, he speaks of death as sleep, and the disciples initially misunderstand what he is saying. The use of "sleep" as a reference to death is found in both the Old Testament (1 Kings 2:10; 2 Chronicles 21:1; Job 14:11-12; Psalm 13:3) and the New (Matthew 27:52; Luke 8:52-53).

John 11:16. The disciples were concerned that Judea was a dangerous place for Jesus, but now Thomas articulates the courage and devotion to face that danger with Jesus. His brave words are reminiscent of the resolve expressed by James and John (Mark 10:38-39), as well as Peter's bold promises at the Last Supper (Mark 14:29, 31).

Earl Marlatt poetically characterized the disciples' devotion: "'Are ye able,' said the Master, 'to be crucified with me?' 'Yea,' the sturdy dreamers answered, 'to the death we follow thee.'"

We know that those disciples were not so fearless and unflinching, however, when the trouble came for Jesus (see, for example, Mark 14:50; Luke 22:54-62). After Christ's resurrection and the Day of Pentecost, though, they showed the mettle to match their words.

John 11:17-19. Because of the climate, as well as limited embalming techniques, the ancient Jews did not leave their corpses unburied for long. Lazarus was likely buried on the day that he died.

Bethany was a small town just across the Mount of Olives to the east from Jerusalem. It was evidently the town where Jesus and his disciples spent their nights during Holy Week. Its proximity to Jerusalem is important to the narrator because "many of the Jews" (11:19) had made the trip, and so were witnesses to this event.

John 11:20-23. It was precisely their confidence that Jesus could heal Lazarus that had prompted Mary and Martha to notify Jesus of his illness. Here, therefore, Martha gives voice to her profound disappointment that Jesus had not come.

It is unclear what hope Martha is expressing when she says, "Even now I know that God will give you whatever you ask of him" (11:22). Within the larger context, it seems unlikely that she had any expectation that Jesus would raise her brother back to life, for she does not immediately latch on to his promise that "your brother will rise again" (11:23), and she resists his later command to open the tomb (11:39).

George Beasley-Murray suggests: "At this point [Martha] affirms her continued confidence in the power of Jesus' intercession for all eventualities. Her brother's death has not destroyed her faith in Jesus." Just as she was affirming her faith that Jesus could have healed Lazarus had he arrived sooner, so she reaffirms her continued faith in his ability going forward.

John 11:24. With a few notable exceptions, the Old Testament does not reflect much belief in an afterlife. The ancient Israelite conception was that the dead went to Sheol, and that it was an undifferentiating place and existence. Rich and poor, wise and foolish, righteous and wicked all ended in Sheol. It was a place of neither torment nor reward. Rather, it was a shadowy, ghostly existence.

During the intertestamental period, however, a strong resurrection expectation grew within Judaism. The Sadducees are notorious for denying it, but most other Jews of Jesus' day embraced the prospect of God resurrecting the dead, and particularly the righteous. This was the hope Martha affirmed.

John 11:25-27. Here is another of the great "I am" statements of Jesus from the Fourth Gospel. In this instance, he redirects Martha's faith from a future event to a present person.

In response, Martha uses three significant terms in reference to Jesus. "Messiah," coming from the Hebrew for "anointed," captured the mounting expectation of Old Testament prophecies about a ruler and reign that would be descended from and reminiscent of David. "Son of God" was a still bolder christological statement, seldom used by others (except demons, as in Luke 4:41) in reference to Jesus until after his resurrection. Finally, "the one coming into the world" (11:27) echoes an important Johannine theme (see also 1:9; 3:19; 6:14).

INTERPRETING THE SCRIPTURE

Tardy Savior

We live in a 9-1-1 culture. Most of us enjoy the proximity and immediacy of help when we need it. In an emergency, we simply pick up a phone—and phones are never far from us, it seems—and within a few minutes, some help has arrived.

Perhaps you have had such an emergency. Because of a loved one's health, an accident, or a fire, you have had to make that urgent phone call. And, moments later, your panic is partly relieved by the sound of approaching sirens. Help is on the way!

But imagine the unthinkable. Imagine those police officers, firefighters, or EMTs seated together in their quarters, playing cards. The alarm sounds, and they hear the quick summary of your need, along with your address. Yet they show no urgency, no movement. "Whose turn was it?" one of them asks, as they continue blithely with their card game.

You're waiting impatiently in your home, desperate to hear the sound of their sirens, but they are shuffling and dealing another hand.

Mary and Martha had sent a poignant and urgent message to Jesus that their brother—"he whom you love"—was sick. It was their 9-1-1 call. Yet Jesus had shown no urgency at all. By the time he arrived, Lazarus had already been in the tomb for four days. Jesus was too late, and the sisters were brokenhearted.

Lament of a Grieving Heart

What's the first thing you say to a dear friend when he or she arrives at a funeral? "Thank you for coming," we cry, as we embrace. "It's so good to see you . . . so good to have you here."

When Jesus arrived to join the mourners following Lazarus's death, however, Martha expressed a very different sort of greeting. "Lord," she lamented, "if you had been here, my brother would not have died" (11:21).

Can we imagine any attendee at a funeral to whom we would say such a thing? Perhaps if those card-playing first responders had not arrived until the day of the funeral, we might say it to them.

This exclamation from Martha is worse, however. In the case of those imaginarily derelict emergency workers, it would only be a professional failure on their part. Tragic, to be sure, but still not the same sort of personal disappointment represented here in this episode with Martha and Jesus.

Jesus' absence—or at least tardiness—was a personal failure. He was both a close friend of the family and a powerful servant of God who had healed countless people throughout the surrounding regions. How could it be, then, that he would not arrive in time to restore his dear friend to health?

Martha's greeting is a personal lament. It is the heartbroken response of a profoundly disappointed woman. Specifically, a woman of faith. And this is where she is a very familiar character to us.

Disappointment requires expectation. You cannot be disappointed if you do not begin with some level of expectation. And the greater the expectations, the more severe the disappointment.

Faith, meanwhile, is a very particular kind of expectation. Faith represents the expectations we have of God. When God disappoints us, therefore, it becomes for us a faith crisis. And at those times, we cry out that quintessential declaration of a disappointed faith: "Lord, if you had been here . . ." (11:21).

Personal Faith

We are struck by the poignancy of Martha's words. And they are poignant not only because of the disappointment that they express but also because of their personal quality. "Lord, if you," she says.

We observe that hers is a very personal statement. She is not vaguely wishing that circumstances had been different—"If only things hadn't happened this way" or "If only the sickness hadn't worsened so quickly." No, her lament is not about circumstances, but about Jesus. There is a personal pronoun attached to her grief.

That shouldn't surprise us, of course. The disappointment is personal because the faith was personal. She didn't trust circumstances; she trusted Jesus.

As the conversation unfolds, however, we discover that her faith needed to be more personal still. "Your brother will rise again" (11:23), Jesus reassures Martha. And she faithfully responds, "I know that he will rise again in the resurrection on the last day" (11:24).

As we noted above, Judaism of the intertestamental period had developed a strong anticipation of an end-of-time resurrection. Martha had latched onto that hope, and so she was not grieving the finality of her brother's death. She clung to the assurance that he would rise again at that climactic event known as "the resurrection."

Amazingly, however, Jesus reframes completely that resurrection hope: "I am the resurrection," he declares (11:25).

Imagine a person hurrying a loved one to the hospital, only to find an individual man standing where the hospital was supposed to be. "We're looking for the hospital," we explain urgently. And he responds calmly, "I am the hospital."

Martha's faith was in a future event: the resurrection. Our faith needs to be more personal, however. For rather than a future event, Martha and we are invited to believe in a present person.

If He, Then I

Throughout our study of John's Gospel, we are examining the marvelous "I am" statements of Jesus. In some instances, it is very clear that what he says about himself carries implications for us. When he says that he is the Good Shepherd (10:11), we recognize that we are his sheep. When he says that he is the vine, it includes the truth that we are the branches (15:5).

Other identifications that Jesus claims for himself, however, do not have such natural or obvious counterparts. If he is the bread of life, for example, what does that make me? If he is the light of the world, then what am I?

And, in this case, where Jesus says that he is the resurrection and the life, what does that mean for you and me?

Jesus answers that question for us. "Those who believe in me, even though they die," Jesus proclaims, "will live" (11:25).

Human beings have become rather expert at postponing death, or in some cases simply prolonging it. We haven't yet found any way to escape it, however. No matter the precautions, the diet and exercise, the quality of health care and coverage, we all live with this certainty: Every human is going to die.

Those who believe in this Jesus, however, live with another certainty. That even though they die, yet shall they live! It is not a generic assumption about an afterlife or a vague notion about the immortality of the soul. Rather, this hope has a name and a face on it. It is a personal faith: faith in the One who is himself the resurrection and the life.

SHARING THE SCRIPTURE

Preparing Our Hearts

Explore this week's devotional reading, found in 1 Corinthians 15:50-58. Paul's stirring words from verses 51, 52, and 53 ring out in sections 47 and 48 of Handel's *Messiah*. We hear the trumpet sounding and rejoice that we shall be raised incorruptible. Handel continues in sections 49 and 50 by taunting death about its sting and victory, which obviously no longer exist. The composer then comes to a resounding hymn of thanksgiving to God in section 51. Listen to this oratorio, if possible. Contemplate how you would express Paul's words in music. Ponder what his words mean for your life.

Pray that you and the adult learners will ponder the meaning of death in the context of Jesus as the resurrection and the life.

Preparing Our Minds

Study the background Scripture from John 11:1-27 and the lesson Scripture from John 11:17-27. Ask yourself: How can we have confidence that death is not the end but a transformation?

Write on newsprint:
- ❑ list of Scriptures for "Explore Jesus' Promise of the Resurrection and the Need for Belief in That Promise."
- ❑ information for next week's lesson, found under "Continue the Journey."
- ❑ activities for further spiritual growth in "Continue the Journey."

Prepare to retell the story of the death of Lazarus from John 11:1-16. Use information from Understanding the Scripture to help clarify events.

LEADING THE CLASS

(1) Gather to Learn

❖ Welcome the class members and introduce any guests.

❖ Pray that the students will find comfort in Jesus' promise of resurrection.

❖ Introduce today's topic of death and resurrection by reading these quotations:

- ■ **At death we cross from one territory to another, but we'll have no trouble with visas. Our representative is already there, preparing for our arrival. As citizens of heaven, our entrance is incontestable.** (Erwin W. Lutzer, 1941–)
- ■ **Death is not journeying into an unknown land; it is a voyage home. We are not going to a strange country, but to our Father's house, and among our kith and kin.** (John Ruskin, 1819–1900)
- ■ **Death is not the end; it is only a new beginning. Death is not the master of the house; he is only the porter at the King's lodge, appointed to open the gate and let the King's guests into the realm of eternal day.** (John Henry Jowett, 1864–1923)

❖ Ask: **In what ways do these quotations affirm or challenge what you as a Christian believe about death and life after death?**

❖ Read aloud today's focus statement: **People often think that death separates us from everything we know. How can we** have confidence that death is not the end but a transformation? Jesus promised that those who believe in him will—even though they die—have a new relationship with God.

(2) Explore Jesus' Promise of the Resurrection and the Need for Belief in That Promise

❖ Set the stage for today's lesson by retelling the story of Lazarus's death as found in John 11:1-16.

❖ Invite three volunteers to read the words of Jesus, Martha, and the narrator from John 11:17-27.

❖ Encourage several people to play the role of Martha as she tells the group how she is feeling about Lazarus's death and about Jesus' absence when the family needed him the most.

❖ Ask: **Despite Lazarus's death, Martha was able to declare her belief that Jesus was the Messiah. What do you think enabled Martha to affirm her belief so strongly?**

❖ Point out that Scriptures give us a firm foundation for believing in the resurrection. Choose volunteers to look up the following passages that you have listed on newsprint, read them aloud to the class, and then discuss what each might tell us about Jesus' resurrection and the promise of our own new life. Ideas are shown in parentheses.

- John 6:40 (Those who believe in Jesus will be raised on the last day.)
- Romans 1:1-6 (Jesus is God's Son, whom God resurrected.)
- Romans 4:24-25 (Jesus "was raised for our justification.")
- Romans 10:9 (Salvation depends on believing that Jesus is Lord and was raised from the dead.)
- Ephesians 1:15-21 (Jesus' resurrection demonstrates God's power.)
- 1 Thessalonians 4:14 (Jesus' resurrection is what makes our own resurrection possible.)

(3) Relate the Statement of Jesus, "I Am the Resurrection," to the Learners' Lives

❖ Note that although Mary certainly believed in the promise of resurrection, many people then and now do not. Invite the students to work with a partner or three-some. Each group is to discuss these questions, which you will read aloud:

(1) **What does it mean in your life to say that Jesus is the resurrection?**
(2) **How would the way you live be different if you did not accept that Jesus was resurrected, which in turn promises life for those who believe?**

❖ Distribute hymnals. Direct students to the section that includes hymns about Jesus' resurrection. Invite the adults to continue working with their groups as they scan these hymns to find words that express or help to shape the learners' beliefs about the resurrection.

❖ Call the groups together and encourage volunteers to announce their selected hymn, briefly state why it "speaks" to them, and then sing an appropriate verse.

(4) Share With Others Our Confidence That We Can Believe in Jesus' Promises and That He Can Make a Difference in Our Lives

❖ Distribute paper and pencils. Encourage the adults to write a brief paragraph about their own belief in Jesus' promises, as evidenced by his resurrection, and how he makes a difference in their lives. Suggest that they review the text for today's lesson from John 11:17-27, as well as the Scriptures studied earlier in the session.

❖ Invite volunteers to roleplay a discussion between two people. One person will use the ideas and Scriptures from his or her paragraph to persuasively share confidence in Christ with the second person, who will act as one who does not share this confidence.

❖ Debrief the roleplay by asking class members to affirm ideas they heard expressed and to suggest other possibilities for helping unbelievers see what a difference Christ can make in their lives.

❖ Conclude by encouraging the students to go forth and share their confidence in Christ with others.

(5) Continue the Journey

❖ Pray that the adults will share with others their confidence in Jesus' promise of resurrection.

❖ Read aloud this preparation for next week's lesson. You may also want to post it on newsprint for the students to copy.

- ■ Title: The Way, the Truth, and the Life
- ■ Background Scripture: John 14:1-14
- ■ Lesson Scripture: John 14:1-14
- ■ Focus of the Lesson: People always try to find direction in their lives. How can we know which way to go? Jesus proclaimed that he was the way people would come to God because he was in God and God was in him.

❖ Challenge the students to complete one or more of these activities for further spiritual growth related to this week's ses-

sion. Post this information on newsprint for the students to copy.

(1) Read Elisabeth Kübler Ross's book *On Death and Dying* to learn about the stages of grief. If someone you know is grieving, see if you can find ideas in this book to help that mourner recognize and go through the process.

(2) Write in a spiritual journal what you believe to be true about death, resurrection, and life after death. This information is for your eyes only, so be absolutely frank before God about what you believe and questions you have.

(3) Encourage someone who is struggling to accept a diagnosis of a life-limiting illness. Share God's good news as it seems appropriate when talking with this person.

❖ Sing or read aloud "Cristo Vive (Christ Is Risen)."

❖ Conclude today's session by leading the class in this benediction: **Go forth rejoicing that God, out of infinite love for the world, gave us Jesus, through whom we have eternal life.**

UNIT 3: THE WORD WILL BE

THE WAY, THE TRUTH, AND THE LIFE

PREVIEWING THE LESSON

Lesson Scripture: John 14:1-14
Background Scripture: John 14:1-14
Key Verse: John 14:6

Focus of the Lesson:
People always try to find direction in their lives. How can we know which way to go? Jesus proclaimed that he was the way people would come to God because he was in God and God was in him.

Goals for the Learners:
(1) to explore how Jesus is "the way" to God.
(2) to claim their life purpose and set their direction.
(3) to make a commitment to follow the way of Jesus.

Supplies:
Bibles, newsprint and marker, paper and pencils, hymnals, paper labyrinth

---

READING THE SCRIPTURE

NRSV
John 14:1-14

¹"Do not let your hearts be troubled. Believe in God, believe also in me. ²In my Father's house there are many dwelling places. If it were not so, would I have told you that I go to prepare a place for you? ³And if I go and prepare a place for you, I will come again and will take you to myself, so that where I am, there you may be also. ⁴And you know the way to the place where

NIV
John 14:1-14

¹"Do not let your hearts be troubled. Trust in God; trust also in me. ²In my Father's house are many rooms; if it were not so, I would have told you. I am going there to prepare a place for you. ³And if I go and prepare a place for you, I will come back and take you to be with me that you also may be where I am. ⁴You know the way to the place where I am going."

I am going." ⁵Thomas said to him, "Lord, we do not know where you are going. How can we know the way?" **⁶Jesus said to him, "I am the way, and the truth, and the life. No one comes to the Father except through me.** ⁷If you know me, you will know my Father also. From now on you do know him and have seen him."

⁸Philip said to him, "Lord, show us the Father, and we will be satisfied." ⁹Jesus said to him, "Have I been with you all this time, Philip, and you still do not know me? Whoever has seen me has seen the Father. How can you say, 'Show us the Father'? ¹⁰Do you not believe that I am in the Father and the Father is in me? The words that I say to you I do not speak on my own; but the Father who dwells in me does his works. ¹¹Believe me that I am in the Father and the Father is in me; but if you do not, then believe me because of the works themselves. ¹²Very truly, I tell you, the one who believes in me will also do the works that I do and, in fact, will do greater works than these, because I am going to the Father. ¹³I will do whatever you ask in my name, so that the Father may be glorified in the Son. ¹⁴If in my name you ask me for anything, I will do it."

⁵Thomas said to him, "Lord, we don't know where you are going, so how can we know the way?"

⁶Jesus answered, "I am the way and the truth and the life. No one comes to the Father except through me. ⁷If you really knew me, you would know my Father as well. From now on, you do know him and have seen him."

⁸Philip said, "Lord, show us the Father and that will be enough for us."

⁹Jesus answered: "Don't you know me, Philip, even after I have been among you such a long time? Anyone who has seen me has seen the Father. How can you say, 'Show us the Father'? ¹⁰Don't you believe that I am in the Father, and that the Father is in me? The words I say to you are not just my own. Rather, it is the Father, living in me, who is doing his work. ¹¹Believe me when I say that I am in the Father and the Father is in me; or at least believe on the evidence of the miracles themselves. ¹²I tell you the truth, anyone who has faith in me will do what I have been doing. He will do even greater things than these, because I am going to the Father. ¹³And I will do whatever you ask in my name, so that the Son may bring glory to the Father. ¹⁴You may ask me for anything in my name, and I will do it."

UNDERSTANDING THE SCRIPTURE

John 14:1. While this verse marks the beginning of a chapter, it comes in the midst of a larger dialogue. John devotes five chapters to the Last Supper scene. This story begins in chapter 13 and includes Jesus washing his disciples' feet, predicting Judas's betrayal, and predicting Peter's denial. Additionally, he has told them that he is leaving and that they cannot come (13:33).

All of these revelations must have been very disorienting and disturbing for the disciples, and so as chapter 14 opens, Jesus speaks reassuringly to them: "Do not let your hearts be troubled."

The instruction to believe both in God and in Jesus is the first hint of a larger theme in this passage. Jesus identifies himself with the Father, and so the disciples are encouraged to trust both.

John 14:2-3. The news of Jesus leaving—and the disciples not being able to go with him—must have been an unsettling prospect. They were his followers. They had left all in order to go with him wherever he went (compare Mark 10:28). Accordingly, this new word was most reassuring. He was not going away permanently, but temporarily. Furthermore, he promised to return "so that where I am, there you may be also" (14:3). Indeed, Jesus tells them that his departure was for their benefit: "I go to prepare a place for you" (14:2).

We are accustomed to hearing the Emmanuel prophecy (Isaiah 7:10-14) read each year around Christmastime, along with the account of its fulfillment in Jesus' birth (Matthew 1:22-23). This is the incarnation truth that Charles Wesley sang: "Pleased with us in flesh to dwell, Jesus, our Emmanuel." The good news of Emmanuel is that "God is with us," and we celebrate it especially at Christmas.

Here at the Last Supper, then, that good news comes full circle. Now the promise is not only that God is with us, but that we will be with God. Our Lord does not merely condescend to our place but raises us up to God's place.

John 14:4-5. Thomas's objection seems reasonable: If they don't know where Jesus is going, they cannot possibly know the way to get there. It was unclear up until this point whether the disciples should have known where he was going. Jesus was more explicit about his destination later (for example, 14:12, 28; 16:10, 28), but at this point the disciples were uncertain about where he was going.

At the same time, Jesus' statement remains true. After all, he did not say that they knew where he was going; he simply said that they knew the way. And it turns out that they did know the way, inasmuch as they knew him.

John 14:6. This is another of the seven great "I Am" statements by Jesus, though in a sense it is three different statements.

Jesus' identification of himself as "the way" is similar to his statements about being "the bread of life" (6:35), "the good shepherd" (10:11), or "the vine" (15:1). They are all tangible images; we could draw pictures of them.

On the other hand, "the truth" and "the life" are more abstract, like "the resurrection and the life" (11:25). These are not tangible objects. Rather, they are concept words—the kinds of words that are not usually accompanied by the definite article. We might speak generally of truth or life, but Jesus identifies himself specifically as "the truth" and "the life."

Meanwhile, Jesus' statement, "no one comes to the Father except through me," recalls his earlier identification of himself as "the gate" (10:7). Just as "whoever enters by [him] will be saved" (10:9), so whoever comes by way of him will come to the Father.

John 14:7. We return to a key theme of this passage, and one of the signature themes of John's Gospel: Jesus' identification with the Father. Jesus makes a one-to-one correlation—to know him is to know the Father.

Because of our well-established doctrine of Christ through centuries of church history, this is a statement we embrace and celebrate. In its original context, however, it would have been scandalous. Indeed, when Jesus had made similar identifications of himself with God in public, his hearers sought to kill him (5:17-18; 8:54-59).

John 14:8-11. Early in John's Gospel, we read, "No one has ever seen God" (1:18). That would have been standard orthodoxy for the Jews of John's day. Now, however, Jesus makes the startling assertion that his disciples have, in fact, seen the Father.

C. S. Lewis famously argued that it is an intellectually ineligible position to conclude that Jesus was simply a great teacher. "A man who was merely a man and said the sort of things Jesus said would not be a great moral teacher," Lewis insisted. "He would either be a lunatic—on a level with the man who says he is a poached egg—or else he would be the Devil of Hell."

This episode features some of Jesus' most dramatic claims. We welcome the grand good news that he shares, and we rejoice in the truth that the Father has been revealed in him.

The encouragement to believe "because of the works" (11:11) recalls the facts that Jesus was doing his Father's work (4:34; 5:17) and that his works bear witness to him (5:36; 10:25).

John 14:12-14. Having spoken of his works, now Jesus looks forward to the works that his followers will do. Their works will be greater (14:12), and yet we see that it is still Jesus working, for he promises that he "will do whatever you ask in my name" (14:13). And we observe that such carte blanche is not for self-gratification or aggrandizement, but "so that the Father may be glorified in the Son" (14:13).

INTERPRETING THE SCRIPTURE

Which Way Are You Going?

Let me ask you a personal question: How good is your sense of direction?

The person with a poor sense of direction, you know, can manage to get lost even in a rather familiar place. I knew a girl years ago who got lost walking home from school—and it wasn't even her first year going to that school. "Familiar," another directionally challenged friend told me, "doesn't make any difference to me. The fact that I recognize all the turns and intersections doesn't make me any less confused by them. It's just a familiar confusion."

Conversely, the person with a strong sense of direction can manage to find his or her way even in a completely new and unfamiliar place. Even when that individual is forced onto some uncharted detour, or is traveling without a map, he or she still has such a strong, innate sense of where the destination is that he or she can navigate without the need for specific turn-by-turn directions.

Just finding a certain town, street, or address, however, is small potatoes compared to the profound matters at stake in this week's passage from John. At issue here is not merely the destination of a given errand or trip. Rather, it is the destination of one's whole life that is in question.

The Father's House

I spent a few years in college as a driver for a restaurant that offered free pizza delivery. In the dark on certain streets, it was sometimes a real challenge to find the address of the house that I was seeking.

Our ultimate destination, by contrast, is marvelously well lit. It is no ordinary house—it is the Father's house. And we know the way.

Though our selected passage from John is separated by a thousand years from Psalm 23, the two texts paint the same picture and bear witness to the same truth. The psalmist, you recall, anticipates that he will "dwell in the house of the LORD for ever" (23:6 KJV). And this is the lovely prospect that Jesus shares with his disciples: the promise of "my Father's house" (John 14:2).

Jesus was emphatic on the point that he was going to his Father (14:12, 28; 16:10, 28). And even on the eve of his crucifixion, when we might think more in terms of Jesus preparing to go to the cross, the author frames the narrative in terms of "going to God" (13:3).

That destination was not exclusive to Jesus, however. Quite the contrary. He assured the disciples that he would prepare a place for them as well, and then return in order to get them. The incarnate Word, who came to dwell among us (1:14), now makes provision for us to go and dwell with him (14:3). Surely this is the fulfillment of the psalmist's lovely hope of dwelling in the house of the Lord forever.

You and I, then, are invited to live our lives with that sense of destination. Our ultimate goal is not a certain title at work or degree in school, neither a corner office downtown nor a desirable address in the suburbs. Our final goal is not to have a comfortable retirement or a prearranged funeral. Rather, you and I live toward a destination, and it is nothing less than the place Jesus prepares for us in the Father's house.

Personal Business

Most destinations require something of a plan. When I was a child, my parents would get out their maps and their magnifying glasses in order to plot out the details of a long family trip. Now, when we plan our family trips, we type in the starting and ending addresses on a computer or GPS device, and the technology plots out our steps and our stops for us. Whether by new methods or by old, however, the trip always requires a plan.

Other destinations are not quite physical addresses, but they still require their own kind of planning. In order to get from where I am to the degree that I want to earn, the weight I ought to lose, or the financial goal I need to achieve, I have to identify the path from here to there. It will not happen simply because I want it to. It will happen because I identify the steps that I need to take, and then take them.

When it comes to our ultimate destination, however, there is no elaborate plan required. This may seem surprising, for our experience tells us that longer trips require longer directions. More miles mean more steps. Yet that paradigm assumes that the journey depends upon things we do. But perhaps this journey does not.

In fact, the way to our ultimate destination is simple and straightforward. We do not need to memorize multiple directions or recall a series of turns. For the way is not an itinerary, it's a person. And according to our text, to know him is to know the way.

Knowing the Way

Our present world is composed of many different peoples and cultures, featuring a broad assortment of world religions. Within that context, Jesus' claim to be "the way, the truth, the life" (John 14:6), as well as the only way to the Father, may seem exclusive, perhaps even prohibitive. But it only seems so when we lose sight of the big picture.

Just as a map features boundaries and borders that a bird does not see when it flies overhead, I believe that God does not see the world as we do. I don't think God views all of the artificial and temporary boundaries of "religions" that seem so real and important to us. Rather, when looking at the beloved world (John 3:16), God saw all of us together as a lost human race. And hopelessly lost, at that, apart from God's own gracious intervention.

Jesus is that gracious intervention by God. Indeed, Jesus is no less than a personal intervention by God's own self. And when we recognize that, then we begin to understand just how open and inclusive God's plan for salvation is.

We misunderstand Jesus if we think of him as just a man making competing claims against other men, whether philosophers, teachers, or founders of religions. No, for Jesus is God incarnate saying, "Here I am!" This is the astonishing truth of the good news found in declarations like these: "Whoever has seen me has seen the Father" (14:9); "the Father and I are one" (10:30); "the Word was with God, and the Word was God" (1:1).

We must not underestimate what is at stake here. The world perceives the issue as a contrast between religious truth claims, or different philosophies vying against one another. The gospel message, however, is that the God who made the whole world came into the world and provided salvation for that lost world by means of Godself.

When Jesus says that no one comes to the Father but through him, therefore, he is not saying something narrow and sectarian. He is not meaning to exclude whole regions of the world that have grown up under the influence of some other teaching. Rather, he is saying something that is *universally inviting*.

We saw this same principle at work when we explored Jesus' statement that he is the resurrection (11:25). We need not look for life's answers in events or plans, in dogmas or directions. All that we need is found in a person. And to know the person is to know the way.

SHARING THE SCRIPTURE

Preparing Our Hearts

Explore this week's devotional reading, found in Matthew 7:13-20. In verses 13-14 Jesus discusses two roads. The way of discipleship leads to life, but the other way leads to death. We can choose which path we will follow. Moreover, as we see in verses 15-20, people are known by their fruits. Those who choose the way of discipleship bear good fruit. Which way have you chosen: the way of the world or the alternative way that leads to life? Give examples of the kind of fruit you are bearing.

Pray that you and the adult learners will be ever mindful of the choices you make, recognizing that one way leads away from God and the other way toward God.

Preparing Our Minds

Study the background Scripture and the lesson Scripture, both of which are from John 14:1-14. When you are looking for direction in life, how can you know which way to go?

Write on newsprint:

❑ information for next week's lesson, found under "Continue the Journey."
❑ activities for further spiritual growth in "Continue the Journey."

Locate a downloadable picture of the labyrinth in Chartres Cathedral at http://zdi1.zd-cms.com/cms/res/files /382/ChartresLabyrinth.pdf. Print a copy for each class member, or ask a class member to do that during the week.

LEADING THE CLASS

(1) Gather to Learn

❖ Welcome the class members and introduce any guests.

❖ Pray that the students will make new discoveries about how Jesus is the way to God.

❖ Distribute copies of the paper labyrinth you have found. Explain the following: **Although labyrinths predated Christianity, Christians have used them for centuries as a way of making a symbolic journey or pilgrimage to God. Unlike a maze, the labyrinth has one way in and one way out. The route may look complicated, but it is impossible to get lost if travelers stay on the path. Entering the labyrinth and tracing the route to the center provides time to release one's burdens and open the heart. Being in the center rosette gives the pilgrim time to rest and commune with God in prayer and meditation. Retracing one's steps to return to the entrance provides time to process any directions or teachings God has given.** Help the adults to encounter the labyrinth by tracing the route with their fingers or pencils.

❖ Discuss these questions:

(1) What surprised you about working with a labyrinth?

(2) Did you find any new directions for your life? (Students need not reveal what these directions are, but do challenge them to follow up and try to get on these new paths.)

❖ Read aloud today's focus statement: **People always try to find direction in their lives. How can we know which way to go? Jesus proclaimed that he was the way people would come to God because he was in God and God was in him.**

(2) Explore How Jesus Is "the Way" to God

❖ Choose one volunteer to read John 14:1-7 and another to read verses 8-14.

❖ Invite the students to state the main message of this passage in their own words.

❖ Post a sheet of newsprint. Encourage the class to identify the questions or concerns raised by the disciples in this passage. Suggest that the students think of other questions or concerns they might have had if they had been present. List all of these ideas. Use information from Understanding the Scripture to help clarify information. Also point out that just as Nicodemus and the Samaritan woman misunderstood Jesus' metaphorical speech, so too did Thomas. The disciple was hearing the word "way" in terms of geography, but Jesus was using the term to refer to the works that he did that revealed who he was in relation to God.

❖ Compare this "I am" saying to those in chapter 10 where Jesus called himself the "gate" and the "shepherd." Through both the "gate" and the "way" one is able to gain access to life with God. Similarly, both the shepherd and Jesus embody the life that one leads in God's presence.

❖ Conclude by reading "Knowing the Way" from Interpreting the Scripture.

(3) Claim Life Purpose and Set Direction

❖ Distribute paper and pencils. Challenge the students to sketch maps of their lives. They may start with straight lines and show intersections along the way where they have made decisive turns that have set them on a particular course. They may wish to label these "roads," though they will not be asked to share them with anyone.

❖ Read "Which Way Are You Going?" from Interpreting the Scripture. Challenge the class to review their maps to see if they are "on course" or have somehow lost their way. Provide a few moments for silent reflection so that the adults can think about the way they need to be going and then either continue along the way or reset their course.

❖ Bring the group together and suggest that the students think about their life purposes. Why are they here? Recognize that some adults will not have given much thought to this question, so do not press them. Prompt the adults to claim their purposes and to compare it to the maps of where they have been going throughout their lives. Challenge them to make changes, even U-turns, so that their directions and the purposes God has for them are in tandem.

(4) Make a Commitment to Follow the Way of Jesus

❖ Recommend that the adults page through their text for this quarter, any notes they have made, and their Bibles to answer this question: **What have you learned about the way of Jesus?** After providing a few minutes for the students to do this review, call on volunteers to answer the question.

❖ Lead the class in this commitment by Saint Richard of Chichester (1197–1253). Read a line and ask the class to echo what you have said. The words will be familiar to some, since they were adapted for the musical *Godspell* and became a hit song titled "Day by Day."

> O most merciful Redeemer, Friend,
>   and Brother,
> May I know thee more clearly,
> Love thee more dearly,
> And follow thee more nearly:
> For ever and ever.

(5) Continue the Journey

❖ Pray that the adults will set their compasses to follow Jesus this week.

❖ Read aloud this preparation for next week's lesson. You may also want to post it on newsprint for the students to copy.

- ■ **Title: Rules for Just Living**
- ■ **Background Scripture: Exodus 22:1–23:9**
- ■ **Lesson Scripture: Exodus 23:1-9**
- ■ **Focus of the Lesson: Everyone desires and deserves justice. How do we act justly toward friend and foe? By treating everyone the same, we reflect the justice of God.**

❖ Challenge the students to complete one or more of these activities for further spiritual growth related to this week's session. Post this information on newsprint for the students to copy.

(1) Review the "I am" statements we have studied this quarter: "I am the bread of life," "the gate," "the good shepherd," "the resurrection and the life," and "the way, the truth, and the life." Reflect on what these sayings teach you about the nature and mission of Jesus. Write insights in your spiritual journal.

(2) Ponder John 14:12-13. How is the community of faith doing "greater works" than Jesus performed? If you believe the church is not doing "greater works," why do you think that is the case? What can be done to bring about change?

(3) Do some interior "housecleaning." If your actions and attitudes do not square with the "way" Jesus revealed, pray that God will help you to change. Be open to that change and do all in your power to make it happen.

❖ Sing or read aloud "Come, My Way, My Truth, My Life."

❖ Conclude today's session by leading the class in this benediction: **Go forth rejoicing that God, out of infinite love for the world, gave us Jesus, through whom we have eternal life.**

FOURTH QUARTER
God Calls for Justice

JUNE 3, 2012–AUGUST 26, 2012

The final quarter for the 2011–2012 year surveys the Old Testament by focusing on the theme of justice. As we will discover, justice relates to God's ongoing relationship with Israel and all peoples of the earth. God's justice embraces righteousness and peace. Moreover, God expects those who rule to care for people as a good shepherd faithfully tends a flock.

The four sessions of Unit 1, "Justice Defined," explore the basic teachings of the law as it is set forth in Exodus, Leviticus, and Deuteronomy. The quarter begins on June 3 with an examination of "Rules for Just Living" as found in Exodus 22:1–23:9, which is part of "the Book of the Covenant." We turn to Leviticus 19:9-18, 33-37 on June 10 to learn about "Living as God's Just People," that is, as people who reflect the holy nature of God. Leviticus 25:8-55, which we will study on June 17, teaches us how to "Celebrate Jubilee" and the new beginning it represents. "The Heart of the Law," which entails walking, serving, loving, and obeying God, is the focus of our lesson from Deuteronomy 10:1-22 and 16:18-20 on June 24.

Unit 2, "Justice Enacted," looks at the justice of God as it is enacted through four of Israel's leaders: Samuel, David, Solomon, and Jehoshaphat. In the session for July 1, "Samuel Administers Justice" from 1 Samuel 7:3-17, the judge calls people to turn to God, who will deliver them. The last words of David, which we will study on July 8 as we read 2 Samuel 22:1–23:7 and 1 Chronicles 18:14, demonstrate that "David Embodies God's Justice." On July 15 we explore 1 Kings 3 and 2 Chronicles 9:8 to hear a dispute between two mothers that "Solomon Judges with Wisdom and Justice." We explore the topic of restorative justice on July 22 as we read in 2 Kings 4:1-37 and 8:1-6 how "A King Acts on a Widow's Behalf." According to our text for July 29 from 2 Chronicles 18:28–19:11, "Jehoshaphat Makes Judicial Reforms" and calls the people back to God.

Unit 3, "Justice Promised," explores assurances of God's justice as found in Psalm 146 and the prophets Isaiah, Jeremiah, and Ezekiel. Exodus 21–23 and Isaiah 58 form the backdrop for our study of Psalm 146:1-10, which as we will learn on August 5, offers "Praise for God's Justice." On August 12 we turn to the beloved words of Isaiah 9:1-7, in which "God Promised a Righteous Lord" who was "a son given to us" (9:6). "God Promised a Righteous Branch," the session for August 19 from Jeremiah 23:1-6 and 33:14-18, examines the prophecy of a just leader who will restore the throne of David. The quarter ends on August 26 with "God Promised to Be with Us," a lesson from Ezekiel 34 that assures the people that one day God will set up a good and just shepherd to replace the self-serving ones who had been oppressively leading the people.

MEET OUR WRITER

THE REVEREND JANICE CATRON

Janice Catron is a Christian educator and ordained minister in the Presbyterian Church (USA), currently serving at John Knox Presbyterian Church in Louisville, Kentucky. Prior to moving to this congregation, she served on the national staff of the Presbyterian Church (USA) for fourteen years in various positions related to education and publication. In conjunction with her publishing house work, Rev. Catron was a member of the Committee of the Uniform Series. She also taught as adjunct faculty at Louisville Presbyterian Theological Seminary in the area of Hebrew Bible.

A native of Mississippi, Rev. Catron received her B.S. from Millsaps College, M.A. from Emory University, and M.Div. from Louisville Presbyterian Theological Seminary, and did her doctoral work at the University of Chicago. In addition to writing for *The New International Lesson Annual*, Janice is the author of *Job: Faith Remains When Understanding Fails* and *God's Vision, Our Calling: Hope and Responsibility in the Christian Life*.

Janice and her husband, Gordon Berg, live in Louisville, where he provides information technology support for a nonprofit educational and counseling facility for emotionally challenged teenage girls. When not working, Janice and Gordon enjoy watching movies together, playing on the computer, and spoiling their cat.

THE BIG PICTURE: ENCOUNTERING GOD'S CALL FOR JUSTICE

The lessons for this quarter come from several books in the Hebrew Bible (our Old Testament), and they include some texts that you probably do not read often. The basic idea in these passages will feel very familiar though. Each one addresses the theme of "justice" in some way, and each affirms the same moral and ethical concerns that we see in Jesus' teachings. Indeed, it is likely that Jesus had many of these texts in mind when he spoke out on behalf of helpless people in his own society. After all, the Hebrew Bible was Jesus' Scripture.

Despite the common theme, however, the texts for this quarter also have some significant differences. They come from a variety of authors and historical settings, so we will have to consider changes in context from time to time. It is interesting to note how the theme of God's steadfast love and abiding justice runs true throughout the ages, regardless of what else may be happening in the world.

The Graciousness of God's Justice

What do you think of when you hear the word "justice"? Perhaps the word "fairness" comes to mind, or the image of blindfolded "Justice" holding her perfectly balanced scales. Perhaps you jump to thoughts of defense of the innocent or punishment for the guilty. Odds are, however, that your initial response falls short of what our Scriptures mean by the term.

In our modern society, justice most often refers both to the process supported by our legal system and also to a broader social and philosophical concept that includes all ethical behavior. While this was also true for the biblical writers, they added a dimension that we tend to overlook outside of Bible studies and mission-based conversations. Within our Scriptures, justice is always rooted in our covenant relationship with God and the love that flourishes there.

The Scripture passages for this quarter bring this home quite powerfully. Here we will encounter laws that, from one perspective, are part of a mundane social justice system. Through the theological lens of Scripture, however, these laws are always set in the context of God's divine justice—a justice that stems from love, grace, and compassion and that is intended for all people regardless of their nationality, race, or status in society. Part of the call to covenant living is the call to live out God's justice as individuals and as a community.

The very language of the Bible makes this clear. There are many words that Scripture associates with justice, but two stand out in the Old Testament. The first is "righteousness," which is often paired with "justice" in the prophetic writings and the Psalms. In Hebrew, the root of this word means "straight" or "true." It's an image that would have resonated with a carpenter like Jesus, because it carries the sense of something (or, in our case, someone) being shaped and crafted to fit perfectly within an intended space. Artists may think instead of intentional lines or musicians of true notes, while those of us who type may think of justified paragraphs. On a literal level, all these examples convey the basic meaning of the word.

In Hebrew culture and religion, however, righteousness came to mean much more as an ethical and theological concept. Out of its root, the word grew to include a sense of being right—or, more important, being put right—with God. Because it also kept the sense of being "true" or "just" as defined above, the term even became synonymous with "having integrity."

The second word associated with justice in the Old Testament is "peace." Today this word usually is used as the opposite of war, thus carrying the basic sense of "an absence of conflict." The Hebrew term is far more comprehensive. The root of the word *shalom* is "safety," and this reflects the notion that we only feel at peace when we also feel safe in the core areas of life. Thus the term indicates the health, well-being, and prosperity both of individuals and of nations. In many prophetic writings it refers to conditions of economic and social justice for all members of the community. In some contexts it means "salvation." In the broadest sense of the word, though, "peace" refers to the contented state of being that comes when relationships are whole and unbroken, whether these relationships are between members of a family, groups in society, or entire nations. It most especially refers to the state of being that comes when covenant relationships are whole and unbroken—and that includes our relationship with God.

Righteousness and peace. Integrity and wholeness. Staying true to God's ways and seeking the well-being of everyone. These are the elements of justice that the Old Testament holds up as essential for the community of faith in every age.

The Gift of God's Law

Because so many of the Scripture passages this quarter include legal codes and prophetic injunctions, it might be helpful to remember the way these texts were viewed in biblical times. All of these passages could be considered commandments or ordinances dictated by God and demanding obedience, and at a fundamental level this holds some truth. According to the Bible, however, we come closer to God's reality when we see these writings as *teachings* or *instructions*. Indeed, this is the real meaning of the Hebrew word torah, which English Bibles tend to translate as "law."

In the Hebrew mind-set, which we see not only in the Old Testament but also in Jesus' teachings as well, Torah is a gift from God, a guide given to humanity to point us toward attitudes and actions that help create the realm of God here on earth. Compliance is mandatory only in the sense that we cannot reap the benefit of this lifestyle unless we choose to embrace it and embody it faithfully. So, throughout these lessons, whenever you see the word "law" think of this in the context of *God's teaching* and see if that makes a difference for your understanding of what the text has to say.

Looking Ahead to This Quarter

The biblical writers maintain that the only way to achieve God's justice is to follow these instructions we have been given regarding how to treat one another. This idea is fleshed out in different ways by the quarter's three units.

Unit 1, "Justice Defined," draws on texts from the Pentateuch (the first five books of the Bible) to set *justice* in the context of God's overall call to act with love and compassion. The four lessons all build on the theological basis of God's sovereign rule. In other words, God owns all there is, even people, so God has the right to say how folk are to be treated. Equally important, God loves and cares for all. The call of the faith community is to care for others as God has cared for us—and to extend this care to those who would otherwise be outside society's notice. In short, the first four lessons show that the goal of divine justice is to enable all people to share in the well-being and wholeness that God intends for everyone.

The five lessons of Unit 2, "Justice Enacted," build on this base by looking at how God's law was supported by key leaders from a little later in the community's history: the judge Samuel, King David, King Solomon, the prophet Elisha, an unnamed king, and King Jehoshaphat. Their stories are told in passages from the Hebrew histories, which include

1–2 Samuel, 1–2 Kings, and 1–2 Chronicles. From the examples lifted up in the texts, we see that true justice carries aspects of deliverance, righteousness, wisdom, compassion, and integrity.

Finally, Unit 3, "Justice Promised," presents four lessons that address the eternal and cosmic elements of God's justice. The selected writings from Psalms and the Prophets reassure us that this gift of justice is rooted in God's eternal reign and that it will be established by the Prince of Peace, our Good Shepherd, who will establish a new covenant with us. In the realm to come, justice will finally be achieved as God has desired all along.

The Theological Grid

The Scripture texts for Unit 3 come from a variety of sources, each with its own background and setting. They share a common theme, but not always a common theology. In contrast, 90 percent of the passages for the first two units have been shaped by a strong editorial hand with a definite theological perspective. Because the core of this thought is found in the Book of Deuteronomy, scholars refer to the set of books from Deuteronomy through 2 Kings as the Deuteronomistic History. Its overall purpose is the theological explanation of why in 587 B.C. Jerusalem was destroyed and Judah came to an end as a nation.

It is common in times of crisis to look back to one's roots for perspective. It is so easy to be changed gradually by the environment in which we are living and not to know that change has taken place. We take for granted that we are living by the things that we confess with our lips, until we review the implications of our faith and discover how far we have drifted from them. The Deuteronomists felt this had happened to the Hebrew people, and they wanted to set the record straight.

Accordingly, their writings emphasize the covenant made at Sinai and the marvelous saving acts of Yahweh. As the Deuteronomistic Historians saw it, it was the obligation of a thankful people to serve their covenant Lord in response to these gracious deeds. The decisive period of the past for them, counter to the thought of other biblical historians, was not the golden age of David's rule but the time of the Exodus. That was when Yahweh had claimed Israel as a special people by great signs and wonders, by terrors and trials and wars, by a mighty hand and an outstretched arm.

Looking back over the people's entire history, the Deuteronomists interpreted the many disasters of military defeat and subjugation to enemies as punishment from God. In their view, because Israel committed idolatry and refused to follow the laws of God that would lead to a just society, the Lord "gave them over to plunderers" and "sold them into the power of their enemies" (Judges 2:14). The victories realized during the original entry into the land would be no more. God would not continue to protect the Hebrew people, because they refused to be loyal (2:20-23). Indeed, the fall of Jerusalem and Judah to Babylon in 587 B.C. was interpreted as God's punishment for these sins (2 Kings 23:26-27).

At one level this theology is helpful. It was neither the weakness nor the injustice of God that had brought about Israel's distress. The people were responsible for their difficulties because they had rebelled against God. By breaking the commandments and going after other gods, Israel was deservedly punished.

The problem comes if this idea is applied as an explanation for every disaster. Some defeats in war are the result of human bungling rather than divine intervention. On the other side of the coin, just because Hitler's troops successfully invaded Europe did not mean that he was God's servant or that Europe was being justly punished. Every difficulty in life cannot and should not be explained as divine retribution. A person's blindness is explained quite differently by Jesus, for example (John 9:1-3). Much caution must be exercised or this theological principle may become a harmful lie.

The "History" of the Histories

When we as modern students pick up a contemporary history textbook—the history of World War II, for example—we tend to expect to find an objective record of the events of that particular period. We expect the facts, with any interpretation presented separately and covered with proper warning. Yet even historians rarely achieve pure objectivity. Moreover, not every historian even tries to be completely objective. They may wish to present the history of World War II from the Canadian point of view or the Italian peasant's point of view. A specific scholar may write one history that traces the impact of Roman Catholicism on events leading to World War II, then later, the same scholar might write another history exploring the impact of antireligious Marxist philosophy on German society in the same period.

Every historical book is presented from a particular point of view. In the case of the biblical writers, they had a definite theological perspective. Their purpose was to write a sacred history, providing specific answers to questions of tremendous importance to the people to whom the writings were addressed: Who are we? What is the meaning of our past? Why have we suffered defeat and deportation? Do we have any future? These are the questions addressed by some of the biblical writers (and editors). Some of these are our questions too.

The Message for Us

When we consider the type of justice that God desires and then we look at the world as it is, we see that the church still has a lot to do. We remember what Jesus said of himself in Nazareth, as he read a passage from Isaiah 61:1-2 that sounds a lot like the texts for this quarter:

"The Spirit of the Lord is upon me,
    because he has anointed me
        to bring good news to the poor.
He has sent me to proclaim release to the captives
    and recovery of sight to the blind,
        to let the oppressed go free,
to proclaim the year of the Lord's favor." (Luke 4:18-19)

We also remember that Jesus told a story centered on acts of compassionate justice such as we find in the law—acts that include feeding the hungry, giving drink to the thirsty, welcoming the stranger, clothing the naked, caring for the sick, and visiting those in prison (Matthew 25:31-46). Jesus' tie to these folk is so complete that he indicates any act of kindness or justice shown to "the least of these" (25:45) is shown to him as well.

In light of these passages, we see that the church gives its best witness to Christ and to God's call for justice when it demonstrates compassion for the oppressed, the brokenhearted, captives, prisoners, and all who mourn. This too the church is doing all over the world. Mission reports are full of stories of Christian hospitals, relief programs, schools, and projects for economic development.

While we are never told of an occasion in which the Hebrew people actually enacted God's laws as they should have—nor the church, either, for that matter—the goal of equality, freedom, and justice was never quite forgotten. On the liberty bell in Philadelphia is inscribed a verse from the Year of Jubilee: "Proclaim liberty throughout all the land unto all the inhabitants thereof" (Leviticus 25:10 KJV). The goal of Christians everywhere is to bear witness to the liberating and just realm of God, in which God's will is done on earth as it is in heaven. All over the world, that is what the church is doing. Thanks be to God!

CLOSE-UP: GOD'S JUSTICE MAKES IT RIGHT

Many people think of justice in terms of Lady Justice—a blindfolded woman holding a scale in one hand (generally, her left) and a sword in the other. The familiar pictures and statues date back to a goddess of the Roman Empire, Justitia. In the scales, she measures the weight or strength of each side of a legal case. One side of the double-edged sword symbolizes reason; the other side, justice. Lady Justice may use her sword for or against either the plaintiff or defendant. First added on a statue created in 1543 in Berne, Switzerland, the blindfold reminds us that justice is always to be fair and impartial.

But is it? Experience often tells us otherwise. Even fair-minded jurors can make tragic mistakes with irreversible consequences. Innocent people have been wrongly imprisoned—even executed. Thanks to advances in technology, DNA tests are more routinely used to help free innocent persons who have been unjustly convicted. "Justice" in our legal system refers to determining guilt or innocence and then meting out punishment to fit the crime. This type of "retributive" justice is considered acceptable because it provides some measure of emotional satisfaction to the victim or victim's family.

The Bible, however, is much more concerned with another kind of justice, one that is rooted in the very nature of God and measured by faithfulness to God's covenant. Such justice cares deeply about relationships, about making things as they should be. This type of justice is illustrated in the phrase "make it right," which is used by Mike Holmes, a meticulous contractor who appears on television to help families whose homes have been damaged by unscrupulous or incompetent builders.

"Making it right" in God's vocabulary has to do with right relationships, both between humans and God and among all humans. God's covenant demands such right relationships. As we discover in this quarter's lessons, those who violate God's law are required to "make it right" by restoring to the victim that which has been taken or damaged. God's justice requires that all people be treated fairly and impartially. Yet the Bible repeatedly identifies groups of powerless people—the widow, the orphan, the poor, the stranger in the land—who need special care because they are on the margins of society. These groups are named not only in the Old Testament but also in the New. In the Gospel of Luke, for example, we find Jesus quoting the prophet Isaiah as he announces his own mission in Luke 4:18-20. Jesus himself will make things right for the poor, the captives, the blind, the oppressed, and he will proclaim Jubilee so that all might have a fresh start. Although Jesus has a special concern for the poor, he is truly the Savior of all. His life, death, and resurrection focus on freeing all who call upon his name. He can make it right (justified) between God and us. Instead of receiving the punishment we are due, we are graciously restored through Christ to a relationship with the God of peace, righteousness, and justice.

FAITH IN ACTION: PRACTICING JUSTICE

Throughout this quarter we are exploring God's justice and how that is to be practiced. Recall that this justice is seen in God's nature and action, embodies the love of God and love of neighbor described in the covenant, and is the yardstick that the prophets used to call people back to faithfulness to God's living. God's justice clearly continues beyond the scope of our Old Testament study as it is enacted in Jesus. He not only taught about justice but modeled it, particularly as he identified with those on the lowest rungs of the social ladder. Moving beyond the days of the Bible, we too are called to love God and love neighbor as part and parcel of faithful discipleship.

Post the following cases on newsprint or read them aloud. Form groups so that the adults may discuss how these cases might relate to people in their own community.

Case 1: Those without adequate shelter

Who are the homeless in your community? While these folks are often stereotyped as "lazy," "shiftless," or "unwilling to work," an estimated 20 to 25 percent of homeless people suffer from some form of mental illness. Approximately 33 percent of homeless adults are veterans who have served in the United States military. Precise numbers are difficult to determine, but many other people are at risk for homelessness because of overcrowded conditions, abuse within the home, job loss, impending foreclosure, or personal financial collapse. Try to determine how many people in your community are homeless. How many shelter beds does your community offer? When are these available? Who is eligible to receive one? How do laws treat the homeless? Where do they spend their days? What can your church do to help these people experience God's justice?

Case 2: Those without adequate food

Who are the hungry in your community, those who lack food one or more days per month? A report released by the Food Research and Action Center in 2010 showed that, according to data collected by Gallup through 2009 from more than 530,000 respondents, "food hardship" is a pervasive problem across the United States. At the end of 2009, approximately 18.5 percent of people experienced food hardship. In homes with children, that figure rose to 24.1 percent. Although some will be able to qualify for the Supplemental Nutrition Assistance Program (formerly food stamps), others earn just a little too much to get this assistance. Where are the soup kitchens in your community? Where are the food pantries? How often can people go to these facilities to receive help? What can your church do to help these people experience God's justice?

Challenge the class members to choose at least one group that is suffering injustice in their community. Suggest that they explore church programs, nonprofit agencies, and legislation to see how the community is assisting those who cry out for justice. Some assistance will be short-term—to give the homeless a safe place to sleep and the hungry a meal. Other assistance must be long-term—to change attitudes and public policies that support conditions in which homelessness and hunger are allowed to exist. God's justice demands that you do whatever you can to "make it right."

UNIT 1: JUSTICE DEFINED
RULES FOR JUST LIVING

PREVIEWING THE LESSON

Lesson Scripture: Exodus 23:1-9
Background Scripture: Exodus 22:1–23:9
Key Verse: Exodus 23:2

Focus of the Lesson:
Everyone desires and deserves justice. How do we act justly toward friend and foe? By treating everyone the same, we reflect the justice of God.

Goals for the Learners:
(1) to explain ways justice was to be executed in the biblical community.
(2) to describe how it feels to be treated unjustly.
(3) to commit to living out the biblical commands for justice.

Pronunciation Guide:
Hammurabi (ham uh rah′ bee)
Torah (toh′ ruh)

Supplies:
Bibles, newsprint and marker, paper and pencils, hymnals, clay

---

READING THE SCRIPTURE

NRSV
Exodus 23:1-9

¹You shall not spread a false report. You shall not join hands with the wicked to act as a malicious witness. **²You shall not follow a majority in wrongdoing;** when you bear witness in a lawsuit, **you shall not side with the majority so as to pervert justice;** ³nor shall you be partial to the poor in a lawsuit.

⁴When you come upon your enemy's ox

NIV
Exodus 23:1-9

¹"Do not spread false reports. Do not help a wicked man by being a malicious witness.

²"**Do not follow the crowd in doing wrong.** When you give testimony in a lawsuit, **do not pervert justice by siding with the crowd,** ³and do not show favoritism to a poor man in his lawsuit.

⁴"If you come across your enemy's ox or donkey wandering off, be sure to take it

or donkey going astray, you shall bring it back.

⁵When you see the donkey of one who hates you lying under its burden and you would hold back from setting it free, you must help to set it free.

⁶You shall not pervert the justice due to your poor in their lawsuits. ⁷Keep far from a false charge, and do not kill the innocent and those in the right, for I will not acquit the guilty. ⁸You shall take no bribe, for a bribe blinds the officials, and subverts the cause of those who are in the right.

⁹You shall not oppress a resident alien; you know the heart of an alien, for you were aliens in the land of Egypt.

back to him. ⁵If you see the donkey of someone who hates you fallen down under its load, do not leave it there; be sure you help him with it.

⁶"Do not deny justice to your poor people in their lawsuits. ⁷Have nothing to do with a false charge and do not put an innocent or honest person to death, for I will not acquit the guilty.

⁸"Do not accept a bribe, for a bribe blinds those who see and twists the words of the righteous.

⁹"Do not oppress an alien; you yourselves know how it feels to be aliens, because you were aliens in Egypt.

UNDERSTANDING THE SCRIPTURE

Introduction. The compendium of laws that constitute this section of Exodus immediately follows the Ten Commandments (Exodus 20:1-21). It is usually referred to as the Covenant Code or the Book of the Covenant (based on the reference in 24:7). The purpose of these verses is to expound on the Decalogue by applying its ten general commands to various specific cases and circumstances within the daily life of the Israelite community.

Exodus 22:1-15. From the perspective of an ancient agrarian community, livestock and land were of incalculable value. A family's livelihood depended on oxen to pull plows, sheep to provide wool and meat, donkeys to haul and transport, and fertile fields and vineyards to grow produce for both eating and trading. Domesticated animals and property were necessary for survival. Consequently, stealing an ox or destroying a field was considered a serious crime. The penalties for such crimes were equally serious. Note that in the case of stolen livestock, the concern of the law is not punishing the thief but restoring the lost property to its owner. The theme of all the

sanctions in this section is restitution, not retribution.

Exodus 22:16-17. Once again, the point of the law here is to provide for restitution. What is at stake in this case, though, is not an animal but a human being—not a man's ox but his daughter. While we might want the Bible to pay some attention to the victim of the crime in this case, we must acknowledge the patriarchal society out of which the law comes. Unmarried female children were key to a family's future. Daughters were valuable assets. Consequently, the violation of a daughter's virginity was foremost an offense against her father. Like the previous laws, this one is concerned chiefly with compensating a property owner's loss. The bride-price (perhaps 50 shekels, as noted in Deuteronomy 22:29) seems designed to accomplish two goals: to restore the family honor, and if the father does not refuse to accept the perpetrator, to clear the way for a man to receive the violated woman as his wife, thus restoring some measure of order to the community.

Exodus 22:18-20. These three verses seem connected only by the severity of the penalty prescribed: death. On closer study, though, this set of laws has assumptions about God at its root. Yahweh is Creator. Yahweh's power is inviolable. Israel's proper relationship to Yahweh includes honoring how the Creator has intended the world to operate. Sorcery is an affront to God's sovereignty because it purports to usurp God's prerogative of power.

Anyone who would play God, as it were, is a threat to God and God's creation. Likewise, anyone who subverts the created order by engaging in sexual relations with an animal distorts God's intentions for human and beast alike, and undermines the foundation of communal life.

Finally, the ultimate idolatrous act—sacrificing to any god but Yahweh—receives the ultimate penalty. The Hebrew term rendered into English as "devoted to destruction" (22:20) refers to the practice described in Deuteronomy 13:12-17 of treating an idolatrous town as "a whole burnt offering to the LORD" (13:16). The punishment is so severe because worship of other gods was considered a dire threat to Israel's relationship to Yahweh and to Israel's acknowledgement of Yahweh's sovereignty.

Exodus 22:21-24. In these verses, the experience of the Exodus is the impetus for treating both resident aliens (those with no legal rights of citizenship in the community) and the socially marginalized (those without the protection of a male head of household) with the same compassion Yahweh showed the Hebrew slaves in Egypt. The consequences of mistreating the widow or the orphan are starkly ironic: The phrase in verse 24, "I will kill you with the sword," means Israel's men will fall in battle, thus leaving their children and wives fatherless, widowed, and vulnerable, experiencing for themselves the struggle of marginalization and the need for compassion.

Exodus 22:25-27. The laws in these verses seem aimed at minimizing the hardships of the poor. Torah puts great emphasis on maintaining social harmony within the Israelite community. The case of the cloak taken in pawn again promotes Yahweh's compassion for those who, at the edge of existence, especially within Israel, cry out for help. The phrasing of the text recalls the Hebrews' plight and God's response in the Exodus event. Essentially, the law's aim is to prioritize concern for the well-being of the community over concern for the viability of the economy.

Exodus 22:28-31. The word in verse 28 translated as "revile" in the NRSV and "blaspheme" in the NIV designates speaking in a way that denies authority and power to God. To curse a temporal leader is to accomplish much the same thing. In both cases, such speech is not constructive but deliberately destructive. There is no place among God's people for that type of trash talk.

The following verses (22:29-31) provide confirmation of God's authority in concrete ways: making required offerings of first fruits, consecrating firstborn sons and livestock to the Lord (see Exodus 13:1-2), and following clean slaughtering protocols (see Deuteronomy 14:21). God's people must acknowledge God's sovereignty and utter holiness. Why? Because God has chosen them to be a holy people.

Exodus 23:1-9. It has been said before, but it bears repeating here: The memory of the Exodus event is what drives the ethical concerns of Torah. Particularly in these verses, justice for all is mandated precisely because once upon a time the people themselves were "aliens in the land of Egypt" (23:9). Whether the venue is a court of law or the back forty of someone's field, the Israelite community was commanded to act righteously and to tell the truth. For a community to thrive and survive, those with power or possessions must not take advantage of the powerless or possessionless. Everyone must be treated fairly. If the poor are in the wrong, even they are not to be given preferential treatment. Moreover, justice cannot be subject to the whims of personality of friendship. An enemy at risk of losing an ox or a donkey—representative of livelihood and survival—deserves to be treated like a friend. For the people called Israel, everyone is a neighbor.

INTERPRETING THE SCRIPTURE

Called to Remember

Making modern application of an ancient legal text like Torah is tricky. Part of the challenge is that the agrarian culture of a bygone age and the technologically driven culture of a postindustrial age present such different contexts for reading passages like those in Exodus 22–23. Today's owners of automobiles and shopper rewards cards find it difficult to take seriously property disputes involving sheep and oxen; yet advocating for justice among the poor and disenfranchised generates immediate attention. When readers today approach the laws in Exodus, the tendency is to read past the quaint ones that involve livestock, to reject outright those that treat rape as a property violation, and to embrace those that deal positively with the poor. Such selective interpretation, though, falls short of a fair appreciation of these Torah texts.

Whether in the broad strokes of the Decalogue or in the specific nuances of case law, Torah's aim was to establish precise boundaries within which the covenant community could order its daily living. The Israelites had been called to be "consecrated" to God (Exodus 22:31). As such, they needed boundaries to set them apart from those nations where people worshiped the rain and prayed to stones, where justice was something to be purchased, where disputes were settled by violence, and where those on the margins were left there to suffer. God had called Israel to be different. In fact, often, even in the law sections of Torah, Israel was reminded of its calling—or rather, Israel was *called to remember*, and out of that theological memory, to live accordingly.

We should also note, however, that much of the material in these verses bears a remarkable resemblance to some of the law codes and legal treatises of other ancient Near Eastern cultures. The Code of Hammurabi—a Babylonian legal text dating from about 1780 B.C.—is one example, and is especially noteworthy for containing a version of the "eye for an eye" principle of retributive justice found in Exodus 21:24-25. These parallels suggest a couple of things: First, Israel's law code is not only precept but also proclamation, testifying to the biblical notion that Yahweh is the Creator God, concerned about all creation, the covenant people as well as those peoples outside the covenant; and second, if Israel is to carry out its charge to bless other nations, it should order its communal life so as to be *distinctive* but *not detached* from those neighbors.

Yahweh Is Lord

Central to Israel's theological memory was the assurance that Yahweh was the Holy One who brought the Hebrew slaves out of bondage in Egypt and established a covenant relationship with them. Because God had acted on their behalf in the past, the laws by which the people of Israel lived were a reflection of the One in whom they trusted and had faith. A just God asked for just ways of ordering the contingencies of living together. That means justice for all of God's people and all of God's creation.

It is crucial to see how much the Exodus laws emphasize restitution. That emphasis clearly reflects the intention of Israel's God: restoring what has been lost, making all things right again, maintaining balance within the community. From the perspective of God—the God who created all things, the God who took great pains to convince the Egyptians to let the Hebrews go and, in the end, effected the people's escape and cared for them in the wilderness—everyone deserves a fair shake. That's why the law says even if your enemy's donkey needs help, you should get over your enmity for the sake of doing the right thing. That's why the law says you cannot show partiality to the poor in court, for in that case, pity is not the same as justice. Remember: Yahweh is Lord of all, friend or foe, and Yahweh desires justice for all, rich or poor.

You Were Aliens in the Land of Egypt

Another key component of Israel's theological memory was the story of Israel's beginning. Once upon a time, a band of Hebrews, enslaved to the powerful and oppressive Egyptians, cried out in their misery. Then God heard their cries and miraculously delivered them from their bondage, bringing them into a new land flowing with milk and honey. It is hard to overestimate the significance of the Exodus for Israel or the extent to which that single event defined the people's self-understanding. From the Bible's perspective, that understanding meant that the way the Israelites interacted with one another, as well as the way they lived among their non-Israelite neighbors, had to reflect the message of the Exodus.

Twice in the Exodus texts for this lesson the phrase "for you were aliens in the land of Egypt" appears (22:21; 23:9). In addition, the law states more than once that God will listen for those who cry for help. The point is that the people's memory of their own oppression should be the very impetus for their treatment of others. God's compassion for the suffering, the poor, the outcast, and the marginalized remains in effect—it did not end with God's deliverance of the Hebrews. In fact, those who benefited from

God's compassion in the past should be uniquely aware of the importance of extending it to others in the future. Of all people, says the law to Israel, "you know the heart of an alien" (23:9).

Still Called to Remember

God's covenant with Israel and Israel's memory of God's deliverance provide the shape of Torah laws as well as an integral component of the church's Scripture. Today, we read these particular Scriptures seeking to discern how God's "covenantal intention" for Israel (to borrow a phrase from Walter Brueggemann) can actually pertain to the shared life of Christian community.

I think about my church. When we made plans for our building, we intentionally set aside space for mattress storage, a shower stall, and a washer and dryer set. The ethical considerations that informed those plans were not made with our church members in mind; rather, they were made out of our commitment to providing regular hospitality to members of the homeless population in our community. The biblical stories of God welcoming and caring for the stranger (or the alien) were put into practice in the way we ordered our congregational life and in the way we made mundane decisions about our property usage.

Such decision making should be routine for God's people today. The Bible says we should not bear a false report, so how do we most certainly tell the truth? The Bible says we should not participate in mob rule at the expense of justice, so how do we stand against the crowd to advocate for what is right? The Bible says we should not oppress a resident alien, so how do we offer respect and neighborliness to those who are not part of us but who live among us in the world?

Remember: God first chose Israel. Remember: God first loved us.

SHARING THE SCRIPTURE

Preparing Our Hearts

Explore this week's devotional reading, found in Deuteronomy 32:1-7. This passage is part of a song that Moses recited to all of Israel. Moreover, it is a lawsuit that God is bringing against the people, who have turned away to worship other gods. Verse 4 highlights the faithfulness, uprightness, and justice of God, referred to as "father" in verse 6. In stark contrast, verse 5 berates the "degenerate children" who have been "perverse." If God were to bring a lawsuit against the contemporary church, what would be the charges against us?

Pray that you and the adult learners will give thanks for the justice of God and do your utmost to live according to that justice.

Preparing Our Minds

Study the background Scripture from Exodus 22:1–23:9 and the lesson Scripture from Exodus 23:1-9. Think about how we can act justly toward both friend and foe.

Write on newsprint:
❑ questions listed under "Explain Ways Justice Was to Be Executed in the Biblical Community."
❑ responsive reading for "Commit to Living Out the Biblical Commands for Justice."
❑ information for next week's lesson, found under "Continue the Journey."
❑ activities for further spiritual growth in "Continue the Journey."

LEADING THE CLASS

(1) Gather to Learn

❖ Welcome the class members and introduce any guests.
❖ Pray that the students will seek to know the biblical understanding of justice.

❖ Write on a sheet of newsprint *Justice is . . .* and invite the class members to give their own definitions. Here are two additional definitions for the group to consider:
- **Justice is nothing other than love working out its problems.** (Joseph Fletcher, 1905–1991)
- **Justice is truth in action.** (Benjamin Disraeli, 1804–1881)

❖ Encourage the adults to discuss which definition(s) fit best with their own understanding of justice.

❖ Read aloud today's focus statement: **Everyone desires and deserves justice. How do we act justly toward friend and foe? By treating everyone the same, we reflect the justice of God.**

(2) Explain Ways Justice Was to Be Executed in the Biblical Community

❖ Select, if possible, nine volunteers, each to read one verse from Exodus 23:1-9.

❖ Form several small groups. Assign each group two or three verses for study. Distribute paper and pencils. Post these questions on newsprint for discussion:
(1) **What is the purpose of this law?**
(2) **How would you restate this law in your own words?**
(3) **What contemporary examples might relate to this law?** (For example, our neighbor may not have a lost donkey, but she might have a lost dog that we could return to its home.)
(4) **How would this law bring greater justice both to the Hebrew people of Moses' day and to your own community?**

❖ Call on a spokesperson from each group to summarize the group's discussion.

❖ Wrap up this portion of the lesson by reading "Yahweh Is Lord" from Interpreting the Scripture. Think for a few moments about the concept of "restitution" by asking: **How might our understanding of justice, and the way justice is meted out, be different if we focused on restitution rather than retribution?**

(3) Describe How It Feels to Be Treated Unjustly

❖ Invite the adults to use one of the following ways to show how they feel when they have been treated unjustly. Give everyone the following three options, but ask only two or three students to perform at a time so that others may observe. Try to give everyone a turn.

- Use body language and facial expressions.
- Drum on a table or other wooden object. Use rhythm and volume to express yourself.
- Knead clay into a shape, or simply use kneading motions to convey your feelings.

❖ Prompt the group to discuss the kinds of emotions they have witnessed. For example, were people angry, fearful, withdrawn, ready to fight, accepting of the situation, resigned?

❖ Culminate this activity by discussing this question: **What do our own reactions to injustice teach us about the importance of living by God's commands for justice?**

(4) Commit to Living Out the Biblical Commands for Justice

❖ Read "Still Called to Remember" from Interpreting the Scripture.

❖ Discuss these two questions from the end of the reading:

(1) **The Bible says we should not participate in mob rule at the expense of justice, so how do we stand against the crowd to advocate for what is right?**

(2) **The Bible says we should not oppress a resident alien, so how do we offer respect and neighborliness to those who are not part of us but who live among us in the world?**

❖ Consider issues in your own community that cry out for biblical justice. Are there instances of bullying in the schools, people afraid to leave their homes due to drug dealers, or other instances where "mob mentality" is making life difficult for others? Are there immigrants who are not being treated fairly? Are the courts working fairly or turning aside from justice? Encourage the adults to tell brief stories of injustices that they have heard about or witnessed.

❖ Provide a few moments for silent meditation. Invite the adults to consider how they can become involved so as to ensure that all people are treated fairly.

❖ Conclude this portion by leading the adults in reading Micah 6:6-8 responsively as their personal commitment to live according to God's standards of justice. Unless each student has a copy of the NRSV, post this reading so that everyone will have the same words.

Left Side: **"With what shall I come before the LORD,**
   and bow myself before God on high?
Right Side: **Shall I come before him with burnt offerings,**
   with calves a year old?
Left Side: **Will the LORD be pleased with thousands of rams,**
   with ten thousand rivers of oil?
Right Side: **Shall I give my firstborn for my transgression,**
   the fruit of my body for the sin of my soul?"
All: **He has told you, O mortal, what is good;**
   and what does the LORD require of you
   but to do justice, and to love kindness,
   and to walk humbly with your God?

❖ **Option:** If you have access to *The United Methodist Hymnal*, consider using

"For Courage to Do Justice," found on page 456.

(5) Continue the Journey

❖ Pray that the adults will strive to live justly, according to the teachings of the Bible.

❖ Read aloud this preparation for next week's lesson. You may also want to post it on newsprint for the students to copy.

■ **Title: Living as God's Just People**
■ **Background Scripture: Leviticus 19:9-18, 33-37**
■ **Lesson Scripture: Leviticus 19:9-18, 33-37**
■ **Focus of the Lesson: People want to feel significant. How do we assure others that they are valued? We treat them with love, justice, and generosity.**

❖ Challenge the students to complete one or more of these activities for further spiritual growth related to this week's session. Post this information on newsprint for the students to copy.

(1) **Investigate injustice in your own community, particularly situations where an entire group of people is being treated unjustly. Work to end this injustice by talking with the people involved, enlisting help from your congregation, and calling legislators to enact laws that would have a positive impact on this situation.**
(2) **Pray for a person or group who suffers from injustice.**
(3) **Be aware of any injustice that you are committing against individuals or groups. Take action to change your own behavior.**

❖ Sing or read aloud "Where Cross the Crowded Ways of Life."

❖ Conclude today's session by leading the class in this benediction adapted from Deuteronomy 10:12-13, the key verses for June 24: **Go forth remembering that we are to fear the Lord our God, to walk in all his ways, to love God, to serve the Lord with all our heart and soul, and to keep God's commandments.**

UNIT 1: JUSTICE DEFINED
LIVING AS GOD'S JUST PEOPLE

PREVIEWING THE LESSON

Lesson Scripture: Leviticus 19:9-18, 33-37
Background Scripture: Leviticus 19:9-18, 33-37
Key Verse: Leviticus 19:34

Focus of the Lesson:
People want to feel significant. How do we assure others that they are valued? We treat them with love, justice, and generosity.

Goals for the Learners:
(1) to cite biblical guidelines that develop compassionate living.
(2) to reflect on situations in which they have been treated with compassion.
(3) to identify a community need and find a way to respond appropriately to it.

Pronunciation Guide:
ephah (ee' fuh)
hin (hin)

Supplies:
Bibles, newsprint and marker, paper and pencils, hymnals, art supplies for a collage

---

READING THE SCRIPTURE

NRSV
Leviticus 19:9-18, 33-37

⁹When you reap the harvest of your land, you shall not reap to the very edges of your field, or gather the gleanings of your harvest. ¹⁰You shall not strip your vineyard bare, or gather the fallen grapes of your vineyard; you shall leave them for the poor and the alien: I am the LORD your God.

¹¹You shall not steal; you shall not deal falsely; and you shall not lie to one another.

NIV
Leviticus 19:9-18, 33-37

⁹" 'When you reap the harvest of your land, do not reap to the very edges of your field or gather the gleanings of your harvest. ¹⁰Do not go over your vineyard a second time or pick up the grapes that have fallen. Leave them for the poor and the alien. I am the LORD your God.

¹¹" 'Do not steal.

" 'Do not lie.

¹²And you shall not swear falsely by my name, profaning the name of your God: I am the LORD.

¹³You shall not defraud your neighbor; you shall not steal; and you shall not keep for yourself the wages of a laborer until morning. ¹⁴You shall not revile the deaf or put a stumbling block before the blind; you shall fear your God: I am the LORD.

¹⁵You shall not render an unjust judgment; you shall not be partial to the poor or defer to the great: with justice you shall judge your neighbor. ¹⁶You shall not go around as a slanderer among your people, and you shall not profit by the blood of your neighbor: I am the LORD.

¹⁷You shall not hate in your heart anyone of your kin; you shall reprove your neighbor, or you will incur guilt yourself. ¹⁸You shall not take vengeance or bear a grudge against any of your people, but you shall love your neighbor as yourself: I am the LORD.

³³When an alien resides with you in your land, you shall not oppress the alien. **³⁴The alien who resides with you shall be to you as the citizen among you; you shall love the alien as yourself,** for you were aliens in the land of Egypt: I am the LORD your God.

³⁵You shall not cheat in measuring length, weight, or quantity. ³⁶You shall have honest balances, honest weights, an honest ephah, and an honest hin: I am the LORD your God, who brought you out of the land of Egypt. ³⁷You shall keep all my statutes and all my ordinances, and observe them: I am the LORD.

" 'Do not deceive one another.

¹²" 'Do not swear falsely by my name and so profane the name of your God. I am the LORD.

¹³" 'Do not defraud your neighbor or rob him.

" 'Do not hold back the wages of a hired man overnight.

¹⁴" 'Do not curse the deaf or put a stumbling block in front of the blind, but fear your God. I am the LORD.

¹⁵" 'Do not pervert justice; do not show partiality to the poor or favoritism to the great, but judge your neighbor fairly.

¹⁶" 'Do not go about spreading slander among your people.

" 'Do not do anything that endangers your neighbor's life. I am the LORD.

¹⁷" 'Do not hate your brother in your heart. Rebuke your neighbor frankly so you will not share in his guilt.

¹⁸" 'Do not seek revenge or bear a grudge against one of your people, but love your neighbor as yourself. I am the LORD.

³³" 'When an alien lives with you in your land, do not mistreat him. **³⁴The alien living with you must be treated as one of your native-born. Love him as yourself,** for you were aliens in Egypt. I am the LORD your God.

³⁵" 'Do not use dishonest standards when measuring length, weight or quantity. ³⁶Use honest scales and honest weights, an honest ephah and an honest hin. I am the LORD your God, who brought you out of Egypt.

³⁷" 'Keep all my decrees and all my laws and follow them. I am the LORD.' "

UNDERSTANDING THE SCRIPTURE

Introduction. The Book of Leviticus continues the story of the people's wandering in the wilderness that began in Exodus. Because it is almost completely composed of ancient laws, many of which are not observed by modern Judaism or Christianity, most people find it a dull and irrelevant read. In fact, though, Leviticus raises some interesting and pertinent questions for the life of faith today. Overall, the book is concerned with how an infinite and holy God can in any way relate to a group of finite and sinful people. The basic answer, which reflects the book's origins among the Hebrew priestly class, is that human beings must show appropriate awe and deference to God both in their worship and in the way they conduct their lives.

Fitting well within this concern, Leviticus 19 describes attitudes and actions appropriate to the people of God. The injunctions come directly from the Lord, relayed through Moses, and they deliberately call to mind the Ten Commandments. Verse 2 expresses the heart of the chapter: "You shall be holy, for I the LORD your God am holy." In other words, we humans are to imitate the model of God's holiness. The Hebrew people are now established in a covenant relationship with God, who delivered them from Egypt (19:36), and this necessitates a new way of life. The chapter further defines covenant behavior in terms of religious (19:3-8) and ethical (19:9-18) considerations. Verses 19-37 continue this theme, mixing together religious and ethical concerns in the laws presented there. Also, as one reads chapter 19 as a whole, it is important to pay attention to the way in which the laws are worded. Writing in *Leviticus* in *Interpretation*, Samuel E. Balentine explains:

> While most of the prohibitions are couched negatively, as behavior that must be avoided, a significant number are stated positively, thereby reiterating the assertion in chapters 18 and 20 that holiness must be manifest in lives that say both yes to what God requires and no to what God forbids. One without the other will never be sufficient to obey God's commandments.

Finally, it is interesting to note that Leviticus 19 falls between two chapters that deal primarily with laws covering human sexual conduct. Leviticus 18 lists prohibited relationships and Leviticus 20 states the penalty for breaking these laws. While this might seem like an odd context for Leviticus 19's instructions for holy living, most scholars

assume the literary structure is deliberate. As Samuel Balentine puts it: "The frame, chapters 18 and 20, insists that the journey toward holiness goes through the ethics of human relationships. The center, Leviticus 19, insists that how humans relate to one another is the measure of their fidelity to God."

Leviticus 19:9-10. The laws regarding the collection of harvest are probably most familiar to us through the story of Ruth. There we read how the landowner Boaz, a righteous man, left plenty of harvest "remainders" for the poor to gather. He followed this ancient law that instructs farmers not to reap from every plant and to leave behind fallen grains and grapes. The law is exceedingly generous in that it covers the "poor" and the "alien." The latter word refers to strangers and foreigners, usually Gentile, who would likely have no support system within Jewish territory. This section of the code, therefore, moves the Jewish community from a mind-set of "taking care of one's own" to "taking care of God's own"—a remarkably broad view, indeed.

Leviticus 19:11-13. These verses forbid dishonesty in any form. Followers of God are not to steal, cheat, or lie. Most especially, they are not to make promises sworn on God's name that they intend to break. Verse 13 repeats the command against fraud or theft and additionally forbids keeping wages until morning. In an economy where laborers received only enough pay for a day's worth of food, this law represents an act of kindness; it allows workers to buy food for themselves and their families at the end of the day, thus ensuring no one goes hungry.

Leviticus 19:14. This seems an odd verse on the heels of economic concerns, yet it carries forward two crucial themes: that of God caring for those who need protection and aid, as well as God's desire that we not take advantage of one another. People within God's community are not to use another's disability as a means of debasing that person. Out of respect for God and for those whom God holds dear, therefore, one does not shout hateful words at someone who cannot hear or put impediments in the way of someone who cannot see.

Leviticus 19:15-16. Verse 15 calls for true impartiality in a court setting. Judges are not to be swayed by awe or fear of the rich or by pity for the poor. Verse 16 continues the theme of acting fairly by prohibiting slander as well as deliberate profit from a person's injury or death.

Leviticus 19:17-18. These verses address the proper attitude one is to have toward family members and neighbors. "Neighbor" here carries the dual sense of both other citizens within one's nation and other members of one's faith because there was no distinction between the two in the life of the Hebrew people. In these relationships, the people of God are to put aside hatred and revenge, acting always with love, instead— a dynamic that sometimes includes reproof (or correction) of another's wrongdoing. Note that Jesus quotes verse 18, a powerful summation of all the Hebrew ethical laws, as part of the "greatest commandment" for all believers (Matthew 22:39; Mark 12:31; Luke 10:27).

Leviticus 19:33-37. Continuing the open-minded concern of verse 10, verse 33 extends the same love for the neighbor to foreigners living within one's national borders. The reminder to the people (19:34) is that they, too, were once foreigners—in Egypt, no less, where they were also helpless and at risk. Moreover, they are to be honest and ethical in all their business dealings. God's call, therefore, is to show compassion and care to others as God has shown it to them. In turn, the people are to obey God's rules.

INTERPRETING THE SCRIPTURE

A New Perspective

At first glance, the laws of Leviticus 19 seem like little more than good sense and basic ethics. It is hard for us to appreciate how truly radical these laws were at the time—or how much they still have to teach us today.

Let us begin with the past. As the lesson for June 3 pointed out, there were many law codes throughout the ancient Near East but few touched on the needs of people on the margins of society. Certainly none addressed concern for the unprotected and the oppressed at the level we see in the laws of the Old Testament.

Here we have some amazing instructions indeed that were basically unprecedented in biblical times:

▶ If you are a landowner, don't make the maximum profit that you can. Choose to make less money and instead give part of your crop to the poor. This tiny loss to you will mean life to others.

▶ Be absolutely fair and honest in all your dealings. Don't take from others through stealing, lying, cheating, fraud, or just plain meanness.

▶ Treat everyone with the same fairness and honesty. Don't bend the rules for someone because of their circumstances, whether good or ill. The rules themselves are designed to be fair—so trust God's design and stick to the plan.

▶ Do not seek to take advantage of a situation when someone is injured or deceased. In those cases, families need your help, not your greed.

▶ Make peace with your own family members and anyone else you know when discord arises. Don't try to get even and don't hold a grudge, but do whatever it takes to make things right so that you can "love your neighbor as yourself" (19:18).

▶ And, by the way, apply all of the above to folks from another country who happen to live in your community. It does not matter that they are not citizens of your nation or members of your faith—God asks you to interact with them according to the divine rules of being human with one another.

▶ Finally, if you happen to be a merchant or a money changer, be honest in the exchange of goods and monies. It's the right thing to do.

Nowhere else in biblical times do we find laws like this, based on a premise of divine love and care. The repeated refrain that runs throughout the passage—"I am the LORD [your God]"—anchors these instructions in the community's covenant relationship with God and in God's own divine nature.

Total Involvement

The Bible teaches that God and the world are inseparable. Some people claim that they can worship God in the quiet of their homes or in the beauty of nature and that they do not need a worshiping community or a witness in the world. Such a view misunderstands the Old Testament view of life with God. The promise of the covenant is not "I have chosen you and you shall be my individual." The promise to which we must respond is given to a community. So if you choose one, you get the other as well. That is not to say that we are not individuals or that our individuality is unimportant, but community does matter.

Consider the following. We may speak of life as taking place on three levels. One level is the life we lead in the privacy of our homes or our hearts. This is the level where one confronts God and hears God's word on a strictly personal basis that penetrates into the soul of our being.

The second level is life as we live it among a small, select group of family and friends. Usually, there is a high trust component and one can begin to ask questions about what it means to be connected to God. This is where the sharing of self starts. Characteristic of this level are statements including the words *I think, I feel, I am touched, I sense, I am grateful.* We make these "I" statements when we feel secure, and in this level we use such statements to try out one another. We find that all the things we discovered in the private, internal level are true for others as well.

The third level is the corporate level. Here we interact with a broader array of people. We may be forced to brush against folks we don't know or like, but here is where we put into practice all that we have articulated in the other levels. This is the level of the church. We need all three levels to maintain the right balance between the strong senses of individuality and community.

The temptation is to go for one level exclusively. Thus we think that regular worship attendance is sufficient Bible study, that giving to the mission of the church will make up for Sunday mornings spent elsewhere, or that activity in an agency that helps people fully satisfies the need to be involved in the affairs of the world. The Bible stresses that our individual response to God must be expressed in relationship to others. Only in this way do we become transformed into the body of Christ in the world—prophetically pronouncing the wondrous deeds of our God and our Creator, telling of God's decision to call us God's own, and attesting to God's love through our lifestyle.

Living Out Our Calling

When we move into a consideration of faith in action today, the intensity of the biblical teachings becomes even clearer. We might well ask what it means for a congregation or an individual Christian today to be faithful to a call from God that says financial gain must not come at the cost of another's detriment. What does it take for us to be faithful as advocates of justice or to have integrity in all our dealings? Given the influx of refugees to our country and ongoing struggles over just treatment for illegal aliens, we certainly need to ask what message these teachings hold for us regarding our attitudes and actions toward "foreigners" in our midst.

These are difficult questions to address, yet the text itself gives us a starting point for theological reflection. We need to begin with what God has done for us, especially in terms of compassion and care. Think of a time when you felt helpless or alone and God reached out to envelop you in care. This might have been through a purely spiritual experience or, more likely, encouraged

through the loving aid of another person. *This* is what Leviticus 19 wants you to recall. In essence the text says, "Remember what it felt like to be anxious and then rescued, afraid and then safe. Now look for ways to accomplish that for others—because God cares for them just as for you, and God is looking to work through you this time to bring relief."

It is a holy calling—and a joyous one when we give ourselves to it completely. Through lives dedicated to bringing God's loving justice to the world, we discover ourselves as part of God's own grand and powerful plan. And, miracle of miracles, we find God through our bringing life where there is death, comfort where there is grief, and hope where there is despair. Thanks be to God!

SHARING THE SCRIPTURE

Preparing Our Hearts

Explore this week's devotional reading, found in Luke 10:25-37, the beloved parable of the good Samaritan. Try to read this familiar story with "fresh eyes" by putting yourself in the place of the priest, Levite, or Samaritan. What do you notice about the injured man—or do you see him at all? What motivates you to react the way that you do? Now think about times when you were (or could have been) a good neighbor to a stranger in need. How did you react? Why? How are you similar to or different from the characters in Jesus' story?

Pray that you and the adult learners will be aware of those in need and do whatever you can to show compassion.

Preparing Our Minds

Study the background Scripture and the lesson Scripture, both of which are from

Leviticus 19:9-18, 33-37. Think about how you ensure that other people feel valued.

Write on newsprint:
- ❏ information for next week's lesson, found under "Continue the Journey."
- ❏ activities for further spiritual growth in "Continue the Journey."

Collect art supplies for a collage, including glue, scissors, magazines that may be cut, and construction paper or posterboard.

LEADING THE CLASS

(1) Gather to Learn

❖ Welcome the class members and introduce any guests.

❖ Pray that the students will reflect today on compassion and the biblical guidelines that undergird compassionate living.

❖ Read this story, which is based on a true situation: **She slipped into the back** pew long before the service started. Ours was a reasonably large congregation, but I knew I had never seen this young woman before. She seemed to appreciate my welcome, but kept her head down and had little to say. She definitely seemed troubled, and the best way I knew to help was to alert a staff person skilled in counseling. My hunch was correct: This woman was homeless and confronting a wall of other issues. Our congregation swung into compassionate action. One of our members had space to take her in while more permanent housing was located. Others did what they could to help meet her needs. I've lost track of this woman, but am grateful that her presence taught us much about compassion.

❖ Read aloud today's focus statement: **People want to feel significant. How do we assure others that they are valued? We treat them with love, justice, and generosity.**

(2) Cite Biblical Guidelines That Develop Compassionate Living

❖ Select a volunteer to read Leviticus 19:9-18, 33-37.

❖ Post newsprint and challenge the group to restate these biblical commands in their own words. Use ideas from the list in "A New Perspective" if the adults seem stumped.

❖ Review the list by asking these questions. Use information from Understanding the Scripture as appropriate to fill in gaps.

    (1) Which of these commands still apply today?

    (2) Which seem difficult to do today? Why?

    (3) Give a concrete example of how you have seen one of these commands recently enacted.

    (4) Viewed as a whole, what makes these commands so important not only to individuals but also to a community?

❖ Wrap up by reading this enacted parable: **A pastor had contacted an actor to**

come to her church before worship on a Sunday morning and sit in the parking lot within easy view of a main door. The actor was told to dress and act as a homeless person. He was not to do anything to frighten the parishioners, but could feel free to ask for help if someone approached him. No one did. Instead, worshipers went inside, some expressing pity for the man, others wondering if the police should be called. When the pastor began her sermon on Leviticus 19, on cue, the apparently homeless man walked down the center aisle as the pastor described why he had come and noted that no one paid any attention to him.

❖ Ask: **How might the congregation have responded, both before and after they learned this person's true identity?**

(3) Reflect on Situations in Which the Learners Have Been Treated With Compassion

❖ Provide a few moments for the adults to recall a specific time when they were treated with compassion.

❖ Call on volunteers to comment on their recollection of this experience, not by describing it in words but by saying a color that reflects how they felt; describing a scene in nature that captures their feelings; singing (or naming) a song that captures their mood; or doing some brief body movements or a dance to demonstrate how they felt.

❖ Conclude by trying to summarize the feelings that were expressed through these actions. Suggest that if being the recipient of such compassion is such a positive experience for them, they may want to help others to experience these emotions by treating someone in need with compassion.

(4) Identify a Community Need and Find a Way to Respond Appropriately to It

❖ Read or retell "Living Out Our Calling" in Interpreting the Scripture.

❖ Set out art supplies, including scissors, glue, magazines that can be cut, and construction paper or posterboard. Invite the adults to think about groups of people in their community who are not being treated with justice and compassion. Encourage them to find pictures of such groups—perhaps children, older adults, people who are part of a racial or ethnic minority, adherents of a different faith than the majority of the community—and arrange these pictures on a collage. If the class is small, work together to create one large collage; if the class is larger, form small groups and ask each one to create a collage. Prompt the adults to talk about why they perceive certain groups are not treated compassionately.

❖ Post the collage(s) and raise this question: **Given the need that we see, how can we respond compassionately to at least one of the groups we see pictured here?** List ideas on newsprint. Poll the class to see who is willing to work on which idea. Perhaps the class as a whole will select one group and focus their energies there so as to meet a need.

(5) Continue the Journey

❖ Pray that the adults will find a way to compassionately meet a need within their community.

❖ Read aloud this preparation for next week's lesson. You may also want to post it on newsprint for the students to copy.

■ **Title: Celebrate Jubilee**
■ **Background Scripture: Leviticus 25:8-55**
■ **Lesson Scripture: Leviticus 25:8-12, 25, 35-36, 39-40, 47-48, 55**
■ **Focus of the Lesson: Some people are oppressed because of the** unjust circumstances into which they are born and in which they live. How can all people be treated fairly regardless of their life circumstances? By observing a Year of Jubilee, those who are oppressed are given the means for making a fresh start.

❖ Challenge the students to complete one or more of these activities for further spiritual growth related to this week's session. Post this information on newsprint for the students to copy.

(1) **Keep a dated journal of acts of compassion that you perform. Review this journal periodically. Do you notice any patterns? What kinds of people are recipients of your compassion? How often do you act with compassion?**

(2) **Research the word "compassion" in a Bible dictionary or concordance. What do you learn about compassion as related to God? What are God's expectations for human compassion? How can you promote compassionate behavior among people you know?**

(3) **Take action this week to show compassion to someone who is clearly "not like you."**

❖ Sing or read aloud "Jesu, Jesu."

❖ Conclude today's session by leading the class in this benediction adapted from Deuteronomy 10:12-13, the key verses for June 24: **Go forth remembering that we are to fear the Lord our God, to walk in all his ways, to love God, to serve the Lord with all our heart and soul, and to keep God's commandments.**

UNIT 1: JUSTICE DEFINED
CELEBRATE JUBILEE

PREVIEWING THE LESSON

Lesson Scripture: Leviticus 25:8-12, 25, 35-36, 39-40, 47-48, 55
Background Scripture: Leviticus 25:8-55
Key Verse: Leviticus 25:10

Focus of the Lesson:

Some people are oppressed because of the unjust circumstances into which they are born and in which they live. How can all people be treated fairly regardless of their life circumstances? By observing a Year of Jubilee, those who are oppressed are given the means for making a fresh start.

Goals for the Learners:

(1) to summarize the principles of Jubilee.
(2) to recall a time when they needed an opportunity to begin again.
(3) to familiarize the participants with community resources available to assist people in making a fresh start.

Pronunciation Guide:

cinquain (sin' cane)

Supplies:

Bibles, newsprint and marker, paper and pencils, hymnals

READING THE SCRIPTURE

NRSV
Leviticus 25:8-12, 25, 35-36, 39-40, 47-48, 55

⁸You shall count off seven weeks of years, seven times seven years, so that the period of seven weeks of years gives forty-nine years. ⁹Then you shall have the trumpet sounded loud; on the tenth day of the seventh month—on the day of atonement—you shall have the trumpet sounded throughout

NIV
Leviticus 25:8-12, 25, 35-36, 39-40, 47-48, 55

⁸'Count off seven sabbaths of years— seven times seven years—so that the seven sabbaths of years amount to a period of forty-nine years. ⁹Then have the trumpet sounded everywhere on the tenth day of the seventh month; on the Day of Atonement

all your land. **¹⁰And you shall hallow the fiftieth year and you shall proclaim liberty throughout the land to all its inhabitants. It shall be a jubilee for you:** you shall return, every one of you, to your property and every one of you to your family. ¹¹That fiftieth year shall be a jubilee for you: you shall not sow, or reap the aftergrowth, or harvest the unpruned vines. ¹²For it is a jubilee; it shall be holy to you: you shall eat only what the field itself produces.

²⁵If anyone of your kin falls into difficulty and sells a piece of property, then the next of kin shall come and redeem what the relative has sold.

³⁵If any of your kin fall into difficulty and become dependent on you, you shall support them; they shall live with you as though resident aliens. ³⁶Do not take interest in advance or otherwise make a profit from them, but fear your God; let them live with you.

³⁹If any who are dependent on you become so impoverished that they sell themselves to you, you shall not make them serve as slaves. ⁴⁰They shall remain with you as hired or bound laborers. They shall serve with you until the year of the jubilee.

⁴⁷If resident aliens among you prosper, and if any of your kin fall into difficulty with one of them and sell themselves to an alien, or to a branch of the alien's family, ⁴⁸after they have sold themselves they shall have the right of redemption; one of their brothers may redeem them. . . . ⁵⁵For to me the people of Israel are servants; they are my servants whom I brought out from the land of Egypt: I am the LORD your God.

sound the trumpet throughout your land. **¹⁰Consecrate the fiftieth year and proclaim liberty throughout the land to all its inhabitants. It shall be a jubilee for you;** each one of you is to return to his family property and each to his own clan. ¹¹The fiftieth year shall be a jubilee for you; do not sow and do not reap what grows of itself or harvest the untended vines. ¹²For it is a jubilee and is to be holy for you; eat only what is taken directly from the fields.

²⁵" 'If one of your countrymen becomes poor and sells some of his property, his nearest relative is to come and redeem what his countryman has sold.

³⁵" 'If one of your countrymen becomes poor and is unable to support himself among you, help him as you would an alien or a temporary resident, so he can continue to live among you. ³⁶Do not take interest of any kind from him, but fear your God, so that your countryman may continue to live among you.

³⁹" 'If one of your countrymen becomes poor among you and sells himself to you, do not make him work as a slave. ⁴⁰He is to be treated as a hired worker or a temporary resident among you; he is to work for you until the Year of Jubilee.

⁴⁷" 'If an alien or a temporary resident among you becomes rich and one of your countrymen becomes poor and sells himself to the alien living among you or to a member of the alien's clan. ⁴⁸he retains the right of redemption after he has sold himself. One of his relatives may redeem him.

⁵⁵[F]or the Israelites belong to me as servants. They are my servants, whom I brought out of Egypt. I am the LORD your God.' "

UNDERSTANDING THE SCRIPTURE

Introduction. The laws of Leviticus 25 take the Fourth Commandment, which sets the Sabbath as a day of rest (Exodus 20:8-11), and expand its concept to include periodic "rest" within agricultural and economic situations. The opening verses (25:1-7) set the stage by declaring every seventh year as a "sabbath" for the land, a time when no one is to plant in a field or to prune a vineyard. Rather, these areas are left alone to recover strength and health. The remaining laws build on the theology of these first seven verses.

Leviticus 25:8-13. These verses decree another kind of rest for the land—a time when its God-appointed stewards will be restored. When the Hebrews first came into Canaan, the land was divided among the tribes according to families. Every family in Judah and Israel owned a particular piece of property. According to the divine plan, no citizen of these nations could ever be utterly impoverished, because every person had a legitimate claim to the land and that claim would be upheld over time.

Leviticus 25:14-17. This passage addresses ethical issues pertinent to leasing one's land. Although permanent title could not be sold (25:23), Hebrew landowners could sell farming rights to their land. In these cases, the duration and pricing of contracts was based on when the next Jubilee Year would occur. Should the contract prove miscalculated, the costs would be adjusted accordingly. The key concern here is that no cheating should occur (25:17), out of respect for the God of this community. As in Leviticus 19 (see Lesson 2 for June 10), the term "neighbor" applies to both other citizens within one's nation and other members of one's faith.

Leviticus 25:18-22. Verses 18-22 reassure the people that God will provide for them. The anticipated worry over food supply (25:20) echoes the people's anxiety in the wilderness over potential starvation (Exodus 16:2-3) and thirst (Exodus 17:1-3). This time, instead of manna from heaven or water from a rock, God promises an exceptional blessing in the form of a sixth-year harvest bountiful enough to provide food for three years. In a pattern typical for the Pentateuch, God responds to people's concerns by providing even more than they ask. The tripled harvest of the sixth year will not only supply food for the sabbatical year, it will also yield enough stores to carry the

people through the next full harvest. This would not come until the ninth year, if planting resumed in the eighth.

Leviticus 25:23-24. God's promise to the people stems from divine love for them. Verse 23 reminds us that God's ability to keep this promise is rooted in divine ownership of the land in question.

Leviticus 25:25-28. The rest of the laws in this chapter address the redemption of property. Verses 25-28 begin this section with a practical application of verses 23-24 by outlining three ways property can be redeemed if someone sells it under economic distress. First, if at all possible, the next of kin (literally, "redeemer") is to buy back the property in the seller's name. If there is no available redeemer, then the original seller has rights to repurchase if he or she finds the funds. Note that this is not a free market exchange; the land is not bought back at current market values. Rather, the original price is prorated and the balance is returned to the buyer, who has no choice in the matter. In this way, the law not only guarantees that land stays within assigned families but it also provides safeguards against anyone profiting from another's misfortune. Finally, in event of no other means of redemption, the Jubilee Year ensures the return of property to the original owner (or nearest relative).

Leviticus 25:29-34. These verses detail redemption rights pertaining to houses. Any house can be redeemed within the first year. After that, redemption laws depend on the house's location—whether that is in a walled city (that is, major urban area), a smaller, unwalled city or village, or a city set aside for the levitical priests (see Numbers 35:1-8).

Leviticus 25:35-38. In the midst of these property laws, we come to instructions regarding family members. What if one relative becomes financially dependent on another? The law suggests that such family members are not to be considered property or prey. These relatives are to be allowed to live within the wealthier family households.

While the text implies that these relatives may contribute to the cost of their room and board as they are able, the law strictly forbids taking advantage of them by loaning money at interest or by charging them for food and shelter "at a profit" (25:37). The section ends with yet another reminder that the land belongs to God, so God can set the terms for residency (25:38).

Leviticus 25:39-43. The next verses concern Hebrew nonfamily members who are indebted to a property owner or head of household. If one cannot pay off the debt financially, then the person (and sometimes his or her family) must pay it off in service as "hired or bound laborers" (25:40), but never as a slave (25:42). In contrast to this section, which speaks of release only in a Jubilee Year, other passages allow for release after six years if the person so chooses (Exodus 21:1-6; Deuteronomy 15:12-18). In any event, the indebted servants are to be treated kindly (25:43).

Leviticus 25:44-46. Although members of the Hebrew community could not become slaves, plenty of others could. These verses specifically list members of surrounding nations as eligible, along with "the aliens residing with you" (25:45). The latter even includes children who may have been born locally. Unlike Hebrew indentured servants, Gentile slaves received no release or protection from the law. They and their families were *property*, a possession to be passed on from one generation to the next (25:45-46). They were also subject to whatever treatment the owner saw fit (25:46).

Leviticus 25:47-55. The final area of redemption includes Hebrews who have "sold themselves" to resident aliens as a result of debt. In these cases, the resident alien is bound by Hebrew law regarding treatment and eventual release. The theological basis for these laws is the same as we saw earlier—like the land, the people belong to God (25:55). For this reason, they cannot be sold in perpetuity and neither are they to be mistreated.

INTERPRETING THE SCRIPTURE

The Fiftieth Year

One of the most interesting laws found in Leviticus concerns the "Jubilee." This special occasion was designed to keep clans—and their land holdings—intact. Underlying the Jubilee law was a radical concept of both property and people: Everything belongs to God, and all transactions should reflect acknowledgment of this reality.

The Year of Jubilee gets its name from the ram's horn, which was used as a trumpet to signal the beginning of this special event. Every seventh year was a sabbatical year, but after every seven-times-seven years, it was time for a festival of celebration and restoration. For most people this was a once-in-a-lifetime occasion, and the Year of Jubilee offered the opportunity to restore what had been taken wrongly, to reevaluate lifetime priorities, and then to celebrate God's grace.

"Celebration" may seem an odd word to use here because this is not celebrating in the normal sense of the word. We tend to think of celebration as a kind of lighthearted activity when people enjoy themselves. In the Year of Jubilee, celebration amounted to an appreciation of others. To celebrate Jubilee was to attempt to give back instead of hoarding for oneself. The origin of such a tradition may have been an attempt to protect the earth from overuse and exploitation, but the laws began to take on a theological significance. They came to be understood as a tangible reminder that it is impossible to own, or even to call one's own, that which belongs to God.

Every Jubilee Year began, appropriately enough, on the Day of Atonement (25:9). As the name implies, this was the day special sacrifice was made for the people's sin. It was a day to contemplate all that one had done against God and neighbor during the past year. Most of all, it was a day on which to celebrate one's liberation from sin. The spiritual slate was wiped clean, so to speak: Each Hebrew started anew. What better day to begin the Jubilee Year, therefore—a time when both land and people were "liberated" from conditions that God did not intend.

The whole concept of Jubilee called for the people to treat others as graciously as God had treated them. The laws were not a functional duty, but a kind of catalyst to make sure that the people were living in harmony with God and with God's creation. The laws of this section of Leviticus interpret God's will, hold it before the people, saying that this is what God is like, and remind people to practice what they preach in regard to loving neighbor as self.

A New Start

Many of us can appreciate the good news of a fresh start represented in this text. There are so many times in life that we wish we could have a "do over" or, like the character in the movie *Click*, be able to hit the rewind button on a remote control and "undo" what we just did. Especially in the economic climate of recent years, though, when so many people are losing jobs or struggling otherwise to make ends meet, the idea becomes quite precious that a home is not lost forever or that one's children are guaranteed an inheritance despite current circumstances.

These were the same concerns faced by people in biblical times. Archaeological data show us that there was a widening gap in Hebrew society over the centuries. For the first few generations after the people entered the land, most towns were fairly uniform. The houses were all basically similar in size and design, indicating that most people shared the same standard of living. Within two hundred years, this had

changed. Towns from the later monarchical period show a definite class system. There were wealthy quarters, with large and well-built homes, and poor quarters, with small houses crowded together.

Other parts of the Bible itself, especially various prophetic writings, tell of the plight of the lower class. Amos describes cruel exploitation of the poor (Amos 2:6-7) and berates the wealthy who oppress them (4:1). Micah speaks of covetous people, presumably wealthy, who seize fields and houses from their rightful owners (Micah 2:2). Isaiah wails against lawmakers who oppress others and who deny justice to the needy and poor (Isaiah 10:1-2). Clearly, there was a need for the Jubilee Year in this society.

Sadly, however, there is no proof that the Jubilee Year was celebrated regularly, if at all, and many scholars maintain that these verses preserve an ideal that was never actually practiced in Israel's or Judah's history. Still, the goal behind the Jubilee speaks to us at a profound level. The laws were designed to counterbalance situations that can lead to a society of only two classes: the rich and the indebted. We in North America are learning all too well what an unhealthy economy this represents. Due to a variety of causes, we are gradually becoming a two-class society, as the "middle" class grows smaller.

Consider for a moment: What would the biblical writer think of current economic conditions in the United States? As this lesson is written, the levels of national and personal debt in the United States are at an all-time high. Because of unemployment and rising health-care costs, personal bankruptcy cases have tripled in some areas. The percentage of those living below poverty level, mostly women and children, is the highest it has been in decades, as is the number of homeless people. Many folk are discovering that they cannot afford to buy houses or to have children under these conditions. The "land of opportunity" is becoming a place where some feel lucky just to survive for another year.

Surely the biblical writer would affirm that the conditions described above do not fit what God wants for people. The Bible witnesses to God's desire for a society where economic justice prevails and the divine order is maintained. Indeed, it is on this theological basis that the specifics of the Jubilee Year were developed.

Our Jubilee

For Christians, the Year of Jubilee takes on a new and significant meaning. It was in the Nazareth synagogue that Jesus, reading from Isaiah 61:1-2, applied these words to himself: "[God] has sent me to proclaim release to the captives, . . . to let the oppressed go free, to proclaim the year of the Lord's favor" (Luke 4:18-19).

The Year of Jubilee has been given to us. We are the captives who have been released and the oppressed who have been set free. The issue is no longer economic debt only, but spiritual debt as well. We who were slaves to sin, cut off from the home we have in God, have been redeemed. Our debt is gone and we are free to start life anew. What greater reason is there to celebrate God's ownership than this?

SHARING THE SCRIPTURE

Preparing Our Hearts

Explore this week's devotional reading, found in Nehemiah 1:5-11. Nehemiah was an Israelite captive who served the Persian king in the trusted position of cupbearer. Having heard about the derelict condition of Jerusalem and its wall, Nehemiah confessed not only his own sins but also those of his family and the people. These sins are rooted in their failure to keep God's covenant. Notice that he did not simply utter a few rote words. No, Nehemiah poured out his heart and soul to God. He recognized God's faithfulness. He was pleading for a fresh start. When have you needed a fresh start? How did God respond to your prayer?

Pray that you and the adult learners will confess your sins and renew your relationship with God.

Preparing Our Minds

Study the background Scripture from Leviticus 25:8-55 and the lesson Scripture from Leviticus 25:8-12, 25, 35-36, 39-40, 47-48, 55. Consider this question: How can all people be treated fairly regardless of their life circumstances?

Write on newsprint:
❑ information for next week's lesson, found under "Continue the Journey."
❑ activities for further spiritual growth in "Continue the Journey."

Familiarize yourself with the Understanding the Scripture portion and "The Fiftieth Year" in Interpreting the Scripture so that you may add information during a discussion for "Summarize the Principles of Jubilee." If you prefer, plan to present a brief lecture to help the adults become aware of the purpose of Jubilee and what was supposed to happen during this holy time.

LEADING THE CLASS

(1) Gather to Learn

❖ Welcome the class members and introduce any guests.

❖ Pray that the students will be challenged to respond to the principles of Jubilee.

❖ List these categories on a sheet of newsprint: *Criminal Injustice, Social Injustice,*

Corporate Injustice. Encourage the students to give examples of such injustices that they have learned about in the media or personally experienced. A criminal injustice, for instance, may occur when a person convicted of a crime such as shoplifting is sentenced to jail time equivalent to that of an armed robber. Social injustices occur, for example, when people are discriminated against because of their race, religion, sexual orientation, gender, or ethnic background. Corporate injustice can occur when a company continues to profit from a product even though it knows the product is harmful.

❖ Read aloud today's focus statement: **Some people are oppressed because of the unjust circumstances into which they are born and in which they live. How can all people be treated fairly regardless of their life circumstances? By observing a Year of Jubilee, those who are oppressed are given the means for making a fresh start.**

(2) Summarize the Principles of Jubilee

❖ Choose a volunteer to read today's lesson Scripture from Leviticus 25:8-12, 25, 35-36, 39-40, 47-48, 55.

❖ Suggest that the adults refer to their Bibles as you discuss the following questions. Use information from Understanding the Scripture to clarify answers or present a brief lecture.

(1) **What is the purpose of the Year of Jubilee?**

(2) **What was supposed to happen in a Jubilee Year?**

(3) **How were family members expected to help one another?**

(4) **How does Jesus claim the idea of Jubilee?** (See "Our Jubilee" in Interpreting the Scripture. Have someone read Luke 4:18-19.)

(5) **Why do you think God would institute the Jubilee?** (Consider that God is the owner of all, and we are only stewards of what is God's.)

(6) **What advantages and disadvantages do you perceive in observing the Year of Jubilee in ancient Israel?**

❖ Conclude with a roundtable discussion in which class members talk about current business and economic structures in light of the Jubilee Year model. Are there ways we could practice Jubilee, at least in some modified form? Who would support Jubilee—and why? Who would lobby against Jubilee—and why?

(3) Recall a Time When the Learners Needed an Opportunity to Begin Again

❖ Read "A New Start" from Interpreting the Scripture.

❖ Challenge the adults to write a cinquain, either individually or in small groups, about Jubilee. Encourage them to think about how they have experienced fresh starts in their own lives. This five-line unrhymed poem follows this format, as shown in the example:

- Line 1—one noun (name of person, place or thing)
- Line 2—two words to describe the noun
- Line 3—three action ("-ing") words
- Line 4—four words expressing feeling about the noun
- Line 5—one-word synonym for the noun in line 1

Jubilee
Hallowed, Holy
Renewing, refreshing, reenergizing
Sign of God's favor
Liberation

❖ Encourage volunteers to read their poems.

❖ Wrap up this section with a time of silent reflection for the adults to consider what opportunities to begin anew have meant to them.

(4) Familiarize the Learners With Community Resources Available to Assist People in Making a Fresh Start

❖ Note that even in societies where economic and business practices make it impossible to practice Jubilee in its biblical form, God's people are still called to care for those in need.

❖ Brainstorm answers to this question: **What resources exist through our church, our denomination, nonprofit organizations, and government organizations to assist people who need to make fresh starts?** Record answers on newsprint.

❖ Discuss these questions:

(1) **What benefit do these organizations offer to those in our community?** (Encourage brief stories of how these organizations make a difference. For example, a Red Cross volunteer may discuss how she is able to help a family whose home was lost to a fire make emergency arrangements and begin to get back on their feet.)

(2) **Which of these programs do you personally support? Why?**

(3) **Would you be willing to mentor someone else who is interested in the outreach work that you do?** (If there are positive responses, encourage people who may be interested in a particular program to stand with the person who is volunteering as a mentor. Recognize that some students are willing to be mentors and to explore a new program.)

❖ Challenge the adults to make a commitment to do whatever they can to help those who need to make a fresh start.

(5) Continue the Journey

❖ Pray that the adults will use community resources to help those who need to make fresh starts.

❖ Read aloud this preparation for next week's lesson. You may also want to post it on newsprint for the students to copy.

■ **Title: The Heart of the Law**
■ **Background Scripture: Deuteronomy 10:1-22; 16:18-20**
■ **Lesson Scripture: Deuteronomy 10:12-22; 16:18-20**
■ **Focus of the Lesson: People respond in various ways to being loved. How should someone respond when he or she is the recipient of love? As recipients of God's love, we are expected to be fair, act justly, and love others.**

❖ Challenge the students to complete one or more of these activities for further spiritual growth related to this week's session. Post this information on newsprint for the students to copy.

(1) **Cancel a debt owed to you and explain to the debtor that you are observing the principle of Jubilee.**

(2) **Research Jubilee USA Network, which focuses on debt reduction and cancellation for poor countries as a matter of justice. Prayerfully consider how you feel about supporting such a group and then respond as you feel appropriate.**

(3) **Research "biblical Jubilee" or "Jubilee Year" in Bible dictionaries or on the Internet. Consider the ways in which the concept of Jubilee is important to Christians.**

❖ Sing or read aloud "Blow Ye the Trumpet, Blow."

❖ Conclude today's session by leading the class in this benediction adapted from Deuteronomy 10:12-13, the key verses for June 24: **Go forth remembering that we are to fear the Lord our God, to walk in all his ways, to love God, to serve the Lord with all our heart and soul, and to keep God's commandments.**

UNIT 1: JUSTICE DEFINED
THE HEART OF THE LAW

PREVIEWING THE LESSON

Lesson Scripture: Deuteronomy 10:12-22; 16:18-20
Background Scripture: Deuteronomy 10:1-22; 16:18-20
Key Verses: Deuteronomy 10:12-13

Focus of the Lesson:
People respond in various ways to being loved. How should someone respond when he or she is the recipient of love? As recipients of God's love, we are expected to be fair, act justly, and love others.

Goals for the Learners:
(1) to investigate ways the people of Israel were to respond to God's love.
(2) to identify times when they extended love to another.
(3) to organize or learn more about a ministry that addresses economic justice needs in the community.

Pronunciation Guide:
Hor (hor)   Levite (lee' vite)
Jotbathah (jot' buh thuh)   Moserah (moh see' ruh)
Kohathite (koh' huh thite)

Supplies:
Bibles, newsprint and marker, paper and pencils, hymnals

READING THE SCRIPTURE

NRSV
Deuteronomy 10:12-22

¹²So now, O Israel, **what does the LORD your God require of you? Only to fear the LORD your God, to walk in all his ways, to love him, to serve the LORD your God with all your heart and with all your soul,** ¹³**and to keep the commandments of the LORD** your God and his decrees that I am

NIV
Deuteronomy 10:12-22

¹²And now, O Israel, **what does the LORD your God ask of you but to fear the LORD your God, to walk in all his ways, to love him, to serve the LORD your God with all your heart and with all your soul,** ¹³**and to observe the LORD's commands** and decrees that I am giving you today for your own good?

commanding you today, for your own well-being. [14]Although heaven and the heaven of heavens belong to the LORD your God, the earth with all that is in it, [15]yet the LORD set his heart in love on your ancestors alone and chose you, their descendants after them, out of all the peoples, as it is today. [16]Circumcise, then, the foreskin of your heart, and do not be stubborn any longer. [17]For the LORD your God is God of gods and Lord of lords, the great God, mighty and awesome, who is not partial and takes no bribe, [18]who executes justice for the orphan and the widow, and who loves the strangers, providing them food and clothing. [19]You shall also love the stranger, for you were strangers in the land of Egypt. [20]You shall fear the LORD your God; him alone you shall worship; to him you shall hold fast, and by his name you shall swear. [21]He is your praise; he is your God, who has done for you these great and awesome things that your own eyes have seen. [22]Your ancestors went down to Egypt seventy persons; and now the LORD your God has made you as numerous as the stars in heaven.

Deuteronomy 16:18-20
[18]You shall appoint judges and officials throughout your tribes, in all your towns that the LORD your God is giving you, and they shall render just decisions for the people. [19]You must not distort justice; you must not show partiality; and you must not accept bribes, for a bribe blinds the eyes of the wise and subverts the cause of those who are in the right. [20]Justice, and only justice, you shall pursue, so that you may live and occupy the land that the LORD your God is giving you.

[14]To the LORD your God belong the heavens, even the highest heavens, the earth and everything in it. [15]Yet the LORD set his affection on your forefathers and loved them, and he chose you, their descendants, above all the nations, as it is today. [16]Circumcise your hearts, therefore, and do not be stiff-necked any longer. [17]For the LORD your God is God of gods and Lord of lords, the great God, mighty and awesome, who shows no partiality and accepts no bribes. [18]He defends the cause of the fatherless and the widow, and loves the alien, giving him food and clothing. [19]And you are to love those who are aliens, for you yourselves were aliens in Egypt. [20]Fear the LORD your God and serve him. Hold fast to him and take your oaths in his name. [21]He is your praise; he is your God, who performed for you those great and awesome wonders you saw with your own eyes. [22]Your forefathers who went down into Egypt were seventy in all, and now the LORD your God has made you as numerous as the stars in the sky.

Deuteronomy 16:18-20
[18]Appoint judges and officials for each of your tribes in every town the LORD your God is giving you, and they shall judge the people fairly. [19]Do not pervert justice or show partiality. Do not accept a bribe, for a bribe blinds the eyes of the wise and twists the words of the righteous. [20]Follow justice and justice alone, so that you may live and possess the land the LORD your God is giving you.

UNDERSTANDING THE SCRIPTURE

Deuteronomy 10:1-5. Recorded as the words of Moses, Deuteronomy 10 describes the second trip up Mount Sinai. Much has happened prior to this ascent, most notably the breaking of the original tablets containing the Ten Commandments, an act of violence on Moses' part when he discovered the people worshiping a golden calf made by his brother, Aaron (Exodus 32:1-6, 15-20). Now God commands Moses to carve out two new tablets and to make an ark (that is, a small portable container) to house them. Moses does so and then carries the blank tablets up the mountain, where God inscribes on them "the same words as before" (10:4). Moses then descends the mountain and, as commanded, safely deposits the tablets in the ark.

Deuteronomy 10:6-9. These verses interrupt Moses' speech with a short travel itinerary that comes from a variant scribal source. A comparison of Numbers 33:30-38 shows some of the same place names in a different order, while Numbers 20:22-29 details Aaron's death on Mount Hor rather than at Moserah (Deuteronomy 10:6). The brief list of sites ends with Jotbathah, which is identified as the place where God "set apart" the tribe of Levi to special service (10:8). The verb translated "set apart" means, among other things, to sanctify someone or something—to make it holy or to dedicate it to a holy purpose. In this case, the role of the priestly Levites encompasses three broad areas. First, they are the official bearers of the ark of the covenant. Numbers 4:4-15 restricts this privilege to a subgroup of Levites, the Kohathites, but here the responsibility is more generally shared. Second, the Levites are to serve as ministers to God by leading worship services and officiating over sacrifices. Numbers 18 describes these duties in some detail, making a distinction between the sons of Aaron and other Levites. According to Numbers 18:2-6, the latter are assistants to those who descend directly from Aaron. Finally, verse 8 of our text says the Levites are to bless the people in God's name. Numbers 6:22-26 contains one such blessing—beautiful words of benediction that Jews and Christians alike have treasured throughout the centuries.

Deuteronomy 10:10-11. Moses' narrative resumes in verse 10, stating that he remained on the mountain for "forty days and forty nights." The count should not be taken literally, however. The phrase is an idiom in Hebrew used to designate a very long time. During this extended stay upon the mountain, Moses apparently begged God to forgive the people, and "the LORD listened" (10:10). Acting once again out of grace and love, God is "unwilling to destroy" the people. Instead, the Lord gives a divine command that the people are to continue their journey to the land of promise (10:11).

Deuteronomy 10:12-19. Having recapped his experiences on Mount Sinai, Moses now addresses the people more directly. The last verses of the chapter (10:12-22) raise questions as to what God requires of the covenant community, and the literary structure of the response seems to be very deliberate. Three statements or injunctions precede the core of the covenant description in verses 17-19, and three follow it. In each case, the first statement outlines in broad terms what God requires, a second highlights the people's place in God's heart, and the final ties the people's call to covenant faithfulness with God's own steadfast keeping of promises.

Calling to mind the better-known imagery of Micah 6:8, this section begins a beautiful description of what God requires. Then the author gives the basis for the call to serve God so completely: The people are to respond in thankfulness out of awareness of the special honor God has granted them. Having pointed out the people's place within the very heart of God, Moses now calls on them to commit completely to the covenant God offers. The imagery of circumcision—the physical sign and seal of the covenant relationship among Hebrew males—is now extended metaphorically to all people in terms of the heart (10:16). As in verse 12, we are to understand this reference to the heart as a call to open one's mind and orient one's will to God and God alone. The section concludes with a summary of the core of the covenant relationship the Hebrew people are to take on.

Deuteronomy 10:20. The author now returns to an outline of actions that fall within covenant expectations. Once again, the call to "fear the LORD" comes first. The covenant community is also to worship God alone (see Exodus 20:1-6) and "hold fast" to their Lord. This latter verb is quite dynamic, in that it means to cling to someone, often in the sense of running closely behind and making sure one does not fall away during pursuit. Finally, the Hebrew people are told to swear by God's name.

Deuteronomy 10:21. This verse echoes verses 14-15 and the statement of how special the people are to God. The people are once again reminded of God's greatness and of God's grace, particularly in terms of the extraordinary acts that God has done on their behalf—acts to which the people themselves are witnesses.

Deuteronomy 10:22. The section ends with a testimony to God's covenant faithfulness. Here we see that the call to commit completely to this relationship with God (10:16) takes power from the reality of God's own commitment. The author points to proof of God's constancy within the existing community itself. God once promised Abraham that his descendants would be as numerous as the stars (Genesis 15:1-6), and now they are. The generational lines from an heir of Abraham to the seventy children born to Jacob in Egypt (see Exodus 1:5) to the current uncountable number of Hebrews is living proof that God keeps divine promises.

Deuteronomy 16:18-20. The commands in this passage reflect life in an established society governed by laws that are overseen by judges and other officials. The text is clear in stating that all who have authority related to Hebrew laws are to act with the same impartiality and integrity that God maintains in relation to justice issues.

INTERPRETING THE SCRIPTURE

A Familiar Concern

What does the Lord require of us? This question, posed by religious leaders and seekers throughout the ages, takes us immediately to the heart of faith in action.

Most of us know the summary of the law found in Micah 6:8:

[God] has told you, O mortal, what
   is good;
   and what does the LORD require of you
   but to do justice, and to love kindness,
   and to walk humbly with your God?

We also know Jesus' reply when asked what is the greatest commandment: "You shall love the Lord your God with all your heart, and with all your soul, and with all your mind" (Matthew 22:37; compare Mark 12:30; see also Luke 10:27). Did you know, though, that both Micah and Jesus probably had part of this week's texts in mind, along with Deuteronomy 6:5, when they spoke? Few of us jump to Deuteronomy 10 when we form our own answers to the question of what God requires, yet perhaps we should.

A quick read through the verses reveals several concepts that are by now familiar to us from Lessons 1 through 3. The text reminds us, for example, of the people's special place within the heart of the Sovereign Creator God and of their call to institute and execute justice on God's terms—justice that is impartial, incorruptible, and all-encompassing (Deuteronomy 10:17; 16:19). Once again we see God's special concern for those on the fringes of society, especially orphans, widows, and "strangers" (10:18-19). As we prepare to celebrate the founding of the United States, these biblical words invite us to consider anew what we mean by the historical declaration of "liberty and justice for all."

What It Takes

From the beginning of the passage, the biblical writer outlines what we need *before* we can start to live out God's justice as a people of faith. First on the list in many translations is "fear." The original Hebrew word really means "awe" or "utmost respect." The starting point for all we do, in other words, is recognizing and honoring who God is.

Next is the instruction to "walk in all [God's] ways" (10:12). Then as now, this phrase is a metaphor for taking on an entire lifestyle. The following two commandments are closely related to this idea as well. The people are told to love God and serve God with all their heart and soul. The word for "serve" also means "worship," while the term "heart" refers to the seat of the intellect and will. When we add that the Hebrew word translated "soul" more generally means "being or breath," then the image becomes one of dedicating our entire self to God.

All this is required, the writer implies, not only for us to keep the commandments but also to ensure we keep them in the right way. God does not want blind or begrudging obedience, but lives of service that are offered out of love and gratitude. We are to live with integrity according to God's covenant instructions, willingly and joyfully, because "God is [our] praise" (10:21).

Partners With God and One Another

Both passages from Deuteronomy make clear two things. The first is that God has more than a passing interest in what happens on this earth. Oppression, exploitation, and injustice are not light matters in God's eyes. Second, God looks to us to be advocates and instruments of the divine goal whenever and wherever we can. We are called to work for justice here on earth, no matter how hopeless the cause may seem at times.

Recognizing and embracing this call, mainline denominations across the globe have devoted themselves to social justice. The United Methodist Church (UMC) itself has developed several unified "Social Principles" that focus on, among other things, eradicating poverty and promoting global health. Giving new words to this ancient concern, the 2008 UMC stance reads, in part:

▶ "We affirm all persons as equally valuable in the sight of God. We therefore work toward societies in which each person's value is recognized, maintained, and strengthened. We support the basic rights of all persons to equal access to housing, education, communication, employment, medical care, legal redress for grievances, and physical protection. We deplore acts of hate or violence against groups or persons based on race, ethnicity, gender, sexual orientation, religious affiliation, or economic status" (from *162 III*).

▶ "We claim all economic systems to be under the judgment of God no less than other facets of the created order. Therefore, we . . . support measures that would reduce the concentration of wealth in the hands of a few" (from *163 IV*).

▶ "We commit ourselves as a Church to the achievement of a world community that is a fellowship of persons who honestly love one another. We pledge ourselves to seek the meaning of the gospel in all issues that divide people and threaten the growth of world community" (from *165*).

Each of these statements bears witness to God's teachings on justice as recorded in Deuteronomy. Each also manifests the sincere belief, held by Christian folks across denominational lines, that our identity as covenant people rests in our willingness to work for peace and justice in God's name.

A Christian's Pledge

Throughout the United States, people will join together in reciting the Pledge of Allegiance on July 4. Based on today's lesson, I invite you to read the following lines from a litany designed as a companion piece to the "UMC Social Creed" and to use them in forming an additional pledge to God. May this pledge serve to inspire you and strengthen you as a citizen of the heavenly realm now and in the days ahead.

Today is the day
God embraces all hues of humanity,
    delights in diversity and difference,
    favors solidarity transforming
      strangers into friends.
And so shall we.
Today is the day
God cries with the masses of starving
    people,
    despises growing disparity
    between rich and poor,
    demands justice for workers in the
      marketplace.
And so shall we.
Today is the day
God deplores violence in our homes
    and streets,
    rebukes the world's warring
      madness,
    humbles the powerful and lifts up
      the lowly.
And so shall we.
Today is the day
God calls for nations and peoples to
    live in peace,
    celebrates where justice and mercy
      embrace,
    exults when the wolf grazes with
      the lamb.
And so shall we.
Today is the day
God brings good news to the poor,
    proclaims release to the captives,
    gives sight to the blind, and
    sets the oppressed free.
And so shall we.

SHARING THE SCRIPTURE

Preparing Our Hearts

Explore this week's devotional reading, found in Micah 6:1-8. In verse 6, the Israelite worshipers want to know what kinds of offerings will please God. They suggest major sacrifices, including firstborn children. But no, this definitely is not what God wants. Read verse 8 aloud with great feeling. Hear what God wants from you. What are you willing to give?

Pray that you and the adult learners will worship by doing justice, loving kindness, and walking humbly with God.

Preparing Our Minds

Study the background Scripture from Deuteronomy 10:1-22 and 16:18-20. The lesson Scripture is from Deuteronomy 10:12-22 and 16:18-20. As you prepare, think about how someone should respond when others have shown love.

Write on newsprint:
❑ information for next week's lesson, found under "Continue the Journey."
❑ activities for further spiritual growth in "Continue the Journey."

LEADING THE CLASS

(1) Gather to Learn

❖ Welcome the class members and introduce any guests.

❖ Pray that the students will be ready to respond to God's love.

❖ Invite volunteers to talk about times when love was unexpectedly, perhaps undeservedly, extended to them. Suggest that they base their stories on these questions:

(1) What were the circumstances?

(2) How did you respond to this gracious outpouring of love?

(3) How did this experience motivate you to extend love to someone else?

❖ Read aloud today's focus statement: **People respond in various ways to being loved. How should someone respond when he or she is the recipient of love? As recipients of God's love, we are expected to be fair, act justly, and love others.**

(2) Investigate Ways the People of Israel Were to Respond to God's Love

❖ Choose two volunteers, one to read Deuteronomy 10:12-22 and the other to read Deuteronomy 16:18-20.

❖ Discuss these questions with the class. Use information from Understanding the Scripture as appropriate.

(1) What do these passages reveal about who God is and how God acts?

(2) What expectations are set forth here for the people of God?

(3) What are God's standards for justice?

❖ Read or retell "A Familiar Concern" from Interpreting the Scripture. As time permits, encourage volunteers to look up and read aloud the Bible passages cited there. Invite the adults to identify other Scriptures with the same theme. Suggest that love,

which reveals itself in justice, is at the heart of God.

❖ Read aloud "A Christian's Pledge" from Interpreting the Scripture. Include the class by gesturing to signal that they are to say "Today is the day" as you begin a stanza. Use another gesture to signal that they are to say "And so shall we" as the stanza ends.

(3) Identify Times When the Learners Extended Love to Another

❖ Read one or more of the following scenarios and encourage the students to respond by describing ways they have extended—or could extend—love to others. If the class is large, form small discussion groups.

Scenario 1: You are on a busy street when a shabbily dressed person approaches you asking for lunch money.

Scenario 2: A neighbor who has often spoken nastily to your children is having car trouble. You know his office is within a block of yours.

Scenario 3: An immigrant family has moved in three houses from yours. You know that God has a special concern for the stranger and alien, but you do not know this family and their immigration status.

Scenario 4: A friend at a party you are attending begins to make jokes and disparaging remarks about a particular group of people. Most who are listening respond with snickers.

❖ Challenge the class to be on the lookout for people to whom they can extend God's love. Encourage them to show God's love to at least one person each day.

(4) Organize or Learn More About a Ministry That Addresses Economic Justice Needs in the Community

❖ Point out that according to our Bible readings, loving God prompts us to love those whom God loves. Notice that in Deuteronomy 10:18-19 three groups of people are called out: orphans, widows, and strangers. In other words, those who are vulnerable to personal, social, and economic injustice are to be especially cared for.

❖ List on newsprint the ministries that your congregation engages in to address economic justice needs. These may be direct service ministries, such as operating a clothes closet, soup kitchen, or a shelter, either within your building or in cooperation with other churches and local agencies. Such ministries usually help people to meet short-term needs. The church may also engage in direct service that offers longer-term assistance, such as Habitat for Humanity. Or you may have ministries that advocate for long-term, systemic change.

❖ Encourage students who are familiar with these ministries to talk about them.

❖ Discuss these questions:

(1) Do you believe that we as a congregation are reaching out to meet the needs of those who are crying out for justice? Explain your answer.

(2) What more can we do to help?

(3) If our members are reluctant to reach out, what steps can we as a class take to help educate and encourage them to become more involved in justice issues?

❖ **Option:** Post newsprint. Help the class to write a litany about love and justice using ideas from today's Scripture reading. Read the litany as a group.

(5) Continue the Journey

❖ Pray that the adults will go forth to address economic justice needs in their community.

❖ Read aloud this preparation for next week's lesson. You may also want to post it on newsprint for the students to copy.

■ **Title: Samuel Administers Justice**

■ **Background Scripture: 1 Samuel 7:3-17**

■ **Lesson Scripture: 1 Samuel 7:3-11, 15-17**

■ **Focus of the Lesson: People want to feel safe. What gives people a sense of security? Samuel taught the people that their security was a direct result of their loyalty and obedience to God.**

❖ Challenge the students to complete one or more of these activities for further spiritual growth related to this week's session. Post this information on newsprint for the students to copy.

(1) **Read Deuteronomy 10:12-13 daily. Try to memorize these words. Evaluate how well you are living up to God's requirements.**

(2) **Research poverty in your community or county. What is the scope of the need? What agencies are trying to help those who lack sufficient food, housing, and jobs? What are churches doing?**

(3) **Spend time with people who may feel lonely, unloved, and forgotten, such as nursing home residents, prisoners, families of prisoners, or patients in long-term psychiatric facilities. Show God's love to them through your actions.**

❖ Sing or read aloud "What Does the Lord Require."

❖ Conclude today's session by leading the class in this benediction adapted from Deuteronomy 10:12-13, the key verses for this week: **Go forth remembering that we are to fear the Lord our God, to walk in all his ways, to love God, to serve the Lord with all our heart and soul, and to keep God's commandments.**

UNIT 2: JUSTICE ENACTED
SAMUEL ADMINISTERS JUSTICE

PREVIEWING THE LESSON

Lesson Scripture: 1 Samuel 7:3-11, 15-17
Background Scripture: 1 Samuel 7:3-17
Key Verse: 1 Samuel 7:3

Focus of the Lesson:
People want to feel safe. What gives people a sense of security? Samuel taught the people that their security was a direct result of their loyalty and obedience to God.

Goals for the Learners:
(1) to explore the biblical story of Samuel's being an administrator of justice.
(2) to recall how they felt at a time when they were rescued.
(3) to identify false gods and make a commitment to set them aside and return to God.

Pronunciation Guide:
Amorite (am' uh rite)	Ebenezer (eb uh nee' zuhr)
Ashtoreth (ash' tuh reth)	Gilgal (gil' gal)
Astarte (as tahr' tee)	Jeshanah (jesh' uh nuh)
Baal (bay' uhl) or (bah ahl')	Kiriath-jearim (kihr' ee ath jee' uh rim)
Beth-car (beth kahr')	Mizpah (miz' puh)
Bethel (beth' uhl)	Ramah (ray' muh)

Supplies:
Bibles, newsprint and marker, paper and pencils, hymnals, map

---

READING THE SCRIPTURE

NRSV
1 Samuel 7:3-11, 15-17

³Then Samuel said to all the house of Israel, "If you are returning to the LORD with all your heart, then put away the foreign gods and the Astartes from among you.

NIV
1 Samuel 7:3-11, 15-17

³And Samuel said to the whole house of Israel, "If you are returning to the LORD with all your hearts, then rid yourselves of the foreign gods and the Ashtoreths and

Direct your heart to the LORD, and serve him only, and he will deliver you out of the hand of the Philistines." [4]So Israel put away the Baals and the Astartes, and they served the LORD only.

[5]Then Samuel said, "Gather all Israel at Mizpah, and I will pray to the LORD for you." [6]So they gathered at Mizpah, and drew water and poured it out before the LORD. They fasted that day, and said, "We have sinned against the LORD." And Samuel judged the people of Israel at Mizpah.

[7]When the Philistines heard that the people of Israel had gathered at Mizpah, the lords of the Philistines went up against Israel. And when the people of Israel heard of it they were afraid of the Philistines. [8]The people of Israel said to Samuel, "Do not cease to cry out to the LORD our God for us, and pray that he may save us from the hand of the Philistines." [9]So Samuel took a sucking lamb and offered it as a whole burnt offering to the LORD; Samuel cried out to the LORD for Israel, and the LORD answered him. [10]As Samuel was offering up the burnt offering, the Philistines drew near to attack Israel; but the LORD thundered with a mighty voice that day against the Philistines and threw them into confusion; and they were routed before Israel. [11]And the men of Israel went out of Mizpah and pursued the Philistines, and struck them down as far as beyond Beth-car.

[15]Samuel judged Israel all the days of his life. [16]He went on a circuit year by year to Bethel, Gilgal, and Mizpah; and he judged Israel in all these places. [17]Then he would come back to Ramah, for his home was there; he administered justice there to Israel, and built there an altar to the LORD.

commit yourselves to the LORD and serve him only, and he will deliver you out of the hand of the Philistines." [4]So the Israelites put away their Baals and Ashtoreths, and served the LORD only.

[5]Then Samuel said, "Assemble all Israel at Mizpah and I will intercede with the LORD for you." [6]When they had assembled at Mizpah, they drew water and poured it out before the LORD. On that day they fasted and there they confessed, "We have sinned against the LORD." And Samuel was leader of Israel at Mizpah.

[7]When the Philistines heard that Israel had assembled at Mizpah, the rulers of the Philistines came up to attack them. And when the Israelites heard of it, they were afraid because of the Philistines. [8]They said to Samuel, "Do not stop crying out to the LORD our God for us, that he may rescue us from the hand of the Philistines." [9]Then Samuel took a suckling lamb and offered it up as a whole burnt offering to the LORD. He cried out to the LORD on Israel's behalf, and the LORD answered him.

[10]While Samuel was sacrificing the burnt offering, the Philistines drew near to engage Israel in battle. But that day the LORD thundered with loud thunder against the Philistines and threw them into such a panic that they were routed before the Israelites. [11]The men of Israel rushed out of Mizpah and pursued the Philistines, slaughtering them along the way to a point below Beth Car.

[15]Samuel continued as judge over Israel all the days of his life. [16]From year to year he went on a circuit from Bethel to Gilgal to Mizpah, judging Israel in all those places. [17]But he always went back to Ramah, where his home was, and there he also judged Israel. And he built an altar there to the LORD.

UNDERSTANDING THE SCRIPTURE

Introduction. The books of 1 and 2 Samuel describe the transition in Israel from a loosely formed, tribal confederacy to a consolidated monarchy. The low point in Israel's history (the last days of the judges) and the high point in Israel's history (the reigns of David and Solomon) happened back-to-back in this period around the turn of the millennium, 1000 B.C. Samuel's ministry spanned this important turning point in the life of the nation.

In addition, dangerous foes surrounded Israel during Samuel's lifetime. The Philistines were a small group of people living on the southwestern plains of Palestine. They were aggressive and well organized. Moreover, they had iron weapons—more effective than Israel's bronze ones—and they had an efficient, permanent army. The tribes of Israel were able to defend themselves against the Philistines somewhat but not completely, so the balance of power tended to swing between these two forces.

At the time our passage begins, a vital national symbol had returned into Israel's hands. The ark of the covenant, the sacred box containing the Ten Commandments, had been captured by the Philistines some time before (see 1 Samuel 4:11). After some years of trouble everywhere the ark was taken, however, the Philistines decided to give it back to the Israelites. It eventually came to Kiriath-jearim, where it stayed until King David brought it to Jerusalem. The story of the ark's journey to Philistine country and back again begins in 1 Samuel 4 and ends with the verses for this lesson (1 Samuel 7:3-17).

First Samuel 7:2 tells how the ark rested at Kiriath-jearim for some twenty years and the people "lamented" for God. The Hebrew seems to imply that they were imploring God's help, apparently because they still felt justifiably threatened by the Philistines. This is the circumstance under which Samuel emerges as the leader who will deliver the people. Such folks throughout Israel's early history are called *judges*, and Samuel will be the last of them. From other biblical sources, we know this particular role primarily involved spearheading actions to deliver the people from military threats.

Samuel was certainly a fitting leader in terms of his devotion to God. His mother had consecrated him to God's service even before he was conceived. As soon as he was weaned, she took him to be raised at the temple in Shiloh (1 Samuel 1:21-28). For the rest of his childhood, he stayed at the sanctuary in Shiloh and assisted Eli the priest with various duties there. Samuel "grew up in the presence of the LORD" (2:21). During the later part of his life, his role as judge was clearly affected by his priestly upbringing. In the verses for this week, we see that Samuel's first order of business was to set Israel right with God. The events that follow seem to represent parts of a covenant ceremony.

1 Samuel 7:3-4. Samuel begins by asking the people to put away all their foreign gods. The charge to "put away" referred both to removing from the heart any devotion to these gods and to disposing of any idols. The plural "Baals" and "Astartes" may signify statuettes of these deities or the worship of individual variations of these deities based on region. Baal was the principal Canaanite god of fertility and also the god of storms. His consort, Astarte, was the goddess of love and fertility and also of war. As a predominantly rural society based on agriculture and husbandry, the Israelites were often tempted to make offerings to any local deity who might be able to increase prosperity. Archaeological remains suggest that worship of Baal and Astarte continued well into the period of the divided kingdoms of Israel and Judah.

1 Samuel 7:5-6. Samuel called for "all Israel" to gather at Mizpah, about four miles northwest of Jerusalem. Such global calls could not be obeyed literally; they occur as a literary device in the Bible to show that the results of any subsequent action will be binding on the whole faith community. Later, after the people have assembled, Samuel has them give an offering of water to the Lord. Offerings of wine were common, so the use of water here may be meant to invoke the image of Israel's wilderness wandering. Then, after the people fast and confess their sin, Samuel "judges" them. The action probably refers to legal proceedings in this instance—hearing cases, settling disputes, and so on. Having been made right with God through the ritual acts of fasting and prayer, the people are now able to be set right with one another.

1 Samuel 7:7-11. The Philistines move to attack the gathering at Mizpah. The people hear of this and ask Samuel to beseech God on their behalf. He does so, and the Philistines are routed by divine intervention. Such action—threat from an enemy, a plea for divine help, and rescue at the hands of a God-given leader—fits a pattern that runs throughout the Book of Judges and thus is fitting for this account of the last "judge" (in this word's meaning of "national deliverer").

1 Samuel 7:12-14. To commemorate the victory, Samuel sets up a standing stone between Mizpah and Jeshanah. He names it Ebenezer ("stone of help") as a testimony to God's aid both then and over the past generations. He and others would have remembered that Ebenezer was the name of the place where the Philistines first defeated the Israelites in a great slaughter (4:2, 10). Now that action has been reversed. Verse 14 goes on to say that Israel recovered all of its territory from the Philistines and even found peace with the Amorites (perhaps here a general term for all other enemies).

1 Samuel 7:15-17. The final verses summarize some of Samuel's other accomplishments. For the rest of his life, he functioned as a circuit judge, traveling to Bethel, Gilgal, and Mizpah before returning home to Ramah. There he served as both judge (in a legal sense) and priest, administering justice and making sacrifices, until setting out on the road for a new round of visits.

INTERPRETING THE SCRIPTURE

A Judge's Role

This week we begin Unit 2 and its focus on how justice was enacted by key leaders in the community of faith. We start with a stirring event in the life of Israel's last judge, Samuel. Gathered at Mizpah under his leadership for a renewal of the covenant with God, the people are attacked by the Philistine army. Thanks to Samuel's prayer and God's intervention, the people not only survive the ambush, they force their enemies to retreat far away.

Given the focus of this quarter, one may wonder what there is to learn about justice from this story of war. To answer this, however, we must put ourselves within the mind of the biblical writer and audience.

This week's text—along with the entire Book of Judges—builds on a particular understanding of the word that we translate as "judge." The original Hebrew word mainly indicates military leaders and community administrators with only minimal, if any, responsibility for legal decisions. Again, we read about a "judge" whom God raises up in times of crisis to lead the people and gain their release from subjugation. Deborah was one such leader (Judges 4–5), Samson another (13–16).

These judges are particularly significant as signs of God's continuing love. They arose at God's initiative when the people were most in need because the Lord "would be moved to pity" (Judges 2:18). Thus the judges indicate God's ongoing concern for Israel. Over and over God would raise up someone to bring the people into safety, security, and prosperity (2:18). The deliverance was very much "this worldly," in the here and now. This is an important reminder that God's love breaks into life now, instead of waiting for some "afterlife" to begin to make a difference.

Within Samuel's lifetime, Israel would have its first king—thus Samuel would be the last of the judges. We know little about him except that he came from a prominent, wealthy family who lived in Ramah, in the hill country of Ephraim. His mother, Hannah, prayed for a son at the sanctuary at Shiloh because she was barren, and she promised to dedicate him to God. Samuel was born to Hannah the next year. When he was weaned, Hannah took him to Shiloh, where she dedicated him as she had promised.

He was reared by Eli, the priest, and assisted in the work at the sanctuary in Shiloh (1 Samuel 2:11-36). After he received a vision concerning the downfall of Eli and his house, Samuel was acknowledged a prophet (3:1–4:1). As our text for this week shows, later in life he served the people as priest, military deliverer, and judge (7:3-17).

The Real Fight

Reading today's passage in its larger context, we see that the real battle Samuel faced was not with the Philistine army but with the Canaanite religion. The Philistines posed a physical threat from which the people wanted relief, but other fears and anxieties had driven them to embrace "baals" and "astartes" as a form of security. Samuel wanted to free the people to experience the true security found only in God.

The word "baal" means "lord." As such, it sometimes was used in a generic sense to address wealthy or powerful men in society, and it also was used at times as a title for God. As a proper name, however, Baal referred to a popular Canaanite god. Mostly known as the god of the storm, Baal represented both the life-giving and life-threatening powers of rain. He and his consort, Astarte, were powerful symbols of fertility in the ancient Canaanite religion. The rituals of this religion—which sometimes included sexual acts designed to stir the deities to fecundity—were intended to ensure that there would be ample crops, thriving flocks, and numerous human offspring.

When the people of Israel left behind the desert wilderness and entered the relatively fertile land of Canaan, they accepted the religion of their farming neighbors as part of the agricultural way of life. There were certain things that one did to grow olives, grapes, or grain. One of these was to set up a small "baal" (an idol honoring Baal). Similarly, a household "astarte" was thought to aid in getting pregnant. Most Israelites did not have the concern of the Deuteronomistic Historians or the prophets for religious "purity." The Israelites believed in the God of the covenant, but they also thought that the little Baal and Astarte figurines couldn't hurt when it came to raising food and having children. Thus Israel was tempted by a religion that seemed to meet very basic personal and communal needs.

Enacting Justice

How different is the religion Samuel represented. While there was concern for childbearing and good harvests, the major emphasis was on caring for one another. In our particular passage today the emphasis is on the single-minded, single-hearted worship of the Lord God. Elsewhere, the tradition also emphasizes our calling to love our neighbor as ourselves. Caring for the powerless, particularly orphans and widows and non-nationals, is a high priority. Thus the religion that developed as a consequence of worshiping the Lord God was quite different in key respects from that of Baal. This is not to say that the Israelites were always faithful or followed their own best understanding, but the theology did produce a different religious tradition than that of the surrounding peoples.

When we try to think about what difference our faith can make, it is not always easy to see. If we look at Christianity's impact on cultures different from our own, it sometimes helps. It is not accidental that Christians have been in the forefront of the effort to improve the place of women in India and China, for instance. It is not coincidence that it was a Reformed Church pastor who started the revolution against Communism in Eastern Europe. Likewise, it is not surprising that some Christians realized many years ago that the social policies of the government of South Africa and other repressive regimes have to be resisted and overturned.

We do not have "judges" now, but it is interesting to note how leaders still do arise to lead God's people. A little-known minister named Martin Luther King Jr. became a national, even international, figure on the basis of work that began in the Birmingham, Alabama, bus boycott. He became an outstanding leader of both whites and blacks in the struggle to ensure the civil rights of all Americans. There are numerous individuals in local communities who rise to particular occasions. They may not gain a national reputation, but they still are leaders of God's people in critical situations. These people remind us that God still hears our cries for help and raises leaders for the occasion.

We also ssee our own responsibility for enacting God's justice in our personal and communal lives. Samuel's model shows us that we are to work toward the good of all and not just our own advantage. We are called to pray for one another and for our world, just as we are called to build communities in which all people feel safe. The final, joyous outcome of accepting this responsibility is that we come to glimpse and even to experience a taste of the perfect justice that will come under the reign of the One who alone is Lord of lords—Jesus Christ our Savior and Friend.

SHARING THE SCRIPTURE

Preparing Our Hearts

Explore this week's devotional reading, found in Ezekiel 18:25-32. Chapter 18 concerns individual retribution. Verse 25 begins the second objection raised, this one concerning what appears to be the arbitrariness of God. Yet that is not the case. In verse 30, God promises to judge us according to our ways and calls us to repent. Clearly God is not interested in seeing anyone die, but rather calls people to turn and live. What is your response to God's call?

Pray that you and the adult learners will recognize and respond to God's call on your lives.

Preparing Our Minds

Study the background Scripture from 1 Samuel 7:3-17 and the lesson Scripture from 1 Samuel 7:3-11, 15-17. Think about what gives people a sense a security.

Write on newsprint:
❑ information for next week's lesson, found under "Continue the Journey."
❑ activities for further spiritual growth in "Continue the Journey."

Locate a map showing Bethel, Gilgal, Mizpah, and Ramah.

LEADING THE CLASS

(1) Gather to Learn

❖ Welcome the class members and introduce any guests.

❖ Pray that the students will seek security in God.

❖ Call on volunteers to define "security" and write their definitions on newsprint. This word has many definitions, including the following ones from *The American Heritage Dictionary of the English Language,* Fourth Edition: "freedom from risk or danger; safety; freedom from doubt, anxiety, or fear; confidence; something that gives or assures safety; a stock certificate or bond."

❖ Ask: **Where do you look for security?**

❖ Read aloud today's focus statement: **People want to feel safe. What gives people a sense of security? Samuel taught the people that their security was a direct result of their loyalty and obedience to God.**

(2) Explore the Biblical Story of Samuel's Being an Administrator of Justice

❖ Read or retell "Introduction" from Understanding the Scripture to orient the students to the history and context of today's session. Also use information from "A Judge's Role" in Interpreting the Scripture to clarify who Samuel was and what his role as a judge entailed. Show the map you have located to mark Bethel, Gilgal, Mizpah, and Ramah, which were the towns on Samuel's circuit (7:16-17).

❖ Choose a volunteer to read 1 Samuel 7:3-11, 15-17.

❖ Use major points from "The Real Fight" from Interpreting the Scripture to explain that Samuel's concerns were with the Canaanite religion.

❖ Suggest that the participants imagine themselves among the Israelite crowd at Mizpah and ask:

(1) **What emotions are overflowing as the Philistines approach?**

(2) **What did you *really* expect Samuel to be able to do?**

(3) **What did you believe about God when you heard a "mighty voice" and realized that the Philistines had been thrown "into confusion" and "were routed" (7:10)?**

(4) **After this amazing encounter with the Philistines, did your view of Samuel change? If so, how was it different?**

(5) **After this encounter with the Philistines, were you eager to return to God and set aside the foreign gods you were worshiping? Why or why not?**

❖ Suggest that the participants imagine themselves as members of the Philistine army and ask:

(1) **What were your expectations as you approached Mizpah?**

(2) **How was your view of Israel's God changed as a result of this encounter?**

❖ Wrap up this portion by asking: **If Samuel were an elected leader, what might his campaign staff say about the work that he does, his character, and the way he leads?**

(3) Recall How the Learners Felt at a Time When They Were Rescued

❖ Form small groups and invite participants to recall times when they needed to be rescued. Perhaps they recall being small children who had become separated from parents. Or maybe they remember being in uncomfortable situations as teens. Possibly they had lost jobs or homes as adults. Some students may wish to tell entire stories, but encourage them to focus on their feelings when they were rescued. How did they feel, for example, when distraught parents found them and held them close for hugs and kisses?

❖ Probe to see if the adults made any changes after these rescues. Did they, for example, decide to stay close to loved ones, particularly in crowds, so as not to become separated again? Ask them to consider how such changes might have given them a greater sense of security.

❖ Conclude this portion of the lesson by asking: **How are the feelings you had about being rescued from danger similar to and different from the feelings you have about Jesus' desire to rescue you from a broken relationship with God?**

(4) Identify False Gods and Make a Commitment to Set Them Aside and Return to God

❖ Distribute slips of paper and pencils. Give the adults a brief time to think of a false god that many people, including some Christians, worship. The students are to sketch a symbol for this false god on their paper, such as a dollar sign to represent money or a thunderbolt to represent power. If they want to identify several false gods, they may create symbols on different sections of their papers.

❖ Invite volunteers to show their symbols and encourage the class to guess their meaning. Ask for a show of hands to identify others who selected the same false god. Display, if possible, these symbols on a wall or bulletin board.

❖ Note that Christians may worship some of these same gods, just as nonbelievers do. Lead the group in reading 1 Samuel 7:3, today's key verse, pointing out that the thrust of the verse is God's deliverance of those who turn toward God.

❖ Provide additional paper for the adults to reflect on the key verse by making a written commitment to put away the false gods that they serve and return to God.

(5) Continue the Journey

❖ Pray that the adults will continue to identify false gods and commit themselves to worship God alone.

❖ Read aloud this preparation for next week's lesson. You may also want to post it on newsprint for the students to copy.

■ **Title: David Embodies God's Justice**

■ **Background Scripture: 2 Samuel 22:1–23:7; 1 Chronicles 18:14**

■ **Lesson Scripture: 2 Samuel 23:1-7; 1 Chronicles 18:14.**

■ **Focus of the Lesson: People want to have a meaningful existence. How do we discover our purpose in life? Acknowledging God's authority in our lives enables us to become the people God created us to be.**

❖ Challenge the students to complete one or more of these activities for further spiritual growth related to this week's session. Post this information on newsprint for the students to copy.

(1) **List strategies that you use to try to make your loved ones and yourself secure. How do these ways support, or seem to question, your sense of security in God?**

(2) **Learn more about policies in place that are to provide for the security of your nation. What evidence do you have that these policies are—or are not—working? How would you compare them to the security that God offered the Israelites?**

(3) **Encourage anyone you can to put away false gods and turn their lives over to the living God.**

❖ Sing or read aloud "Leaning on the Everlasting Arms."

❖ Conclude today's session by leading the class in this benediction adapted from Deuteronomy 10:12-13, the key verses for June 24: **Go forth remembering that we are to fear the Lord our God, to walk in all his ways, to love God, to serve the Lord with all our heart and soul, and to keep God's commandments.**

UNIT 2: JUSTICE ENACTED
DAVID EMBODIES GOD'S JUSTICE

PREVIEWING THE LESSON

Lesson Scripture: 2 Samuel 23:1-7; 1 Chronicles 18:14
Background Scripture: 2 Samuel 22:1–23:7; 1 Chronicles 18:14
Key Verse: 1 Chronicles 18:14

Focus of the Lesson:
People want to have a meaningful existence. How do we discover our purpose in life? Acknowledging God's authority in our lives enables us to become the people God created us to be.

Goals for the Learners:
(1) to describe the results of being an instrument of God's justice.
(2) to reflect on what it means to act justly as a way of worshiping God.
(3) to create a written summary of their own lives as agents of justice.

Pronunciation Guide:
Mephibosheth (mi fib' oh sheth)

Supplies:
Bibles, newsprint and marker, paper and pencils, hymnals, optional recording of Randall Thompson's "The Seven Last Words of David" and appropriate player, research tools (such as Bible dictionary, concordance)

READING THE SCRIPTURE

NRSV
2 Samuel 23:1-7
1 Now these are the last words of David:
   The oracle of David, son of Jesse,
     the oracle of the man whom God
       exalted,
   the anointed of the God of Jacob,

NIV
2 Samuel 23:1-7
1These are the last words of David:
   "The oracle of David son of Jesse,
   the oracle of the man exalted by the
     Most High,
   the man anointed by the God of Jacob,
   Israel's singer of songs:

the favorite of the Strong One of Israel:
2 The spirit of the LORD speaks through me,
    his word is upon my tongue.
3 The God of Israel has spoken,
    the Rock of Israel has said to me:
One who rules over people justly,
    ruling in the fear of God,
4 is like the light of morning,
    like the sun rising on a cloudless
        morning,
    gleaming from the rain on the grassy
        land.
5 Is not my house like this with God?
    For he has made with me an
        everlasting covenant,
    ordered in all things and secure.
Will he not cause to prosper
    all my help and my desire?
6 But the godless are all like thorns that
        are thrown away;
    for they cannot be picked up with the
        hand;
7 to touch them one uses an iron bar
    or the shaft of a spear.
And they are entirely consumed in
    fire on the spot.

1 Chronicles 18:14
**14 So David reigned over all Israel; and
he administered justice and equity to all
his people.**

2"The Spirit of the LORD spoke through me;
    his word was on my tongue.
3The God of Israel spoke,
    the Rock of Israel said to me:
'When one rules over men in
        righteousness,
    when he rules in the fear of God,
4he is like the light of morning at sunrise
    on a cloudless morning,
    like the brightness after rain
    that brings the grass from the earth.'
5"Is not my house right with God?
Has he not made with me an everlasting
        covenant,
    arranged and secured in every part?
Will he not bring to fruition my salvation
    and grant me my every desire?
6But evil men are all to be cast aside
        like thorns,
    which are not gathered with the hand.
7Whoever touches thorns
    uses a tool of iron or the shaft of a spear;
    they are burned up where they lie."

1 Chronicles 18:14
**14David reigned over all Israel, doing
what was just and right for all his people.**

UNDERSTANDING THE SCRIPTURE

2 Samuel 22:1. The passages for this week summarize the reign of King David, mostly in poetic form. Chapter 22 is a hymn of praise that we also know as Psalm 18. While there are small differences between the two versions, the text is generally the same. The occasion for the song is God's deliverance of David from all enemies, including the previous king, Saul. In that regard it appears out of place here at the end of David's life story. Ancient writers often

inserted songs or poetry into prose accounts for effect, considering artistic integrity more important than chronological consistency.

2 Samuel 22:2-4. The psalm begins with images of God designed to promote a sense of safety: rock, fortress, refuge, and so on. The psalmist declares that God is his savior and therefore worthy of praise. The opening verses specifically mention deliverance from violence, and certainly David's life had plenty of that. As a warrior, he fought the Philistines and other marauders. As a rising political star, he had skirmishes with Saul, who actively sought to take his life. As king, David continued to fight wars and also quelled rebellions, the worst of which led to the death of his son Absalom.

2 Samuel 22:5-16. God is in the temple above when David's cry for help comes. Telling of God's subsequent descent to earth, the following verses borrow heavily from images of God's presence in Exodus and other Scriptures. Earthquakes, smoke, and fire are all part of such epiphanies. We also see images associated with the power of storms.

2 Samuel 22:17-20. This same God is the One who saves the psalmist. Note that the description of the deliverance is full of intentional contrasts. The God who comes on the waters of the storm to save David does so by lifting him out of the "mighty waters" that represent threat, chaos, and death (22:17). The defeated enemies, too mighty and strong for the king, are no match for the power of God (22:18). They present a sudden and unexpected attack when David is already in distress, but God is steadfast and constant then and always (22:19). The end result is that God brings David out of the constraints of fear and danger into "a broad place" of safety and rest (22:20). All this the Lord does because David is God's delight.

2 Samuel 22:21-25. The next lines launch into a vindication of the king. Underlying these verses and those of the next section is a concept found elsewhere, for example in Psalm 1 and various proverbs (for example, Proverbs 10:3; 12:2): God rewards the righteous. David declares, in a sense, that God's deliverance is his due because he has been blameless and faithful in all ways. The king's salvation is thus tied to his righteousness and cleanliness in God's eyes, though the reader knows that David has not been truly blameless. It is worth mentioning that other Scriptures, notably the books of Job and Ecclesiastes, offer a different theological perspective. There is a strong biblical strain that sees our commitment and dedication as *God's* due for divine acts of undeserved mercy and grace. In this vein, some suggest that David's words would better be rendered as "I was faithful to God because I trusted God would be faithful to me. Now that God's faithfulness has been proved, I have even more reason to be faithful than before."

2 Samuel 22:26-31. The theme of divine retribution—God rewards the good and punishes the evil—continues in this passage. The psalmist describes God's relationship with people in terms of action and response—in other words, God treats individuals according to how they themselves act. Verse 28 picks up the theme of reversal that runs through much of the Bible in saying the humble are lifted up while the proud are brought low. This part of the psalm harkens back to the song of Samuel's mother, Hannah, which began this particular historical saga (1 Samuel 2:1-10). David ends this section by praising the strength and the refuge he has in God.

2 Samuel 22:32-43. The empowerment described in verse 31 now gains shape in terms of God's preparation of David for war. The king declares that, with God's help, he is now swift of foot, strong with the bow, shielded from harm, and virtually unbeatable in battle. While most of us would be more comfortable with a spiritualized account of the gifts God provides such as those found in Ephesians 6:10-17, these verses reflect the reality of David's world. Hostile groups surrounded Israel's territory and constantly vied for control. War was continual, yet David managed to meet and grow in God even under those circumstances.

2 Samuel 22:44-46. This reference to a military victory over all enemies may refer to events after David became king.

2 Samuel 22:47-51. The psalm erupts into a song of praise to God. David celebrates all that God has done for him and promises to extol God's name "among the nations" (22:50). Verse 51 appears to be a late addition to the poem, perhaps inserted by an editor. The language shifts from a direct personal address to God to the descriptive language of a third-party observer. The verse ends with a declaration of God's steadfast love "to David and his descendants forever."

2 Samuel 23:1-7. Note that verse 1 names David as the "son of Jesse," which (along with the reference to "the God of Jacob") establishes him within Israel's tribal history. Moreover, he is "the man whom God exalted" (23:1), most notably by becoming God's anointed king, and he is no less than God's favorite. This passage contains another hymn of praise, this time presented as David's last words. The psalm begins in verse 2 with prophetic intensity in that David says that the words are *God's* words. He then uses beautiful images from nature to describe the effect of one who rules with justice like God's. This is followed by a celebratory section on the everlasting covenant God has made with David and his descendants.

1 Chronicles 18:14. This verse sums up David's reign concisely with the statement that "he administered justice and equity to all his people." The source for this text is 2 Samuel 8:15.

INTERPRETING THE SCRIPTURE

Insights from Hindsight

The passages for this week look back on the long and successful reign of King David. Both the psalm of 2 Samuel 23 and the brief summary in 1 Chronicles 18:14 affirm that David was a king who truly represented God's justice on earth.

If you have ever studied David before, then you know that the story is not so simple. He was a gifted and passionate man, a charismatic leader, and a true lover of God. Yet he was also hotheaded, sometimes heartless, and prone to do as he wanted without thinking of the consequences.

David is one of those Old Testament characters who demands attention. Other kings may or may not interest us. A prophet's predicament may inspire or depress us. Various other figures from the stories heard in childhood still entrance us, but it is David whom everyone remembers. What do you recall best about David? Why do you think he is such a popular Old Testament character?

For many people, David's appeal comes from his humanness. He is in many ways much like us. He is no cardboard church school figure, but a complex person who responded to the demands placed on him in ways we might not expect of a good biblical example. In his humanness he does things we might have done, but somehow we expect more of him. For instance, was he really generous with Saul's heir, Jonathan's son Mephibosheth (2 Samuel 9:1-13), or was that just a good way to keep an eye on him? What difference does it make? Was David really pious in his acceptance of his son's death (12:15-23), or was it an attempt to impress his followers? Scholars don't agree on these points. We know, though, that this king who ruled during Israel's golden age experienced both success and failure. In short, David was a very human hero. He stood before God in all his strength and weakness.

Here at the end of his life, however, we are invited to remember all that God accomplished through David both *because of* and *in spite of* who he was. It is a message of grace that touches us all. As with David, God can use our gifts to make the world a better place—even despite our worst qualities.

Thus, we can take courage. No matter what life brings our way, no matter what situations we find ourselves in, we are not alone. God is there, working in and through us in ways that we don't expect, staying constantly involved in human affairs.

A Bigger Picture

Because the texts for this week are so complimentary about David's reign, scholars speculate that they were written long after he died. This is more than a mere case of memories growing fonder with the passage of time: The people of the divided kingdoms, Israel and Judah, suffered under a series of bad kings for many generations. After three to four hundred years of increasing economic oppression and perverted justice, they looked back more and more to David's rule as the only era when both king and people "got it right." Stories survived of David's less-than-faithful actions, but overall his reign came to symbolize the best of what it meant to live into God's promise that "I will be their God, and they shall be my people" (Jeremiah 31:33).

This is perhaps why justice runs as such a strong theme through both passages. Historical accounts of the later rulers that we find in 1–2 Kings and 1–2 Chronicles, along with the Prophetic Books, tell us how far both kingdoms fell from the ideal spelled out in Hebrew law. The picture we receive is both horrific and, sadly, familiar.

Consider a few examples from the prophet Amos regarding what was happening in Judah. The law forbade charging interest for loans to fellow citizens and specified very lenient repayment practices, yet Amos saw good, hardworking people being sold into slavery for failing to repay debts that hardly amounted to the cost of a pair of cheap shoes (Amos 2:6). The law required sexual restraint and modesty, but Amos saw young women being sexually abused by foolish youths and by the elders, who should have been the girls' protectors (2:7).

The prophet saw other women, privileged and well fed, lounging in luxury and enjoying fine wines while their servants struggled to survive without basic necessities (4:1). Adding even more insult to injury, some wealthy people were blending their acts of oppression with acts of worship—they lay in the sanctuary on poor people's unreturned cloaks and bought sacramental wine with fines imposed on those least able to pay (2:8; see Exodus 22:25-27).

Similar accusations run through other prophetic writings as well. Micah, for example, describes the effect of an uncaring elite class on the poor and oppressed in vivid imagery. Micah 3:9-12 specifically blames the political and religious leaders for what has happened, culminating in the charge: "Its rulers give judgment for a bribe, its priests teach for a price, its prophets give oracles for money; yet they lean upon the LORD and say, 'Surely the LORD is with us!'" (3:11). Prophets, priests, and judges (who are also sacred figures here) have in the most literal sense sold out. Micah 7:1-6 then describes the effect on the populace of the destruction of their life's social and economic fabric. Worst of all, Micah stresses the deliberate, intentional nature of the crimes committed by the powerful. They lie awake and scheme, and eagerly carry out their plots when morning breaks. They do this because they can; they are conscious of their power and use it (2:1-2).

It is no wonder that the people looked back to David's reign with longing, investing it with all the ideals of God's covenant calls to a just society. When we see our passages for today in this light, they can take on a new significance for us. They become more than historic documents that chronicle a fortunate period somewhere in the distant past. Instead, we are able to see them as reflections of a community of faith that, like ours, is wrestling with a desire for justice and an uncertainty about how to bring it about.

Good News for Today

When we look back on David's reign as this week's texts describe it, there is a word of hope for us and for the world. Regardless of how the passages may exaggerate David's perfection as king, he was nonetheless a true vessel for God's justice in countless ways. If we genuinely long to be a part of God's justice, too, then God can use us effectively as well. As individuals and faith communities, we can be transformed by God into instruments of justice.

Part of this transformation, of course, happens when the word of God is written on our hearts. The rest comes when we intentionally and actively seek to change the structures of injustice that keep people from the wholeness and well-being that God intends for all. Like David and the prophets, we are called to free those exploited by our society's drive for power. Like people of faith throughout the ages, we rejoice when we see God working through us for these ends.

SHARING THE SCRIPTURE

Preparing Our Hearts

Explore this week's devotional reading, found in Isaiah 32:1-8. Here the prophet speaks of an ideal king whose reign will be marked with righteousness and justice. Note the kind of world people will live in when this king rules. How would you describe an ideal ruler? How would people be affected by this monarch's administration?

Pray that you and the adult learners will continue to watch and wait for God's ideal ruler.

Preparing Our Minds

Study the background Scripture from 2 Samuel 22:1—23:7 and 1 Chronicles 18:14. The lesson Scripture is from 2 Samuel 23:1-7 and 1 Chronicles 18:14. As you prepare the lesson, think about how we discover our purpose in life.

Write on newsprint:
❑ information for next week's lesson, found under "Continue the Journey."
❑ activities for further spiritual growth in "Continue the Journey."

Locate, if possible, a CD of Randall Thompson's anthem "The Last Words of David." Have a CD player on hand. Or, if you have the capability, play a YouTube version, but be sure to preview and select one with good sound and tone, as well as an unhurried pace.

Find in your church or public library several Bible concordances and dictionaries. Bring as many as possible to class.

Prepare the suggested lecture for "Describe the Results of Being an Instrument of God's Justice."

LEADING THE CLASS

(1) Gather to Learn

❖ Welcome the class members and introduce any guests.

❖ Pray that the students will recognize the fruits of being instruments of God's justice.

❖ Read these words of former Secretary-General of the United Nations, Dag Hammarskjöld (1905–1961): **On the day I first really believed in God, for the first time life made sense to me, and the world had meaning.**

❖ Invite the participants to talk with a partner or small group about this quotation. How do these words square with their own experiences? Encourage them to talk about how their relationship with God gives their lives meaning and purpose.

❖ Bring the groups together and read aloud today's focus statement: **People want to have a meaningful existence. How do we discover our purpose in life? Acknowledging God's authority in our lives enables us to become the people God created us to be.**

(2) Describe the Results of Being an Instrument of God's Justice

❖ Present the lecture you have created from all of the portions of 2 Samuel 22 in Understanding the Scripture. Your purpose is to set the stage for today's reading.

❖ Choose a volunteer to read 2 Samuel 23:1-7.

❖ **Option:** Play Randall Thompson's exquisite rendition of "The Last Words of David." Talk with the group about how the words of verses 3-4 (quoted from the King James Bible) and the music fuse to create the image of a just ruler. (Note that some class members may have, as your editor does, fond memories of singing this in a high school choir or other choir. They may want to comment on what this music means to them.)

❖ Ask: **What do you learn about David from his last words?**

❖ Follow up on this question by forming groups and distributing whatever study resources you have located, along with paper and pencils. Suggest that students who have Bible concordances consult them too. Ask the groups to find information to support the assertions in verse 1 that David was "the man whom God exalted," "the anointed of . . . God," and "the favorite of the Strong One of Israel" (or as the King James Version says, "the sweet psalmist of Israel").

❖ Wrap up this portion by bringing the groups together to report whatever they found. Ask:

(1) **How does this additional infor-** mation broaden our understanding of David?

(2) **Did you find any references that would argue against the assertions made in the passages we are studying? If so, what were they? How do they present a more rounded picture of David?**

(3) Reflect on What It Means to Act Justly as a Way of Worshiping God

❖ Read these three Scripture texts:

■ **So now, O Israel, what does the LORD your God require of you? Only to fear the LORD your God, to walk in all his ways, to love him, to serve the LORD your God with all your heart and with all your soul, 13and to keep the commandments of the LORD your God and his decrees that I am commanding you today, for your own well-being. (Deuteronomy 10:12-13,** key verses for June 24)

■ **The days are surely coming, says the LORD, when I will raise up for David a righteous Branch, and he shall reign as king and deal wisely, and shall execute justice and righteousness in the land. (Jeremiah 23:5,** key verse for August 19)

■ **He has told you, O mortal,**
    what is good;
   and what does the LORD
    require of you
  but to do justice, and to love
    kindness,
   and to walk humbly with your
    God?
  (Micah 6:8)

❖ Discuss these questions:

(1) **What relationship do you see between these calls for just living and the way we are to worship God?**

(2) **What changes might we as individuals and as a congregation need to make in how we live in**

order to worship and serve God more faithfully?

(4) Create a Written Summary of the Learners' Lives as Agents of Justice

❖ Distribute paper and pencils. Invite the learners to fold their papers in quarters so that they have four blocks per side. They are to label each block as a decade of life: birth–ten, eleven–twenty, twenty-one –thirty, and so on until they reach the decade of their current age (or age eighty). Encourage them to write confidentially something in each block about how they acted as an agent of justice in each of their life decades.

❖ Lead the class in reading today's key verse from 1 Chronicles 18:14. Suggest that this verse could be read as an epitaph for David, who ruled with justice.

❖ Allow a few moments for the learners to review what they have written and consider whether they believe God views them as agents of justice. They are not to share their thoughts or written work. Invite the learners to write an epitaph that could be used to sum up their own lives.

❖ Choose volunteers who would like to share their epitaph with the group.

(5) Continue the Journey

❖ Pray that the adults will work to be agents of justice.

❖ Read aloud this preparation for next week's lesson. You may also want to post it on newsprint for the students to copy.

■ **Title: Solomon Judges with Wisdom and Justice**

■ **Background Scripture: 1 Kings 3; 2 Chronicles 9:8**

■ **Lesson Scripture: 1 Kings 3:16-28; 2 Chronicles 9:8**

■ **Focus of the Lesson: People need a just and wise mediator when life presents unjust situations. To whom may we go to receive justice? Because of Solomon's relationship with God, he was able to make just and wise choices.**

❖ Challenge the students to complete one or more of these activities for further spiritual growth related to this week's session. Post this information on newsprint for the students to copy.

(1) Speak out for an individual or group who has been denied justice. Use whatever influence you have to ensure that these people are treated justly.

(2) Paint or imagine a picture of "the sun rising on a cloudless morning, gleaming from the rain on the grassy land" (2 Samuel 23:4). How does this image help you to envision the just ruler that God chose to reign?

(3) Explore the treatment of immigrants or racial minorities in your community. Are they being treated with the kind of impartial justice that God demands? If not, what can you and your church do to change this situation?

❖ Sing or read aloud "La Palabra Del Señor Es Recta" ("Righteous and Just Is the Word of Our Lord").

❖ Conclude today's session by leading the class in this benediction adapted from Deuteronomy 10:12-13, the key verses for June 24: **Go forth remembering that we are to fear the Lord our God, to walk in all his ways, to love God, to serve the Lord with all our heart and soul, and to keep God's commandments.**

UNIT 2: JUSTICE ENACTED

Solomon Judges With Wisdom and Justice

PREVIEWING THE LESSON

Lesson Scripture: 1 Kings 3:16-28; 2 Chronicles 9:8
Background Scripture: 1 Kings 3; 2 Chronicles 9:8
Key Verse: 1 Kings 3:28

Focus of the Lesson:
People need a just and wise mediator when life presents unjust situations. To whom may we go to receive justice? Because of Solomon's relationship with God, he was able to make just and wise choices.

Goals for the Learners:
(1) to examine the story of Solomon and the two women who came to him seeking justice.
(2) to reflect on the value of wise intervention.
(3) to identify a chronic community dilemma that could be resolved by justice tempered with wisdom.

Pronunciation Guide:
Gibeon (gib' ee uhn)

Supplies:
Bibles, newsprint and marker, paper and pencils, hymnals

READING THE SCRIPTURE

NRSV

1 Kings 3:16-28

¹⁶Later, two women who were prostitutes came to the king and stood before him. ¹⁷The one woman said, "Please, my lord, this woman and I live in the same house; and I

NIV

1 Kings 3:16-28

¹⁶Now two prostitutes came to the king and stood before him. ¹⁷One of them said, "My lord, this woman and I live in the same house. I had a baby while she was there with me.

gave birth while she was in the house. [18]Then on the third day after I gave birth, this woman also gave birth. We were together; there was no one else with us in the house, only the two of us were in the house. [19]Then this woman's son died in the night, because she lay on him. [20]She got up in the middle of the night and took my son from beside me while your servant slept. She laid him at her breast, and laid her dead son at my breast. [21]When I rose in the morning to nurse my son, I saw that he was dead; but when I looked at him closely in the morning, clearly it was not the son I had borne." [22]But the other woman said, "No, the living son is mine, and the dead son is yours." The first said, "No, the dead son is yours, and the living son is mine." So they argued before the king.

[23]Then the king said, "The one says, 'This is my son that is alive, and your son is dead'; while the other says, 'Not so! Your son is dead, and my son is the living one.'" [24]So the king said, "Bring me a sword," and they brought a sword before the king. [25]The king said, "Divide the living boy in two; then give half to the one, and half to the other." [26]But the woman whose son was alive said to the king—because compassion for her son burned within her—"Please, my lord, give her the living boy; certainly do not kill him!" The other said, "It shall be neither mine nor yours; divide it." [27]Then the king responded: "Give the first woman the living boy; do not kill him. She is his mother." **[28]All Israel heard of the judgment that the king had rendered; and they stood in awe of the king, because they perceived that the wisdom of God was in him, to execute justice.**

[18]The third day after my child was born, this woman also had a baby. We were alone; there was no one in the house but the two of us.

[19]"During the night this woman's son died because she lay on him. [20]So she got up in the middle of the night and took my son from my side while I your servant was asleep. She put him by her breast and put her dead son by my breast. [21]The next morning, I got up to nurse my son—and he was dead! But when I looked at him closely in the morning light, I saw that it wasn't the son I had borne."

[22]The other woman said, "No! The living one is my son; the dead one is yours."

But the first one insisted, "No! The dead one is yours; the living one is mine." And so they argued before the king.

[23]The king said, "This one says, 'My son is alive and your son is dead,' while that one says, 'No! Your son is dead and mine is alive.'"

[24]Then the king said, "Bring me a sword." So they brought a sword for the king. [25]He then gave an order: "Cut the living child in two and give half to one and half to the other."

[26]The woman whose son was alive was filled with compassion for her son and said to the king, "Please, my lord, give her the living baby! Don't kill him!"

But the other said, "Neither I nor you shall have him. Cut him in two!"

[27]Then the king gave his ruling: "Give the living baby to the first woman. Do not kill him; she is his mother."

[28]When all Israel heard the verdict the king had given, they held the king in awe, because they saw that he had wisdom from God to administer justice.

2 Chronicles 9:8

[8]Blessed be the LORD your God, who has delighted in you [Solomon] and set you on his throne as king for the LORD your God. Because your God loved Israel and would establish them forever, he has made you king over them, that you may execute justice and righteousness."

2 Chronicles 9:8

[8]Praise be to the LORD your God, who has delighted in you [Solomon] and placed you on his throne as king to rule for the LORD your God. Because of the love of your God for Israel and his desire to uphold them forever, he has made you king over them, to maintain justice and righteousness."

UNDERSTANDING THE SCRIPTURE

1 Kings 3:1-2. This week's story picks up with the reign of Solomon, son of David and Bathsheba. Verse 1 establishes that the kingdom is prospering so far. Solomon has secured peace with Egypt through a marriage to Pharaoh's daughter, and many building projects are underway in Jerusalem. Verse 2 then mentions a concern: The Temple is not yet built, so the people are still going to hilltop shrines ("high places") to make sacrifices.

1 Kings 3:3-7. In verse 3 we read that Solomon himself went to a popular "high place" in Gibeon, about seven miles northwest of the city of Jerusalem, to make a sacrifice to Yahweh. There the Lord appeared to him in a dream and said, "Ask what I should give you" (3:5). The wording is significant because it introduces a theme of "ask" and "give" that is echoed throughout the passage. Verses 6-9 contain Solomon's humble reply. First he credits David's qualities as the reason he now has the throne at God's hands. Then Solomon acknowledges his own inadequacy and seeks God's help. Contrary to the word translated "child" in verse 7, Solomon was not actually a child when he came to power. The Hebrew word literally means "youth" or "adolescent." Solomon had already married the Egyptian princess and had a one-year-old son. We know this because according to 1 Kings 11:42-43 and 14:21, Solomon had a forty-one-year-old son when he died, after reigning forty years. The implication of the word "child" is that Solomon felt himself to be immature, insignificant, and unimportant.

1 Kings 3:8. Solomon's next words also need explanation. He spoke of the people he would govern as "so numerous they cannot be numbered or counted" (3:8). This sounds to modern ears as if the population of Israel was in the millions, which is inaccurate. The Hebrews did not use numbers for mathematical accuracy only. Numbers were also chosen for effect or for symbolic meaning. The

people of Israel, under Solomon, were not nearly as many as implied, but this further illustrates how overwhelmed Solomon felt.

1 Kings 3:9. The key to this passage is in Solomon's request. By calling himself "servant" (3:8, 9), Solomon brings to mind Moses, Abraham, and David—all of whom are called "servants of the LORD." He firmly connected himself to Israel's history and to the Davidic dynasty. Next, Solomon asked for "an understanding mind," followed by the ability "to discern between good and evil" (3:9). In the Hebrew, he literally asked for "a listening heart." First we listen, then we discern. The meaning of the word "heart" in Hebrew is not confined to the emotions, as in modern Western thought. In Hebrew, the heart is the center of understanding. It includes thought and the ability to reason, as well as being the center of purpose and resolve. Solomon was asking for the ability to truly understand his people. He wanted to be able to listen and to make wise, sensitive decisions while governing them. He was asking for good judgment.

1 Kings 3:10-14. Solomon was not asking merely for the ability to judge wisely in legal disputes, however. He was asking for a deeper wisdom, an ability to discern wrong from right, evil from good, falsehood from truth. He was asking for the kind of wisdom we find described in Proverbs and in Job—wisdom that comes only as a gift from God. The request pleased God greatly. "Indeed, I will give you wisdom! And I will also give you wealth and fame and long life. There will never be another king like you," said God, in essence.

1 Kings 3:15. On waking, Solomon goes back to Jerusalem to make sacrifices before the ark of the covenant. The parallel passage in 2 Chronicles 1:13 omits the detail about sacrifice, so some scholars suggest this was added in the Kings account by an editor who wanted to show Solomon's immediate conversion to more orthodox behavior after his dream.

1 Kings 3:16-28. The story of the two women who both claim to be a child's mother is perhaps the best known of all the examples of Solomon's wisdom. Similar accounts of a dual claim to parentage resolved by a wise and crafty judge exist in folklore from other countries as well, but the biblical tale overtly declares *this* judge's wisdom to be a gift from God. Moreover, this divinely granted wisdom is specifically tied to the ability to "execute justice" (3:28). Indeed, the passage lifts up God's justice as something out of the ordinary. Solomon is a king, expected to deal with administration and law on a national level, yet here he shows concern for a local family matter. Moreover, the two litigants are not only women but prostitutes (3:16)—both categories that should put them beneath the king's notice or regard. Nonetheless, Solomon invites them into his presence, listens personally to their accounts, and invites their input into determining a solution. In all these actions, according to Richard D. Nelson, the author intends us to see a truth about God's own standards:

> One hallmark of God's justice is that it is fair to all, even to a pair of disreputable prostitutes. . . . It is justice for the outcast which transcends what may be objectively fair. It is justice for a woman in a man's world. One who has read the Bible's whole story, including John 8:3-11, recognizes that this tale about Solomon displays the genuine character of God's justice in a wisdom that goes beyond mere cleverness. Where such justice is done today, the wisdom of God may be perceived to be at work.

2 Chronicles 9:8. Another famous story associated with Solomon is the visit of the queen of Sheba (9:1-12). Sheba (or Saba) was probably located in the Arabian Peninsula in the area of modern Yemen. After testing the king and seeing all that he has attained, the queen declares that he is as wise as his fame indicates. Verse 8 is part of her speech in praise of Solomon. She praises God for setting Solomon over Israel, thus ensuring justice and righteousness for the realm.

INTERPRETING THE SCRIPTURE

The Historical Setting

Solomon seemed to have been "born with a silver spoon in his mouth." He never launched a major military campaign. After getting supplies and workers from King Hiram of Tyre to help build the Temple, Solomon concluded his payments (after twenty years) by giving Hiram "twenty cities in the land of Galilee" (1 Kings 9:11). By these standards, Solomon may not seem to have been a strong ruler. Yet he is remembered as the wisest of kings. Why would this be?

Certainly Solomon was a decisive king. He executed or exiled his rivals, including his own brothers. He cemented relationships with neighboring kingdoms through treaties and marriages. For example, he married a daughter of the powerful Egyptian pharaoh (1 Kings 3:1). Solomon was also a major builder. He fortified cities and military bases, constructed a palace complex north of Jerusalem, and built the Temple in Jerusalem, which housed the ark of the covenant. By the standards of the day, this Temple was a large and magnificent structure. Sacrifices, feast days, and special festivals—all central to Israel's worship— were focused on the Temple in Jerusalem during Solomon's reign.

Trade and the economy flourished under King Solomon. He commissioned a fleet on the Red Sea to sail to Arabia and East Africa to bring back wealth. He taxed the caravans traveling through Israel, and he shared in the wealth of the sea trade with Tyre. The queen of Sheba came all the way from Arabia just to see the splendor and magnificence of his court. When she arrived, she was overwhelmed, exclaiming, "Your wisdom and prosperity far surpass the report that I had heard" (1 Kings 10:7). Solomon's reign was not only stable and prosperous, it was also splendid. This success led, in part, to Solomon's reputation for wisdom.

God's Wisdom

Solomon and others saw wisdom as a quality of mind and heart that enables a person to live fully, abundantly, and in tune with God. In the ancient Near East, being wise included being successful in the world and being able to counsel others to success. Wisdom could be acquired, even for the simple, by a religious attitude and conscientious efforts. Yet wisdom was also a quality apart from natural human ability. True wisdom was something given to humans as a gift from God.

According to Scriptures, wisdom is a necessary component in living as God wants us to live. Here are several passages that help us understand wisdom from the biblical point of view:

Exodus 31:2-6. In Hebrew, wisdom is basically "skill or talent." It is both the ability and the intelligence necessary to create a work of art.

1 Kings 3:16-28. Wisdom is good judgment, knowing the very best way to solve a problem or decide an issue.

Proverbs 2:1-6. Wisdom is understanding, insight, and knowledge. More important, it is knowledge about the ways of God's will.

Proverbs 9:10. Wisdom begins by "fearing the LORD"—that is, by admitting our dependence on God and by serving our Lord faithfully and with respect.

Matthew 7:24-27. The wise person is one who hears and does the words of Jesus—the person who knows the importance of a good foundation in life.

Matthew 25:1-13. Wisdom is knowing what the consequences will be from our actions. It is the ability to look ahead and be prepared.

The most basic idea of wisdom in the Bible is that it is a gift from God that helps us understand what God expects of us and how we can live rightly as God's children. Wisdom is common sense, gained through practical experience and through our understanding of God as revealed in Jesus Christ. It is skill in living as God wants us to live.

Justice and Wisdom in Action

The story of Solomon and the baby is a great example of God's wisdom and justice in action. On a surface level we can see how compassion weaves through the process as an integral component. Solomon meets these women and personally hears their case, even though they are not only women but also prostitutes. He models what we have already learned from God's instructions to the faith community—that justice is for all God's people, regardless of status. Compassion also runs strong in Solomon's wise judgment: A loving woman receives a child, and a child receives a caring mother.

It is easy to find ourselves on both sides of the situation as presented by the women and Solomon. Each of us knows what it is like to be in a painful situation without any real insight as to how to resolve the problem. In those circumstances, we know what a blessing it is to receive wise guidance—even in the form of an opinionated push—that helps in reaching a solution. In addition, many of us have been asked for guidance, whether or not we feel ready to give it.

Here we can learn from Solomon. Remember that prior to this he had asked God for wisdom. We canpray for God's presence and assistance when nothing is wrong. Such prayers help us, like Solomon, to be open to God's Spirit when we really need it. Solomon also shows us thatit is not enough to be open to God's compassion and discerning wisdom. We also must be willing to take action, or a just resolution to the problem may never come about.

The Remaining Challenge

The dominant theme throughout Solomon's reign was wisdom. As we have seen, "wisdom" in ancient Hebrew thought means understanding life from a universal perspective. It is observing the "marketplace" issues of life and being able to put them into a wider context. Wisdom is an ability of thoughtful discernment. It holds common sense in tension with passionate trust in God. It is being able to discern the strands of truth amid the tangle of lies.

This week's scene of wise justice in action can be a model for us. In times of crisis, transition, or conflict, we can seek out God and ask for insight. When we genuinely open ourselves to God's presence and wisdom through prayer and meditation, God will answer.

The good news is that when others come to us for guidance or discernment, we are not left "orphaned," as the Gospel of John puts it. We have the "Spirit of truth" (John 14:17-18).

As Christians, we have an ultimate, eternal, and ever-present offer of wisdom through our knowledge of Jesus Christ. For if knowledge of God is wisdom, as Proverbs tells us, then in Christ we have wisdom, because in Christ, God is revealed. Furthermore, we are enabled through our faith in Christ to come into the presence of God and seek wisdom. Our search will not be futile.

In our society today, the need for compassionate justice runs deep. Solomon's story gives us hope that we too can be vessels for God to use to set things right. Such justice may not change the immediate circumstances; it may not erase the pain or right the wrongs of the world. Nevertheless, God's wisdom will give us the strength to deal with pain, the courage to face adversity, and the depth of character to rely on God in the midst of life's buffetings. God willing, it will also help us to bring the blessing of God's wisdom and justice to others.

SHARING THE SCRIPTURE

Preparing Our Hearts

Explore this week's devotional reading, found in Psalm 37:27-34. This acrostic psalm is also a poem that teaches a basic lesson of wisdom: "Do not fret" (37:1). Instead, we are to be patient, to "wait for the LORD" (37:34) and trust God. Today's reading extols the virtues of justice and righteousness—and those who practice doing good. Note verse 32. Why do you think that the wicked seek to destroy the righteous? What examples of this behavior do you see?

Pray that you and the adult learners will act with God's wisdom and justice.

Preparing Our Minds

Study the background Scripture from 1 Kings 3 and 2 Chronicles 9:8. The lesson Scripture is from 1 Kings 3:16-28 and 2 Chronicles 9:8. Think about who you would go to if you needed a mediator to resolve a situation with justice.

Write on newsprint:
❑ information for next week's lesson, found under "Continue the Journey."
❑ activities for further spiritual growth in "Continue the Journey."

Plan a brief lecture to introduce background from 1 Kings 3 for "Examine the Story of Solomon and the Two Women Who Came to Him Seeking Justice." Use information from Understanding the Scripture in the sections for verses 1-15.

LEADING THE CLASS

(1) Gather to Learn

❖ Welcome the class members and introduce any guests.

❖ Pray that the students will be aware of how they bring justice to others.

❖ Note that many communities have mediation centers to help individuals and groups resolve conflicts. Perhaps your community has such a center that you could mention as a potential resource for the students or people they know. Read this description of mediation from www.mid shoremediation.org/FAQsAboutMediation. html: **"Mediation is a voluntary, confidential process in which two neutral mediators help two or more people find win-win solutions to their conflict. A community mediation is conducted by highly trained volunteers. Community mediators guide the participants through a process that helps identify problems, generate solutions and create agreements acceptable to both."**

❖ Ask: **If you needed to find a just solution to a conflict, what kind of person would you seek out to mediate the dispute?**

❖ Read aloud today's focus statement: **People need a just and wise mediator when life presents unjust situations. To whom may we go to receive justice? Because of Solomon's relationship with God, he was able to make just and wise choices.**

(2) Examine the Story of Solomon and the Two Women Who Came to Him Seeking Justice

❖ Use the lecture you have prepared to introduce the session. First Kings 3:1-15 records the story of Solomon asking God for wisdom to govern the people. Beginning in verse 16 we find a poignant example of how Solomon relied on God's wisdom to render a just decision.

❖ Invite four volunteers to read the parts of a narrator, Solomon, the first woman, and the second woman from 1 Kings 3:16-28.

❖ Discuss these questions:
  (1) **Based on their testimony alone, which woman's argument seems more compelling?** (Likely the students will not be able to choose, since the women were alone and there was no definitive evidence.)
  (2) **Had you been present when Solomon ordered that a sword be brought, what would you have expected him to do?**
  (3) **As the story unfolds, what was Solomon's real purpose in calling for the sword?** (He correctly assumed that the real mother would want the child to live and, therefore, protest his killing.)
  (4) **Read aloud today's key verse from 1 Kings 3:28. Why do you suppose that the people attributed Solomon's decision to God's wisdom?** (Read 2 Chronicles 9:8, where the queen of Sheba remarks on God setting Solomon on the throne to "execute justice and righteousness.")
  (5) **Can you think of any decisions, particularly by a political leader, that seemed to be as wise as Solomon's decision was? If so, describe the decisions.**

❖ Wrap up by using the Scripture references in "God's Wisdom" under Interpreting the Scripture to summarize what God's wisdom is and how it operates in our lives. If time permits, call on volunteers to read the listed passages.

(3) Reflect on the Value of Wise Intervention

❖ Distribute paper and pencils. Encourage the adults to recall a time in their lives when they needed someone to intervene on their behalf. Without writing anything about the situation itself, the participants are to write words or phrases to describe the outcome of wise intervention. For example, such intervention may *correct a misunderstanding, diffuse a potentially explosive situation,* or *facilitate reconciliation.*

❖ Collect the papers. Either read a representative sample yourself, or shuffle and redistribute papers so that the ideas are presented by people who did not write them.

❖ Ask: **Given that from our own life stories we can point to positive outcomes of wise intervention, what steps can we take to become wiser and better mediators of justice?**

(4) Identify a Chronic Community Dilemma That Could Be Resolved by Justice Tempered With Wisdom

❖ Read or retell "The Remaining Challenge" from Interpreting the Scripture.

❖ Invite the adults to keep in mind that "the need for compassionate justice runs deep," as you read and discuss this case study. If the class is large, form small groups so that more people may present their ideas.

A small town that had thrived for decades found itself in deep economic distress when the manufacturing plant that had employed many residents was shuttered. The product that the plant made had become obsolete, and there was no economical way to retool the factory. Young adults who had planned to stay in the town where they grew up were forced to leave to find work, as their elders struggled with unemployment and the loss of homes. Your church, which is also struggling but believes firmly in God's wise and compassionate justice, wants to find ways to help the community re-create itself. What words of wisdom do you have to share at a town hall meeting?

(5) Continue the Journey

❖ Pray that the adults will work toward justice in their own community.

❖ Read aloud this preparation for next week's lesson. You may also want to post it on newsprint for the students to copy.

■ **Title: A King Acts on a Widow's Behalf**

■ **Background Scripture: 2 Kings 4:1-37; 8:1-6**

■ **Lesson Scripture: 2 Kings 8:1-6**

■ **Focus of the Lesson: People who are estranged from their families may long to return home. How is it possible to go home again? By acting in a benevolent manner, we can offer hope to those seeking justice and restoration.**

❖ Challenge the students to complete one or more of these activities for further spiritual growth related to this week's session. Post this information on newsprint for the students to copy.

(1) Read Bertolt Brecht's *The Caucasian Chalk Circle*, **a play based in part on Solomon's judgment of the case of the two mothers. How is this play similar to and different from the biblical version? What ideas does it evoke for you regarding justice?**

(2) Recall that both women in today's Scripture were prostitutes. Research prostitution and sex trafficking. What drives these lucrative, often illegal practices? Check with local law enforcement officials to see if these practices are affecting your community. Act with other church members to bring about justice for those who are being exploited.

(3) Identify at least one person who exudes God's wisdom. Talk with this individual to learn how he or she appropriated this wisdom. Try to adopt ideas from this person and imitate his or her lifestyle.

❖ Sing or read aloud "Lord, Whose Love Through Humble Service."

❖ Conclude today's session by leading the class in this benediction adapted from Deuteronomy 10:12-13, the key verses for June 24: **Go forth remembering that we are to fear the Lord our God, to walk in all his ways, to love God, to serve the Lord with all our heart and soul, and to keep God's commandments.**

UNIT 2: JUSTICE ENACTED

A King Acts on a Widow's Behalf

PREVIEWING THE LESSON

Lesson Scripture: 2 Kings 8:1-6
Background Scripture: 2 Kings 4:1-37; 8:1-6
Key Verse: 2 Kings 8:6

Focus of the Lesson:
People who are estranged from their families may long to return home. How is it possible to go home again? By acting in a benevolent manner, we can offer hope to those seeking justice and restoration.

Goals for the Learners:
(1) to trace the sequence of events in the life of the Shunammite widow.
(2) to describe how they feel when something lost has been restored to them.
(3) to be aware of situations in which restorative justice is required and do whatever is possible to bring a just resolution.

Pronunciation Guide:
Elisha (i li' shuh)   Naboth (nay' both)
Gehazi (gi hay' zi)   *shalom* (shah lohm')
Gilboa (gil boh' uh)   Shunammite (shoo' nah mite)
Issachar (is' uh kahr)   Shunem (shoo' nuhm)
Jehoram (ji hor' uhm)   Uzziah (uh zi' uh)
Jeroboam (jer uh boh' uhm)   Zarephath (zair' uh fath)

Supplies:
Bibles; newsprint and marker; paper and pencils; hymnals; colored pencils, crayons, or markers in a variety of colors

---

READING THE SCRIPTURE

NRSV
2 Kings 8:1-6
¹Now Elisha had said to the woman whose son he had restored to life, "Get up

NIV
2 Kings 8:1-6
¹Now Elisha had said to the woman whose son he had restored to life, "Go away

and go with your household, and settle wherever you can; for the LORD has called for a famine, and it will come on the land for seven years." [2]So the woman got up and did according to the word of the man of God; she went with her household and settled in the land of the Philistines seven years. [3]At the end of the seven years, when the woman returned from the land of the Philistines, she set out to appeal to the king for her house and her land. [4]Now the king was talking with Gehazi the servant of the man of God, saying, "Tell me all the great things that Elisha has done." [5]While he was telling the king how Elisha had restored a dead person to life, the woman whose son he had restored to life appealed to the king for her house and her land. Gehazi said, "My lord king, here is the woman, and here is her son whom Elisha restored to life." [6]When the king questioned the woman, she told him. **So the king appointed an official for her, saying, "Restore all that was hers, together with all the revenue of the fields from the day that she left the land until now."**

with your family and stay for a while wherever you can, because the LORD has decreed a famine in the land that will last seven years." [2]The woman proceeded to do as the man of God said. She and her family went away and stayed in the land of the Philistines seven years.

[3]At the end of the seven years she came back from the land of the Philistines and went to the king to beg for her house and land. [4]The king was talking to Gehazi, the servant of the man of God, and had said, "Tell me about all the great things Elisha has done." [5]Just as Gehazi was telling the king how Elisha had restored the dead to life, the woman whose son Elisha had brought back to life came to beg the king for her house and land.

Gehazi said, "This is the woman, my lord the king, and this is her son whom Elisha restored to life." [6]The king asked the woman about it, and she told him. **Then he assigned an official to her case and said to him, "Give back everything that belonged to her, including all the income from her land from the day she left the country until now."**

UNDERSTANDING THE SCRIPTURE

Introduction. The great prophet Elijah has ended his time on earth, and his protégé Elisha has now become the primary prophet in Israel (2 Kings 2:1-15). Sandwiched between stories of war, we find a number of accounts of Elisha's miracles. Such reports give proof of the prophet's power as coming from God. Second Kings 4 contains four miracles that the prophet Elisha performed during the reign of the Israelite king Jehoram. These are multiplying the widow's oil (4:1-7), raising the Shunammite's son (4:8-37), purifying a pot of stew (4:38-41), and feeding a hundred men (4:42-44).

2 Kings 4:1-7. Unlike Elijah, Elisha belonged to a group known as "the com-

pany of prophets." These folks lived in community together, apparently with families, and were bound by their common work as prophets. Now just as Elijah had ministered to the desperate need of a widow at the point of death in Zarephath (1 Kings 17:8-16), Elisha brings deliverance to the widow of one of this company. With no source of income, her children are in danger of debt slavery (see Exodus 21:7; compare Leviticus 25:39-46; Deuteronomy 15:12-18; Jeremiah 34:8-16). Fittingly, the single oil jar that symbolizes the widow's poverty miraculously becomes the source of her new abundance. This first miracle demonstrates Elisha's concern for the poor.

2 Kings 4:8-10. The second miracle parallels an Elijah story found in 1 Kings 17:17-24. The current tale involves a "wealthy" woman in Shunem, a town in the territory assigned to Issachar at Shiloh (Joshua 19:18), near Mount Gilboa (1 Samuel 28:4). The term translated "wealthy" also indicates she was "notable," and it can include being known for one's piety. Certainly she was a model of hospitality. The first time she meets Elisha, she offers him a meal. Subsequent visits lead her to build an actual guest room for him and his servant, Gehazi.

2 Kings 4:11-17. When Elisha asks the woman what he might do for her in return, she indicates she lacks nothing. The offer to speak to authorities perhaps indicates a chance to be more protected and secure, but she declines this as unnecessary. The servant then points out to Elisha the lack of a child, echoing a strong biblical theme of an older, barren woman miraculously bearing a son. The woman's initial response to the promise of this gift indicates how deeply she longs for it—and how difficult it is for her to concede its possibility. Verse 17 then briskly states that all has happened as Elisha promised.

2 Kings 4:18-23. Some years later, the boy goes with his father to the fields and becomes ill. Most commentators suppose he suffered a case of sunstroke or heatstroke. His father, seeing the seriousness of the situation, instructs his servant to carry the child to his mother, but after a few hours sleeping on her lap, the little boy dies. Then the Shunammite woman does a strange thing. She quietly takes the boy's body up to Elisha's room, lays him on the bed, shuts the door behind her, and goes out to her husband. She asks him for a donkey so she can get to Elisha quickly. Oddly, the father does not inquire about the child's health nor does she tell him what happened. He simply asks why she wants to go now, when it was considered more fitting to visit prophets on a holy day. Her reply invites him to trust her and not delve deeper. In Hebrew it is a single word, *shalom* (meaning "peace"), which the NRSV rightly translates as an idiom meaning, "It will be all right" (4:23).

2 Kings 4:24-31. The woman sets out after Elisha in haste. He notices her from a distance and sends his servant to ask what is wrong. She replies to Gehazi as she had to her husband, saying nothing but "Shalom." It is only when she reaches Elisha that she says more. Rather than ask for help, though, her words are an accusation—in essence, "Why did you give me a child only to have me lose him?" Elisha immediately sends Gehazi ahead with his staff and instructs him to lay it on the boy's face. This reflects a tradition that a staff acts as a medium for a prophet's power, such as we see with Moses (Exodus 4:1-5; 14:15-18; 17:1-7). Elisha and the mother follow more slowly. Gehazi returns and meets them along the way with a report that the child's condition is unchanged. The language of verse 31 indicates that the boy is dead, but Gehazi perhaps softens the report for the mother's sake.

2 Kings 4:32-37. When he arrives and finds the child dead, Elisha closes himself in the room for privacy. First he prays, then he stretches himself out over the boy completely. Miraculously, the child's flesh warms, but he is not yet truly alive or awake. Elisha paces the room, perhaps to restore his own body heat, and then bends over the child again. This time something happens: The child sneezes seven times and opens his eyes. (In the Bible, seven signifies completion, totality, and perfection.) The story abruptly ends with the call of the mother and Elisha's presentation of her now-living son. She falls at the prophet's feet in gratitude, and then takes her son and leaves with him—perhaps to go to his father with the good news of recovery.

2 Kings 8:1-6. In verses that may be a continuation of chapter 4, Elisha continues his aid of the Shunammite woman by advising her to live elsewhere for seven years in order to avoid an impending famine. Upon her return from Philistia, where she had sojourned, the once wealthy woman learns she has lost everything. She appears before the king just as Gehazi is regaling the king with the details of Elisha's miracles on her behalf. The woman then appeals to the king for help in words that recall the Elijah story of Naboth's vineyard (1 Kings 21:1-16). When the king learns of her distress he rec-

tifies the situation by restoring all she has lost, plus the revenue she would have earned over the seven years. In her previous story, the Shunammite had refused Elisha's offer to use his influence with the king on her behalf (2 Kings 4:13). Now, even in his absence, the influence of the prophet with the king is the decisive factor in the Shunammite's situation.

INTERPRETING THE SCRIPTURE

The Prior Story

This week we consider an account of compassion extended to a woman and her son by both a prophet and a king. Scripture lifts up both parts of the story as an example of God's justice done rightly.

Second Kings 4:8-37 tells how Elisha, spiritual heir to the great prophet Elijah, received exceedingly gracious hospitality from a wealthy woman in Shunem. In return, he prayed that her barren years might end, and she was indeed blessed with a son soon after. Later, when her child became deathly ill, the woman sought out the prophet for aid. As his predecessor Elijah had once done for a widow's son (1 Kings 17:17-24), Elisha was able to draw on God's power to restore the child to life.

The passage for today seems to pick up where the story in chapter 4 left off. We read that Elisha warns "the woman whose son he had restored" (8:1) to settle in another country for seven years in order to avoid a famine coming to her homeland. She does so, taking her entire household, only to return to an unexpected state of homelessness. Apparently, her house and land had been taken over by another in her absence, and she has lost everything she counted on to support herself and all who depend on her. Because this is a matter to be settled within the legal

system of the day (and because she is of the wealthy class), the woman goes to the king for aid.

At the moment of her arrival, the king is asking Elisha's servant, Gehazi, about the great deeds the prophet has done. The writer invites us to see this timing not as coincidence but as providence. Just as Gehazi is telling about the revival of the woman's son, in she comes! Moved by the woman's current plight, and perhaps swayed by her connection to the prophet, the king not only supports the return of her property but also of all income that she would have earned in seven years if she had stayed at home.

The king's actions reflect the call to justice that we have seen throughout the texts for this quarter. The woman in the story who had once been "wealthy" (4:8) is no longer wealthy or powerful in any way. As far as we can tell, she comes before the king with no lands or money—only a plea for what is rightly hers. Because this text does not mention her husband, many commentators assume he has died in the intervening years. If this is so, then she is not only homeless but also a widow, and therefore of special concern within God's call for justice. The happy ending of this story is more powerful in this light, because we see compassion in action for "the least of these" (Matthew 25:40).

No Home, No Justice

The situation in 2 Kings 8 fits what we know of life in Judah during the eighth century B.C. For example, the prophet Micah writes of the injustices he saw:

They covet fields, and seize them;
    houses, and take them away;
they oppress householder and house,
    people and their inheritance. . . .
The women of my people you drive out
    from their pleasant houses;
from their young children you take away
    My glory forever. (2:2, 9)

This state of affairs arose from changes in the social structure that, sadly, paved the way for human greed to take hold. For many centuries, Israel and Judah had been agricultural countries, and most families were able to support themselves with grain, vineyards, and livestock. City-dwelling merchants and the ruling class were a small minority. During the years when Uzziah ruled in Judah (783–742 B.C.) and Jeroboam II ruled in Israel (786–746 B.C.), however, the balance of power shifted from the rural countryside into the urban centers. Wealthy merchants and speculators gained enough economic power to buy up large tracts of rural land, and the farmers and herders were left without means of support. More and more country people crowded into the cities, looking for work. The situation was similar to current problems that developing nations have in many parts of the world today.

Certainly, within North America we still struggle with issues related to the loss of financial security and the resultant homelessness. The National Coalition for the Homeless reported in 2009 a dramatic increase in homelessness in the United States over the past two decades, made worse by a high rate of foreclosures during the recent economic crisis. This agency estimates that there are 3.5 million people without homes in this country, 39 percent of whom are children. The exact number is hard to estimate, however, and may be higher because this group of people frequently seeks shelter in places that researchers cannot effectively search—places such as automobiles, campgrounds, tents, boxes, caves, or boxcars. Clearly, our work for compassionate justice still has much to accomplish.

At Home With Justice

The story of the restored woman in 2 Kings not only opens our eyes to current issues regarding land and justice but it also presents another powerful theological theme as well. God's justice and the woman's celebration of it both center on the gift of security and peace associated with the safety of *home*. It is an image that speaks to our own hearts.

Despite all the problems within his own society, Micah foresaw a day when everyone would receive this blessing. He prophesied that all people would one day live under their own vine and their own fig tree, holding their land secure, undisturbed, and with some measure of prosperity. It's an image of an ideal future, in which God will rule over all peoples, bringing justice and peace to the world and security to those who now can only wait in hope (Micah 4:4-5).

We find ourselves strengthened and encouraged to keep working toward this vision because we believe the promise is for all people, ourselves included. God will one day bring us home to a place of rest and safety, a place where we can dwell forever. We have another promise as well, though—one that guarantees we are not "homeless" in these days of waiting for God's final plan to be fulfilled.

Although we may not yet live at home with God in perfect peace and security, Jesus promises that as long as we are here on earth, he and God will make their home with us (John 14:23). The writer to the Ephesians puts it this way:

So then you are no longer strangers and aliens, but you are citizens with the saints and also members of the household of God, built upon the foundation of the apostles and prophets, with Christ Jesus himself as the cornerstone. In him the whole structure is joined together and grows into a holy temple in the Lord; in whom you also are built together spiritually into a dwelling place for God. (Ephesians 2:19-22)

As the body of Christ in the world, we can take on the continued fight for justice because of the gifts we receive from our Lord Jesus himself—deep compassion, commitment to what is right, and a steadfast faith in God's power to work wonders in the human heart.

SHARING THE SCRIPTURE

Preparing Our Hearts

Explore this week's devotional reading, found in Luke 15:11-24. The story of the prodigal son's return home is perhaps one of the most beloved in the Bible. Can you imagine yourself as the son seeing your dad running to greet you? What emotions well up as you stand in the father's sandals and strain to see the child you thought was dead nearing home? How does the father restore his errant son to the family?

Pray that you and the adult learners will be as willing as the father to restore loved ones who have severed ties to family and home.

Preparing Our Minds

Study the background Scripture from 2 Kings 4:1-37 and 8:1-6. The lesson is from 2 Kings 8:1-6. How can you help those in need of justice to be restored?

Write on newsprint:
❑ information for next week's lesson, found under "Continue the Journey."
❑ activities for further spiritual growth in "Continue the Journey."

LEADING THE CLASS

(1) Gather to Learn

❖ Welcome the class members and introduce any guests.

❖ Pray that the students will seek to know God more fully.

❖ Read this story that appeared on www.revcom.us: **Forced by hurricane Katrina to leave her childhood home in the Saint Bernard Housing Development (New Orleans), Loretta Lyons desperately wanted to return home. Listen to her story in her own words: "They're paying the rent for us now, but what's going to happen to me when the 12 months is over? I'm going to be on the street somewhere. I lost everything I had. I don't have anything, anything. I was on the first floor. I'm not able to buy a house or anything, but I do want to come home and there's plenty of people in Houston who want to come home to New Orleans. There's a whole lot of talk out there about the Louisiana people. When I got to the employment office I tell them I've worked all my life. They tell people on the TV that Texas has a lot of jobs for you. When I go to the unemployment office they see I'm from Louisiana, and they tell me, 'oh, we don't have no jobs.' I need a job, I need a home, and I want to come back to Louisiana, to New Orleans. FEMA money is never gonna take care of the people. You done lost your job, lost your home, lost everything."**

❖ Discuss this question: **What emotions and cries for justice do you hear in Loretta Lyons's voice?**

❖ Read aloud today's focus statement: **People who are estranged from their families may long to return home. How is it possible to go home again? By acting in a benevolent manner, we can offer hope to those seeking justice and restoration.**

(2) Trace the Sequence of Events in the Life of the Shunammite Widow

❖ Read or retell the first two paragraphs of "The Prior Story" and the first paragraph of "No Home, No Justice" from Interpreting the Scripture to familiarize the students with the events that led to the Shunammite widow's homelessness and the social setting.

❖ **Option:** Pretend to be the Shunammite woman. Use information from Understanding the Scripture to tell your story from the time you first met the prophet Elisha until the time your land was restored to you. (If you are male, enlist a female class member early in the week and ask her to prepare to do this monologue.)

❖ Select a volunteer to read 2 Kings 8:1-6.

❖ Ask this question: **Where do you see the hand of God in this story?**

(3) Describe How the Learners Feel When Something Lost Has Been Restored to Them

❖ Distribute paper (preferably unlined) and colored pencils, crayons, or markers. Invite the students to fold the paper into thirds vertically. In the center space they are to draw the outline of something valuable to them that once was lost but later was returned to them. On the left side, they are to use color to show how they felt when they realized that their treasure was missing. On the right side, they are to use color to show how they felt when this treasure was restored to their keeping. Some adults may choose to put their colors in geometric or other patterns, but the emphasis here is on the color and its intensity.

❖ Invite each learner to turn to a partner and talk about why this object held such significance for her or him. The partner will likely be able to discern the pain of loss and joy of return just from the colors.

(4) Be Aware of Situations in Which Restorative Justice Is Required and Do Whatever Is Possible to Bring a Just Resolution

❖ Encourage the adults to name situations in which restorative justice is required. List their ideas on newsprint. Here are some possibilities:

  ■ Homes are being foreclosed on without proper review, leaving some homeowners who have paid their bills properly in a nightmarish situation.

  ■ Families faced with a serious or long-term illness are pushed over the financial edge with mounting medical bills.

  ■ Poor residents disproportionately have landfills and other waste sites as "neighbors."

  ■ Certain potential voters receive automated phone calls designed to keep them away from the polls.

  ■ Convicted felons who are later proved innocent may still languish in prison for extended periods of time before they are released.

❖ Invite the class members to comment on any situations about which they have personal knowledge, without going into great detail or naming parties involved.

❖ Consider with the group whether one or two of the listed injustices are prevalent in your community.

❖ Discuss these questions:
  (1) As a class, what actions can we take to advocate for an end to this particular injustice?
  (2) What can we do to help those who have been treated unjustly?

(5) Continue the Journey

❖ Pray that the adults will seek opportunities to bring justice to those in need.

❖ Read aloud this preparation for next week's lesson. You may also want to post it on newsprint for the students to copy.

- ■ **Title: Jehoshaphat Makes Judicial Reforms**
- ■ **Background Scripture: 2 Chronicles 18:28–19:11**
- ■ **Lesson Scripture: 2 Chronicles 19:4-11**
- ■ **Focus of the Lesson: People want to be judged fairly. How can we expect to receive justice? When human judges adhere to God's standards and fearlessly apply God's laws, there is no perversion of justice.**

❖ Challenge the students to complete one or more of these activities for further spiritual growth related to this week's session. Post this information on newsprint for the students to copy.

(1) Read Robert Frost's "The Death of the Hired Man." What does this poem suggest to you about restoring family—and family-like—relationships?

(2) Research conditions in the Palestinian territories of Israel. What are the current and historic issues that have led to people being displaced from their homeland? What solutions can you suggest that would lead to justice for Palestinians and Israelis?

(3) Identify a person who is working through the legal matters of an estate. Offer moral support. Continue to encourage this person to claim what is rightfully his or hers.

❖ Sing or read aloud "Whom Shall I Send?"

❖ Conclude today's session by leading the class in this benediction adapted from Deuteronomy 10:12-13, the key verses for June 24: **Go forth remembering that we are to fear the Lord our God, to walk in all his ways, to love God, to serve the Lord with all our heart and soul, and to keep God's commandments.**

UNIT 2: JUSTICE ENACTED

JEHOSHAPHAT MAKES JUDICIAL REFORMS

PREVIEWING THE LESSON

Lesson Scripture: 2 Chronicles 19:4-11
Background Scripture: 2 Chronicles 18:28–19:11
Key Verse: 2 Chronicles 19:6

Focus of the Lesson:

People want to be judged fairly. How can we expect to receive justice? When human judges adhere to God's standards and fearlessly apply God's laws, there is no perversion of justice.

Goals for the Learners:

(1) to examine the appointment and work of judges under King Jehoshaphat of Judah.
(2) to consider what it means to be treated fairly or unfairly.
(3) to compare and contrast human justice and divine justice.

Pronunciation Guide:

Abijah (uh bi' juh)
Amariah (am uh ri' uh)
Aram (air' uhm)
Asa (ay' suh)
Asherah (uh shihr' uh)
Baasha (bay' uh shuh)
Beer-sheba (bee' uhr shee' buh)
Ephraim (ee' fray im)
Hanani (huh nay' nie)

Ishmael (ish' may uhl)
Jehoshaphat (ji hosh' uh fat)
Jehu (jee' hyoo)
Micaiah (mi kay' yuh)
Naboth (nay' both)
Ramoth-Gilead (ray muhth gil' ee uhd)
Rehoboam (ree huh boh' uhm)
Tyre (tire)
Zebadiah (zeb uh di' uh)

Supplies:

Bibles, newsprint and marker, paper and pencils, hymnals, news story of high-profile trial

---

READING THE SCRIPTURE

NRSV
2 Chronicles 19:4-11

⁴Jehoshaphat resided at Jerusalem; then he went out again among the people, from

NIV
2 Chronicles 19:4-11

⁴Jehoshaphat lived in Jerusalem, and he went out again among the people from

Beer-sheba to the hill country of Ephraim, and brought them back to the LORD, the God of their ancestors. ⁵He appointed judges in the land in all the fortified cities of Judah, city by city, **⁶and said to the judges, "Consider what you are doing, for you judge not on behalf of human beings but on the LORD's behalf; he is with you in giving judgment.** ⁷Now, let the fear of the LORD be upon you; take care what you do, for there is no perversion of justice with the LORD our God, or partiality, or taking of bribes."

⁸Moreover in Jerusalem Jehoshaphat appointed certain Levites and priests and heads of families of Israel, to give judgment for the LORD and to decide disputed cases. They had their seat at Jerusalem. ⁹He charged them: "This is how you shall act: in the fear of the LORD, in faithfulness, and with your whole heart; ¹⁰whenever a case comes to you from your kindred who live in their cities, concerning bloodshed, law or commandment, statutes or ordinances, then you shall instruct them, so that they may not incur guilt before the LORD and wrath may not come on you and your kindred. Do so, and you will not incur guilt. ¹¹See, Amariah the chief priest is over you in all matters of the LORD; and Zebadiah son of Ishmael, the governor of the house of Judah, in all the king's matters; and the Levites will serve you as officers. Deal courageously, and may the LORD be with the good!"

Beersheba to the hill country of Ephraim and turned them back to the LORD, the God of their fathers. ⁵He appointed judges in the land, in each of the fortified cities of Judah. **⁶He told them, "Consider carefully what you do, because you are not judging for man but for the LORD, who is with you whenever you give a verdict.** ⁷Now let the fear of the LORD be upon you. Judge carefully, for with the LORD our God there is no injustice or partiality or bribery."

⁸In Jerusalem also, Jehoshaphat appointed some of the Levites, priests and heads of Israelite families to administer the law of the LORD and to settle disputes. And they lived in Jerusalem. ⁹He gave them these orders: "You must serve faithfully and wholeheartedly in the fear of the LORD. ¹⁰In every case that comes before you from your fellow countrymen who live in the cities—whether bloodshed or other concerns of the law, commands, decrees or ordinances—you are to warn them not to sin against the LORD; otherwise his wrath will come on you and your brothers. Do this, and you will not sin.

¹¹"Amariah the chief priest will be over you in any matter concerning the LORD, and Zebadiah son of Ishmael, the leader of the tribe of Judah, will be over you in any matter concerning the king, and the Levites will serve as officials before you. Act with courage, and may the LORD be with those who do well."

UNDERSTANDING THE SCRIPTURE

Introduction. First and Second Chronicles were originally one history. Like the books of Samuel and Kings, the text had been divided into two parts long after the original was complete. In modern Bibles, 1 Chronicles records the history of Israel from Adam through the reign of King David, while 2 Chronicles tells of the years from Solomon's reign through the return from exile in Babylon. Jewish tradition teaches that most of Chronicles was written by Ezra and completed by Nehemiah.

Our passage for this week falls within 2 Chronicles 10–36, most of which is about the kings of Judah. (The Northern Kingdom of Israel is rarely mentioned.) The Chronicler focuses on how various kings promoted—or failed to promote—proper ritual and worship. Toward the end of the history, the writer blames the country's fall to Babylonia on those kings who failed in their religious duties. Jehoshaphat is commended for being one of the few kings who fought for reform, although chapter 18 records a problematic alliance with King Ahab of Israel (see also 1 Kings 22:1-35).

Ahab is remembered as one of the worst kings in the Bible—and also as husband of the notorious Jezebel. After he married this Phoenician princess to cement an alliance, Ahab allowed her to set up a temple in honor of Baal-Melkart, the god she had worshiped back in Tyre. Worship of Baal soon became the most popular religion in Israel. Other examples of Ahab's failure to live faithfully as king include his attempts to steal the vineyard of his neighbor Naboth (1 Kings 21:1-16).

Like many other kings of Israel, Ahab often fought against the forces of Syria, which threatened his northern border. Despite two successful engagements against that country, however, he worried after the prophet Elijah said he would meet a fearsome and bloody death. Because of a prophecy made by Micaiah, Ahab especially feared for his life when he joined with King Jehoshaphat of Judah in further warfare against Syria.

2 Chronicles 18:28-34. The setting for the battle is Ramoth-Gilead, a town in northern Trans-Jordan. This area had been hotly contested by Israel and Aram for centuries. Trying to avert disaster, Ahab enters the battle at Ramoth-Gilead in disguise. This leaves Jehoshaphat as a key target for the enemy, since he chooses to go into battle wearing his royal robes (18:29). King Aram had given the order to attack only the king of Israel. When the warriors see Jehoshaphat, they assume him to be the king of Israel and go after him. Unlike the writer of 1 Kings, the Chronicler says in verse 31 that Jehoshaphat's subsequent loud cry was actually a prayer to God for help— a prayer that God answered. Thus the

Chronicler attributes Jehoshaphat's escape from death to God's deliverance as well as the keen eyesight of the charioteers, who eventually realize they are not approaching Ahab after all (18:30-32). It is then that a stray arrow catches Ahab, who subsequently dies of his wounds (18:33-34).

2 Chronicles 19:1-3. Chapter 19 records reforms made by Jehoshaphat and may have been included by the Chronicler as a stark contrast to Ahab's rule. The material is the Chronicler's own; it does not appear in 1 Kings. This account begins with Jehoshaphat's safe return to Jerusalem. There he encounters the prophet Jehu son of Hanani, who may or may not be the person of the same name who prophesied almost fifty years earlier to King Baasha of Israel (1 Kings 16:1-4). A seer named Hanani appears in 2 Chronicles 16:7-10, where he prophesies to King Asa of Judah. In the current verses, the prophet condemns Jehoshaphat for his partnership with Ahab and yet commends his efforts to remove "the sacred poles" from the land. These poles, dedicated to the Canaanite fertility goddess Asherah, would have been wooden pillars or even living trees.

2 Chronicles 19:4-7. These verses, which record details of Jehoshaphat's reform, are missing from the parallel account in 1 Kings 22:41-50. In 2 Chronicles we read that Jehoshaphat, whose residence is in Jerusalem, tours the country and encourages the people to return to the Lord. He appoints judges throughout the kingdom and gives them instructions on how to be a good judge. (Deuteronomy 16:18-20 shows this judicial system is in accordance with the Mosaic law.) Once again, we are reminded that God's justice is pure, impartial, and not subject to corruption.

2 Chronicles 19:8-11. In addition, the king also appoints Levites and priests and clan leaders to serve as judges in Jerusalem. In verse 8, the name "Israel" designates the Southern Kingdom of Judah, which the Chronicler thought of as the true Israel (see

11:3). The instructions given to the judges and other leaders in verses 9-10 bring us back to the Chronicler's own theological view of God's justice. Writing in *First and Second Chronicles*, Paul K. Hooker highlights this understanding:

Justice in the sense apprehended by the Chronicler is finally not punitive or even corrective; it does not seek ultimately to punish the wrong-doer for past crimes or to induce him or her to contemplate the error of his or her ways. Rather, for the Chronicler justice is preventative. It stands as a buffer between human sin and divine wrath. By warning the sinner of the full consequence of his or her act, the judge not only sets to right individual inequities but also shields the whole community from divine wrath. Justice, in this sense, is an extension of grace rather than its opposite as is often thought. It is God forestalling the consequence of our actions so that the actions might be rectified.

INTERPRETING THE SCRIPTURE

The Biblical Setting

According to 1 Kings 22:42, at the age of thirty-five Jehoshaphat became the fourth King of Judah, ruling for nearly twenty-five years (873–849 B.C.). One account of his reign is given in Second Chronicles 17–20, in which he appears as a king who mostly prospers because of the good things he does—and who gets punished those few times he fails to follow God's ways. In particular, this week's passage contains an interesting detail of his reforms not found in the history of 1–2 Kings.

The Chronicler wrote after the Babylonian Exile. Although the date of composition has been debated over the years, evidence in the text, particularly the genealogy of David listed in 1 Chronicles 3 that extends into the fourth century B.C., suggests that the book was written in the first half of the fourth century. In spite of the return of a remnant to Israel, the Temple was destroyed, and the state of Israel was demolished. Jerusalem was a shambles, and the people held varying views as to what it meant to follow God faithfully. There was fear among some, for example, that marriage to non-Jews would dilute the faith. In the eyes of the Chronicler, the people of Israel were losing their sense of identity as a covenant people. This called for drastic measures.

The Chronicler responded to the situation by writing a history of Israel to confirm God's sovereignty. Thus, the Chronicles describes God's miraculous efforts to save the chosen people time after time. In this interpretation of history, Judah and Jerusalem are holy congregations, even without an independent state. God was continuously in control of history, and there was an all-encompassing divine plan for the people of Yahweh. The details of Jehoshaphat's reform are included as a concrete example of the kind of nation that God calls the community of faith to be.

The Historical Reality

As we have seen, though, neither Israel nor Judah achieved God's goals for the nations very often. The early half of the eighth century was a period of peace and great wealth for Israel and Judah, a time of profitable trade with foreign empires with unfortunate social consequences. Along with goods came a higher standard of living and luxury for the upper classes. Wealthy individuals invested in land and built palaces and summer homes. This was often done through economic manipulations and seizing land from the poor. There was a general indulgence in luxurious living, as well as injustice and brutality toward those of lesser means.

Religious conditions in Judah were not much better. Trade brought in not only new products but also new ideas, and there was a push to accept these foreign philosophies and religions. The first two kings of Judah, Rehoboam (922–915 B.C.) and Abijah (915–913 B.C.), supported the old habit of mixing Hebrew and Canaanite worship that had prevailed in the latter days of Solomon, and now an increase in tolerance led to an acceptance of other deities as well. In response, the third king, Asa, tried to introduce reforms, and this effort was continued by his son, Jehoshaphat.

Second Chronicles records how Jehoshaphat tried to restore the purity of the Hebrew religion by removing elements of other religions (19:3). In addition, he reconnected the people to the original intent of the covenant laws by restoring the judicial system. Harkening back to the instructions found in the Pentateuch, he put judges in place with the solemn charge to be impartial and take no bribes (19:7), reminding them that they were stewards of God's justice (19:6). He even appointed judges among the priestly families (19:8), who tended to live apart from others, to see that they had recourse to justice as well.

The Challenge of Always Reforming

Folks who study church life these days often see a typical pattern that goes like this: Churches are born with a vision. They know what they are about and where they want to go. The enthusiasm and faith that initiated their life carries them forward into new territory, and an organization is created to facilitate the dream. The organization establishes programs that enhance, uphold, and support the original vision. Eventually, though, the programs become traditions. They become entities unto themselves with a life all their own. The vision is obscured— distorted by the very programs created to uphold it. The "way things have always been" begins to take precedence over the

real vision. This is a very comfortable stage for those who have long been part of the organization. Unfortunately, the organization itself usually begins to decline in this stage. The vision on which it was founded— and that spurred it to maturity—evaporates. Programs fizzle. Members begin to get bored or angry, and they drift away. A church without a vision, clinging to meaningless traditions, dies.

Fortunately, the death of a vision does not always mean the death of the church. Churches can recapture their vision. *"Ecclesia reformats, semper reformanda"* was a motto of the Protestant Reformers: "The church, reformed, always being reformed." That means that a church must constantly renew its vision. Periodically, the vision must be dusted off and held up and checked for needed repairs. Jehoshaphat did that for Judah. The nation's dream had not weathered the storms of political intrigue, economic struggle, and religious syncretism. Jehoshaphat's reforms offered the nation a resurrected vision.

This model applies to people too. When we lose sight of our vision—the objectives that give our lives meaning and the goals that give us courage—we die. Fortunately, the death of a single vision or dream is not the end for Christians. We are called often to reform our personal vision. Living means experiencing a continual process of death and resurrection. Relationships, positions, ages, careers, and a host of other life experiences may be said to "die." They pass out of our lives, never to return. Resurrection comes when we build a new structure of meaning after the "death," when we claim a renewed, recaptured, revitalized vision. It comes when we accept a new dream. Resurrection happens for us when we are willing to make necessary changes—to reform our lives and our personal traditions.

Sometimes, when we have lost a dream in life—no matter what form it took—we slip into a pattern of harmful daily habits or a lifestyle that doesn't fit who we really are. We become numb to our inner discontent, mired in a sense of hopelessness over how unfair the whole situation is. Sometimes a jolt, a crisis, or a prophetic word of truth is necessary to awaken us. King Jehoshaphat offered his people that jolt through the dramatic shift back to the basic principles of justice that God's law had always upheld. The Chronicler wrote of Jehoshaphat that he walked in his father Asa's way, "doing what was right in the sight of the LORD" (2 Chronicles 20:32). Unfortunately, though, "the people had not yet set their hearts upon the God of their ancestors" (20:33). Jehoshaphat had made inroads to return to a more just society, but the people did not completely change their ways so as to focus fully on God.

Christ offers us that jolt through his life, death, and resurrection. If we keep the focus of our lives on Christ, on the vision of Christ's atoning love and embodiment of justice, then our lives have ultimate meaning. We are able to determine the direction of our lives with renewed confidence and courage, because our vision is of truth. We do not lose sight of our priorities in the midst of life's turmoil because our vision remains clear before us—guiding, shaping, and inspiring us to bring good news to the poor, to let the oppressed go free, and to proclaim God's favor to all (see Luke 4:18-19).

SHARING THE SCRIPTURE

Preparing Our Hearts

Explore this week's devotional reading, found in James 2:1-5. As James speaks of people who show partiality, he is also saying that those people have become judges of others. Playing favorites is not an appropriate way for Christians to behave. Such partiality stems from injustice in that an individual or group is considered somehow better than another. Examine your own heart. Do you show partiality? In what ways?

Pray that you and the adult learners will be open to treating all persons with fairness and equality.

Preparing Our Minds

Study the background Scripture from 2 Chronicles 18:28–19:11 and the lesson Scripture from 2 Chronicles 19:4-11. Consider this question: How can we expect to receive justice?

Write on newsprint:

❑ information for next week's lesson, found under "Continue the Journey."
❑ activities for further spiritual growth in "Continue the Journey."

Plan a brief lecture as suggested under "Examine the Appointment and Work of Judges Under King Jehoshaphat of Judah" to introduce today's session.

Locate media coverage of a high-profile legal case to be discussed under "Compare and Contrast Human Justice and Divine Justice."

LEADING THE CLASS

(1) Gather to Learn

❖ Welcome the class members and introduce any guests.

❖ Pray that the students will feel the Spirit's leading as they encounter the Scriptures today.

❖ Invite the participants to tell brief stories about courtroom cases they have witnessed, perhaps as jurors, observers, or television viewers of shows such as *Judge Judy, Judge Joe Brown,* or *The People's Court.*

❖ Ask: **As you have seen or been part of these cases, what principles seemed to be most important as each case was tried and a verdict was reached?**

❖ Read aloud today's focus statement: **People want to be judged fairly. How can we expect to receive justice? When human judges adhere to God's standards and fearlessly apply God's laws, there is no perversion of justice.**

(2) Examine the Appointment and Work of Judges Under King Jehoshaphat of Judah

❖ Present a brief lecture from "Introduction" through "2 Chronicles 18:28-34" in Understanding the Scripture. Also use "The Biblical Setting" and "The Historical Reality" in Interpreting the Scripture to provide background information for today's lesson.

❖ Select a volunteer to read about Jehoshaphat's judicial reforms as recorded in 2 Chronicles 19:4-11.

❖ List on newsprint God's expectations for a judicial system of God's people.

❖ **Option:** Choose someone to read aloud Deuteronomy 16:18–17:13. Compare this passage to 2 Chronicles 19 to determine how the passages are similar to each other.

❖ Note that Jehoshaphat establishes a two-tiered system: judges in the local cities and a tribunal in Jerusalem.

(3) Consider What It Means to Be Treated Fairly or Unfairly

❖ Invite each student to tell a partner or small group about a time when he or she was treated unfairly. What about this incident hurt him or her? How did this incident cause him or her to treat others differently?

❖ Note that although we all have recollections of unfair treatment, our situations likely pale in comparison to persons who have been wrongly arrested, convicted, and

imprisoned for crimes they did not commit. Read this story of Alton Logan, which *60 Minutes* correspondent Bob Simon reported on in March 2008 and updated in May 2008: **Although Alton Logan's mother and brother testified that he was home asleep when police claim he killed a security guard at a Chicago McDonald's in 1982, Logan was convicted and sentenced to life in prison. Three eyewitnesses identified him as the killer, but Logan had not committed this terrible crime. Even before he was convicted, however, two attorneys for another man, Andrew Wilson, knew that Logan was innocent. Their client had confessed to them. But the way the judicial system in the United States works, laws governing client confidentiality prevented the two attorneys from releasing this information. Even if they had spoken, their testimony would not have been allowed in court because it violated client-attorney privilege. One lawyer did, however, get Wilson's permission to tell what they knew after his death. And so, finally, the truth that Alton Logan knew—and the truth that his brothers Tony and Eugene also knew all along—set him free. Sadly, their mother did not live to see him released. Even more tragic, an innocent man, now age fifty-four, had spent twenty-six years behind bars for a crime that two attorneys knew he had not committed.**

❖ Discuss these questions:

   (1) **Given that client-attorney confidentiality is important, are there situations in which this should be set aside to tell the entire truth?**

   (2) **What changes need to be made to our legal system to keep innocent people from being unjustly treated?** (This might be an appropriate time to consider the death penalty, which Alton Logan nearly received. He could have been executed for a crime he did not commit, had not two jurors refused to hand down that sentence.)

(4) Compare and Contrast Human Justice and Divine Justice

❖ Read or retell the news article you have found about a high-profile legal case that has been resolved. Students may have information to add. Probe the class to see if they believe the case was decided fairly, particularly in light of the Alton Logan case. Then ask: **How do you think this case would have been handled differently if the judge (and jury, if applicable) took heed of 2 Chronicles 19:6 (today's key verse)?** "Consider what you are doing, for you judge not on behalf of human beings but on the LORD's behalf; he is with you in giving judgment."

❖ **Option:** Repeat this discussion with another article you have located.

❖ Post newsprint and write the words *Human Justice* on the left and *Divine Justice* on the right. Draw a line down the center. Pose these questions for discussion:

(1) **Based on the case(s) we have reviewed and other knowledge you have of our judicial system, what would you say are the hallmarks of human justice?**

(2) **Based on the Scriptures we have reviewed and prior discussions we have had about justice, what would you say are the hallmarks of divine justice?**

❖ Invite the learners to reflect on this question: **How are we as the church—and I as an individual—called to enact the justice of God?** Choose volunteers to share their reflections.

(5) Continue the Journey

❖ Pray that the adults will strive to act as stewards of God's justice.

❖ Read aloud this preparation for next week's lesson. You may also want to post it on newsprint for the students to copy.

■ **Title: Praise for God's Justice**
■ **Background Scripture: Psalm 146:1-10; Exodus 21–23; Isaiah 58**
■ **Lesson Scripture: Psalm 146**
■ **Focus of the Lesson: People appreciate receiving lasting justice. Where can we look to find unshakable justice? God is the source of steadfast justice.**

❖ Challenge the students to complete one or more of these activities for further spiritual growth related to this week's session. Post this information on newsprint for the students to copy.

(1) **Look for opportunities to enact justice. Encourage those who have not been acting justly to follow God's ways and treat people fairly.**

(2) **Recall that Jehoshaphat made judicial reforms. What reforms would you like to see in your judicial system? What needs to happen to make it fairer for all people, not just those who have the money to afford a pricey lawyer?**

(3) **Search the Internet to find stories of people who have been wrongfully convicted of crimes they did not commit. See if there is anything you can do to help bring about justice for any of them.**

❖ Sing or read aloud "O Day of God, Draw Nigh."

❖ Conclude today's session by leading the class in this benediction adapted from Deuteronomy 10:12-13, the key verses for June 24: **Go forth remembering that we are to fear the Lord our God, to walk in all his ways, to love God, to serve the Lord with all our heart and soul, and to keep God's commandments.**

UNIT 3: JUSTICE PROMISED
PRAISE FOR GOD'S JUSTICE

PREVIEWING THE LESSON

Lesson Scripture: Psalm 146
Background Scripture: Psalm 146; Exodus 21–23; Isaiah 58
Key Verses: Psalm 146:5, 7

Focus of the Lesson:
People appreciate receiving lasting justice. Where can we look to find unshakable justice? God is the source of steadfast justice.

Goals for the Learners:
(1) to discover the many ways God cares for God's human creations.
(2) to accept that God is faithful and just to those who place their hope in God.
(3) to show thanksgiving for God's help by helping others.

Supplies:
Bibles, newsprint and marker, paper and pencils, hymnals

READING THE SCRIPTURE

NRSV
Psalm 146:1-10
1 Praise the LORD!
  Praise the LORD, O my soul!
2 I will praise the LORD as long as I live;
    I will sing praises to my God all my
    life long.
3 Do not put your trust in princes,
    in mortals, in whom there is no help.
4 When their breath departs, they return to
    the earth;
    on that very day their plans perish.
5 **Happy are those whose help is the God**
    of Jacob,
    whose hope is in the LORD their God,

NIV
Psalm 146:1-10
1 Praise the LORD.
  Praise the LORD, O my soul.
2 I will praise the LORD all my life;
    I will sing praise to my God as long as I
    live.
3 Do not put your trust in princes,
    in mortal men, who cannot save.
4 When their spirit departs, they return
    to the ground;
    on that very day their plans come to
    nothing.
5 **Blessed is he whose help is the God of**
  Jacob,

431

⁶ who made heaven and earth,
    the sea, and all that is in them;
who keeps faith forever;
⁷ **who executes justice for the oppressed;**
who gives food to the hungry.
The LORD sets the prisoners free;
⁸ the LORD opens the eyes of the blind.
The LORD lifts up those who are
    bowed down;
  the LORD loves the righteous.
⁹ The LORD watches over the strangers;
  he upholds the orphan and the widow,
  but the way of the wicked he brings to
    ruin.
¹⁰ The LORD will reign forever,
  your God, O Zion, for all generations.
Praise the LORD!

whose hope is in the LORD his God,
⁶the Maker of heaven and earth,
  the sea, and everything in them—
  the LORD, who remains faithful forever.
⁷**He upholds the cause of the oppressed**
  and gives food to the hungry.
The LORD sets prisoners free,
⁸ the LORD gives sight to the blind,
  the LORD lifts up those who are bowed
    down,
  the LORD loves the righteous.
⁹The LORD watches over the alien
  and sustains the fatherless and
    the widow,
  but he frustrates the ways of the wicked.
¹⁰The LORD reigns forever,
  your God, O Zion, for all generations.
Praise the LORD.

UNDERSTANDING THE SCRIPTURE

Psalm 146. This joyous psalm praises God for divine help. Along with Psalms 147–150, it begins and ends with the word *hallelujah* (literally, "praise the LORD"). Verses 1-2 are a personal expression of praise, rather than a corporate one. Verses 3-4 highlight God's power by pointing out the inadequacy of humans, regardless of their earthly status. Verses 5-9 show the gracious intent of God's help, offered to all. This includes those who most need it, which we see in a catalog of familiar groups—the oppressed, hungry, imprisoned, blind, and so on. The list ends with specific reference to strangers (aliens), orphans, and widows. Verse 10 closes the psalm with another statement of praise.

Introduction to Exodus 21–23. These chapters belong to a section known as the Covenant Code or Book of the Covenant, which spans Exodus 20:22–23:19. The laws reflect a settled rural society heavily dependent on agriculture and husbandry. Archaeological evidence indicates that many of these laws originated elsewhere; the Hebrew community adapted them from other cultures over time as seemed practical and appropriate.

Exodus 21:1-11. This section addresses the rights of slaves (see also Deuteronomy 15:12-18). While similar to other legal codes throughout the ancient Near East, these verses also highlight Israel's particular concern for *all* people, including women (wives) and both male and female children.

Exodus 21:12-27. Here the laws move to general prohibitions and restitutions designed to protect people. Note the distinction between murder and manslaughter, which includes a place of refuge for someone who commits the latter (see Numbers 35:12; Deuteronomy 4:41-43; 19:1-13; Joshua 20). Verses 20-25, known as the *lex talionis* ("law of retaliation") are meant as a mercy. It limits vengeance to what is equitable rather than allowing it to escalate as other legal systems did.

Exodus 21:28–22:17. The laws in this section deal with property and restitution. Just as Exodus 21:12-14 allows for unintentional killing, these laws also consider harm that arises from carelessness rather than intent (21:28-36). Other categories of law apply to theft (22:1-4), neglect (22:5-6), trusteeship (22:7-15), and bride price (22:16-17).

Exodus 22:18–23:9. The collection now turns to various social and cultic laws. Verses 18-20 reflect practices associated with other religions (and thus prohibited for the Hebrews). Verses 21-24 underscore God's care for resident aliens, widows, and orphans. Verses 25-27 prohibit financial gain at another's expense. Verses 28-31 cover the homage that is due to God. Chapter 23 starts with issues related to justice, including fair and honest actions in court (23:1-3, 6-8) and care for property that belongs to an enemy (23:4-5). Verse 9 closes this section with another command to treat resident aliens fairly.

Exodus 23:10-19. This "cultic calendar" echoes texts found in Exodus 34:18-26, as well as Leviticus 23:1-44 and Deuteronomy 16:1-17. It begins with instructions regarding a sabbatical year for the land, which is designed to benefit the poor (Exodus 23:10-11). Then comes a statement on sabbath observance and its connection to caring for living creatures (animal and human) under one's authority. Verses 14-17 concern the proper celebration of harvest festivals. The final verses (23:18-19) ban practices that were common in Canaanite worship.

Exodus 23:20-33. These final verses of chapter 23 speak of an angel (or messenger) sent to guide the people (23:20-22). In Hebrew scripture, "angel" often refers to a manifestation of God's own person (for example, Genesis 16:7-14). Verses 23-33 then describe the protection that will come from God's presence as the people travel through various territories. This includes a cessation of sickness and other bodily ills within Israel (23:25-26). These blessings are quickly followed by a horrifying description of the destruction of all enemies (23:27-30). The language of holy war may disturb modern Christian readers. As commentator J. Gerald Janzen helpfully reminds us:

> This passage raises profound issues about cultural imperialism with a religious base, about genocide and ethnic cleansing, and about religiously fueled intolerance. It is easy to read a passage like this as sponsoring such things and then either to act accordingly in one's own time and place or to repudiate the passage as well as a Bible that contains such passages. Such interpretations are too simple. The scriptural story, as it goes on, progressively transforms these themes until in Jesus Christ they become transformed radically. . . . The transformation that Jesus Christ brings to these issues has to do with *how* the battle is waged [against the forces of injustice in the world].

Verse 31 describes an expanded and idealized Promised Land. The boundaries outlined here include territories that were never part of Israel. The chapter concludes with a blunt reminder that the people are to be allied with God and God alone. Other people and their gods will have the effect of becoming a "snare," so for that reason these other people are not allowed to inhabit the land God has promised to the covenant people.

Isaiah 58. Isaiah 58 presents a stark contrast between actions that are righteous and those that are unrighteous, set in the context of true versus false worship in the practice of fasting. The people claim to seek God and think they are demonstrating their righteousness and humility by fasting, but God indicts their self-serving actions. These purportedly righteous people are oppressing their workers and quarreling. Fasting itself is not being condemned in this passage; the problem is the hypocritical way the people practice this ritual. This chapter goes on to detail what God truly desires: Injustice is to be replaced by kindness and justice as embodied in such acts as sharing food with the hungry, clothing the naked, and otherwise tending to "the needs of the afflicted" (58:10). Isaiah likens these acts of mercy to a light that shines in the darkness (58:10; see also 42:6-7). The chapter closes with a promise of strength and abundance from God, along with a call to strict observance of the sabbath day. This latter emphasis was common in postexilic Jewish writings.

INTERPRETING THE SCRIPTURE

An Old Song

"Praise the Lord!"

Thus begins and ends each of the last five hymns in the Book of Psalms. Represented by the simple Hebrew word *hallelujah*, this call to thankfulness is a joyous reminder of all God has done, is doing, and will do for the sake of the world. In keeping with the theme of our last four lessons, "Justice Promised," Psalm 146 intertwines our praise to God with moving images of divine justice.

The psalmist sings of God's justice in terms that are quite familiar by now. Running throughout the verses are echoes of theological concepts we have heard before in this study. God the Creator, Sovereign Lord of all there is, "executes justice for the oppressed" (146:7). This same almighty God feeds the poor, sets prisoners free, brings sight to the blind, and lifts up those who are bowed down (146:7-8). Lest we forget the full scope of God's compassion, the psalmist adds a reminder that God watches over resident aliens in the land, as well as orphans and widows (146:9).

Even while inviting us to reach back through history to when God's teaching was first shared with the community of faith, the psalmist also looks ahead to the day that God's justice will be implemented perfectly. The psalmist is so sure of this outcome that he actually puts these future events into the present tense, as if they are already accomplished. Thus the psalmist celebrates the majesty and love of God by proclaiming divine justice and righteousness, encouraging us to consider the role we play in bringing these to fruition.

The Psalmist and Us

We can connect to this psalm in many ways. For example, like the psalmist, we experience moments in which we are so aware of God's care that our hearts overflow with praise and gratitude—and sometimes we express these feelings through songs and poetry. Certainly, our lives are enriched by the gift of others' creative output in the many different forms of vocal and instrumental music, as well as books and other media. Many people love the fact that Psalm 146 does more than remind us to praise God—it reminds us to sing our praise in joy!

Most of all, we take assurance from the psalm's promise that what we see today is not all there is. Many of us can cite examples of times when, to use the language of the psalms, the wicked prospered and the righteous suffered. The news is full of stories of those who profit through wrongdoing. No matter where we look, we see acts of injustice every day. In these joyous verses, the psalmist reminds us that this is not the end of the story.

The Call to Righteousness

Like the biblical prophets, the psalmist connects God's justice with our righteousness. As elsewhere in the Hebrew Scriptures, "righteousness" is not something one does, but something one has as an integral part of one's nature. Being righteous means being shaped in the image of Christ. It means being in tune with God in our deepest heart of hearts. It means accepting that God is in control of our lives.

Righteousness is not an action to be performed; it is a state of being with God.

The psalmist also suggests that righteousness involves knowing where true power and control lie—which is with God, of course. Some worldly appearances to the contrary, the only control we humans have is in choosing to give control to God. We can decide to obey God. We can decide whether we will trust in the unreliable, mortal rulers of this world—or trust in God's love and power for our lives. We can choose to do justice and love kindness. We cannot control events outside ourselves, but we can control whether or not we offer ourselves to God as a living sacrifice. We can control whether transient things of this world give our lives meaning, or whether a right relationship with God gives our lives meaning. This is not to say that human beings have no initiative or freedom of choice. On the contrary, the whole purpose of freedom of choice is to enable us to choose to be just and righteous—to choose God and God's ways.

The Challenge to Do Justice

"Justice" is a much bandied-about word in the modern world. We fight wars for justice. Our courts are overloaded with people seeking justice. It is a concept that most of us appreciate and seek to practice. Yet, in truth, the task seems enormous when we look at the world situation. When it comes to our Christian calling, we wonder: How can one do justice in a world where armies annihilate whole villages? How can one do justice in a nation where police officials practice violent racial discrimination? How can one do justice where big businesses seem to be out to destroy one another—and many unsuspecting individuals become "collateral damage"? How can one do justice in cities and states where local laws are often influenced by wealthy citizens seeking advantage—or, at the very least, seeking not to be disadvantaged or inconvenienced in some way?

Psalm 146 seemingly answers such questions with a question of its own: Why would you *not* fight for justice when you know God is behind it? For the psalmist, doing justice means not despairing in the face of injustice, but working to right the wrong. It means not giving up, but maintaining our own integrity in the face of enormous opposition. Doing justice means taking a stand for what is right. Perhaps we begin in small ways at first—by refusing to join in a conversation that promotes racial or gender degradation, by reevaluating a career that promotes violence or environmental damage, or by courageously taking a stand on a controversial issue. We do what we can, trusting God to do the rest.

The ways in which we can each work for justice are as varied as our unique interests and gifts. Some of the greatest strides to work for a better life for all, which is what God's justice aims for, have come when a sense of urgency got stirred up in someone who chose to act on it. Every neighborhood clothes closet or homeless shelter is an example of this, as are large organizations like Rainbow PUSH Coalition, Jobs with Justice, and Amnesty International. There are many other groups of this nature, in which people have been called to quicken society's conscience and to advocate for new attitudes and laws that provide greater justice for all. In the very variety of needs and responses, we are assured that each of us has something to offer, without which the whole would not be complete. The promise is that as long as we each do our part, then God will work through all of us collectively to make a difference.

Keep up the fight, says the psalm, in essence. Keep it up as if it were already won, because in a sense it is. Keep up the fight, and keep singing your songs of thanks and praise to God, the source of our victory. Praise the Lord!

SHARING THE SCRIPTURE

Preparing Our Hearts

Explore this week's devotional reading, found in Luke 4:16-21. In these familiar words Jesus introduces his mission to his hometown synagogue members in Nazareth. Verses 18-19 combine Isaiah 58:6 and 61:1-2 to announce Jesus' concern for justice. Anointed by the Spirit, he proclaims good news to the poor, the release of captives, the return of sight to the blind, the release of the oppressed, and the Year of Jubilee. Through Jesus, this amazing reversal prophesied by Isaiah "has been fulfilled" (Luke 4:21). How does Jesus bring about justice in your life? What have you been called to do to enable others to be treated justly?

Pray that you and the adult learners will pledge yourselves to do all you possibly can to ensure that every person is treated with justice.

Preparing Our Minds

Study the background Scripture from Psalm 146; Exodus 21–23; Isaiah 58. The lesson Scripture is from Psalm 146. Ask yourself: Where can I look to find lasting justice?

Write on newsprint:

❏ information for next week's lesson, found under "Continue the Journey."
❏ activities for further spiritual growth in "Continue the Journey."

Familiarize yourself with the information from Understanding the Scripture for Exodus 21; 22; 23; and Isaiah 58. You may need to add some of this information to the discussion near the end of "Discover the Many Ways God Cares for God's Human Creations."

Check out websites for programs listed under "Show Thanksgiving for God's Help by Helping Others." Also provide information for ministries in your community that help needy persons.

LEADING THE CLASS

(1) Gather to Learn

❖ Welcome the class members and introduce any guests.

❖ Pray that the students will celebrate God's care for humanity.

❖ Read this story from www.iyjl.org/?p=1544 about Rosalba Feliz, who immigrated to the United States as a teenager: **At age thirteen Rosalba came with her family to the United States as an undocumented immigrant. She realized in high school that she needed, as she calls it, "a 9-digit number," a Social Security number that would allow her to pursue her dream of becoming a police officer. Despite help from empathetic police officers, she could not fulfill her goal until her legal status could be changed. Without a change in the immigration laws, she had no hope and was, as she states, "growing old with no future." She had made up her mind to return home to the Dominican Republic, but then she heard about "The Dream Act." Believing that a productive future might be possible, one in which she could "become a part of society and as [a] police officer help [her] community," she decided to stay and fight for her dream.**

❖ Ask: **Where do you see justice—or injustice—in this story?**

❖ Read aloud today's focus statement: **People appreciate receiving lasting justice. Where can we look to find unshakable justice? God is the source of steadfast justice.**

(2) Discover the Many Ways God Cares for God's Human Creations

❖ Introduce Psalm 146, one of the "Hallelujah Psalms" by reading or retelling "An Old Song" from Interpreting the Scripture.

❖ Distribute hymnals with a Psalter and invite the participants to read Psalm 146 responsively.

❖ **Option:** If you do not have hymnals that include a Psalter, enlist a volunteer to read Psalm 146 from his or her Bible.

❖ Distribute paper and pencils. Encourage the adults to read Psalm 146 silently and slowly, making note of any words or phrases that grab their attention.

❖ Invite volunteers to state the word or phrase that they found most striking and to explain why the word caught their attention.

❖ Form four groups. Assign each group one of these background chapters: Exodus 21; Exodus 22; Exodus 23; or Isaiah 58. Each group is to scan its assigned chapter and look for common points between that chapter and Psalm 146. What does each have to say about God's perspective on justice?

❖ Bring the groups together so that they may report on the points they found most important. (Be prepared to add information about any of these chapters from Understanding the Scripture.)

❖ Conclude by asking: **In what ways do you see Jesus fulfilling Psalm 146:7-9?**

(3) Accept That God Is Faithful and Just to Those Who Place Their Hope in God

❖ Distribute hymnals if you have not already done so. Invite the adults to work with a partner or in a group of three to identify hymns related to God's faithfulness and justice. Examples include "Great Is Thy Faithfulness," "The King of Love My Shepherd Is," "God Will Take Care of You," and "He Leadeth Me: O Blessed Thought." The partners are to read aloud to each other verses that seem particularly meaningful to them.

❖ Call everyone together. List hymns on newsprint as groups name them.

❖ **Option:** Sing a verse or two of each hymn that has been named.

(4) Show Thanksgiving for God's Help by Helping Others

❖ Recall that Psalm 146 lauds God for being faithful and just. This psalm names vulnerable groups in society: the oppressed, those who hunger, the prisoner, the poor, the stranger, the widow and orphan.

❖ Read James 2:14-18 and remind the adults that we show our faith in God by acting as God acts.

❖ Talk together about a class project that would help others and include individuals from the congregation and the community. Encourage the adults to suggest projects they are familiar with that your church is not currently engaged in. Here are some possibilities:

- **CROP Hunger Walk**—sponsored by Church World Service to raise money for hungry people: www.churchworldservice.org/site/PageServer?pagename=crop_main.
- **Stop Hunger Now**—provides dehydrated meals, which groups pack, for children in schools and orphanages around the world: www.stophungernow.org/site/PageServer?pagename=progs_os.
- **Habitat for Humanity**—works with local affiliates in the United States and around the world to build safe, decent, affordable homes for those willing to put sweat equity into the home: www.habitat.org/.
- **Prison Fellowship**—founded by Chuck Colson to help inmates come to know Jesus and turn their lives around, thereby restoring peace to communities: www.prisonfellowship.org/prison-fellowshiphome.

❖ Call for those who are willing to investigate one or more of the projects to raise their hands. Encourage them to report back what they discover about the projects that interest them and how the class can become involved.

(5) Continue the Journey

❖ Pray that the adults will commit themselves to helping others in grateful response to the help they have received from God.

❖ Read aloud this preparation for next week's lesson. You may also want to post it on newsprint for the students to copy.

■ **Title: God Promised a Righteous Lord**

■ **Background Scripture: Isaiah 9:1-7**

■ **Lesson Scripture: Isaiah 9:2-7**

■ **Focus of the Lesson: Discouraged people look for hope. Where can we find hope? Our hope is found in the coming Messiah who established a just and righteous kingdom.**

❖ Challenge the students to complete one or more of these activities for further spiritual growth related to this week's session. Post this information on newsprint for the students to copy.

(1) **Read Psalms 146; 147; 148; 149; 150, one per day. These are known as the "Hallelujah [or Hallel] Psalms." Note that each of these psalms begins and ends with "Praise the LORD!" As you** read each psalm, offer praise to God because of who God is.

(2) **Think about how people are treated in your community. Ask yourself: What would Mother Teresa or Dr. Martin Luther King, Jr., say to us about the justice with which certain groups are treated? What changes do we need to make? How can I work with others to initiate this change?**

(3) **Rewrite Psalm 146 in your own words. Think deeply about the meaning of this psalm, perhaps reading it in several translations before you write your own version. Read it aloud as you enthusiastically praise God.**

❖ Sing or read aloud "Immortal, Invisible, God Only Wise."

❖ Conclude today's session by leading the class in this benediction adapted from Deuteronomy 10:12-13, the key verses for June 24: **Go forth remembering that we are to fear the Lord our God, to walk in all his ways, to love God, to serve the Lord with all our heart and soul, and to keep God's commandments.**

UNIT 3: JUSTICE PROMISED

God Promised a Righteous Lord

PREVIEWING THE LESSON

Lesson Scripture: Isaiah 9:2-7
Background Scripture: Isaiah 9:1-7
Key Verse: Isaiah 9:6

Focus of the Lesson:
Discouraged people look for hope. Where can we find hope? Our hope is found in the coming Messiah who established a just and righteous kingdom.

Goals for the Learners:
(1) to contrast the Israelites' despair during their enslavement with their hope in the righteous reign of God.
(2) to identify elements from the Scripture text that give them hope today.
(3) to organize a class project that offers hope to the hopeless.

Pronunciation Guide:
Lachish (lay' kish)
Midian (mid' ee uhn)
Sennacharib (suh nak' uh rib)
shalom (shah lohm')

Supplies:
Bibles, newsprint and marker, paper and pencils, hymnals, optional copy of Handel's *Messiah* and appropriate player

---

READING THE SCRIPTURE

NRSV
Isaiah 9:2-7

2 The people who walked in darkness
   have seen a great light;

NIV
Isaiah 9:2-7

2The people walking in darkness
   have seen a great light;

those who lived in a land of deep
  darkness—
  on them light has shined.
3 You have multiplied the nation,
    you have increased its joy;
  they rejoice before you
    as with joy at the harvest,
    as people exult when dividing
      plunder.
4 For the yoke of their burden,
    and the bar across their shoulders,
    the rod of their oppressor,
    you have broken as on the day
      of Midian.
5 For all the boots of the tramping warriors
    and all the garments rolled in blood
    shall be burned as fuel for the fire.
6 **For a child has been born for us,**
    a son given to us;
  authority rests upon his shoulders;
    and he is named
  Wonderful Counselor, Mighty God,
    Everlasting Father, Prince of Peace.
7 His authority shall grow continually,
    and there shall be endless peace
  for the throne of David and his kingdom.
    He will establish and uphold it
  with justice and with righteousness
    from this time onward and
      forevermore.
  The zeal of the LORD of hosts will
    do this.

on those living in the land of the shadow
  of death
  a light has dawned.
3You have enlarged the nation
  and increased their joy;
they rejoice before you
  as people rejoice at the harvest,
as men rejoice
  when dividing the plunder.
4For as in the day of Midian's defeat,
  you have shattered
the yoke that burdens them,
  the bar across their shoulders,
  the rod of their oppressor.
5Every warrior's boot used in battle
  and every garment rolled in blood
will be destined for burning,
  will be fuel for the fire.
6**to us a child is born,**
  to us a son is given,
  and the government will be on his
    shoulders.
And he will be called
  Wonderful Counselor, Mighty God,
  Everlasting Father, Prince of Peace.
7Of the increase of his government and
    peace
  there will be no end.
He will reign on David's throne
  and over his kingdom,
establishing and upholding it
  with justice and righteousness
  from that time on and forever.
The zeal of the LORD Almighty
  will accomplish this.

UNDERSTANDING THE SCRIPTURE

Introduction. Many scholars assert that the book of the prophet Isaiah comes to us from three different worlds. The first 39 chapters speak of conditions in the eighth century B.C., when the Assyrian Empire, ruthless and bent on expansion, had cast its shadow over everything. The tiny kingdom of Israel was crushed by this powerful nation in 722–721 B.C., not to come to life again until modern times. Judah survived as a little land, surrounded by a hostile empire.

Chapters 40–55 reflect different conditions and are written in a different style. By the time this part of the book was written, Assyria had been succeeded by Babylon, and Judah as a nation had been swallowed up by this new menace in the year 587 B.C. Jerusalem and the Temple had been destroyed, and the better part of the population carried off into exile. These chapters are thought to have been written toward the end of that period of exile, 550–540 B.C. The writer saw clearly that a new leader was emerging, Cyrus of Persia, who would conquer Babylon, expand the empire, and then allow the exiles to go home.

The last part of the book (chapters 56–66) seems to come from a still later time. These chapters fit into the difficult time of rebuilding, after the exiles had returned to Jerusalem.

The background to Isaiah 9 is a time of crisis in the original Isaiah's lifetime (according to many scholars, approximately 730 B.C.). Several years before, the armies of Syria and Ephraim (Israel) had invaded Judah. Chapters 7–8 relate how Isaiah counseled King Ahaz to trust in God in that situation (7:4). Failure to do so could lead to Judah's sharing of Israel's prophesied downfall (7:8, 17-18). As it was, Ahaz hedged his trust by buying the high-priced protection of Assyria (2 Kings 16:7-9). Some scholars interpret Isaiah 8:16-18 to represent the prophet's "withdrawal" from counseling Ahaz, based on the king's decision to throw in his lot with the Assyrians. The following verses (8:19-22) convey a sense of impending doom similar in spirit and message to the earlier oracles that Isaiah pronounced against his own people (1:21-23; 5:1-13). The scene is a foreboding one as chapter 8 ends: All is hunger and darkness, anger and despair. Faces turn to seek some sense of direction or guidance, but find only gloom. Despair reigns—but not forever.

Isaiah 9:1. Isaiah 9:1 introduces a reversal of this dire situation. The judgment of the "former time" will be no more. The "way of

the sea" refers to the trade route stretching southwest from Damascus through Galilee and along the coast to Egypt. God will transform this favored highway of invading armies, including those of Assyria, to a way made glorious by God.

Isaiah 9:2. Beginning with verse 2, the prophet offers God's promise of light to those shadowed by Judah's grief. This verse has become a familiar litany in the church's worship at Advent, particularly at candlelight services that mingle the words with symbols of light. When Isaiah speaks of light shining in a land of "deep darkness," his choice of Hebrew wording is identical to that used in a much older psalm intended to bring comfort to the despairing: "Even though I walk through the *darkest valley*, I fear no evil" (Psalm 23:4, italics added).

Isaiah 9:3-5. One component of the despair faced by Isaiah's audience was uncertainty over the covenant's continuity. If such judgment as Isaiah had earlier announced came to pass, did that mean God had deserted the people or ended the covenant? In previous passages, Isaiah answered this concern with God's promise that a remnant would continue (1:9; 4:2-6). In this passage, the prophet draws on words and themes directly related to the covenant. "You have multiplied the nation" (9:3) recalls the fundamental promise of the covenant to Abraham and Isaac and Jacob (Genesis 17:2; 26:24; 28:3). The imagery of Isaiah 9:4-5 arises from the fate of their neighbors, and the fear for their own lives. The people's joy emerges from an anticipated destruction of the oppression and militarism that currently weighed on them.

Isaiah 9:6. In glorious language, Isaiah prophesies the birth of a Davidic heir who will restore the nation's status and pride. Prophets often named their children to make a point—Hosea did so (Hosea 1:2-9), and so did Isaiah (Isaiah 7:3; 8:1-5)—and here in verse 6 the names of the child are quite significant. They reflect the people's hope for an ideal king, a hope that later evolved into the expectation of a messiah. The names for this child indicate a complete and perfect human ruler: This one will reign with wisdom ("Wonderful Counselor"). The term "Mighty God" can be translated "Divine Hero," meaning the person acts with God's own power to bring deliverance. "Everlasting Father" conveys both the king's loving, watchful concern for the people and the promise that this ruler's care will never fade. Finally, this "Prince of Peace" will bring God's *shalom* to the people. This Hebrew term means far more than an absence of war. Rather, it indicates complete and holistic health for the entire community, including social and economic well-being that extends to everyone.

Isaiah 9:7. In this text's concluding verse, Isaiah explicitly mentions what may have been the most endangered aspect of God's covenant at that time: the Davidic kingship. Samuel's warning of what kings would bring upon the land (1 Samuel 8:9-18) proved all too true in Israel and Judah's subsequent history. However, God promised David a dynasty established forever (2 Samuel 7:12-13, 16). With the Northern Kingdom of Israel poised on ruin's edge, and with Assyria threatening to undo Judah's kingdom, the Davidic promise of an everlasting throne must have seemed frail at best. Consequently, Isaiah's underscoring of that promise in Isaiah 9:7 serves as affirmation that God's covenant remains trustworthy.

INTERPRETING THE SCRIPTURE

The Background of the Birth

"For unto us a Child is born, unto us a Son is given." With those words from Isaiah 9:6 Handel's *Messiah* breaks into some of the most joyful music ever written. Almost always, hearing them sung brings hope and joy to our hearts. Perhaps studying them can bring us something of these feelings too.

Invasion, defeat, charges of conspiracy, terror, corrupt leadership—the background of Isaiah's hymn is not hopeful or joyful at all. The chapter preceding it ends, "They will look to the earth, but will see only distress and darkness, the gloom of anguish; and they will be thrust into thick darkness" (8:22). If there were a musical prelude to Isaiah's song, it would include the sound of "the boots of the tramping warriors," and if there were a backdrop, it would be "garments rolled in blood" (9:5).

Precisely what war the prophet meant is debated, but there was enough horror in the last half of the eighth century B.C. that almost any year in that period can be defended as a date for this prophecy. At one point, Syria and Israel ganged up on Judah, invading it and so terrifying weak King Ahaz that we are told his heart "and the heart of his people shook as the trees of the forest shake before the wind" (7:2). Isaiah's oracle might come from that event or it could be a bit later, when Zebulun and Naphtali, tribes of Galilee, were gobbled up by the Assyrian invaders (9:1).

Perhaps Isaiah's words came from those desperate days when Samaria had fallen and the armies of Sennacharib slaughtered town after town until they reached the very gates of Jerusalem. That Assyrian emperor has left us a carving vividly depicting his siege of Lachish, the largest city in Judea after Jerusalem. The carving shows his huge army camped around Lachish's fortress walls, building ramps to climb over the walls and readying a battering ram to knock the walls down. Some Israelites, trying to escape, are shown impaled on sharp poles, left hanging there as horrible examples for the people of the city. Some are already being led off into slavery.

No wonder the prophet wrote of "gloom" and "darkness" (8:22). Nonetheless, in that dark time he was to sing a song of irrepressible hope and dawning joy.

The Prince of Peace

Using what scholars call "the prophetic perfect," Isaiah described the coming deliverance as though it were already accomplished. "Those who lived in a land of deep darkness—on them light has shined" (9:2). In the prophet's vision, the nation was pictured as if it had already been rescued. What has accomplished this? "A child has been born for us, a son given to us" (9:6). For Isaiah, this son was the sign of salvation.

Consider the four names of this child. Note, by the way, that these are not names given the child simply by his parents. These are what people who know this one will call him:

- Wonderful Counselor—The Hebrew word translated "wonderful" is sometimes used of God. Centuries later, Plato pointed out that what we most want in a ruler is wisdom and good counsel. This king has wisdom from God, and he can give us divine guidance.
- Mighty God—Cautious scholars carefully insist that Isaiah is not really calling this promised ruler God, the divine self. They note that the Old Testament sometimes used this term to describe heroic human beings. Granted, Isaiah is speaking poetry, but he is coming about as close as an Old Testament writer could come to describing a person who is God incarnate.
- Everlasting Father—The best-loved

kings have often been called fathers of their realms, and the best-loved queens have been called their nations' mothers. The name is a symbol of the love of the people for the sovereign. Even more, it is a symbol of the sovereign's eternal love and care for the people.

- Prince of Peace—There will be no more crunch of the "boots of the tramping warriors" nor the gruesome sight of "garments rolled in blood" (9:5). With the coming of this child "there shall be endless peace" (9:7).

This descendant of David will use divine authority to establish firmly the throne that seemed to be tottering in Isaiah's day. Furthermore, his kingdom will be established "with justice and with righteousness" (9:7). In the first chapter of the Book of Isaiah the prophet had pleaded with the people:

> Seek justice,
>   rescue the oppressed,
> defend the orphan,
>   plead for the widow. (1:17)

At last, by God's doing, a government concerned for the poor will be established. The prophet declares in hopeful expectation: "The zeal of the LORD of hosts will do this" (9:7).

What Child Is This?

Who was this child of whom Isaiah spoke? It was obvious that he was to be king, for he would sit on "the throne of David" (9:7). Probably the hope had already grown by Isaiah's day that someday there would come the great descendant of David about whom Nathan, David's advisor, had prophesied (2 Samuel 7:11-16). God, it was said, had made a covenant with David that his dynasty would rule forever (2 Samuel 23:5). Perhaps Isaiah was recalling that promise.

Scholars have made varied guesses about

whom Isaiah meant. Some propose that he sang these words of hope when good King Hezekiah was born. Others suggest that the song was composed for that same king's inauguration, "birth" being a figure of speech for the beginning of his reign. Still others believe this was a song repeated at the inauguration of *every* king, a kind of all-purpose patriotic hymn. King after king was born and king and after king was inaugurated in hope, but none of them fit the measure of this melody.

Exactly what Isaiah expected, we can never know for sure. What we do know is this: Long after there were no more kings on the throne in Jerusalem, devout Jews still sang this song. The fifth-century A.D. rabbi who composed a targum (or paraphrase) on this poem inserted a word to describe the kingly figure. He called him, in Hebrew, *messiah*; the Greek translation would be "Christ." Faithful Jews believed that someday this promised king would come.

As Christians, we believe we know what God ultimately had planned. The last years of the era called "B.C." were also a time of "distress and darkness" (Isaiah 8:22). King Herod was so terrified he might lose his throne that he murdered even his own sons, because he thought they might be plotting against him. Many were ready to "curse their king" (8:21). In the middle of the night, Zealots plotted revolution. Often they turned to false messiahs. Their desperate intrigues, however, never had a chance. Rome stood ready to slaughter any who might rebel.

There were, however, some who were ready to "turn their faces upward" (8:21; compare with Matthew 2:2). They saw a star. Even in a distant land they had heard of the promised "King of the Jews." They did not find him in Herod's palace, but at Bethlehem they learned new meaning for Isaiah's words: "For a child has been born for us, a son given to us" (Isaiah 9:6). May we ever be faithful vessels for his gift of light and joy!

SHARING THE SCRIPTURE

Preparing Our Hearts

Explore this week's devotional reading, found in John 8:12-19. In one of the familiar "I am" statements, Jesus tells us that he is the "light of the world" (8:12). If we follow his light, we "will never walk in darkness" (8:12). Consider the stark contrast between light and darkness. What advantages are there to living in the light? Rate your life on a "brightness scale," using zero for total darkness and ten for brightest light. Are you where you want to be? If not, what steps will you take to move closer to the source of light?

Pray that you and the adult learners will move ever closer to the full light of God.

Preparing Our Minds

Study the background Scripture from Isaiah 9:1-7 and the lesson Scripture from Isaiah 9:2-7. Consider this question: Where do you look for hope when you feel discouraged?

Write on newsprint:
- ❏ information for next week's lesson, found under "Continue the Journey."
- ❏ activities for further spiritual growth in "Continue the Journey."

Locate a recording of Handel's *Messiah* and an appropriate player if you choose the option under "Identify Elements from the Scripture Text That Give the Learners Hope Today."

LEADING THE CLASS

(1) Gather to Learn

❖ Welcome the class members and introduce any guests.

❖ Pray that the students will find hope as they encounter the righteous reign of God.

❖ Make a list of groups of people (no individual names) who may be discouraged and lack hope. Here are some ideas: *those who are unemployed, those who are homeless, those who cannot make ends meet, those in broken relationships, students who are performing poorly in school, patients who are seriously ill and their families, those who have experienced an unwanted life change.*

❖ Ask: **Where might these discouraged people seek hope?**

❖ Read aloud today's focus statement: **Discouraged people look for hope. Where can we find hope? Our hope is found in the coming Messiah who established a just and righteous kingdom.**

(2) Contrast the Israelites' Despair During Their Enslavement With Their Hope in the Righteous Reign of God

❖ Set the scene by reading or retelling "The Background of the Birth" from Interpreting the Scripture. Add information from "Introduction" from Understanding the Scripture.

❖ Invite the students to imagine themselves as slaves in a foreign country and ask:

(1) **How might your situation as a captive slant your current view of God?**

(2) **How might your current situation shape your expectations for the future?**

❖ Choose a volunteer to read Isaiah 9:2-7.

❖ Post a sheet of newsprint with these two headings: *Reasons for Despair* and *Reasons for Hope.* Encourage the class to review the reading and call out reasons from the text for despair and hope. For example, life in "deep darkness" would

have caused despair, whereas life lived in the light would be cause for hope. Similarly, oppression would cause despair, though the broken rod would bring hope.

❖ Relate this study to Jesus, in whom Christians see this passage fulfilled, by reading or retelling "What Child Is This?" from Interpreting the Scripture.

❖ Compare the description of the righteous king in Isaiah 9:2-7 with two other passages from Isaiah that Christians have also interpreted as being related to Jesus: Isaiah 7:14; 52:13–53:12. First, have volunteers read these two Scriptures. Then ask: **As you consider all of these references, what kind of picture emerges about the One who will bring in the righteous reign of God?**

(3) Identify Elements From the Scripture Text That Give the Learners Hope Today

❖ **Option:** Play "For Unto Us a Child Is Born" from Handel's *Messiah.* Discuss how this music enriches the biblical words.

❖ Use information from "The Prince of Peace" in Interpreting the Scripture to unpack the meanings of each term used to describe this child given for the people.

❖ Distribute paper and pencils. Invite the adults to write a brief paragraph—even words or phrases, if they prefer—to describe the kind of reign that this child will inaugurate.

❖ Encourage the students to talk about their perceptions of life as it will be when this ideal "prince of peace" comes to rule. Here are some questions to ask that the adults may have considered as they wrote their paragraphs:

(1) **What will the government look like in this realm?**

(2) **If this government were to have a budget, what would be the priorities?**

(3) **How will the leadership be different from that which we have known?**

(4) **How will people be treated by the ruler and by other people?**

❖ Conclude by asking: **How does the thought of this ideal reign give you hope for today?**

(4) Organize a Class Project That Offers Hope to the Hopeless

❖ Note that in most jurisdictions school will begin in just a few weeks. Many students dread the return to school, not because of class assignments or homework but because they lack proper clothing, shoes, and school supplies. They may feel that other students are looking down on them; they may even be bullied.

❖ Suggest the following steps to encourage the class to offer proper equipment, self-esteem, and hope to those students who are unable to afford what they need.

(1) **Decide what the class can do. Can they purchase school supplies, clothing, or shoes? Can they enlist help from the congregation, perhaps collecting some gently used clothing?**

(2) **Select someone to contact local schools or the board of education to determine where help is needed. This class spokesperson should then speak with the school principal to get detailed information about what is needed. Many schools have specific lists of supplies for each grade.**

(3) **Set up boxes to collect supplies. Ask several class members to oversee the collection.**

(4) **Deliver the supplies (or clothing) to the school by the date designated by the school.**

❖ Wrap up this portion of the lesson with a few moments of silent prayer for those students who will receive the supplies.

(5) Continue the Journey

❖ End the silent time by praying aloud that the adults will do what they can to offer hope to those who feel hopeless.

❖ Read aloud this preparation for next week's lesson. You may also want to post it on newsprint for the students to copy.

- ■ **Title: God Promised a Righteous Branch**
- ■ **Background Scripture: Jeremiah 23:1-6; 33:14-18**
- ■ **Lesson Scripture: Jeremiah 23:1-6; 33:14-18**
- ■ **Focus of the Lesson: Leaders may betray the people whom they serve. Where do we find leaders whom we can trust? God promises to send leaders who will administer justice in God's name.**

❖ Challenge the students to complete one or more of these activities for further spiritual growth related to this week's session. Post this information on newsprint for the students to copy.

(1) **Research an ongoing conflict. Where in the world do people live in darkness and need to see the light of the Savior's hope? Offer prayer. Do whatever else you can to help these people.**

(2) **Make a commitment to work for peace in your own community, perhaps through a church ministry or nonprofit organization.**

(3) **Contemplate today's key verse, Isaiah 9:6. What difference does it make in the way you live your life that "a child has been born for us"?**

❖ Sing or read aloud "Christ Is the World's Light."

❖ Conclude today's session by leading the class in this benediction adapted from Deuteronomy 10:12-13, the key verses for June 24: **Go forth remembering that we are to fear the Lord our God, to walk in all his ways, to love God, to serve the Lord with all our heart and soul, and to keep God's commandments.**

UNIT 3: JUSTICE PROMISED
GOD PROMISED A RIGHTEOUS BRANCH

PREVIEWING THE LESSON

Lesson Scripture: Jeremiah 23:1-6; 33:14-18
Background Scripture: Jeremiah 23:1-6; 33:14-18
Key Verse: Jeremiah 23:5

Focus of the Lesson:
Leaders may betray the people whom they serve. Where do we find leaders whom we can trust? God promises to send leaders who will administer justice in God's name.

Goals for the Learners:
(1) to explore the benefits of being under the leadership of a righteous shepherd.
(2) to identify a situation in which they were betrayed by a trusted leader.
(3) to investigate ways people are trained for leadership roles in the church.

Pronunciation Guide:
Abiathar (uh bi′ uh thahr)   Jehoiakim (ji hoi′ uh kim)
Adonijah (ad uh ni′ juh)   Josiah (joh si′ uh)
Anathoth (an′ uh thoth)   Megiddo (mi gid′ oh)
Baruch (bair′ uhk)   Nebuchadnezzar (neb uh kuhd nez′ uhr)
Hilkiah (hil ki′ uh)   Phinehas (fin′ ee uhs)
Jehoahaz (ji hoh′ uh haz)   Zedekiah (zed uh ki′ uh)
Jehoiachin (ji hoi′ uh kin)

Supplies:
Bibles, newsprint and marker, paper and pencils, hymnals

READING THE SCRIPTURE

NRSV
Jeremiah 23:1-6

¹Woe to the shepherds who destroy and scatter the sheep of my pasture! says the

NIV
Jeremiah 23:1-6

¹"Woe to the shepherds who are destroying and scattering the sheep of my pasture!"

LORD. ²Therefore thus says the LORD, the God of Israel, concerning the shepherds who shepherd my people: It is you who have scattered my flock, and have driven them away, and you have not attended to them. So I will attend to you for your evil doings, says the LORD. ³Then I myself will gather the remnant of my flock out of all the lands where I have driven them, and I will bring them back to their fold, and they shall be fruitful and multiply. ⁴I will raise up shepherds over them who will shepherd them, and they shall not fear any longer, or be dismayed, nor shall any be missing, says the LORD.

⁵**The days are surely coming, says the LORD, when I will raise up for David a righteous Branch, and he** shall reign as king and deal wisely, and **shall execute justice and righteousness in the land.** ⁶In his days Judah will be saved and Israel will live in safety. And this is the name by which he will be called: "The LORD is our righteousness."

Jeremiah 33:14-18

¹⁴The days are surely coming, says the LORD, when I will fulfill the promise I made to the house of Israel and the house of Judah. ¹⁵In those days and at that time I will cause a righteous Branch to spring up for David; and he shall execute justice and righteousness in the land. ¹⁶In those days Judah will be saved and Jerusalem will live in safety. And this is the name by which it will be called: "The LORD is our righteousness."

¹⁷For thus says the LORD: David shall never lack a man to sit on the throne of the house of Israel, ¹⁸and the levitical priests shall never lack a man in my presence to offer burnt offerings, to make grain offerings, and to make sacrifices for all time.

declares the LORD. ²Therefore this is what the LORD, the God of Israel, says to the shepherds who tend my people: "Because you have scattered my flock and driven them away and have not bestowed care on them, I will bestow punishment on you for the evil you have done," declares the LORD. ³"I myself will gather the remnant of my flock out of all the countries where I have driven them and will bring them back to their pasture, where they will be fruitful and increase in number. ⁴I will place shepherds over them who will tend them, and they will no longer be afraid or terrified, nor will any be missing," declares the LORD.

⁵**"The days are coming," declares the LORD, "when I will raise up to David a righteous Branch,** a King who will reign wisely and **do what is just and right in the land.** ⁶In his days Judah will be saved and Israel will live in safety. This is the name by which he will be called: The LORD Our Righteousness."

Jeremiah 33:14-18

¹⁴" 'The days are coming,' declares the LORD, 'when I will fulfill the gracious promise I made to the house of Israel and to the house of Judah. ¹⁵" 'In those days and at that time I will make a righteous Branch sprout from David's line; he will do what is just and right in the land. ¹⁶In those days Judah will be saved and Jerusalem will live in safety. This is the name by which it will be called: The LORD Our Righteousness.' ¹⁷For this is what the LORD says: 'David will never fail to have a man to sit on the throne of the house of Israel, ¹⁸nor will the priests, who are Levites, ever fail to have a man to stand before me continually to offer burnt offerings, to burn grain offerings and to present sacrifices.' "

UNDERSTANDING THE SCRIPTURE

Introduction. The fall of Jerusalem occurred in 587 B.C., and many people consider this to be the most pivotal date in the Old Testament. Everything written before that time points ahead to the catastrophe of the exile. Everything afterward seeks to explain and interpret it. It so happens that the long ministry of Jeremiah falls on both sides of that event, making him a fairly unique figure in Israel's history—the hinge joining *what was* with *what came to be*.

A great deal of Jeremiah's ministry took place in those decades when time was running out for Judah. This means that much of his prophecy was heavy with warning of the coming disaster. In general, though, the book is divided more by literary concerns than chronology. Chapters 1–25 are autobiographical, consisting mostly of Jeremiah's own prophecies. Chapters 26–45 have mostly biographical material compiled by Jeremiah's scribe, Baruch. Chapters 46–51 contain oracles against nations that were hostile to Judah. The final chapter, which is very similar to 2 Kings 24:18–25:30, recounts the fall of Jerusalem.

We know little of Jeremiah himself. He began his career in 627 B.C. (Jeremiah 1:2), just five years before King Josiah began his extensive reforms of the religious and social system. Jeremiah apparently approved of this program, because we do not hear from him again until after Josiah's death at the battle of Megiddo in 609 B.C. The biblical history records how the people returned to worshiping foreign gods soon after Josiah's death. They might have been swayed otherwise if Josiah's successor, his son Jehoahaz, had been a good king and able to keep the throne. The Egyptian king who defeated Josiah took Jehoahaz as a prisoner, however, and put his brother Jehoiakim on the throne. Under Jehoiakim's leadership, the people quickly deserted the worship of God that Josiah had fought to establish.

Jehoiakim caused trouble for Judah in more ways than one. He not only led the people astray religiously but he also took risky political chances. The history of Jehoiakim's reign shows that he often sought to further his own power and advantage. He served the Egyptian king who appointed him only as long as Egypt seemed strong. Jehoiakim quickly switched allegiance to Babylon, however, after it proved to be more powerful than Egypt. Then, after three years as Nebuchadnezzar's vassal, Jehoiakim saw an opportunity to rebel, so he did. Thus we can see how Jeremiah had much to address during his key years as a prophet.

Jeremiah 23:1-4. This oracle falls within a larger section of prophecies related to the royal house (21:11–23:8). It begins with a condemnation of Israel's kings, referred to metaphorically as "shepherds." (See next week's lesson for more information on this image.) Counter to their ultimate responsibility as representatives of God, the kings have misled the people and caused them to stray off the paths of righteousness and justice. They have not led the people in their charge in caring ways. Accordingly, God announces intentions to attend to the sheep that have been scattered across the landscape of ancient Near Eastern nations (that is, "the remnant," 23:3), claiming them again as God's people. God will gather them and bring them back into the fold in their own land, where they will be fruitful and multiply. Once the people have been returned to their own land, God will raise up shepherds who will truly shepherd them. Because of such divine action, the people will not be fearful again.

Jeremiah 23:5-6. The text then focuses on the promise of a leader from the line of David whom God will raise up. This shepherd/king, referred to as a "righteous Branch" (23:5), will rule in justice and righteousness. (Compare Zechariah 3:8 and 6:12, where "Branch" appears as a messianic title.) Appropriately, this king is named "The LORD is our righteousness" (23:6). This designation indicates that God's own desire for justice and righteousness will come to fruition through this king, and Israel will dwell in safety at last. Moreover, according to commentator John M. Bracke:

> This vision of Judah's future is a play on the name of Judah's last king before the exile, King Zedekiah. Zedekiah's name in Hebrew means "The Lord is righteousness," but it is clear in the Book of Jeremiah that the prophet did not think Zedekiah was righteous (21:1-2; cf. 34:1-6; 37–39). However, Jeremiah imagines that day when there will be a king of the house of David who will be what Zedekiah's name falsely claims, an embodiment of the Lord's righteousness.

Jeremiah 33:14-18. These verses present a variation of Jeremiah 23:5-6. Here we read of an eternal line of Davidic kings who will follow the rule of the one designated as a "righteous Branch." In contrast to Jeremiah 23, however, it is not a king who will be called "The LORD is our righteousness," but the city of Jerusalem. Part of Jeremiah's vision in 33:14-18 is that the city itself will become a place of justice, an earthly locale that mirrors heavenly justice. The covenant community that lives in this city understands itself to be in relationship with God and neighbor. Verse 17 refers to kings of the Davidic line who will rule, while in verse 18 we read that God promises an unbroken line of levitical priests. This idea of government by both a king, who is the agent of God's rule, and the priests, who are to offer sacrifices, is also seen in Haggai 1:1; 2:2; and Zechariah 4:11-14. This righteous rule, promised by God, will be fulfilled in the coming days.

Summation. Taken as a whole, the oracles of Jeremiah 23:1-6 and 33:14-18 offer assurance to the people that God will honor the covenants made with Israel's royal and priestly leaders (see 2 Samuel 7:14-16; Numbers 25:10-13). Moreover, God will honor these promises forever. All future generations of Israel can count on these promises unconditionally. Age after age, the community of faith will be marked by an ongoing experience of the mercy of God.

INTERPRETING THE SCRIPTURE

Jeremiah's Story

Today's passages from Jeremiah continue the theme of God's justice that is to come. Here we see the promised justice embodied in a "righteous Branch" from David's line, a king who will be a good shepherd over God's flock.

Jeremiah was born sometime between 652 and 645 B.C. He was from the town of Anathoth, which was located in the territory of Benjamin, about three miles northeast of Jerusalem. It was known as a town where priests lived. The ancient name of Anathoth has been preserved in today's modern town of Anata; the ruins of the original town are located about half a mile southwest of Anata at the archaeological dig known as Ras el Kharuba.

Little is known about the personal life of Jeremiah, other than he was the son of Hilkiah, who was a priest and possibly from the family of Abiathar. Abiathar was the priest of King David (see 1 Samuel 22:20-23; 30:7). David's son, Solomon, banished Abiathar to Anathoth for supporting Adonijah for king instead of Solomon (1 Kings 2:26-27). According to tradition, Abiathar was a descendant of Phinehas, the son of Eli. Eli was priest at Shiloh when

Samuel was dedicated as a child to God's service. If this family connection is true, then knowledge of the covenant relationship between God and Israel was most likely passed on to Jeremiah from a family lineage of individuals who were intimately involved in serving God.

Jeremiah began his prophetic work as a young man during the thirteenth year of King Josiah's reign (627 B.C.). Some scholars think Jeremiah was around twenty years old at this time. At first, he used his young age as a reason to reject God's call to the vocation of prophet, but God overrode this objection during a powerful vision. Although Jeremiah was an unwilling prophet in the years to come, he experienced the might of God in this call, and he went forth as a changed person.

Jeremiah prophesied to Judah until its last days before the Babylonian captivity (587 B.C.). He worked during the reigns of five Judean kings—Josiah, Jehoahaz, Jehoiakim, Jehoiachin, and Zedekiah. All in all, he prophesied for a total of about forty years. He dictated much of the book from which we read to his faithful secretary, Baruch. Jeremiah is often referred to as the "weeping prophet" because of the feelings he had concerning the judgment that was about to fall on Judah and because of how he felt about the difficulty of his task.

The Struggle for Justice

One of the reasons there are so many social and self-help programs for the poor in the world is that there is an inequality of opportunity between those who have and those who have not. Overcoming this inequity is one of the founding principles of the Western democracies. In the United States, for example, this is symbolized by the Statue of Liberty. The poem by Emma Lazarus, with the words "Give me your tired, your poor, your huddled masses yearning to breathe free," captures the meaning of this great symbol of freedom.

The inspiration drawing many to the shores of the United States has been that here all will have equal opportunity. Some people may think that we Americans are dreaming if we think that this will ever be true, but it is a worthy vision. For Christians, for the people of the covenant, this is our vision also and always has been. We are not allowed to ignore the poor and wretched of the earth, for Christ died for us all. To be a Christian is to claim the poor, the oppressed, and the exploited as our brothers and sisters.

It was this same doctrine of fairness and justice for all that Jeremiah preached to the people of Judah during the time when our texts were written. He was appalled at the dishonesty of his nation's leaders, and he spoke words of condemnation to those citizens who closed their eyes to what was happening. He tried to convince the wealthy that it was their obligation to turn away from exploiting the poor for their own advantage and share their wealth and economic opportunity with them. More than condemning, Jeremiah tried to give a vision of what life could be like if the people were willing to change. He rooted this vision in God's promise of a just and righteous king—a king that we celebrate as Jesus Christ.

What Can We Do?

In both passages for this week, Jeremiah describes a day when all people will live in safety and well-being. He received this vision of a blessed future during a time when Judah was wracked with social and moral evils, yet the vision became more real to him than what he saw in the world. On the strength of God's promise, Jeremiah was able to overcome despair and keep speaking out for the changes he knew God desired.

Like Jeremiah, most of us are keenly aware of social and ethical evils today. We are aware of the crime, divorce, and suicide rates. We are constantly confronted with drug problems, homelessness, abuse—

spousal, child, parental, animal, and environmental—and the escalating manifestations of violence. Money talks, and power is misused. At times it seems that the fabric of our lives and society is unraveling right before our eyes in our families, neighborhoods, nations, and world.

We know that the problems and evils of our age are not pleasing to God. We also know that our relationship with Christ involves witnessing to the love and justice of God for all of God's creation. We honor and respect men and women who dedicate their lives to speaking out on matters of public concern. We remember leaders such as Gandhi, Dorothy Day, Dietrich Bonhoeffer, Simone Weil, Dag Hammarskjöld, and Martin Luther King Jr., who left us example after example of addressing issues of social justice. We think of Mother Teresa, Gustavo Gutiérrez, Václav Havel, Pope John Paul II, and Dorothee Soelle, who serve as exemplars for many of us on ways to address matters of public concern. We are aware of the multifaceted work that goes on day after day by such organizations as Habitat for Humanity and Goodwill Industries International. Many of us can think of other individuals and organizations that not only work hard to address the many ills of our society but also manifest God's love, justice, and peace in their stance of living. We name this stance "Christian ethics."

If anything, Jeremiah's message to us is encouragement not to give up hope. Under the leadership of our Good Shepherd, we can and will accomplish justice in this world. So we keep working to see that all people have a fair share in the riches of this earth. We keep raising our voices on behalf of *all* God's flock, regardless of race, creed, or any other category that tends to separate us from one another. We keep sharing our conviction that God is with us, calling us to care and to share. Most of all, we keep trusting God's promises and God's grace.

SHARING THE SCRIPTURE

Preparing Our Hearts

Explore this week's devotional reading, found in Psalm 33:1-5. After opening with words of praise, the psalmist describes God's word as "upright" and God's work as being done faithfully (33:4). Moreover, God loves "righteousness and justice" (33:5). Everyone benefits because God's "steadfast love" fills the earth (33:5). Think about the many descriptions and examples we have seen throughout this quarter of God's justice and righteousness. How do the ideas in Psalm 33 add to or reinforce what you already know? Give thanks for the goodness and greatness of God.

Pray that you and the adult learners will praise the Lord of love, justice, and righteousness.

Preparing Our Minds

Study the background Scripture and the lesson Scripture, both of which are from Jeremiah 23:1-6 and 33:14-18. As you read, think about where you can find trustworthy leaders.

Write on newsprint:
❑ information for next week's lesson, found under "Continue the Journey."
❑ activities for further spiritual growth in "Continue the Journey."

Option: Invite a respected church leader or the pastor to discuss how leadership training is conducted in your congregation. There may be people in the class who could do this, but contact them ahead of time to let them know this issue will be discussed so that they can be prepared. Set a time limit. Let this person or persons know that providing handouts or ways to find further information would be appreciated.

LEADING THE CLASS

(1) Gather to Learn

❖ Welcome the class members and introduce any guests.

❖ Pray that the students will give thanks for good and just leaders.

❖ Post newsprint on which you will write the answers to this question: **What criteria do you use to determine whom you will vote for during a political election?** Once the students have suggested ideas, review them. How might these ideas be grouped? Likely some will concern the candidate's policies; some, the candidate's ethical and moral standards; others, experience; and still others, past performance in elected and professional positions.

❖ Ask: **When you have taken your criteria into account and cast your vote accordingly, what are your expectations if your candidate is elected?**

❖ Read aloud today's focus statement: **Leaders may betray the people whom they serve. Where do we find leaders whom we can trust? God promises to send leaders who will administer justice in God's name.**

(2) Explore the Benefits of Being Under the Leadership of a Righteous Shepherd

❖ Read or retell "Jeremiah's Story" from Interpreting the Scripture and "Introduction" from Understanding the Scripture to help the students learn more about this prophet and his ministry.

❖ Select two volunteers, one to read Jeremiah 23:1-6 and another to read Jeremiah 33:14-18.

❖ Discuss these questions:
  (1) What are the traits of a poor shepherd?
  (2) What are the traits of a good shepherd?

  (3) What are God's intentions for the sheep?

❖ Distribute paper and pencils. Invite the adults to sketch a branch, which they will label "righteous Branch" (Jeremiah 23:5, today's key verse, and 33:15). Then they are to draw small "limbs" shooting off from the branch. On each of those "limbs" they will write a word describing the "righteous Branch" that today's readings suggest. Words will vary but they may include *king, wise, just, one who saves, righteous, one who provides safety, "the LORD is our righteousness."*

❖ Encourage the participants to share their sketches with a partner or small group. As they reflect on the words they have selected, encourage them to discuss the benefits they see in living under this "righteous Branch" whom God promised to raise up from the shepherd David.

(3) Identify a Situation in Which the Learners Were Betrayed by a Trusted Leader

❖ Read this information: **Trusted leaders—even trusted church leaders—can betray the people they are called to serve. Such betrayals occurred in Jeremiah's day, and they continue to occur, though perhaps in different ways, in our day. One particularly serious betrayal is that of a church leader abusing a child physically, sexually, or psychologically. No church is immune from such a possibility, though the Roman Catholic Church has often been in the news, in the courtroom, even in bankruptcy court due to allegations of child abuse. Other church leaders have been accused of mishandling church finances. The marital infidelity of a church leader may also create chaos within a congregation.**

❖ Invite the learners to speak in general terms about a time when they felt betrayed by a trusted leader, such as a church official, teacher, coach, or employer. Suggest that to protect privacy they avoid names and geographical locations. Encourage adults who continue to feel harmed by this abuse to talk with a counselor or seek legal redress, or both. Be supportive, but make clear that such serious problems cannot be solved within the classroom.

(4) Investigate Ways People Are Trained for Leadership Roles in the Church

❖ Introduce the guest you have invited to discuss leadership training in your congregation. Even if this person is known to the group, or perhaps is even a class member, be sure everyone knows why he or she has been asked to speak.

❖ Listen to the speaker's presentation and review any handouts. Encourage the class to ask questions. Here are some ideas for points that may not have been covered:

(1) **What spiritual qualities do you look for in all leaders?**

(2) **Please give us examples of some gifts you look for as you match leaders with specific positions.**

(3) **What methods do we use to train these leaders?** (For example: Are they given books? Do we hold a training workshop? Do we provide mentors? Do new leaders work with a team of more experienced leaders?)

❖ Conclude by thanking the leader for speaking with the class. Let the leader know how much his or her work is appreciated and benefits the entire congregation.

(5) Continue the Journey

❖ Pray that the adults will prayerfully consider whether God is calling them into positions of leadership and, if so, that they will act on that calling.

❖ Read aloud this preparation for next week's lesson. You may also want to post it on newsprint for the students to copy.

■ **Title: God Promised to Be with Us**

■ **Background Scripture: Ezekiel 34**

■ **Lesson Scripture: Ezekiel 34:23-31**

■ **Focus of the Lesson: People are searching for tranquillity and wholeness. Where can these things be found? A lasting**

relationship with God and an assurance that God is with us meet our deepest need.

❖ Challenge the students to complete one or more of these activities for further spiritual growth related to this week's session. Post this information on newsprint for the students to copy.

(1) **Consider your expectations for governmental leaders. Thomas Jefferson explained the First Amendment of the U.S. Constitution in an 1802 letter to the Danbury Baptist Association this way: "I contemplate with sovereign reverence that act of the whole American people which declared that their legislature should 'make no law respecting an establishment of religion, or prohibiting the free exercise thereof,' thus building a wall of separation between Church & State." How does this "wall of separation" create opportunities and challenges for Christian leaders?**

(2) **Investigate some clergy scandals that have damaged not only the pastor but also a congregation. What would you say to these shepherds about the way they have harmed their flocks?**

(3) **Consider how volunteer leaders are trained in your congregation. Are they given enough information and solid role models to lead God's people? If you sense gaps, what suggestions can you make to help the church do a better job of training its leaders?**

❖ Sing or read aloud "Jesus Shall Reign."

❖ Conclude today's session by leading the class in this benediction adapted from Deuteronomy 10:12-13, the key verses for June 24: **Go forth remembering that we are to fear the Lord our God, to walk in all his ways, to love God, to serve the Lord with all our heart and soul, and to keep God's commandments.**

UNIT 3: JUSTICE PROMISED

GOD PROMISED TO BE WITH US

PREVIEWING THE LESSON

Lesson Scripture: Ezekiel 34:23-31
Background Scripture: Ezekiel 34
Key Verse: Ezekiel 34:23

Focus of the Lesson:
People are searching for tranquillity and wholeness. Where can these things be found? A lasting relationship with God and an assurance that God is with us meet our deepest need.

Goals for the Learners:
(1) to analyze the new covenant between God and God's people.
(2) to identify situations in which they find peace and wholeness.
(3) to respond to God's presence in their lives.

Pronunciation Guide:
Torah (toh' ruh)

Supplies:
Bibles, newsprint and marker, paper and pencils, hymnals, meditative instrumental music and appropriate player

---

READING THE SCRIPTURE

NRSV
Ezekiel 34:23-31

23I will set up over them one shepherd, my servant David, and he shall feed them: he shall feed them and be their shepherd. 24And I, the LORD, will be their God, and my servant David shall be prince among them; I, the LORD, have spoken.

NIV
Ezekiel 34:23-31

23I will place over them one shepherd, my servant David, and he will tend them; he will tend them and be their shepherd. 24I the LORD will be their God, and my servant David will be prince among them. I the LORD have spoken.

²⁵I will make with them a covenant of peace and banish wild animals from the land, so that they may live in the wild and sleep in the woods securely. ²⁶I will make them and the region around my hill a blessing; and I will send down the showers in their season; they shall be showers of blessing. ²⁷The trees of the field shall yield their fruit, and the earth shall yield its increase. They shall be secure on their soil; and they shall know that I am the LORD, when I break the bars of their yoke, and save them from the hands of those who enslaved them. ²⁸They shall no more be plunder for the nations, nor shall the animals of the land devour them; they shall live in safety, and no one shall make them afraid. ²⁹I will provide for them a splendid vegetation so that they shall no more be consumed with hunger in the land, and no longer suffer the insults of the nations. ³⁰They shall know that I, the LORD their God, am with them, and that they, the house of Israel, are my people, says the Lord GOD. ³¹You are my sheep, the sheep of my pasture and I am your God, says the Lord GOD.

²⁵" 'I will make a covenant of peace with them and rid the land of wild beasts so that they may live in the desert and sleep in the forests in safety. ²⁶I will bless them and the places surrounding my hill. I will send down showers in season; there will be showers of blessing. ²⁷The trees of the field will yield their fruit and the ground will yield its crops; the people will be secure in their land. They will know that I am the LORD when I break the bars of their yoke and rescue them from the hands of those who enslaved them. ²⁸They will no longer be plundered by the nations, nor will wild animals devour them. They will live in safety, and no one will make them afraid. ²⁹I will provide for them a land renowned for its crops, and they will no longer be victims of famine in the land or bear the scorn of the nations. ³⁰Then they will know that I, the LORD their God, am with them and that they, the house of Israel, are my people, declares the Sovereign LORD. ³¹You my sheep, the sheep of my pasture, are people, and I am your God, declares the Sovereign LORD.' "

UNDERSTANDING THE SCRIPTURE

Introduction. A contemporary of Jeremiah, the prophet Ezekiel went to Babylon in 597 B.C. as part of the first deportation, which comprised key Judean leaders. He was apparently included in this first group of folks removed to the land of their conquerors because he was a priest from Jerusalem. (His language and imagery show great familiarity with the rituals and procedures of the Temple in Jerusalem before its destruction.) He served as a prophet during this time of exile, and he remained in Babylon until at least 571 B.C.

Overall, the Book of Ezekiel is divided into two main parts. The first is full of prophetic warnings (Ezekiel 1–24). The second part, written after the destruction of Jerusalem in 587 B.C., contains condemnation of the nations that profited by Israel's misfortune (Ezekiel 25–32) and oracles of hope and restoration (Ezekiel 33–48). Our text for today comes from this latter section. In addition, we see three main themes throughout the book as a whole and in Ezekiel 34 itself—reassurance of God's presence with the people, a belief that the moral and ethical lapse of Judah's religious and political leaders brought consequences, and a focus on the nature of legitimate leadership in the restored community that is to come. Note that throughout the chapter, Ezekiel refers to "Israel"—by which he means all of the Hebrew people, regardless of tribe or original citizenship in the political kingdoms of either Israel or Judah.

A key image in Ezekiel 34 is that of the "shepherd." Reflecting the pastoral life of the people, much emphasis was given to sheep and shepherd imagery in both Testaments. The role of the king was often described as shepherd to the flock (see Psalm 78:70-72). However, most of the prophetic usages depict shepherds who fail to act as they should. No earthly anointed one (king) measured up to all the expectations, and the people looked more and more for an Anointed One to come from God. In the same way, the earthly shepherds (kings) did not measure up, and the people looked more and more for a Good Shepherd to come from God. The most completely developed images of God as Good Shepherd are found in Psalm 23, John 10, and this chapter from Ezekiel.

Ezekiel 34:1-10. As we saw in the previous lesson, one powerful common thread in the prophets' messages before the exile was that the leaders of the people had not given proper leadership. As bad as it was for the people to go astray, it was worse for the leaders to corrupt them and lead them astray. Hosea had condemned the priests for neglecting the law (Hosea 4:4), railed against priest and king (5:1), and denounced princes and kings (13:10). Micah had accused the leaders of injustice (Micah 3:1-3, 9), saying that even the prophets were leading the flock astray (3:5).

Similarly, Isaiah said the key problem was that of leadership (Isaiah 1:22-23), and he called for judgment on the leaders (10:1-4). A complete change was necessary, one in which God would restore corrupt judges and counselors to the righteous state they had at the beginning (1:26). Jeremiah cried out against faithless shepherds (Jeremiah 23:1-4), and Zechariah amplified the theme of the sheep being scattered when the evil shepherds are struck down (Zechariah 11:4-17; 13:7). All prophets, priests, and kings of the establishment fell under the scrutiny of the prophets of God, and they were found wanting.

Ezekiel strongly picks up on this theme, describing the rulers of "Israel" (that is, the Hebrew people) as shepherds who do not tend to the flock. They do not protect, lead to safe pastures and good watering places, seek the lost, nurse the hurt, and so on. Rather, the shepherds feed themselves on the flock; they are fat, clothed with the sheep's wool, and have slaughtered the flock with no thought to their responsibility as shepherds (Ezekiel 34:3-6). The assault of Babylon on Israel was like wild beasts on the flock, because the shepherds were not faithful. Now God will act against the wicked shepherds (34:7-10). Moreover, God will rescue the sheep, who had fallen prey to the very shepherds who were supposed to protect and care for them.

Ezekiel 34:11-16. Ezekiel makes it clear that God will be the shepherd to rescue and care for the ravaged people. God will seek them out where they have been carried in oppression. God will gather them and lead them back to security (see Isaiah 40:11). Many beautiful texts from the Book of Psalms spring to mind, in which God is depicted as Shepherd. "The LORD is my shepherd" (Psalm 23:1); God has made us, "we are his people, and the sheep of his pasture" (Psalm 100:3); and others such as Psalm 95:7, which speaks about the Israelites as being "the people of his pasture, and the sheep of his hand."

Ezekiel may have known of Jeremiah's words (Jeremiah 23), and so he amplifies the concept of God's bringing the flock back from exile, leading them to safety, tenderly caring for them as a good shepherd (Ezekiel 34:11-16). The concern here is for the flock, the people. They have been betrayed by the leaders and have suffered much. There is no notion here that God will appoint more and better earthly shepherds. Rather, God alone will take up this enterprise and do what shepherds are called to do: search for the lost who have been scattered, retrieve those who have strayed, care for the injured and weak.

Ezekiel 34:17-31. The chapter closes with God's judging between good and bad sheep (34:17-22), words about the messianic shepherd (34:23-24), and a prophecy of the covenant of peace to come (34:25-31). That the Messiah would come as the Good Shepherd is a theme prominently picked up in the New Testament. (See especially John 10 and Revelation 7:17.) It was with this deep background of imagery in their minds and hearts that the early disciples heard Jesus talking of judging the sheep, of a new covenant, and of himself as the Good Shepherd.

INTERPRETING THE SCRIPTURE

Israel's Shepherds

With the study of Ezekiel 34 we come full circle. We began this series of studies with a people chosen and blessed to be God's servants of justice in the world, a people directly governed and cared for by God. The Exodus from Egypt had marked them as peculiarly Yahweh's possession. The commandments gave expression to how a people chosen and blessed by God should live—as God's representatives, shepherds for the flock of the world, seeing that all people were cared for properly.

By the time Ezekiel made the prophecy in chapter 34, his home kingdom had fallen to invaders and he was living in exile along with all the other key leaders of Judah. As Ezekiel and other prophets saw it, a large part of the reason for the failure of the nation was the abuse of power by the leaders of the people. Kings, false prophets, and false priests, all acting out of self-interest, had contributed to Israel's downfall. Israel was like a flock of sheep without a shepherd, and Ezekiel takes the shepherds to task. They have fed themselves instead of the sheep; they have not cared for the sick and the lame nor sought the lost (34:4). They have cared only for themselves. Therefore Yahweh will replace them as Shepherd of the flock (34:11-16).

Ultimately, Yahweh will care for the chosen people through a new shepherd, the descendant of the house of David (34:23).

The true nature of God's rule over the people is to be expressed in the form of a loving, caring shepherd who puts his own life on the line for the flock. Yahweh will gather the people together again and breathe new life into their dead bones, thereby giving the people a new spirit and a new heart willing to be faithful. God will then establish with them an eternal covenant of peace (Ezekiel 34:25; 36–37). So for the exiles, disillusioned and despairing, the old national hope is transformed. It depends on a new saving act of God that will take place in the future. The King/Messiah who is to come will be the Good Shepherd of a transformed flock.

A Covenant of Peace

From the beginning of this study we have seen how peace, especially as the Old Testament understands it, is a vital element of God's justice. After all, God designed Torah as a gift to guide us in ways that bring safety, well-being, and wholeness to everyone. In this week's passage, the promise of a coming "covenant of peace" (34:25) includes all three of these elements.

First, the people will feel physically secure since there will no longer be wild animals to harass them. These "wild animals" are metaphorically seen as instruments of God's judgment elsewhere in Ezekiel (5:17; 14:15, 21; 33:27). Second, the people will enjoy an abundance of food as the land again becomes fruitful. Finally, the

Israelites will also be protected from hostile nations that oppress them. To a people exiled from home, feeling that their identity and existence are quite fragile, these were potent words. Moreover, these words surely reminded them of the blessings promised in Leviticus 26:4-13.

As with most covenant agreements, however, this new arrangement involves both gifts and expectations. So the promise of peace is intended, in part, to help the Hebrews rehear and reclaim their call as the people of God. From Ezekiel's perspective, once the people were settled in safety, they would then be free to pursue peace on both a spiritual and a social level, dedicating themselves to the embodiment of God's plan for the community of faith. As a restored and now safe community, they would at last be able to create a just society here on earth where all are treated humanely, granted access to the basic necessities, and allowed to share in the security that God has provided.

The truth of how this works rings true to us. We know that, all good intentions aside, we cannot do our best to bring peace or wholeness to any situation when we are under duress ourselves. When we suffer from physical or emotional attacks (coming from our own selves or externally from others), the stress of financial woes, or other circumstances in life that threaten our well-being, we stand in need of peace ourselves. Of course, God can still work through us in such circumstances, but we tend to be better agents for God when we can throw ourselves wholeheartedly into the service at hand. This was the future that Ezekiel held out for his people.

In this passage, Ezekiel simultaneously reminds us of God's promise and our call. The guarantee of God's presence, salvation, and peace is real and sure. When we find ourselves "exiled" in some way, we can trust that God is at work to bring us home. During those times when we are blessed

with peace, however, God expects us to respond in gratitude and love by actively seeking to spread this gift to others.

Shepherds of Peace

So we consider today the questions that arise for us out of Ezekiel's message to his community. How do we live as a people of God within this covenant of peace? How do we live under God's direction and guidance with Jesus as our Shepherd? How can we be effective instruments of peace and wholeness?

Ezekiel would be quick to say, first of all, that this is something we do together. As the body of Christ, we can be transformed into shepherds who not only care for one another but also are equipped to take on care for the world. In this way, we and the world move one step closer to the wholeness found in God's perfect peace.

When we think of ourselves as shepherds within God's covenant of peace, the time-honored words of Saint Francis of Assisi seem as appropriate now as when they were written in the thirteenth century:

> Lord, make me an instrument of
> thy peace;
> where there is hatred, let me sow love;
> where there is injury, pardon;
> where there is doubt, faith;
> where there is despair, hope;
> where there is darkness, light;
> and where there is sadness, joy.

Certainly this prayer is helpful as we seek to serve as instruments of peace in our households and neighborhoods, schools and workplaces. A kind word, a bit of flexibility, a neighborly concern for those we encounter can promote and encourage goodwill and peaceful coexistence. A listening ear can do more to bring about reconciliation than hundreds and hundreds of meaningless words.

In households, even households of one person, peace can be the hub of life, the center of all that goes on, affecting family members and friends alike who seek a restful haven. When the spirit of quiet calmness pervades a home, people will come for ministry.

"You are my sheep, the sheep of my pasture, and I am your God, says the Lord GOD" (Ezekiel 34:31). Resting on this promise, we may not know exactly what the future brings, but we trust that the God of the future will meet our needs and make all things right.

SHARING THE SCRIPTURE

Preparing Our Hearts

Explore this week's devotional reading, found in Psalm 23. If you have memorized this beloved psalm, repeat it from memory. Which images comfort and speak peace to you? Try reading this psalm from a translation other than one you memorized. What new images or ideas arise? What words would you use to describe this shepherd?

Pray that you and the adult learners will give thanks for the Good Shepherd who tenderly cares for you.

Preparing Our Minds

Study the background Scripture from Ezekiel 34 and the lesson Scripture from Ezekiel 34:23-31. Reflect on where peace and wholeness can be found.

Write on newsprint:

❑ information for next week's lesson, found under "Continue the Journey."

❑ activities for further spiritual growth in "Continue the Journey."

Locate some meditative instrumental music and an appropriate player. You may want to use calming natural sounds, such as a babbling brook or rustling leaves.

Prepare a brief presentation as suggested under "Analyze the New Covenant Between God and God's People."

LEADING THE CLASS

(1) Gather to Learn

❖ Welcome the class members and introduce any guests.

❖ Pray that the students will appreciate the covenant that God has with them.

❖ Play some meditative instrumental music and invite the readers to close their eyes and relax. After a few moments read aloud Psalm 23, preferably from the King James Version. Continue to let the music play for a brief while after you finish reading.

❖ Invite the students to comment on whatever they could see, hear, touch, smell, or taste as you read the psalm. Encourage them to describe the mood that this psalm evokes in them.

❖ Read aloud today's focus statement: **People are searching for tranquillity and wholeness. Where can these things be found? A lasting relationship with God and an assurance that God is with us meet our deepest need.**

(2) Analyze the New Covenant Between God and God's People

❖ Transition from the Good Shepherd of Psalm 23 by asking a volunteer to read Ezekiel 34:23-31.

❖ Identify characteristics of the Good Shepherd found in verses 23-24.

❖ Form small groups to further investigate the image of the Good Shepherd as it appears in the New Testament. Assign one or more of these passages to each group: Matthew 9:36; 18:12-14; Luke 15:1-7; John 10:1-18; 21:15-17.

❖ Call on a spokesperson from each group to identify at least one characteristic of the Good Shepherd that they found in their assigned reading.

❖ Bring the contrast between good and bad shepherds into focus by presenting information from "Introduction" and "Ezekiel 34:1-10" in Understanding the Scripture and "Israel's Shepherds" in Interpreting the Scripture. Be sure to point out that the bad shepherds neglected the needs of the people and focused on meeting their own needs and whims. Help the class to see why God's people so desperately needed a good shepherd.

❖ Distribute paper (preferably unlined) and pencils. Invite the adults to listen again as you read about God's promised covenant of peace from Ezekiel 34:25-31. Encourage them to sketch one or more scenes to illustrate what the world will be like when all are at peace. Suggest that those who prefer not to draw simply write a description in their own words.

❖ Form groups of three so that the adults may show and discuss their ideas with others. Encourage them to talk about action the church might take to help facilitate this coming time of peace.

(3) Identify Situations in Which the Learners Find Peace and Wholeness

❖ Suggest that the learners turn over their papers and write answers as you read this list of partial statements:

(1) **When I am feeling stressed and out of sorts, I can re-center myself by listening to _____.**

(2) **The color _____ tends to rev me up, whereas the color _____ tends to help me slow**

down and enjoy a relaxing moment.

(3) **The smell of _____ brings back warm childhood memories and tends to comfort me.**

(4) **My favorite comfort food is _____.**

(5) **If I could go anywhere in the world to find peace and quiet for a calming vacation, I would go to _____.**

(6) **If I could change one thing in the world to make it a more peaceful and hospitable place for all of God's creatures, I would _____.**

❖ Listen to answers from volunteers. Note any common themes among the responses.

❖ Read "A Covenant of Peace" from Interpreting the Scripture.

❖ Wrap up this activity by asking the adults to compare their feelings to these answers to the feelings that the covenant of peace discussed in Ezekiel 34:25-31 brings to mind. Ask: **What do your answers suggest about the kinds of situations in which you find peace and wholeness?**

(4) Respond to God's Presence in the Learners' Lives

❖ Discuss these questions from "Shepherds of Peace" in Interpreting the Scripture:

(1) **How do we live as a people of God within this covenant of peace?**

(2) **How do we live under God's direction and guidance with Jesus as our Good Shepherd?**

(3) **How can we, individually and as the church, be effective instruments of peace and wholeness?**

❖ Challenge the class members to respond to God's presence in their lives by taking these steps, which you will read aloud:

- **Step 1: Close you eyes and imagine yourself in a place where you feel especially peaceful and close to God. Look around. Take in the sights and sounds.** (pause)
- **Step 2: Envision Jesus walking toward you and sitting down next to you. Tell him about something in your life that is disrupting your peace.** (pause)
- **Step 3: Listen to his words of hope and comfort.** (pause)
- **Step 4: Thank Jesus for his promise of peace in your life.** (pause)
- **Step 5: Open your eyes and return your attention to the group**.

(5) Continue the Journey

❖ Pray the prayer of Saint Francis of Assisi, found under "Shepherds of Peace" in Interpreting the Scripture. Or, if you have access to the entire prayer, perhaps in your hymnal, invite the class to read this prayer in unison to close not only today's session but also this quarter.

❖ Read aloud this preparation for next week's lesson. You may also want to post it on newsprint for the students to copy.

- **Title: Faith Calls for Perseverance**
- **Background Scripture: Hebrews 10:19-31**
- **Lesson Scripture: Hebrews 10:19-31**
- **Focus of the Lesson: People wonder about, may even envy, others who feel secure about their spiritual lives. What security is available? The writer of Hebrews tells us that our sins can be forgiven because of the blood of Jesus and**

that we can experience the presence of God in a new and life-giving way through faith.

❖ Challenge the students to complete one or more of these activities for further spiritual growth related to this week's session. Post this information on newsprint for the students to copy.

(1) **Identify someone who needs a shepherd's tender care. Do whatever you can to help meet this person's needs.**

(2) **Look at some elected leaders through the lens of the Good Shepherd. What evidence do they give of being good leaders? What evidence do they give of being poor, even abusive, leaders? Call or write to at least one of these leaders to commend or condemn his or her support of certain legislation or policies.**

(3) **Walk a labyrinth or trace the route around a handheld one. Ask God to help you to dispel stress and worry and be enfolded in God's love and peace. How does the labyrinth experience help you to meet your deepest needs?**

❖ Sing or read aloud "The King of Love My Shepherd Is."

❖ Conclude today's session by leading the class in this benediction adapted from Deuteronomy 10:12-13, the key verses for June 24: **Go forth remembering that we are to fear the Lord our God, to walk in all his ways, to love God, to serve the Lord with all our heart and soul, and to keep God's commandments.**